The History of Communication

Robert W. McChesney and John C. Nerone, editors

WCFL, Chicago's Voice of Labor, 1926–78

WCFL

Chicago's Voice of Labor, 1926–78

Nathan Godfried

UNIVERSITY OF ILLINOIS PRESS

Urbana and Chicago

© 1997 by the Board of Trustees of the University of Illinois
Manufactured in the United States of America
1   2   3   4   5   C   P   5   4   3   2   1

This book is printed on acid-free paper.

Library of Congress Cataloging-in-Publication Data
Godfried, Nathan.
    WCFL, Chicago's voice of labor, 1926–78 / Nathan Godfried.
        p.   cm. — (The history of communication)
    Includes bibliographical references and index.
        ISBN 0-252-02287-4 (alk. paper). — ISBN 0-252-06592-1
    (pbk. : alk. paper)
        1. WCFL (Radio Station : Chicago. Ill.)—History. 2. Labor
    radio stations—Illinois—Chicago—History. 3. Labor
    movement—Illinois—Chicago—History. I. Title. II. Series.
    HE8698.G63   1997
    384.54'06'57734—dc20   96-10132
                                                                    CIP

To Beth and Isaac

CONTENTS

Illustrations follow 130

ACKNOWLEDGMENTS

Like any project that has taken more than a decade to complete, this work has led its author on a convoluted, exciting, and exhausting journey. Along the way, I have enjoyed the assistance of many people. Manjunath Pendakur and David Roediger offered their insights into mass media and labor history, as well as suggestions on sources and consistent enthusiasm for the project. Manji deserves special credit (or blame) for pushing me into the field of mass communication history. Henry Binford and Mark Tolstedt provided helpful ideas during the book's early stages. Thomas McCormick deserves thanks for stimulating my interest in labor history many years ago and for being a good friend.

I owe a deep intellectual debt to Robert W. McChesney, coeditor of the History of Communication series for the University of Illinois Press, and to Steven J. Ross. These scholars carefully read the manuscript and offered thoughtful and constructive criticisms. To the extent that I successfully incorporated their suggestions, the book's analysis and narrative benefited significantly. The weaknesses and errors that remain are my responsibility.

Summer research grants and a sabbatical from Hiram College supported part of the research for and writing of this project. Librarians and archivists at the Chicago Historical Society, the State Historical Society of Wisconsin, the Labor-Management Center at Cornell University, the New York Public Library, Hiram College Library, Tamiment Library, and the George Meany Archives made my task easier. Ward L. Quaal, Leslie F. Orear, Irwin E. Klass, Morris S. Novik, and the late Joseph M. Jacobs graciously shared their experiences and knowledge with me. I wish to thank my colleagues at Hiram College and at the University of Maine—especially Dixon Slingerland, Roland Layton, Wilson Hoffman, and Alex Grab—for their conviction that quality teaching and scholarship work together. To the creative and enthusiastic students in my popular culture, radical history, and twentieth-century courses at Hiram, I owe a special debt for forcing me to rethink fundamentals and clarify ideas. Richard L. Wentworth and Becky Standard have provided excellent editorial assistance.

I wish to acknowledge the love of learning and commitment to social justice that the Rabinowitz family—especially my late mother, Sylvia, and her sisters Deborah and Diana—instilled in me. My father, David—a rank-and-file organizer of the Building Service Employees' Union—has shown, by example, the promise of working-class life. Most of all I thank my wife, Beth McKillen. She has helped me at every stage of this project, listening to ideas, reading drafts, and offering critical comments that strengthened the analysis. Her own exceptional work on Chicago labor and its democratic impulses has provided the best possible model for me to emulate. This book is dedicated to her and to our son, Isaac, who makes our outfield complete.

PREFACE

The central value of historical understanding is that it transforms historical givens into historical contingencies. It enables us to see the structures in which we live and the inequality people experience as only one among many other possible experiences. . . . Once you surrender the fixed older forms of historical explanation and process, the future becomes open. It then becomes even more important to analyze and examine the history of those structures and ideologies that shape our lives.

—Herbert Gutman

Historians have described and analyzed the efforts of labor activists and others to build a movement during the early twentieth century that would secure greater rank-and-file control over the workplace and achieve industrial democracy. Scholars also have examined the demise of that movement during the course of the century.[1] An important and neglected battlefront of this war for workers' control was fought in the arena of the mass media and popular culture. During the first third of the century, local trade unions, city federated labor bodies, and radical organizations, building on the tradition of a labor and radical press, attempted to guarantee a place for workers in the newly emerging media of motion pictures and broadcasting. Elements within the labor and radical movements also sought to develop a working-class culture or, at the very least, to enhance working-class consciousness while building alternative and oppositional cultures to that of bourgeois America. Although these efforts vacillated, they continued through much of the century. Proponents of a labor press, radio, and film considered the new mass media not simply as tools in the struggle with capital and the state but as "a locus of, and one of the stakes in, that struggle."[2]

Conventional wisdom—Herbert Gutman's "historical given"—holds that the American mass media, operating in a private enterprise structure, allow relatively open access to all interested parties and grant success to those participants who best respond to market forces. The supporters of this system perceive U.S. mass media as the inevitable products of a natural evolutionary process and, therefore, as the best of all possible worlds. They "celebrate the media status quo" and praise the media's freedom, objectivity, diversity, public access, and social responsibility. They dismiss as cranks or extremists those individuals or groups that have criticized, challenged, or obstructed in any way the natural development of the capitalist media.[3]

Such a perspective, however, ignores fundamental contradictions and tensions in mass media development in the United States.[4] Most important, the conventional wisdom has neglected or obscured the power struggle waged between the groups in society that owned the means of cultural and ideological production (e.g., broadcasting, newspaper, and movie facilities) and those who, refusing to accept their role as mere consumers of culture, challenged the corporate media structure.[5] This study seeks to transform the "historical given" of corporate broadcasting and its manipulation of popular culture into a "historical contingency" by examining how a segment of the organized labor movement developed its own radio station in an effort both to *contest* the influence of mass media and mass culture on the working class and to *use* the mass media and culture in the interest of workers.

The Chicago Federation of Labor (CFL) established WCFL, its own radio broadcasting station, in 1926. Originally conceived as part of a media web (newspaper and press service) that was to aid in the campaign for a labor party during the early twenties, WCFL did not materialize until after that movement's death. CFL officials nevertheless pushed ahead with efforts to create an alternative to the emerging corporate radio structure. From its inception, WCFL encountered opposition from unsympathetic commercial broadcasters and state regulators and from indifferent and sometimes hostile national labor union officials. Indeed, WCFL's history revealed a dialectical relationship between it and the trade union movement, the corporate radio world, and the federal government.

While WCFL was the only radio station in the nation owned and operated by a labor organization, it was not the only manifestation of labor or radical challenges to the institutional structure or the cultural and ideological products of corporate broadcasting. The Socialist party, for example, established a radio station in New York City in 1927. Named after Eugene V. Debs, WEVD dedicated itself to becoming "a fighting, militant champion of the rights of the oppressed." Well into the thirties, WEVD officials urged the labor community to make use of the station's facilities and offered to assist trade unions in educating and organizing workers.[6] The San

Francisco Labor Council and the St. Louis Central Trades and Labor Union, among other groups, considered creating their own radio stations to "broadcast the worker side of current events." The radical American Fund for Public Service also planned to purchase its own broadcasting outlet in 1925.[7] Trade unions in Baltimore, Paterson, Memphis, Seattle, and elsewhere secured time on commercial stations, often sponsoring popular entertainment along with short talks on the history and goals of the labor movement. All these groups knew, as officials of the Women's International League for Peace and Freedom noted in 1925, that radio was "developing as a very much more important way of reaching large numbers of people than the newspapers which they have learned to distrust."[8] With the new opportunities the advent of FM broadcasting in the forties afforded, the United Automobile Workers and the International Ladies' Garment Workers' Union established their own, albeit short-lived, radio stations. Both the American Federation of Labor (AFL) and the Congress of Industrial Organizations (CIO) sponsored radio programs and news commentators between 1940 and 1960.[9] WCFL thus was part of a broader struggle on the part of organized labor to gain access to the airwaves.

The "Voice of Labor" began as a listener-supported station, emphasizing popular entertainment and labor and public affairs programming. A host of internal contradictions and external pressures changed it, by the end of the thirties, into a commercial station—that is, one dependent on advertising and mass entertainment programming for its survival. Having succumbed to the "laws" of the marketplace, WCFL maintained its labor connection by securing trade union sponsorship for "popular" programming and providing some time for labor announcements and labor analyses of contemporary events. By the fifties and sixties labor radio had redefined its service to Chicago trade unions as funding its own operations and general federation activities by maximizing profits. This led to a program format designed to attract the most rapacious consumer audience and, consequently, big-spending advertisers. Successful for a short time, this transformation ultimately failed and led to the station's sale in 1978. Reconciling the apparent conflict between its commitment to serve labor and its need to heed market forces comprised a significant element in WCFL's long struggle to survive.

WCFL was a relatively small broadcasting station throughout much of its history. It never achieved the level of success—as measured by financial profits, institutional development, technological advancement, or programming innovation—reached by national radio networks (e.g., the National

Broadcasting Company and the Columbia Broadcasting System) or by powerful independent stations (e.g., the *Chicago Tribune*'s WGN); nor did WCFL emerge as one of the chief agents for organizing workers in Chicago. An examination of the history of WCFL, nevertheless, enhances our understanding of a number of issues crucial to labor, mass media, and popular culture history.

WCFL's development paralleled and exemplified important changes in the organized labor movement during the twentieth century. Labor radio's rise and fall highlight local labor organs' dialectical relationship with the national AFL, the corporate sector, and the government. Alan Dawley has suggested that an analysis of labor's struggle with government and business in the twentieth century may be divided into three eras. The period through the twenties was dominated by corporate business, not just in the economy, but throughout society. Here the government served to bolster the needs and interests of big business, functioning first as a "promotional state" and then as a "cooperative state." In this environment, the level of class conflict was relatively high as workers attempted to reduce the "emerging social order['s] . . . inequalities of wealth and power."[10] AFL officials sought to improve the standing of workers by cooperating with "enlightened" leaders in the corporate and state sectors. This meant, among other things, acquiescing to the emerging corporate broadcasting structure. But Chicago labor officials rejected this strategy and built their own alternative mass media outlet. WCFL's early development revealed local labor's resistance to both corporate broadcasting and its supporters among the AFL hierarchy. Local labor sought not just to receive information and mass culture produced by business but also to become a potential producer of its own culture through its own institutions. The extent to which this potential was or was not realized constitutes the heart of this study.

The second era identified by Dawley, from the thirties to the early seventies, was characterized by a state-mediated "social compromise" between labor and capital. "Although capital retained those managerial prerogatives most vital to the profit motive, workers for the first time entered a *corporate* existence, enjoying privileges and prerogatives recognized in law (Wagner Act, Social Security, wage and hour laws) and custom."[11] After a brief spurt of labor radicalism, conservatism grew in the labor movement—part of the price of the "corporatist compromise." Before making its peace with the state and the corporate sector and while undergoing its own metamorphosis into a commercial radio station, WCFL had its last hurrah as an independent voice for workers during the Great Depression and the New

Deal. With the end of World War II and the solidifying of the corporatist compromise, WCFL retained few of the characteristics of labor radio. It no longer challenged the direction or strategy of the AFL hierarchy, preferring instead to fulfill the corporatist dream at home in Chicago. By the time the great compromise collapsed in the seventies—marking the emergence of a third period in which corporations and the state launched a new offensive against workers—labor radio, like the organized labor movement at large, was weak and unable to respond to the changed circumstances.[12] The story of WCFL thus offers insights into the shifting fortunes of organized labor over the course of the twentieth century.

A study of WCFL also highlights the complex interaction among broadcasting's "industrial structure, . . . political environment, and . . . cultural product."[13] Because WCFL's history parallels the history of broadcasting in the United States, its story clarifies some of the crucial business and regulatory developments in the industry, especially during the twenties and thirties. While radio broadcasting may have acquired much of its corporate, private capital, and mass consumer characteristics by 1922,[14] it is a mistake to assume that such corporate control was absolute or uncontested. Unions and working-class communities, among others, resisted and challenged commercial broadcasting, although the struggle varied in intensity over time.[15] Thus the story of WCFL reveals the process of resistance and adaptation.

As in the context of the labor movement and the broadcasting industry, WCFL's history overlaps and intersects important changes in twentieth-century American popular culture. The concept of popular culture has posed problems for those seeking to understand the working-class experience in the United States. Lawrence W. Levine has defined popular culture as culture that is "widely disseminated, and widely viewed or heard or read" and has argued that it constitutes a "process of interaction" between texts, which contain multiple meanings, and audiences with "complex amalgams of cultures, tastes, and ideologies."[16] Popular culture is "contested terrain" between producers and consumers. Creating culture in a capitalist society requires capital and those who have "the capital to mass produce and mass market cultural forms" possess the power to set their own agenda.[17] An economic elite may seek to manipulate society by producing cultural commodities and leisure activities that reinforce and legitimize the dominant group's values, ideology, and power. But "audiences are not passive, inert receptacles"; they continually reinterpret "popular culture in ways different from the intended meanings."[18]

A number of historians have examined how working-class audiences have received and perceived popular culture, how they have given new meanings to the dominant messages of the mass media, and how some have formed their own alternative or oppositional cultures.[19] The following study contributes to this ongoing exploration by addressing two interrelated questions: How have trade unions "attempted to combat the influence of mass culture on the workers" and How have they tried "to make use of mass culture in the interest of the workers"?[20] In the minds and hearts of its creators and supporters, WCFL promised to realize labor's hope that radio would serve progressive ends. The history of WCFL addresses the central tension between the "utopian possibilities" offered by working-class movements, mass media, and popular culture on the one hand and their "actual practices" on the other.[21]

Labor's response to the rise of radio broadcasting in the twenties very much grew out of the way in which workers and trade unions had dealt with other mass media—particularly the print media—in the preceding decades. This history of WCFL therefore begins with a brief examination of the interrelationship between organized labor and the print media prior to 1925. It then explores the rise of radio broadcasting, radio's impact on popular culture, and radio's initial interaction with workers. The chronological analysis of WCFL naturally divides into the era dominated by Edward N. Nockels (1925–37) and the era of William Lee (1946–78), with an interregnum (1937–46). Each chronological section of the study will describe and analyze how CFL officials conceptualized labor radio, its structure, its cultural products, and its role in American society in general and the organized labor movement in particular. These sections will consider how and why the CFL's efforts to create labor radio engendered conflicts or alliances with the national organized labor movement (the AFL and the CIO), the executive branch of government (including the Federal Radio Commission and the Federal Communications Commission), Congress, and the corporate broadcasting world (the National Broadcasting Company, the National Association of Broadcasters, and local Chicago stations). WCFL's changing programming and relationship with its audience remain important components of this study, but require a caveat. Broadcasting networks and major independent stations have left behind ample artifacts of their programming—in the form of transcriptions, recordings, or scripts. WCFL, with a few exceptions, however, did not. Analyzing WCFL's cultural products in the same way that one might critique the music, drama, comedy, and news of NBC, CBS, or WGN thus becomes hazardous. This study will attempt to address questions of programming through the use of secondary source descriptions and critiques of WCFL shows and the small number of extant scripts from the "Voice of Labor."

Labor and the Mass Media to 1925

Chicago radio station WCFL, the "Voice of Labor," began its five decades of broadcasting during the summer of 1926. Although local trade unions had first raised the need for labor radio three years earlier, the larger forces that shaped WCFL dated back at least to the turn of the century and stretched beyond the confines of Chicago. Labor radio grew out of the efforts of workers, immigrants, and radicals to confront the dominant political, social, economic, and cultural institutions of U.S. society. In the context of the early twentieth century, this meant dealing with the newly emergent corporate capitalist political economy and its concomitant mass commercial culture. As the independent radical Scott Nearing noted in 1922, those who controlled the majority of "property" created society's "governing ideas and motives" and manipulated education, the press, and other institutions to justify the "great inequalities in wealth in the community."[1] Working-class movements responded to the dominant structure and its ideology in two ways: They sought to amend or alter dominant institutions, to make them more responsive to the needs of the majority of the population. Attempts to reform or reshape the system from within often coincided with working-class efforts to build an alternative to the dominant structure. A labor press, labor education, labor movies, and "labor capitalism" all paved the way for labor radio.[2] Such alternative structures, while "separate and distinct from the dominant society," did not necessarily oppose or threaten the dominant system.[3] Even those institutions that began as both alternative and oppositional often changed over time. The story of WCFL reveals such an evolution and begins at the intersection of corporate capitalism and mass culture, on the one hand, and working-class movements and their alternative and oppositional institutions, on the other.

. . .

During the closing decades of the nineteenth century the nation faced severe economic crises and potential class warfare. Recurring economic depressions, massive immigration, rapid urbanization, and working-class and farmer upheavals (e.g., the Great Railroad Strike of 1877, the Haymarket incident in 1886, the Populist movement, the Homestead Strike in 1892, the Pullman Strike in 1894) shocked the nation's business and intellectual elites. In particular, class-conscious capitalists representing the emerging large and concentrated corporations demanded a new order, social cohesion, and a rationalized political economy. These captains of industry and finance believed that long-range stability, "class harmony and organic unity were essential to society and could be secured if the . . . functional groups" of business and labor "were imbued with a conception of mutual rights and obligations."[4] They modeled this class cooperation on the structure with which they had intimate contact—the corporation. By the early twentieth century, many of these same corporate elites came to recognize the vital role that the state might play in regulating political structures and manipulating power alignments in order to minimize class conflicts and maximize capital accumulation. Responding to the challenges of the period and the efficient model offered by the new corporate form, capitalists of large-scale enterprises and state officials developed a theory of social order and political structure that historians have labeled "corporatism."[5]

Corporatism proposed to wed the elites of large, hierarchical, functional groups—capital, labor, and agriculture—and state leaders into an informal and, at times, formal "public-private power-sharing arrangement." Advocates of this system argued that a community of interests, aims, and ideals united labor, capital, and the state. In particular, they believed that increased production and the expansion of markets, sources of raw materials, and investment outlets would bring prosperity and full employment to all Americans and an end to the possibility of class war at home.[6] Their commitment to maximizing production and marketplace expansion led inexorably to efforts to create more and larger corporations as the vehicles of acquisition.

As in most sectors of the economy, corporate formation and economic centralization and concentration increasingly became the norm in the realms of communication and culture. Ken Ward has explained that "in the nineteenth century the press became the first medium capable of reaching a mass audience through a combination of technological improvements in the production and distribution of newspapers and fundamental developments in their financial organisation."[7] The large-circulation press grew quickly after 1870 due to new technologies such as the telegraph and underwater cables, efficient railroad and postal services, and the development of news agencies. Unlike its predecessor, which relied either on political party subventions or high prices to stay afloat, the new press depended on commercial advertising for its profits. By the early 1900s, much of the newspaper press had entered the field of corporate finance, and vice versa; it experienced mergers and consolidations, which eliminated weaker papers and centralized the control of the American press in fewer and fewer hands. The newspaper world adopted scientific management and other methods to enhance organizational efficiency and weaken the power of labor. A newspaper trust, for example, had formed in Chicago by the 1890s. The publishers of the city's leading "general interest" dailies colluded to "control costs, avoid potentially crippling competition, and impose their terms upon" local unions. In Chicago as elsewhere, "large-circulation newspapers had become industrial enterprises in their own right."[8]

Like the press, the theater, motion pictures, and other entertainment and information vehicles fell under corporate control. Hundreds of local and isolated independent stock companies performed throughout the country before 1870; but these gave way, by the turn of the century, to a highly centralized commercial theater located in New York. This theater separated management from production, developed a standardized product aimed at the audience's lowest common denominator, and sought monopoly control.[9] Vaudeville experienced similar concentration. In 1901, over 90 percent of the country's most important vaudeville theaters (sixty-two of sixty-seven) formed "a classic oligopoly" aimed at lowering production costs—including performers' salaries—countering the formation of an actors' labor union and limiting "competition among members by carving up the country into protected territories for each circuit." Entrepreneurs in vaudeville applied "the principles of industrial standardization and mass production to popular entertainment" by regulating the time limits of each performance (seven to twenty minutes), ensuring that each act fulfill a specific task, and developing an overall "performance system" to "manipulate the expectations and desires of the audience."[10]

Movies, "the first of the modern mass media," evolved from short film-strips on narrow subjects, viewed through peephole machines, to multireel films portraying complex stories that were projected onto large screens at huge movie theaters. In 1896 vaudeville theaters began showing movies as one of the acts on their bill cards. Within a decade and a half, nickelodeon theaters—designed to show motion pictures—numbered more than ten thousand and attracted some 26 million Americans across the nation each week. The majority of these audiences came from the working-class communities in urban areas.[11] Initially a small business operation, the motion picture industry became a part of corporate America by the end of World War I. While sixty companies made over two thousand films in 1912, only eight companies made 90 percent of the eight hundred films produced yearly during the 1920s. These eight giants followed the lead of the short-lived Motion Picture Patents Company (1908–18), which had sought to control all aspects of the industry—from the production of raw film, motion pictures, and projecting equipment to the distribution and exhibition of films.[12] During the second decade of the twentieth century, Hollywood's "future moguls" (Adolph Zukor, William Fox) "merged mass production to mass distribution for the first time in motion picture history." They controlled the industry by integrating "supply (the stars), production (the studios), and distribution (the key theaters)." Building a system based on an expensive star system, elaborate productions, and luxurious movie palaces meant that "only giant firms could compete."[13]

Corporate capitalism transformed and developed cultural forms and leisure activities into commodities and devised methods to sell them to consumers. Mass media and culture served to reinforce and to legitimize the prevailing political, economic, and social structure in the country; mass-produced cultural commodities glossed over society's inequities and conflicts. The newspaper press, for example, became a key vehicle for creating images of society that would offend the smallest number of consumers. By constructing "areas of agreement, rather than differences, between individuals in its readership," a popular newspaper helped "to create the ideas of 'the mass', rather than serving the individual groups of people already in existence."[14] Thus large-circulation newspapers not only represented the corporate model but they also promoted the ideology of a harmony of interests among different classes and sectors of U.S. society, while rationalizing society's economic and political inequalities.

The movie industry also reflected the corporate order with its assembly-line techniques, specialization, and mass production; but it too created an image of being a responsible institution and "catering to the needs and desires of the American people." Movie themes attempted to regenerate middle-class ideals in the context of the transition from Victorian to modern values. Films reaffirmed the importance of individualism in a corporate era while luring audiences with "luxury, fun, and freedom." By utilizing people's "free time," movies helped to diffuse frustration and thereby helped, as one industry official put it, to "avoid any revolution against our economic system." Most important, films, movie stars, theater palaces, and Hollywood itself stressed the quest for private fulfillment through consumption; thus they "helped to legitimize the consumption economy."[15]

Vaudeville grew out of, and away from, an older popular culture rooted in local custom and tradition and reciprocity between artist and audience. It became a new modern popular culture.[16] Seeking a mass audience, vaudeville provided something for everyone—comics, crooners, jugglers, puppets, dancers, magicians, and so on—and tended to thrive in large cities with diverse populations. With its emphasis on tasteful and proper shows for middle-class men and women and their families, and through the use of relatively inexpensive ticket prices, vaudeville "incorporated" larger audiences than the legitimate theater. Entrepreneurs sought to suppress the differences within their audiences and touted vaudeville as an egalitarian institution, the "realization in popular entertainment of American democratic ideals."[17]

The early twentieth-century movement toward concentration and centralization and the production of an ideology subservient to a corporatism-in-the-making should not be overstated—especially in the realm of mass media and popular culture. Mass communications in the early 1900s "lagged behind other industries in terms of . . . technical sophistication, centralization, and national integration" and remained relatively open and competitive. Prior to the advent of electronic media, "almost any organized and determined group, sect, or party could command significant means of ideology production by running a printing press, renting a headquarters and meeting hall, speaking on the labyrinth lecture circuit, and otherwise moving into the marketplace of ideas."[18] Steven Ross has explained that "the modest cost of making a one or two-reel film . . . allowed a wide range of reformers, religious organizations, manufacturers, and government agencies to make movies advancing their various causes."[19] During the Progressive Era, on the one hand, industrial firms supported company auditoriums, drama clubs, plays, and pageants in an effort to maintain a quiescent work force, and, on the other hand, ethnic, socialist, and labor communities created their own theaters, plays, and pageants with the goal of giving "working people more political power and cultural influence."[20] A significant advocacy movement for societal reform within the newspaper and periodical world—"muckraking"—also developed during this period. On the eve of World War I, therefore, a myriad of newspapers and journals, combined with an ever-rising literacy rate, as well as film and theater, helped to sharpen ideological struggle in the United States.[21]

World War I and the Bolshevik Revolution produced an opportunity for government and business, at the local and national levels, to eliminate or repress "deviant ideologies." Seeking to silence the pacifists, socialists, and labor radicals who challenged U.S. entry into war, the Woodrow Wilson administration initiated, according to Robert Justin Goldstein, "a program of repression that matched or exceeded wartime repression even in clearly totalitarian countries such as Germany and Russia." The postwar Red Scare provided another opportunity for the defenders of the status quo to suppress radical and labor newspapers, magazines, and films.[22] As effective as these efforts were, they failed to destroy entirely the existing working-class media and cultural institutions or the desire on the part of radicals, progressives, and labor to create new ones. Ideological struggle continued into the twenties.

Alternative working-class media and culture developed simultaneously with their dominant or mainstream counterparts. Some leaders of working-class movements hoped to reform corporate capitalism's ideological and cultural institutions, and hence their products, by cooperating with and operating through the dominant socioeconomic and political system. Others desired to create separate and distinct worker-led media and cultural institutions. The latter group recognized that while capitalist media treated their audiences as passive consumers, alternative institutions would seek an active and positive relationship with their audiences. Building alternative media also required an independence from the finances and controls of other societal forces.[23]

Functioning within a capitalist society, however, demanded that even alternative media and cultural organs secure funding and follow standard business practices. Organized labor's effort to raise capital and create business ventures posed serious dilemmas for the movement. The frequency of "trade union capitalism" increased significantly during the twenties. These activities rested on the assumption that "labor must accept the institutions of a capitalistic society and work, through capitalistic methods, toward a new social order."[24] Business unionists, typical in the American Federation of Labor, favored labor capitalism because it helped to institutionalize trade unionism within the capitalist system while still serving the needs of workers. Labor radicals and progressives saw labor capitalism as a tool to bring about, as the International Ladies' Garment Workers' Union (ILGWU) hoped, the "ideal of a co-operative commonwealth in which industry is in the hands of the producers and in which production is motivated not by the seeking of profits but the desire to serve the needs of the people." Opponents of labor capitalism warned that becoming involved in business diverted attention and energy away from the primary purpose of trade unions—using the strike to organize workers and to secure power for the working classes.[25]

From New York to Chicago to Seattle, local unions and federated city labor bodies nevertheless established their own banks, insurance companies, cooperative housing, retirement homes, recreational buildings, union label stores, and newspapers during the twenties. Labor banks, for example, appeared in Seattle, Chicago, Cleveland, and New York, among other cities. The Amalgamated Clothing Workers of America (ACWA), which had established a labor bank in both Chicago and New York by 1924, contended that such banks served union members, the union itself, and the labor movement at large. By removing their money from capitalist banks and placing it in labor banks, workers simultaneously weakened the former and strengthened the latter.[26]

Labor banks and other labor businesses had financial, industrial, and social goals. But "labor-capitalist propaganda enterprises," as Dana Frank has explained, while following typical business techniques, aimed for ideological, not financial returns on investment. The creators of Seattle's Federated Film Corporation, for example, recognized that motion pictures appealed to the masses, that they provided an easy way for the labor movement to gain access to large audiences, and that they offered a means of converting workers into unionists. Financed by Seattle's metal trades, mill workers, painters, and central labor council, the film company produced militant, radical, and educational films highlighting labor's point of view.[27] Across the nation, radicals and workers founded film companies to counter the antiunion propaganda of the movie industry and industrial sector. They made "movies that offered positive portrayals of worker cooperatives, industrial and trade unionism, socialism, and government ownership of industry."[28]

The inherent contradictions between employing capitalist methods to support alternative media were most acutely felt in the labor press. Two writers of the labor scene in 1920 explained that many labor weeklies had become private business enterprises "just as dependent on big advertisers as are the capitalist papers themselves."[29] Elliott Shore, in his study of the Socialist organ, the *Appeal to Reason,* argued that J. A. Wayland, its editor, considered the paper as "first and foremost a business enterprise" and therefore "made the necessary compromises to stay in business." Wayland accepted advertisements because they allowed the paper to expand and to attract more subscribers. But once radical or labor publications accepted advertising, "they took with it a whole style of commercial speech that directly undercut the message of the movement they embraced."[30]

Advertising did not necessarily mean the undermining of the alternative press's positions on industrial relations or politics. Advertisers often had little interest in, or impact on, the editorial policy of a particular paper or journal. A number of periodicals secured advertising revenue from firms that were politically sympathetic with organized labor or from labor unions themselves. But, as Oscar Ameringer, editor of the dissident weekly the *Illinois Miner,* noted in 1924, labor papers that restricted advertising to these sources drew "their support from a field comprising less than 5 per cent of the total business of a community." The vast majority of potential advertisers may have opposed the labor press on political principle, but more likely they found that the labor press's insufficient circulation made it an undesirable advertising medium. Norman Thomas, head of the Socialist party and editor of the *New York Leader,* believed, however, "that in ordinary times a labor paper, without compromising its principles, can get considerable advertising, *provided it can first get enough circulation among workers who can be reached only through its columns.*"[31]

Securing a massive readership posed a constant problem for the labor and union presses. Ameringer explained that the former served workers as a whole, while the latter served their respective organizations. J. B. S. Hardman, editor of the *Advance,* a publication of the ACWA, considered the labor press to be a "mouthpiece" for "a more or less clearly-defined philosophy or ideology." But Ameringer contended that the value of the labor press rested in its ability to influence "the great masses outside of the ranks of labor, without whose assistance or consent organized labor must remain forever a more or less helpless minority."[32]

By definition, union publications were more narrowly orientated than the labor press, concentrating on immediate conditions and representing the policies of the unions that published them. Ameringer criticized trade union officials for reducing "their journals to mere barkers for their personal political ambitions," denying the rank and file the opportunity to question or challenge leadership policies, and ignoring the principle of freedom of the press. The best of the official trade union papers lacked outside readers; the worst were ignored by their own members.[33] Ameringer and other observers often lamented that union publications proved too narrow in their coverage. Workers might have consulted their union papers for information on "hours and wages and the politics of organization," but they continued to "take clues on economics, politics, philosophy, art and science from the general press."[34] This narrowly defined conception of the role of a union press often coincided with the "bread and butter" and business unionism characteristic of many craft unions and the AFL. The AFL's own publication, the *American Federationist,* begun in 1894, prided itself on functioning as "a safe adviser and practical exponent of trade unionism."[35]

To the extent that labor and radical publications eluded the commercial demands of the marketplace, remained close to their immediate communities, and sought to broaden their approaches to working-class and trade union issues, they retained their potential as alternatives to the dominant print media. As editor of the *Advance,* Hardman tried to "feed . . . the mind and the imagination of" his readers, to "encourage and stimulate discussion of union problems," to "relate the trade union to the labor movement and to correlate it with labor and social advance everywhere," and to "represent and reflect most matters which interest the group of which the union members are a part."[36] In Seattle, over sixty local unions and the Central Labor Council held stocks that financed the *Union Record.* At least during the early twenties, "tens of thousands in union funds . . . flowed into the *Record,*" which performed a broad array of crucial educational and informational services for Seattle labor.[37] The various foreign-language papers of the ACWA had the advantage of strong support from the union's large ethnic rank and file. Foreign-language paper editors in general, by virtue of "their birth and environment, by their social position and economic status," often remained close to the people they served. By keeping advertising to a bare minimum, the trade union and working-class immigrant and radical publications remained honest to the spirit of a labor press.[38] Relatively free from the self-imposed constraints of the marketplace, immigrant labor journals such as the ILGWU's *Justice* (in both Yiddish and Italian editions) and the ACWA's *Advance* (English), *Industrial Democracy* (Polish), *Fortschritt* (Yiddish), and *Il Lavore* (Italian) were distinguished by "the wide range of subjects treated and the effort to deal with these subjects from a broad social viewpoint."[39]

The supporters and organizers of a labor and union press insisted that labor needed its own vehicles for disseminating its ideas and information to workers and the general public. As trade unions grew in size and strength, and in particular as national trade unions formed, a labor press became essential. The "spoken word became insufficient to supply the members" with organizational information or "with the ideas necessary to strengthen their cohesion."[40] Through the labor press's stories, acknowledged the AFL in 1909, "the same thought can be impressed upon thousands of minds, in widely scattered communities, at the same time."[41] Thus labor newspapers and other publications became popular to bolster the fight for the rights of workers across the nation. Monthly and weekly labor periodicals grew in number from approximately 100 nationwide in 1870 to 300 by 1919 to over 570 by 1940.[42]

Under certain circumstances, labor publications enhanced or created a common feeling of identity among workers (class consciousness). Newspapers became institutions for immigrant working-class communities to bolster "ethnic identity, articulating common concerns, and mobilizing the group[s] politically in defense of [their] interests."[43] The ethnic press, according to Ken Fones-Wolf and Elliott Shore, could either reinforce immigrant group solidarity or assist in assimilating "upwardly mobile immigrants." The latter process occasionally meant supporting "class solutions to problems of unequal distribution of wealth and power in the United States."[44]

The labor press also served to offset the growing power and propaganda of the capitalist press. Local and national labor officials recognized that the capitalist press provided only superficial coverage of labor news and usually took a hard antilabor stance in their editorials, as well as in their "news" stories. Media critics throughout the twentieth century have acknowledged, as Stephen Haessler explained, that "newspapers do not reflect 'public opinion,' they reflect the views of those who own and control them." Or, in the distinctive words of the *New Yorker* magazine writer A. J. Liebling, "freedom of the press is guaranteed only to those who own one." The AFL understood this fundamental principle of the mass media, frequently praising the labor press for "saying the right word at the right time to place labor's side before the world upon any given controversy or point at issue."[45]

Since at least the late nineteenth century, trade union, immigrant community, and radical political critics of the American media had warned about how the concentrated and profit-oriented mass media supported the socioeconomic status quo. "Isolated" in the city and in their jobs, workers became dependent on newspapers for almost all their information. That dependence gave more power to the printed medium because the press could provide or withhold information and thereby influence "the social viewpoint of the reader." Observers of the labor movement in the early twentieth century contended that the profit motive forced the media to give "prominence to such news and opinion as may justify the existing social order, as will suggest that its fundamentals are eternal." Whether immigrant or native-born, America's working classes recognized that the nation's press and film industry were business enterprises comparable to any industrial corporation.[46] The noted liberal editor Oswald Garrison Villard lambasted the *New York Times,* the *Chicago Tribune,* and other corporate newspapers for purveying the news that interested or served the needs of their owners and editors.[47]

Class warfare and the antagonism between the capitalist media and working-class and radical movements intensified during the opening decades of the twentieth century, reaching new heights by the twenties.[48] The media industry's accelerated rate of concentration and centralization, as it caught up with the rest of corporate industrial America, contributed to this conflict. In the area of motion pictures, for example, Steven Ross has explained that "the antilabor, anti-Left films of this era paralleled . . . the emergence of the movie industry as one of the nation's largest industries and the protracted drives to unionize the industry's workers."[49] A similar situation developed in the new field of radio broadcasting. "The rapid rise of a centralized electronic media" stimulated a "consensus of normality."[50] Mass media owners accelerated the process of concentration in part to maximize their profits, but also to "inculcate and defend" their socioeconomic and political agenda and to regulate and often repress the expression of ideas they deemed dangerous to the established order.[51] Radio was to play a vital role in this effort.

Radio broadcasting seemed to explode onto the American scene during the early twenties. KDKA, the Westinghouse Electric Company's experimental station in Pittsburgh, secured a special license to broadcast in October 1920. It began operation by providing the returns of the Harding-Cox presidential election. The publicity surrounding KDKA's successful broadcast led other companies and groups into the field of entertaining and informing the American people. During 1921, the Department of Commerce issued twenty-eight broadcasting licenses. By 1925 there were 571 stations operating in the United States. "With almost stunning suddenness the radio has become a power boundless in possibilities for good or evil," observed *Outlook* magazine in March 1924. A writer for *Scribner's Magazine* described radio's "world-broadening and boundary obliterating mission."[52] This rendition of the rise of radio broadcasting is fine, as far as it goes. As Susan Douglas has demonstrated, however, "complicated social and technical processes" of the early twentieth century produced the "sudden" radio broadcasting "boom" of 1922. Corporate, government, and "amateur" constituencies, as well as the press, helped define the goals and functions of radio broadcasting well before its mass appeal.[53]

Like much of the nation's mass media and culture at the turn of the century, radio was an amalgamation of new technology and entertainment. The rise of mass entertainment—evident in dime novels, comic strips, amusement parks, vaudeville, and movies—was a product of technological innovations, industrialization, corporate capitalism, urbanization, and mass internal and external population migration. All these conditions allowed for the widespread manufacture and dissemination of cultural products. Entrepreneurs sought to develop mass consumer markets for these various leisure and cultural activities, in other words, to commercialize American culture. Within this milieu, radio broadcasting developed.[54]

Radio began as a vehicle for point-to-point communication. Guglielmo Marconi and other researchers developed a telegraph system without wires at the end of the nineteenth century. Carrying a coded message—usually the dots and dashes of Morse code—through the air, the wireless radio excited the imagination of both business officials and military and naval leaders. The latter sought government control over the wireless for reasons of national security, while the former wanted private control and profits. Although the press claimed that the wireless would end the communication monopoly held by Western Union (telegraph) and American Telephone & Telegraph (telephone), those very firms, in addition to Marconi and other radio manufacturers, raced to privatize the airwaves and establish their own monopolies. As early as 1915, AT&T president Theodore N. Vail indicated his company's desire to control wireless technology in order to protect AT&T's telephone interests and to reach the "unassimilated masses" with the message that monopoly capitalism could obviate industrial and class conflict and make all the people in the world "as harmonious as the mythical happy family."[55]

Initially, however, only vicious financial, patent, and legal battles characterized the corporate and state rivalry over radio. The Radio Corporation of America emerged from this extended battle at the end of 1919. A state-sanctioned monopoly, RCA virtually controlled radio telegraphy in the nation. Through a series of special arrangements negotiated between 1919 and mid-

1921, RCA, General Electric, Westinghouse Electric, AT&T, and United Fruit Company created a corporate alliance that controlled radio technology. The radio trust remained fixated on radio's use as a "long-distance, point-to-point communication between specific senders and receivers" and virtually ignored the instrument's potential use for a wider audience.[56]

Radio broadcasting became a distinct possibility well before the advent of RCA. In the fall of 1906, the American scientist Lee De Forest developed a vacuum tube, the three-element grid audion, which made it possible to pick up, amplify, and oscillate the human voice. De Forest's innovation turned the wireless telegraph into a wireless telephone and soon raised the idea that the radiophone might send out music and talk to more than one listener. De Forest himself probably conceived of radio broadcasting in the winter of 1906–7, considering it both as a way of providing music—especially opera—and speech to "the culturally and economically excluded" and as a way of making money by selling his own radio apparatus.[57] Although hampered by financial and legal problems, De Forest engaged in a series of experimental broadcasts from 1907 onward. Other inventors and amateur radio operators joined him in transmitting music (live and recorded), lectures, poetry readings, and informational talks. After constructing a 125-foot tower on the roof of his factory in 1915, De Forest began broadcasting phonographic music and, eventually, concerts, football games, election returns, and advertisements.[58]

De Forest's audience consisted of middle-class young men and boys who experimented with radio and "who didn't merely listen but communicated feverishly with each other." These radio enthusiasts comprised a grassroots network, eventually forming the American Radio Relay League in 1914. Amateurs viewed the airwaves as a new frontier of exploration and development. They criticized government and business efforts to monopolize the wireless, using democratic rhetoric to declare the air free and a public resource.[59] Most important, amateurs spread the concept of radio as a broadcasting medium. Although the Radio Act of 1912 relegated them to the low end of the electromagnetic spectrum, amateurs continued to expand their listening and sending activities. On the eve of the U.S. entry into World War I, the nation was home to 13,581 licensed amateur sending stations and an estimated 150,000 unlicensed receiving stations. Shut down by the government in April 1917, amateur radio operators did not disappear, but served in communication positions in the armed forces, where hundreds of other recruits received radio training. With the resumption of civilian radio operations, the Commerce Department licensed 6,103 amateur stations in 1920 and 10,809 in 1921.[60]

By the early twenties, amateurs and their followers already had helped to construct a nascent broadcasting network and audience. As the radio boom developed, department stores, electrical manufacturers, newspapers, utility companies, and other enterprises often transformed amateur stations into commercial ones in an effort to create favorable publicity for themselves or to enhance the sales of their services or products. Colleges and universities sought out amateurs to help create educational stations. Cultural entrepreneurs had developed mass public amusements, but radio amateurs demonstrated that some people preferred their information and entertainment in private, away from open public spaces. Amateurs, according to Susan Douglas, "were the first subculture of Americans, during the explosive rise in public entertainment, to spend much of their leisure time at home, using a new communications technology to entertain themselves and others." Radio broadcasting thus "went public in the privacy of the home."[61]

Given the widespread and growing interest in radio broadcasting, it is not surprising that the radio trust would become intrigued with what the amateurs had accomplished. The Westinghouse Electric Company was not yet a member of the radio trust when it received a special license from the Commerce Department to initiate a broadcasting service in October 1920. Pittsburgh station KDKA went on to broadcast music and the presidential election returns. Westinghouse provided broadcasting services primarily to sell its radio receiving sets. It thus portrayed radio listening as something for the masses, not just for enthusiasts with technical knowledge. Over the course of the next year, KDKA increased its power in an effort to reach a wider area of radio receivers and experimented with different types of broadcasts to attract more listeners. With the success of KDKA and the acquisition of important radio patents, Westinghouse joined the radio trust in June 1921. Before the end of the year, the company had established additional stations in Newark, New Jersey (WJZ), Chicago (KYW), and Springfield, Massachusetts (WBZ). AT&T started WEAF in New York and inaugurated toll broadcasting in 1922. The radio trust thus co-opted "the amateur vision of how radio should be used." It used the ether "for commercial ends," seeking "to promote cultural homogeneity, to mute or screen out diversity and idiosyncrasy, and to advance values consonant with consumer capitalism."[62]

The print media, having already entered the realm of big business by the twenties, praised the role of corporate capitalism in radio. Newspapers and magazines portrayed radio as so new and complex that "only large corporations with their vast resources and experience in efficiency and management could possibly tame it."[63] Commenting on radio's "social destiny," the press noted the medium's ability to "promote cultural unity" in the country by linking together millions of towns and homes; spreading mutual understanding among the urban poor, isolated farmers, and the uneducated; and using English as a universal language to overcome ethnic divisions. According to the press, radio could obliterate class distinctions in the nation by bringing high culture and information to the masses. This also would undo all the supposedly bad effects of other mass entertainment forms such as movies, amusement parks, and dime novels.[64] The press simultaneously legitimized corporate control over radio and "cast radio as an agent of altruism, restored democracy, and individual control." Radio became a democratic agent, a leveler of class differences, and a mechanism to spread education, improve politics, and enhance religion. As Susan Douglas has explained, press "references to democracy and to audience participation equated consumption with power."[65] The promulgation of such myths, nevertheless, helped to intensify the appeal of radio broadcasting among a host of corporate, civic, and religious leaders, as well as the general public. Leaders of the nation's largest trade union federation fell within this group.

As in most national issues, the American Federation of Labor's stance on the mass media reflected its corporatist position. AFL leaders such as Samuel Gompers and William Green, embraced the productionist policies advocated by the captains of industry and finance and by government officials. They favored policies designed to increase the absolute size of America's economic pie, while acquiescing to a division of the pie that guaranteed a disproportionate allocation to the corporate capitalist sector. Like corporatists in business and government, national labor leaders rejected concepts of class struggle, abandoned demands for democracy in the workplace, and ignored distributionist strategies aimed at reallocating wealth and power in society. Trade union officials promised a responsible, predictable, and peaceful work force in exchange for a growing economy, nominal welfare reforms from the state, and token participation in policy making.[66]

As noted above, the AFL favored a labor press to educate workers and the public concerning "the cause of labor." AFL conventions frequently urged affiliated unions and the rank and file to support the labor press's valuable service. But the federation never viewed the labor press as a substitute or alternative to the papers or periodicals published by the capitalist sector. The labor press concentrated on protecting and expanding workers' rights and on helping the mainstream press to understand correctly the trade union point of view.[67] During the early twenties, for example, leaders of the AFL rejected pleas from local unions for the establishment of a daily AFL newspaper chain throughout the country. Local leaders urged the creation of this alternative and oppositional labor press to counter the antiunion propaganda of the capitalist media. In 1922, however, the AFL Executive Council dismissed such arguments by alluding to its limited resources and concluding that the AFL had to make decisions based on "utility, expediency, and business judgment." AFL officials hoped that the expanded work of its "Information and Publicity Service will result in a constantly improving standard of accuracy in daily newspapers even though not owned or controlled by Labor."[68] Given financial constraints, AFL leaders chose to work within the capitalist media to convey labor's message, rather than developing an alternative to challenge the system.

At the same time that it rejected creating a daily labor press as economically nonviable, the AFL viewed as too costly and impractical efforts by various trade union and radical organizations "to create a permanent oppositional cinema" to offset the biased portrayals of labor unions and workers in capitalist sector movies. The AFL refused to finance independent movie productions, although it did fund and supervise one film project in 1925.[69] Within this context, it is not surprising that the AFL hierarchy judged that the possibilities of a labor broadcasting system outside of the corporate structure did not warrant the appropriation of scarce funds.

Throughout the twenties, leaders of the AFL concurred with the radio industry and the federal government that the emerging commercial system served the interests of all groups in society. As early as 1924, the AFL Executive Council decided not to act on a report estimating the cost of installing and maintaining a radio broadcasting station at AFL headquarters in Washington, D.C.[70] At its annual convention in 1925 the AFL formally rejected a proposal to establish its own radio station. The federation acknowledged the growing significance of broadcasting for organized labor, but held that local trade unions could purchase time on existing radio stations.[71]

AFL president William Green, like Gompers before him, emphasized labor collaboration with capital and the state. His strategy called for convincing business and political leaders and the general public that organized labor was a respectable and patriotic American institution. Green pushed for union-management cooperation.[72] In the realm of broadcasting this meant accepting the nascent commercial broadcasting system and working with it, not against it. If business firms advertised and sponsored programs on commercial radio, organized labor could do likewise. As Green often noted, "ownership of a station is not necessary in order to have time allocated for discussion of the problems of workers."[73] AFL leaders embraced a vision of the dominant ideology that defined the apparatus of a particular mass medium as "neutral." They failed to recognize that radio in the United States was a product of American capitalism. Financial limitations, reinforced by its cooperative corporatist ideology, led the AFL to miss an opportunity to develop its own communications structures.

Not all local trade unions or city central bodies agreed with the AFL hierarchy. Labor leaders in Chicago, New York, Seattle, and elsewhere worried that the immense power and influence of the mass media, which resided in the hands of the business sector, threatened labor union and working-class interests. They questioned, to some extent, the corporate media contention that marketplace choices meant democracy, that consumption meant power. These same leaders, together with their unions, sought to create their own media web. Unlike their counterparts in the national labor federation, union leaders in Chicago questioned the "neutrality" of radio technology. They intuitively understood, as numerous scholars have explained since, that "communications are intimately integrated into the totality of relations of production and social relations." Radio, according to Susan Douglas, was a "social construction"—the product of inventors, corporations, and the press working within the capitalist environment of the early twentieth century.[74] Leaders in the CFL understood this problem to an extent. Seeking to create an alternative to the dominant broadcasting system, they hoped that labor ownership of a radio station might overcome the inherent limitations of operating in the capitalist marketplace and yield a usable popular culture.

The Creation of WCFL, 1925–26

When rejecting a proposal to establish its own radio station in 1925, the AFL argued that local trade unions could purchase time on existing broadcasting outlets. This decision reflected, in part, an Executive Council determination that the AFL's limited resources were better utilized elsewhere.[1] But two other issues influenced the decision. By the middle of the decade, officials had concluded that labor weakness and employer hostility required abandoning all remnants of labor militancy and accepting a strategy of "advertis[ing] the virtues of trade unionism." William Green, who succeeded to the AFL presidency upon Samuel Gompers's death in 1924, "packaged and marketed the new AFL, and . . . took his product door-to-door . . . to anyone willing to listen."[2] Labor officers preferred not to challenge the capital sector but to follow its lead. If business firms advertised and sponsored programs on radio, organized labor could do the same. The decision not to fund a radio station also revealed a clear lack of vision on the AFL's part. While many individuals and firms perhaps overstated radio's potential during the early twenties, AFL leaders consistently misunderstood the new medium. At best, the AFL hierarchy perceived radio as an electronic bulletin board.

The experience of local labor, progressive, and radical groups in the interwar period demonstrated the inadequacy of the AFL's policy of cooperating with commercial broadcasters. Attempting to buy airtime relegated trade unions to a second-class status vis-à-vis capital. It forced labor to accept small favors bestowed by the radio industry and the state. The Socialist party leader Norman Thomas observed in 1926 that organized labor and liberal groups "have rarely been able to get hearings over established stations. Part of the difficulty lies in the high charge for broadcasting; part of the difficulty in direct censorship."[3] In 1939, the National Association of Broadcasters made explicit what had been an unwritten rule for over a decade: Stations should not air trade union views because the "discussion—or dramatization—of labor problems . . . is almost always of a controversial nature. Even the so-called facts about labor . . . are usually challenged."[4] Thus U.S. trade unions struggled to educate and inform the public about labor and working-class issues via an unsympathetic and often intransigent commercial radio system.

The CFL challenged commercial broadcasters, federal regulators, and conservative national labor officials by creating its own broadcasting outlet. Radio station WCFL emerged in a complex economic, social, and political environment in which national forces interacted with local Chicago and internal CFL conditions. Local labor leaders and the rank and file felt a special need for a "voice of labor" in the context of the rough and tumble of Chicago city politics—exacerbated by Prohibition and its concomitant intensified vice and corruption—and a generally hostile business and state climate for both existing trade unions and future organizing efforts. The antiunion sentiment so prevalent in the union town of Chicago—and reflected in a variety of union-busting efforts by major employers and the government—had its national parallel. The AFL's weak and lackluster policies did little to alter this situation. Set against this backdrop, the creation of WCFL seems quite remarkable. Equally significant was the vision of WCFL's creators; they conceptualized labor radio both negatively, as a way to counter the propaganda of the capitalist media, and positively, as a way to shape working-class culture and consciousness. This chapter describes the opening battle the CFL waged in 1925–26 to establish labor radio. That campaign illustrates key developments in the U.S. broadcasting system, the labor movement, and the relationship between radio and the working class.

• • •

Under the leadership of President John Fitzpatrick and Secretary Edward N. Nockels, the CFL attempted to continue a long-established, but dying tradition within the U.S. labor movement. During the early part of the nineteenth century, city and state federations of labor had played a vital role in the development of organized labor. As Sidney Lens explained, these organizations "had called strikes, organized boycotts, raised funds for relief, undertaken new organizational ventures and handled labor's political and legislative activity." Close to the rank and file, and drawing delegates from most of the local unions in the area, city and state central bodies "were the dynamos that ran the labor movement."[5]

But the boom in industrial capitalism and the emergence of concentrated and centralized corporations necessitated the formation of similarly structured national trade unions. The growing power of individual national unions and of the combination of these unions (into the AFL) at the end of the nineteenth century and the beginning of the twentieth increasingly removed the labor movement from the rank and file. National unions pressured their local affiliates to get city and state federations to join the AFL. While once enjoying an independent existence, local federated bodies soon found their power and initiative "being emasculated" inside the AFL.[6]

Size and power constituted only one aspect of the division between local labor bodies and the AFL. National labor officials feared "reform-minded workers" at the local level "who might reject traditional doctrines and established leaders."[7] Samuel Gompers and William Green emphasized narrow economic goals for workers and labor collaboration with capital and the state. They perceived rank-and-file workers "primarily as consumers" and sought "to negotiate the price of labor."[8] This bread and butter and business unionism assumed that labor and capital shared a harmony of interests in maintaining and expanding the capitalist system. Capital and labor presumably played equal roles in an open, pluralist, and competitive society based on reasonable profit and social justice for all. In this scheme, the state appeared as a neutral umpire. To achieve their goals, AFL leaders organized skilled workers, developed union-management cooperation, participated in the two-party political system, and maintained the federation's centralized and hierarchical structure. Throughout the twenties, the AFL sought to convince business and political leaders and the general public that organized labor was a respectable and patriotic American institution.[9]

While national labor leaders rejected theories of class conflict and advocated the socially and economically conservative policy of business unionism, many local labor leaders and the rank and file did not. Alan J. Singer has shown that even during the conservative and "lean years" of the twenties, when workers battled and often lost to industry's union-busting campaigns, rank-and-file laborers became "working-class conscious, identifying as members of a social and economic class with distinct political organization and goals." Singer concluded that "many of the radical ideas and strategies that gave direction to worker struggles during the 1920s were proposed, developed, and implemented, by rank and file leaders who were both workers and intellectuals, and who had deep roots in the labor movement."[10] Such a description certainly fits Fitzpatrick and Nockels and helps to explain why, under their direction, the CFL "probably held out longest in its efforts to maintain independence" from the AFL and why the CFL could be considered a distinctly class-conscious organization.[11]

Fitzpatrick and Nockels fit the important strata of rank-and-file leaders that Antonio Gramsci referred to as "organic intellectuals."[12] Utilizing Gramsci's concept, the historian George Lipsitz has provided an appropriate description of the working-class organizers and thinkers of the CFL: "Organic intellectuals direct the ideas and aspirations of their class even though they hold no formal status or employment as 'intellectuals.' Social action constitutes the indispensable core of their activity. Organic intellectuals not only analyze and interpret the world, they originate and circulate their ideas through social contestation."[13] Contemporaries of the Fitzpatrick-Nockels team frequently acknowledged the "pioneering" nature of the CFL. According to one longtime associate of the CFL, the federation's president and secretary made up "the most active, the most untiring, the most militant sponsors of organized labor." Another Chicago labor activist recalled the two men as "definitely . . . cutting edge people" and "fireballs" during the twenties.[14] As organic intellectuals, Fitzpatrick and Nockels learned "about the world by trying to change it," and they changed the "world by learning about it from the perspective of the needs and aspirations of their social group." By challenging corporate interests on many levels, they hoped to "expose the gap between" the illusion of class harmony and "the real conflicts and antagonisms that divide" society.[15]

Both Fitzpatrick and Nockels had deep roots in Chicago's working-class communities and unions. Born in Ireland in 1871, John Fitzpatrick emigrated to the United States in 1882. He worked in the Chicago stockyards, including a sojourn on the killing floor. While still an adolescent, the Irish immigrant became a journeyman horseshoer, an active member of the Horseshoers' Union, and a union organizer. He quickly won the respect of his working-class brothers and sisters and the attention of local union officials. Fitzpatrick first served as CFL president between 1895 and 1901; reelected in 1906, he held the presidency until his death in 1946. Contemporary friends and enemies agreed that Fitzpatrick was "a man of exceptional intellect, idealism, and integrity."[16] They also found him, as labor lawyer and longtime acquaintance Joseph M. Jacobs remembered, an "absolutely dynamic" leader, "labor through and through in every pore of his being." Fitzpatrick would "brook no opposition on the merit and value of the American trade union movement."[17]

Fitzpatrick accepted the "permanence of a working class" and "sought an equitable share of America's rewards for the worker."[18] His program included widening the base of the trade union movement, democratizing its institutions, and strengthening its political power. Under Fitzpatrick's guidance, the CFL became, as Chicago union officials Joseph D. Keenan and Lillian Herstein later recalled, a "sort of . . . open forum where each union came down to report." CFL meetings, "blue with smoke," served as a "great debating society" and as a "coordinator" for the various components of the Chicago labor movement. But more than this, the CFL under Fitzpatrick attempted to organize unskilled workers (industrial unionism as opposed to craft unionism), to shift power and control from national unions and the AFL to local federations and affiliates, and to create a viable labor party. Constructing a media web controlled by labor constituted one means of implementing this overall program.[19]

As president of a major city labor federation, Fitzpatrick clearly recognized how commanding news and public opinion could strengthen the labor movement and its various causes. Controlled by business interests, however, the commercial press and radio aimed at "making a profit and establishing conservative thought-control."[20] Chicago possessed several examples of this tendency, but "no newspaper in America," as George Seldes wrote in 1938, had "such an unbroken record of labor-baiting as the *Chicago Tribune.*" During the railroad strike of 1877, the newspaper's editors, who favored the importation of scabs, urged the police and militia to shoot strikers without warning. During the Haymarket incident in 1886 the *Tribune* led other newspapers in demanding a quick trial and execution of the anarchists. Throughout the industrial unrest of the late nineteenth century and the early twentieth, the *Tribune* never hesitated to condemn workers and to uphold capitalists' sacred prerogatives.[21]

During World War I, Fitzpatrick and CFL secretary Edward Nockels planned to build a media web consisting of a labor newspaper and a news service, later joined by a broadcasting station, which would help to inform, educate, and organize labor and the general public and thus offset the pro-business propaganda of the *Tribune* and its counterparts. When the CFL's weekly *New Majority* first appeared in January 1919, it proclaimed that the city's "toilers should have their own newspaper, upon which they can rely for the truth about things of interest to workers and in which they can find expression of their point of view."[22] Later in 1919, the *New Majority* and over thirty other publications pooled resources to form the Federated Press. Modeled after the Associated Press and the United Press, this press service supplied labor periodicals with accurate news from across the country and around the world. At its high point in 1923, the Federated Press served seventy-five publications and two hundred local trade unions, with foreign branches in England, Belgium, Russia, Holland, Scandinavia, New Zealand, and Australia.[23]

Fitzpatrick's efforts at reform found little favor with the AFL leadership, which consistently opposed independent local thought on trade union matters. Samuel Gompers viewed local bodies as necessary evils and "intrinsically irresponsible." The CFL, in particular, had violated Gompers's sacred policy of refraining from independent political activity and subordinating political power to economic action. By supporting an independent labor party during the early twenties, Fitzpatrick and the CFL came under increasingly hostile criticism and pressure from the AFL hierarchy.[24] The *New Majority* made no secret about its class-conscious orientation, nor did the Federated Press. Gompers viciously attacked the latter institution, characterizing it as "one of the greatest menaces to the advancement" of the U.S. trade union movement because it opposed AFL policies, criticized AFL officials, and supported the Industrial Workers of the World and the government of the Soviet Union. Matthew Woll, AFL vice president, condemned the Federated Press for allowing communists to have access to its services. "The Federated Press," contended Woll, "lends itself continuously to the spreading of doctrines subversive of the best interests of the American working people as expressed in the bona fide trade union movement."[25]

The first two filaments of the CFL's media web emerged while Fitzpatrick was still committed to reforming trade unionism in the country. By the midtwenties, however, Fitzpatrick's reform movement broke under AFL pressure, the nation's general atmosphere of political conservatism, and the betrayal of William Z. Foster and the communists in the Labor party. Faced with the option of disappearing from the labor scene or acquiescing to the AFL's conservative rule, Fitzpatrick chose the latter. In 1924, the *New Majority* became the *Federation News* as editorial policy shifted away from its formerly independent radicalism. The paper no longer officially subscribed to the Federated Press, although it published selected press materials well into the thirties. It relied instead on the International Labor News Service— part of the AFL's Information and Publicity Service.[26] While bowing to the

AFL on the issue of the news service and newspaper, the CFL continued to push for a labor radio station.

The need for labor alternatives to the corporate media did not disappear because of the CFL's problems. Business efforts to suppress labor unions by means of court injunctions, police and militia repression, and "welfare capitalism" intensified in the middle part of the twenties. Supreme Court rulings in 1921, 1925, and 1927 virtually outlawed secondary boycotts and made it impossible for unions to secure a national closed shop for the purpose of protecting union standards and wages. In Chicago, various businesses employed the "American Plan"—a form of industrial paternalism— to ensure the open shop. When this failed, they resorted to the use of yellow dog contracts, spies, blacklisting, court injunctions, preemptory dismissals, and violence. When some five thousand dress and cloak makers of the Chicago Ladies' Garment Workers' Union engaged in a general strike in February 1924, the employers, assisted by the state's attorney and the courts, used injunctions and hired thugs to break the walkout.[27] Chicago's mainstream print media and infant radio industry gave scant attention to the plight of labor under these repressive conditions.

Broadcasting in Chicago, as elsewhere in the nation, reflected the interests of those who owned the means of radio production. An assortment of newspapers, hotels, manufacturers, and department stores had established radio stations in the city by 1925. These outlets overwhelmingly provided musical programs as a way of gaining listeners and thereby enhancing the good name of station owners or the sale of their products or services. The city's first station, KYW, which opened in November 1921, initially broadcasted only Chicago Civic Opera performances six days a week. As the opera season came to an end in March 1922, however, Westinghouse Electric Corporation, which owned the station, realized that it needed new programs to maintain audience interest in radio and hence boost the sales of its radio apparatus. Often a station's very call letters served a promotional function—as was the case with *Chicago Tribune* station WGN ("World's Greatest Newspaper") or Sears Roebuck and Company station WLS ("World's Largest Store"). Although KYW, WGN, WLS, and the *Chicago Daily News's* WMAQ periodically aired news bulletins, informational or educational programming constituted a fraction of the normal broadcast schedule and virtually ignored issues of organized labor. Chicago's radio pioneers had little desire either to report on or to deal with trade unions. KYW made radio history in 1924 when it hired nonunion pianists, thus fomenting the first strike by the musicians' union against a radio station.[28]

Union leaders in Chicago recognized, by 1925, that they faced a dilemma: Their need to communicate labor's position to both workers and the general public continued unabated, but the print and emerging broadcast media seemed unable or unwilling to perform that function for them. They thus chose to continue efforts to gain access to the mass media, even as they abandoned a labor party. Originally conceived in the era of Fitzpatrick's labor reform movement, the broadcasting station did not materialize until after that movement died. The major force behind the creation of the radio station was not Fitzpatrick, but Edward Nockels.

Friends and acquaintances described Edward Nicholas Nockels as impulsive, hard-headed, a man of strong convictions, a fighter.[29] Born in Dubuque, Iowa, in 1869, the son of a cooper, Nockels spent most of his childhood in St. Paul, Minnesota. After getting through the fifth grade "by the skin of his teeth," Nockels quit school and went to work. Arriving in Chicago by the late 1880s, Nockels served an apprenticeship as an electrical worker. He helped organize the Gas and Electrical Fixture Hangers' Union in 1891 and became its business agent two years later. When the Pullman strike erupted in 1894, Nockels supported the American Railroad Union. He reorganized his own union as a local of the International Brotherhood of Electrical Workers in 1895 and remained its business agent until his election as the CFL's secretary in 1903. He held the latter position until his death in 1937. Like Fitzpatrick, Nockels played a prominent role in many of Chicago's crucial labor battles during the opening decades of the twentieth century, including organizing efforts among construction workers, teamsters, meatpackers, and steelworkers. Nockels's health occasionally posed a problem for his friends and family. A diabetic, Nockels suffered an attack during 1921 so severe that his doctor wanted to amputate one of his legs. Fitzpatrick and other friends refused to allow this and "hauled him off" to a sanitarium in Battle Creek, Michigan. Nockels remained there for several months. Placed on a very strict diet, he returned to Chicago and his union activities. But his work remained listless until the idea of labor radio rejuvenated him.[30]

"More excitable and more radical than Fitzpatrick, [Nockels] rushed into projects earlier and stayed with them longer than his companion."[31] Radio became a project almost exclusively identified with Nockels. John Fitzpatrick admitted in 1926 that "the C.F.L. executive board was not all enthused as to the radio project and I also practically deserted the secretary."[32] Frank P. Walsh, a close friend of Nockels and a supporter of WCFL in many of its legal battles, apologized to Nockels in 1928 for not providing "more help on your radio matters. I know that they are the interests that lie closest to your heart at the present time."[33] Despite tremendous obstacles, Nockels dedicated himself to securing a voice of labor over the airwaves.

Several concerns drew Nockels to crusade for labor radio. The "radio mania" of the early twenties produced eloquent journalistic pieces on the promise of broadcasting. Print media profusely praised radio for its potential to overcome class, ethnic, and cultural divisions within society and to improve everything from politics to religion to musical tastes.[34] Like many of his contemporaries, Nockels probably believed parts of this fanciful speculation and democratic rhetoric. In his various speeches, he constantly referred to the "revolutionary" possibilities of the medium and its fate "to become the unrivaled master" of human civilization. If radio could overcome divisions within the working class, it offered a means for enhancing worker solidarity and class consciousness. Nockels rejected the idea that radio could fulfill its glorious potential under the domination of corporate capitalism. If radio possessed even a fraction of the power its advocates claimed for it, then it was crucial that commercial forces not monopolize the medium. The threat of corporate-controlled radio and the corresponding elimination of worker or popular inputs motivated Nockels to act. Coming on the heels of the unsuccessful labor party movement, labor radio also may have appeared as the last attempt to continue the reform movement initiated by Fitzpatrick. Always eager to engage in a good fight, the battle over who would control radio seemed a natural outlet for the CFL secretary. At the very least, Nockels saw a labor radio station as a thorn in the side of corporate monopolies, state bureaucrats, and even the AFL hierarchy. In an atmosphere of corporate, state, and AFL conservatism, the decision to build a labor radio station was itself, as Nockels remarked, a "revolutionary action."[35]

·   ·   ·

The odyssey of labor radio began not with Nockels, however, but rather with a grass-roots call for action. In March 1923 at a regular CFL meeting, representatives from the local pressmen's union observed that broadcasting had become a popular means of publicity. Unfortunately, the "enemies of organized labor" utilized radio "for the spreading of anti-union propaganda." Delegates passed a resolution calling on the federation to investigate the possibility of establishing a labor radio station. But the CFL executive board made no immediate effort to study the subject. In February 1924, delegates from the Commercial Portrait Artists' Union renewed the call for a radio station. A lengthy discussion among CFL delegates led to a consensus to adopt "radio as the most modern means of communicating labor's message to the people."[36]

At this point, CFL officials discussed the matter of radio with Samuel Gompers. The AFL president explained that the Executive Council had already investigated the possibility of establishing a station in Washington, D.C., estimated the initial construction cost at seventy-five thousand dollars and annual operating expenditures at forty thousand dollars, and concluded that such a station would not provide a significant return on the large investment. Illness prevented Nockels from contesting this assessment. By the time Nockels had returned to work, Gompers had died and William Green had become the new AFL president. The change in national leadership, however, produced no new insights by the AFL hierarchy.[37]

Not deterred by the AFL's dismissal of the idea, Nockels continued to investigate the possibility of labor radio. While in Washington, he consulted with officials of the Brotherhood of Electrical Workers who believed "it quite feasible" to develop a radio station. Nockels learned that the Brotherhood of Locomotive Engineers had considered constructing a broadcasting station at their Cleveland headquarters. Under Nockels's direction, the CFL executive board finally initiated a feasibility study. When, in the spring of 1925, a special meeting of Local 194 of the Painters' Union again raised the radio question, the issue became the centerpiece of discussion at a subsequent CFL meeting. Fitzpatrick reported that one hundred thousand dollars might cover the initial cost of erecting a broadcasting station. Noting that he had to suspend forty-one local unions several years earlier because they failed to pay a five-cent assessment, Fitzpatrick doubted whether the federation could raise the required funds. Nevertheless, CFL members instructed the executive board to consult with the Illinois State Federation of Labor (ISFL) on the question of establishing a radio station.[38]

Fitzpatrick and Nockels met with ISFL vice president Victor A. Olander in October 1925. The three men concluded that they needed additional information before committing the CFL to a radio project. They hired radio expert William J. H. Strong to study the issue of labor and radio. Strong, a former adviser to the Republican National Committee on political broadcasting, served as president of the Chicago Council of Associated Technical Engineers. In the spring of 1925, Strong had failed to raise the funds needed to purchase a broadcasting station in Chicago on behalf of his organization. At the same time that he consulted with CFL officials about radio, Strong apparently hoped to work out some arrangement whereby his organization and the CFL might jointly share a broadcasting outlet.[39]

Strong's report on radio assumed that the labor federation was "serious" about broadcasting and that "entertainment is not its primary objective." Submitted in mid-November, the report argued that the CFL would derive "very distinct and great benefit" by properly using radio to educate the public in the principles of trade unionism, develop the interest of union members, facilitate union growth, nurture the development of progressive economics, and support political candidates friendly to labor. The CFL could purchase airtime from some stations, "but there is no guaranty of permanency in this."[40] Strong concluded that "it was entirely a practical and safe proposition for organized labor to enter the radio field."[41] Advising against building a new broadcasting station, he recommended that the CFL purchase an existing outlet and create a special nonprofit corporation to control the station. Strong warned that radio "is rapidly becoming restricted" and that "those who would get 'on the air' have no time to lose."[42]

CFL delegates discussed the Strong report at length at a December 1925 meeting. The author answered questions on such matters as financing, advertising, and securing radio receivers. Surprisingly, the discussion failed to touch on the important subject of programming. When the talk ended, CFL members moved that Nockels and the executive board ascertain whether local unions would assist in financing a radio station. The entire subject would then be referred to the executive board with "full power to act."[43] But events outside of Chicago forced CFL leaders to rush ahead into the radio field.

During the early twenties Secretary of Commerce Herbert Hoover, using power ostensibly derived from the Radio Act of 1912, brought broadcasting within the domain of the Commerce Department.[44] Hoover acted on the premise of mutual cooperation between his department and the private sector. In the absence of comprehensive federal legislation, a series of national radio conferences (1922–25) helped to develop an informal (and extralegal) framework for creating order and efficiency in broadcasting. At the 1924 conference, industry leaders urged Hoover to clear the crowded air lanes, which were utilized by some 530 radio stations, a five-hundred-fold increase since 1921. A year later, Hoover announced that the number of broadcasting stations (571) had reached a "saturation point." With the full support of the 1925 radio conference, Hoover ordered a freeze on the issuing of broadcasting licenses.[45]

Meanwhile, although the AFL hierarchy had rejected a call for a national labor radio station, convention delegates instructed the Executive Council to investigate the feasibility of trade unions securing time on established broadcasting stations. In late November, William Green wrote to state and local federations requesting their officials to "get in touch with the proper authorities of the broadcasting station in your vicinity to find out whether arrangements can be made locally to carry out the spirit and intent of the . . . proposal." Green's letter to the CFL listed twenty-one stations in the Chicago area that might sell airtime to labor.[46] In the weeks that followed, Nockels contacted several local stations, but not in response to Green's order. Instead of inquiring about the availability of airtime, Nockels asked station managers the "price for the purchase or control of their stations."[47] In early December, Nockels sent the Strong report to Green, informing the AFL chief that the city federation planned to establish its own radio station. The CFL executive board had decided "that the use of radio by leasing time from stations not controlled by the Federation is too costly, uncertain, and quite impossible as a business proposition, and that the control of a station by the Federation is essential if radio is to be used by Trade Unions."[48]

Upon receiving word of the CFL's plans, AFL officials consulted the Commerce Department. They learned that the department no longer issued new licenses for broadcasting stations—especially in the "over-burdened" Chicago market. Green passed the "bad" news back to Nockels and recommended that he visit the Federal Building in Chicago, where the Superintendent of Radios "would furnish you with detailed information showing how extremely crowded Chicago is in the matter of broadcasting stations and the impossibility of issuing new licenses there for some time to come." The AFL president insisted on being "kept fully advised to subsequent movements of your organization upon this matter."[49] AFL officers worried about the CFL's tendency toward independent action. The unsuccessful labor party episode had irked the AFL hierarchy earlier in the decade. More recently, the CFL endorsed the Amalgamated Clothing Workers of America, a non-AFL union that had seceded from the AFL-chartered United Garment Workers. The AFL considered the ACWA illegitimate, but CFL leaders praised it as a "militant and progressive" body and as a distinguished friend of the Chicago labor movement. National union officials decided to monitor the CFL's independent activity regarding radio.[50]

The AFL's request for information alerted the Commerce Department to the CFL's plans for operating a radio station. Acting Secretary Stephen Davis notified the CFL in mid-January 1926 that "all wave lengths available are in use." He saw "no possibility of providing an operating channel" for the proposed station and thus ruled that "a license can not be issued." Davis cited the Fourth National Radio Conference recommendation that no further licenses be issued until there had been a substantial reduction in the number of broadcasting stations.[51] While issuing no new licenses, the Commerce Department did allow the transfer of licenses when broadcasting facilities were bought and sold. In other words, "the license ran to the apparatus" and when the apparatus changed hands, the Commerce Department approved the transfer of the license. Thus when *Liberty* magazine, a link in the *Chicago Tribune* media chain, wanted a radio station in Chicago, it merely purchased an existing licensed station for fifty thousand dollars and secured federal recognition of the sale and transfer of the license. Nockels and the CFL objected to such machinations, not only because the *Tribune* empire already controlled WGN, but also because organized labor was ill-equipped to play successfully the game of selling licenses to the highest bidder.[52]

Nockels quickly challenged the Commerce Department's freeze policy. He informed Davis that the CFL's plans "have been consummated and we are now negotiating for the erection of a broadcasting station." Nockels continued: "We were rather astonished to learn that labor is to be excluded from the free air. We have been informed that WEAF of New York has a wave length throughout this country all for itself, and to think that when our station is erected that a license can not be issued for its operation is almost beyond our belief."[53]

By picking on station WEAF in New York, Nockels identified an appropriate example of the nation's commercial radio system. Owned and operated by AT&T, WEAF had introduced the concept of "toll" broadcasting in 1922 and had become the key link in an expanding chain of radio stations. In the early years of the decade, AT&T had formed an alliance with General Electric, Westinghouse, and the Radio Corporation of America based on an exclusive sharing of valuable patents in the radio production field. That alliance began to erode, in part, as each member sought to dominate the field of broadcasting. AT&T vice president A. H. Griswold bluntly stated what his counterparts secretly sought for their corporations: "The Bell System desires to monopolize broadcasting."[54] Herbert Hoover, who was "more willing to risk the development of private monopoly or oligopoly than federal control," actively cooperated with the alliance members. Their compliance with his extralegal system of regulation made the system work; and that regulation, not surprisingly, supported the policies and needs of the large corporations.[55]

Nockels recognized and understood all of this. His letter to Davis questioned the authority and legitimacy of the "so-called 'national radio conference.'" "Our information is that these interests are attempting to gain a monopoly of the air." In a direct assault on those "interests," Nockels requested a license for a labor radio station to be "assigned one-half of the wave length of WEAF, of New York," and with five thousand watts of power.[56] In this and future correspondence, Nockels implied that the CFL would establish a labor station with or without the Commerce Department's approval.

Government officials remained unmoved by Nockels's challenge. Acting Secretary Davis explained that the department licensed stations on a first-come-first-serve basis and that Chicago already had more than its share of wavelengths. To take WEAF's exclusive frequency would deprive New York of radio time and give it to the saturated Chicago market. In a clever play with words, Davis defended his boss by asserting that the secretary "has no right under existing law to select the individuals who should exercise the broadcasting privilege." Davis assured Nockels that the department did not discriminate against labor organizations. The situation, lectured Davis, "is by no means as simple as it may appear to anyone not wholly conversant with it."[57] Having already questioned the legitimacy of the National Radio Conference, warned of the specter of radio giants monopolizing the air, and asserted the CFL's right to secure a license, Nockels ignored Davis's remarks.

Nockels did not shy away from a direct confrontation with the state over either the issue of labor's access to the airwaves or the threat posed by an emerging "radio trust." In early March 1926, radio engineer William Strong represented the CFL at a series of hearings before the Senate Committee on Interstate Commerce. The committee was investigating a bill, proposed by Clarence C. Dill of Washington, that promised to address the outstanding problems facing the nation's nascent radio industry. When Dill asked Strong whether the CFL favored the government owning all radio stations, the radio engineer replied in the negative. But the government, explained Strong, had to regulate all radio stations, declare radio "to be a public utility," and halt the development of a monopoly in the radio field. To keep radio "democratic," Strong insisted that all people had to have access to all kinds of stations. This could be achieved by establishing a large number of stations with small power allocations and by limiting commercial advertising.[58] Although none of these recommendations became part of the proposed radio legislation, they did become the foundation of subsequent CFL arguments before state agencies and committees. While the battle in Washington had just begun, more immediate problems faced Nockels in Chicago.

William Strong had advised the CFL to purchase an existing radio station rather than construct one—in large part because of the difficulty of securing a broadcast license. In early 1926 the CFL considered buying three possible stations, ranging in price from $85,000 to $285,000. Negotiations dragged through February and March. Before withdrawing from negotiations in late February, Station WHT offered to sell its license for $285,000 or to allow the CFL to use its facilities for one hour a day for three hundred days a year for $25,000. Station WENR remained in the bidding, but its cost hovered around $200,000, well beyond the meager assets of the CFL.[59] Apparently blocked by the high cost of purchasing a radio station, federation officials jumped at a new opportunity, which emerged in March 1926, to build their own radio station.

During World War I the U.S. Navy had made use of Chicago's Municipal (Navy) Pier that stretched out into the waters of Lake Michigan. Among other things, the navy had installed wiring necessary for radio equipment in the towers at the end of the pier. Much of this wiring apparently remained intact in 1926. Fitzpatrick and Nockels wished to take advantage of this situation and asked the city's approval to use the towers for a broadcasting facility.[60]

CFL officials first approached the mayor with their request. Chicago mayor William E. Dever's relationship with the city's labor movement was ambiguous at best. His efforts to act as a neutral third party, or at least as a representative of the public, in labor-capital disputes initially won him union approval as an honest broker. But when Dever refused to get involved in a stormy battle between the superintendent of the Chicago Public Schools and the Chicago Teachers' Federation and as he developed more cordial relations with the city's business class, labor officials became concerned. When Fitzpatrick and Nockels inquired about the Navy Pier towers, Dever avoided the issue and referred them to the city's corporation counsel. CFL leaders never sought the latter's opinion and instead went to Alderman Oscar F. Nelson.[61]

A longtime vice president of the CFL, Nelson had risen in the ranks of the National Federation of Post Office Clerks. Admitted to the Illinois bar in 1922, Nelson won a seat on the Chicago City Council as a North Side Democrat in 1923. Despite his party affiliation, Nelson had more in common with former Republican mayor William Hale (Big Bill) Thompson than with the Democratic Dever. Nelson, a longtime advocate of labor radio, brought the issue before the city council in late March 1925. There he secured an "unexpected" unanimous council vote directing the commissioner of public works to permit the CFL to lease the north tower at the end of Navy Pier for a proposed radio station transmitter. In return for a ten-year lease, the CFL promised to pay one dollar a year and to make the station available for municipal broadcasts. Whether Dever agreed with the deal is unclear, but, as contemporary political observers knew, the mayor would not use his veto prerogative "against a powerful labor organization."[62] With a transmitting tower firm in hand, Nockels purchased the necessary apparatus and had it shipped to Navy Pier. Workers from various CFL trade unions erected the transmitter antenna and installed the equipment for a radio studio. Nockels and Victor Olander were present when technicians turned on the power and tested the transmitter for the first time on June 19, 1926. The cost of construction and equipment totaled less than fifty thousand dollars.[63]

Generating money to pay even this relatively small expense highlighted the difficult problem of financing the station. On January 29, 1926, the Illinois Secretary of State granted a charter to the Chicago Federation of Labor Radio Broadcasting Association and its nine directors: Nockels, Fitzpatrick, Oscar Nelson, James C. Petrillo of the Chicago Federation of Musicians, William A. Neer of the Teamsters' Joint Council, John H. Walker of the Illinois State Federation of Labor, Margaret A. Haley of the Chicago Teachers' Federation, Samuel Levin of the ACWA, and Charles F. Wills of the *Federation News.* The association immediately asked Nockels and Strong to request financial assistance from the American Fund for Public Service—in the range of $100,000–$200,000—for the establishment of labor radio. The New York–based organization, founded in 1922 by Charles Garland and dedicated to financing progressive and radical causes, was sympathetic to the idea of developing a radio station devoted to working-class and "minority" interests. The fund had just recently failed to purchase its own radio outlet in New York City. Support for the concept of labor radio notwithstanding, the Garland Fund rejected the CFL request. Members of the board of directors gave no specific reason for the unfavorable ruling, but they apparently determined that they would be unable to secure the "kind of control" that they usually sought in such situations. This was the very reason that the fund had given in 1925 for refusing to finance the station proposed by Strong's Associated Technical Engineers.[64]

Even before receiving the rejection from the Garland Fund, Nockels had begun developing an alternative funding scheme for labor radio. At a February 1926 CFL meeting, he unveiled a plan that asked affiliated unions voluntarily to assess their members twenty-five cents every three months for two years. The first year's assessment of one dollar per member would purchase equipment and build a station. The second year's assessment would go to an endowment fund, the interest from which would maintain the station "permanently without any further cost to the local unions." A representative of Carpenters' Union Local 141 immediately announced that his union's members were so committed to the establishment of a labor radio station that they would support such an assessment. In a letter to all affiliated unions, Nockels and Fitzpatrick urged "prompt action on this most important event in the history" of the American labor movement.[65]

In subsequent explanations of the financial and organizational structure of the radio station, Nockels assured interested unions that the CFL Radio Broadcasting Association, as specified in its charter, was a not-for-pecuniary-profit operation. It would sell neither stocks nor bonds, but instead rely on voluntary subscriptions. The CFL would totally own and control the station, with its executive board electing the station's board of directors. Members of the radio board would come from those organizations levying the two-dollar assessment. This structure paralleled the operation of the CFL itself.[66]

The first major response to the funding strategy came not from a Chicago union, but from William Green. The AFL Executive Council questioned the CFL's plan to levy an assessment upon the membership because it appeared to violate the AFL regulation that "all special assessments should only be declared upon a referendum vote of the unions affiliated." In addition, Matthew Woll worried that the separate organ to purchase and maintain the station—i.e., the CFL Radio Broadcasting Association—would not be under proper "trade-union supervision." Green demanded an explanation from the CFL. In a conciliatory letter to Green, Fitzpatrick suggested that AFL officials had misunderstood the situation. The CFL executive board recommended "a voluntary assessment and this recommendation was carried by a unanimous vote. This is a voluntary assessment for such organizations that agree to it." In an effort to ease AFL fears, Fitzpatrick promised that the CFL "will not pursue any course contrary to the requirements" of the AFL. Green thanked Fitzpatrick for the clarification and dropped the matter.[67]

Having temporarily quieted the AFL watchdogs, the CFL returned to the task of securing voluntary assessments from local unions. The federation's newspaper became a key instrument in stimulating support for the radio project. Nockels offered those union members who contributed the two-dollar assessment a free one-year subscription to the *Federation News*. According to circulation manager Charles Wills, it cost the paper $2.06 to send the paper to one person for one year, so "the Two Dollars went to the Broadcast Station and $2.06 came out of the *Federation News* to meet the obligation of the contract entered into with organizations subscribing to the radio station. We made *The Federation News* the 'extra bar of soap,' as it were." The *Federation News* also inaugurated a radio column in April 1926 entitled "Labor Radio News." Written by the CFL's new radio engineer, L. J. Lesh, the column guided readers through the mechanics and economics of radio. It also reported on the development of WCFL.[68]

Nockels used the pages of the *Federation News* to emphasize the importance of a broadcasting station for the trade union movement. Time and again he explained that "the sole purpose of the venture is to advance the principles of trade unionism, to acquaint the public with economic conditions as they affect labor today, and to tell the true state of affairs with reference to present day issues, frequently beclouded by the daily press." Combating the "subsidized press" and its distortion and omission of facts concerning labor became a major rationale for supporting labor radio. The CFL station would ameliorate the deficiencies of the commercial press and broadcasters by presenting information on prospective labor legislation, proceedings in the national and state legislatures, international labor activities, local employment conditions, and local labor organizing. Nockels insisted that labor radio would be owned by the contributors to a voluntary fund and would serve the entire working class, both organized and unorganized.[69]

Advocates of WCFL conceptualized the station as combining the functions of both the labor and the trade union press. Lesh contended that "the giant voice of radio [could] tell the world and particularly the whole working class what is going on and how . . . problems can be solved." Nockels explained that "the radio will provide means for the local unions to send messages to their members and all of organized labor promptly, and have a more lasting effect on the memories of their rank and file than printed notices, etc., and newspaper announcements which they might overlook."[70] CFL officials, trade union delegates, and the rank and file centered their discussions on the value of labor radio as an organizing and news medium. This, after all, was what would distinguish labor radio from commercial broadcasting. But Nockels and his colleagues assured the Chicago rank and file that "music and entertainment will offset the heavy ammunition."[71]

Entertainment programming figured prominently in the thinking of CFL officials. In response to a question at a CFL meeting in early May, Nockels stated that "about 75 per cent of the broadcasting time would be devoted to entertainment." This was crucial for a number of reasons. All the talk about reaching out to the wider working-class community in the Chicago area meant little if labor radio could not attract listeners. To do this, WCFL would have to offer more than a diet of labor officials speaking about industrial relations and trade union issues. A *Federation News* editorial acknowledged in late February that labor had to have its own radio station "to facilitate the necessary education of the public to labor's problems," but that this was possible only "if the heavy ammunition will be combined with a few numbers in a lighter vein." Nockels repeatedly promised delegates that WCFL would give them a "show" for their contributions. This meant that not only would WCFL counter the propaganda of the *Chicago Tribune* but also that WCFL's own labor propaganda would make up just one part of a program filled with a variety of high quality entertainment.[72]

Labor radio, through its efforts to entertain, educate, and inform laborers and their families, could help to build working-class solidarity in Chicago, or so WCFL supporters hoped. One of Lesh's early columns argued that "radio is the thing that will bring the workers together on a united front."[73] Both Lesh and Nockels wanted workers to listen to labor radio not just when their unions made announcements but throughout the day. If labor radio was to help facilitate working-class solidarity, it needed to become a part of working-class life. A cartoon drawn by Lesh that appeared in a May issue of the *Federation News* depicted one of the proposed uses of labor radio. A construction worker sat on a girder of the steel frame of a new building. With the city skyline in the background, the worker took his lunch break—a lunchbox at his side and a pipe in his hand—while listening to a nearby radio. The balloon above the radio speaker said "W.C.F.L. Broadcasting" followed by musical notes. Within a year this vision of labor radio was realized when Cigarmakers' Union Local 14 announced that it had a radio in its shop and "that the men tune in [WCFL] and listen during the day." The union urged other workshops to install their own radios.[74] In the spring of 1926, however, the focus of attention rested on mobilizing Chicago area unions to agree to the voluntary assessment.

At the end of March, the five thousand members of Chicago Typographical Union Local 16 voted for the first-year assessment of ten thousand dollars for the station. Other unions followed the CTU's lead. By mid-April, Nockels reported that twenty-four unions, comprising about twenty-eight thousand members, had voted to pay the two-dollar assessment. Within weeks, an additional seventeen thousand workers in fourteen unions had made pledges. According to Nockels, a total of seventy-five local unions with a combined membership of approximately fifty-seven thousand had voluntarily contributed to WCFL by the late spring. Unions ranging in size from the eight-thousand-member Bricklayers' Union Local 21 to the ten-member Rope Splicers and Repairmen's Union supported labor radio because they viewed it as a way to inform the public about the labor movement and to bring unorganized workers into the ranks of the organized. The American Society of Composers, Authors, and Publishers granted a free license to WCFL to broadcast all copyrighted music—thus saving the CFL a substantial amount of money in fees and royalties. Unions such as the Bakers' Union, which already had used motion pictures "as a means of advertising our union label," viewed radio as another mechanism by which to expand consumer-oriented labor campaigns. Those in the forefront of workers' education in Chicago also recognized the important role radio could play in such programs. The progressive ACWA, for example, although not affiliated with the AFL, contributed ten thousand dollars to WCFL.[75]

Nockels embraced these contributions to the fledgling radio station, but realized that the majority of CFL affiliates remained indifferent to the concept of labor radio. Only 30 percent of the CFL's affiliated union members agreed to the voluntary assessment by the end of the year.[76] A few unions, like Machinists' Union Local 337, voted unanimously against the assessment, believing that any available funds should be used directly in organizing the nonorganized workers in various trades. A majority of those local unions not responding in any manner to the call for contributions remained preoccupied with their own needs or uncertain as to the advantages that labor radio offered them.[77] Trade union apathy remained a dilemma for Nockels and WCFL throughout the decade. But as spring turned to summer in 1926, the outlook for a broadcasting station owned and operated by organized labor seemed promising. Improving the forecast was a court decision concerning another Chicago radio station, WJAZ.

Eugene F. McDonald, president of the Zenith Corporation of Chicago, owned and operated WJAZ. The Commerce Department limited WJAZ broadcasts to two hours a week on a wavelength shared with a General Electric station in Denver. Opposed to Hoover's attempt to rule radio as a "supreme czar," McDonald challenged Hoover's regulatory framework by jumping to an unoccupied Canadian frequency in December 1925. The Commerce Department sued Zenith for "pirating" a wavelength and operating for unauthorized periods of time. In April 1926, the U.S. District Court of Northern Illinois ruled that the Radio Act of 1912—the only federal statute regulating radio—did not empower the commerce secretary to refuse a license, assign hours, limit power, or specify and restrict wavelengths.[78] CFL officials hailed the Zenith ruling as undermining both radio czar Hoover and the "air monopoly."[79]

The ruling gave Nockels the legal precedent he needed to secure both a license and a preferred wavelength for WCFL. CFL officials had long argued that the Commerce Department did not have the power to refuse the granting of a license. William Strong reminded a Senate committee in March 1926 that "the law says it is mandatory upon the department to issue a license." In May, Nockels announced that the CFL would defy the federal agency and broadcast without a license. "We are quite willing," Nockels declared, "to have the matter taken to court." Frank Walsh prepared to serve as WCFL's counsel in the event of a court battle.[80]

The Zenith ruling also opened the way for Nockels and the CFL to "hijack" the 610 kilocycle wavelength—the clear and strong wavelength assigned to AT&T station WEAF. As late as May 1926, the Commerce Department hinted that it would sue the CFL if the latter began unauthorized broadcasting. In June, the federal radio inspector in Chicago approved WCFL's equipment and technical setup. Nockels simultaneously prepared to inaugurate broadcasts and to fight for a radio license, linking the CFL's plight to the larger issues of "freedom of the air" and the radio monopoly. A confrontation seemed inevitable.[81] On July 8, however, the Justice Department publicly concurred with the Zenith decision. Hoover abandoned all efforts to supervise radio and urged stations to engage in self-regulation. Four days later the Commerce Department granted a broadcast license to the CFL, explaining that it would "issue licenses only for stations which are fully equipped and ready to operate." On July 27, 1926, WCFL began regular broadcasts from 6:00 to 10:00 P.M., Tuesday through Saturday, on a wavelength of 610 kilocycles and with one thousand watts of power. The following month, WCFL acquired an AT&T license to use patents and telephone facilities for remote control. Broadcast hours soon expanded to include two hours on Sunday afternoon.[82]

• • •

The "Voice of Labor" began its broadcast operations from a small set of offices located in the north tower at the east end of Navy Pier. A reception room and a generator occupied the lower level of the tower. Upstairs one could find a small cork-lined studio—covered with a gold leaf finish—and the WCFL transmitter, with heavy plate glass separating the two. WCFL had negotiated a contract with Charles Frederick Stein for the use of a grand piano. In return for free use, repair, and tuning, WCFL agreed to play the piano regularly and to announce periodically that the station exclusively used a Stein grand piano. Station engineer Lesh explained to the readers of his column that the small pier facilities eventually would "be supplemented by a larger studio probably in the loop district where we will be able to accommodate full orchestras and send music over to the pier by means of remote control telephone equipment." Indeed, Lesh mentioned a plan for fifteen outside microphones "scattered over the city at strategic points such as Union headquarters, theatres, and other sources of voice and music."[83]

In an effort to fulfill this multiremote broadcast plan, WCFL officials made special arrangements with two Chicago hotels. These deals also served to provide WCFL with "winter quarters." Station personnel acknowledged that the studio—situated as it was at the end of a pier stretching far out into Lake Michigan—was "rather inaccessible in the winter." Indeed, a blizzard in the first winter of broadcasting left the technical crew and one staff singer stranded on the pier until a horse and sleigh could rescue them. The Alamo Hotel and Cafe, located at Wilson Avenue and the lake, agreed to cover the cost of building a studio and reception room next to its famous dance floor. Its orchestra would provide music for WCFL and, in return, the station would give free promotion for the cafe and hotel. Station officials secured a second Stein piano for their Alamo studio and remote broadcasting began there in September. A month later, WCFL opened a second remote studio at the Brevoort Hotel, located at West Madison Street in the Loop. Such arrangements between broadcast stations and hotels and hotel orchestras were common in Chicago during the early twenties. WGN, for example, had a similar deal with the Edgewater Beach Hotel and the Drake Hotel.[84]

Labor radio officials conceptualized and developed their program ideas in light of the shows aired by Chicago's other radio stations. The bulk of this programming between 1921 and 1926 revolved around classical, dance, and ensemble music, popular songs, musical comedy, opera, and doses of vaudeville. WCFL programs followed suit with contralto vocalists, an assortment of Irish tenors, pianists, special ethnic festivals, and vaudeville acts. A typical vaudeville act was "Little" Joe Warner, a "character" singer and "dialect" comedian with a repertoire of Jewish monologues, Italian dialect numbers, and "darky syncopated revival" songs.[85] Acknowledging that WCFL's schedule resembled that of its city counterparts does not mean that the program ideas of WGN and WLS constituted the sole inspiration for the Voice of Labor.

As WCFL's general manager, Nockels promised to offer a first-class program that would be "entertaining and educational at the same time." This effort to combine entertainment and education, as well as information and propaganda, reflected existing trade union practices and traditions. The idea of holding "large assemblies devoted to music and brief lectures," for example, had been a crucial component of the worker education campaign of the Chicago branch of the ACWA. During 1921–22, the union sponsored "ten combined concerts and lectures . . . with the finest music and speakers," attracting some fifteen thousand people to each event.[86] Labor Day parades and celebrations also served to entertain and educate large numbers of workers and the general public.[87] Nockels and other WCFL officials believed that radio could use the same format to supplement these mass public gatherings.

As early as March 1926, Nockels described a daily labor show, airing between 6:00 and 7:00 P.M., that would contain "vocal and instrumental selections" of music "intermingled with short talks and news of interest to the working people."[88] WCFL's opening night of broadcasting on July 27, 1926, began with "CFL Bulletin and Talks Hour" at 6:00 P.M. John Fitzpatrick discussed how "labor will use this station to tell its story," and Victor Olander followed with a talk on the importance of the trade union movement as manifested in the miners' union. Interspersed with the speeches were piano selections, a flute solo, a performance by the WCFL ensemble, and a contralto solo by Vella Cook.[89] In the weeks and months that followed, the "Bulletin and Talks Hour" presented discussions of the American Plan, the British coal industry and the plight of British miners, the fight against the Bread Trust, a report on the Paissaic textile strike, the origins of Labor Day, the yellow dog contract, the prospects for radio legislation in Congress, the organization of white-collar employees, and a history of the Carpenters' Union, among other topics. Speakers included representatives from the Trades Union Label League, the British Miners' Federation, the United Textile Workers of America, the Chicago High School Teachers' Council, and, of course, the CFL.[90]

Despite the scope and variety of these talks, station officials lamented the relatively weak trade union participation in labor radio. The engineer and columnist L. J. Lesh perhaps exaggerated this concern in August 1926 when he wrote that "except for a few [announcements of] picnics, baseball games, and infrequent talks on labor subjects, Federation hour from six to seven at WCFL is a good deal of a flat tire." Nevertheless, Nockels and other station staff frequently reminded CFL affiliates that the daily 6:00–7:00 P.M.

time slot was available for any announcements and other information that unions might wish to broadcast. They welcomed and solicited rank-and-file ideas and suggestions on the station and its programming. Nockels urged delegates at a September CFL meeting to take WCFL postcards and to distribute them to union members, family, and friends. "In this way, the C.F.L. hopes to arrange the [labor] program as nearly as practicable to the needs and desires of the great rank and file of labor."[91]

CFL officials assumed that local labor and community groups would submit appropriate news and information to the station for broadcast. In 1927, Nockels invited the officials of local, national, and international trade unions affiliated with the AFL to send WCFL "a statement . . . telling . . . the accomplishments of the [respective] union . . . and making some reference to the value of trade unionism in general." Many unions responded, including the ILGWU in New York.[92] Meanwhile, in the offices of the CFL, staff members skimmed over labor publications from all over the country and clipped out items of possible interest to WCFL listeners. But Nockels and his colleagues never considered developing a system of correspondents and reporters to go out and collect information from local unions. Even if they had conceived of such a system, a tight operating budget limited the station staff to a handful of engineers, announcers, and program managers. As it was, Nockels and others pulled double duty as officers in the city labor federation and managers of the radio station.[93]

The relative newness of radio and an uncertainty regarding its possible uses also explain the Chicago labor community's hesitation toward WCFL. Some individual trade union leaders had imaginative ideas for labor radio, but many others—perhaps the majority—were unsure what to do with a broadcasting outlet. Even those who had pushed for the creation of labor radio often narrowly defined its functions. At a meeting of Painters' Union Local 275 in late December 1926, for example, members proposed rescinding their union's voluntary assessment for WCFL. Complaints abounded concerning the station's music, general programming, and time of labor talks. But the major objection came from members who "seemed to feel that the labor station should be on the air for nothing else than the spreading of propaganda, preferably radical propaganda." Anton Johannsen, who represented WCFL at the meeting and who held "radical" credentials, told the painters that the station was open to their union, but that they had never availed themselves of the broadcasting facilities. While the union ultimately decided to continue its financial support for labor radio, questions remained regarding the functions of WCFL.[94]

The weak participation of local unions in programming affairs disappointed WCFL officials, but the lag in union financial support threatened the station's survival. Just before going on the air in late July, WCFL had received some $29,000 in contributions from local unions, while expenditures amounted to only $17,000. But after a month of broadcasting, regular expenses had increased to $23,892. Although donations totaled $37,525.50 by October, WCFL nevertheless operated at a deficit of $5,127 during the last three months of 1926. Well before the end of the year, however, Nockels and his colleagues had begun contemplating supplemental financing schemes.[95]

The labor editor Oscar Ameringer once observed that if publishing plants owned by labor would print the stationery, literature, and journals of the large international unions, they could secure enough legitimate profits "to subsidize" "a real labor press."[96] Nockels formulated a similar scenario for labor radio. At an October CFL meeting, Nockels announced plans to operate a radio telegraph from WCFL. Constructing two new transmitters and installing shortwave equipment would help WCFL to establish a communications network—linking Chicago with other key cities. Lesh contended that WCFL Radio Telegraph would pay for itself by handling the heavy and steady telegraphic traffic of large companies located in Chicago and other urban areas. The station also could handle telegrams to and from labor headquarters across the nation. Regular traffic over the WCFL radio telegraph station began on November 12, with business links to Buffalo, Cleveland, Detroit, Duluth, and Sheboygan. With the installation of a radio telegraph utilizing short wavelengths, Nockels hoped to send and receive telegrams from all over the world.[97] But these hopes were never realized for both financial and technical reasons, and WCFL was forced to look for other funding sources.

From the advent of labor radio, station officials had recognized the need for some advertising. In the fall of 1926, Lesh admitted that WCFL had "slipped into the broadcast game with very little grief." But in order to serve organized labor and the larger working-class community and to maintain the listening public's goodwill, WCFL would require additional power and "superior" programming. "Such programs cost a lot of money," argued Lesh, and either WCFL would pay for them (sustaining programs) or commercial accounts would cover the expenses (sponsored programs). Lesh recommended building up commercial accounts.[98] John Fitzpatrick elaborated on this theme in a Christmas Eve address over WCFL. The CFL president asked for "toleration" from the federation's members and friends "in the struggle to finance and operate this station." WCFL already reserved and would continue to reserve certain hours for trade unions; indeed, the Voice of Labor would give local unions as much time as they desired. But the balance of airtime would be sold in order to make WCFL self-sustaining. Fitzpatrick cautioned that "we may be forced to do many things that under ordinary circumstances we would not do." The CFL, for example, would stand by all the labor programming over the station, but it would not and could not "be held to subscribe or advocate the thoughts or views" of those who bought time over WCFL.[99] The use of sponsored programming and advertising did not sit well with many trade union members.

In an effort to generate greater labor interest in the station and, to a lesser extent, ease its financial burden, Nockels decided to hold "a big blow-out to celebrate the official opening" of WCFL and to highlight its "enormous possibilities." The general manager envisioned the "Radio Frolics" as "an old-fashioned barn dance with jazz music and a cafeteria supper." He promised a memorable occasion with prominent labor and political leaders, comedians, motion picture and radio stars, music, and a masquerade ball. Local unions purchased blocks of one hundred tickets for $75.00, while single tickets for adults cost $1.00 and $.50 for children. Any profits from the event went to help support the Voice of Labor. Nockels pushed the gala event at CFL meetings and the *Federation News* ran large advertisements touting the promised appearance of George Jessel, Sam Jaffe, Jeannette McDonald, and other entertainers. The Radio Frolics took place at the Ashland Auditorium on Saturday, December 11, from 2:00 P.M. to 2:00 A.M. Officials estimated the crowd at just under eleven thousand. The celebration generated some revenue for WCFL, clarified the purposes of the station to the public, and provided the participants with a good time.[100] CFL officials decided to make the Radio Frolics an annual event.

• • •

In less than a year Edward Nockels had created a radio station out of nothing. At the first Radio Frolics, and indeed throughout the last half of 1926, local and national union representatives credited Nockels with bringing about "a miracle." They acknowledged how the establishment of labor radio continued the CFL's pioneering tradition. Soon after WCFL's first broadcast in late July, several CFL delegates noted that their unions had remained skeptical regarding the labor radio project, but now that Nockels had pulled it off, they would be willing to pay their assessment. James Cahill of Pressmen's Union Local 3, one of the first supporters of labor radio, congratulated Nockels and the CFL for doing "the job." At the same time, however, Cahill and others registered disappointment over the failure of the AFL to promote the CFL's broadcasting station.[101]

AFL negligence, if not outright disdain, of WCFL concerned both Nockels and Fitzpatrick. Given the financial problems plaguing the nascent station, both men realized the boost that only AFL legitimation could give it. Formal AFL approval of, and participation in, WCFL might supply the station with the prestige necessary to secure more local and national backing. Badly weakened by its clash with the AFL hierarchy earlier in the decade, the CFL now sought the AFL's blessing. CFL officials invited AFL participation and input in the early development of WCFL, but received only token acknowledgment of the project. AFL secretary Frank Morrison visited WCFL's facilities in June and later announced that the national organ supported the CFL effort and opposed a monopoly of the air. At the AFL convention in October 1926, CFL delegates asked for and received a formal convention endorsement for the station. The powerful Committee on Resolutions, however, referred to the Executive Council the CFL's request for AFL participation in the control and management of WCFL. "Any such participation," declared the committee, "must be under such terms and conditions as the Executive Council itself may determine."[102]

Despite the suspicion of the AFL hierarchy, Nockels continued his efforts to increase national and international labor officials' interest in labor radio and to secure the national labor federation's financial and political support for WCFL. When times seemed particularly unstable—for example, when financial problems intensified or when the radio trust or federal government pursued partisan plans to modify the broadcasting system—and WCFL's future seemed most endangered, Nockels proposed that the CFL transfer ownership of labor radio to the AFL.[103] WCFL's future survival thus hung not only on its relationship with local Chicago unions but also indirectly with the AFL leadership in Washington, D.C. From 1927 onward, developments outside of Chicago increasingly determined WCFL's fate.

The Promise of Labor Radio, 1927–28

The Voice of Labor emerged as an informal federal regulatory system crumbled, new national radio networks formed, advertising's role in funding radio operations increased, and the new medium's promise to transform society persisted. WCFL and Chicago labor leaders hoped to meet the challenges and to exploit the opportunities that these larger conditions and forces posed. Struggling with problems of regulation, finance, and programming in 1927 and 1928, they sought to realize their goal of serving the union movement, the working class, and the general public.

· · ·

The 1926 Zenith decision and attorney general's ruling—denying that the Commerce Department had the right to refuse a license, assign hours, or limit power—facilitated the establishment of WCFL. But the undermining of Herbert Hoover's regulatory structure also opened the gates for everyone seeking to enter or improve their position in the radio field. During 1926 the number of radio stations operating in the United States increased from 528 to 719. Federal radio inspectors reported that 62 stations had altered wavelengths and another 63 had unilaterally increased power.[1] Near anarchy in the Chicago airwaves forced the city council to appoint a commission of representatives of the area's leading broadcast stations, including WCFL, to study limiting power, dividing time, and extending the broadcast band. All groups in the chaotic radio field—corporations, amateurs, educators, and labor—recognized, however, the inadequacy of local efforts and the need for federal regulation. Pressure for a new radio act intensified through the last half of 1926.[2]

The CFL sought radio legislation that would protect organized labor's stake in the new medium. Several interrelated issues—monopoly, property rights, and freedom of speech—concerned CFL leaders. Since the beginning of its campaign to secure a broadcasting outlet, the CFL had attacked RCA and AT&T as the real air pirates, insisting that these monopolists had "no divine right to assume that the air is their personal property."[3] At hearings on a radio bill proposed by Senator Clarence Dill in early 1926, engineer William Strong explained how commercial stations legally denied labor access to their broadcasting facilities. Advertisers warned stations that "if you take union stuff we won't let you take any of our advertising." Making radio democratic thus required a multitude of different stations broadcasting on low power, with strict limits on advertising and on patents for radio equipment.[4]

Nockels urged inhibiting the growth of radio's "monopolistic octopus." Denying property rights on the air would aid in this effort. Restricting the influence and power of the Commerce Department, which Nockels viewed as the protector of the radio trust, also would hinder the octopus. Organized labor opposed a bill proposed in early 1926 by Maine representative Wallace H. White because it granted to the commerce secretary wide discretionary powers to regulate radio. The Schenectady (N.Y.) Trades Assembly feared that a commerce secretary "allied with the enemies of organized labor . . . , could make it absolutely impossible for our ideals and program to be broadcasted." William Strong voiced these same anxieties to the House committee considering White's bill in March. The Dill measure had the advantage of eliminating the commerce secretary and substituting a regulatory commission. Nockels worried, however, that "experts competent to sit" on the commission were "already financially linked with radio." CFL officers hoped that a commission might include among its members "someone sympathetic to Labor interests," perhaps the president of the AFL or the attorney Frank P. Walsh.[5] Wherever the CFL looked, monopolists of the air appeared ready to conquer small stations like WCFL and all of radio.

Congress passed an "emergency" radio bill in February 1927. The Radio Act of 1927 was not a "reform" law, but a "compromise between those who wanted an independent agency and those who wanted to keep regulation in the Commerce Department." As Robert W. McChesney has explained, the act sought to address "the short-term business problems of the broadcasters" while "ignor[ing] any discussion of fundamental broadcasting policy."[6] The law created the temporary Federal Radio Commission (FRC) and granted the agency exclusive power to grant licenses, classify all stations, assign wavelengths, provide equitable geographic distribution of facilities, and so forth. Designating the electromagnetic spectrum a valuable natural resource to be conserved, the 1927 act made broadcasting a privilege rather than a right. The FRC would grant, renew, and transfer licenses on the undefined basis of the "public interest, convenience or necessity." The act denied the FRC "the power of censorship" over radio stations and prohibited all interference with "the right of free speech." Sixty days after the law's passage, all existing licenses were automatically terminated.[7] WCFL and 730 other stations had to reapply for broadcasting licenses and wavelengths.

In its license application, WCFL confronted the ambiguous question: "Why will the operation of this station be in the public convenience, interest, and necessity?" Nockels claimed that labor radio met the test criteria because of the station's location, ownership, method of financing, audience, operating principles, and programming. Located in the nation's second largest city and near the country's geographical and population center, WCFL had access to a large audience of both industrial and agricultural workers. It held the potential, "with adequate power," to serve not only Chicago but also the state, the nation, and "the entire North American Continent." Regarding financial matters, WCFL's manager explained, with more confidence than existing conditions justified, that labor radio would "have abundant financial support, solely from voluntary contributions from listeners, to whom this station makes a special appeal." WCFL, after all, was "owned, supported and operated by and for the workingmen and farmers" of North America, who numbered more than five million. Nockels contended that while the method of financing via voluntary contributions might not be practical for other stations, it was the "soundest method" for WCFL, "by reason of its principles and clientele."[8]

WCFL sought neither pecuniary profit nor any political advantages and operated solely for public service. Nockels emphasized that WCFL provided the only outlet in the nation "through which labor can proclaim its principles and ideals. All other leading stations are owned by Capital, and speak the voice of Capital." Station staff conceded that the bulk of airtime "is devoted to entertainment, chiefly musical in character." Yet the application stressed the trade union, educational, and civic value of WCFL programs. One hour a day focused on subjects of interest to labor. Programs for farmers included reports on market and crop conditions, weather forecasts, and government studies. Frequent educational talks provided information for the general public. The City of Chicago could use WCFL without charge between 10:00 A.M. and 12:00 P.M. for public addresses or announcements. Local unions also used WCFL as their official broadcasting medium. "Surely, in the entire United States," argued WCFL, "there should be one unlimited station which speaks primarily the voice of the workshop and the farm."[9]

While considering the applications of WCFL and other stations, the FRC held public hearings to solicit ideas for new regulatory policies. Nockels suspected the five radio commissioners of colluding with the radio trust because they possessed technical, business, and government experience, but lacked any labor background. The appointment of W. H. G. Bullard as chairman of the commission probably most worried Nockels. As the officer in charge of naval radio operations for many years, Bullard also oversaw the formation of RCA and served as the government's representative on its board of directors. John F. Dillon also had government service as a Commerce Department radio inspector. Both Dillon and Bullard, however, died shortly after their appointment to the FRC. Orestes H. Caldwell, an engineer and editor of various radio publications, and Henry A. Bellows, a station manager from Minneapolis, both served on the commission for relatively short periods. The other commission members during 1927–28 included Eugene Sykes, a former Mississippi supreme court justice, Sam Pickard, an educational broadcaster from Kansas and radio director for the Department of Agriculture, and Harold A. Lafount, a receiving set manufacturer in Salt Lake City.[10] Whatever real or imagined danger posed by these commissioners, Nockels intended that they understand organized labor's position regarding radio broadcasting.

Speaking before the FRC on March 30, 1927, WCFL's general manager reiterated organized labor's opposition to property rights on the air and maintained that radio benefit all people and not become a source of profit for only private or political interests. WCFL, as a listener-supported station, of course, "is for public service and in the interest of the people." "Only stations built and maintained by the listening public should be entitled to use the air, which Congress itself declared to be 'public property.' What right has an individual or corporation to use and exploit public property for profit?"[11]

As the FRC approved licenses and assigned wavelengths in the spring of 1927, it gave little thought to Nockels's argument, but concentrated instead on temporarily "accommodat[ing] all the existing 733 stations through the sharing of the ninety frequencies." Given their technical and occupational backgrounds, the commissioners adhered to the practices and policies that Hoover had set at the national radio conferences; they favored those stations "with prior experience, superior equipment, and financial resources."[12] Commissioner Caldwell later explained that the FRC favored "good-behavior" stations that consistently put "out programs in the public service." These broadcasters—composed almost entirely of giant corporate and independent commercial stations—possessed high-quality technical facilities and extensive financial resources. By bestowing upon them exclusive nationwide wavelengths with unlimited time and high power allocations, the FRC enhanced the already privileged position of these stations. Smaller stations owned and operated by religious, educational, municipal, and other noncommercial organizations, "suffered with weak frequencies, shared wave lengths, and small power allocations."[13]

A provision in the 1927 act requiring all stations to reapply for their licenses worried the WCFL manager. FRC statements that it had no immediate plans to engage in a full-scale reallocation of frequencies or elimination of stations did not allay Nockels's fear that the powers-to-be meant to destroy the Voice of Labor. Thus Nockels, in mid-March 1927, offered to donate WCFL to the City of Chicago on the conditions "that the station be located in the proposed civic hall and that it be municipally owned and operated." Nockels apparently believed, albeit briefly, that it was better for WCFL to continue as a municipal station—so long as it remained open to the workers of the city—than lose its license as a labor station.[14] As it turned out, this was an unnecessary worry on Nockels's part. WCFL fared well with the FRC. In May, the commission renewed WCFL's license and its fifteen hundred watts of power, but shifted its wavelength from 610 to 620 kilocycles. Labor radio now shared its wavelength, and hence time, with station WLTS—owned and operated by Chicago's Lane Technical High School. WCFL officials expected WLTS "to be a congenial companion." WLTS received airtime Monday through Saturday between 9:00 and 10:00 A.M. and between 2:00 and 4:00 P.M. WCFL retained the 10:00 A.M.–2:00 P.M. and 4:00 P.M.–12:00 A.M. time slots, Tuesday through Saturday, and various hours on Sunday.[15]

Nockels believed that WCFL's adequate wavelength, its intermediate position between privileged corporate stations and disadvantaged nonprofit outlets, and its unique labor orientation obliged the station to speak out on national radio issues. WCFL would fight all manifestations of the radio trust—from chain broadcasting to patent pools to advertising—because radio held the potential of serving the "common people of America," of placing the "needs of humanity above all other considerations," and of "favoring the man against the dollar."[16] This position on radio fit into the CFL's critique of corporate capitalism. Nockels and Fitzpatrick, according to Steven Sapolsky, acted as twentieth-century "radical Jeffersonians," interpreting "society . . . as one vast, virtuous majority that suffered injustice" at the hands of a narrow minority of corporate monopolists.[17] Nockels contended that radio equipment manufacturing firms and the National Broadcasting Company (created in the fall of 1926) and the Columbia Broadcasting System (formed in the spring of 1927) sought to eliminate all competition in the ether by charging high fees for the use of their patented equipment and by producing expensive programming. A widely accepted de facto property right in the air for existing stations made it almost impossible for any except wealthy firms to enter the radio field.[18]

Nockels feared not merely the potential for a corporate monopoly over communications technology (telegraph, telephone, radio) in the United States but also a corporate monopoly over the nation's cultural and ideological production. Radio stations owned by big business or controlled by the two networks already engaged in "outright propaganda or delusive special pleading." A greater danger resided in their "chiefly entertainment" programming, which kept the "'Sweaty night-cap' masses pleased and contented," thus making it easier for the radio trust to secure profits from advertising, the sale of radio receivers, and royalty fees on patents.[19] Fitzpatrick and Nockels urged Congress to investigate a radio monopoly that poured millions of dollars into broadcasting "wonderful music and entertainment with which to lull the people to sleep while, with their . . . perfumed silk gloves, they will be able to pick the pockets of the people for all time to come."[20]

This challenge to the radio trust stations did not necessarily represent a philosophical or aesthetic opposition to popular entertainment programming. Rather it reflected an understanding that the networks could, as Nockels explained, "put out a program impossible to compete with, and . . . spend more money in one week on such a program, then [sic] the cost of building a new station." Nockels did not doubt that these programs would be of the "very highest class," but if people listened exclusively to the networks, it would "deprive all other stations of their listeners." Without viable alternatives, the corporate radio sector could create and perpetuate "mass thought."[21] The only way to secure protection against corporate domination of both radio technology and radio's cultural products resided in developing a powerful alternative and oppositional radio station.

Nockels had grandiose plans for labor radio, envisioning it as a national station. An exclusive wavelength, unlimited time, maximum power, and shortwave capability would enable WCFL to launch a national campaign against the corporate giants. At the same time, these improvements would enhance WCFL's service to organized labor and the general public. Soon after receiving a new license in May 1927, WCFL officials looked for a suitable location outside of the city limits for the construction of a superpower station. Nockels urged all national, state, and central labor bodies to write to the FRC requesting an exclusive wavelength and maximum power for the Voice of Labor. A tour of super-station sites in Long Island (WEAF), New Jersey (WJZ), Pittsburgh (KDKA), and Schenectady (WGY) reinforced Nockels's conviction that financing remained a major obstacle. By the summer of 1927, the CFL already had invited Wisconsin, Iowa, Indiana, and Illinois farm organizations to join labor radio for two dollars per member. Nockels urged all trade unions to "take advantage of . . . radio, not for commercial purposes, but for the sole purpose of defending and giving service to the labor movement." "Since this is going to be a super station," Nockels told CFL members in early August, "we expect to take the Radio situation up with the international organizations for their co-operation and assistance in order that they may come in and make use of this new wonderful science."[22]

In January 1928, WCFL applied to the FRC for an increase in power to ten thousand watts, with an option to go to fifty thousand watts. A month later Nockels wrote Commissioner Sam Pickard that WCFL required a new frequency (770 kilocycles) because the station might want to enhance its power beyond the ten thousand watts requested in January. "We are exceptionally interested," noted Nockels, "in securing satisfactory reception of our station in the vicinity of Washington, wherein is located our national headquarters." Acting without a response from the FRC, Nockels and his colleagues planned to erect a superpower broadcast station utilizing fifty thousand watts—sufficient to make WCFL "heard throughout the length and breadth of the land." In May 1928, the CFL purchased a one-hundred-acre tract of land twenty-two miles west of Chicago as a site for WCFL's nationwide transmitting station.[23]

A clear channel and superpower transmitter made up one way to spread WCFL's message across the country; shortwave broadcasts offered another. Nockels considered short wavelengths "invaluable" because "with about 1000 watts, we can relay WCFL programs around the world with less than one-third the cost of a broadcast station." In 1927, WCFL asked the FRC for permission to receive and use a short wavelength for broadcasting purposes. Nockels explained that a shortwave channel would allow WCFL to broadcast programs around the country to substations—built by local labor bodies at nominal cost—for rebroadcast. This would obviate the expensive use of telephone and telegraph wires controlled by the corporate giants.[24] In addition to shortwave broadcasting, WCFL personnel tinkered with broadcasting television signals. Edward Nockels became the first subject broadcasted by WCFL's experimental television apparatus in June 1928.[25]

Shortwave and television experimentation notwithstanding, WCFL's immediate technical problem in 1927 remained inadequate studio facilities at Navy Pier. Temporary studios at local hotels functioned adequately during the winter of 1926–27, but the WCFL staff wanted more permanent surroundings. In February, the Brunswick-Balke-Collender Company—a national dealer in phonograph equipment, records, and radio sets, as well as bowling alley, billiard, and pool table supplies—signed an agreement with the CFL allowing the federation to lease the entire seventh floor of its building at South Wabash Avenue in the Loop. Here the CFL established a new studio for WCFL, as well as offices for itself and the *Federation News*. The decade lease required that the CFL pay a rental fee of one dollar per year "in consideration of which the name Brunswick-Balke-Collender Company will be announced by our radio station at stated periods." In exchange for free publicity, Brunswick provided WCFL with two broadcast rooms, access to artists who recorded under its label, and the use of Joe Lyons, the director of Brunswick's recording laboratories, as the new WCFL music director.[26]

WCFL inaugurated its new studios in early May with special programs and publicity. Musical performances arranged by Lyons alternated with addresses by Fitzpatrick, Olander, Nockels, and others praising the new surroundings and improved programming. To emphasize the new professionalism of labor radio, WCFL paid for a full-page advertisement in the May 4 edition of *Variety*. Editors of the show business trade journal observed that this was the "first full-page advertisement from a radio station dwelling upon the professional or show aspect of radio." The WCFL announcement listed artists and staff members by name and identified them all as professional talent. According to *Variety*, New York advertising and broadcasting executives perceived "the advertisement . . . as another of the links that is drawing radio into the business of public entertainment, which is show business."[27] WCFL officials certainly had every intention of presenting quality "public entertainment"—preferably with a labor twist—to their audience.

Entertainment programming dominated the schedules of commercial radio stations. A study of nine prominent broadcasting stations—including Chicago stations WGN, KYW, WMAQ, and WBBM—in July 1928 revealed that, on average, 79 percent of the available airtime went to musical shows and comedy sketches and only 21 percent went to news, information, religion, and education.[28] Labor radio only marginally improved on this record, allotting approximately 25 percent of its airtime for informational, educational, and religious programs. During the first week in June 1928, for example, 6.5 hours (10 percent) of WCFL's 64 hours of total airtime went for labor programs and another 10.75 hours (17 percent) went for information, education, or religious programs.[29]

WCFL officials turned to entertainment programming for a number of reasons. Labor radio could serve organized labor only if workers and their families listened to it. While some unionists perceived of labor radio as merely a propaganda arm of the Chicago labor movement, Nockels understood that "no one will listen to speeches all the time." WCFL staff also recognized that workers and their families were not monolithic. As station engineer L. J. Lesh observed in his *Federation News* radio column: "We must remember that there are persons who actually enjoy a ten cent vaudeville theatre and many who prefer burlesque to grand opera. The old question of 'high-brow versus low brow' will continue to provide an interesting debate among broadcasters and the palpitating public." If WCFL was to become *the* station of Chicago's working-class, it had to offer a variety of labor and entertainment programs, to integrate labor messages and labor news into the entertainment, and to make listeners feel that the station was their institution, open to their suggestions and serving their needs both at the workplace and at home.[30]

The task of formulating labor and entertainment programming and finding or developing the necessary talent fell to Nockels and his assistants. WCFL business manager Franklin C. E. Lundquist, a union musician for over a decade and a participant in the early development of Chicago radio, knew his way around the city's broadcasting and entertainment industry. Under his direction, WCFL secured a license from the American Society of Composers, Authors, and Publishers allowing the station free use of members' works; acquired a collection of sound effects equipment—everything from duck quacks and horses' hoofs to rifle shots and wind whistles; negotiated for the free use of a twenty-five-thousand-dollar Barton organ; and hired Eddie Hanson, the star organist for the Balaban and Katz theaters in Chicago, to perform daily recitals.[31]

Finding talent to fill the airwaves proved difficult. Even given the services of recording artists who used the Brunswick studios, the Voice of Labor required additional singers, musicians, comedians, and announcers to fill its program schedule. An assortment of amateur and aspiring musicians and singers offered their services to WCFL—and station managers often used them. R. L. Redcliffe, a member of the executive board of Cement Workers' Local 76 and the booking director for the American Entertainers Exchange—a talent agency affiliated with WCFL—helped supply some radio artists.[32] Labor radio also hired the National Radio Audition Corporation to conduct a nationwide search for radio talent. To facilitate this search, the company made a short motion picture about WCFL, presumably to be shown in the theaters where the company would hold auditions. In the movie, first shown on July 29, 1927, Nockels escorted the audience on a tour of WCFL facilities at Navy Pier and the Brunswick Building. After viewing the studios, station artists—including announcer Maurice Wetzel, pianist Doris Schenk, and the syncopation team of Ford and Wallace—gave brief performances. There is no evidence that the movie fulfilled the goals of making "two million people . . . familiar" with WCFL or generating a "great quantity of excellent new talent," but it did demonstrate the CFL's willingness to use one mass medium to promote another.[33]

WCFL's entertainment shows fell into familiar categories. Musical programs—varying from classical and opera to popular dance and jazz—dominated its schedule and that of hundreds of other radio stations. Like other broadcasters, WCFL initially encouraged musicians to play without compensation. James C. Petrillo, president of the Chicago Federation of Musicians, convinced Nockels, however, that radio stations "are no more entitled to free music than to free rent" or "free electric power." Nockels promptly complied with Petrillo's request and employed an orchestra for WCFL.[34] The station also made arrangements with local orchestras affiliated with specific night clubs or restaurants to broadcast their music. Lundquist's pickup of the Savoy Ballroom orchestras brought dance music to WCFL's listeners from one of Chicago's most popular African-American night clubs. During the summer months, WCFL broadcasted the Sunday afternoon civic band concerts from Navy Pier. Labor radio also aired some "stage shows" from the Granada Theatre on the Far North Side of the city.[35]

Comedy skits followed music as the most frequently scheduled programming. Usually two or more actors combined to present humorous songs and jokes. The *Federation News* described "School Days," which aired on Monday evenings, as "a half hour of burlesque and banter, sharply drawn character portrayals of the variety that inspires caricatures." The show's humor derived from the interplay of an assortment of ethnic stereotypes, including the "confused and confusing schoolmaster with a Teutonic lingo," the students with the "Celtic temperament" or "Stockholm brogue," and the requisite Italian and Jewish characters. Instrumental and vocal selections provided periodic respites from the puns and convoluted syntax that made up the bulk of the dialogue.[36]

The coverage of sporting events, although a small part of the schedule, nevertheless became an important segment of WCFL programming. The *Federation News* columnist Paul R. Cline hosted a daily twenty-minute show in mid-1927 in which he commented on major sports, including labor sports activities. WCFL covered sporting events whenever the opportunity arose. Such was the case of the Dempsey-Tunney boxing match at the city's Soldier Field in the fall of 1927. The Chicago Park Commission's decision to give NBC the exclusive right to broadcast the fight generated a strong protest from Nockels, who accused the commission of "unfair discrimination" and NBC of seeking a "monopoly of the air." Nockels successfully pressured the two parties to allow WCFL to broadcast the fight too.[37] A radio trade journal acknowledged, in the fall of 1927, that improved facilities and equipment, fine musical talent, and quality announcers had made WCFL into "an instrument of public service and a builder of good will for labor" in Chicago.[38] But WCFL also distinguished itself by reshaping traditional entertainment forms within a working-class context and producing programs that reflected the needs and concerns of Chicago's workers.

The first attempts to bring together labor interests and entertainment programming came in mid-1927. Beginning in June and continuing for about five months, the Voice of Labor announced—both over the air and in the *Federation News* radio schedule—that popular musical programs came to the listening public through the "courtesy of" particular labor unions. These were not "sponsored" programs in the sense that trade unions paid for a specified show's airtime or its performing talent, but rather these were "sustaining" programs produced and paid for by the station from the voluntary assessments of local labor unions. WCFL thus provided free publicity for the teamsters, bakery workers, hotel and restaurant employees, high school teachers, and the many others who had voluntarily contributed to labor radio.[39]

"Own Your Home Hour," which aired Monday through Saturday in different evening time slots during the fall and winter of 1927, illustrated another effort to merge popular programming forms and labor interests.

Directed by the Chicago Ideal Homes Council, the program combined musical selections with talks on home financing, construction, and decoration. It offered cash awards to the letters best describing, in five hundred words or less, "My Ideal of a Home." Music, informational talks, and essay contests were familiar radio fare by 1927, but the message here was unique. The council's desire to stimulate single-family home construction in the metropolitan area reflected the profit interests of building companies and, perhaps, a general business sense that home ownership made for a more stable, if not pliable, work force. Chicago building trades naturally favored the expansion of construction opportunities for their members. But the CFL also supported this concept because working-class immigrant families had been sacrificing for decades in order to own their own homes. Their actions may have echoed European immigrants' wish for land or, more likely, a desire to protect against "the precarious quality of their existence." Whatever the reasons, workers considered home ownership important. "Own Your Home Hour" reflected the conviction of CFL leaders that home ownership contributed to the health and happiness of workers and their families. Providing entertainment and expert information on constructing the ideal home became a public service. The station even erected its own Ideal Home in Lombard, Illinois, broadcasting the cornerstone laying ceremony in November 1927.[40]

Labor festivities in general and Labor Day in particular offered another opportunity for Nockels to develop programming that joined traditional celebrations with modern broadcasting. When the CFL decided not to sponsor its own parade in 1927, Nockels chose to recreate the traditional Labor Day parade on radio. Station announcer Wetzel, business manager Lundquist, and two assistants fashioned an imaginary "old time parade" complete with marching bands, banners, floats, and speeches. With appropriate sound effects and a live band in the studio, Wetzel described two hundred divisions of union members marching from the Water Tower down Michigan Avenue, through Grant Park, and into Soldier Field before a reviewing stand occupied by city, state, and national labor officials and public dignitaries. Local unions, at Nockels's request, had sent the station descriptions of the number of their members who would march, what instruments they would play, and the messages carried on their banners or floats. Staff artists performed special numbers during the course of the parade. The imaginary labor parade generated thousands of cards and letters praising the program; the station repeated the show in 1928.[41]

The advent of labor radio and the success of the first WCFL Radio Frolics in December 1926 renewed a CFL interest in using collective social gatherings and leisure activities to strengthen the organized labor movement. Labor Day provided the perfect setting for a program that would simultaneously publicize labor's goals to a wider audience, enhance worker solidarity, and entertain the public. In 1927 and 1928, CFL officials reclaimed the holiday—which they believed had been usurped by employers and company unions—by replacing the parade with a Labor Day demonstration in Soldier Field. For a one-dollar admission, workers and their families could enjoy dancing, animal acts, boxing matches, soccer and baseball games, clowns, concert bands, parachute jumping, radio performers, and fireworks. The Soldier Field celebration also contained the obligatory speeches by prominent labor and political figures. Nockels's 1927 speech elaborated on the purpose of WCFL and the danger posed by the air monopoly. Each gala occasion ended with an evening ball and reception at the Navy Pier auditorium. Net proceeds went to support the operation of WCFL, which, of course, broadcasted the festivities. Some fifty-two thousand men, women, and children attended the 1927 Labor Day celebration; another sixty thousand participated in the 1928 affair. CFL officials considered these Labor Day activities important and devoted much time and effort to organizing them.[42]

The establishment of WCFL on Navy Pier and the reinvigorated Labor Day celebrations demonstrated Nockels's concern with both the socioeconomic and cultural needs of Chicago's working class. Worried that people had not taken full advantage of the downtown lakefront for recreation and socializing, the CFL negotiated with the city in April 1927 to use the auditorium on the pier for summer dances and entertainment. WCFL informed "the people that a wonderful recreation center is at their disposal during the summer months and that merely by an outlay for carfare, they can take their families and their lunch baskets and enjoy the lake breezes, the excellent music, dancing and other entertainment." Drawn to the lakefront by "good entertainment, a fine orchestra, and other attractions," Nockels and Fitzpatrick hoped the gathering of workers and their families would foster class allegiances.[43]

When Nockels talked about how WCFL could serve the labor movement, he defined "service" and "labor" in the broadest ways possible. "Labor" referred not just to the organized trade union movement but to all workers, their families, and the communities in which they lived. "Service" meant providing "not only entertainment but information; not only music but science, history, economics, and all the other things that make for human welfare." Service also meant permitting trade unions and labor organizing campaigns as much access to WCFL as necessary.[44]

Opening its facilities to those people and groups who could not afford to buy airtime, WCFL invited progressive politicians, academics, and community leaders and organizations to address important economic and social issues over the air. Each week, the Public Ownership League of America examined the advantages of municipal ownership of local transportation companies while the Illinois League of Women Voters lectured on child labor, health, and political issues. The Infant Welfare Society of Chicago, the Union Motor Club, and the Juvenile Protective Association, among other groups, utilized WCFL. Civic and religious leaders used labor radio to appeal for public assistance during natural disasters, such as the spring 1927 flooding along the Mississippi River that forced hundreds of people from their homes. Community-oriented programming also included readings of plays, stories, and poems for "shut-ins" and occasional celebrations for a city neighborhood, suburb, or nearby town—such as a special "Waukegan Night" show in March 1927. The Radio League of Reconciliation sponsored the Reverend William Baily Waltmire's attack against the capitalist industrial order and his demand that the church "challenge the autocracy of modern industry."[45]

The vital difference between labor radio and commercial stations resided in programming that served the trade union movement. From the outset, WCFL set aside an evening time slot—the name of the show changed frequently—for a discussion of labor issues, news, and announcements. Talks by various labor and farm groups often appeared in this time period. In the summer of 1927, the fifteen-minute "Labor News Flashes" joined the schedule. This program provided a "boiled-down version of the news matter and feature articles furnished to the Labor press by [the] International Labor News Service," an affiliate of the AFL. In addition to the labor hour, WCFL provided weekly blocks of time—fifteen to thirty minutes—to the bakers, the printing trades, and other unions.[46]

The Chicago Trades Union Label League took full use of WCFL facilities. League president Harry E. Scheck, one of the original supporters of labor radio, presided over a weekly show that combined entertainment with lectures on the importance of purchasing goods and services with the union label. Scheck's daughter occasionally read the poem "The Union Label Girl," and WCFL staff comedians, announcers, and singers performed. For the New Year's Eve show in December 1928, Scheck wrote a "spirited" sketch in which the daughter of a trade unionist (Scheck's daughter) befriended a strikebreaker (Scheck), teaching him about the dangers of the open shop and the need for union-made goods. Scheck frequently asked members of the Label League to volunteer to appear on the program; he welcomed "criticisms, good, bad, or indifferent"; and he solicited suggestions for "diversified" programs. Responses to the show, either by mail or at league meetings, indicated that listeners enjoyed the music and songs and found "the short but interesting speeches on various subjects to be very acceptable."[47]

Nockels invited local and national labor leaders to voice their opinions on contemporary social, economic, and political issues over labor radio. Anton Johannsen, president of Carpenters' Union Local 1367, for example, discussed the Sacco-Vanzetti case in May 1927. WCFL continued to broadcast nightly statements defending the two anarchists until just before their execution in August.[48] *Federation News* managers frequently addressed the WCFL audience on the importance of the labor press. R. L. Redcliffe from the cement workers, Charles F. Wills from the CFL Executive Board, and Harry Winnick from the Retail Clerks' Association also presented regular labor talks.[49] Various trade unions accepted Nockels's offer to broadcast five-hundred-word statements outlining their achievements and commenting on the value of trade unionism in general. The ILGWU's statement, "Triumph of Garment Workers through Idealism," aired on a July evening in 1927.[50]

Trade union shows over WCFL followed predictable formats—straight talks or lectures interspersed with musical selections and skits. Labor organs occasionally arranged exclusive entertainment programs. In early 1928, the Label League offered an hour of "high-class entertainment," including musical acts, comedy teams, a monologue artist, and a poetry reading. The popular and costly show led Scheck to observe that future programs would require financial help from unaffiliated unions.[51] WCFL also aired special union gatherings such as the annual spring banquet of the Moving Picture Operators' Union, held in April 1928 at a local hotel ballroom and including theatrical talent and a seventeen-piece orchestra. Franklin Lundquist declared the broadcast "an unusual success" because it placed the union "before the public eye"; and he promised that WCFL always would be "open as a medium of publicity for our unions." The Bakery and Confectionery Workers' International Union produced its own one-hour show in early May, featuring vocal selections performed by the Chicago Bakers' Singing Society and the Singing Section of the Ladies' Benevolent Society and a short talk, "Labor's Struggle and Labor's Song." Officials hoped to demonstrate that bakery workers were "prompted by loftier aspirations" than making dough.[52]

A major function of WCFL was to serve the labor community in times of crisis. Any union that "was on strike or had a story to tell the public, [was] given free time on the air." WCFL broadcasted a major benefit, in March 1928, for the families of striking coal miners in Ohio, Pennsylvania, and West Virginia. Station artists and local theater and radio talent sang, played jazz, and performed dramatic sketches, while John Fitzpatrick explained the strike issues. The broadcast generated thirty-five hundred dollars in donations from local unions and individual workers.[53] When gardeners and florists in Chicago locked out their employees in the spring of 1928, WCFL offered twice a day descriptions of the union's plight and requested a public boycott of flower purchases. The effectiveness of the WCFL-led boycott became evident when the employing businesses sought a court injunction against the Voice of Labor.[54]

Unions that utilized WCFL for their strikes or organizing campaigns seemed satisfied with the results. The *Federation News* business manager Charles Wills contended that WCFL "had done more to get information out about the union label than all the efforts of the C.F. of L. since its inception." Bakers' Union Local 2 decided to help finance WCFL after the station had assisted in the union's campaign against two recalcitrant baking firms. The Toledo (Ohio) Central Labor Union thanked WCFL in May 1928 for exposing the unfair employment conditions at a local business firm, thereby helping to correct problems there. The Iowa State Council of the Brotherhood of Carpenters and Joiners described the station as a "progressive enterprise" and urged its members "to give WCFL our full cooperation and support."[55]

Praise for WCFL's various entertainment, civic, religious, and labor programs also came from nonunion sources. High school students seeking material for term papers and class speeches turned to the Voice of Labor. Unemployed workers wrote to WCFL seeking advice and job information. Letters came from listeners in Wisconsin and Minnesota and as far away as California. Audience members with no immediate interest in labor developed attachments to the station and sought assistance from it. One woman, who listened to WCFL for several hours every evening, requested WCFL's aid in rectifying a complaint she had concerning a faulty stove and an uncooperative store. Another listener wrote to praise WCFL's "wonderful programs," especially the "clean, educational, and entertaining" discussion shows.[56]

Determining WCFL's overall popularity in 1927–28 remains problematic, laudatory letters notwithstanding. On the one hand, the staff's public claims of audience approval were self-serving. On the other hand, radio surveys and polls that highlighted WCFL's unpopularity obscured as much as they revealed. Early radio audience studies, directed by trade industry magazines, radio stations, or advertising agencies, often used simplistic techniques and sets of criteria defined by the commercial broadcasting industry. The trade journal *Radio Broadcast,* for example, polled its readers—60 percent of whom were radio dealers, engineers, or skilled technicians—in the spring of 1927 asking which stations in their area should be allowed to continue on the air and which ones should be eliminated. Chicago readers named Westinghouse station KYW and *Chicago Tribune* station WGN as the most popular broadcasting outlets and rated WCFL as "wholly unpopular."[57]

Another 1927 survey of Chicago radio assessed radio's usefulness as an advertising medium. Pollsters interviewed one thousand owners of radio sets in the city and found that four stations ranked far ahead of all the others as good advertising vehicles. Although the survey did not specify the winners or losers, WCFL obviously fell into the latter category because, as the study explained, "each leading station appealed to all classes of listeners" through musical and sports programming. By definition, a station with a "class following" could not become a "leading station."[58] A fall 1928 telephone survey of 49,139 Chicago residents conducted by the Great Lakes Broadcasting Company (owner of WENR) identified the city's top stations as WENR, KYW, WGN, WMAQ, WLS, and WBBM. Only 1,068 respondents (2 percent) specified WCFL as their first choice among the twenty-four radio stations in the area.[59] Telephone surveys, however, proved unreliable because a greater percentage of middle- and upper-class homes had telephones than did working-class homes.[60] Audience surveys of the late twenties confirmed what commercial radio stations, networks, and advertisers wanted to believe: The most "popular" radio outlets in Chicago and elsewhere were those with wealthy benefactors, advertising bases, and overwhelmingly entertainment-oriented program schedules.[61]

Nockels paid little attention to commercial radio surveys, yet he remained concerned about the composition of WCFL's audience. Commenting on the letters that the station had received as of the spring of 1928, Nockels declared that "there are more people listening in and writing in, who do not belong to the organized labor movement, than those who belong to unions."[62] Station officials feared that a substantial segment of the labor movement remained ignorant of or, even worse, ambivalent toward the Voice of Labor. CFL leaders launched a campaign to increase worker interest in and support for WCFL during early 1928. *Federation News* articles and editorials lamented organized labor's shortsightedness and its tendency to underfinance "its own ventures." The labor movement needed both WCFL and the national broadcasting system proposed by Nockels because only labor radio could offset the radio trust's "deliberate distortion of facts" and "harmful propaganda." Workers had to "give liberal support to WCFL and respond to the request of financial aid without hesitation."[63] Nockels reminded CFL delegates of radio's potential and of its significance for labor: "Radio is just as important to the lives and welfare of the people as is life insurance or sick benefits."[64]

Labor radio would prove crucial to the welfare of workers and trade unionism if it remained responsive to workers' needs, if it manifested the kind of democratic decision-making that the CFL had always valued. Nockels favored having CFL members form an advisory committee to "tell the [station] directors what they want done and then . . . send out the suggestions for a referendum vote." The CFL conducted a referendum vote on the question of when to schedule the labor talks hour; approximately twenty-nine thousand union members participated.[65] CFL delegates also voted in the spring of 1927 to require a referendum vote among the station's contributors before management took "final action . . . on any proposal affecting WCFL." This requirement came in the wake of Nockels's unilateral offer to donate WCFL to city hall. Local unions, which had voluntarily allocated scarce resources to support labor radio, felt that Nockels should not have the power to make such decisions without consulting them.[66] Later in the year, Nockels asked listeners to express their preference for a continuation of "silent night" in Chicago. Begun in the early twenties, silent night was the policy of suspending local broadcasts for one night so that listeners might pick up stations in other cities (a practice known as "DX-ing"). As network programming expanded in the late twenties, long-distance listening declined and silent nights disappeared. Chicago's commercial radio stations contended that silent night resulted from an agreement among station managers, and thus could be terminated at their discretion, but WCFL considered it a pact between stations and listeners.[67]

To maintain the working relationship among the station, its union patrons, and its audience, Nockels sought to avoid controversy. But free speech and censorship disputes inevitably arose. Among the more embarrassing cases was an uproar over medicine shows. The American Medical Association criticized WCFL in 1928 for "agitating" the air with an assortment of quacks. The head proofreader at the AMA, a member of Chicago Typographical Union Local 16 and a supporter of labor radio, lamented "that the station should be delivered over to quacks and charlatans when there must be so many really scientific and valuable lectures that could readily be obtained." Dr. Percy L. Clark and his Institute of Santology generated the most controversy over WCFL. Dismissing all medicines as "poison" and all medical procedures as unnecessary, Clark offered special diets and Santology oil as a cure for everything from asthma and diabetes to rheumatism and smallpox. In addition to the AMA's formal condemnation of Clark, several trade union delegates pushed for his removal from the airwaves. A member of the Chicago District Diagnosticians' Association denounced Clark's opposition to vaccinations and serums, as well as "the aspersions which he casts upon the entire medical profession." Nockels defended Clark's right to express his opinion over the air and reminded members of the medical fraternity that they could challenge Clark by buying airtime under the same terms as he did. The CFL secretary did concede that Clark should not abuse the courtesy that WCFL extended to him.[68]

Another controversy arose during the winter of 1927–28 when the station sold airtime to two area churches whose preachers used the facilities to denounce labor's demand for a forty-hour work week. Fitzpatrick had warned local unions that keeping WCFL alive might force the CFL to engage in questionable tactics and that the CFL would not be responsible for the views of those who purchased time over the station. At a subsequent CFL meeting, however, delegates insisted that labor radio cancel its contracts with the designated churches and recommended that the CFL appoint an advisory committee to oversee WCFL. Nockels bluntly responded that "if you don't want to hear the sky pilots, turn the little knob." Fitzpatrick, more tactful than his friend, explained that "our farmer friends [say] that their wives greatly appreciate in general what the preachers broadcast." Oscar Nelson asserted that the effort to remove the preachers was a communist-inspired "attack on church use of the radio." Despite their defense of free speech and a promise to debate the forty-hour-week issue with the clerical critics, WCFL officials canceled a contract with one of the offending churches in mid-February.[69]

A series of talks by the president of the Public Ownership League of America, Carl D. Thompson, generated another free speech debate in the fall of 1927. Criticizing the city administration's policies regarding municipal ownership of local transportation companies, Thompson outraged Chicago mayor William Thompson, who called the station to complain. Carl Thompson's comments also annoyed transport union officials who were negotiating with the city traction companies. A secret alliance between union leaders and utility king Samuel Insull made the former sensitive to criticisms of the status quo and wary of proposals for public ownership of the transport system. The unions asked Nockels to halt Thompson's radio attacks temporarily. When Thompson refused to tone down his commentary, Nockels discontinued the talks. Shocked by Nockels's unusual action, Thompson charged that there was "somebody behind it."[70] At a subsequent CFL meeting, delegates accused Nockels of acting at the request of the mayor. Nockels angrily responded that the streetcarmen's union had requested a halt to the program during wage negotiations and before the incident with the mayor. "No one controls this station," asserted Nockels, "except the unions who contribute to its support."[71]

A cynical delegate dismissed WCFL's rhetoric regarding free speech over the air as spurious and asked whether the CFL leadership would allow a communist to speak over the station. Fitzpatrick answered that WCFL "is open to communists just as it is open to everyone." Any worker, no matter how affiliated, having "something to say that furthers the labor movement and Americanism, can say it over WCFL."[72] It was unlikely that CFL officials, many of whom blamed communist machinations for undermining the labor party movement earlier in the decade, would accept the possibility that a communist's message might benefit either labor or the nation. Indeed, just weeks earlier the executive board, in a report on the station's defense of Sacco and Vanzetti, warned against using WCFL for communistic propaganda. The principle of free speech was not absolute, but open to interpretation by rank-and-file workers and WCFL officers. Nockels nevertheless remained committed to adhering to a certain level of participatory democracy in the federation and the radio station. Conceding that contributing unions controlled WCFL, he insisted that "any controversy regarding the use of the station by a speaker was up to the discretion of such locals, and could be settled by a referendum vote."[73] Free speech controversies weakened WCFL efforts to widen its audience and to secure the funding necessary to carry out station operations.

WCFL faced two financial problems throughout this early period: Funding "normal" station operations, which escalated with the growing competition of radio networks, and providing for Nockels's grandiose plans for labor radio. Although Nockels wanted an alternative to commercial radio, he modeled labor radio on the structure of the corporate system. He wished WCFL to become "big" and "powerful"; to reach all across the nation via enhanced power, a clear channel, and shortwave relay stations; and to offer listeners high-quality programming with top-notch talent. The financial demands for such an operation clearly would surpass the meager revenues of WCFL.[74]

Transforming WCFL into "one of the finest super-power" radio stations in the nation required FRC authorization to increase power to fifty thousand watts and the acquisition of requisite equipment and facilities. Nockels believed that achieving the latter objective would facilitate securing the former. In the spring of 1928, he launched a campaign to fund and construct a new studio and transmitter. The FRC had ruled that WCFL could not increase its power until it situated its transmitter at least twenty miles outside of Chicago. John G. Clay's Laundry and Dye House Drivers' Union Local 712 loaned the CFL approximately forty-eight thousand dollars in 1928 to help purchase one hundred acres of land near Downers Grove, Illinois, some twenty-two miles west of Chicago. Nockels planned to reserve twenty acres of the purchase for the new broadcasting station and to subdivide and sell the remaining eighty acres as home building lots. The net proceeds, Nockels hoped, would finance the construction of the new station. Fulfilling the dream of a national radio station inexorably drew the CFL further into the world of "labor capitalism." Chicago labor began selling real estate in order to finance a radio station that would compete successfully with corporate broadcasters.[75]

A more immediate problem than funding the future expansion of WCFL was meeting the daily station expenses of equipment maintenance, program production, and talent. These costs grew steadily during 1927–28. WCFL spent approximately $2,044 in wages for its artists in December 1927, but during the first six months of 1928 the average monthly expenditure on radio talent was $2,437. Rapidly expanding radio networks—NBC and CBS—with their vast financial resources, technical capabilities, and talent pools overwhelmed WCFL and exacerbated its precarious financial position. WCFL's operating deficit at the end of 1926 was $5,127; in December 1927 it totaled $7,510.85.[76]

The initial funding scheme for WCFL called for CFL-affiliated unions and other interested labor, farmer, cooperative, and public interest groups to assess each of their members one dollar per year for two years. Nockels hoped that these one-time voluntary assessments would pay for the construction of the station and create an endowment to cover present and future operating expenses. During 1927–28, approximately 150 local unions paid quarterly radio assessments, including $419.00 from Bakery Drivers' Union Local 734, $15.00 from Broom and Whisk Makers' Local 29 and $60.00 from Building Service Employees' Union Local 19. Two nonaffiliated unions had donated the largest single, lump-sum amounts in 1926: $16,000 from the Bricklayers and $10,000 from the ACWA. Smaller quantities trickled in from area trades and labor assemblies and sympathetic individuals. The Union Motor Club, a group of union workers and car owners, promised to donate $.50 for each fully paid member enrolled in the club between June 1927 and June 1928. Although Nockels and other Chicago labor leaders appreciated these contributions, they realized that only 30–33 percent of the CFL's membership had agreed to the assessment and that, over time, these payments declined. In June 1927, voluntary assessments from unions brought in $9,020.25; from mid-October to mid-November 1928, they totaled only $3,932.00. Nockels admitted to AFL officials that while WCFL took in $152,938.02 during the fiscal year ending on October 15, 1928, "less than $40,000 was contributed by local unions." During its first year of operation, over 90 percent of WCFL's income came from trade union contributions, but by the end of 1928, less than 30 percent did so.[77]

CFL leaders continually urged union support for WCFL, arguing that commercial broadcasters discriminated against working-class organizations. Even when labor or progressive groups gained access to the air, networks and local stations retained the power to censor what these groups had to say. WJZ, lead station in the NBC Blue network, for example, abruptly cut off a speech by Victor Berger in April 1927. Just as the Socialist leader charged that capitalists controlled American politics, education, and broadcasting, WJZ technicians literally removed his microphone and switched to a church service. The station denied charges of censorship, claiming that Berger's program had exceeded its designated time limit. In Paterson, New Jersey, the owner of WODA objected to the "communistic" tone of a local typographical union speaker and "pulled the switch" on the talk.[78]

Such incidents made John Fitzpatrick wonder why state federations and the AFL "are all sitting back and not making a move to take advantage of" labor radio. Admonishing two-thirds of Chicago's unions for failing to do their fair share, he contended that if all the locals paid their assessments, "we would have little or no trouble in maintaining the labor station."[79] Union leader Redcliffe reiterated these sentiments, arguing that WCFL's "unlimited benefit" to organized labor "should be sufficient cause for all the Local Unions to come to the material and financial assistance of the Station." WCFL was "in danger of being silenced, curtailed, or commercialized," warned Redcliffe, "because Locals fail in their duty to support the project, and to pay a voluntary assessment."[80]

CFL leaders often alluded to the parsimony of trade unions. In discussing the possibility of creating a national chain of labor owned and controlled movie theaters across the nation and of producing pro-labor films, the editor of the *Federation News* cautioned that such an ambitious and desirable educational project could succeed only with generous union aid. "Labor's unpardonably rotten support of the labor press throughout the country and its absolute tightwadedness in so far as the first labor radio station (WCFL) is concerned, is not at all encouraging."[81] Nockels and Fitzpatrick also referred to the inability of trade union leaders "to see beyond their own noses" and to finance adequately vital labor activities. "Capital views [labor's] strange and almost suicidal apathy and foolhardy closefistedness with some glee," concluded the *Federation News.* The CFL repeatedly emphasized the immeasurable publicity value of the labor press and radio and insisted that spending money on WCFL was an investment in the labor movement itself.[82]

Untouched by these pleas, a majority of Chicago-area trade unions remained ambivalent toward labor radio. Unions that helped finance WCFL usually declared their reasons for doing so, but those unions that chose not to assist the station rarely offered a public explanation. The weak economic and political position of much of organized labor during the late twenties certainly exacerbated the poor financial health of local unions, making the allocation of scarce resources to labor radio appear a luxury. CFL accusations that some local labor organizations lacked imagination and foresight regarding radio also contained a germ of truth. Although Nockels and other station staff had tried to educate the labor community regarding the operation and purpose of labor radio, certain labor groups continued to perceive WCFL solely as a propaganda vehicle or electronic bulletin board. Whatever the reasons, labor's relatively weak support for WCFL forced Nockels and his colleagues to find supplementary funding sources.

A long-standing desire on the part of the CFL for a labor-farmer alliance suggested another revenue source. Labor and agricultural leaders often referred to the division between the country's "producers"—workers and farmers—and the nation's "exploiters"—bankers and industrialists. Although the Farmer-Labor party of the early twenties had disintegrated, CFL leaders hoped for a revival of cooperation between the two groups.[83] Radio seemed a likely point of agreement because farming organizations, like labor unions, feared a broadcasting system dominated by corporate capitalists. Few radio stations had developed in rural areas and many farmers felt that the programming of centralized radio networks, originating as it did in metropolitan centers, would constitute a "form of urban cultural imperialism." Nockels understood the farmers' need for radio service and believed that WCFL could fulfill that need, while simultaneously linking together rural and urban interests. WCFL thus placed the "Farmers' and Co-Operators' Night" after the CFL's own program on Wednesday evenings. Labor radio also regularly covered market, weather, and crop conditions; aired government reports and statistics on agriculture, horticulture, and livestock; and presented occasional talks on subjects of special interest to farmers. Iowa senator Smith W. Brookhart, for example, occasionally spoke over WCFL on the need for farmer-labor cooperation.[84]

WCFL began discussions with Wisconsin, Iowa, Indiana, and Illinois farm organizations in the winter of 1927. Business manager Lundquist and CFL delegate Johannsen described plans to establish a labor super station to an executive board meeting of the Farmers' Union of Iowa. The board appeared interested in the project, agreeing to pay the voluntary assessment if the superpower station ever materialized.[85] In July 1928, the FRC rejected the Iowa group's efforts to purchase its own broadcasting outlet. According to farm union president Milo Reno, Commissioner Sam Pickard explained that if the farmers made an arrangement with the CFL, the FRC would grant WCFL super-station status with a clear wavelength and approval to use fifty thousand watts of power.[86] Soon thereafter, the Farmers' Union of Iowa signed a contract with WCFL, agreeing to assess its sixteen thousand members one dollar per member for three years in return for a voice in WCFL's operation and the station's quarterly radio magazine. The farm union also promised to raise the issue of WCFL before the National Convention of Farmers' Organizations scheduled to meet in Denver. With a combined membership of eighty-seven thousand, a commitment by this body would strengthen labor radio's financial fortunes. The prospect of a farmer-labor coalition on labor radio and an array of other issues excited both Nockels and Fitzpatrick.[87] But it also highlighted the disappointing support that WCFL received from the labor movement. Using the deal with the Iowa farmers to prod local labor to action, Nockels warned that without a more enthusiastic trade union response to WCFL, "I am afraid the farmers will have more affiliations with this station than the labor organizations."[88]

As he developed a strategy for bringing farmer groups into WCFL, Nockels conceived of a radio magazine that would provide timely articles on radio issues and help to link WCFL listeners' associations. In the fall of 1927, Nockels announced the publication of *WCFL Radio Magazine,* a quarterly periodical with a yearly subscription price of $1.25. During its first years the magazine operated at a deficit, but by 1929 it generated a small income (approximately $5,600) for the station.[89]

A richer source of revenue for WCFL came from the annual Radio Frolics and Labor Day celebrations. The first Radio Frolics, held at the end of 1926, raised $2,069.38 for the station. Nockels decided that holding an annual event would generate income for WCFL and provide an opportunity for the labor community to socialize. Musicians, singers, comedians, and actors from WCFL and Chicago area theaters donated their time and talent. Those paying the $1.00 admission price in December 1927 enjoyed a "hot jazz band and a waltz and two-step orchestra," listened to speeches, and competed for free radio sets. Widely publicized in the federation's newspaper, as well as on WCFL, the Frolics drew several thousand people in 1927 and 1928. The 1927 event contributed $4,392.98 to station operations. Tickets to the Labor Day celebrations in Soldier Field also contributed to WCFL's coffer.[90]

WCFL developed two other major income sources during 1927–28. Rental income—derived from outside use of WCFL equipment and studios—made up about 13 percent of the station's total revenue during the first half of 1928. More important was income derived from advertising and commercially sponsored programming. This type of financing presented fundamental problems that Nockels recognized and understood from the outset. The more dependent the station became on "selling time," the more it would need to attract large audiences by developing entertainment programming and scheduling it in desirable time periods. Increases in commercial programming inevitably would decrease the time available for labor shows. While aware of this dilemma, Nockels nonetheless watched as sponsored programs and advertising revenue became increasingly important for WCFL's survival. In June 1927, the station reported earning only $375.40 from advertising; but during the first half of 1928, WCFL brought in, on average, $3,236.44 per month in advertising revenue (or about 30 percent of total monthly income). Major sponsors included radio equipment manufacturers and distributors, "medical" practitioners, finance companies, department stores, groceries, jewelers, heating companies, cleaners, and laboratories. Even as WCFL's reliance on advertising grew, Nockels hoped to ameliorate its impact by securing more labor input.[91]

Existing problems notwithstanding, CFL leaders remained optimistic about labor radio's future in the summer of 1928. They hoped to shape program concepts and messages that would assist organized labor and expand the station's audience. But as they explored new ways in which WCFL could spread its message to the American public, government and corporate radio bureaucrats developed a frequency allocation scheme that endangered the Voice of Labor.

. . .

During 1927 and 1928, the commissioners and staff of the FRC worked at establishing a national radio system based on the vague test of "public interest, convenience, and necessity." With the assistance and encouragement of commercial radio groups such as the National Association of Broadcasters, the FRC reasoned that the public interest required the most economical, efficient, and full use of the limited available frequencies. The public interest also demanded that radio serve the "general public" rather than "special interests." Adequately financed broadcasting stations, endowed with advanced technology and the skilled staff to use it, provided continuous service and thus passed the public interest test. These same stations, owned and operated by large business organs, sold airtime and developed programs aimed at the largest possible audience. Thus the FRC concluded that large commercial stations best served the public. Religious organs, civic groups, educators, and trade unions, on the other hand, constituted special interests. Radio stations under their direction served small, select audiences and suffered from underfinanced and poorly equipped facilities and personnel. In its reallocation scheme presented in the fall of 1928, the FRC rewarded commercial stations with clear wavelengths, unlimited time, and high power.[92]

On August 30, 1928, the FRC issued General Order No. 40, designed to solve interference problems. The order classified all ninety-six available frequencies, between 550 and 1,500 kilocycle, into four categories. One category set aside six channels, each 10 kilocycles wide, for Canadian use. Another set aside forty clear stations—eight in each of five radio zones—with power ranging from five thousand to fifty thousand watts. Another thirty-five channels, seven per zone, became regional stations. Situated between one thousand and fifteen hundred miles apart, these stations had less than one thousand watts of power. The remaining fifteen channels, three per zone, went to low-power (one-hundred- to five-thousand-watt) local stations. Reallocation meant a bonanza for the nation's commercial stations because they received all the clear channels and the bulk of the regional frequencies.[93]

The new allocation shifted WCFL to a 970 kilocycle wavelength and reduced its power to one thousand watts. WCFL shared its new channel with station KJR in Seattle, Washington. The FRC required that the Voice of Labor cease broadcasting at sundown on the Pacific coast so as not to interfere with KJR. WCFL thus halted programming during the evening hours when its target audience of working people was most likely to listen to radio. For the next thirty months, Nockels and the CFL waged a battle against the FRC's reallocation scheme. At FRC hearings, in Congress, and in court, WCFL representatives accused the FRC of conspiring with the radio trust to silence labor's concerns.[94]

Nockels set the tone for WCFL's campaign at a CFL meeting in early October 1928. "Labor does not seek special privileges," he argued, "but it does ask for the same consideration that others get." When the FRC placed WCFL on the 620 kilocycle frequency and reduced the station to fifteen hundred watts in May 1927, labor did not object because "other stations were being treated in the same manner." WCFL recognized the need for reallocations to alleviate the interference problems, but it hoped that there would be equal treatment for all stations. Nockels believed that FRC members had promised to give WCFL a clear channel and maximum power. Instead, WCFL received less time and less power, limiting the station's ability to reach beyond a radius of one hundred miles and depreciating labor's investment in radio.[95] The FRC's favorable frequency, time, and power decisions regarding "the corporation-owned stations, power trust stations, and newspaper trust stations" constituted a "deliberate conspiracy" to eliminate WCFL from the ether. Reporting to the CFL executive board in December, Nockels explained that the FRC appeared "to be falling in line with these vested interests" by eliminating WCFL and other stations and giving the clear-channel stations a monopoly of the air.[96]

Nockels charged the FRC's general counsel and a key figure in the reallocation scheme, Louis G. Caldwell, with a conflict of interest. Immediately before and after the reallocation decision, Caldwell served as a member of the *Chicago Tribune*'s law firm. *Tribune* radio station WGN received one of the forty clear channels as did Westinghouse station KYW (leased by the Hearst newspaper chain) and WMAQ owned by the *Chicago Daily News*. Chicago's only three clear, unlimited channels thus went to major newspapers. Because those journalistic enterprises represented the dominant ideology of corporate capitalism, Nockels could find "no reason on earth" why these papers "and all the papers in the country should [not] be on one channel."[97]

WCFL officials warned of a movement toward a communications monopoly in the country, pointing to the already close links between the telegraph, telephone, and cable monopolies and the growing press trust. In a letter sent to all members of Congress in January 1929, Nockels and Fitzpatrick described how the radio trust, with combined assets of $3 billion and control over important radio patents, owned and operated eleven stations with an aggregate power of 220,000 watts. More importantly, the trust held exclusive use of seven of the forty clear channels. Public utility, insurance, and various manufacturing and merchandising companies owned and operated another twenty-two clear stations. By denying organized labor the right to secure one clear channel with adequate power and time, the FRC, according to Nockels and Fitzpatrick, had demonstrated its "crass disregard and contempt" for American workers.[98]

The CFL, unlike the AFL, never accepted industry and government arguments that private commercial stations would provide the labor movement with better broadcasting services than a labor owned and operated outlet. Local union officials responded that workers and farmers did not have free and equal access to the commercial press and radio. Inhibiting WCFL's operations thus constituted, according to one union officer, a "grim and insidious danger" to workers' "economic, social and domestic liberty."[99]

Soon after the reallocation announcement, Nockels launched a campaign to rectify WCFL's poor position. This campaign included demands for a clear channel, at least twenty-five thousand watts of power, unlimited time, and two shortwave channels, to facilitate day and night relay broadcasting services. Nockels revived his plan to broadcast WCFL programs to a series of small local stations that would rebroadcast the programs to their communities "without paying tribute to the long distance telephone wires." The exorbitant costs of using AT&T's wires, argued Nockels, made nationwide broadcasting "too expensive for any organization that is not heavily capitalized and is able to handle a lot of advertising."[100]

Sharing the 970 kilocycle frequency with Seattle's KJR, with the consequent loss of prime broadcast hours, forced WCFL to seek another wavelength. Commenting on his strategy years later, Nockels admitted that "in order to get a hearing [before the FRC] WCFL was compelled to enter . . . a law suit against some one designated Station in Chicago, and . . . to show by a preponderance of evidence" that WCFL better met the public interest test than the targeted station. In November 1928, he petitioned the FRC for unlimited time on the relatively clear channel of 770 kilocycles—a wavelength then occupied by Chicago station WBBM. Nockels submitted a complicated plan to shift WBBM, a CBS affiliate, to another frequency and to move or eliminate other stations in order to accommodate WCFL's needs. By juxtaposing WBBM's profit orientation with WCFL's commitment to serve the public interest, CFL officials hoped to win approval for their application.[101] While petitioning the FRC for time, channel, and power changes, WCFL planned to lobby Congress to alter the administrative policy of a supposedly independent commission.

Securing national legislation required far more political clout than the CFL possessed; it necessitated the input of the AFL. Fearing that the FRC reallocation scheme and the growing power of corporate radio meant the death of labor radio, Nockels intensified his efforts to secure an AFL commitment to WCFL. Until 1928, however, the AFL Executive Council had extended only rhetorical backing to the CFL's radio enterprise. Nockels offered to "appoint this Radio Station as [the AFL's] official broadcasting station" at the end of 1926 and again in 1927 and 1928, but the AFL Executive Council refused to lend its name to the project. The CFL invited all national and international union leaders to speak over WCFL when they visited Chicago, but only a handful took advantage of the offer.[102] At the AFL convention in 1927, delegates from Chicago proposed that all affiliated unions establish a "radio fund" that would be "maintained by 25 cents per member per quarter" and would be used by the unions to finance "a chain of broadcasting radio stations." The fund obviously could have supported WCFL's operations. The Committee on Resolutions, however, struck out the proposal, agreeing only to authorize the Executive Council to reexamine the issue of labor broadcasting. CFL representative Anton Johannsen asked the same convention to "commend the *WCFL Radio Magazine* for subscription to all those interested in radio." The Committee on Resolutions sent the resolution to the Executive Council for further study—where another possible financial boost to WCFL died.[103]

AFL suspicion of the CFL and labor radio reflected the national organ's preoccupation with creating an image for itself as a cooperative institution and thereby gaining admittance to the policy-making councils of government and business. The leadership of the AFL sought to secure economic benefits for organized labor by playing the mass media game with its corporate- and state-formulated rules. Any trade union action that might smear the image of a respectable, responsible cooperative labor movement immediately came under AFL scrutiny. Prior to 1924, the CFL leadership had held a distinctly class-based critique of corporate capitalism linked to local labor and ethnic communities.[104] This class-based analysis suffered severe setbacks during the early twenties, but it never entirely died. Nockels retained some of this analysis in his efforts to build WCFL, and AFL officials consequently maintained a wary eye on WCFL's challenge to commercial radio.

Preoccupied with WCFL's survival and recognizing the importance of securing AFL backing for a fight in Congress and the FRC, Nockels embraced a risky strategy. Appearing before the AFL Executive Council in

October 1928, he explained his desire to "indicate to [the] Radio Commission that the [labor radio] project has the hearty support of the" AFL and its affiliated unions. He offered the AFL yet another chance to participate in WCFL. The Executive Council agreed to read a report by WCFL attorney Hope Thompson on the history of WCFL and "to inquire into the trusteeship of WCFL and what property right if any the American Federation of Labor has in it."[105] Acting on these positive overtures, Nockels offered the AFL an "equitable interest" in all of WCFL's properties and property rights. He promised that even if the CFL's charter lapsed or the AFL withdrew the charter, title to all station property rights would automatically transfer to the AFL. In exchange, Nockels expected the council to join the battle against the FRC and the radio trust. Nockels hoped to identify WCFL as a part of the AFL and himself as the AFL's legislative representative on broadcasting issues. Such designations might enhance labor radio's case before Washington authorities. Vice President Matthew Woll found the proposal quite proper "in view of the further support sought to increase the service and values of these properties and enterprises." The Executive Council authorized further investigation of the situation and requested additional information about WCFL.[106]

Nockels replied to Woll's inquiry with characteristic bluntness:

> [The CFL] is willing at any time to turn over the entire Station and all of its property, wave length, equity, etc. to the American Federation of Labor, if that body wishes to take ownership, management and control of the Station. If not, then we are willing to have the AFL supervise, or censor, or appoint representatives to participate in the management, . . . or, in fact, to do anything that in its judgment will further the interest of organized labor in the perpetuation and use of this Station. . . . We are entirely willing to submerge our identity and to have this Station made the Station of the AFL.[107]

Having thus prostrated himself before the AFL hierarchy, Nockels asked that the entire organized labor movement publicly and materially support WCFL's demands. Appropriate AFL action would make WCFL "one of the most powerful instruments for publicity, education, entertainment and for offensive and defensive propaganda that it is possible for the human mind to conceive."[108]

It remains unclear to what extent AFL officials bought Nockels's hyperbole. The CFL's willingness to share the potential economic and political rewards of the radio station with the AFL attracted some AFL oligarchs to the cause. But Woll and others continued to worry about CFL radicalism and the financial complications of getting involved with labor radio. If the AFL took equity in the radio station and if something happened that forced the revocation of the CFL charter, who would get the radio station properties? Woll believed that "the local unions would have prior claim" to those assets. William Green, fearing that "there might be difficulty in securing control on account of the protest of affiliated unions," remained convinced that the federation should avoid the "tremendous obligation" of ownership. The Executive Council finally decided that Woll should continue investigating the possibility of AFL participation in the ownership of labor radio, but with the understanding that the AFL "may exercise censorship supervision of the programs that are broadcast from WCFL."[109]

At the same time, AFL leaders realized that they had little choice but to defend WCFL and protect the labor movement from outside attack. The union hierarchy continued to question the viability of a labor owned and operated radio station, but it asserted labor's right to have the option to create and maintain such a station. At the 1928 convention, the Executive Council formally opposed "any movement which will tend to weaken our position in this field." Council members recommended that affiliated unions assist WCFL in its fight against the FRC and, in the event these efforts failed, that "steps be taken to bring the entire matter to the attention of the Congress." In using whatever influence it might have in Congress, and in urging affiliated unions to support WCFL's petitions in the FRC, the AFL protected the name of the organized labor movement. In return for these favors, WCFL had to promise "to adhere strictly to the principles and policies" of the AFL.[110]

William Green's commitment to an independent labor radio system went only as far as his collaborationist ideology would take him. AFL leaders acknowledged that the FRC's reallocation scheme discriminated against WCFL and favored commercial interests. They also admitted that radio as a field of publicity might fall under the control of a few corporations "which will then be able to dictate what may or may not be broadcast." But the AFL hierarchy maintained that labor's legitimate place in broadcasting "will not be denied by intelligent, public-spirited citizens." The growth of vast nationwide radio networks—which Nockels feared as part of a radio monopoly—could serve organized labor's cause. AFL officials still urged trade unions to secure airtime via established commercial stations. Green firmly believed that, as in other fields of the political economy, labor would participate equally and harmoniously with capital in the development of broadcasting.[111] Indeed, Green had already taken steps in this direction before the fall of 1928.

In February 1927, Green became a member of the Advisory Council of the National Broadcasting Company. A creation of RCA head Owen D. Young, the advisory council included prominent educators, corporate officials, religious figures, and a women's club president. Ostensibly designed to monitor and evaluate NBC programming, the council never heard a complaint from a single listener or criticized any network policy. The council's annual meetings did offer Green an opportunity to rub elbows with state and corporate luminaries such as Elihu Root, Charles Evans Hughes, and Dwight W. Murrow. Thus Green vicariously participated in radio broadcasting policy making. Green told the AFL Executive Council in the fall of 1928 that his only duties were "to express views as to what would make broadcasting more pleasing." Each year the council met to praise "the notable" achievements of NBC and each year Green profusely thanked NBC for the best music and entertainment and for allowing AFL officers to broadcast Labor Day addresses. Indeed, the AFL chief believed that his association with the council helped to make NBC's facilities available to labor.[112] Green preferred this cordial relationship with the dominant media over Nockels's confrontational approach.

• • •

The CFL had struggled from 1925 through 1928 to create and maintain a labor radio station in a hostile environment. By controlling radio technology, corporations eventually turned broadcasting into a profit-making venture. These same firms assumed the role of "custodians" of the air, "presenting themselves as acting out of benevolent, farsighted paternalism." The state, through legislative action and executive manipulation, determined that it had the power to resolve disputes in the electromagnetic spectrum; and it inevitably gave "preferential treatment toward the technologically most powerful (and richest) commercial stations," while "marginaliz[ing] . . . smaller, noncommercial stations."[113] The results were a radio industry and state regulatory agency that defined public interest, convenience, and necessity in terms of private property rights and profits and that had little interest in ensuring equal access to radio facilities for varying views and opinions.

WCFL emerged within this developing system as a self-proclaimed nonprofit, listener-supported station, dedicated to serving the interests of workers and their communities. It struggled in this environment to produce programming that would both entertain and enlighten its working-class audience; to maintain, as much as possible, a democratic decision-making structure; and to secure independent sources of financing. But FRC Order No. 40 in the fall of 1928 posed a major challenge to the Voice of Labor. Nockels had long warned organized labor of what the corporate broadcasting structure might do. The stakes, according to Nockels, were immense because the enemies of organized labor better understood the importance of labor radio than labor itself. As early as December 1927 Nockels noted:

> I know that Labor is much more respected than it ever has been before. I know that you don't hear over the air as much propaganda against labor by the other side as you did before we had our own radio station, because of the knowledge that we have the means of making reply. . . . We reach people who can't read, or who can't see and we get our message across, it is wonderful. This is a radio age. For less than one-half of one per cent of what it would cost to establish newspapers throughout the land, we are reaching people and telling them about organized labor. . . . There is nothing more important to the welfare and the happiness of the labor movement in this age than radio.[114]

THREE

Clear-Channel and Other Battles, 1929–32

The promulgation of Federal Radio Commission General Order No. 40 produced an intense conflict between the formidable corporate broadcasting world and its challengers. On one side congregated the national radio chains (NBC and CBS) and their affiliates, advertising agencies, independent commercial stations, and the FRC; and on the other side stood the "displaced and disadvantaged nonprofit broadcasters."[1] WCFL and the CFL became important combatants in this struggle, loosely aligned with the religious, agricultural, and educational organizations that also opposed the emerging corporate order. Echoing Edward Nockels's critique of the radio trust, officials of the Association of College and University Broadcasting Stations (predecessor to the National Association of Educational Broadcasters) condemned high-powered commercial station monopolization of the forty clear channels. These radio educators shared WCFL's assessment that FRC rulings and regulations created an environment conducive for corporate domination in the ether. They held that only independent educational stations, like independent labor stations, offered a bulwark against corporate radio's voracious appetite for profits, its incessant advertising, its endless entertainment programming, its insidious consumer propaganda, and its implicit and explicit censorship.[2]

WCFL's battle for a clear channel, full time, and maximum power took place within this larger war over the future of American broadcasting. But while labor radio shared with nonprofit broadcasters a common assessment of the corporate radio industry, WCFL officials kept the needs and goals of organized labor in the forefront of their thinking. Nockels believed it crucial that workers and their organizations have guaranteed access to the nation's airwaves. Thus he challenged the FRC's allocation scheme in Congress and the courts, demanding a clear channel—the one used by Chicago station WBBM—for WCFL. At the same time, Nockels and his radio staff tried to develop programming that would serve Chicago workers and their families and the organized labor movement. The next chapter details the evolution of WCFL programming and financing between 1929 and 1932. This chapter explores the national political and economic struggle for labor radio.

• • •

Under Nockels's direction, organized labor initiated a two-front war against the FRC in early 1929. In Congress, CFL and AFL representatives lobbied for legislative action to ameliorate WCFL's situation. WCFL attorney Hope Thompson told a House committee in January that the radio trust did not deserve "all the cream" of broadcasting frequencies. When the FRC granted clear channels to high-power stations owned by an exclusive group of firms or individuals, argued Thompson, it helped to create a monopoly. To remedy this situation, the FRC had to provide a clear channel and full time to WCFL. Thompson explained that although the CFL owned the station, WCFL received support from the "entire labor movement" of the nation and that the AFL ultimately controlled the operation.[3]

Senators and representatives from Illinois and surrounding states heard similar arguments from their constituents. At the request of Nockels and John Fitzpatrick, midwestern labor and farm groups sent delegations to Washington to testify on WCFL's behalf, wrote to their representatives to protest FRC decisions, or passed resolutions supporting WCFL. Also at Nockels's request, trade unions and private citizens across the nation sent telegrams and letters to Congress praising WCFL's service to labor communities, criticizing the greedy radio trust, and lamenting how the FRC denied a "square deal" to organized labor. These grass-roots messages argued that WCFL was "entitled" to the same advantages the FRC bestowed on stations owned by corporations, newspapers, and utilities.[4] CFL and AFL pressure on the legislative branch produced some results. As the *New York Times* reported in late January 1929, several legislators "took up the cudgels" for WCFL and promised to act on the matter if the FRC remained intransigent.[5]

Nockels launched the second front of his campaign against the FRC in

April 1929. With formal FRC hearings on WCFL's frequency requests scheduled for midmonth, Nockels appealed for help from city central labor bodies across the nation. The CFL secretary asked that each organ send its own fifty-word telegram to the FRC demanding that the commission grant WCFL an exclusive clear channel of 770 kilocycles, unlimited time, a boost in power, and two shortwave frequencies.[6] Attending various labor conventions, such as that of the National Women's Trade Union League of America, Nockels argued that WCFL belonged not to the CFL but to the entire labor movement. Radio's great potential for the "future welfare and education of the people" required the dismantling of corporate capital's control over the medium; this necessitated a strong WCFL and assistance from the labor movement. Rose Schneiderman, president of the Women's Trade Union League, assured Nockels that the convention would consider his request, which it did by passing a resolution condemning the FRC and endorsing the cause of labor radio.[7] With the moral backing of the WTUL and other labor bodies, Thompson opened the case for WCFL before the FRC.

Thompson told the commissioners that shifting WCFL's frequency to WBBM's frequency would diversify radio programming. While acknowledging the quality of WBBM's popular shows, Thompson expressed "little patience with the theory that radio is to be just for entertainment." He insisted that WCFL would refuse a license if forced to air only musical programs and denied the right to explain the aims of organized labor. FRC chairman Ira Robinson, a former judge, rejected WCFL's assessment that commercial broadcasters, directly or indirectly, propagandized capitalist values and goals through entertainment shows and advertisements. Obfuscating the issue, he declared that if labor bodies broadcasted direct propaganda, then capital should receive the same privilege. When the chairman suggested that a scarcity of available shortwave frequencies made the CFL's strategy for a labor broadcasting chain unworkable, Thompson reminded Robinson that WCFL had requested such frequencies as early as 1927. "Robinson looked very anxious," described one reporter, because the FRC had "been giving away short waves during the past two years" to AT&T and other radio trust members. AT&T, of course, had a vested interest in preventing the development of wireless telephony and the linking of radio stations without wires. Thompson threatened to challenge AT&T's "possession of this privilege as a violation of the Radio Act" and to force it to surrender some of its "loot." As to the question of trade union access to commercial radio, Robinson suggested that "when Congress stamped the spectrum as belonging to the public," it created a licensing system that guaranteed private ownership of stations in addition to public access. But the WCFL attorney felt confident that the present law did not require station owners to satisfy all access demands. Moreover, the lack of rate regulation meant that stations could make the cost of access to their facilities "prohibitive." Robinson predicted that, over time, judicial action would resolve these problems. Labor officials wanted a clear-channel station in the interim.[8]

Approximately seventy-five labor officials joined technical experts to support WCFL's case before the FRC. Keeping its word to endorse the WCFL petition, the AFL sent representatives to testify at the hearings. Secretary Frank Morrison, Vice President Matthew Woll, and President William Green told the commissioners that the labor movement had as much right to own a radio station as did corporate interests. *Labor* editor Edward Keating explained that the commercial media approached "all industrial problems from the viewpoint of the employer of labor," thus ignoring the views of 90 percent of the American public. Selma Borchardt, vice president of the American Federation of Teachers, refuted the FRC's view of labor as a special interest: "Labor is not a special interest, but a special approach to the general interest."[9] Morrison reassured the commission that the AFL was not a radical working-class organization and that its brand of trade unionism meant "industrial cooperation and understanding," not industrial strife. WCFL, as an AFL affiliate, would broadcast responsible programs.[10] Neither the conciliatory statements of Morrison, Woll, and Green nor the sharp criticisms of Keating and Borchardt could offset the commercial radio campaign against WCFL.

The two stations most affected by the WCFL proposal—WBBM in Chicago and KFAB in Lincoln, Nebraska—condemned WCFL's service to labor, while praising their own service to "the great listening public." Both stations portrayed WCFL's current programs as inadequate at best, and inappropriate and offensive at worst. Ralph Atlass, one of the owners of WBBM, hired an agency to transcribe several days of WCFL programming and entered hundreds of pages of these transcriptions into the official record of the hearings. WBBM argued that on one broadcast day, WCFL gave labor only 66 minutes of airtime, but provided quacks and patent medicine shows with 81 minutes and advertising, in general, with 583 minutes. Thompson dismissed this information as misleading, noting that the sample day was atypical and that WCFL had its own extensive file on programming. He pointed out that commercial stations damned WCFL both for broadcasting labor propaganda and for not broadcasting labor programs.[11]

Supporters of organized labor who observed the FRC hearings disagreed on how the FRC would rule. Laurence Todd, a correspondent and columnist for the Federated Press Service, saw no legal or other reason why the FRC would refuse WCFL's request. "Refusal would not only be difficult to explain," wrote Todd, but it would arouse national protest and would produce a federal court battle. He predicted a favorable decision that would lead, within a few months, to WCFL "broadcasting serious discussions of the people's struggle for bread, in competition with jazz and stock market quotations."[12] Chicago unionist Ben F. Ferris, on the other hand, recalled that he walked away from the hearings convinced "that there was a conspiracy to keep WCFL from getting what it asked."[13] Such pessimism reflected a troublesome aspect of the hearings.

FRC staff members, representatives of the corporate radio industry, and even leaders of the AFL struggled to make it appear as if their positions reflected honest differences of opinion within a generally harmonious structure. The hearings, however, revealed a power conflict between labor and capital over broadcasting. KFAB's attorney staked out the position of the owners of radio when he argued that the FRC should evaluate a radio station not based on the "personal, financial or private interests of those who send" out the programming—that is, the producers—but on "the welfare of those who receive it"—the consumers. Hope Thompson reversed the equation, contending that the FRC should concentrate on the owners of the means of radio production, on those who had the power to determine the limited choices available to the listening (consuming) public. While KFAB and WBBM highlighted the "classless" character of their audience, WCFL emphasized the class character of the overwhelming majority of radio stations in the nation—owned and operated by corporations or individuals seeking profit.[14]

WCFL's potential to become a propaganda and organizing vehicle for the working class made it dangerous. It was one thing to have a commercial radio station that presented the usual music, drama, and comedy and offered limited time to trade unions. It was an entirely different situation, as the Federated Press reporter Todd noted, if a labor-owned station might "send strike appeals into the homes of millions of people and tell of crimes committed by company gunmen." If WCFL sought to report on strikes, unemployment, corporate waste, and corruption, and if it sought "to build the labor movement and carry on its propaganda for a higher standard of life for everyone," then it "opened a new vista of possible stirring up of public opinion." Nockels's arguments and actions implied a battle for power;

they emphasized that the FRC and the radio trust wished to silence labor radio because it challenged the vested interests and privileges of organized capital. Within the context of this all-pervasive, but rarely acknowledged, class struggle, the FRC issued a ruling.[15]

On May 20, 1929, the FRC denied WCFL's application for a license to operate full-time on 770 kilocycles with fifty thousand watts of power. The commissioners ruled that the changes requested by the CFL failed to meet the test of the public interest, convenience, and necessity. Within a month Nockels had increased pressure on Congress for a legislative remedy to the FRC curse while Thompson appealed the FRC decision to the District of Columbia Court of Appeals.[16] Nockels was particularly outraged that, as it denied WCFL's requests, the FRC approved the petition for increased power by Chicago station KYW (1,020 kilocycles). Owned by Westinghouse—a member of the radio trust—and operated by the Hearst corporation—a member of the newspaper trust—KYW received a power boost to fifty thousand watts. Another fifty-thousand-watt Westinghouse station, KDKA in Pittsburgh (980 kilocycles), already blanketed WCFL broadcasts outside of Chicago. Now KYW threatened to do the same with WCFL's local operations. Adding insult to injury, the FRC also approved a clear channel and fifty thousand watts of power to Chicago station WENR (870 kilocycles)—controlled by Samuel Insull's utility empire. Nockels took the FRC decision as further evidence of the federal government's collusion with corporate interests. As these events unfolded, an incident in the summer belied the FRC contention that commercial stations "would afford organized labor better broadcasting service than they could secure from a station of their own."[17]

President Frank Gillmore of the Actors' Equity Association had arranged with Los Angeles station KMTR to broadcast a series of talks outlining the union's willingness to arbitrate a contract with Hollywood motion picture producers. Having paid the station's regular time rates, Gillmore arrived at the KMTR studio to broadcast the union's message. Station officials informed Gillmore that "higher powers" (the Motion Picture Producers and Distributors of America and its head, Will Hays) had intervened and prohibited him from speaking. The FRC dismissed Gillmore's formal protest, asserting that it lacked the power to interfere with such broadcasting decisions. Critics of the FRC and commercial broadcasting had a field day with the KMTR incident. For many the case demonstrated that certain stations were "controlled by those whose sympathy is with the employers," that commercial radio did indeed censor labor, and that state regulators acquiesced to all of this. The *Federation News* ridiculed the myth promulgated by business and government leaders that American broadcasters willingly provided labor an opportunity to use their microphones.[18] WCFL officials probably agreed with Laurence Todd's commentary on the KMTR case: "[The FRC] commissioners have served the radio trust handsomely, in delivering to it a virtual monopoly of the use of the ether in this country. If the radio trust uses this control, handed to it by a government commission, for gagging the labor movement and glorifying the big anti-union corporations throughout the United States, Commissioner [Eugene O.] Sykes will lose no sleep."[19]

After consulting with the AFL Executive Council, Nockels had WCFL's lawyer file written arguments with the Court of Appeals in early June 1929. Thompson argued that in refusing to grant WCFL the frequency of WBBM, the FRC perpetuated the "unlawful theory" that "priority in time of operation establishes a vested interest in a radio frequency." He reiterated the reasons why the station needed and deserved a clear channel and increased power, emphasizing the station's continuing service to the labor community and the general public and its role in opposing a dangerous radio monopoly.[20]

The FRC's defense rested on two pillars. Attorneys described the agency as a group of experts who carried out purely technical tasks in a professional manner. "Radio is [a] highly technical subject," asserted FRC lawyers, and assigning channels a technical matter. Modifying WCFL's frequency meant a series of channel shifts leading to the closing down of Nebraska station KFAB. That action would exacerbate the already inequitable distribution of transmitting facilities in Illinois and Nebraska. The FRC insisted that it made its decision in an objective manner. By denying WCFL's application, the agency merely fulfilled its technical and statutory obligations as outlined in the Radio Act of 1927 and the Davis Amendment of 1928.[21]

FRC attorneys also pointed to what they considered the fundamental weakness of WCFL's case: The CFL represented a special interest group that, by definition, did not pass the public interest test. "All stations should cater to the general public and serve public interest as against group or class interest," asserted the FRC. With a finite number of frequencies, the commission could not give each special interest group that asked for one its own exclusive channel. The commission refused to allocate facilities for "class" stations. If a legitimate reason existed for labor radio, testified the FRC, station WCFL fell short of fulfilling it. According to the commission, WCFL gave as much time to advertising "medicine of questionable value" as it did to programs of interest to organized labor. Even when it had a desirable frequency, WCFL failed to air more than sixty-six minutes of strictly labor programs in a twelve-hour broadcast day. The FRC contended that WBBM rendered a superior service to the people of Chicago while most of WCFL's programs failed to serve the public interest. Finally, the FRC maintained that since "enough" stations across the nation broadcasted labor programs, there was little need for a radio station dedicated to working-class causes.[22]

While dismissing as irrelevant WCFL's programming, the FRC admitted that it ignored the numerous petitions and resolutions submitted in support of the station. The FRC regarded such public correspondence as lacking "facts." In testimony before a congressional committee, former FRC general counsel Louis G. Caldwell described how "packing cases" of what he labeled "valueless" affidavits and letters swamped the commission during its early years. Yet, Commissioner Orestes H. Caldwell later lamented how the FRC often lacked detailed information on listener popularity and how the commission relied on "a lot of hearsay." "I fear," admitted Caldwell many years later, "we did a *great* many injustices to the stations when we assigned their relative positions." Nockels could not have agreed more.[23]

The FRC's ruling against WCFL in May, and its diatribe against the station before the court of appeals in June, forced even conservative labor organs to acknowledge, as Nockels stated, the FRC's "poorly disguised hostility toward organized labor." The International Labor News Service, a semiofficial news service of the AFL, withdrew its own application for continental and transoceanic short wavelengths—which it wanted to use in the transmission of trade union news. According to the service's editor and manager, Chester M. Wright, the FRC's treatment of WCFL "showed a degree of prejudice against organized labor that precluded any expectancy of fair play, square dealing or equity." The FRC's determination that the dissemination of trade union news violated the public interest led an increasing number of business unionists to question whether that agency could be trusted with providing an "enlightened guidance of radio's future."[24]

Critics of the AFL found the federation's new dissatisfaction with commercial broadcasting somewhat ironic. Harvey O'Connor, a Federated Press correspondent, challenged the FRC's contention that "labor unions are no more important than churches, fraternal societies or the Ku Klux Klan." But he also understood how such a characterization of organized labor derived from the policies, practices, and ideology of the AFL. O'Connor argued that the identification of organized labor as a special interest naturally flowed from "the beautiful civic-mindedness of many labor officials who have insisted that labor is but one among a multitude of organizations, humble in its aspirations, dreaming not of a social order based on workers' rule but of a 'legitimate' place in a static society along with the W.C.T.U., the U.S. Chamber of Commerce and the Knights of Pythias."[25] Although such criticism struck at the heart of organized labor's problems, few AFL officers chose to discuss it, let alone act upon it. Indeed, the AFL drew an entirely different lesson from the FRC decision than did O'Connor.

AFL support for WCFL, never strong in any material way, dissipated after the FRC ruling. The powerful Executive Council and Committee on Resolutions continued to allow delegates at national meetings to pass resolutions supporting WCFL's bid for a clear channel. At the 1929 convention, for example, the officers of some forty national and international unions submitted a resolution calling on Congress to enact appropriate legislation on WCFL's behalf. At the same convention, however, the Executive Council issued a strongly worded resolution urging all levels of the labor movement to take advantage of every opportunity to send their message "through *whatever* broadcasting station may be available for the purpose."[26] The AFL hierarchy never abandoned its conviction that the capitalist broadcasting system could serve labor's interests; if trade unions produced "well planned radio programs," they would enhance "labor's standing in the community." In its best corporatist logic, the AFL asserted that "broadcasting that conforms to the ethics of [the] advertising business, presenting the facts as to labor's position, would make for that mutual understanding of related problems that promotes industrial peace in the community."[27]

Several CFL delegates challenged this position, preferring O'Connor's assessment. Radicals and progressives within the CFL had long questioned the AFL's collaborationist strategy in general and its commitment to labor radio in particular. At a CFL meeting in February 1929, for example, delegates from three unions insisted that "a simple [AFL] endorsement [of WCFL] will not do the work." Harking back to the CFL's glory days a decade earlier, these labor activists demanded that Fitzpatrick and Nockels expand efforts "in behalf of political action for the working people." Linking together WCFL and political education, the delegates called for a Labor party to "change the present system of production for profit to one for production for use."[28] The CFL's conservative voices dismissed these arguments and Nockels himself remained silent. Forced to balance the goal of an independent radio outlet with the burden of obeying the AFL, Nockels focused on WCFL's survival.

As he waited for the appeals court to hear oral testimony, Nockels pushed ahead with the campaign to secure a legislative remedy to WCFL's problems. Congress, having passed the Radio Act of 1927, claimed a legitimate interest in that act's implementation. Nockels understood that the various efforts of enlightened corporate capitalists to create informal power-sharing arrangements with the state were far more successful in the executive branch of government than in the legislative branch. To the extent that pluralist forces still operated in the American political setting, they were strongest in Congress. Here it was still possible for labor to have an impact on the thinking of individual representatives and senators, although it was easier for lobbyists to block legislation than to create it.[29]

Nockels's attempt, as he described it, to "panhandle" Congress to secure a clear channel for WCFL produced some results by the fall of 1929. Illinois's two Republican senators, Charles S. Deneen and Otis F. Glenn, supported WCFL. Both men recognized the need to hold together different groups, as one reporter described it, in the "horrors" of the Illinois political environment and especially in Cook County, where one found "a vast brood, a swarming and struggling litter of petty local machines." In this context it was important for them to maintain friendly relations with organized labor. Nockels felt confident that, with his lobbying effort, the Senate would "give us an even break with any other station on the air."[30]

In January 1930, the Senate Committee on Interstate Commerce heard Hope Thompson testify on the radio trust's threat to the public. The WCFL attorney used the opportunity to plead the station's case. Refuting the reasoning of FRC chairman Ira Robinson, Thompson noted that "every station is engaged in propaganda all the time." Broadcasting programs reflecting the "serious intellectual challenge of labor"—including political and scientific discussions—better served the public interest than "tickling a million people." The FRC, according to Thompson, had done little to ameliorate the "'national intellectual prostitute' of chain station rubbish." Asserting that the legislative branch did not have the "guts" to battle the powerful and influential radio trust, Thompson goaded Congress to act on this matter.[31] Nockels, who also appeared before the committee, urged the Senate to approve legislation that would restructure the FRC, providing labor and agriculture with their own representatives on the commission. He concluded that Congress had to "recover this priceless treasure . . . from monopolistic control by a few corporations who are using it for private profit."[32]

FRC officials and industry representatives also testified before the Senate committee. Chairman Robinson dodged questions about why WCFL had been denied a clear channel by asserting that he did not favor "the doctrine of cleared channels," preferring instead regional ones. Commissioner Harold LaFount said that he dismissed WCFL's case because the station spent only ten-twelve minutes a day for labor messages and the bulk of its programming resembled that of commercial stations. Senator Smith W. Brookhart of Iowa responded that he had personally heard WCFL air "extensive programs in the interest of labor." When Brookhart and Senator Burton K. Wheeler of Montana then pressed LaFount on the legitimacy of organized labor's request for a clear channel, the radio commissioner weakly suggested that WCFL might apply for one of the clear channels in Chicago and wait for the FRC to "determine whether or not they could put the channel to a greater beneficial use." Commissioner Charles Saltzman asserted that WCFL simply did not deserve WBBM's channel. When asked whether he had ever voted to take frequency, time, or power away from RCA or "power trust" radio stations, Saltzman replied that no "case has ever come up like that." National Association of Broadcasters president William S. Hedges found contemptible all talk of a radio monopoly, insisting that the public benefited when newspapers owned radio stations in the same town.[33]

The mere threat of congressional interference in the broadcasting field forced the FRC to make some conciliatory moves toward WCFL. As early as November 1929, the FRC had offered WCFL an opportunity to experiment with a new wavelength, 1,280 kilocycles. The new channel permitted WCFL to broadcast full-time as a regional station. In another attempt to mollify labor, the FRC granted WCFL the privilege of broadcasting shortwave programs under the call letters W9XAA on wavelength 6,080 kilocycles. WCFL experimented with 1,280 kilocycles during December 1929, but found it unsatisfactory—it was "chuckfull of heterodyne and whistles"—and returned to 970 kilocycles in January 1930. A month later, the FRC permitted WCFL and W9XAA to operate temporarily until 9:30 P.M. in order to determine the extent of interference between WCFL and KJR. While accepting these offers, Nockels conceded nothing. No channel between 1,200 and 1,500 kilocycles, argued Nockels, "will be acceptable to the Labor Movement, because that is down in . . . the 'dumps.'" WCFL wanted a clear channel in the band from 550 to 1,000 kilocycles; Nockels explained: "We are going to insist and intend to fight on getting back that which was stolen from us, namely, our original wavelength of 620 kilocycles with unlimited time and sufficient power."[34]

The FRC restrictions on WCFL's broadcasting hours and on its power usage greatly hindered the station's opportunity to serve Chicago-area labor. During the summer of 1929, listeners complained that interference by superpower stations in Chicago and elsewhere virtually drowned out labor talks and discussions over WCFL. These complaints continued into 1930. WCFL's weekly broadcast time declined by 21 percent between the summer of 1928 (sixty-three hours) and the winter of 1929 (fifty-one hours).[35] This demonstration of labor radio's weakened effectiveness became an important part of the effort to mobilize the organized labor movement behind WCFL's legal and legislative agenda.

Nockels took every opportunity to galvanize the troops. The *Federation News* kept the radio story before the trade union movement's collective eye. In April 1930, as the court of appeals prepared to hear oral testimony on WCFL's case, Nockels wrote an article that appeared, in slightly modified form, in a number of labor periodicals. The CFL secretary rated the acquisition of "one radio wavelength with a nation-wide network" as labor's most important goal after securing the right to organize, and he predicted that "whoever controls radio broadcasting in the future will eventually control the Nation." The radio trust and the great newspaper chains, according to Nockels, were engaged in an unprecedented movement "to seize control of the means of communication and to dominate public opinion." Equally unprecedented was the federal government's "crass disregard and contempt for the rights of those who toil." Protecting the public interest, convenience, and necessity required the presentation of "the serious problems of life . . . , not from one viewpoint, but from many groups and many points of view." Nockels asked the American labor movement to pressure Congress to protect the national interest—the interest of workers and farmers—by enacting legislation setting aside three clear channels. The federal government would hold those channels, in perpetuity, for all the people. One channel would go to public groups to disseminate educational and other information of national concern. Farmer organizations would control a second channel for the benefit of agriculture. Finally, the government would designate a third frequency to the labor organizations most representative of workers' interests.[36]

On April 7, 1930, the District of Columbia Court of Appeals heard oral arguments in the case *Chicago Federation of Labor v. Federal Radio Commission*. On May 5 the court upheld the FRC policy decision to deny increased power, unlimited time, and the 770-kilocycle frequency to WCFL. Chief Justice George E. Martin accepted the FRC's reasoning that "meritorious" stations such as WBBM and KFAB should not "be deprived of broadcasting privileges when once granted to them . . . unless clear and sound reasons of public policy demanded such action." The court praised WBBM, in particular, for consistently furnishing "equal broadcasting facilities to all classes in the community," while noting that WCFL's past record "has not been above criticism." Thus no public interest would be served by shifting the 770-kilocycle channel from the two stations to WCFL.[37] The court ruling embraced the myth that commercial radio represented the public interest, while a labor radio station reflected a specific class bias. FRC decisions favoring corporate capitalists did not reflect "class partiality," but a commitment to serve the "national interest."[38]

Within days of the court ruling, Illinois representative Frank B. Reid introduced a resolution in the House that required the FRC to assign three clear channels to the Departments of Agriculture, Labor, and Interior. The heads of the respective departments would designate appropriate stations in the country to use the clear broadcast channels. Reid intended that the Labor Department's channel go to WCFL. House Resolution No. 334 never emerged from the floor of the House, but a similar measure made progress in the Senate.[39]

Senator Otis F. Glenn offered an amendment to the 1930 radio bill. It ordered the FRC to assign a clear channel with unlimited time and sufficient power "to the owner or owners of the broadcasting station or stations approved by the recognized labor organizations, which in the opinion of the Commission are most representative of" the nation's labor interests. On February 17, 1931, the Senate approved the radio bill and the Glenn amendment and sent them on to a House conference committee. Nockels and WCFL endorsed the measure, arguing that it served the public interest and undermined the radio monopoly. Nockels warned that big business already controlled a "preponderance of the nation's daily press"; if it dominated the air, "it acquires an absolute dictatorship." The FRC's failure to remedy the situation necessitated that Congress protect organized labor's right to be heard over the airwaves. Utilizing similar logic, nonprofit groups also agitated for national legislation that would allocate a set percentage of radio channels for their exclusive use. As the CFL lobbied to enact the Glenn amendment, college broadcasters supported Ohio senator Simeon D. Fess's Bill, which called for reserving at least 15 percent of all channels for educational broadcasting. Network and independent stations vigorously opposed congressional interference on behalf of labor and other groups.[40]

WCFL faced a powerful array of commercial radio supporters. Trade journals had long dismissed complaints of a radio monopoly, pointing to the hundreds of radio stations operating in the country. Commercial radio served "the public without discrimination" or censorship. According to *Radio Broadcast,* "there are plenty of stations with liberal views sufficient to entertain all but the most rabid and extreme." To the extent that censorship plagued the industry, it derived from onerous government regulations. Acknowledging that special interest groups should have access to radio facilities, *Radio Broadcast* contended that workers, socialists, vegetarians, atheists, Mormons, and so on did not need or deserve exclusive channels. The corporate radio industry denounced attempts by WCFL and other entities to make radio the "tool of any class or grouping of society."[41]

Commercial broadcasters desired formal legislative or judicial action to recognize and protect their alleged vested and permanent private right to wavelengths. *Radio Broadcast* provided the prevailing economic logic for this position. It noted that ninety-seven broadcasting corporations reported a combined income of over $73 million in 1930; of those stations, thirty had netted just under $10 million and fifty-eight others reported operational losses totaling $1,181,127. The trade journal suggested that congressional interference in the radio field would endanger "the stability of the profitable groups." Explaining that in order for broadcasting to expand, "the operations of those engaged in it must continue to show a profit," the journal complained that the FRC did too little to protect the investment of radio broadcasters.[42]

The commercial broadcasting system's strongest backer was the National Association of Broadcasters (NAB). Created in 1923, the NAB voiced the interests of middle-range and large commercial stations, advertisers, and the networks. NBC and CBS officials dominated the NAB executive committee during the early thirties. The NAB praised the American system as the best in the world because, among other things, it directly reflected "what the great mass of American people want." Broadcasters "must render a public service not only under the law, but also in order to hold" the audience. The NAB could find no evidence of programming having been "sacrificed to profit" and it dismissed criticisms of monopoly and censorship as the wild ravings of special interest groups.[43] Trade association officials helped prepare the industry's recommendations for frequency reallocations in 1927 and 1928 and the FRC adopted their basic concepts. Not surprisingly, the NAB and WCFL rarely agreed on anything. In 1928 NAB officials ejected WCFL for ostensibly failing to pay dues. Nockels contended that the expulsion came as a result of WCFL's call for a federal investigation into the radio trust. WCFL attacked NAB members for supporting the "establishment of perpetual ownership of property rights in wave lengths." When the

NAB proposed a national educational radio program in January 1929, Nock-els characterized it as an example of "mass education, mass thought, mass production." WCFL's general manager believed that both the NAB and the radio trust wanted "to be dictators of what the public should hear and see and know." He later portrayed NAB officials as "stool-pigeons" for the corporations and lobbyists for the "trust press over the air."[44]

One member of the NAB and the trust press posed a particular problem for labor radio. Long-standing conflicts between the *Chicago Tribune* company and the CFL raged over city politics and industrial relations; these carried into the field of broadcasting. The *Tribune's* radio station, WGN, had one of the nation's forty clear channels and frequently requested power increases (up to fifty thousand watts). WGN and the *Tribune* company favored property rights in the air and sought legislation that would guarantee such proprietary privileges. On the other hand, media mogul Robert R. McCormick despised all government regulations that impinged on the sanctity of the private marketplace. He considered the 1927 Radio Act "a fool law" and believed that "self-interest" would "dictate fairness over the radio if ethics" did not. Ethics aside, McCormick's media empire manipulated the revolving door that connected the FRC to boardrooms of the corporate broadcasting world.[45]

In 1925, McCormick's law firm in Chicago chose an attorney to study the radio industry and law. Within a few years, Louis G. Caldwell became recognized as a "brilliant young attorney with a unique insight into the technical problems of radio." From July 1928 until the spring of 1929, Caldwell served as the FRC's general counsel. He helped formulate and implement the 1928 frequency reallocation scheme. In that plan, Caldwell's former employer received a clear channel (720 kilocycles) with unlimited time. Upon resigning from the FRC, Caldwell returned to the *Tribune*-WGN law firm. He remained in Washington "to see that WGN got the best in radio, and on McCormick's terms." Frequently called to testify before the FRC and congressional committees or to serve as a consultant on international and domestic radio boards or to head various private organs' radio committees (e.g., the American Bar Association's Committee on Communications), Caldwell emerged as one of the nation's preeminent specialists on radio law. His lobbying efforts soon included work as head of the Clear Channel Broadcasting Service. Composed of twenty-six of the nation's most powerful stations and armed with an annual war chest of some $260,000, the service became "the most powerful radio lobby in the capital." With Caldwell at the helm, it maintained the lucrative "*status quo* among clear-channel plum-holders."[46] Louis Caldwell's influence on the development of American broadcasting in the twenties and thirties led some critics of the system to wonder whether radio industry officials had conspired from the beginning to "dominate the sources of legal opinion in America with relation to radio." There is no doubt that Robert McCormick and other pioneer broadcasters recognized the need to develop specialists who would protect basic capitalist values in the new communications field.[47]

Caldwell reflected the views and the values of corporate radio and especially those of McCormick. He condemned both political interference in the operations of the FRC and the FRC itself as obstacles to the proper working of the private radio market. He vehemently denied the existence of a radio trust and characterized such public protests against the radio industry as "uninformed." Ever the scientific manager, Caldwell insisted that the radio experts (lawyers and engineers) should make radio policy according to the "mandates of radio physics" and not according to economic, social, or political demands of special interest groups. The perfect servant of power, Caldwell conveniently divorced radio broadcasting in the United States from its socioeconomic setting. He firmly believed that his treatment of broadcasting issues was rational, objective, and imminently fair.[48]

When looking for another Chicago station to challenge—as a way to get a new hearing for WCFL before the FRC—Nockels naturally gravitated toward a representative of the corporate broadcasting system. Owned by a traditional enemy of organized labor, possessor of a clear channel, and recent applicant for increased power, WGN was the perfect choice. The fact that the station was represented by an attorney whose use of the revolving door between the government and business sectors raised ethical questions—at least in the eyes of Nockels—made WGN an even more attractive target. In September 1930, Nockels formally applied to the FRC for WGN's clear wavelength of 720 kilocycles, unlimited time, and fifty thousand watts of power.[49]

WCFL's application clashed with an earlier WGN request for the maximum power of fifty thousand watts. In December, FRC chief examiner Ellis A. Yost accepted Caldwell's argument that the FRC permit all clear-channel stations to use maximum power. Yost approved the applications of WGN, WMAQ (owned by the *Chicago Daily News*), and WBBM, declaring that "it is a waste of potential broadcasting resources to limit cleared channel stations to less than 50,000 watts." Clear-channel stations were "qualified for high power and service to the public." Thus the FRC examiner recognized Caldwell's implicit argument that clear-channel station investments mandated maximum power and, hence, maximized profits. Stations not privileged enough to possess a clear channel did not deserve increased power. Yost recommended against WCFL's request for the WGN channel. A *Tribune* editorial praised Yost for his "fine courage and a grasp of the broad principles of public service."[50]

The FRC examiner's negative report on WCFL seriously weakened the station's application. Equally devastating was the lingering fatal illness of WCFL's attorney, Hope Thompson, which forced the CFL to seek continued postponements of the FRC hearings. After securing new legal representation—William B. Rubin—WCFL asked the FRC, on April 14, 1931, for additional time to prepare for the hearing. The FRC agreed and scheduled a new hearing for mid-May. But the very next day, April 15, in the absence of any representative from WCFL, Caldwell contended that any further delay in deciding the Chicago stations' requests for increased power was inconsistent with their right to due process of law and "inconsistent with the principles of fair play." FRC commissioners concurred, vacated their order of the previous day, and, thereby, rejected WCFL's application. WCFL protested the commission's action, but to no avail.[51] A few days later, as the FRC heard Caldwell's closing arguments demanding increased power for WGN, the issue of WCFL reemerged. Caldwell attacked WCFL's programs as "an insult to the honest labor people of Chicago," its title (the Voice of Labor) as undeserved, and its efforts to secure congressional legislation mandating a clear channel for labor as "a vicious piece of class legislation."[52]

Caldwell's attack and the FRC's abrupt action once again sent WCFL to Congress. John Fitzpatrick's assessment made after the announcement of Yost's recommendation in late 1930 seemed most appropriate in the spring of 1931: "It is not over. The radio commission has been playing along with the *Tribune* all of the time. We will not seek justice from it—but go directly to Congress." Nockels had known for almost a year that WCFL would have to lobby for legislation in order to secure its clear channel.[53] But corporate resistance to legislative action proved formidable.

In the fall of 1931, the American Bar Association's Standing Committee on Communications denounced all legislative efforts aimed at setting aside fixed percentages of broadcasting facilities for special interest groups.[54] The ABA committee consisted of four attorneys whose clients included RCA, NBC, and nine radio stations. Chaired by Louis Caldwell, the committee echoed familiar industry arguments regarding the sanctity of the private-property, profit-driven broadcasting system. Caldwell and his colleagues explained that the limited broadcast spectrum made it impossible to allow every business or school of thought to operate a station. Reallocating frequencies to labor and other narrow interest groups threatened the elimination of anywhere between 30 and 240 existing stations, depending upon what category of frequencies and stations would be reassigned. Such a reallocation would mean that some communities might lose broadcasting service, that station owners would suffer catastrophic financial losses, and that the listening public in general would sacrifice quality service. Caldwell found the benefits of this scheme, in the form of improved educational and public service, "questionable" at best. The specter of increasing government control over broadcasting proved as frightening to committee attorneys as the loss of private property and profits. They concluded that commercial broadcasting in the United States was far superior to government broadcasting in Europe and that U.S. programs "imperfect as they may be, are by far the best in the world."[55]

A few days before formally presenting this report to the 1931 ABA convention in Atlantic City, New Jersey, Caldwell held an open meeting to discuss the committee's findings. A sparse and relatively silent audience apparently concurred with much of the analysis and recommendations of Caldwell and his colleagues. Washington, D.C., attorney John W. Guider, who would join Caldwell's committee in 1932, warned that if Congress passed legislation granting WCFL a clear channel, "it is going to be a big job to take it away. It will be a lot easier to prevent it."[56] Only S. Howard Evans, representing the *Ventura Free Press,* challenged the report and its authors. The small California daily had undertaken a national attack on the radio trust and, in particular, on advertising over the air. Ostensibly directed at freeing airtime for education, information, and public service, the campaign reflected the intensifying competition between radio and newspapers for advertising dollars.[57] Evans attacked Caldwell's assertion that the proposed legislation to set aside clear channels to labor, education, and so on directly violated the property rights of existing station owners. Evans continued: "I cannot escape the conviction that the rights of the public in radio must be supreme. The people own the air. It is not enough to say that they are protected because they do not need to listen to programs they do not like. They should be entitled to a positive control over the kinds of programs which are broadcast."[58] Such criticisms inevitably hinted at the impropriety of committee members who simultaneously defended commercial radio, while receiving "attractive legal retainers from broadcasting stations."[59]

Caldwell certainly had realized that someone would make this indictment against him and his colleagues during the convention. Indeed, even before the ABA convention began, the CFL and educational organizations had launched attacks against Caldwell. The official organ of the National Committee on Education by Radio, *Education by Radio,* noted in late August 1931 that Caldwell accepted "larger retainer fees from commercial broadcasting companies" than any other lawyer in the country. "Is it ethical practice or is it legal racketeering," asked the education journal, "for a man with a selfish interest at stake to use a great civic organization like the ABA to promote his gain contrary to the public good?"[60] Nockels, who had frequently raised similar questions, asked his friend and progressive lawyer Frank Walsh to attend the meeting as WCFL's representative and to denounce both the ABA report and Caldwell.[61]

Caldwell received moral support from what appeared an unlikely source. Whether by coincidence or planning, S. August Gerber, the manager of New York radio station WEVD, attended the open meeting. Gerber's station, owned and operated by the Debs Memorial Radio Fund, an affiliate of the Socialist party, had been fighting a license battle with the FRC for some time. Gerber acknowledged that Caldwell was representing WEVD before the FRC, but insisted that the attorney's interest in the station was not pecuniary. Without commenting on the merits of the ABA report, Gerber testified that Caldwell was a man of integrity and that the report did not reflect a conflict of interest on his part. Caldwell had good reason to appreciate Gerber's defense.[62] Here a representative of a leftist political party, certainly no friend of the radio trust, portrayed Caldwell as a defender of minority groups' access to the airwaves, thereby making Caldwell appear as a "neutral" and "objective" technician seeking the best for national broadcasting.

When Caldwell finished the formal presentation of his committee's report to the assembled convention on September 18, Frank Walsh immediately attacked the dangers of an air monopoly. The extreme concentration of clear channels in the hands of private radio equipment manufacturers, publishing firms, and merchandising companies, argued Walsh, could produce "predigested" information, homogenized programming, and the limitation, if not suppression, of free discussion. Recounting the long and difficult struggle waged by WCFL against the corporate giants and the state bureaucracy, Walsh explained labor radio's support for the Glenn amendment and its court battle with WGN. He also pointed out the *Chicago Tribune*'s long-standing bitter hatred of the CFL and WCFL and Caldwell's position as attorney for both the newspaper and its radio station. Taking all this into consideration, Walsh urged the ABA to refrain from taking a position on the pending radio legislation.[63]

Having denounced the committee's radio report, Walsh yielded the floor to his opponent. Caldwell acknowledged that he and his colleagues represented radio stations, but he insisted that because the proposed legislation under question was not directed at any individual station, there was nothing unethical about the committee's findings. Walsh countered that stations such as WGN stood to lose if Congress enacted the Glenn amendment. Caldwell dismissed Walsh's other objections to the committee report, emphasizing the committee's deep concern with maintaining freedom of discussion in the air. Keeping the air free, lectured Caldwell, depended on every broadcaster being "a public utility available to all schools of thought." By implication, WCFL represented narrow special interests and therefore threatened the free ether.[64] The Caldwell-Walsh clash at the ABA convention did not alter the ABA report. It did lead, however, to the addition of Walsh to the Standing Committee on Communications. Walsh assured Nockels that his new position would allow him to serve as WCFL's "proxy in radio matters" within the ABA.[65]

Periodically during 1930 and early 1931 the FRC permitted WCFL to continue its broadcast day beyond the time of sunset on the West Coast. These temporary tests were to determine the extent of interference between WCFL and Seattle station KJR. In late September 1931 the commission authorized WCFL to operate full-time on 970 kilocycles. Mainstream press reports depicted the decision as a victory for WCFL, but Nockels quickly clarified that the FRC had merely provided "provisional relief in the matter of time." KJR's new owners, the National Broadcasting Company, retained the right to protest—for any reason—the simultaneous use of the 970-kilocycle band and thus block the full-time operation of WCFL. In any event, the FRC decision left unresolved "all important" questions of a clear channel and increased power. These issues, observed Nockels, remained "to be settled through action either by the Federal Radio Commission or the Congress that created it."[66]

WCFL's efforts to secure a redress of its grievances via the legislative branch received support from educational organizations and the AFL. Among the former groups, the National Committee on Education by Radio (NCER) proved the most sympathetic to labor radio's cause. Organized at the end of 1930, the NCER grew out of a series of conferences held by representatives from the National Education Association, the Association of Land-Grant Colleges, and the Association of College and University Broadcasting Stations, among other organs. Financed by the Payne Fund and headed by Joy Elmer Morgan, the NCER embraced many of the same analyses and recommendations advanced by Edward Nockels. The committee, for example, attacked the radio trust for its insatiable desire for "private profit and gain" and its ultimate goal of securing "vested rights in the air." Morgan insisted that education was not a special interest and therefore deserved its own broadcasting outlets. Denying that commercial radio provided ample time for cultural and educational programs, the NCER endorsed the Fess bill, which called for setting aside 15 percent of all radio facilities for use by educational institutions. The NCER argued that commercial stations retained the power to censor speakers or materials, to penetrate shows with "insidious advertising," and to deny education sufficient or suitable hours.[67] Although the NCER never established formal ties with WCFL, the FRC and the broadcasting industry viewed both movements as dangerous to the status quo.

At the AFL convention in November 1931, delegates petitioned Congress to pass legislation granting organized labor "its proper share of the radio channels, wave lengths, and facilities equal to that of any other firm, company, corporation or organization." By 1931 such petitions had become commonplace and signified only the AFL hierarchy's qualified support of WCFL. More revealing of the AFL leadership's thinking regarding radio was the Executive Council's argument that labor must recognize and utilize "the facilities placed at its disposal from time to time by the national chains and the local stations." Seeking cooperation with the corporate sector, AFL leaders embraced the newly formed National Advisory Council on Radio in Education (NACRE). The council offered to arrange a national "broadcast of Labor's contribution to the public welfare in various fields of endeavor."[68]

The AFL hierarchy's enchantment with the council was hardly surprising. Funded by John D. Rockefeller Jr. and the Carnegie Corporation, the council dedicated itself to the educational use of radio. But unlike the NCER, the NACRE rejected the idea that educators needed their own exclusive channels to make use of radio. Levering Tyson, NACRE secretary, condemned the NCER, especially its role in the "asinine" Fess bill. Council members believed that the commercial broadcasting system afforded ample opportunities for educational programs and they urged the industry to regulate itself or face encroachments by "a loony Congress."[69] Thus the council and the AFL leadership shared a commitment to working with the capitalist broadcasting system. In the spring of 1932, CBS agreed to broadcast, on Sunday afternoons, a series of half-hour programs entitled "Builders of America—An Epic of American Labor" directed jointly by the NACRE and the AFL. Labor-corporate cooperation appeared to have reaped rewards as William Green, Matthew Woll, and an assortment of other union officials prepared to talk about the history of the American labor movement over national radio.[70] This victory came as the AFL believed it had settled the issue of WCFL.

Although Congress had defeated the Glenn amendment in 1931, the CFL renewed efforts to legislate a solution to labor radio's problems in January 1932. West Virginia senator H. D. Hatfield and Boston representative William P. Connery each introduced a bill in their respective bodies authorizing the FRC to assign to labor a clear channel for broadcasting.[71] Nockels planned to focus labor and public support behind the two bills. WCFL attorney William B. Rubin urged workers and union leaders to write to their representatives in Congress and demand passage of the pending legislation. Pointing to the reciprocal relationship between labor and WCFL, Rubin noted that labor radio could be workers' "greatest" and "strongest ally" only if they supported the station.[72]

Nockels believed that securing rank-and-file and labor leadership support for WCFL was necessary to gain passage of clear-channel legislation and to continue the attack against the *Chicago Tribune*, WGN, and Louis Caldwell. By early 1932, Nockels may well have become obsessed with Caldwell. Writing to Walsh, Nockels explained that WCFL would ask Congress for the 720-kilocycle channel. "Our claim is that it was unethical for Caldwell to accept the General Counselship of the FRC when the *Tribune*'s interests were involved, and that it was Caldwell who wrote General Order No. 40 for the Commission which makes it impossible under the rules of the Commission to ever dislodge the *Tribune* from its ill-gotten gains."[73] Nockels understood that taking such action would cause "some gnashing of teeth." Caldwell, already in Washington to lobby against the two bills, had warned Congress that granting "a channel to a group, whether educational, labor or otherwise, will destroy the best broadcasting system in the world." Passage of such legislation would set the precedent for other special interests to acquire their own national clear channels. Nockels anticipated that if Congress passed a bill giving WCFL the *Tribune*'s wavelength, Caldwell would immediately seek an injunction claiming confiscation of property and property rights.[74]

In March 1932 a subcommittee of the Senate Committee on Interstate Commerce held hearings on the Hatfield bill. The arguments, pro and con, were familiar. Harry Shaw, president of the NAB, opposed the legislation because it catered to one special interest group and opened the door to others. He assured committee members that the NAB opposed the bill on "principle" and not because it involved labor per se.[75] Shaw concurred with the FRC that the bill established a "dangerous precedent" by allowing Congress to "usurp the power of allocating facilities it already has vested in the Commission." The FRC further refuted the allegations of bias and unethical behavior raised by the CFL and the AFL, attacked the special class interest of WCFL, and reiterated that "all stations should cater to the general public and serve the public interest as against group or class interest."[76]

Organized labor then "paraded its stars" before the Senate committee. Nockels, Rubin, and AFL executives Matthew Woll and John P. Frey testified in favor of the Hatfield bill.[77] Rubin reversed industry and government arguments, contending that the FRC had allocated clear channels along "class" lines by assigning the limited frequencies to commercial and industrial groups. Failing "to assign to labor a national cleared channel is class administration." Moreover, General Order No. 40 constituted "censorship of the air, limiting free speech, arbitrarily exercised by" the FRC. Nockels emphasized how the FRC had "trampled on the rights of labor" and how organized labor came to "Congress for a fair break."[78]

The hearings again raised the controversial issue of property rights on the airwaves. Harry Shaw insisted that although broadcasters had invested millions of dollars in their stations, they signed away their property rights to secure licenses. Station owners did not have a "vested right" because every six months they had to apply for a renewal of their licenses. Michael J. Flynn, the legislative representative of the AFL, countered that the FRC virtually rubber-stamped license renewals, making them, in practice if not in spirit, permanent. Shaw denied this, asserting that broadcasters deserved private property protection for their frequency, power, and time allocations and that passage of the Hatfield bill would further erode the already limited rights of broadcasters. Flynn responded that the nonprofit groups seeking clear channels worked "for the common welfare of this country," that "they constitute 90 percent of the people of this country," and that they therefore deserved access to the airwaves.[79]

These debates came to an end in late March when the Senate subcommittee abruptly halted its hearings, postponing them indefinitely. Fearing that organized labor might have enough influence to secure passage of the bill, radio industry and FRC officials sought a deal with the CFL that would preempt congressional action.[80] Informal negotiations began among the FRC, the National Broadcasting Company (owner of KJR), the AFL, and the CFL. Nockels, however, continued to act as if WCFL's salvation would come at the hands of Congress. He requested that Rubin prepare a detailed response to Caldwell's criticisms against WCFL—in particular, the accusation that WCFL never served the interests of labor. Nockels was incensed with the "maliciousness of this man" who had insisted before the FRC that WCFL "has never given and does not now give, any appreciable time to the interests of Labor." As late as mid-April, Nockels still hoped that Congress would grant WCFL its clear channel of 720 kilocycles and thus break the powerful control of the radio trust and the FRC.[81]

Tensions between WCFL and the radio trust also continued unabated in the ABA's Standing Committee on Communications. In early April, committee chair Caldwell solicited the CFL's views regarding radio's "legal and legislative problems." Nockels could not believe the audacity of a man who denounced WCFL's performance as a labor station while inquiring as to its views on radio legislation. Tired of dealing with "this boy," Nockels asked the AFL to condemn Caldwell and the ABA for "going out of [their] way in taking sides against" the Hatfield bill. Walsh, who promised to "keep my eye on the committee," suggested that Nockels "write a sizzling letter to the gentleman in your own polite but forcible way." In the end, Nockels dismissed Caldwell's invitation as "an idle gesture" and questioned the "propriety" of an ABA radio committee led by WGN's attorney. WCFL's manager once again challenged the legitimacy of the ABA's position on radio legislation, dictated as it was by individuals who derived personal enrichment from the broadcasting industry and who recommended policy that protected their income source.[82] These attacks by labor on the legal and financial foundations of commercial broadcasting stopped suddenly in the late spring of 1932.

On May 17, 1932, the FRC authorized WCFL to increase its power from fifteen hundred to five thousand watts and to operate for an unlimited time on its present frequency of 970 kilocycles. In exchange for these concessions, the AFL abandoned its legislative lobbying campaign to secure a clear channel. NBC, as owner of KJR, consented to full time for WCFL on the 970-kilocycle band. The deal took effect on May 27.[83] By securing labor's withdrawal from the legislative arena, the corporate radio networks and stations eliminated the dangerous precedent of recognizing a congressional right to allocate broadcast frequencies for educators, religious organizations, and other nonprofit groups. Corporate broadcasters vehemently opposed any and all congressional efforts to interfere with what they considered their private business sphere. The spring 1932 deal was, as Robert McChesney has written, "a major triumph for the commercial broadcasters."[84]

The difficult question to answer remains why Edward Nockels agreed to this arrangement. Some industry and government officials feared that Congress was on the verge of passing the Hatfield bill. Nockels consistently had argued that such legislative action offered the only long-term solution to WCFL's plight. Yet the manager of labor radio did not push ahead with the legislative option. The *Federation News,* which had thoroughly and prominently covered the ongoing war between WCFL and the broadcasting industry and the FRC, only briefly mentioned the ostensible peace agreement. A small boxed article appeared in the back pages of the June 4, 1932, issue with the headline "Labor Wins Victory in Long Air Fight." A terse statement indicated that WCFL had won its six-year war for a clear channel and increased power. The article informed Chicago workers that organized labor would not press for national legislation to assign labor an exclusive wavelength.[85] Neither Nockels nor any other CFL official offered an explanation of the negotiations or the final settlement. The *Federation News's* cryptic discussion of the "deal" suggests that Nockels was less than satisfied with the arrangement.

WCFL's manager acquiesced to the deal because it appeared the best solution at the time. Corporate radio had mounted a widespread and intense attack on the Hatfield bill. The industry had far more resources and hence influence with both the FRC and selected groups in Congress than organized labor. Many progressive and leftist critics of American broadcasting believed that WCFL could never achieve equity with the corporate stations and networks because, as the socialist *New Leader* explained, "power inevitably goes to great wealth."[86] While there appeared an opportunity for WCFL and the CFL to overcome this obstacle in the spring of 1932—and push the Hatfield bill through Congress—it was an opportunity predicated on strong political and financial support from organized labor, especially the AFL. It was precisely this prerequisite that worried Nockels.

Support from the AFL hierarchy was neither firm nor deep. Michael J. Flynn, the AFL legislative representative, acknowledged in the spring of 1932 that, for some time, AFL officials considered Nockels "a pest" because of his continual demands that they support WCFL. With the depression reaching new depths and with working-class families in need of food and shelter, the AFL could not divert scarce funds to the radio project or any other media operation. The economic crisis forced dramatic reductions, for example, in the number of reporters for the AFL's International Labor News Service, which now relied on local affiliates to supply information on important labor, economic, and industrial relations events. Although trade unions might depend "upon the activities of Ed Nockels and his associates to keep labor in the forefront of radio activities," Flynn admitted that the unions had "but little cash with which to reimburse them."[87] The AFL's weak support for WCFL also derived from the corporatist ideology of AFL leaders, which held that labor did not require its own broadcasting outlet, but could rely on the corporate stations and networks to provide access to the airwaves. The AFL considered the compromise that it brokered with the FRC and NBC a triumph.[88]

The same economic problems that plagued the AFL's media operations hindered the CFL as well. As the next chapter will explain, the depression played havoc with the finances of both the CFL and WCFL. The fight against commercial broadcasters and the FRC drained valuable energy, resources, and time from the CFL. Labor radio's legal expenses, for example, doubled over the course of 1929, from $2,763 for the first half of the year to $5,495 for the second half. Continuing the battle in Congress beyond the spring of 1932 would have threatened whatever resources WCFL had left. Without AFL financial support, Nockels could not carry on the legislative battle. Nockels concluded that WCFL had to fight for the best conditions that it could obtain and, in the spring of 1932, the AFL-brokered deal with the FRC and NBC seemed to be the best option. Aside from securing unlimited time and increased power, Nockels assumed that WCFL finally had won firm AFL support. For the next several months CFL officials talked of renaming the station WAFL, reflecting the presumed increased role of the national federation in labor radio.[89] But this expanded role for the AFL never materialized.

· · ·

The CFL's prolonged battle with the radio industry and federal regulatory system, much to Nockels's chagrin, had discouraged other labor groups from entering the field of broadcasting. The AFL's International Labor News Service withdrew its application for continental and transoceanic short wavelengths because it feared the FRC's bias against organized labor. For similar reasons, the St. Louis Central Trades and Labor Union decided against establishing its own radio station in the spring of 1930. During a lengthy debate, opponents of the plan cited "the man-killing struggle which the CFL has waged with the reactionary and pro-trust FRC." Knowing that the commission gave "private commercial stations a monopoly of good wave lengths" and fearing that "the money-bossed" FRC would assign a local labor station with the same "back-alley wave bands" given to WCFL, the Missouri labor organ decided instead to rely on commercial broadcasters who might be friendly to labor.[90] Despite the move by St. Louis and other unionists to use commercial radio stations, Nockels remain convinced that if "the chain stations get control of the air, they will have a hundred and one excuses for not giving us any time on the air. [The labor movement must] be able to say when, where, and how we are to go on the air, Labor does not want to be dependent upon the radio trust and trust-kept newspapers and 'air hogs' in order to get our message into the homes of the people, as made possible by radio."[91] In this context, Nockels and the CFL felt obligated to guarantee the survival of WCFL because it represented labor's only hope to keep alive the dream of "democracy in radio broadcasting."[92]

That dream withstood a terrible pounding during 1929–32. WCFL attorney William Rubin concluded that "the big interests, the anti-laborites with a far sightedness beyond that of most . . . labor leaders . . . knew that WCFL would be a mighty power for the cause of labor if it ever had the right to fully function. So, by various and dubious means and methods, they started out to stint its growth and keep WCFL busy with its own affairs." He lamented that while preoccupied with "fighting for its own existence and growth," WCFL was "of little service to the cause of labor."[93] This analysis explains at least part of WCFL's difficulty in concentrating on the development of innovative programs for its working-class audience. As the next chapter suggests, however, such an analysis underestimates the important services that WCFL did provide workers, their families, their unions, and their communities.

FOUR

"Something Different into Our Lives": Programming, 1929–32

The 1929–32 battle revealed that corporate broadcasters and the FRC had little respect for labor radio, feared its potential role in industrial disputes, and sought to obstruct its development. *Radio Broadcast* demanded the elimination of WCFL from the ether, claiming it presented inferior programs, interfered with clear-channel station WEAF, and represented a "class" station. The trade journal implied that the FRC's inability to remove WCFL from the air threatened the legitimate business interests of broadcasters.[1] WCFL officers, sensitive to the attacks on the quality of their programming and operations, attempted to outmaneuver the radio trust by mixing public service and educational fare with music, vaudeville, and sports, but presumably not in the same proportions as on commercial stations. They also remained committed to keeping the station open to the labor movement and working-class interests.

The Great Depression further hindered these admirable goals. Drastic wage cuts, massive layoffs, bank and business failures, and increasing poverty took its toll on the organized labor movement. Unemployment in Chicago grew from 11 percent in 1930 to over 28 percent in 1932. Local unions "found 35 to 60 percent of their membership out of work." Even those fortunate workers who kept their jobs saw their incomes fall. The average weekly wage for those employed in Chicago's manufacturing industries fell from $31.16 in 1929 to $20.20 in 1932. John Fitzpatrick recognized that unemployment and lower wages had "badly handicapped" Chicago's labor movement.

For many unions striking against wage cuts "or for organizational purposes seemed suicidal."[2] Economic hardships thus exacerbated labor radio's formidable political problems. WCFL attempted to finance and produce quality programs for workers within this larger context and in competition with commercial broadcasters.

. . .

Contemporary surveys of commercial radio programming during the late twenties and early thirties revealed the dominance of music and vaudeville-style entertainment. A study of 206 commercial radio stations during one day in December 1932 found that 87.5 percent of all airtime went to music and vaudeville shows.[3] An investigation of the program schedules of WGN, WMAQ, KYW, WBBM, and five other stations over the course of ten years (1925–34) revealed the same skewed programming. In July 1929, for example, these stations devoted, on average, 77 percent of their airtime to entertainment shows (including sports) and only 20 percent to news, information, and educational programming. The averages for July 1932 were more unbalanced—81 percent and 16 percent respectively. Disaggregating the statistics for July 1934 revealed that WGN led the other eight stations in sports programming (14.56 percent of its airtime) and it trailed all stations in educational shows (0 percent).[4] Talk shows providing beauty, cooking, and health hints slightly improved the program distribution statistics for the networks. In January 1929, the musical, comedy, dramatic serial, and variety programming of the NBC Red and Blue networks and CBS constituted 64 percent of airtime; in January 1932 entertainment programming amounted to 73 percent of airtime.[5]

Increased sponsorship of programs and the expansion of advertising also distinguished independent and network radio during 1929–32. Virtually all radio programs fell into one of two categories—sustaining or sponsored. In the former category, a station provided the facilities and arranged for the talent, but received no revenue or profit. Radio stations or networks sustained programs in order to showcase them and secure a sponsor or, in a smaller number of cases, to demonstrate that commercial radio could provide "quality" shows in the public interest. In sponsored programs, advertisers paid for a station's facilities and time and talent. The sale of airtime produced revenue and profit for the station or network.[6] Sponsored programs on the networks averaged 75 percent of total airtime by January 1931 and all of these shows were entertainment programs. Of the network's remaining 25 percent of airtime, 13 percent went to sustained entertainment programs and 12 percent to nonentertainment fare—the latter comprising all of the network's nonentertainment shows.[7]

WCFL's program schedules for 1929–32 differed little from that of its Chicago or network rivals. Music and comedy and, to a lesser extent, sports dominated the schedule. For its 1931 license renewal, WCFL estimated that 75 percent of the station's monthly programming was devoted to entertainment and 25 percent to labor, agricultural, educational, and religious shows. A review of labor radio's schedule for three weeks in 1931, however, discloses that only 12 percent of WCFL's total broadcast time went to nonentertainment programming. Unlike the networks, where 75 percent of airtime went to sponsored programming, WCFL's commercial shows made up only 34 percent of the available airtime.[8] These data seem to reinforce the accusations of federal authorities and commercial competitors that WCFL provided no significant service to Chicago's working classes. But aggregate statistics obscure as much as they reveal and demand a closer examination of program content.

Edward Nockels and his staff tried to schedule programs that would attract listeners in general, and a working-class audience in particular. Determining audience desires, however, proved problematic. Station officials repeatedly solicited comments regarding labor radio from area trade unions and WCFL listeners. Requesting feedback from the listening public was not unique to WCFL; radio station managers throughout the twenties relied upon letters from listeners to learn about audience reaction to programming and advertising.[9] WCFL programmers responded not only to listeners' letters but also to an array of conflicting and contradictory influences. The suggestions of different groups of listeners, the offerings of network and independent radio stations, the needs of organized labor, the demands of advertisers, and the grandiose plans of Nockels combined to produce a broadcast schedule of sharp extremes.

Religious and educational shows constituted a small portion (approximately 4 percent) of WCFL's schedule during the 1929–32 period. Primetime religious talks by ministers and missionaries or afternoon meditation shows joined special Christmas and Easter broadcasts and the usual Sunday church services.[10] The League of Reconciliation's Dr. Copeland Smith, pastor of Chicago's Grace Methodist Episcopal Church, hosted several religious discussion programs over WCFL. Smith also developed an educational program entitled "Biographies in Bronze." The series, which originated at WMAQ but moved to WCFL in early 1929, examined a variety of historical figures with a focus on the explorers and settlers of North America. Smith considered radio lecturing a poor educational technique and preferred instead "the idea of two folks talking out their problems." Recognizing that "tired [working] men and women must have their information served to them palatably," Smith sought to coat "the pill of knowledge . . . with the sugar of interest." "Biographies in Bronze" utilized two speakers—Smith and WCFL announcer Harold O'Halloran—and humor and music—the WCFL orchestra played "music illustrative of the period" under discussion—to inform its audience.[11] The series represented one of WCFL's rare regular educational programs for either adults or children.[12]

Labor radio's most important children's program was the "Junior Federation Club," a thirty-to-sixty-minute show scheduled six afternoons a week. Conceived by business manager Franklin C. E. Lundquist in 1928 and supported by the teachers' unions and the Chicago Board of Education, the show offered "music, poetry, science, current events, and other activities . . . put on the air by the students themselves in their own way." Classes from elementary and secondary public schools as well as individual students performed musical numbers, recited poetry, and described their school activities on the air. Student teachers from the Chicago Normal College would read stories. References to the CFL and labor-related contests brought labor issues into the show. The Chicago Trades Union Label League, for example, rewarded those children who saved the most trade union labels, while the Chicago Chapter of the League for Industrial Democracy, working with teachers' unions, offered high school students cash prizes for the best essays on economic and political subjects. The show's regular cast included WCFL musicians and singers, with announcer O'Halloran (Daddie Hal) and then program director Henry Francis Parks (Uncle Henry) serving as the master of ceremonies. Children became members of the club by sending in their names, ages, and addresses, notes on what they liked to do and their program preferences, and snapshots of themselves. Station officials welcomed parental comments on the program.[13]

The "Junior Federation Club" became a success. Thousands of letters from Chicago youngsters flooded WCFL as club membership grew from fourteen thousand at the end of 1929 to forty thousand by the following fall. O'Halloran read the letters over the air and the *Federation News* printed samples of the mail and snapshots of the children. In December 1928, the club sponsored a Christmas party for four hundred children, giving away gifts donated by various unions.[14] Station staff planned an extravagant Christmas party for 1929, hoping to enhance the image of WCFL and organized labor among children, their parents, and the general public. Nockels explained:

We are going to give the children a treat that no other institution has given before. The Street Car Men's Union is contributing the use of their hall. . . . We will have WCFL artists there to entertain them and we will broadcast the program. Candy and other things that children like will be distributed and the kids are sure to have a good time. We want them to know that the Labor Movement is their best friend. The station is making many friends not only for itself, but for the Labor Movement as a whole, and we believe it is good propaganda to educate our school children as to what the Labor Movement means.[15]

Chicago unions and businesses, responding to appeals made over WCFL, donated toys, food, trees, decorations, and cash for the celebration. Close to ten thousand children and their parents filled the hall to capacity. One CFL official observed that the children enjoyed two hours of entertainment and received "all the goodies they could eat and gifts to take home, and they were not asked to listen to propaganda of any kind, but just to have a good time and be happy."[16] The party generated positive publicity for WCFL and the CFL, thus prompting station and labor officials to sponsor a similar event in 1930. John Fitzpatrick commended not only the Christmas party but also WCFL and the "Junior Federation Club" program. The club, according to the CFL president, had "a tremendous membership reaching into the homes of our people and out into the community, centering their eyes on the labor movement."[17]

The "educational" program "WCFL Radio Study Club" also aimed to improve labor's standing in the community. Created in the fall of 1929, the show offered theoretical and practical information on constructing radio and television receivers. By mailing a postcard to the station, "students" received free lessons on how to build a battery-operated radio receiver. The correspondence course and the radio program attracted hundreds of children and adults. A majority of the students had no labor affiliation, so tracts dealing with the organized labor movement's history, aims, and accomplishments accompanied the radio lessons.[18] Although the "Junior Federation Club" and the "Radio Study Club" enhanced WCFL's public image and proved popular, the bulk of WCFL's schedule remained far less distinctive.

WCFL entertainment programming was similar to that of commercial radio. Musical programming dominated the WCFL schedule during 1929–32, with 52 percent of the station's airtime going to such shows—compared to 55 percent of network time. Music permeated every part of labor radio's schedule, from the morning exercise and wake-up program to travelogues.[19] Significant turnover characterized WCFL's staff of classical and popular musicians and singers over this period. The station carried a variety of dance orchestras and popular music shows from the "Merry Garden Ballroom" to "Tin Pan Alley." Staff organists and pianists provided the core of music during the broadcast day. Al Carney, a musician with vaudeville, theater, and radio experience, became staff organist in 1929. His daily programs—"Your Hour" (audience requests), "The Old Time" (music twenty or more years old), "Novelty Pianologues" (humorous tunes), and musical weather reports—earned him "a considerable following."[20]

Henry Francis Parks, who joined the station in the fall of 1929, became the major influence on WCFL's music programming. A noted musician, composer, and music critic, Parks wrote columns on music for national magazines and the *Chicago Daily News*. Entering the radio business in 1923, when broadcasters needed multiple talents to survive, Parks developed into a one-man radio station—functioning as commercial agent, station manager, engineer, program manager, announcer, and pianist. He became a versatile member of the WCFL staff—hosting the "Junior Federation Club," providing piano accompaniment for a variety of singers on different daily shows, serving as station announcer, and occasionally working the control board. Believing that WCFL would win its battle for full time, a clear channel, and maximum power only by broadcasting "quality" programs, Parks sought to diversify and improve WCFL's musical offerings. One of his shows offered condensed versions of grand operas performed by the WCFL orchestra and the opera department of the American Conservatory of Music. Parks structured the program to make it accessible to people who knew little or nothing about opera—including translating performances into English to help "WCFL listeners to completely understand everything" that transpired. The station also carried performances of the Metropolitan Opera via the NBC network. Parks augmented nonclassical music programs by using electrical transcriptions on the "Golden Hour of Music" and expanded station efforts to develop new musical talent.[21]

Comedy, the other staple of both labor and corporate radio, drew heavily from burlesque and vaudeville. But unlike the networks and independent stations, WCFL could not afford to employ high-priced national vaudeville talent. Thus labor radio, according to *Variety*, preferred "to hitch its bandwagon to the recruits from an earlier day vaudeville" and to "revamp and etherize" old routines. It became the "only local station of major dial rating where a vaudevillian can . . . get a crack at the mike and a reasonable opportunity for development."[22] Veteran comedians inundated the WCFL schedule. Twenty-year vaudevillians Billy Doyle and Ned Becker developed a comedy patter routine, "Adolph and Rudolph," for WCFL in December 1929. The six-day-a-week, fifteen-minute program derived its humor from a stereotyped Dutch dialect. Despite *Variety*'s complaint that the "unexciting" and "third rate" comedy script delivered "hardly a laugh," Doyle and Becker secured the sponsorship of a local clothing store.[23] WCFL sustained vaudeville shows such as the "Tripoli Trio," an Italian instrumental-singing-comedy act, in order to attract a commercial sponsor. Other performers gave "their services gratis on . . . the hope it will bring them some club work."[24]

Only a handful of the sustained comedy shows secured sponsors. Texas Guinan, a performer who once declared herself "the Most Fascinating Actress in America," directed a thirty-minute show over WCFL in late 1931. Her "shocking" material and "rough and ready" humor frightened most advertisers, according to *Variety*. On the other hand, Guinan attracted new listeners to WCFL, while picking "up some suckers" for her club act. A *Federation News* columnist admitted in 1931 that the daily half-hour "Hooligan Time" was "neither dignified nor punctilious," but did offer versatile and popular performers.[25] WCFL's "Happiness Hour," on Monday nights, offered a "curious collection of amateurs" who would never have made it inside the door of another station. These "freak ether" acts nevertheless generated much comment in Chicago radio circles because of their very oddity.[26]

With the national production of "Amos 'n' Andy" in August 1929 and "The Rise of the Goldbergs" later in the year, NBC introduced a new form to radio programming. These shows presented continuing plots and repeating characters in nonmusical drama or comedy formats. Radio drama on the networks doubled during the 1929–32 period. Although this programming often lacked quality actors and good writers, it forced WCFL and other independent stations to develop their own dramatic serials.[27] Labor radio occasionally aired lectures on drama and offered dramatic readings. It sustained an amateur group, the Players Guild of Evanston, which performed for thirty minutes on Thursday evenings in the spring of 1931. The *Federation News* touted the six-member cast as "one of the best [dramatic groups] in the country." But *Variety* lambasted the program for its weak performances and "amateurish writing," suggesting that WCFL aired the guild players only to "grab enough listeners from [their] suffering relations who are forced to listen in." The trade journal warned that "some day even the family may rebel."[28] WCFL also sustained "Suburban Sally," a fifteen-minute show that aired three evenings a week and featured Marion Gibney, a stock company actress from suburban Oak Park. The program centered on "the every day happenings in the life of all families," but "humorless" gags and "pathetic" heart appeal never secured it a commercial sponsor. "Hello Marie" followed the stories of a telephone operator, bell hop, and reporter in a metropolitan hotel. It remained on the WCFL and NBC schedules from late 1931 into the spring of 1932.[29]

Labor radio received a few programs from NBC. The unique WCFL-NBC relationship began in the fall of 1927 when WCFL carried the Tunney-Dempsey championship bout from Soldier Field, thereby circumventing NBC's exclusive broadcast of the match. Eighteen months later, WCFL leased NBC facilities to broadcast Herbert Hoover's presidential inauguration ceremonies. This cooperative venture soon led to an agreement between the Voice of Labor and NBC that allowed the former to purchase and broadcast selected programs from the NBC Blue network. NBC interest in labor radio derived from its marketing and distribution strategies in Chicago and elsewhere. Short of their own radio network, WCFL staff recognized the need to have some access to a chain in order to pick up national political events and to vary program offerings. WCFL slowly incorporated a few Blue network music and variety shows, as well as information programs, into its schedule. The station relied on NBC for broadcasts of talks by national political figures, the World Series, the Kentucky Derby, championship boxing matches, and speeches by AFL officials. WCFL officials carefully limited the use of network programming because of financial reasons. NBC, on average, supplied only 5 percent of WCFL's total weekly programming during this period.[30]

Foreign-language and ethnic shows with entirely home-grown entertainment consistently ranked among the most popular programs on the WCFL schedule. Ethnic neighborhoods defined the city of Chicago and its environs and workers were as likely to be organized according to nationality as according to skill or industry.[31] WCFL's ethnic programs reflected such diversity, but they did more. They demonstrated a continuing CFL commitment to make the federation a center of ethnic activity. Elizabeth McKillen has argued in a slightly different context that the CFL leadership considered ethnic and class goals as complementary. During the high point of their progressive union organizing and political campaigns (1914–24), Fitzpatrick and Nockels rejected the AFL's assimilation strategies and attempted to use the ethnic concerns of workers to bring them into a labor party. Although these efforts failed, the policy of linking ethnic concerns with class-conscious actions continued in a modified form with WCFL's ethnic hours.[32]

Recognizing the importance of the ethnic dimension in working-class

Chicago and seeking to expand the WCFL audience, station officials introduced and maintained more than seven ethnic or nationality "hours," including German, Lithuanian, Polish, Italian, and Jewish programs, during
1928–32. *Variety* commended WCFL's ethnic shows for serving, "unofficially,
the foreign-speaking population of Chicago." Broadcast usually on Sunday
afternoons or evenings, these ethnic hours consisted of music, dancing,
singing, occasional dramatic skits, conversation, and public announcements
of ethnic festivals and community meetings. WCFL sustained a few of these
programs, but local businesses sponsored the majority. Ritter's Furniture
Store sponsored a Polish program over WCFL beginning in December 1929.
Variety praised the show's music as a "wholesome departure from the mo-
notonous pops heard from the regulation radio bands." In cooperation with
various local German-American groups, Julius Klein, editor of a German-
language newspaper, founded WCFL's German radio hour in December
1928. Klein established a second German variety program, sponsored by
local businesses, in April 1931. "Spanish Hour," supported by a Spanish-lan-
guage periodical in Chicago, presented singers and musicians from Mexi-
co and Central America.[33]

WCFL's "Jewish Hour," originated by Harry Winnick, an official of the
Retail Clerks' Association, and sponsored by local Jewish businesses, first
appeared on Friday evenings in early 1930. The program initially featured
the city's leading Jewish musicians, including cantors, instrumentalists, and
folksingers with "schmaltz." Winnick later introduced short dramas and
comedies. Under the direction of Hyman Novak, four cast members—including Novak's young daughter—performed Yiddish plays. Although the
program's producers promised to keep interruptions to a minimum, *Variety* complained that "more than half of this hour was taken by weary and
long drawn commercial announcements." The trade magazine also criticized the poor talent and writing; questioned the use of English for the
advertisements and Yiddish for the program; and condemned the show for
divesting Yiddish plays of meaning and action by condensing them into
twenty minutes. Nevertheless, "The Jewish Hour" remained an important
part of WCFL's Friday night schedule for over eighteen months.[34]

The most famous and longest running of all WCFL's nationality programs was the "Irish Hour." Introduced in June 1930, the "Irish Hour" became the domain of Maurice Lynch, the CFL's financial secretary. As director and announcer, Lynch combined Gaelic and modern Irish songs,
clogging, and a little Irish history in an hour of "pure entertainment." Tom
Ennis performed folk tunes on the Irish Union Pipes, while Lynch's nieces

danced and various WCFL artists sang. *Variety* labeled the show as "Irish with a vengeance" and noted that Lynch spoke with "a brogue of the traditional thickness of a Dublin fog." The Street Car Men's Union Local 241 helped WCFL to sustain the program and keep it "free from commercialism." The "Irish Hour" ran for 1,176 Sunday evenings until its termination in March 1953—a tribute to both its producers and the Irish community that supported it. All the other ethnic hours had been discontinued years earlier as "the demand for these programs declined."[35]

WCFL responded well to the perceived special needs of Chicago's ethnic communities, but its record with African Americans proved far less exemplary. The CFL's relationship with Chicago's African-American community had been complex and contradictory. Fitzpatrick tried to organize black workers in the city's stockyards and steel mills during the World War I era. Although, as James R. Grossman has explained, the leaders of the CFL "lacked the overt, conscious, and malicious racism displayed by [Samuel] Gompers, most leaders of craft unions, and most other Americans," they nevertheless were unable "to transcend the racial ideology" of their generation.[36] Like most commercial broadcasters, the CFL's radio station exploited African-American stereotypes.

Following the lead of the popular network show "Amos 'n' Andy," WCFL developed its own minstrel and "Negro dialect" programs. "Pencil and Eraser" and "Speed and Lightning" continued the American theatrical tradition of using white comedians in blackface to portray "jovial characters." Station artists Harold O'Halloran and Burt Squire played "Pencil and Eraser" for fifteen minutes, six nights a week. A white brother team portrayed "Speed and Lightning" and, according to WCFL publicists, "their colored dialect is really amusing as they encounter untold difficulties during their travels of the States." *Variety* found the gags old, but generally liked the comedy skits and the performers' "harmonizing of pop ballads." WCFL publicized "The Night Court" as "an entertaining and wholesome adaptation of the minstrel show idea with a mock court as a setting." Prisoners brought before the docket "state their case and wind up with a blackout gag delivered by the droll-speaking judge."[37] One African-American artist, Clifton Moore, wrote and starred in his own fifteen-minute minstrel show six days a week. The *Federation News* described Moore as a talented musician (guitar, banjo, and harp), poet, and writer and as a genius at mimicry, "particularly of his, the colored, race."[38]

Although African-American actors were virtually absent from WCFL comedy shows, black singers and musicians figured prominently in station musical programs. Broadcasts from the Savoy Ballroom, "centrally located in the heart of Chicago's exclusive colored settlement," featured two of Chicago's best orchestras. Shelby Nichols, a "baritone of exceptional ability," appeared every Saturday afternoon in 1930 on WCFL's "Timely Topics" show. "Showboat," a forty-five-minute program that originated from a Chicago cafe located at Clark and Lake Streets, offered "Louis Armstrong and his famous band and no one less than Stepin Fetchit, America's leading colored comedian." WCFL also aired the "Harlem Harmony Hounds," an African-American quartet that favored the musical style of the Mills Brothers, and Cab Calloway's Cotton Club orchestra via NBC. According to WCFL, the talent of black musicians and singers derived from "the heritage of a race endowed with deep musical feeling and consciousness."[39]

The ethnic hours and much of WCFL's other entertainment programs used a significant proportion of local talent. Independent stations often drew on area singers, musicians, comedians, and actors to fill their schedules. The ethnic hours employed talent from Chicago's neighborhoods and suburbs. Vella Cook, a native Chicagoan, had sung at area weddings, banquets, funerals, and other social functions before joining WCFL in 1926. She was the first soloist heard over labor radio and became one of the station's most versatile performers. "When artists didn't show up, [Cook] did the entire program. . . . If it was a German one, then Vella was German, likewise Scotch, or Yiddish. There wasn't a nationality she couldn't do on a few minutes notice."[40]

WCFL's open door for local talent afforded black musicians vital access to radio. White musicians' unions controlled negotiations with the large radio networks, denying African Americans their fair share of radio jobs. Smaller stations such as WCFL offered opportunities for local black performers. Both the Harlem Harmony Hounds and the Melody Mixers consisted of black teenagers from Chicago neighborhoods. Eddie Johnson, later to become a noted jazz saxophone player and band leader, began his professional musical career as a member of the Melody Mixers performing a daily fifteen-minute program over WCFL. According to Johnson, "our reputation as singers spread fast as a result of the [WCFL] radio show." Local performers thus sought airtime either to secure sponsors for their programs or to generate more work in the Chicago area.[41]

This reliance on a local talent pool continued even as network-affiliated stations grew in number and became enmeshed with the "national" artists of NBC and CBS. Program manager Henry Parks proudly noted that station staff had patiently taught promising young singers how to perform over the radio and had discovered new talent through regular auditions. Working-class Chicago produced its fair share of new talent for WCFL: John Reddington, "Chicago's Entertaining Fireman," played the harmonica and tap danced; the "golden voiced tenor" Walter Duffy delivered milk; Erna Waterhouse, a member of the Bindery Women's Union, sang everything from "heavy classical pieces to . . . simple and light folk songs"; Mary Idelson, a Forest Park Library employee, acted in comedy skits on the "DeLux Variety" program; and Rocco Dabicci, a "wily and capable" salesman, sang Italian folk music on the "Junior Federation Club" and "Timely Topics."[42] The use of local talent helped labor radio maintain its links with the area's working-class communities.

Believing that workers also loved their sports, the WCFL staff made every effort to broadcast sporting events and news. During the spring of 1929, business manager Lundquist arranged for labor radio to broadcast all the home baseball games for the Chicago Cubs and Chicago White Sox. This was not an exclusive contract because other stations in Chicago also carried the games. Nevertheless, baseball broadcasts over WCFL had little trouble finding business sponsors and large audiences. Station announcer Burt Squire assisted John O'Hara, a former minor league ball player and newspaper reporter, in providing play-by-play coverage. Baseball games occupied a significant percentage of the WCFL schedule in the spring and summer months. During the week of June 29–July 5, 1929, for example, coverage of the Sox and Cubs made up over 19 percent of WCFL's airtime. With the Chicago Cubs winning ninety-eight games behind the power hitting of Roger Hornsby and Hack Wilson in 1929, local stations covering baseball chose to broadcast the Cubs' out-of-town games by tickertape rather than pick up the White Sox home games. WCFL, however, remained at Sox Park to broadcast the play-by-play. "This loyalty to contract, insisted upon by Mr. Nockels, forever endeared WCFL to Mr. [Charles A.] Comiskey," owner of the White Sox. The following season Comiskey named WCFL the "official" White Sox station. WCFL did not ignore the Cubs, however. When the team went on to win the National League Pennant and play the Philadelphia Athletics in the 1929 World Series, labor radio aired the first two games played in Chicago and carried the remaining three games from Philadelphia via the NBC network.[43]

Although baseball game broadcasts became the cornerstone of the WCFL sports' schedule, the station covered other athletic activities. Labor radio aired all the home football games of the University of Chicago in 1930 and picked up the Notre Dame–Army game at Soldier Field at the end of November. WCFL easily found commercial sponsors for these athletic events.[44] NBC provided WCFL with occasional heavyweight championship bouts. The station also carried an electrically transcribed program sponsored by a tobacco company and featuring former boxing champion Jim Corbett recounting past ring contests and commenting on the contemporary boxing scene. Patrick Horgan, editor of *Turf World*, supplied listeners with daily horse racing information in 1932.[45]

WCFL's entertainment programming included an assortment of miscellaneous talk or information shows. Tips on gardening, cooking, and beauty care filled afternoon time slots. Morning wake-up and exercise shows included weather information, market reports, and some music. Medical "information" shows such as the "Restoro Health Institute" and "Health Talk" continued into 1929. Laura Patterson's "Shut-In Hour" offered readings of appropriately inspiring personal stories such as Helen Keller's autobiography. Labor radio picked up the independently syndicated "Chevrolet Chronicles," heard over 120 stations, in 1930–31. Captain Eddie V. Rickenbacker, the World War I flying ace, introduced the war reminiscences of decorated American veterans and war correspondents.[46] Although these and other entertainment programs were vital to WCFL, the station insisted that its alternative public affairs programming and its oppositional labor programs set it apart from corporate broadcasters.

Once again the issue of the quantity and quality of alternative and oppositional programming becomes important. WCFL allocated, on average, only 8 percent of its airtime between the summer of 1928 and the summer of 1932 to labor, agricultural, civic, educational, and informational programming.[47] Although a small part of the total, this programming served a vital function within Chicago's progressive and working-class communities. Supporters of labor radio consistently cited the station's indispensable publicity value, especially as an alternative to the capitalist media. CFL vice president and city alderman Oscar F. Nelson noted in the spring of 1929 that even if WCFL cost a million dollars to build and operate, it was money well spent "if for no other reason than we can talk back to the *Chicago Tribune* and the *Chicago Daily News* and every other newspaper that undertakes to misrepresent Labor." As local governments throughout Cook County faced bankruptcy in 1929–30, the Chicago business community and their media blamed public officials for wasting tax money and thereby causing the financial crisis. WCFL and the *Federation News,* however, explained how tax dodging by big business contributed to the financial problems of local governments. While the corporate media urged the appointment of business elites to take over public duties, the labor media denounced efforts by business to become "dictators without portfolio," setting up "quasi-public bodies" and usurping the authority of elected officials.[48]

Edward Nockels developed a cordial working relationship with a variety of progressive political and social movements, organizations, and individuals in Chicago and elsewhere, offering them free use of station facilities. These activists, in turn, praised WCFL for its assistance in educating and informing the public. The Iowa farmers' union president called WCFL "an absolutely essential publicity agency that has become indispensable to the farmers." Socialist party officials appreciated WCFL's "thoughtfulness" in broadcasting a "splendid memorial service" in 1929 for their longtime leader Victor Berger. A few years later, the party's League for Industrial Democracy presented the "Forum of the Air" series over WCFL, which discussed the causes of and solutions to unemployment.[49] Local union leaders and the *Federation News* attested to labor radio's "limitless scope and power" and its ability to help solve labor's problems and simplify "every phase of labor's activities." Progressive speakers such as Rev. J. W. R. Maguire and the attorney Meyer Fink offered weekly commentaries on economic, political, and labor issues. Fink's rapidly delivered, but persuasive speeches analyzed the utility monopoly in Chicago, social security, corporate law, and other contemporary issues. Fink considered WCFL "by and far [Chicago's] most liberal and advanced" station.[50]

In theory the Voice of Labor echoed the nonpartisan political policy of the AFL, refusing to endorse any political party. In practice WCFL readily allowed liberal and leftist politicians throughout the Midwest to use its facilities to publicize their candidacy for office. Lillian Herstein, head of the Chicago Teachers' Federation and a member of the CFL executive board, ran as a Farmer-Labor party candidate for Congress in 1932 and discussed her platform over WCFL. In aldermanic elections, Oscar F. Nelson effectively used WCFL to counter the political clout of local businesses that manipulated WGN, WBBM, and WMAQ in an effort to gain control of the city council. Labor radio also provided airtime for the supporters of attorney William B. Rubin, who ran in the Democratic party primary for governor of Wisconsin. When a candidate for the bench in Milwaukee failed to gain access to *Milwaukee Journal* radio station WTMJ after the newspaper and the station attacked him, he conducted his political campaign over WCFL.[51] Progressive causes such as the movement to free Tom Mooney also gravitated to the Voice of Labor, which broadcasted fund-raising shows and news of mass meetings.[52]

Nockels attempted to secure international figures to address the WCFL audience. When British prime minister Ramsay MacDonald considered a visit to the United States in the fall of 1929, Nockels asked the Socialist party to use its influence to get MacDonald to travel to Chicago and give an address over WCFL. Nockels argued that a speech by the head of the British Labour party would benefit the U.S. labor movement and "would do much to increase the friendly spirit of the unions towards the [Socialist] Party." Although MacDonald never journeyed to Chicago, the first president of the Irish Republic did visit in March 1930. John Fitzpatrick proudly escorted Eamon De Valera to the WCFL studios, where the Irish leader spoke on creating a daily newspaper for Ireland.[53]

Station staff also attended to local and national civic affairs. WCFL placed microphones in the Chicago mayor's office and the city council chambers in March 1929 hoping, as the *Federation News* explained, that officials would talk honestly to the people of Chicago on important subjects "which are often misrepresented by the daily press." Two years later, WCFL inaugurated a daily afternoon news summary. City sealer Joe Grein conducted a series of talks in 1931–32 that exposed weight and measure racketeers in Chicago. Given the importance of the 1932 presidential election, WCFL devoted over sixty hours to covering the national conventions of the Democratic and Republican parties. The station also sustained expert discussions of crime, child welfare, and unemployment and relief as the depression worsened.[54]

In its continuing effort to incorporate farmers' concerns into its schedule, WCFL offered daily agricultural market reports and opportunities for officials of farming organizations to voice their concerns and ideas. Gail Wilson, a former staff worker on the National Women's Trade Union League of America, supervised the fifteen-minute "Farm Talks" segment every afternoon. Under the auspices of the Farmers' Union of Illinois and the Farmer-Labor Exchange of Chicago, the program broadcasted "workers who have accomplished some measure of success in agriculture, in the co-operative movement or in trade unionism." Wilson also commented on important agricultural issues. To assist consumers, "Market Place," a daily morning program that began in March 1932, incorporated daily market reports on the best buys in fresh meat, vegetables, and fruits, and hints on how to prepare foods. Station staff hoped to help housewives find inexpensive foods and to assist "the independent grocer and butcher . . . to compete more favorably with the highly organized chain stores."[55]

The Voice of Labor sustained the vast majority of its public affairs programs, while seeking sponsors for entertainment programming. But the distinctions between sustaining and sponsored programs blurred when applied to labor shows. WCFL gave free airtime to labor unions and working-class organizations to make important announcements during strikes, boycotts, lockouts, and organizing drives. It also cooperated with local unions to produce shows that educated, informed, and entertained the audience. These programs used various formats to explore themes and issues of importance to working-class communities and organized labor. A final category developed slowly over the course of the thirties and involved individual labor unions paying for the station's facilities and for program production. These shows resembled the format and content of commercial programs on the networks and independent stations, but instead of selling specific goods or services, trade unions "sold" their good names or their political and economic agendas.

A small group of Chicago trade unions and labor officials made regular and extensive use of WCFL. Harry Winnick of the Retail Clerks' Association, Charles F. Wills of the CFL Executive Board, and L. P. Straube of the *Federation News* business office frequently gave radio addresses on trade union, economic, and political issues.[56] The Chicago Trades Union Label League continued to sponsor its own show and urged all local trade union leaders to make use of the airtime. The Label League took its program seriously. When business manager Lundquist informed the league that its program would air at 6:15 P.M. instead of 7:15 P.M., league members objected because "organized workers do not care to tune in on the radio until they have had their evening meal and in most cases 6:15 is too early." Lundquist acquiesced and the label show retain its later time slot.[57]

President Harry E. Scheck considered WCFL of invaluable assistance to the various campaigns of the Label League. A national union label campaign opened in April 1931 over WCFL with an address by George W. Perkins, president of the AFL's Union Label Trades Department. The thirty-minute program also included musical numbers—a rendition of "Don't Forget the Union Label, It's Your Friend" and "Stand by the Union Label"—and the recitation of "Union Label Girl." WCFL's orchestra manager agreed to play "Stand by the Union Label" at least once each day during the month of April.[58] As the depression deepened and weakened Chicago businesses, including the union label store, WCFL urged workers to increase their purchases of union products. Commercial radio stations, fearing the hostility of national advertisers, refused to join WCFL in publicizing another campaign to "buy Chicago products."[59]

Unions that used WCFL during noncrisis periods tended to provide programming that explained the functions and benefits of the organized labor movement. The Chicago Printing Trades Unions offered two series of talks over WCFL in 1931. The first centered on the humanitarian activities of the respective unions, examining pension and mortuary benefits, aid to the unemployed, and educational programs. A second series explained how the unions' economic and social functions contributed to the printing industry and to the entire nation. Other labor groups and individuals followed with talks on workers' education, leisure, the depression, and public works projects.[60]

CFL leaders inaugurated a new organizing drive in the summer of 1929 with "an educational program over WCFL." The series of fifteen-minute talks entitled the "History of Labor" aired on Saturday evenings and explained the history of the AFL and the advantages and benefits of trade unions to unorganized workers. Special programs continued this educational effort. In May 1930, for example, WCFL celebrated the one hundredth birthday of Mother Jones with a musical tribute and speeches emphasizing her militancy and class-consciousness. WCFL repeated these themes in two memorial programs after Jones's death in late November. Yet another memorial to Mother Jones in May 1932 again used music, poems, and speeches to stress labor's need for agitation, struggle, and organization.[61]

Such programs notwithstanding, commercial radio observers criticized WCFL for producing boring "labor propaganda talks." *Variety* lambasted Scheck's weekly fifteen-minute program, for example, condemning the straight lectures as intense and humorless and recommending that they "be made interesting first and proselyting second." The trade paper asserted that only small audiences would listen to Scheck's "harangue on the union label" or to L. P. Straube's commentary on "present-day social problems." The "tired farmer or worker," contended *Variety,* was "not anxious to listen to serious business at 7:15 p.m., just when he has finished his supper" and prepared to relax.[62] Such an assertion, however, ignored the context of individual working situations, workers' home life, and the particular programs in question. Industrial conflicts, for example, stimulated substantial worker interest in labor radio as a source of information and analysis. Even *Variety* admitted that forceful speakers with topics of immediate concern for workers and their families generated dedicated audiences. Joe Grein's reputation as "Chicago's fighting City Sealer and friend of the housewives" earned his Tuesday evening show during the 7:00 hour "considerable popularity with hoi poloi."[63]

A few WCFL sustaining labor education and information shows experimented with different formats. Occasionally a union would celebrate a special event or anniversary by producing thirty or sixty minutes of music, singing, and labor talk.[64] One labor talk show, a conversation between station announcer Joe Plunkett and L. E. Keller, head of the Brotherhood of Railway Employees, supposedly took place on a train traveling from Chicago to St. Louis. Sound effects indicating a moving train provided a backdrop for a discussion of railroad wage reductions. When the train "stopped" in St. Louis, a German band provided a musical interlude. According to the reviewer for *Variety,* the program was "well routined and maintained interest throughout."[65] But such deviations from straight talk or interview formats on labor shows were rare.

WCFL broadcasted a significant number of speeches by AFL officials, especially on Labor Day and other appropriate occasions. These talks usually avoided alienating "the undifferentiated listening public." The historians Michael Kazin and Steven J. Ross have suggested that AFL speakers over radio "portray[ed] themselves as representatives of the general public and defenders of the American way of life." Their talks emphasized organized labor's achievements in worker efficiency, increased consumption, and so on, and labor's legitimate role in the nation's economic, social, and political life. By toning down class conflict rhetoric, radio speeches by the AFL hierarchy moved organized labor to the center of "political discourse."[66]

A majority of WCFL's labor programs were designed to educate the general public and unorganized workers about the labor movement and thus reflected the business unionist and corporatist ideology that dominated the AFL speeches. In explaining the need for WCFL in February 1930, Charles Wills argued that labor radio programs demonstrated to the general public "that Labor has something fundamental in its program, like the five day week, a living wage, etc." This helped counter the "lying propaganda" of the business media, which had led the public "to believe that our program contains only dynamite."[67]

WCFL, like the *Federation News,* however, remained wonderfully diverse and relatively open to conflicting opinions during this period. The pages of the weekly newspaper printed the conservative commentary of William Green, Matthew Woll, and Frank Morrison, on the one hand, and the radical analysis of Harvey O'Connor, Jessie Lloyd, Scott Nearing, and Carl Haessler, on the other.[68] In a similar fashion, the CFL's radio station aired both corporatist assessments of labor's proper role in the political economy and more progressive and radical examinations of contemporary problems. Official CFL acquiescence to general AFL policy notwithstanding,

Nockels remained enough of a rebel to allow local unions and commentators to challenge the national federation. Union and nonunion speakers offering militant class-conflict analyses over WCFL often came to the microphone during times of labor crisis.

Trade unions and their supporters flocked to WCFL in times of industrial disputes, lockouts, strikes, and organizing drives. Two strikes in particular highlight the utility of labor radio in times of crisis. Radio stations had employed musicians to provide live music for their audiences since the late twenties. The Chicago Federation of Musicians, in the winter of 1931–32, demanded new contracts that would give its members a six-day work week without changing their pay. When the commercial stations refused, the musicians threatened to strike. Labor radio settled with the union and the two bodies then agreed that WCFL would broadcast the music of the thirty-two striking orchestras and bands around the clock—alternating every thirty minutes or so. Fearing a massive loss of advertising revenue due to the substitution of phonograph records for live bands and annoyed at the thought of WCFL airing their musicians in a marathon session, the members of the Chicago Broadcasters' Association yielded to the union's demands.[69]

A bitter strike between Chicago theater owners and the Moving Picture Operators' Union in the fall of 1931 led to a struggle for public opinion. Chicago newspapers and radio stations, which depended heavily on the advertising revenue of area theaters, refused to offend the owners by even acknowledging the workers' side of the conflict, let alone providing airtime for the strikers. WCFL gave union officials the public forum they required to get their story out to the general membership and population. Although the employers threatened to seek an injunction against WCFL, the station continued to attack scab labor. Upon settling with the theater owners, the union donated five thousand dollars to the Voice of Labor.[70]

WCFL, without a doubt, served a vital propaganda and information function for labor during crisis periods, and a small number of dedicated unions utilized the station to good effect for general educational purposes during times of relative industrial peace. "The CFL Bulletin Board," the daily (except Sundays) evening time slot open to all labor organizations wishing to broadcast messages, offered trade unions an unprecedented opportunity to discuss their activities, to recruit or instruct new members, and to educate the public on important social, economic, and political issues.[71]

Trade union use of WCFL nevertheless disappointed CFL officials. During the eight-day period in February 1929 when WBBM had paid for a transcription of all WCFL programming, only two unions made announcements over the bulletin program: The Boot and Shoe Workers' Joint Council publicized a boxing contest and the printers notified the rank and file of an important union meeting. The bulk of the bulletin board show went to weather and market reports, promotions for WCFL programs, a synopsis of the latest issue of the AFL's *American Federationist*, notices of educational and political talks in the Chicago area, and reports on missing persons.[72] Nockels and other CFL officials remained frustrated by this failure of local unions to take advantage of the opportunities offered by WCFL. Opponents of WCFL recognized this problem and used it to attack the station. During the FRC hearings in April 1929, lawyers for the commercial stations criticized Nockels for labeling programs as labor shows when they contained little or no labor material. Nockels did not deny this, but explained that "I gave labor all the time they *wanted* and *asked for,* in every particular. Never was there a time when [WCFL] was not open to labor free of cost, . . . any time they wanted it."[73]

Federation officials had no definitive answer as to why trade unions remained apathetic toward labor radio, but they saw this phenomenon as part of a larger problem facing the labor movement. Harry Scheck commented that workers rationalized their weak participation in the union label store by complaining about the store's poor location, inadequate parking, and lack of desired goods. But Scheck believed "that the great majority of the members of our movement are fast asleep and totally unaware of some of the most important principles" of trade unionism.[74] A CFL committee examining the labor press lamented in 1930 that "even our own membership are becoming lax, not caring what happens," as demonstrated by poor attendance at union meetings and delegates who failed to report to their unions. Charles Wills noted that only a small percentage of the city's labor movement participated in union events such as the WCFL Radio Frolics and Labor Day celebrations. Most important, labor organizations ignored the necessity of a labor press "except where they have run into keen conflict with employers and stand a chance of being put out of existence."[75] Wills continued: "In such cases, our editor has found representatives of such organizations at our door so regularly and with so much material concerning their own affairs, that if he printed all their offerings, there would be hardly a chance to write anything else than the story of their own particular affairs."[76]

A report on the possibility of establishing a daily labor newspaper exposed the union apathy dilemma. At the request of CFL delegates, John

Fitzpatrick had appointed a group to investigate the issue. The committee held lengthy discussions on the issue and reported to the federation in May 1930. Although committee members acknowledged the utility of a labor daily, they suggested that the CFL consider three issues before moving forward on the proposal. As a first step, affiliated unions had to fulfill their existing obligations to support the weekly *Federation News*. Committee members also raised the need to eliminate, or at least modify, "the hypocritical attitude toward advertisers, a handicap that would, if permitted by any private press, put such a paper on the financial rocks in short order." The committee concluded that "the financial requirements necessary for the establishment of a daily paper involves the consideration of *our radio station* which, as a publicity agency, possesses even greater virtues than a daily paper, and here again, your committee was confronted by the *obvious evidence of apathy* which has no logical excuse to offer for its existence."[77]

A number of delegates spoke to the issue of the labor movement's "apathy" regarding the labor media. The *Federation News's* L. P. Straube lamented that workers supported the enemy press every time they bought a morning daily for two cents or an evening newspaper for three cents. In the midst of a depression, why would workers allocate their scarce resources on the products of the newspaper trust and ignore labor's own weekly paper and radio? Some delegates suggested that renewing labor militancy was a prerequisite to securing rank-and-file support for labor media; others argued that successful labor newspapers and radio themselves would "awaken the old militancy." CFL representatives also clashed over who would take the lead on these issues: Was it first necessary to get union officials committed to a plan of action before the membership could be expected to become interested or did the impetus have to come from the rank and file?[78] These questions plagued the CFL throughout the thirties and hindered efforts to develop WCFL.

The analogy between the labor press and labor radio was a strong one. Just as trade unions ignored the labor press except in crisis situations, so did organized labor neglect WCFL except when confronted with workplace disputes. Years earlier, representatives from Typographical Union Local 16 had suggested that organized labor's rank and file simply had little comprehension of the radio situation in the country. Labor activists who did understand the stakes involved had to educate the general membership and "wake up" the labor movement. William Rubin and several CFL delegates argued that union leaders also lacked vision and failed to understand the utility of labor radio or the labor press. They acknowledged that labor's enemies had a better sense of the potential of WCFL than labor itself. Nockels and his supporters thus engaged in a continuing effort to educate the labor movement about radio. One union officer's exhortation that "we should never overlook and never forget that we must continually agitate and organize among the unorganized" applied to labor radio: WCFL officials continually had to agitate and organize among those who did not understand the importance of labor's voice.[79] Raising labor's awareness and appreciation of labor radio was crucial not only for the well-being of organized labor but also for the financial health of WCFL.

Nockels tried to create and maintain a nonprofit, listener-supported radio station. As he explained several times: "We are for the man as against the dollar whenever there is a clash of interests. We operate solely for public service and not at all for pecuniary profit."[80] But obstacles ranging from union apathy to the worsening depression to the plans for a national labor radio network to the growing costs of station operations to intensified competition with commercial networks all served to undermine efforts to keep WCFL free from commercial pressures.

Station operating expenses climbed throughout the 1929–32 period. The cost of wire rentals, for example, rose from $1,843.99 during the first six months of 1929 to $2,766.64 for the same period in 1930. The combined wages of studio artists and Navy Pier technicians increased by 12.5 percent, from $30,024.76 to $33,767.08, during 1929. Expenditures for necessary repairs, replacements, and supplies also increased from $2,860.91 during the first half of 1929 to $5,045.43 during the first two quarters of 1930. The overall cost of operating WCFL during January–June 1929 reached $54,793.10, while in the same period in 1930 the station's expenses totaled $61,753.09.[81]

As costs rose, station income from noncommercial sources failed to keep pace. Given that only one-third of Chicago-area unions voluntarily contributed to WCFL and given that station costs continued to grow, WCFL officials quickly realized that Nockels's original financing plan could not support labor radio in the future. Offering union members subscriptions to the new *WCFL Radio Magazine* became one way to generate supplemental annual income from trade unions; net proceeds from the subscription price helped fund station operations. Although a variety of Chicago unions— including those of the printers, bakers, railway workers, building service employees, teachers, carpenters, and teamsters, to name just a few—continued their financial support for WCFL, their total donations stagnated or fell. During the first six months of 1929, union contributions to the station totaled $6,835; between January and June 1930, donations reached only $3,844; and by the first half of 1931 they had plummeted to less than $2,000.[82]

Proceeds from WCFL Radio Frolics offset some of the decline in revenue from union contributions. Profits from the annual celebration reached $8,250 in 1929, $13,046 in 1930, $11,350 in 1931, and $10,400 in 1932. Financial secretary Maurice Lynch feared that the "hard times" facing union members would erode their participation in the frolics; but both the 1930 and 1931 affairs exceeded his expectations. Upon learning that the 1930 Frolics generated a decent profit, Nockels, who had been in Washington, D.C., for two months fighting for WCFL, wired Lynch: "Send me some dough."[83] Income derived from the Radio Frolics, however, could not by itself counteract increasing expenditures. Although the 1929 Frolics generated enough cash to pay the station's legal fees for the year, the station nevertheless suffered a net loss of $22,338, compared with a $4,496 deficit the previous year.[84] Only increases in advertising revenue allowed WCFL to survive the depression.

Sponsored programming had been an important component of WCFL since its inception. Station business manager Franklin Lundquist often explained to union officials that "WCFL simply could not exist on labor patronage alone, because not all of the organizations in the Chicago Federation patronize and support it." WCFL had to sell commercial accounts if it were "to leave a balance sheet in black ink." Under Lundquist's direction, WCFL established the Union Broadcast Service to concentrate on "allocating the time assigned for commercial sponsorship and providing specialized service of every kind desired by advertisers." Carl P. McAssey, who headed the sales office, became the leading advocate for increased advertising and sponsored programming. Arguing that labor radio could not survive in the commercial radio world as a listener-supported station, he urged WCFL to accept sponsored shows as long as the shows and sponsors did not violate the station's principles and ideals.[85]

Sports, ethnic shows, and a few music-variety programs usually found ready sponsors. But selling the rest of WCFL's schedule proved difficult. Advertisers historically had avoided working-class periodicals because they considered the readers weak consumers. Prospective radio sponsors held a similar outlook toward a labor audience. Compounding this problem were complaints about WCFL's limited range and its poor sound quality. Lundquist pointed out that business "prejudice and bias against any sort of labor patronization" had cost WCFL much support. In addition, WCFL refused airtime to businesses that had practiced unfair labor policies.[86] The station did encourage businesses employing union labor to advertise and sponsor programs. Charles McMorrow, an official of the Boot and Shoe

Workers' Union, for example, helped arrange for the Florsheim Shoe Company—a union employer—to advertise over the station in 1929. McAssey denied that union members were weak consumers. Following the lead of one WCFL advertiser, McAssey and his staff insisted that the station's audience comprised "the best paid and most constantly employed working people in America, not only able but willing to buy" quality merchandise.[87]

The sponsored programming and advertisements that made their way into the WCFL schedule left much to be desired. McAssey's sales team occasionally wandered from the principles and ideals of organized labor and, in at least one instance in 1932, received a warning from the CFL Executive Board to "exercise greater care in acceptance of advertising not conforming to organized labor's best interests." Nevertheless, WCFL managers learned from their *Federation News* colleagues that it was fiscally irresponsible to limit advertising only to concerns that were 100 percent union.[88]

WCFL's sponsors were more likely to engage in excessive commercialization than in outright antilabor behavior. Under the rubric of entertainment programming, businesses often presented fifteen- to sixty-minute sales pitches. The "Leiter Store Program," which aired for thirty minutes at 7:30 P.M. twice a week during early 1929, offered brief musical interludes between prolonged descriptions of the shopping bargains available at its downtown department stores. Throughout 1930–32, a significant proportion of WCFL's morning schedule went to programs such as "Lane Bryant Shopping News," "Evans Furriers," and the "Radio Shoppers Club," all of which duplicated the format of the Leiter show.[89] Henry Parks's "whimsical tinkle of the keys" for a retail furrier in May 1931 only came "between long and tedious readings on bargains on furs." A reviewer for *Variety* lamented that "on a 15-minute program less than a third of the time is devoted to the piano romancing."[90] *Variety* also condemned the daily "Bart Fur Factory" for its "perfunctory" orchestra music and its unabashed "direct merchandising." While WCFL shunned the label of commercial station, its advertisements were among "the frankest and least restrained of any in town."[91]

As the depression worsened, network competition intensified, and station expenses rose, WCFL became more dependent on advertising revenue. Station income from advertising increased by over 62 percent between the first half of 1929 and the first half of 1930—jumping from $39,782 to $64,525. Advertising revenue already totaled $77,496 in 1929, or over 70 percent of the entire station income for the year.[92] Nockels knew that WCFL could not survive without advertising. The sponsored portion of WCFL's schedule steadily grew and the sustaining segment shrank. When WCFL decided in April 1932 to suspend the political commentary of Meyer Fink, Nockels explained that the "prime reason . . . was because the time could be sold and as you know we are in great financial need and every dollar counts." Even before terminating Fink's program, station staff had pressured the liberal Chicago attorney to ease his criticisms of utility companies because "of a certain advertising contract."[93]

The desire to realize Nockels's dream of a nationwide labor radio network, even in the context of the Great Depression, intensified the search for more commercial advertisers for WCFL. Nockels and Lundquist believed that a clear channel, unlimited power, and shortwave broadcast capacity would make WCFL "national in its scope of activity." Once workers "from Maine to California" could hear the Voice of Labor, "then and only then, could WCFL reasonably expect the support of every local throughout the United States." Lundquist contended that "if such a Utopian desire could be attained, WCFL could disdainfully refuse any and all forms of commercial patronage."[94] CFL officials held that advertising was a necessary evil; it would help establish the super station that, in turn, would bring national recognition and financing and thus eliminate dependence on advertisers.

Believing that a superpower WCFL was a realistic goal, Nockels and his staff pushed ahead with plans to improve existing studio facilities, build a new transmitting station, and develop shortwave capabilities. They attempted all this even as the depression wreaked havoc on the Chicago working class. Having outgrown its facilities in the Brunswick building by 1931, the CFL negotiated with the American Furniture Mart Corporation for space in its building located at Lake Shore Drive and Huron Street. Officials worked out a deal similar to the existing one with the Brunswick company and moved the offices of the federation, the newspaper, and the radio station in late August. The formal dedication of the new WCFL facilities took place on September 25, 1931, with an assortment of music, including performances by artists from the Polish, Jewish, Irish, and German ethnic hours in the new Sam Gompers studio. Earlier in the year, WCFL had purchased a new fifteen-hundred-watt transmitter from RCA and installed it at Navy Pier.[95] Shortwave broadcasting experiments continued throughout this period. Having secured FRC approval to use its shortwave transmitter, W9XAA, WCFL began broadcasting test programs in November 1929. The following fall, WCFL began international broadcasting experiments. By early 1931, letters from Europe, Central America, and the Caribbean indicated good daytime reception of WCFL programs.[96]

Edward N. Nockels, the father of labor radio. Nockels guided WCFL during its most militant period (1926–37). (Photo by Burke and Koretke, ICHi-26119, courtesy of the Chicago Historical Society)

491.5 METERS

500 WATTS

W—C—F—L
THE CHICAGO FEDERATION LABOR
BROADCAST STATION LOCATED ON
THE MUNICIPAL PIER, CHICAGO, ILLINOIS

Workers from various Chicago trade unions erected a transmitter and installed the equipment for a WCFL studio in the north tower at the east end of Navy Pier in 1926. WCFL began regular broadcasts on July 27, 1926. This illustration is from the CFL letterhead, circa 1926. (Courtesy of the Chicago Historical Society)

In 1927 WCFL broadcasted the Labor Day celebration at Soldier Field sponsored by the CFL. The festivities simultaneously publicized labor's goals to a wider audience, enhanced worker solidarity, and entertained the public. For a one-dollar admission, workers and their families enjoyed dancing, animal acts, soccer and baseball games, clowns, concert bands, and fireworks. All proceeds supported labor radio. (Photo by Burke and Koretke, ICHi-20832, courtesy of the Chicago Historical Society)

The centerpiece of Ed Nockels's plan for a nationwide radio system was the con-
struction of a superpower station. Nockels purchased land near Downers Grove
in mid-1928, set aside twenty acres for the future transmitter, and subdivided the
remaining land into building lots. A real estate company advertised the lots in the
Federation News, June 22, 1929, 9. Nockels wanted to use the proceeds from the
real estate sales to finance the construction costs of the new station but the Great
Depression quickly undermined his scheme. (Courtesy of the Chicago Historical Society)

THE AIR MUST REMAIN FREE. IT MUST NOT BE HARNESSED, METERED AND METED OUT TO THOSE WHO CAN PAY A BIG PRICE AND EXACT A BIGGER TOLL.

"The Air Must Remain Free," cartoon in *Federation News,* September 7, 1929, 1. This cartoon portrayed the organized labor movement, helped by WCFL, as a solitary defender of the public's right to freedom of the air. Aligned against labor and the public were powerful vested commercial interests and the federal government's own regulatory body. (Courtesy of the Chicago Historical Society)

"Am I Not as Important . . . ," cartoon in *Federation News,* April 12, 1930, 1. WCFL and CFL officials contended that Federal Radio Commission Order No. 40, issued in the fall of 1928, unfairly allocated the nation's forty clear channels to stations owned and operated by corporate interests, thereby denying organized labor the right to secure one clear channel with adequate power and time. (Courtesy of the Chicago Historical Society)

Ed Nockels (*left*), Alderman Oscar Nelson (*center*), and CFL president John Fitz-patrick (*right*), the founders of WCFL, spoke over the radio station during the La-bor Day celebration at Soldier Field in 1930. (From the *Federation News,* courtesy of the Chicago Historical Society)

"STAKING OUT HIS CLAIM"

"Staking Out His Claim," cartoon in *Federation News,* February 7, 1931, 2. This cartoon reflected the WCFL perspective that the radio industry and the Federal Radio Commission had defined public interest, convenience, and necessity in terms of private property rights and profits; that it had ignored the need for ensuring equal access to radio facilities for varying views and opinions; and that it therefore demonstrated contempt for workers and the general public. (Courtesy of the Chicago Historical Society)

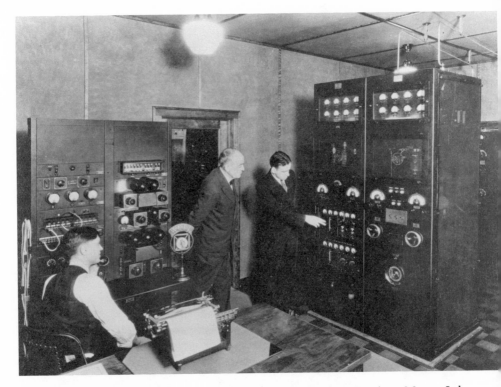

In the fall of 1931 WCFL moved its studios to the American Furniture Mart at Lake Shore Drive and Huron Street. Maynard Marquardt (*right*), WCFL's engineer, explains the operation of equipment to Ed Nockels (*center*), as J. J. Kurilla (*left*) looks on, April 4, 1931. (Photo by Thos. Coke Knight, Inc., ICHi-26121, courtesy of the Chicago Historical Society)

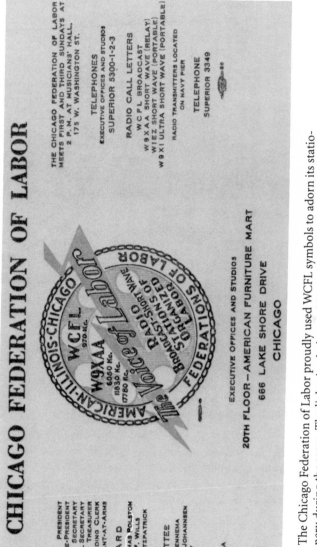

CHICAGO FEDERATION OF LABOR

OFFICERS

JOHN FITZPATRICK - - - PRESIDENT
OSCAR F. NELSON - - VICE-PRESIDENT
E. N. NOCKELS - - - SECRETARY
MAURICE LYNCH - FINANCIAL SECRETARY
ARTHUR E. OLSEN - - TREASURER
HARRY E. SCHECK - READING CLERK
CHAS. HAYMAN - SERGEANT-AT-ARMS

EXECUTIVE BOARD

GEORGE BENDEL   W. THOMAS POLSTON
PAUL B. DAVID   CHAS. F. WILLS
LILLIAN HERSTEIN   JOHN FITZPATRICK
        EDW. N. NOCKELS

LEGISLATIVE COMMITTEE

F. A. ACKERMAN   J. G. BENNEMA
MEYER ADELMAN   ANTON JOHANNSEN
        ELIZABETH A. GRADY

E. N. NOCKELS
        GEN. MGR. WCFL · W9XAA

THE CHICAGO FEDERATION OF LABOR
MEETS FIRST AND THIRD SUNDAYS AT
2 P.M. AT MUSICIANS' HALL,
175 W. WASHINGTON ST.

TELEPHONES
EXECUTIVE OFFICES AND STUDIOS
SUPERIOR 5300-1-2-3

RADIO CALL LETTERS
W C F L BROADCAST
W9XAA SHORT WAVE (RELAY)
W1EZ SHORT WAVE (PORTABLE)
W9XI ULTRA SHORT WAVE (PORTABLE)

RADIO TRANSMITTERS LOCATED
ON NAVY PIER

TELEPHONE
SUPERIOR 3349

EXECUTIVE OFFICES AND STUDIOS
20TH FLOOR—AMERICAN FURNITURE MART
666 LAKE SHORE DRIVE
CHICAGO

The Chicago Federation of Labor proudly used WCFL symbols to adorn its stationery during the 1930s. The lightning bolt stood for both radio waves and electricity. (Courtesy of the Chicago Historical Society)

Ed Nockels developed a cordial working relationship with a variety of progressive political and social movements, organizations, and individuals, offering them free use of WCFL facilities. This painting depicts the International League for Peace and Freedom address by Jane Addams over WCFL on May 4, 1935. (Photo by Frank Willming, ICHi-26120, courtesy of the Chicago Historical Society)

William Lee became president of the CFL upon John Fitzpatrick's death in 1946. A quest for power and a commitment to business unionism characterized Lee's reign as CFL chief (1946–84). WCFL continued to serve the publicity interests of the CFL as illustrated here by Lee's radio speech at a banquet, circa the 1950s. (ICHi-26122, courtesy of the Chicago Historical Society)

A close personal friend of William Lee, Richard J. Daley found WCFL a consistent supporter of his political campaigns and programs through his tenure as mayor. In 1956, Daley celebrated WCFL's thirtieth anniversary with a plea for labor support for his clean-up Chicago campaign. (From the *Federation News,* courtesy of the Chicago Historical Society)

The 1950s and early 1960s proved to be the most profitable era in the history of WCFL in part because of local sports programming. William Lee attributed much of the station's financial success to the formation of a ten-state regional network to cover the Chicago White Sox baseball games. Here Bob Rhodes (*far left*), a station sports commentator, and Ralph Kiner, a commentator and former major league all-star player, chat with Roy Sievers of the White Sox in 1961. (From the *Federation News,* courtesy of the Chicago Historical Society)

The centerpiece of Nockels's plan for a nationwide labor radio system was the construction of a superpower broadcasting station. With funds borrowed from the Laundry and Dye House Drivers' Union, Nockels had purchased one hundred acres of land near Downers Grove in mid-1928. CFL officials set aside a twenty-acre plot for the future site of the fifty-thousand-watt broadcasting station, WCFL's shortwave and television transmitters, and experimental laboratories. They subdivided the remaining eighty acres into 72 business sites and 258 home building lots and hired a real estate company to prepare the property for sale. Nockels hoped to finance a significant part of the construction cost of the new radio station—estimated at one hundred thousand dollars—with the proceeds from the property sales. The remainder of the construction costs would come from national labor organizations once the labor radio network began coast-to-coast operations.[97]

Nockels's vision for the "WCFL 50,000 Watt Radio Broadcast Station-Labor Park-Subdivision" was grandiose. Influenced by the elaborate housing and transportation scheme developed by the ACWA in New York City, Nockels hoped to create a self-contained working-class community around the radio station complex. He saw the sale of relatively inexpensive housing lots to union members as an important service offered by the CFL to workers. In addition, the radio station's power plant—necessary to guarantee that the government or business could not eliminate WCFL from the air—would provide cheap electricity for the surrounding community and demonstrate the efficacy of "public ownership" of utilities. Nockels envisioned that working-class home owners would substitute the lower-priced electricity for gas as a source of heating and that this expanded use of electricity would eventually help cover the estimated one-hundred-thousand-dollar cost for the power plant. Beginning in the spring of 1929, CFL officials promoted the sale of property in the Labor Park-Subdivision as a good investment for unions or individuals, as a valuable service to workers wanting new, affordable housing, and as a way to support labor radio. Fitzpatrick, Nockels, Lundquist, and a dozen other labor officials, as well as a few union locals, became the first to purchase lots.[98]

At a meeting of the CFL in June 1929, Nockels explained his plan and, in a dramatic gesture, moved to transfer the title of the Downers Grove land, which had been in his name, to the federation, to be held in trust for the members. He estimated the property's value at "a half million dollars, to say nothing of what your broadcast station is worth and will be worth within the next year or two." CFL officials planned to "ask one hundred or more labor organizations that . . . have some money . . . to buy one or two or three lots for their organization to hold for themselves, or to sell to their members or others, in order that we may immediately take the money accruing from the sale of the lots" to construct the new fifty-thousand-watt station. Charles Wills of the *Federation News* and the Building Service Employees' Union pointed out that by buying a lot a union had "an opportunity to contribute to the radio station and still at the same time have a title deed to a piece of property that is bound to increase in value when the station is on its way to completion." Lillian Herstein proclaimed that in turning over the property's title to the CFL, Nockels "was really giving the Federation much more than a half million dollars, since he gave them the most fundamental thing in human life and liberty—an instrument for the freedom of expression."[99]

Critics of labor capitalism, noting that the CFL already had problems with its ongoing businesses (*Federation News* and WCFL), questioned the outcome of this experiment in "real estate and radio station financing."[100] Nockels denied that either the radio station or the real estate deal were "commercial" ventures. "We are not interested in profits," he contended, but rather "in the condition of workers and the compensation they shall receive." The real estate–radio operation sought to protect "the labor movement against the encroachment of Capital and the vested interests" by giving "Labor its chance to take the offensive when necessary, instead of always having to be on the defensive." Nockels insisted that unions could do whatever they desired with the lots—hold them for their own use or resell them to union members or to the general public, either at cost or at a profit.[101]

Several Chicago-area unions inspected the Labor Park during the summer of 1929. They found that residential lots sold for $1,250–$1,500 and business lots for $1,600–$2,250. The terms of payment seemed reasonable: Unions paid 25 percent of the price in cash, with the balance spread over three years; individuals put down 10 percent cash and had three and a half years to pay the balance. Although the post office clerks, carpenters, and other local unions decided to purchase individual lots, the majority of labor organizations remained uncommitted; some were wary of investing in real estate, others were too weak financially to make the down payment.[102] The onset of the Great Depression effectively undermined Nockels's elaborate funding scheme and the WCFL property remained virtually untouched for the next three years.

Only in the summer of 1932, in the aftermath of the FRC-NBC deal, did the CFL Executive Board vote to proceed with the construction of the foun-

dation of a broadcast building and antenna towers, as well as a water supply system, in Downers Grove. Lacking both the funds and FRC approval
to construct a fifty-thousand-watt station, WCFL sought financing for a
five-thousand-watt transmitter. Ground-breaking ceremonies took place on
August 1. To a rain-soaked assembly of labor and political dignitaries, Nockels recounted WCFL's long struggle for survival and described the planned
new station and its potential for unrivaled national and global service.
WCFL publicists continued to wax eloquently about a future super radio
station in the Chicago suburb: "Behold—once a grazing prairie, mighty
labor is transforming it into an Eden of ethereal waves where one may par-
take of the apple of wisdom without suffering banishment."[103] But depression-era financial crises delayed both the construction of the new facilities
and FRC approval for increased power. One year after the ground-breaking ceremony, Nockels was still trying to negotiate a $150,000 loan to finance
the station. Actual construction of the fifty-thousand-watt broadcast transmitter at Downers Grove was delayed for over a decade.[104]

· · ·

Labor radio's fight for a clear channel took place in less than ideal circumstances; and Nockels remained less than fully satisfied with the outcome of
the 1929–32 battle. Nevertheless, the bureaucratic, legislative, and legal struggles themselves were significant for several reasons. WCFL's stand against
representatives of corporate radio provided a rallying point for Chicago's
trade unions and, to a lesser extent, the national labor movement. Moreover, labor radio's clash with big business and government publicized important messages that the CFL wished to convey to different audiences:
Nockels and his associates hoped to alert the labor movement to the usefulness of labor radio in influencing national economic and political affairs
and, at the same time, to educate the general public and especially unorganized workers to the merit of the labor movement itself. The "publicity
value" of the Voice of Labor derived not solely from the station's programming but also from WCFL's very existence.[105] Labor radio's continued operation in the face of overwhelming opposition and its fight for equal treatment among the nation's mass media helped to enhance and to spread the
cause of organized labor.

An important facet of WCFL's publicity function was its role in aiding
and linking together other labor institutions and traditions and presenting
them to the larger community. Labor radio supported the Chicago Trades
Union Label League's various educational campaigns and the union label

store. Two traditions and institutions in particular relied heavily upon WCFL: Radio Frolics and Labor Day celebrations. The first WCFL Radio Frolics held in December 1926 celebrated the creation of labor radio; subsequent events in 1927–29 functioned as supplemental income sources for the station. In the midst of the battle with the FRC and the broadcasting industry, CFL officials decided to make the Frolics into a permanent annual celebration. Charles Wills, chairman of the CFL Radio Frolics Committee, explained in January 1930 that while the Frolics celebrated the nation's only labor broadcasting outlet and helped "to maintain our radio station and meet the expenses of our fight for a clear channel and unlimited time," it also showed the critics of organized labor "what kind of people we are."[106]

The 1930 Radio Frolics attracted approximately ten thousand workers, their families, and friends to an evening of entertainment and food, including music, dancing, and comedy performed by WCFL ethnic artists and Chicago theatrical stars.[107] Impressed by the success of the event, John Fitzpatrick observed how WCFL had brought "something different into our lives." Labor radio offered all of Chicago's workers a common reference point through its programming of traditional Labor Day ceremonies and new celebrations such as the Frolics, the CFL-sponsored summer band concerts on Navy Pier, and Junior Federation Club activities. Fitzpatrick continued:

> Before the advent of WCFL we used to go on our separate ways and have our own social affairs. That was all right for the various organizations, but here, in the last few years, we have been developing something fine that permeates the entire labor movement, reaching out not only to the families of the members, but to their friends and associates as well, and they come to an affair of this kind and they find it is a very pleasing and enjoyable one, in agreeable surroundings, and it helps the labor movement considerably.[108]

CFL officials did not "expect the 1931 Frolics to be anything like the financial success that it was a year ago, on account of the continued depression . . . , but we do expect it to be as great a success, socially." When a crowd of some nine thousand attended the event, Fitzpatrick again commented on "how the activities of this Federation . . . and of WCFL appeal to the rank and file of the labor organizations and the public."[109] The WCFL Radio Frolics not only supplemented the station's income but it also created a setting that strengthened social ties among workers and enhanced labor's image in the community.

Like the Radio Frolics, Labor Day activities had a multiple impact on the workers of Chicago and, like the Frolics, they became closely linked with WCFL. The advent of labor radio revitalized the celebration of Labor Day in Chicago during the late twenties and early thirties. Attracting some one hundred thousand people in 1930 and seventy-five thousand in 1931, the CFL's Labor Day activities entertained and educated workers and the general public. Labor Day had always been "a day on which unionists defined themselves in confident tones to the nation at large"; and the Chicago celebrations rejoiced in organized labor's accomplishments. The huge programs, carefully planned by CFL delegates and held at Soldier Field, included band concerts, fireworks, automobile and motorcycle races, trade union parades, performances by WCFL staff artists, children's parades, and, of course, speeches by prominent labor officials. At the same time, these mass events served as protest demonstrations, particularly in 1930 and 1931, against the severe unemployment plaguing the city and nation. WCFL publicized and broadcasted the event, emphasizing both its entertainment and political contexts. Nockels also saw the Labor Day celebration at Soldier Field as a way of enticing workers and their families to the city's lakefront and exposing them to the area's extensive recreational and educational opportunities. CFL officials finally hoped that ticket sales to the event would generate additional income for labor radio.[110]

Through its labor programming, ethnic hours, the Junior Federation Club, the use of local talent, and the broadcasting of social and political events such as the Frolics and Labor Day celebrations, WCFL made itself a community and grass-roots institution. Its moments of crass commercialization and growing reliance on advertising notwithstanding, labor radio performed a valuable service to Chicago's working classes by promoting and strengthening, as Lizabeth Cohen has argued in a similar context, "ethnic . . . and working class affiliations."[111]

Tangled Web, 1932–37

The spring 1932 deal between organized labor and the FRC required an end to union support for special legislation to guarantee a clear channel for labor radio. Educational broadcasters had hoped that a successful labor effort to reserve clear channels for its use would set the precedent for the passage of the Fess bill. When the AFL and the CFL withdrew from the legislative crusade, some advocates of educational radio felt betrayed. Officials of the Ventura Free Press, for example, quietly condemned what they characterized as the "graft and corruption" of the Chicago labor movement and questioned the CFL's fitness "to operate any kind of a radio station even with 5 watts." S. Howard Evans, who had supported WCFL and had attacked the ABA's stands on the Glenn amendment and the Fess bill in 1931, now dismissed the role of labor in radio reform, arguing that it never was in a position either to aid or hinder that movement.[1] Such sentiments, while understandable on an emotional level, misread the complexity of the situation in Chicago and Washington.

WCFL's compromise with the FRC and NBC came as economic conditions rapidly deteriorated in Chicago. By May 1932, a full 40 percent of the city's work force was unemployed and 130,000 families received relief assistance—compared to 13,000 two years earlier.[2] As most unions fought for their very survival, they relegated labor radio to a second- or third-tier concern. This came at just the time that radio, especially network radio, became an increasingly important fixture in American life and, consequently, a growing source of profits for corporate owners. Edward Nockels recognized these conflicting forces at work and sought to do whatever was necessary to secure labor radio's continued existence. Such a commitment led him to weave a tangled web of compromises and deals with the most unlikely of partners.

· · ·

Nockels and the CFL only temporarily abandoned their war against the commercial broadcasting system in 1932. They did not consider the arrangement with the FRC and NBC a permanent solution to the problem of WCFL and the radio trust. Indeed, a year after the deal, FRC secretary Herbert L. Pettey ordered WCFL to explain why the FRC should extend the station's "special experimental authorization" to broadcast after sunset in Seattle. Nockels feared that the FRC request "is a fishing expedition and no matter how we make it out, somewhere along the line, we will be refused the Special Authorization."[3] Thus Nockels continued his battle for a clear channel, increased power, and unlimited time. The changing political environment in 1932–34 provided Nockels and his counterparts in the nonprofit radio alliance with what they presumed was a friendly and supportive administration in the White House.

Organized labor first responded to the Democratic presidential candidate, Franklin D. Roosevelt, with equal measures of ambivalence and skepticism. Although the New York governor's campaign devoted great attention to poverty, unemployment, and other working-class problems, it never mentioned unions or the right to organize and bargain collectively. Roosevelt's appointment of Frances Perkins as secretary of labor, who lacked a union background, incensed AFL leaders. But the attitudes of union officers and rank-and-file workers changed as the New Deal created relief and reform mechanisms such as the Federal Emergency Relief Agency, the National Recovery Administration, and the Works Progress Administration. Workers came to see Roosevelt, the New Deal, and the Democratic party as meeting their needs. The relationship between the New Deal and the labor movement remained, as James R. Green has written, "a complex one" as "worker militancy and the threat of radicalism pushed the New Deal to the left," while "government actions and policies helped the new unions gain a foothold in basic industries."[4]

The National Industrial Recovery Act, including section 7(a), which recognized the right of workers to organize unions and to engage in collective bargaining with leaders of their own choosing, proved important to the labor movement. In addition to helping workers to organize, the act out-lined a program to achieve industrial reorganization and planning. The National Recovery Administration (NRA), headed by Hugh S. Johnson, required businesses to form trade associations on an industrywide basis. These organs would draw up codes of fair and unfair business practices and establish machinery capable of achieving some degree of economic plan-ning—for example, controlling prices of raw materials and finished goods and setting production quotas. Although labor and consumers had repre-sentation on the code authorities, business leaders dominated the formu-lation of industry codes. Johnson believed that the NRA constituted a form of industrial self-government and hence its success rested on business ex-ecutives. With regard to workers, Johnson believed that as "partners of management in the general producer interest," they had the right to orga-nize; yet he opposed strikes and other labor organizing tactics.[5]

Although CFL officials resisted the pro-business orientation of the NRA and its administrator, they believed that it offered them an opportunity to expand trade unionism and to improve working conditions and benefits in Chicago. Fitzpatrick joined the Chicago Recovery Committee, if for no other reason than to keep an eye on the local business association. The CFL studied how to organize Chicago's unorganized workers under the provi-sions of the NRA. Nockels became the labor advisor to the radio broadcast-ing industry in its effort to create an industry code.[6]

As labor advisor, and later as a member of the Code Authority for the Radio Broadcasting Industry, Nockels worked to enhance the position of labor radio, while challenging the NAB and the radio trust. The NAB for-mally submitted a proposed code for the broadcasting industry in late August 1933. Dismissing the proposal as meaningless, Nockels noted that the labor wage provisions reduced wages instead of maintaining or raising them; that the unfair practice clauses would perpetuate existing unfair prac-tices and sanction new ones; and that the proposed Code Authority placed too much power in the hands of the networks, their affiliates, and their advertisers. After consulting with Actors' Equity, the American Federation of Musicians, and the Brotherhood of Electrical Engineers, Nockels asked WCFL attorney Benjamin F. Goldstein to draw up an alternative code that would protect labor. As a radio station, WCFL had the right to submit modifications to the basic code. On behalf of John Fitzpatrick and WCFL, Goldstein presented labor's proposal at hearings on the radio code held in late September. Although unable to secure all the desired changes, Nockels did help to modify the radio industry's code.[7]

From his vantage point on the Code Authority, Nockels opposed NAB and network efforts to consolidate power in their own hands. The code agency had, among other responsibilities, the tasks of implementing the code and investigating alleged violations to it. To facilitate the latter function, Nockels proposed creating local or district committees to investigate and report on code violations. This proposal and a corollary suggestion that the Code Authority create an efficient system of local self-regulation reflected Nockels's interest in a decentralized system to enhance the power of local groups and to circumvent the power of the corporate radio industry. Although the Code Authority initially voted to adopt Nockels's resolution in September 1934, it revoked this decision in November. Nockels blamed the defeat on the machinations of "some Star Chamber session conducted and controlled" by "astute officials" of the NAB who sought to entrench their organization and to control "the situation locally as well as nationally." By defeating the plan for "efficient cooperation through localized units" of the Code Authority, the NAB succeeded in keeping power in the central body where industry leaders sat in control.[8] The experience of Nockels and Fitzpatrick with the NRA may have reinforced their suspicions of working with industry officials, but it did not undermine their growing faith in Roosevelt and the New Deal.

The CFL, like other labor bodies, initially approached Franklin Roosevelt with caution. Chicago teachers' head Lillian Herstein supported Norman Thomas for president in 1932 because she "couldn't see in Franklin D. Roosevelt . . . any promise for fundamental changes in the economic system that had thrown us into depression."[9] During the 1932 elections, the *Federation News* extensively covered local elections, but provided virtually no space to the presidential campaign. WCFL proudly announced that it aired Roosevelt's speeches in Chicago in July, but this had more to do with the *way* that WCFL carried the speech (it experimented with a portable shortwave system) than with the candidate's message. Roosevelt, for his part, paid little attention to Fitzpatrick and Nockels, despite their reputations as "absolutely honest, able and influential [leaders] in the labor movement."[10]

But as the New Deal slowly addressed some of the nation's industrial problems and as workers began to identify with the Democratic party, the CFL came to embrace and defend President Roosevelt's recovery program. When Robert R. McCormick's *Chicago Tribune* and William Randolph Hearst's Chicago newspapers attacked Roosevelt and the NRA in 1933, the *Federation News* and WCFL denounced the attacks and supported the administration.[11] In 1934, Nockels ran in the Democratic party primary election for representative of the Tenth Congressional District. His platform revolved around protecting the interests of workers and supporting President Roosevelt's programs.[12] By 1936, WCFL had committed its facilities to securing Roosevelt's reelection. Nockels requested, for example, that NBC, from which WCFL received national political broadcasts, feed labor radio "any and all available speeches of President Roosevelt in preference to the broadcasts of the Republican National Convention or any other conflicting broadcast."[13]

Nockels hoped that WCFL support for Roosevelt would build goodwill with the president and thereby protect and improve the station's position in radio. He viewed the anti-NRA and anti-Roosevelt campaign as part of corporate America's opposition to progressive change. Another manifestation of this reactionary movement was the FRC's increasing harassment of WCFL—especially in regard to the 1932 deal. As early as July 1933, Nockels had asked Frank Walsh to introduce him "to the powers that be" in Washington in order to show the FRC "that we had some very good friends in the present administration" who supported a clear channel for labor radio.[14] In the fall, Nockels sent Walsh evidence of Chicago's anti-Roosevelt media, explaining that when these forces "get ready to attack our station, or if the FRC refuses to give us what we are entitled to, I want you to be in a position to get the word across to President Roosevelt and his secretary, Louis Howe, so that they will know who their friend has been in and out of season in Chicago." Convinced that NBC and CBS opposed Roosevelt and the NRA, Nockels wanted Walsh "to put in a good word with the President . . . that Labor's radio station is the only one that is going the route, especially in Chicago, and that WCFL should be given consideration for their loyalty to the administration when questions of interest affecting Labor's station come up."[15] Certainly such considerations were not beneath the president. Roosevelt needed radio to generate public support for his legislative programs.[16] Whether he would respond to the needs of WCFL was another matter.

Educational, agricultural, and religious broadcasters, as well as organized labor, embraced the New Deal's reform atmosphere. But Roosevelt made no significant move to alter the radio status quo in 1933. As the historians Philip Rosen and Robert McChesney have explained, the broadcasting networks had provided the president and his administration important access to the nation's airwaves so the White House had no wish to antagonize commercial radio with radical regulatory changes. Seeking an opportunity to restructure the broadcasting system, the nonprofit reformers grasped at Roosevelt's proposal to replace the 1927 Radio Act. The president asked Congress in early 1934 to combine the regulation of telegraphs, telephones, cables, and radio under a single communications commission.[17]

At a CFL meeting in February, Nockels introduced a resolution calling for a revamping of the nation's communication system. Arguing that telephones, telegraphs, and radios should not be controlled by private interests, Nockels proposed that the federal government assume control by creating a regulatory board with representatives from management, labor, and the general public.[18] Although not raising the issue at this forum, the CFL secretary recognized that reformulating the regulatory system might create the opportunity to reallocate clear broadcasting channels to nonprofit associations. Nockels did not publicly lead this renewed assault on the radio trust. Appearing before the Senate Committee on Interstate Commerce, which held hearings on the proposed communications bill in March 1934, Nockels testified only to the AFL's position on AT&T's telephone monopoly. The proposal for reallocating all frequencies, wavelengths, power, and time assignments and granting 25 percent of those facilities to educational, religious, agricultural, labor, cooperative, and other nonprofit groups came from Father John B. Harney, who represented New York radio station WLWL.[19] Using Harney's proposal as their base, Senators Henry D. Hatfield of West Virginia and Robert F. Wagner of New York introduced an amendment to the communications bill after the close of Senate hearings. A lively battle commenced.[20]

Nockels worked behind the scenes to find sponsors for the amendment. At a CFL meeting in April he told members that securing clear-channel stations for labor, religious, educational, and farm movements would "do more to destroy the monopoly and dictatorship of the air than anything else." Here was a concrete way to obstruct corporate radio's efforts from securing property rights in the air. Although Nockels urged trade unions across the nation to write to their representatives in Congress, he lamented organized labor's poor response. "It is often discouraging and disappointing to find how little response we get from our affiliated organizations when we call upon them for cooperation."[21]

When the House of Representatives Committee on Interstate and Foreign Commerce finally held hearings on the communications bill, Father Harney again raised the reserved-channel reallocation scheme. In written testimony to the committee, Nockels recounted the troubled history of WCFL and the development of the radio trust. He explained how the NAB sent out a cryptic telegram to all stations warning that passage of the Wag-

ner-Hatfield proposal would mean the cancellation of all licenses in ninety days. The telegram implied that station owners might not regain their
licenses and thus lose their capital investments. Attacking the NAB as a
"stool-pigeon" of the trust, Nockels lamented how the industry's oligopolistic elements "never fail to hide behind the skirts of the small stations,"
making it appear as though the trust's interests actually serve the "interest
of the little fellow." Nockels urged the House committee to disregard the
NAB-induced telegrams of protest against the amendment. Failure to enact the legislation, according to Nockels, would allow the radio trust to
maintain and increase its dangerous "stranglehold on the facilities of the
air."[22] In a letter to Robert Wagner in May, Nockels reiterated these arguments and insisted that "an equitable reallocation should be one of the main
purposes of the proposed communications commission."[23]

WCFL's effort to secure passage of the Wagner-Hatfield amendment included direct appeals to the White House. In late May 1934, Nockels asked
Louis Howe to hand deliver a three-page, single-spaced letter to the president. The letter reminded Roosevelt of the "relentless opposition" to the
New Deal and how "WCFL has stood alone in its unqualified support and
endorsement of your policies and your Administration." In closing, Nockels noted that the president could learn more about WCFL from Frank
Walsh who could substantiate "our claim for recognition as an effective
influence, not only in this community but throughout the central west."[24]
About a week later, Nockels informed Walsh about the pending legislation,
urging the attorney to become familiar with the material "because, as I said
before, I may have to be calling on you for a helping hand." The WCFL
manager was anxious and annoyed that "everybody has a drag with the
President" except labor. He accused FRC secretary Pettey, who had been the
director of radio publicity for the Democratic National Committee, of serving the interests of network radio owners, acting unfriendly to labor, and
aiming "to cause us trouble in the future." Nockels asked Walsh to prepare
for a major conflict.[25]

Unfortunately for Nockels, the battle already had ended by late May.
Whatever the state of preparedness of labor and other nonprofit groups for
winning clear radio channels, the opposition proved formidable. Nockels's
warnings concerning the radio trust's ability to co-opt small independent
stations and its ability to define the proper boundaries of the debate went
unheeded. For more than a year, the NAB had been engaged in an exhaustive effort to defend commercial broadcasting from all critics. The NAB's
Broadcasting in the United States, published in 1933, for example, was a 191-

page propaganda piece extolling the benefits and achievements of America's commercial and private broadcasting system, including its enhancement of free speech, democracy, individualism, and competition and its production of the greatest entertainment in the world.[26] In the end, the NAB, *Broadcasting* magazine, NBC, and CBS worked strenuously to convince station owners and a majority of legislators that the Wagner-Hatfield amendment would seriously undermine, if not destroy, this best of all possible broadcasting systems.

When the Senate finally turned to debate the Wagner-Hatfield amendment in mid-May, its members appeared sharply divided. Clarence C. Dill, one of the pioneers in radio legislation, vigorously opposed the reallocation scheme and urged his colleagues to postpone action pending a study of the idea by the new communications commission. The Washington senator perceptively argued that the so-called nonprofit religious and educational associations would have great difficulty in maintaining noncommercial stations in a commercial broadcasting structure. Even if nonprofit organizations secured clear channels and maximum power and time, without an independent source of funding, they would have to become commercial to survive in the capitalist marketplace. Indeed, the proposed amendment acknowledged this situation by authorizing the nonprofit stations "to sell air time in the commercial field sufficient to pay for the maintenance of the stations." Dill concluded that it was "bad policy" for Congress to become involved in this allocation scheme. Maine senator Wallace H. White added that the amendment would create havoc in the well-functioning broadcasting system and threaten it with destruction.[27]

Supporters of the amendment, led by Wagner and Hatfield, emphasized the issues of fairness, access to radio, and the lack of educational programming on commercial stations. But several senators remained torn between the two sides. Senator Simeon D. Fess of Ohio had sponsored the 1931 bill to allocate 15 percent of all airtime for educational purposes and initially had spoken in favor of the amendment; but now he voiced doubts. Perplexed legislators found Dill's proposal that the new commission study the reallocation idea an easy way of avoiding congressional complicity in the undermining of commercial broadcasting. With this safety valve, senators defeated the Wagner-Hatfield amendment by a vote of 42 to 23 (with 31 senators not voting). Fess voted against the amendment. The House debate over the reallocation scheme proved nonexistent, as only one representative rose to address the legitimate radio interests of religious, labor, farming, and educational groups.[28]

The communications bill sped through both houses of Congress during the late spring of 1934 and the president signed it on June 20. Taking effect on July 1, the Communications Act abolished the FRC, established the Federal Communications Commission (FCC), and granted the new body virtually all the powers the Radio Act of 1927 had given to the FRC: The authority to classify stations, assign wavelengths, inspect equipment, and issue and renew licenses according to the public interest, convenience, and necessity. The new law's only concession to the critics of commercial radio was section 307(c), which required that the FCC study and submit recommendations regarding the proposal that Congress pass a law allocating fixed percentages of broadcasting frequencies to specified types of nonprofit radio programs or to persons associated with nonprofit activities. The new commission, two of whose members were carryovers from the FRC, scheduled hearings for the fall of 1934.[29]

Having lost the battle for a diversified radio system in Congress, the reserved-channel forces had lost the war. The newly created FCC worked with virtually the same statutory base as the old FRC. Commissioners generally accepted the nation's broadcasting structure and remained reluctant to change policy. Hampson Gary, a Washington attorney and new commissioner, informed the NAB in mid-August that the FCC would build on the policies and practices of the FRC and engage in evolutionary, rather than revolutionary change. Sounding more like a spokesman for the radio industry than the supposedly impartial chair of the FCC's Broadcast Division, Gary declared the U.S. broadcasting system "one of the finest in the world." He assured the industry that it was neither desirable nor necessary for the FCC to exercise "bureaucratic control" or to "dictate what manner of entertainment or discussion shall go on the air." Such comforting comments notwithstanding, commercial radio prepared a detailed and massive defense.[30]

A few days after Gary's speech, the NAB sent an urgent message to radio stations across the nation warning them that they would be on trial at the FCC hearings. The association requested information from each and every station in order to prepare the industry's defense. Among other things, the NAB asked station owners to describe any arrangements they might have made on behalf of educational institutions, civic or charitable organizations, religious bodies, political organizations, public health services, and labor or farm groups. Stations were to indicate whether or not the service rendered was free of charge. If the station charged a fee, the NAB wished to know whether the fee was a regular commercial rate or merely an operating charge to cover actual cost.[31] The NAB collected data and sworn testimony from 269 stations and assembled some ten thousand pages of material to present at the FCC hearings.

NAB managing director Philip G. Loucks, acting as the industry's chief defense counsel, brought the station survey information before the FCC's Broadcast Division in mid-October. His witnesses included station and network officials as well as representatives of religious, educational, and civic groups who had used commercial radio to air their public service programs. The NAB hoped to prove that the private radio system cooperated with all the groups vying for exclusive channels of their own, provided the best program service in the world, and contributed to national economic recovery by stimulating consumption and assisting commerce. "Our testimony will show that any change, however slight, in the present system is undesirable from the standpoint of the public and disastrous from the standpoint of broadcasters and the vast majority" of "special interest" organizations.[32]

Station and network executives went to great lengths to outline the advantages that organized labor derived from the existing system. Henry A. Bellows, former commissioner of the FRC and current chairman of the NAB Legislative Committee, offered four representative letters from labor groups praising the cooperation of local radio stations.[33] More impressive than vague letters of recommendation from the hinterland were the testimonies of CBS executive Frederic A. Willis and NBC president Merlin H. Aylesworth. Both network officials read letters or reports written by AFL president William Green to bolster the industry's case that it met the broadcast needs of organized labor. In one letter, Green praised CBS for broadcasting the series "American Labor and the Nation" and for allowing the federation to use its facilities on Labor Day and during the AFL's annual convention. "This cooperation has been tendered without limitation of any kind," wrote Green. "It has been an educational service of a high order."[34]

Green offered an equally laudatory analysis of NBC's service to labor. Aylesworth inserted into the record of the hearings the complete set of NBC Advisory Council reports. Each document contained Green's comments on NBC's assistance to organized labor. In the 1934 report, Green waxed eloquent on NBC's high standards of excellence, finding it difficult to determine "on what date [NBC] reached its highest point in perfection of service." After noting the usual network willingness to broadcast Labor Day speeches and parts of the AFL convention, Green concluded that NBC "has steadfastly maintained the great democratic principle of free speech."[35] Corporate radio used Green's words to undermine the call for an independent and diversified broadcasting system.

The radio industry's unified and exhaustive defense of its commercial base followed the incoherent and contradictory testimony of nonprofit groups. Religious and educational organizations failed to coordinate their arguments or to reach a consensus on solutions to their various problems. One educational broadcaster suspected that the FCC might be willing to give educators seven or eight channels, if the commission did not then have to take care of labor and religious groups. Some nonprofit group leaders attempted to mollify commercial operators by affirming their belief in the American system. Withholding criticism of commercial radio, an educational leader confined his discussion to the advantages that might accrue from establishing a chain of nonprofit stations. Already working against a well-organized industry and facing a passive state organ, the reserved-channel proponents did little to assist what was rapidly becoming a quixotic cause.[36] Exacerbating the task of the nonprofit groups was the inconsistent policy of organized labor.

Nockels reiterated to both Chicago unions and AFL leaders that breaking the radio monopoly necessitated reallocating clear-channel frequencies to labor, education, and other nonprofit organizations. During the late summer of 1934, some union officers informally discussed the possibility of using the upcoming FCC hearings, and the apparent division among religious and educational groups, to demand as many as eleven new channels for organized labor. The AFL hierarchy considered what the creation of a nationwide labor network—with broadcasting facilities in most large cities—would mean for accelerating trade union organizing and consolidating gains made under the NRA.[37]

As the hearings on reserved channels opened in Washington, D.C., in early October, the AFL annual convention began in San Francisco. Delegates appeared overwhelmingly in favor of substantially changing the corporate broadcasting system. Four convention resolutions dealt with the issue. Resolution 171, submitted by AFL secretary Frank Morrison, required that the AFL petition the FCC and Congress to allocate not less than 50 percent of all radio facilities to nonprofit organizations or associations. Representatives from six state federations of labor proposed (Resolution 200) that the AFL "militantly" oppose any allocation of more than 50 percent of radio to private profit organizations and that it vigorously protest any FCC member who consented to such a division. Resolution 122 dealt specifically with WCFL and demanded that the FCC assign labor radio to a clear channel of 970 kilocycles, with unlimited time and maximum power. The resolution also formally "commended the courage, persistence and constructive, farsighted policy which led the Chicago Federation of Labor to establish station WCFL." The most radical of the proposals, Resolution 192, contended that because broadcasting belonged to the people, it should not be used or controlled by private interests as a means of profit or propaganda. This resolution, offered by the state federations of Washington and Oregon, demanded that the AFL lobby for legislation to nationalize radio broadcasting in the United States.[38] The powerful Committee on Resolutions endorsed and sent on to the Executive Council Resolutions 171, 122, and 200. Not surprisingly, it rejected the idea of nationalizing radio stations throughout the country. The National Committee on Education by Radio and other critics of the radio status quo commended the federation's "forward-looking position" as reflected in its convention resolutions.[39]

As the FCC hearings came to a close in November, the AFL's national legislative representative finally appeared. William C. Hushing inserted into the record the resolutions passed at the recent AFL convention. He outlined the problems of radio station WCFL, insisted that the station deserved to have a clear channel, and expressed the desire of rank-and-file workers throughout the nation to hear the Voice of Labor. Hushing's testimony clearly conveyed the AFL convention's desire to have Congress set aside frequencies for labor, education, and other nonprofit groups.[40]

On November 12, just four days after Hushing testified, William Green attended the FCC hearings. In a surprise move, Green refuted the earlier testimony, explaining that Hushing did not know about the AFL Executive Council's action at a meeting held *after* the convention adjourned. AFL leaders had always felt uneasy attacking corporate broadcasters. Just a year earlier, the AFL convention had given its blessings to the radio industry's advertising practices, thereby sanctioning broadcasting's commercial structure.[41] Green and others remained committed to furthering the image of the AFL as a responsible and cooperative labor organization and this meant working with, not against, the system. The Executive Council had reconsidered the resolutions and instructed Green to take whatever action he deemed appropriate. Green withdrew the AFL resolutions from further consideration by the FCC and asked the FCC to disregard the testimony of Hushing. The AFL president wanted the FCC to act only on the AFL convention resolution dealing with the labor radio station. Denying any financial interest in WCFL, Green urged the FCC to recommend that Congress set aside channel 970 kilocycles as a clear channel, with unlimited time and power. Broadcast Division Chairman Gary and Vice Chairman Thad H. Brown informed Green that although their division considered such requests, this specific petition was irrelevant to the issue of the hearings. The commissioners did agree to give Edward Nockels, who spoke briefly after Green, two weeks to consult with various AFL bodies and to present a formal brief to the FCC. Thus ended the participation of the AFL and the CFL in the hearings. Thus concluded the FCC hearings themselves.[42]

The FCC's report to Congress in January 1935 recommended that the legislative branch take no action regarding the allocation of frequencies to nonprofit organizations. According to the commissioners, commercial radio was willing and able to provide time for educational, religious, labor, and other nonprofit needs.[43] A forceful statement by the organized labor movement in favor of the reserved channel proposal would not have altered the FCC's final report. Nevertheless, the AFL's abrupt and complete abandonment of the nonprofit cause further weakened that movement's already tenuous position.

The AFL shift in position reflected a change in tactics, not in principle. Green, Woll, and other leaders desired reaching a corporatist compromise with business and government. They did not wish to jeopardize an already beneficial relationship with the radio networks—a relationship that the hearings accurately described. Indeed, in the aftermath of the hearings, the AFL and CBS resumed a two-year joint effort, with the cooperation of the National Advisory Council on Radio in Education and the Workers' Education Bureau, to present "Labor Speaks for Itself!" This program's fourth series (the first and second had aired in 1932 and the third in 1934) consisted of ten fifteen-minute broadcasts and aired over the CBS network on consecutive Friday evenings in the fall of 1935. Program themes included economic security, the National Labor Relations Act, labor standards, workers' education, the AFL, and dictatorship and democracy.[44] Satisfied with this kind of access to the nation's airwaves, AFL oligarchs never seriously sought a redivision of the electromagnetic spectrum. They endorsed WCFL's demand for a clear channel because it was the least they could do to demonstrate token support for one of their own city labor bodies.[45] While AFL actions derived from straightforward concerns, the relative silence of the CFL and Edward Nockels regarding the FCC hearings stemmed from a far more complicated array of forces.

The Voice of Labor endured a hectic period during 1933–35. In addition to battles with Congress and before the FCC, WCFL faced challenges and opportunities posed by commercial broadcasters and obstacles created by the AFL. Nockels searched for ways to guarantee WCFL's survival and continued development as a service for and a tool of the nation's working class during the depths of the Great Depression. The WCFL manager believed that, under the circumstances, the ends justified the means. Whatever potential paths to success Nockels uncovered—regardless of their condition, who built them, or where they might lead—he tried them all. Nockels frequently led WCFL down two or more paths at once. Such was the case during 1933–35: While pressuring the FCC for a clear channel, he simultaneously negotiated a complicated deal with NBC and planned WCFL's own regional network.

. . .

WCFL had maintained a business relationship with NBC since 1929 when the labor station began taking selected programming from the Blue network. The use of NBC programs did not inhibit Nockels from continuing his assault on the radio trust—of which NBC was a principal component. In December 1929, for example, Nockels accused NBC and the rest of the radio trust of trying "to prohibit any one with independent notions from securing the air and talking to the people." The movement toward toll and chain broadcasting, in which NBC took the lead, limited public access to a public resource and restricted freedom of speech by requiring people to pay to use the radio. Before a Senate committee in early 1930, Nockels questioned whether "it is in the public interest, necessity, and convenience that practically the entire Nation should receive its radio programs from the city of New York, and that such programs should be selected and determined by two or three corporations." NBC had no interest in the public welfare; instead it wanted "to make money, to acquire power, and to control . . . this unparalleled new means of communication." Nockels remained convinced that NBC's clout stopped "us from getting a 40-hour week written into" the NRA code for the radio industry. When RCA became the target of antitrust action in 1931, Nockels demanded that the FRC deny license renewals to NBC-owned stations because their parent company had violated the Radio Act's antimonopoly provisions.[46]

NBC officials, for their part, developed a multisided strategy toward labor radio and organized labor. They found WCFL and its manager beneath contempt and suspected everything that Nockels did. When WCFL engineers requested technical assistance, NBC officers usually refused, criticizing the station's inability to do anything on its own.[47] WCFL's failure to pay for the sustaining programming it secured from the network exacerbated the relations between the two. By February 1933, WCFL owed NBC $2,381.25. Niles Trammell, vice president in charge of NBC's central division, warned

Nockels that failure to pay his current bills would lead to WCFL's removal from the network. Privately, Trammell admitted that NBC "probably would never get the money from the voice of labor." But this was not necessarily a bad thing because, as he told NBC vice president Frank M. Russell, NBC should hold the debt over Nockels's "head until such time as we wanted something from him."[48]

The network took an entirely different approach to the AFL. NBC and its parent company, RCA, were both practitioners of corporatist policy, willing to cooperate with "responsible" labor leaders such as William Green and Matthew Woll.[49] Green's presence on NBC's National Advisory Council demonstrated part of this cooperation. This spirit also manifested itself in the behavior of NBC president Merlin H. Aylesworth, who often publicly displayed the fairness of his network. Socialist party leader Norman Thomas acknowledged his own role as NBC's "pet radical" during the thirties, explaining that he "had been valuable to the N.B.C. as a proof of [its] liberalism." Radio commentator H. V. Kaltenborn observed that Aylesworth occasionally "takes particular care to allot radio time to some well-behaved liberal or radical speaker like Norman Thomas, and then advertises this concession widely and vigorously."[50] The harmonious relationship between the AFL hierarchy and the NBC boardroom helped to clear the way for the spring 1932 deal in which NBC and its Seattle affiliate, KJR, agreed to allow WCFL to broadcast beyond sunset on the West Coast. This concession represented a temporary privilege granted by the FRC and NBC to WCFL; it was not a permanent right won by labor radio. NBC bestowed the privilege, in part, to placate the AFL leadership and maintain capital-labor cooperation and, in part, to assure that friendly relations with WCFL would protect the company's business interests in Chicago.

With the Red and Blue networks, NBC required at least two full-time outlets in the lucrative Chicago market. As of 1934, the network possessed WMAQ, which carried NBC Red programs, and WENR, which aired the Blue schedule. NBC owned a half interest in WMAQ, with an option to purchase the other half by November 1934. The network had purchased WENR in 1931, but the station shared its frequency (870 kilocycles), and hence time, with WLS. The latter station, owned by Burridge D. Butler and the Prairie Farmer Publishing Company, lacked its own transmitter and thus, through a contractual arrangement with NBC, used the WENR transmitter. When negotiations to renew the WENR-WLS contract began, NBC opposed Butler's proposed revisions. Network officials contended that WLS made "more money today than any other fifty kilowatt transmitter in the country, with the probable exception of WLW [in Cincinnati]." Trammell described Butler as "a bull-headed individual" destined to cause trouble. Anticipating a breakdown in negotiations, Trammell recommended that NBC develop other options and "train our guns accordingly."[51]

Of the various options that Trammell outlined in the early spring of 1934, only one seemed viable. If NBC could gain control of WCFL's operation and management, then the company could do one of two things: It could lease WCFL to Butler "for a consideration and the exclusive use of his share of 870" or it could sell WENR to Butler and "place all of our programs on WCFL, and increase the power of the [WCFL] transmitter." An NBC take-over of WCFL, concluded Trammell, "would fortify our position in Chicago."[52] Trammell and Frank Russell, who initiated talks with labor officials, hoped to manipulate NBC's collaborative relationship with the AFL hierarchy and the deteriorating financial situation of WCFL to the network's advantage.[53]

Throughout the spring and summer of 1934, NBC officers negotiated with representatives of both WLS and WCFL. Discussions with Butler were difficult, but the network concluded a satisfactory contract with WLS by September.[54] A resolution to the WLS problem did not mean the end of discussions with labor. On the contrary, negotiations with labor representatives intensified during the fall of 1934 as network officials sought to enhance both their Chicago and national markets. Russell's contacts with "responsible" labor officials revealed that they recognized WCFL's need for a "better plan of operation." But Nockels resisted NBC's efforts to lease labor radio's facilities.[55]

Like their colleagues in the NAB, NBC executives worried about the fall 1934 FCC hearings and the effort on the part of "special interests" to extend government control over radio. Russell, among other NBC officials, warned of "certain elements in the labor movement" who favored legislation "detrimental to the best interests of the American system of broadcasting." The labor leaders, who Russell never named, had approached Senators Wagner and Hatfield and helped produce the dangerous amendment to the Communications Act. Russell was certain that "in the main these activities have been carried on *without* the encouragement of officials of the American Federation of Labor."[56] NBC president Aylesworth, RCA president David Sarnoff, and their subordinates firmly believed that the AFL hierarchy shared their conviction that commercial broadcasting by serving mass audiences served the public interest. The threat from the "special interests" and from irresponsible critics such as Nockels, however, forced NBC to act.

Aylesworth suggested that, in preparing for the hearings, NBC tone down its commercialism, removing possibly offensive advertisements from its broadcasts; improve the quality of its sustaining programs; and present "the real facts about American broadcasting."[57]

It was in this environment that Nockels contacted NBC in September 1934 and informed Aylesworth that the CFL and the AFL soon would demand that the FCC grant WCFL a clear channel on 970 kilocycles. Nockels promised that WCFL would not interfere with station KJR; and he asked Aylesworth if NBC "will resist this position." An annoyed NBC president responded that the network had "always cooperated with the" AFL and would continue that policy by permitting the "principal executives of organized labor" to use radio. Aylesworth's reference to the union elite obviously excluded Nockels. Criticizing CFL ineptness, Aylesworth pointed out that NBC had allowed WCFL to broadcast with a five-thousand-watt transmitter in order to test interference with station KJR, but that WCFL had failed to do so. The NBC chief failed to understand WCFL's desire to make 970 kilocycles into a clear channel. But he also feared that a CFL request to the FCC to make 970 kilocycles into a regional channel would mean open competition for the frequency. It was far preferable for WCFL and KJR to cooperate and jointly use the channel than to invite FCC interference.[58]

In the fall of 1934, as the FCC Broadcast Division held its hearings on section 307(c) of the Communications Act, Nockels shifted his position on cooperation with NBC. It is possible that the powerful network's promised concessions overwhelmed Nockels's aversion to the radio trust. It is doubtful, however, that Aylesworth's arguments alone swayed Nockels. The Chicago labor leader remained primarily concerned with labor radio's survival, and that seemed endangered in the latter half of 1934. Pending the formation of the new FCC and the conducting of hearings, most stations had their licenses renewed for six months. The FCC, however, renewed WCFL's license for only ninety days because of complaints of "inferior program service," probably a reference to what *Broadcasting* magazine identified as "questionable medical programs." Russell of NBC observed that organized labor feared that the FCC might use this opportunity to eliminate WCFL from the spectrum. Green's effort to keep AFL Resolution 122 before the FCC thus seemed designed to afford "some measure of protection to the very existence of WCFL."[59]

Russell, who attended the FCC hearings for NBC, characterized Green's testimony as a "great victory for American radio." When he withdrew most of the resolutions previously passed by the AFL convention, Green made, according to Russell, "the significant statement that he did not think additional radio legislation was necessary" to guarantee labor access to the broadcasting system. Russell assured his superiors that Green's action meant "that no element of Labor will participate in legislation against the existing system when Congress convenes in January." As for Green's support for a clear-channel WCFL, Russell remained "sure that it will not be dangerous to our interests" because while Green "spoke in support of WCFL," he did so "in a manner which I do not consider serious."[60]

NBC president Aylesworth accepted most of Russell's analysis, but continued to distrust Nockels. He agreed that the AFL hierarchy probably supported the remaining resolution out of a desire to guarantee the continued operation of WCFL. On the other hand, Aylesworth remained skeptical of the motivations of Nockels. "I think certain representatives of labor" will attempt to spread ownership of radio stations by AFL affiliates throughout the nation, "all to be located on 970 and with a directional antenna with a limitation of power so that the labor stations on 970 would not interfere with each other." Such an arrangement might cause havoc with other stations, including NBC affiliates, on nearby frequencies. "The 970 channel should be watched very closely by all of our people," concluded Aylesworth.[61]

Such worries soon became irrelevant. Within three weeks of Green's testimony before the Broadcast Division, NBC officials Trammell, Russell, and Mark Woods had reached an "understanding" with Nockels, WCFL sales manager Carl P. McAssey, and attorney Benjamin F. Goldstein. According to the preliminary agreement, NBC promised to furnish WCFL with free, nonduplicated sustaining service; to sell, without charge, local commercial and national spot programs for WCFL at regular card rates less an advertising agency commission; to "make available the facilities of one of its networks for one fifteen minute period [AFL] program once a week"; to pay the cost of WCFL debts to RCA for equipment and installation (approximately $47,756); to furnish without cost to WCFL other equipment (e.g., microphones, amplifiers, speakers); and to acquiesce to an AFL attempt to petition for a local station in Washington, D.C. To help WCFL permanently protect the frequency of 970 kilocycles, NBC negotiators suggested that WCFL apply to build stations located at Fort Worth, Texas, and Albany, New York. The AFL would hold title to the 970-kilocycle wavelength, but the AFL/WCFL would lease, at the charge of $1 per year, the stations and frequency to NBC for a period of twenty-five years. NBC would build and maintain the stations and situate them so as not to interfere with WCFL's service. NBC also promised to provide thirty minutes of free time daily on these stations for labor programs sponsored and supervised by the CFL.[62]

From the perspective of NBC negotiators, the proposed arrangement offered advantages to both the network and labor radio. Mark Woods, who helped to negotiate the "understanding" for NBC, argued that labor benefited from the cancellation of its debt to RCA, the use of one NBC network for a weekly AFL program, access to half-hour sustaining programs in upstate New York and Texas for local labor groups, and NBC sustaining program service for WCFL. NBC would benefit from having a Blue network station in Albany with projected annual profits of $199,970. The establishment of another NBC outlet in Texas would allow for an intricate manipulation of stations and equipment that would ultimately produce an extension of NBC's basic Red network to Tulsa and Fort Worth and its basic Blue network to Oklahoma City and Dallas. Woods calculated the potential profits of such a development at $243,619 per year. In terms of the Chicago market, NBC could extend its Blue network sustaining service to WCFL when WENR was not on the air.[63]

Despite the enthusiasm of regional and middle-echelon NBC officers, New York executives and legal personnel objected to aspects of the proposed deal. Aylesworth, while attracted to many of the deal's benefits, worried about the role Nockels would play in developing and supervising labor programs for broadcast over the Blue and Red networks. The NBC president did not mind complying with the requests of William Green, but "I would not want to see a series of Labor programs offered to our Associated stations under the immediate direction of Nockels, originating in Chicago, and in the form of attacks on employers, etc."[64] Such reservations ultimately became moot when NBC legal counsel, A. L. Ashby, declared the proposed deal "obviously illegal." In blunt memoranda to company officials, Ashby explained that the tentative agreement "is clearly a trafficking in frequencies which violates both the letter and spirit of the Communications Act." NBC chairman David Sarnoff vetoed the deal.[65]

The negotiations with NBC revealed how far Nockels was willing to go to guarantee the survival of the Voice of Labor. He apparently believed that the arrangement with NBC would absolutely secure the 970-kilocycle frequency for WCFL, protecting it from various competitors, even while forcing labor radio to lease the frequency to NBC in eastern and southern markets.[66] By the late spring of 1935, several organizations had petitioned the FCC for the 970-kilocycle channel. Hearst Radio, Incorporated, wanted it for a proposed station in Albany, New York; the ILGWU announced its desire to build a radio station in New York City on the same frequency; and a Texas company sought the channel for a station in Dallas. The Hearst empire also attempted to purchase WCFL from the CFL in 1934.[67] Although these dangers passed, they illustrated the precarious position of the Voice of Labor.

Continuing financial problems, exacerbated by the Great Depression, also dictated that Nockels secure greater stability for WCFL. Insufficient funds forced the CFL to postpone development of its superpower station at Downers Grove. Fearing that further delays in the construction of that station would lead the FRC/FCC to deny WCFL petitions for increased power and time, Nockels pushed ahead in the spring of 1934 with a scheme to build a station only one-fifth the size of the one originally planned. Even this scaled-back structure would cost the federation some sixty-one thousand dollars to build, equip, and connect to studios in Chicago, plus four hundred dollars per month for electricity. Station officials welcomed any arrangement that eased the financial burden of this project.[68]

The extent to which the AFL might have influenced Nockels's decision to follow this strategy is unclear, although it certainly applied some pressure on Nockels to compromise with NBC. WCFL's precarious position in 1934 made AFL support for the station all that more important to Nockels, who understood the collaborative relationship between the AFL hierarchy and the leaders of commercial radio. Even as NBC and WCFL concluded their deliberations in early 1935, the AFL-NBC quid pro quo reached new heights. William Green thanked Aylesworth in early 1935 for sending him "the gilt-edge pass to all NBC Studios" and then requested that the network provide time for a weekly fifteen-minute sustaining program developed by the AFL. The NBC president responded that the network would "be delighted to cooperate with your office and the AFL" and that the proposed program, "with careful planning," should render a great public service.[69] A few months later, Aylesworth, under attack from congressional critics who accused him of helping electric power companies to propagandize the airwaves, sought Green's help. "I am certain that you above all others know the sympathetic attitude of the NBC toward Labor. Certainly the American Federation of Labor has the freedom of the air over the NBC. . . . I have such a high regard for your fairness and integrity that I know when the opportunity comes, you will use your influence to see that an unfair and libelous statement of this character is frowned on."[70] Thus the powerful radio network made concessions to organized labor and, in exchange, received labor's assistance in protecting the status quo. That Nockels, a longtime critic of the broadcasting industry's manipulation of labor, should acquiesce to this collaborative arrangement only demonstrates the CFL's growing adherence to the conservative policy of the AFL.

Even if one acknowledges the serious threats to WCFL's survival that surfaced during the thirties, the proposed NBC deal was the height of hypocrisy because it contradicted two fundamental principles of the CFL and WCFL. In the course of making the deal, Nockels circumvented a democratic decision-making process that had once been the pride of the labor federation. Since 1927 when Nockels unilaterally offered to donate WCFL to the city of Chicago, CFL leaders had agreed that proposed changes to WCFL would require a binding referendum vote of the local unions that had contributed to the station.[71] The 1934 deal with NBC would have dramatically changed WCFL's situation, but Nockels never brought the issue before a CFL meeting or discussed it in the *Federation News*. On the contrary, he and other leaders restructured the relationship between local unions and the radio station, reducing the opportunities for a rank-and-file discussion or vote on the station's future.

The CFL Executive Board altered WCFL's legal and financial structure during 1934. Officers had set the stage in mid-1933 by amending the CFL constitution to allow for the incorporation of WCFL. Arguing at the time that WCFL was "a commercial proposition," John Fitzpatrick explained that other labor organs with established businesses such as insurance funds and housing projects had separated these activities from their trade union functions to protect their members under the law. In the fall of 1934, a nonprofit corporation took over all the assets of WCFL and a profit-oriented corporation oversaw daily station operations. The nonprofit body issued "income bonds," or stocks, to unions that had contributed to the construction and maintenance of the station; in effect, it reimbursed the local unions' original "investments" in the station. Nockels and Fitzpatrick became trustees for the CFL's own stock in the station for a period of twenty years.[72] The new structure met legal requirements and facilitated the paying off of debts associated with construction of the Downers Grove broadcasting facility. But this arrangement also imposed another level of bureaucracy between the radio station and individual unions and thereby limited the rank and file's direct participation in station operations and policies.[73]

In addition to violating at least the spirit of the CFL's democratic principles, the proposed deal also undermined the heart of WCFL's attack on the radio trust. Nockels and the CFL had condemned WGN and other commercial stations for buying and selling radio licenses during the twenties.

Yet here was labor radio treating the public airwaves as if they were the private property of private interests. Although Nockels had doubts about the deal, it was NBC's recognition of its blatant illegality that scotched it.

WCFL was not much better off in the spring of 1935 than it had been three years earlier. Although the nation had a new communications act and commission, radio broadcasting rested firmly in the hands of powerful, concentrated private corporations. The Voice of Labor continued to share the 970-kilocycle frequency with NBC affiliate KJR; it could broadcast throughout the day, but only at the acquiescence of NBC and the FCC. In the aftermath of the failed deal, NBC executives still hoped to manipulate the Chicago radio market to their advantage and therefore hoped to keep the labor station within reach. They maintained contact with WCFL by providing it with free sustaining services and by nurturing their relationship with the AFL hierarchy.[74]

The story of WCFL's failed deal with NBC had a strange and confusing subplot. At the same time that Nockels negotiated an elaborate programming and frequency arrangement with a network power, he attempted to connect WCFL to a new challenger to NBC and CBS. In March 1933, the radio comedian Ed Wynn announced plans to establish an alternative radio network. The Amalgamated Broadcasting System was to encompass some one hundred stations nationwide. Wynn's network sought to attract the best talent and to relegate commercial messages to brief announcements immediately prior to and following a program. As radio stations and the newspaper industry launched the first battles in a radio-press war, Wynn also promised close cooperation with the press.[75]

Nockels requested information about the nascent network as it set up offices in New York City during late March 1933. Wynn replied that as soon as Amalgamated opened its seaboard network it would expand westward and would welcome an agreement with WCFL. By the time Amalgamated opened its fifteen stations along the Atlantic coast in late September, Nockels had arranged with the firm's general manager, Ota Gygi, for WCFL to become "the key station out of Chicago for the system when it comes this way." Nockels attended the lavish inaugural festivities, which marked both the beginning and the end of the third network. Amalgamated suffered from too many artists and too few sponsors. Wynn resigned his figurehead position as president on October 25, and the entire system ceased operations four days later. A legal battle then ensued over the system's scarce assets.[76]

Amalgamated's real operational head, Ota Gygi, emerged from the debacle relatively unscathed and willing to try a smaller version of the project.

Gygi, as one network official noted, seemed determined to "become a radio executive or bust." He hoped to create regional networks around the country and eventually to unite them in a national chain. In the spring of 1934, Gygi met with Nockels in Chicago. By June the two radio enthusiasts had agreed to make WCFL the key outlet for Gygi's midwestern chain of independent radio stations. Programs would originate in Chicago at WCFL and then be fed out via wire to thirty stations in Wisconsin, Illinois, and Indiana. WCFL prepared to develop programming for the tristate network by hiring a new program director with radio and motion picture experience. Colby N. Harriman set out to guide WCFL's program department away from a labor orientation and toward a "balance of programs for all audiences."[77]

Gygi and Harriman put together a sixteen-hour, seven-days-a-week broadcasting schedule. Musical shows would make up 67 percent of the week's programs; literary, dramatic, or educational shows, 17 percent; news and commentary, 7 percent; specialized programming for women and children, 5 percent; and miscellaneous shows, 4 percent. The network promised to place advertisements (never to exceed ninety seconds) at the beginning and ending of programs and at the seven-minute mark. While seeking national sponsors, Gygi hoped to play on local station pride and secure local advertisers.[78] As Gygi later recounted: "After signing sixteen stations, obtaining commitments for that many more for a tri-state network . . . ; with unlimited opportunities for expansion, with contracts amounting to one and a half million dollars minimum in time as exchange for programs and wires and with the Federation of Labor as partner, things seemed pretty sweet."[79]

Originally scheduled to begin broadcasting on October 1, 1934, wire difficulties postponed the opening of the new midwestern network until December. As the year ended, and after several other false starts, WCFL indefinitely postponed the opening of the Affiliated Radio Network. Officials publicly explained that they wished to wait until WCFL's new five-thousand-watt transmitter could go into service. But negotiations with NBC, then under way, offered WCFL a more promising path to success. By early 1935 the entire chain idea disintegrated. WCFL released Gygi, but kept Program Director Harriman, whose task now became to "concentrate on WCFL as an individual station and [to] slough off all matters regarding a possible regional network at this time."[80]

Although outraged by what he considered the CFL's betrayal, Gygi never adequately clarified why WCFL abandoned him. One explanation went that, in violation of previous agreements and understandings, Nockels sought to use the network "as a buffer and excuse for labor propaganda and for unionization" of the affiliated stations. When the participating station owners learned of this, the "dream evaporated."[81] Gygi also contended that Nockels offered NBC part ownership in the network in exchange for NBC programming. Niles Trammell rejected the offer, explaining, as Gygi recalled, that "anyone who could commit stations to a network plan presented an obstruction, hinderance [*sic*] and danger, no matter how small." At that point, according to Gygi, WCFL decided to go ahead with its own deal with NBC, leaving Gygi in the lurch.[82]

Each of these alternative explanations holds a germ of truth. Nockels looked for the best possible deal to guarantee WCFL's survival and success. Weighing the options as of December 1934 and January 1935, Nockels deemed the NBC offer the more secure of the two. As for the criticism that Nockels intended to use the network to broadcast labor propaganda and to unionize radio stations, one must acknowledge that labor propaganda was in the eye or ear of the beholder. Business officials readily recognized labor propaganda, but not business propaganda. Nockels never tried to conceal that labor radio aimed at serving the labor movement. A regional network, headed by WCFL, would have to provide time for working-class discussions and trade union announcements. At WCFL, Nockels and the CFL supported a union work force with union contracts. The CFL undoubtedly wanted to spread this to the other members of the network, although neither Gygi nor the CFL explained how this might occur. In any event, by the spring of 1935, two more attempts to protect and develop labor radio had failed: Securing a clear channel via a deal with NBC and creating a regional network with WCFL as the center.

• • •

Nockels's failures on the business front perhaps explain his desire to return to the burning issues of labor radio's early years: Monopoly of the air, public domain versus private property, and media access. During the latter half of 1935 and throughout 1936, Nockels turned his attention to these larger problems of labor and broadcasting, leaving the daily operations and finances of WCFL to staff personnel. The CFL leader remained committed to a diversified and democratic broadcasting system in the United States. He regarded radio as the "last great public domain," warned of the increasing threat posed by FCC–radio trust collaboration, and contended that WCFL offered an alternative to the dominant system. Indeed, the dangers posed by the radio industry's centralization and concentration necessitated an independent labor radio station with a clear channel and maximum power.[83]

The depression and attendant financial problems had delayed, until June 1935, WCFL's efforts to bring its power up to the already approved level of five thousand watts. A year later, however, the ever-optimistic Nockels petitioned the FCC for permission to increase WCFL's power to fifty thousand watts.[84] This demand again raised the problem of interference with Seattle station KJR. NBC officials sought to resolve this complex situation because of their investment in KJR and their recurring problems with Burridge Butler, the obstinate owner of WLS. As late as November 1936, NBC executive Niles Trammell still argued that one solution for the network's problems in Chicago was to "acquire by purchase or by lease WCFL or WGN."[85] In any event, network officials sought to maintain a reasonably friendly working relationship with labor radio.

After meeting with representatives from both KJR and WCFL, NBC announced in late December 1936 that, pending FCC approval, it would allow WCFL to shift to a cleared channel on 1,020 kilocycles and to increase its power to fifty thousand watts. Nockels rejected the offer as spurious. The 1,020-kilocycle frequency experienced considerable interference from Canadian and Mexican stations. More importantly, Nockels objected to the deal because it manifested a fundamental problem with corporate radio— and a flaw in AFL president Green's policy of collaborating with capital and the state. NBC, with apparent FCC approval, had made a unilateral offer to grant a special favor to organized labor. The network consulted with neither the CFL nor the AFL.[86] Favors granted from above, Nockels understood, could just as easily be withdrawn. He insisted that organized labor, the working class, and the public at large could not rely on the good graces of the profit-oriented, private broadcasting system for access to the public airwaves; they needed an independent voice.

Nockels's rejection of the NBC proposal and his insistence on securing full power on the 970-kilocycle wavelength continued to make the WCFL general manager the target of radio industry attacks. *Broadcasting* magazine, noting WCFL's endless "clamoring for a clear channel," implied that the fickle labor movement had rejected a generous and substantial offer made by the industry. *Variety* dismissed as laughable Nockels's demand for fifty thousand watts of power and his complaints "that commercial broadcasters badly treated educators, labor organizations, and other non-profit outfits." WCFL could not complain about corporate radio, contended *Va riety,* because of its own abysmal record of broadcasting an inadequate percentage of labor and educational programs.[87]

Industry officials denounced Nockels's demand for increased power because it required a bewildering shifting of frequencies. WCFL's application to the FCC recognized that if it received the 970-kilocycle wavelength as a clear channel, with fifty thousand watts, it would interfere not only with Seattle's KJR but also with Pittsburgh's KDKA (980 kilocycles). Therefore, the application asked that Boston station WBZ (990 kilocycles) and KDKA exchange frequencies and that Seattle's KJR be assigned 980 kilocycles with WBZ. NBC officers correctly concluded that Westinghouse Electric, the owner of KDKA, "will unalterably oppose any suggestion in this direction and in this they will have the support of the entire industry."[88] This latest battle in Nockels's continuing war with the FCC and the radio industry over a clear channel coincided with a study made by the FCC's Broadcast Division and Engineering Department.

FCC hearings began in the fall of 1936 seeking data on the "corollary social and economic" impact of power and frequency allocations.[89] The usual cast of players with their well-worn routines came to testify in Washington. Representatives from the Clear-Channel Group, for example, argued that the allocation problem was a "technical" question: "How best to divide up and regulate the use of the broadcast band so as to provide a maximum of good reception" over the most area and for the most people. Louis Caldwell testified that the obvious answer to the "technical" question was to protect the position of clear-channel stations by maintaining and increasing their broadcast power advantage over regional and local radio outlets. Local and regional stations countered that they best served rural and urban needs and deserved improved power and frequency allocations from the FCC.[90]

Nockels's comments to the FCC staff also summarized the positions he had taken during the preceding decade of struggle. What was unique about Nockels's testimony, however, was his refusal to consider the questions of power and frequency allocations as technical issues. Labor recognized the need for the FCC to secure engineering and scientific data and to obey certain engineering rules. But "we never believed that the [FCC] should disregard the social, educational and economic considerations that broadcasting involves." Nockels insisted that decisions regarding radio station allocations were fundamentally economic, social, and political. America's workers, contended Nockels, defined the "public interest, convenience, and necessity" standard as "that which contributes to the health, comfort and happiness of the people and that which provides wholesome entertainment, increases knowledge, arouses individual thinking, inspires noble impulses, strengthens human ties, breaks down hatred, encourages respect for law, aids employment, improves the standard of living, and adds to the peace and contentment of mankind."[91] One could argue that Nockels held an idealistic vision of radio, seeing the medium primarily as one of social uplift. The corporate broadcasters, on the other hand, perceived radio primarily as an advertising medium with the goal of getting people to buy corporate goods, services, and ideology.

From Nockels's vantage point, the FCC and its predecessor had pursued an "erroneous" policy of "cutting . . . a monstrous melon into forty luscious slices" and then passing them out to the selfish "gluttons of monopoly."[92] As of the fall of 1936, CBS, NBC, and the Mutual Broadcasting System manipulated more than 50 percent of the total facilities then available on clear-channel assignments. Superpower stations, according to Nockels, literally drowned out regional and local stations and, because of their tremendous cost and concomitant need for advertising, led to increased commercialization among all radio stations. Granting the clear-channel stations the five hundred thousand watts that they sought would only exacerbate an already intolerable situation. "In times of national emergency, controversy, strikes, lockouts, and disagreement," warned Nockels, corporate controlled superpower stations would "surely disseminate propaganda the like of which this country has never yet experienced, with the result of further clipping and controlling by sheer power and brute force the intellectual and economic soul of this country."[93]

Concluding that the electromagnetic spectrum belonged to all the people, Nockels recommended three possible ways both to guarantee a fair distribution of the spectrum and to defeat the radio monopoly's threat to American free speech: Reallocating wavelengths; limiting all stations to a power of ten thousand watts, thus making them all local stations; or authorizing the government to seize and operate all radio stations in the country. "Labor hopes and trusts that the necessity for the last named alternative will not be forced upon us, but we are . . . thoroughly in favor of complete government control and operation in preference to complete control and operation by trusts, press, magazines, radio networks and their closely allied interests."[94]

The heart of Nockels's commentary was lost on the FCC staff members in charge of the hearings. Ignoring Nockels's criticisms and proposals, they only wished to know what detailed suggestions Nockels could make with reference to the engineering principles of allocation.[95] In the final report, issued in July 1937, the Engineering Department authors interpreted Nockels's testimony "to be basically a warning to keep the channels of radio broadcasting available to all groups of society and all legitimate schools of thought so that no single group will be denied the ability to reach the public on any fundamental social principle." Although this concern figured into Nockels's assessment, it constituted but one part of a larger critique, which the authors of the report dismissed. Echoing corporate ideology, the FCC technocrats asserted that the commercial base of American broadcasting guaranteed free speech and access to all interested parties and that the competitive network system had "made the world's finest programs available to thousands of communities, large and small, programs which they prefer and which they would be unable otherwise to enjoy."[96]

FCC technicians provided the quintessential corporate defense of network radio's free speech and public access argument:

> There is no evidence that the 3 national chain companies, the 25 regional network groups, and the 303 stations affiliated with networks have *combined for the purpose* of controlling the channels of mass communication in a manner inimical to the interest of the public. . . . Their past record of performance with respect to the use of their facilities has been liberal, particularly for the discussion of public questions. It is also well known that the facilities of the three major chain companies are used in active competition.[97]

Characterizing the networks' record with regard to public policy discussions as "liberal" and "competitive" was disingenuous. NBC and CBS displayed their openness and fairness selectively. When criticism of the network system reached a crescendo and especially when disaffected groups went to Congress seeking regress for their grievances, only then did the radio giants "serve" the public interest. When outside pressures subsided or when profits declined, the diversity and openness of the radio system became an illusion.[98] Just six months before the FCC report became public, the American Civil Liberties Union published a detailed collection of case studies of censorship in American broadcasting.[99] The FCC engineers chose to ignore this body of evidence that contradicted the conventional wisdom. They did concede, however, that if further study revealed faults within the existing system, then "the Commission can undoubtedly influence *voluntary* changes from the broad standpoint of public interest, convenience, and necessity."[100]

The FCC report simplified the decade-long ideological and political battle between Nockels and Caldwell. FCC technicians rejected Nockels's indictment of the American broadcasting system and embraced Caldwell's defense of the same. Interestingly enough, Nockels and Caldwell shared some assumptions about American broadcasting. Each man was a radio enthusiast, a firm believer in the power, importance, and hence responsibility of the new medium. Caldwell told the NAB convention in 1930 that broadcasting "has a social and cultural importance overshadowing any other development of twentieth century civilization." Just months earlier, Nockels spoke of how radio "revolutionizes our world" and "is destined to become the unrivaled master of human destiny."[101]

Both men also hailed the importance of free speech over the air and condemned censorship. But here their assessments of broadcasting diverged sharply. While Nockels accused commercial broadcasters of censoring the opinions of workers, radicals, and progressives, Caldwell singled out government censorship. The WGN attorney found "private censorship" a "bewildering" concept, preferring instead "editorial selection." Drawing an analogy between the broadcast and print media, Caldwell contended that "some one must determine what shall go to make up the daily broadcast program, for there is a physical limit to the number of hours of a station's daily operation. Some one must make a selection of material of interest and importance to the public."[102] When the government established the public interest, convenience, and necessity standard for broadcasters to meet, it raised the problem of how to measure the success with which stations adhered to the standard and this, in turn, led to government censorship by default. The First Amendment to the Constitution prohibited the "evil" of government censorship. Caldwell preferred "private censorship"—editorial selection—over government censorship. He always took care to note "the *supposed* evils of private censorship" and to explain that the necessary and sufficient safeguard against such evils "is provided by *competition* between the various agencies of mass communication." Because the Radio and Communications Acts explicitly prohibited broadcast monopolies, competition in the medium was assured.[103]

Thus for Caldwell, the FCC engineers, the NAB, NBC, and CBS, private radio station censorship was not censorship at all; it was merely the natural and practical operation of the marketplace. These same interests asserted that the predominant power of two or three networks and of an increasing number of clear-channel stations controlled by a decreasing number of corporate owners did not constitute monopoly; it was competition. In this context, the FCC report reinforced, if nothing else could, the need for Edward Nockels's challenges to the propagandists of the American radio system. Ironically, the report appeared several months after Nockels's death.

Labor Radio and Working-Class Culture, 1932–37

Edward Nockels's efforts to protect and enhance WCFL's operations during the midthirties reflected his conviction that labor radio could play a valuable role in the lives of workers and their unions. Nockels perceived WCFL as both a symbol of trade unionism and a service to working-class communities. WCFL's mere presence symbolized an alternative to the business-owned mass media and an oppositional force in American politics and culture. By producing and broadcasting entertainment, civic, educational, and labor programming WCFL served as a propaganda and organizing tool for the trade union movement and contributed to the formation of a working-class culture. But guaranteeing that WCFL fulfilled these functions required that labor radio establish itself as a superpower station, which, in turn, required defeating the considerable power of radio "monopolists, the kept press and all that army of greed."[1] In this endeavor, WCFL officials found themselves trying to balance the station's labor orientation with the ever-increasing demands of commercial broadcasting.

As the Great Depression reached new depths this balancing act became increasingly difficult. The long period of economic crisis and concomitant loss of advertising and subscriptions forced CFL leaders to consider temporarily suspending publication of the *Federation News*.[2] Those conditions also led Nockels to hold a second fund-raising benefit for WCFL in the fall of 1932. Acknowledging that "the depression has hit WCFL, as it has other industries," Nockels hoped that a well-attended benefit would put labor radio "on a plane of equality" with other stations. Although the November dance at the Chicago Coliseum drew some twenty-two thousand people and generated ten thousand dollars for WCFL, the station's financial woes continued unabated.[3] These problems, the increasing demands that organized labor placed on WCFL, and the continuing goal of creating a superpower station combined to force CFL leaders to consider controversial and often short-sighted ways to guarantee the station's survival. Through all the machinations with corporate networks and state agencies, however, programming and financing issues remained constant.

· · ·

WCFL managers and staff disagreed over the proper course of action that would produce a viable labor radio station. Nockels believed that securing a superpower, clear-channel position was a prerequisite to improving programming and fulfilling the economic, political, and ideological goals of labor radio. Thus he pushed ahead with deals that he thought would ease the financial problems restraining the construction of a fifty-thousand-watt transmitter in Downers Grove and he continued to pressure the FCC to grant WCFL maximum power, full time, and a clear channel. WCFL's business and programming managers, on the other hand, contended that improving the station's entertainment programming was the prerequisite for building a sizeable audience that would attract advertisers. These sponsors would subsidize the development of better programs and equipment, which would maintain an audience to receive labor's economic, political, and ideological messages.

The responsibility for upgrading the station's entertainment shows fell to the program directors, most of whom were knowledgeable about radio and the entertainment industry, but not necessarily the trade union movement. Malcolm Eagle, a former vaudeville showman, joined the Voice of Labor in the middle of 1934. Assigned the task of invigorating WCFL's tired variety programs, he brought a standard vaudeville style to the airwaves with "Sher Bloomers," a fast-paced program with good comedians and a fine singer, and "WCFL Variety Revue," a sixty-minute, four-act sustaining feature.[4] Colby N. Harriman—production manager, director, and writer for several motion picture companies and radio stations—also joined WCFL in 1934. Originally a part of the station's deal with Ota Gygi, Harriman remained after the regional network plan disintegrated. As WCFL's head program director, Harriman defended sponsored broadcasting and pushed for the commercialization of WCFL, the use of high production values, and the need to "attract and hold a large and varied audience." WCFL needed "show-manship"—defined by the entertainment industry as "the art of holding the interest of the greatest number of people with the least possible effort." Properly developed programs would "strike an average taste level" with "an emotional kick" and with sincerity. Harriman contended that well-prepared, presented, and balanced programming would help WCFL become "the voice of the people" and not just "the voice of labor."[5]

An important "progressive step" in WCFL's development, according to Harriman, was the increased use of NBC programs. The quantity of NBC programs aired over WCFL increased between 1932 and 1937, but whether these shows raised the overall quality of WCFL's schedule is debatable. In September 1932, WCFL carried an average of one hour of NBC program-ming during a normal seventeen-hour broadcast day: Thirty minutes of "Cheerio," an inspirational morning talk show, fifteen minutes of music in the afternoon, and fifteen minutes of the "Vic and Sade" comedy soap op-era. In the midst of the NBC-WCFL negotiations in December 1934, labor radio aired two to three hours of network shows per day, including several late night popular band music programs and daytime comedies. The fol-lowing spring, WCFL carried a high of three and one-quarter hours of shows from the Blue network each day, including the "National Farm and Home Hour," an afternoon talk and variety program. Although its deal with NBC collapsed, WCFL continued to air two or more hours of NBC shows per day during the next two years. NBC accepted this arrangement because the Blue network required an additional Chicago outlet for some of its shows.[6]

Although WCFL carried a selection of NBC's "important international broadcasts, radio personalities, notable events and affairs of the moment," the vast majority of the shows were mediocre entertainment. "Honeyboy and Sassafras," a fifteen-minute daytime "Negro dialect" comedy show, fea-tured two blackface comics who performed particularly "old-fashioned and racially insulting" routines. WCFL aired a number of NBC's nondescript "light music" features during the day and at night, including "The Jesters" and "Three X Sisters." Sales Manager Carl P. McAssey nevertheless praised the "NBC sustaining features which have set a standard" against which all other sustaining and commercial programs would be judged.[7]

Under the direction of Harriman, McAssey, and Business Manager Franklin Lundquist, WCFL's programming increasingly resembled, and oc-casionally matched, the quality of network radio entertainment. Music and music variety shows dominated the schedule. A typical weekday broadcast included jazz, classical music, "hillbilly" music, popular dance bands, and an assortment of soloists. WCFL frequently auditioned new musical talent and aired selected programs as showcases for the amateur musicians.[8]

A majority of labor radio's music came from live performances, but a significant proportion derived from recordings. The use of disc jockeys to play electrical transcriptions and records had become an important part of commercial radio by the midthirties because it cost less than paying for live music and because it diversified a station's musical offerings. WCFL had practiced this format since its early days, especially in its morning wake-up shows and some of its talk and religious programs. Labor radio also had used transcriptions of syndicated shows.[9] Two WCFL programs fit into the "deejay" format during this period: "Morning Music" and "Red Hot and Low Down." The former aired in 1933 for forty-five minutes six days a week and offered a range of musical styles. Sports announcer Bob Hawk hosted "Red Hot and Low Down," which began in 1932 and ranked among the most popular radio shows in Chicago for four years. Hawk recalled that combining popular musical recordings and witty talk "was real corn, but people loved it."[10]

Listeners also enjoyed the live music and variety available on WCFL's ethnic shows. Ethnic and foreign-language programming made up 6 percent (400 minutes) of WCFL's total 7,080 minutes of airtime during an average broadcast week in 1934 and 4 percent (300 minutes) in 1936. Polish, Lithuanian, German, and Swedish programs remained on the WCFL schedule, with the "Irish Hour" continuing its reign as the most popular of the genre. *Variety* contended that these sentimental foreign-language programs appealed to "the average laboring man from Europe." But while "ethnic identity continued to have meaning in the daily lives of Chicago workers during the 1930s," other class, political, and cultural forces impinged on workers' consciousness. A decade of restrictive immigration policies, the emergence of second- and third-generation ethnic Americans, and a reorientation of ethnic institutions gradually made ethnic programming less and less important.[11]

Immigrant and native-born workers followed WCFL's coverage of Chicago-area athletic events. Bob Hawk's play-by-play of the Chicago White Sox and Chicago Cubs remained a big attraction—even though several other stations carried the games. In 1935, WCFL introduced pregame interviews of players, managers, and umpires from the field via special wire. Labor radio also aired Northwestern University football games and the Christian Youth Organization's weekly boxing matches. Hawk and John

O'Hara presided over a nightly sports review show. WCFL later added NBC sports reporter Clem McCarthy's commentary show to its schedule.[12]

When not catering to Cubs and White Sox fans during summer afternoons, WCFL's daytime broadcasts consisted of light music, variety, and talk shows. The latter category usually included advice and self-help shows aimed at a female audience. Local firms selling household goods or services sponsored food and cooking, mental and physical health, beauty, gardening, and general "homemaking" shows. Beauty shops sponsored series telling women how to improve their appearance while the Homemakers' Service Bureau produced "Homemakers Round Table" (1936), a combination of talk, advice, and musical selections. WCFL carried NBC's "Women's Review," a thirty-minute afternoon show that also dispensed homemaking information. "For Women Only," a fifteen-minute street-reporter show, placed announcer Don Norman in downtown Chicago at midday, where he asked women shoppers questions submitted by WCFL listeners. Women wrote, directed, and performed in most of these shows. Indeed, WCFL afforded women significant opportunities in program development and production. Gail Wilson directed the important "Farm Forum"—arranging for speakers, interviewing expert labor and farm guests, and offering market and news reports. Helen Lochrie directed the Thompson Beauty Shop program as well as the popular comedy sketch "Night Court." Women entertainers and artists were well represented in the station's music and variety shows.[13]

Although WCFL boasted an early example of a dramatic series aimed primarily at women—"Great Love Affairs of All Time," directed by Shirley Linder in late 1932—it never developed its own extensive schedule of soap operas.[14] Network radio experienced an explosion in the number of daytime women's serial dramas—from four shows in January 1933 to twenty-eight in January 1937. The networks, emerging "as a national mass-marketing medium for large corporations," found that narrative drama attracted large audiences. Industry officials believed that housewives determined and made most family purchases and that those housewives spent the greatest amount of time in the home, where they easily could be reached by radio broadcasts. Soap operas thus developed as "merchandising vehicles" in which the needs of the sponsor shaped narrative and character development and aimed at selling products to female consumers. National manufacturers of household goods placed their advertising money in network serials because the potential audience vastly surpassed that on local stations.[15] It is not surprising, therefore, that WCFL failed to develop daytime women's dramatic series like those on the radio chains. This did not mean, however, that WCFL ignored drama programming.

Chicago lacked the theatrical and motion picture stars, found in New York City and Hollywood, who became major attractions on network variety and comedy programs. The city did have an abundant supply of local dramatic talent and this helped it to become "a center for the production of radio drama." It took at least a decade, however, for radio to develop and train its own accomplished writers and actors and even then they "produced formulaic stories for formulaic series." Radio networks with ample capital usually found it easier than local independent stations to secure the services of skilled scriptwriters and actors for dramatic plays and serials. This left stations such as WCFL searching for amateur theater talent.[16]

WCFL's regular drama productions relied heavily on amateur theater groups and therefore varied in theme and quality. "Little Theatre" groups, such as the Ilka Diehl Players and the Footlight Players, produced original skits or playlets with love or mystery themes. When Howard T. Keegan, a former actor and theatrical producer with experience in NBC's Chicago studios, joined the program department in mid-1932, he introduced and directed a series of dramatic skits. One typical serial was "The Run Around." Written by a Chicago newspaper reporter and directed by WCFL commentator and *Federation News* reporter Phil Friedlander, the serial dramatized the "experiences of the most beautiful and richest coed in the world [who] suddenly loses her fortune and is forced to shift for herself." Starring a senior at the University of Chicago, the show depicted the heroine's attempts "to make a name and a living for herself in the field of radio." Although the show touched on an appropriate depression-era theme (people facing financial ruin and personal adversity) and gave an inside look at radio production, it never secured a sponsor and lasted for only a few months in mid-1936. WCFL gave trial runs to many other serials, but few survived for any length of time.[17]

Labor radio's rapid turnover of sustaining entertainment shows reflected managerial efforts to develop programs that would attract paying sponsors. Accelerating the station's commercialization, in turn, would help pay for improved entertainment and additional and better equipment, thus giving WCFL a more competitive edge in regional and national markets. But as the sponsored portion of the total schedule slowly increased during the middle of the thirties, so did tensions within WCFL over goals and tactics. On the one hand, labor progressives and leftists remained concerned with labor solidarity and with making WCFL an important tool in expanding trade union organizing activities and developing working-class culture and consciousness. On the other hand, business unionists became preoccupied with making WCFL more profit oriented.

Chicago radio stations engaged in an intense competition for improved frequency, power, and time in order to reach a potentially huge radio market and thereby attract more sponsors and increase advertising rates. A study by the Columbia Broadcasting System in 1933 estimated over 7.5 million radio listeners in the metropolitan area.[18] Nockels hoped to reach a significant portion of this audience by improving the station's technical facilities and, in particular, building a super station at Downers Grove. Indeed, WCFL's general manager remained convinced that maximum power and a clear channel would solve labor radio's problems. A superpower and clear-channel WCFL, together with the shortwave station W9XAA, would reach an "extensive" national and international audience. More importantly, WCFL would provide "intensive" coverage to the metropolitan Chicago area and the surrounding countryside, reaching the homes of those poor workers and farmers with "small or inefficient receiving sets." Increased power would help WCFL to pay its debts, especially to those labor organizations that contributed to the station. Maximum power and the subsequent clear reception of the WCFL signal also would lead to "a corresponding improvement in programs."[19] But the deepening depression frustrated Nockels and his colleagues, forcing them to scale back their plan for the superpower station and eventually settling for the construction of a five-thousand-watt transmitter. Chief Engineer Maynard Marquardt continued experimenting with short- and ultrashortwave transmissions in an effort to conduct remote broadcasts without the use of expensive telephone wires. These technical advancements impressed many in the radio industry, but WCFL required more money in order to continue them and, eventually, to realize the dream of a fifty-thousand-watt station.[20]

The CFL made several attempts to alleviate WCFL's economic problems in the midthirties. A business reorganization during the middle of 1934 created the WCFL Cooperative Broadcasting System and the WCFL Operating Company. The latter for-profit corporation took responsibility for the station's daily operations. The former "not for pecuniary profit" corporation took control of all of WCFL's assets and issued $150,000 worth of income bonds to compensate those unions that had contributed to the station's construction and to encourage other union investors in WCFL. Bondholders would receive the face value of the bonds paid out of the net income of the corporation, but only "after all debts now existing or to be incurred by said company in connection with the construction of the new broadcasting station near Downers Grove, Illinois, are paid off."[21] By the middle of 1935, the WCFL Cooperative Broadcasting System still owed two of its creditors, the CFL and the *Federation News*, approximately $21,709. Nockels proposed that the federation unilaterally cancel this debt. Although some delegates wondered why the CFL was turning over "its surplus cash to the radio station instead of using it for organizing purposes," Nockels insisted that this was merely a bookkeeping transaction. Defenders of Nockels's proposal testified to the great benefits that labor derived from WCFL.[22] The unanimous adoption of the resolution, however, did not substantially alter labor radio's financial plight.

Although Nockels believed that securing maximum power and a clear channel were the prerequisites to rectifying WCFL's problems, he acquiesced in a concurrent effort to boost the station's advertising revenue and listening audience. The first step in this campaign involved hiring Carl P. McAssey as sales manager of WCFL's commercial department in January 1933. McAssey, a salesman at the station for two years, immediately added seven more people to his department and inaugurated an aggressive campaign to find sponsors for WCFL entertainment programs. New clients, including a fuel company, a laundry, a beauty shop, a dressmaking school, a finance company, and a cemetery, joined WCFL. But many area businesses remained skeptical about advertising over labor radio and, in particular, about its audience.[23]

Radio industry officials reinforced these reservations by belittling WCFL's programming, sponsors, and "large working class audience." *Variety* asserted that labor operated WCFL "with very little taste or discrimination." It ranked WCFL dead last when evaluating eight Chicago radio stations in 1934 on the "basis of showmanship, merchandizing, program creation, and general popularity within [the] community."[24] In a review of a fifteen-minute program starring Grace Wilson, the magazine derided the singer and her accompanist and then explained that the show's sponsor, a resort hotel in upstate New York, chose WCFL because it wanted to reach "the lower brackets of the population." Aimed at laborers, the show was "not big time" entertainment, but definitely "a lower class effort" with "an overload of talk and plugging."[25]

McAssey attempted to counteract this negative image of WCFL by inverting industry criticisms. In a large advertisement in the October 1, 1933, issue of the trade journal *Broadcasting,* and in an article in the *Federation News,* McAssey told prospective sponsors that WCFL was the "most effective independent local station in the Chicago territory" precisely because of its labor audience. Within WCFL's listening area of approximately ninety miles resided some 1.5 million members of organized labor and their families—a potential market of 6 million consumers. He implied that these union families all listened to labor radio and that, despite the deepening economic depression, these people held jobs and wanted to spend their money. Indeed, these workers were "110.9% better paid than other groups according to Government Reports." WCFL offered advertisers the best return for their investment—low commercial rates, "complete-intensive-economical coverage of [the] rich Chicago market," and the "unique [union] audience." McAssey also insisted that WCFL's programs were "of sufficient variety" as "to appeal to people of every class and in every walk of life."[26]

Another obstacle hindering McAssey's efforts to "sell" WCFL came from progressives seeking to reform American broadcasting and, more importantly, from certain CFL leaders who remained ambivalent about the commercialization of WCFL. For some time, political activists, intellectuals, and educators had condemned corporate broadcasting for excessive advertising and profiteering. Such criticisms helped launch the radio reform movement of the first third of the decade.[27] Although his attacks against commercialism fluctuated over time, Nockels remained, in principle, a staunch opponent of this foundation of the broadcasting industry. But Nockels also recognized the dilemma of operating an alternative and oppositional station in a capitalist system: The "operation of a high power, modern radio station in competition with a large number of other broadcasting stations by no means hampered financially, involves a tremendous expense" and requires, therefore, that "we accept a certain number of commercial programs." While encouraging listeners to patronize WCFL's advertisers, Nockels reiterated that labor radio "is not operated for profit" and apologized when station policy decisions favored short-term financial gains over long-term ideological and cultural needs.[28]

McAssey and Business Manager Lundquist displayed no such ambiguity regarding WCFL's commercialization—nor could they. Chronic financial problems forced the business staff to conduct a dual sales job: "Sell" labor radio to reluctant advertisers and "sell" advertising to a skeptical labor movement. While Nockels attacked American radio, McAssey's staff praised it as the best in the world and attributed that greatness to advertising. "Advertising is the basis for existence in American radio," argued sales officials, and "advertising rightly done needs no apology from any of us." McAssey wrote in 1933 that WCFL had reached the point where its audience deserved more extensive entertainment "than the contributions of labor." WCFL needed programming comparable to the "commercially sponsored programs on other stations." Conceding that labor radio was already a commercial station, McAssey urged WCFL to become more competitive with the other independent and network broadcasting outlets in Chicago. Accomplishing its primary objective of serving organized labor required that WCFL turn a greater profit.[29]

McAssey's arguments reflected the U.S. broadcasting industry's dependence on advertising, ratings, and profits. The law of commercial broadcasting, firmly established by the midthirties, "dictated that an audience should be placated" with popular programming. Competing within this environment necessitated that WCFL allot more time to securing sponsors and hence to programming that sponsors wished to support. In a speech over WCFL in November 1933, the station's business manager admonished those people who criticized radio programs for containing "too much advertising." This demonstrated, according to Lundquist, "a spirit of ingratitude." If Americans wanted to continue enjoying "free" programming, then it was "only fair to expect" that the broadcasters were "entitled to . . . very necessary revenue." Echoing the words of network radio executives, Lundquist concluded that American commercial radio gave listeners "the best in music, inspiring lectures, drama, and comedy," and all "without being taxed one penny."[30]

While Nockels steadfastly opposed overcommercialization, McAssey and Lundquist made a heavy commitment to advertisers. They promised prospective sponsors that the sales department was "constantly on the lookout for ways and means of improving our service to advertisers and also of placing before [them] the many advantages of the use of WCFL as an advertising medium." Sales officials sanctioned blatant advertising shows such as "Dr. Springer's Forum" and "The Merchants' Prosperity Hour." Dr. Curtis H. Springer presided over two fifteen-minute programs each day: The evening broadcasts offered commentary on economic, social, and political topics and the daytime programs promoted the sale of his health products. "The Merchants' Prosperity Hour," ostensibly a "novel idea in radio advertising," aired six days a week for a total of almost four hours. It contained a heavy sales pitch, relieved only by infrequent organ music. The sales staff defended this type of programming, while assuring Chicago labor that commercial programs would not contain anything "in conflict with the principles and ideals" of WCFL or the CFL.[31]

Despite the limits necessitated by the marketplace, WCFL remained committed to public service. While one may dispute WCFL's self-proclaimed number of public interest and educational broadcasts—McAssey put the total at 3,329 in 1933–34 and Nockels claimed over 5,000 in 1935–36—WCFL did serve the community.[32] Labor radio mounted successful campaigns against real estate and insurance fraud, unfair utility charges, and organized crime in Chicago. Under the direction of Gail Wilson, the midday "Farm Forum" included important market information and farming news as well as interviews with prominent agricultural and labor officials. The Utility Consumers and Investors' League of Illinois, with CFL backing, launched a series of radio talks over WCFL in 1933 aimed at educating the general public on the utility issue and urging consumers to fight for reasonable rates and effective regulation. Paul H. Douglas, a professor of economics and president of the league, explained the connection between high utility rates and reduced wages with the prolongation of the depression. Roundtable discussions of important social, economic, and political problems also emanated from WCFL studios. From December 1935 through March 1936, WCFL aired weekly debates among college students on topics such as minimum wage and maximum hour legislation.[33]

The Voice of Labor, as well as the *Federation News,* remained remarkably open to different and conflicting opinions on labor-related issues. A commitment to free speech had been a distinguishing characteristic of the CFL for decades and it continued well into the thirties. The *Federation News,* for example, carried the AFL news service reporter Joseph Wise's stories attacking the Communist party and red-baiting the head of the Federated Press, Carl Haessler, while, at the same time, publishing Federated Press stories, including those written by Haessler.[34] In a similar vein, while Matthew Woll denounced the country's communists in a series of talks entitled "The Red Invader" aired over WCFL, leftists such as Sarainne Loewe received airtime to criticize red-baiters as counterproductive and to urge labor solidarity.[35]

The Voice of Labor also became the home of a number of interesting political commentators, including Phil Friedlander, the Reverend J. W. R. Maguire, Barratt O'Hara, and Ira Latimer. Friedlander, a columnist for the *Federation News,* reported on Chicago's Century of Progress Exposition in 1933 and 1934 and, as the "Voice of the Air," covered the 1934 racketeering trial of members of Local 712 of the Laundry and Dye House Drivers' Union. Father Maguire of St. Viator College began his Sunday evening talks on economic and labor issues in 1932. His strong support for organized labor and the New Deal, and his equally vigorous criticism of big business and its press minions, earned the labor priest a popular following throughout the midthirties.[36]

Former Illinois lieutenant governor Barratt O'Hara's talks over WCFL commenced in 1933 and continued into 1937. At their height, these fifteen-minute commentaries aired six evenings a week and covered "hot subjects on which a servile press maintains a discreet silence or . . . distorts the truth." O'Hara, a strong supporter of the New Deal and organized labor, analyzed, among other subjects, the huge discrepancy between the salaries of business executives and the wages of workers, the banking sector's control of industry, New Deal programs, and the importance of the labor movement in Chicago industry and economy.[37] A series of O'Hara radio talks denouncing the real estate bond market in the spring of 1934 generated a protest demonstration of twenty thousand irate bondholders in downtown Chicago. Although the only publicity for the demonstration came from O'Hara's broadcasts, protesters came from Illinois, Wisconsin, Michigan, Indiana, and Iowa.[38] O'Hara estimated that he had received approximately twenty-five thousand dollars worth of free airtime during his first year on WCFL. If he had been forced to rely on a sponsor, O'Hara did not believe "they would have left me entirely free and independent." Only WCFL allowed him to speak "the truth as I found it and believed in it." O'Hara praised CFL leaders for their wisdom and humanity.[39]

Every Friday during 1935–36, Ira Latimer commented on the week's news from a labor perspective. A doctoral candidate in sociology at the University of Chicago, Latimer came to WCFL with solid progressive political credentials. His father, a former socialist, served as the Farmer-Labor party mayor of Minneapolis during the midthirties. Latimer had traveled extensively throughout Europe, Asia, and the United States and began broadcasting while a student at Ohio State University. His news commentaries over WCFL began in March 1935 (a weekly column in the *Federation News* started in April). Although occasionally delayed by a late running baseball game, Latimer put "on some exceedingly interesting and informative programs," according to Nockels. His shows covered an array of local, national, and international issues, from health insurance and vocational guidance to the NRA and the Tennessee Valley Authority, from French nationalism and Nazi policies to trade unionism and a labor party.[40]

Latimer's talks linked together domestic and foreign policies, providing an intriguing and often radical perspective on contemporary events. In the fall of 1935 he announced that his program would henceforth give greater attention to "Labor news comments" for WCFL's labor audience.[41] Indeed, from October 1935 to the spring of 1936, Latimer expanded his commentary on labor issues and devoted considerable time to discussing the important role that the labor media, especially WCFL, played in the organized labor movement and in progressive reform. Like other advocates of the labor media, he warned that the effort of "fascist Chicago newspapers" to dominate "public opinion and public information" served only "their financial masters" and endangered "American liberty and our traditional republican form of government."[42] The labor movement needed "to control public opinion and to win the professional and middle classes and farmers" to its "side in the struggle with Organized Business." As a prerequisite, however, "far more workers need[ed] to become regular listeners of WCFL." Latimer urged local unions to "report important union news to Labor's radio audience" and he encouraged workers to have their unions make "fullest use" of WCFL and to get their friends and relatives to listen.[43] Sharing the commitment of many activists to develop a working-class culture, Latimer pleaded with workers to attend union meetings; read the labor press; see labor ballet, drama, and movies; and listen to labor radio.[44]

Nockels and Fitzpatrick, among other organic intellectuals, had waged a war for the hearts and minds of the working class for some time and their main weapons had been labor media, labor celebrations, and labor education. The creation of the CFL Speakers' Bureau marked an important development in the struggle. Established with CFL support, the bureau, among other things, aimed at developing a "working class psychology to stimulate and train trade unionists to become effective organizers and courageous, intelligent leaders of labor." The bureau offered a "progressive and educational" program that included "classes, discussions, [and] lectures" and furnished speakers for various organizations and organizing campaigns. Sarainne Loewe, secretary of the Speakers' Bureau, emphasized that the bureau sought people who had a practical, not a theoretical, knowledge of trade unionism.[45]

Loewe herself combined the attributes of an organic intellectual steeped both in theory and practice. "A dynamic speaker and [a] tireless" organizer, she played a leadership role in CFL organizing campaigns during the midthirties and became "the darling" of the federation.[46] In many ways, Loewe advocated a progressive leftist ideology that had characterized CFL leaders of a decade earlier. Dividing the world between workers and bosses, she talked about the necessity of abolishing the profit system and endorsed a dual working-class strategy of using strikes to fight economic battles and a labor party for political contests. She declared that the Speakers' Bureau "frankly takes the viewpoint of the worker as the basis for all its teachings. Its purpose is to advance the interests of labor—the vast majority of the nation in every way." In August 1935, Loewe joined three hundred other trade unionists to form the Labor Party of Chicago and Cook County. The new organ opposed "the political parties supporting capitalism" because "in the struggle between capital and Labor, there can be no such thing as a 'non-partisan' position."[47]

A firm advocate of labor radio, Loewe frequently argued that local trade unions should acknowledge WCFL's great service to organized labor by using and supporting the station.[48] The bureau had its own regular fifteen-minute Tuesday evening show during 1934–36. Loewe and other activists discussed a variety of issues affecting the workers of Chicago and the world, emphasizing the need for labor solidarity in the face of the ideological and economic power of capitalism. In September 1934, Loewe condemned both the Communist party's efforts to destroy AFL unions—while ostensibly building new revolutionary ones—and the AFL's "equally unprincipled attacks . . . on communism." Urging labor to oppose the party's destructive tactics, she also reminded unionists "that [communists] are workers and they are fighting the same common menace as all other workers, namely, lowering of living standards. The police and the employers must not be used by one labor faction against another. Officers of labor unions who help to incite police and boss supported raids on communists or any other workers are committing a shameful breach of working class solidarity that the whole labor movement will suffer for in the future."[49]

Loewe explained that red-baiting inevitably became labor-baiting, that both had links to fascism, and that the persecution of the "reddest Reds or the most conservative unionists should meet with the united and determined opposition of all workers and workers organizations."[50] In her New Year's message broadcast over WCFL in late 1935, Loewe exhorted "the workers of Chicago . . . to unite and organize regardless of race, color or creed, regardless of whether you are employed or unemployed; whether you wear a white collar or black overalls. The strength of those who do the world's useful work lies in their numbers and in the fact that they are indispensable. This strength can only be realized through organization."[51]

The CFL Speakers' Bureau believed that "the present situation calls for progressive labor education and this idea dominates its radio talks as well as its various classes." Under Sarainne Loewe's direction, the bureau expanded and integrated its educational and broadcasting activities. The bureau's weekly talk program over WCFL presented labor material that had "a decided educational value" in and of itself. At the same time, the program stimulated interest in the bureau's courses in public speaking, labor economics, labor history, and parliamentary law. Workers who successfully completed these courses could, beginning in the spring of 1935, receive instruction in broadcasting and "speak for the Bureau over radio station WCFL."[52] Loewe initially taught this new class called "Radio Composition and Broadcasting." By instructing students on how to write radio talks and providing them with experience before the microphone, Loewe and WCFL's staff announcers helped "to develop capable writers and radio speakers for the labor movement."[53]

Officially renamed The Federation Labor School in June 1935, the bureau's education program introduced a new course on labor drama in early 1936. This class responded to the challenge of making labor education entertaining as well as informative and of reaching as wide an audience as possible. Labor School officials hoped "to work up a series of plays and skits based upon the struggles of the labor movement" and then to make those plays "available for union meetings and labor organizations."[54] Labor drama also contributed to a labor culture that would aid unionists in the "work of organizing, educating, bargaining, [and] building a stronger" labor movement. Given the multiethnic and multiracial composition of Chicago's working class, the trade union movement needed a labor culture in which "various colors, accents and languages [would] mingle." Bureau officials worried that "a trade unionist thinking only of wages and hours without getting into the swing of union work and union play may fail in a crisis."[55]

The drama class met on Wednesday evenings for two hours during the first half of 1936. William Schaeffer of the Elevator Operators and Starters' Union taught the class and also wrote the group's first play. *The Company Union* portrayed a group of workers who, frustrated with the company union, built their own labor organization and conducted a strike that won both union recognition and a contract. During rehearsals, class members suggested changes in dialogue and direction and occasionally revised entire scenes. The drama group performed the play at several union halls during the spring of 1936. In May, the Speakers' Bureau broadcasted the play over WCFL hoping to teach labor "the value of [using] drama in putting over trade union propaganda. One little play of this kind . . . is worth a hundred speeches of propaganda."[56] Such efforts to bring drama to workers in their union halls and over WCFL constituted one part of a larger movement toward workers' theater during the thirties.

The Great Depression, the New Deal, and the revival of radical politics and working-class organizing accelerated the growth and development of workers' theater. Increasing from approximately twenty-one groups across the nation in 1930 to four hundred by 1934, the labor drama movement served multiple functions.[57] As the historian Colette Hyman has argued, the plays of workers' theater were both descriptive and prescriptive; they reflected the "received notions and lived experiences" of the workers who wrote and attended the plays and they revealed those workers' "idealized conceptions" of a world they wished to create. Workers' theater thus served as an alternative vehicle for radical political activity, becoming a theater of class struggle. The CFL's drama group, among many others, demonstrated that workers' theater was also a democratic theater in which workers could write and revise, act and direct. Daniel Friedman's study of workers' theater concluded that "at no time were regular American working people viewing plays, debating aesthetics, acting, and writing shows in such numbers or with such enthusiasm" as they did during the thirties.[58]

Theatre Union, founded in 1933, manifested one type of workers' theater. Created by artists who believed that unions formed the vanguard of societal change, the group produced "plays of overtly propagandistic proletarian content," depicted "economic and social problems experienced by the majority of Americans," and made those plays "available to audiences unable to pay Broadway prices." By the end of its second season (1934–35), half a million people had attended the theater's four productions. Even the *New York Times* praised the Theatre Union's "honorable record for enterprise and originality" and its "creditable pioneering among new, unexploited audiences."[59]

Chicago workers also developed their own viable social theater during the thirties.[60] Workers who formed the Chicago Repertory Group, for example, were "so intensely interested in building up a labor theater that they devote all of their free time to this end, frequently working late into the night with the prospect of a hard working day ahead. This group has been presenting plays and sketches before labor unions, [the] unemployed, and at strikes throughout the summer."[61] Seeking to combine "the struggles and ideals of organized labor with the skill and sensitivity of creative art," the Chicago Repertory developed into the "most important labor theatre in the city" during the decade. It maintained low ticket prices (35–75 cents) and offered special discounts for blocks of seats purchased by trade unions, making it possible for workers and their families to attend. Repertory productions included musical satires ridiculing the antilabor stance of the Hearst press or the efforts of city authorities to ban "profane" social plays. The group performed famous works such as Clifford Odets's *Waiting for Lefty* and Albert Maltz's *Black Pit* as well as lesser-known pieces, all of which emphasized "the lives and struggles of working class people" and challenged "the anti-labor forces of war and fascism."[62]

With its focus on the working class, the Repertory Group thought it appropriate to secure a formal endorsement from the CFL. In the fall of 1936, Alice Evans explained to CFL delegates that the theater (including motion pictures), together with the press and radio, constituted the "three great agencies of propaganda" that shaped public opinion. Because the CFL had undertaken the difficult job of educating the public on labor issues, it needed to utilize all three media. Workers might attend union meetings, listen to WCFL, and read the *Federation News*, but they "then go to the movie or vaudeville show and applaud" a performance that tells "us to be satisfied with 'plenty of nothing' or enjoy an anti-labor play. Isn't it just as important to have entertainment with a labor slant, as it is to have . . . a copy of the *Federation News* in your pocket?" Acknowledging that Chicago's "cultural movement" did not possess the funds necessary to produce labor films, Evans argued that the labor theater would have to produce plays "which could reach thousands—if not millions—of people." Workers' theater thus required and deserved backing from organized labor. Evans noted that "the Chicago Federation of Labor Players" and individual union leaders—including John Fitzpatrick, Samuel Levin (ACWA), and Lillian Herstein— already supported the Repertory Group. CFL delegates officially endorsed the Chicago Repertory Group, allowing its representatives to visit local unions and sell tickets.[63]

The *Federation News* also recognized the importance of labor drama and inaugurated the "Workers' Theatre" column in 1935. Drama Editor Cecil Robinson praised the valuable contributions made to working-class culture by the workers' theater movement of Chicago. He reviewed plays written or performed by local groups, explored developments in workers' theater, and explained the social, artistic, and political importance of these cultural institutions. Readers of Robinson's column learned of the raw enthusiasm and "vitality of expression" of working-class theater, of the occasionally weak tempo and less than biting satire of its productions, and of the efforts of African-American players and the workers' theater movement to remedy the lack of a "powerful social theatre . . . [in Chicago's] Negro culture."[64]

Given the commitment of many CFL leaders to both labor theater and labor radio, it would seem natural that the two components of labor culture and propaganda would develop a close working relationship. Wishing to reach a wide working-class audience with their plays, some workers' theater members considered radio "a dramatic medium of great value, particularly to those denied any other theater."[65] WCFL occasionally aired the productions of the Labor School's drama group. In the spring of 1936, WCFL broadcasted a serial written by George V. Martin of the Federal Theater Project's Theater No. 1. The production, under the joint supervision of Theodore Viehman, director of Theater No. 1, and R. Calvert Haws, WCFL program director, aired three mornings each week. Both the *Federation News* and WCFL kept Chicago laborers informed of workers' theater performances in the area—whether offered by the Chicago Repertory Group, the Federal Theater Project, the touring Brookwood Players, or the New Theatre League's midwest festival. During February and March of 1937, members of the Chicago Repertory Group collaborated with WCFL in presenting a series of dramatic and informational sketches. Each skit dealt with a different aspect of the newly devised Social Security system. Written by experts hired by the AFL's Workers' Education Bureau, the minidramas made their premier over WCFL on Tuesday evening, February 16, 1937. Lillian Herstein helped to coordinate the various productions.[66] Linkages such as these notwithstanding, a close and regular cooperative relationship between labor radio and workers' theater never materialized in Chicago.

A number of structural problems inhibited an alliance between labor radio and workers' theater. In general, the link between "legitimate" theater and commercial radio took a relatively long time to develop. Commercial radio's voracious appetite for profits and the prejudices of sponsors and advertising agencies obstructed the development of "serious" plays written especially for radio. Broadcasting industry officials believed, as a 1937 how-to book on radio writing succinctly put it, that "your radio audience, in mass, has a mental age of about fourteen"; that writers should avoid trying to educate the audience when attempting to entertain them; and that they should "steer far clear of the sophisticated type of entertainment if you are aiming at a capacity audience." Just as the radio industry neglected the theater as a source of programming, "skilled theatre workers . . . [failed] to understand, much less master, the difficulties and opportunities" of radio.[67]

The mutual prejudices that permeated the worlds of commercial radio and theater and that obstructed a meaningful interchange between the two carried over into the realms of labor radio and workers' theater. Many theater people simply had little understanding or use for radio. Even those individuals in workers' theater who perceived radio's potential preferred direct interaction with their audiences. They chose to bring their ideological and political plays to workers in the union halls, at labor celebrations, or on picket lines. Financial problems exacerbated these obstacles. On the one hand, the small operating budgets of workers' theaters precluded them from purchasing airtime over WCFL. On the other hand, the demands for free broadcasting slots from unions, organizers, and political activists overwhelmed labor radio, relegating gratis time for workers' theater to a low priority. Nevertheless, even the tentative links between labor radio and labor theater prove significant when placed within the context of WCFL's other efforts to build trade unionism and a working-class culture during the thirties.[68]

WCFL's commitment to both the Radio Frolics and Labor Day celebrations, for example, contributed to bolstering working-class consciousness and solidarity in Chicago. Radio Frolics continued to serve as a major social event for area workers, as well as a source of additional revenue for WCFL. Responding to financial problems exacerbated by the Great Depression and to demands for greater participation in the annual event, the Frolics' planning committee expanded the affair in 1933. The main ballroom of the Street Car Men's Building became the location of an entertainment extravaganza using WCFL talent as well as performers from other Chicago radio stations. Members of WCFL's popular ethnic hours furnished over a quarter of the entertainment program, which WCFL broadcasted from 8:00 P.M. to 1:00 A.M. At the same time, hundreds of people inundated the three dance halls on the second floor of the building, where orchestras played waltz, popular, and country music.[69]

The Frolics entertained Chicago's workers and their families throughout the decade. Orchestras offered a variety of musical options for dancers, radio and theater artists entertained thousands in the ballroom, and WCFL broadcasted the event to those who could not attend. WCFL's advertising manager and program director produced the Frolics during this period. In 1934, the AFL, in an effort to strengthen ties with the White House, sponsored a series of charity presidential parties throughout the country, with the proceeds going to the Infantile Paralysis Foundation. Nockels protected the Frolics' primacy in organized labor's social calendar by arguing that the CFL not solicit local unions to purchase tickets for the presidential party "because all such soliciting must be done for the . . . Frolics" in order to maximize returns for WCFL.[70] In an effort to resolve overcrowding and to generate more revenue for WCFL, organizers changed the structure of the celebration in 1936 and 1937, offering two evenings of entertainment instead of one: Saturday night dances and Sunday night music and comedy. The 1936 Frolics attracted a combined crowd of fifteen thousand people.[71]

Labor Day celebrations, like the Radio Frolics, enhanced working-class socializing and solidarity, while bringing attention to WCFL. The 1932 festivities included a parade down Michigan Avenue to Grant Park and Soldier Field. Five divisions of marchers, including local unions, marching bands, and speakers, participated. At the stadium, the marchers and spectators reviewed "Labor's army of unemployed followed by massing of trade union banners." The protest demonstration against unemployment continued with addresses by labor and civic leaders. A spectacular pageant, "The Call of Labor," then followed. After these ceremonies, the assembled crowd left the stadium and entered the Century of Progress International Exposition grounds for a special entertainment program. An evening dance at Navy Pier ended the day. Labor radio carried selected parts of the long Labor Day celebration. The elaborate 1932 festivities allowed workers both to express their feelings regarding inept government and business responses to the depression and to rejoice in the achievements and promises of the labor movement.[72]

Labor Day organizers linked the 1933 and 1934 celebrations to the Century of Progress Exposition. The 1934 event covered two days and incorporated elaborate musical presentations, a ball, circus acts, movies, a water carnival, and speeches. Important local and national luminaries such as Senator C. C. Dill, John H. Walker of the Illinois State Federation of Labor, Father J. W. R. Maguire, and New York mayor Fiorella LaGuardia addressed the large crowd and a larger WCFL radio audience. WCFL also secured a speech from Upton Sinclair, who was passing through Chicago. The noted author had just captured the Democratic nomination for governor of California on the platform of ending poverty in the state.[73]

Organized Labor Day celebrations came to an abrupt halt in 1935 because of a free speech controversy involving Father Charles E. Coughlin. Father Coughlin had preached traditional sermons over the radio for several years before venturing into political commentary. By the midthirties the Catholic priest had developed a large following for his right-wing political and religious fundamentalist messages. Coughlin's populist style and his attacks against international bankers attracted some labor officials and rank-and-file members to his campaign. Progressives and leftists within the labor movement, including the left wing of the CFL, however, remained suspicious of him. "Many of us believe," wrote one Chicago unionist in June 1935, that Coughlin's "movement is one of the many Fascist tendencies, conscious or unconscious, now developing here." Opponents of Coughlin insisted that his movement was not labor-based, but an expression of the middle class and small businesses and that "in reality" the movement might be "the bitterest enemy of labor rather than its friend."[74] Despite such labor ambivalence toward Coughlin, the CFL came to the radio priest's defense in mid-1935.

The Chicago Park Commission decided in the spring of 1935 to reject Father Coughlin's request to use Soldier Field for a rally of his National Union for Social Justice. Commissioners ruled that the city parks could not "be used for the dissemination of propaganda on political and economic subjects of a controversial nature." Coughlin challenged this restriction in the courts, winning in the lower courts and losing on appeal.[75] The CFL quickly entered the fray, in part because of the issue of free speech and in part because officials suspected that the *Chicago Tribune*'s Colonel McCormick had influenced Robert J. Dunham, the park commissioner, to deny the permit. Labor leaders pointed to the Park Commission's use of the *Tribune* law firm in its legal battle with Coughlin. Nockels, in a move meant to annoy the *Tribune* as much as anything else, offered Coughlin free airtime over WCFL in order to address the people of Chicago. Several WCFL commentators, including Barratt O'Hara, denounced the Park Commission's decision.[76]

As this conflict raged, the CFL applied for a permit to use Soldier Field for a Labor Day celebration. With the *Federation News* and WCFL defending Father Coughlin's right to free speech, park commissioners feared that the CFL might invite Coughlin to speak at the Labor Day rally. The commission insisted on seeing a full schedule for the event before it would grant the permit. Meeting with CFL officers in late July, Dunham reiterated that the city would not allow speakers to discuss controversial economic or political issues in its parks and warned that if the CFL could not abide by that rule then it could not use Soldier Field. Astonished CFL leaders replied that the CFL's "very purpose . . . was to deal with economics which were surely controversial, and we could not permit any censorship of our discussion or our speakers on this subject." Given the federation's long and steadfast support for free speech, free press, and free assembly, Fitzpatrick and his colleagues refused to "submit to any form of censorship over our Labor Day Celebration." They turned down an offer giving them access to the stadium if they promised not to invite Coughlin to speak. Dunham then refused to grant the CFL a permit, effectively destroying the 1935 celebration.[77]

The cancellation of the 1935 celebration at Soldier Field left federation officials with only one way to mark Labor Day. WCFL became the centerpiece of Labor Day festivities in both 1935 and 1936. Labor radio aired an assortment of speeches, a dramatization of the history of the labor movement, music, recitations, and even a rare recording of Sam Gompers. Detailed coverage of an imaginary parade and a history of the Chicago labor movement supplemented the other Labor Day programs on WCFL in 1936. These productions helped to maintain some labor solidarity during these years. WCFL's finest hours of service to organized labor, however, came during times of labor crisis.[78]

. . .

Strikes, lockouts, court injunctions, mass arrests, and similar actions presented WCFL with great challenges. In the midst of the Great Depression, and after a decade of relative inactivity on the part of labor, came a wave of militant working-class actions that challenged American business and stimulated union organizing campaigns. Labor militancy manifested itself not only in strikes against capitalist enterprises but also in actions for or against the state and established trade unions. The battle within the AFL between craft and industrial unionists—a battle that eventually produced a new labor organization, the Congress of Industrial Organizations—was as bitter as any between labor and capital. Equally intense was organized labor's participation in national politics, especially its growing commitment to Franklin D. Roosevelt and the Democratic party, and in national legislative and judicial procedures dealing with labor's right to organize and bargain collectively.[79] The days when station managers lamented the lack of labor news and union use of radio facilities seemed ancient history by 1935.

With plenty of crises to motivate workers, community activists, and trade unions to ask for WCFL's help, labor radio found itself inundated with requests for airtime. Unfortunately, it lacked the financial resources, staff, and time to meet all the demands made upon it. When a Chicago local of the ILGWU requested airtime from WCFL in early 1936, Nockels responded that while the station favored the local's proposal, "each request must be sanctioned by the President of the International." The Chicago local of the ILGWU received such support and WCFL provided the airtime.[80]

A strike in Janesville, Wisconsin, in 1936, which pitted Carpenters' Union Local 836 against the Utley Construction Company, provided another example of how labor radio allocated scarce resources to local trade unions. The company, seeking to undermine the union by hiring strikebreakers, advertised for carpenters in Chicago newspapers. Union officials asked WCFL to tell its audience about the ongoing strike and the efforts of the company to hire scabs. The district council of the Brotherhood of Carpenters and Joiners urged WCFL not to grant the request of a little "jerk water town" because "it might result in our members compelling us to make unreasonable requests of WCFL, which would embarrass us and WCFL as well." In explaining WCFL's decision not to assist the union, Nockels noted that the local had not gone through proper channels and that in any event "we are unable to make announcements of this nature over WCFL . . . because we could not possibly find the necessary time to put all such announcements on the air."[81] Indeed, by 1936–37, WCFL had introduced a new level of bureaucracy with which all individuals and groups had to contend before they could secure airtime.[82]

As long as unions and individual activists went through the proper channels, WCFL imposed no censorship or time limit or cost on those who wished to use the airwaves. Like many broadcasters, WCFL had required that speakers present their transcripts to station officials *before* airtime, but labor radio waived this requirement during labor crises.[83] Joseph M. Jacobs, a labor attorney and activist in the Chicago area, frequently used WCFL to inform workers of the important labor battles taking place in their community, battles that local and network corporate broadcasters chose to ignore. Jacobs, who represented a variety of workers seeking to exercise their right to organize, spoke over WCFL on October 10, 1935, for example, and described the grave situation in Terre Haute, Indiana. State officials had aligned with employers to impose martial law or, as Jacobs vividly characterized it, "a vicious military fascist dictatorship" on the city in order to quash a labor strike. "The only medium whereby we could bring these issues to the public," recalled Jacobs, "was through station WCFL."[84]

Jacobs's contention that only WCFL offered an outlet for labor activists during crisis situations was valid. Although the network giants NBC and CBS and several local radio stations allowed selected trade union and radical leaders to use their facilities, they refused to do so when issues of a "controversial" nature were the topic. Hammond, Indiana, station WWAE allowed the Lake County Central Labor Union to produce a daily program, during the winter of 1934–35, that included orchestra music and speeches and provided the public with an overview of organized labor's aims and objectives. Milwaukee station WTMJ sold airtime to the Socialist party in 1934 for a fifteen-minute Sunday talk program that expounded on basic socialist theories and philosophies. But when the Federated Trades Council of Milwaukee wanted to inform the public about an ongoing strike in 1937, local stations refused access to their facilities arguing that the talks were "too controversial." WCFL broadcasted the council program.[85] Barred from commercial radio, labor organizers turned to WCFL, becoming, in the process, committed supporters.

WCFL's role in an AFL organizing campaign during 1935 amply demonstrated the power of radio controlled by and for labor. This campaign revolved around the effort of workers at a chain of "dental parlors" in Chicago to organize a union. The company's refusal to recognize the union provoked a strike and boycott of the parlors. WCFL informed the public about the strike, indicating that the company was nonunion and suggesting that workers and their families patronize other dentists. Because a large portion of the company's clientele consisted of working-class people, the firm found WCFL's participation in the boycott particularly threatening and sought an injunction against the station. A lower court issued a temporary injunction. In November, however, the Illinois Appellate Court overturned the lower court decision, upholding the right of organized labor to strike and to conduct a legal boycott via radio. The decision reaffirmed the potential of labor radio.[86]

In addition to allocating free airtime to unions to make announcements during crises, WCFL set aside time for labor organizations to present their own programming. The Chicago Joint Council of Bakery and Confectionery Workers, for example, supervised a number of educational and informational programs in its campaign against nonunion bakeries. Its 1936–37 radio campaign, which featured economic and political discussions by Barratt O'Hara, led to a significant increase in the patronage of union bakery shops and in the employment of union workers.[87] The Chicago Trades Union Label League's close association with WCFL continued with broadcasts of the league's weekly fifteen-minute program. When, in 1933–34, the Label League faced a national antiunion label propaganda drive, WCFL gave the organization multiple daily spots as well as use of "Labor Flashes" to make important announcements.[88] WCFL supported talks by prominent labor and civic leaders under the auspices of the Chicago Teachers' Federation during 1932–34. The union praised WCFL for its assistance in fighting for better public schools in the city.[89]

Requests for airtime over WCFL came from a plethora of local unions and organizing campaigns. Faced with limited time slots and growing commitments to advertisers, officials imposed restrictions on access to WCFL's facilities. Local 712 of the Laundry and Dye House Drivers' Union and selected other unions, however, received special consideration from WCFL. A strong and constant backer of WCFL since the station's inception, Local 712 had advanced Nockels the money necessary to purchase land in Downers Grove for the construction of a superpower station. It renewed the mortgage when the depression undermined WCFL's real estate plan, making it impossible for the station to repay its debts. Local 712 reaped the re-wards of this generosity when government officials indicted its officials on charges of racketeering and corruption in 1933–34. Chicago's commercial media had a field day portraying not only Local 712 but virtually all area labor organizations as rackets. Phil Friedlander's "Voice of the Air" program over WCFL provided Chicago listeners with labor's perspective on Local 712's trial—a necessary antidote to the unsympathetic and slanted cover-age by the commercial press. CFL officials granted Local 712 as much free airtime as they needed to counteract media propaganda and promised: "If it became necessary to give Local No. 712 time on the air that conflicted with a commercial program, there isn't an advertiser who could persuade us to withhold that time from the union. We are with them all the time and all the way."[90]

Providing free airtime to unions, whether in crisis or noncrisis situations, was an important function of labor radio. But given the tremendous de-mands made upon WCFL by labor organs seeking access to the airwaves, and given the difficult commercial and financial pressures under which the station operated, WCFL had to find new ways for unions to use its facili-ties. Station managers increasingly encouraged local unions to become "sponsors" of their own popular shows, thus resolving the basic contradic-tion between commercial programming and service to the labor commu-nity. But difficult questions remained as to whether union sponsors could integrate their labor messages into a popular radio format or, avoiding the connection at all, keep the union message and the entertainment separate.

Since the inception of labor radio, program directors attempted to give a distinctly labor twist to popular entertainment genres. Such was the case in 1937 as contest or quiz shows replaced amateur programs "as the most pop-ular form of audience participation programming." Like amateur hours, quiz shows entertained listeners and afforded them the opportunity to control, in a sense, the content of the programming. "Professor Quiz," which appeared on CBS in 1936, and "Uncle Jim's Question Bee" awarded small cash prizes (around ten dollars) to those participants best capable of "answering gener-al information questions."[91] Following this lead, the *Federation News* spon-sored the "Federation News Question Bee" over WCFL during early 1937. Contestants answered questions about labor history and problems, and the winners received cash awards of ten dollars. Announcers Don Norman and Major Holmes presided over the Saturday and later Monday evening shows, giving a sales pitch for the newspaper at the beginning, middle, and end of each program. In addition, during the first few shows, the newspaper's business manager Charles F. Wills briefly explained the history and significance of the organized labor movement to the listening audience. This experiment in popular programming was short-lived, falling from the schedule in March 1937. But the *Federation News* continued to sponsor entertainment shows, shifting to a musical variety format in April.[92]

The first effort by a local union to sponsor a popular program that had no direct connection with labor issues, but nevertheless aided in a union organizing campaign, aired in the spring of 1936. During the depression, Chicago-area milk producers had expanded the use of chain grocery stores and the sale "of bulk milk at nonunion depots around the city" in an effort to cut their distribution costs. The Milk Wagon Drivers' Union counteracted this threat by launching a strike against milk depots employing nonunion drivers and inaugurating a new commercial radio program aimed at children. Virtually identical to dozens of children's shows on commercial networks and independent stations, the "Pioneer Trading Post" aired over WCFL weekdays at 6:15 P.M. R. Calvert Haws, the WCFL program director who helped develop the show for the Milk Wagon Drivers' Union, purposely chose a format that would attract the ultimate consumers of milk. By dramatizing the stories of the American pioneers, creating a radio club, and conducting contests, the sponsors hoped "to make children union-minded and to bring patronage to the union men working in the dairy industry." Within ten weeks of the first broadcast some twenty thousand children had joined the Pioneer Trading Post Club. Chicago-area children could secure club membership applications only from union milk drivers. Those children who lived in homes not served by union drivers complained to their parents, who in turn complained to local dairies. As a result, thirty-two dairies voluntarily signed with the union, putting some seven hundred union drivers back to work. Labor officials estimated that the percentage of milk handled by union employees had jumped from 80 to 92 percent over the course of two and a half months.[93]

"Pioneer Trading Post" opened up a relatively untouched avenue for trade unions interested in using the radio to further their goals. By the end of the thirties several other unions had followed the milk drivers' lead, with mixed results. Rather than producing programs that examined specific labor themes or analyzed political and socioeconomic problems or responded to immediate community concerns, unions sponsored entertainment programs similar to those on the radio networks. They then "advertised" their organizations as some commodity, "selling" their good names and goodwill to the community.

The inauguration of popular programming sponsored by labor unions marked an important change in a radio station that had undergone many alterations in its first decade of existence. By 1937, WCFL was no longer a community-based-and-supported radio station. Advertising, not voluntary contributions from Chicago area workers, financed the bulk of station operations. WCFL's programs mimicked network shows and a significant percentage of WCFL's schedule came directly from NBC Blue's selection of sustaining programs, especially light musical, variety, and talk shows. Although the station remained open to labor announcements and labor news analyses, advertising concerns dictated that more time went to sponsored programming. WCFL was well on the road to treating its listeners, not as partners in a cooperative effort, but as consumers. It had begun to resemble the very system it sought to oppose.[94]

By the midthirties, the United States had developed a broadcasting system characterized by centralized and concentrated networks producing programs aimed at a mass audience for a profit. Edward Nockels and a host of other labor, educational, political, and intellectual leaders lambasted this system for its failure to educate and inform, its tendency to censor ideas dangerous to the status quo, and its effort to legitimize itself and the general capitalist system. Commercial broadcasters rarely attended to the concerns of workers. When they did respond to labor's needs, usually under the threat of government intervention—via new legislation or antitrust action—they did so in a patronizing manner and for the goal of maximizing profits.[95]

It is important to note, however, the dialectical forces working within the capitalist broadcasting system. Broadcast media have tended to serve the "psychological and cultural needs" of workers.[96] The historian Lizabeth Cohen has argued that network radio during the thirties helped to pull "workers out of their isolated cultural communities and [gave] them more experiences in common with other workers." By providing workers with "common cultural experiences," network radio "made them feel part of a larger, citywide and particularly national culture." Building cultural unity and class identity was a crucial prerequisite to creating national industrial unions such as those comprising the CIO.[97] Thus the very broadcasting structure that denied to organized labor a fair hearing and manipulated union access to its facilities helped to shape a cultural environment that facilitated industrial union organization.

Although network radio programming contributed to the development of a national culture, which in turn undermined the cultural and ethnic divisions among workers, it simultaneously weakened the ability of workers to battle the nation's corporate capitalist structure. In the thirties, network radio destroyed the opportunity for groups or individuals critical of American capitalism to gain access to the air, except on the conditions laid down by corporate broadcasters. The economic, political, cultural, technical, and ideological power of the radio networks constantly endangered the survival of alternative broadcasting outlets. Even the FCC could not ignore this problem indefinitely. In 1938, the commission finally agreed to consider the problem of how the radio networks limited diversity on the airwaves. It took until 1941 for the agency to complete its massive investigation of the monopoly aspects of "chain broadcasting." The FCC's dramatic findings called for, among other things, the breakup of NBC's network empire and substantial changes in the affiliate relationship at CBS.[98] Edward Nockels would have embraced the report with great enthusiasm, if he had been alive.

· · ·

On Saturday afternoon, February 27, 1937, Nockels prepared for yet one more trip to Washington, D.C., to confront the FCC on the issues of increased power for WCFL and the dangers posed by the radio trust. Taking a break from his tasks, Nockels went to a favorite restaurant on South Wabash Avenue near the CFL offices. There he suffered a fatal heart attack.[99] Nockels's death saddened labor activists everywhere. Upon learning the news, Frank Walsh grieved that Chicago had lost a man of "fine intelligence, gentile nobility of character and infinite courage." Walsh telegrammed Roosevelt's secretary, requesting the president to say a word about Nockels. "I do not exaggerate," wrote Walsh, "when I say he was the most respected and beloved man in the labor movement in the United States and recognized by all of Chicago as one of its most useful citizens."[100] Similar sentiments came from all over Chicago. At Nockels's funeral, the Reverend J. W. R. Maguire said of his friend: "His death was like his life, sudden and impulsive, for Ed Nockels was a man of impulses, some of which may at times have been unwise and imprudent, but all of which were righteous and noble."[101] Eulogies for Nockels inevitably included references to his "dream and pride," WCFL. The attorney William B. Rubin wrote that Nockels "loved and lived for his cause. He gave to the world the first Labor radio broadcasting station." Even technocrats at the FCC acknowledged, while never really comprehending, the "many valuable and thought-provoking contributions" that Nockels had made to the discussion of radio broadcasting.[102]

Edward Nockels's importance to WCFL cannot be overstated. For twelve years he had provided the leadership necessary to keep the station operating—despite countless problems. As his colleagues often noted, labor radio would have been impossible without him. During WCFL's early days, observers praised Nockels for his "prophetic vision." One *Federation News* writer contended that a study of radio's usefulness affected Nockels "as the biblical version of Heavenly splendor affected Saul of Tarsus. Both saw the light and a vision of limitless possibilities that justified the dedication of their energies to the task of eventual realization."[103] But while Nockels's belief in the revolutionary potential of radio remained constant, his conceptualization of labor radio was never as straightforward or as rigid as his admirers thought.

Nockels presented two alternative and somewhat contradictory visions of an American broadcasting system. He devoted the last decade of his life to building a national labor broadcasting system founded on a superpower, clear-channel WCFL with shortwave capabilities. A labor radio network, he assumed, would be strong enough to counteract the influence of corporate radio in the battle for the hearts and minds of the American public. At the same time, however, Nockels remained attracted to a vision that redefined American broadcasting, that emphasized a decentralized and democratic broadcasting structure. His last testimony before the FCC in 1936 emphasized the importance of a diversified and democratic radio system based on a multitude of local stations with low power. These arguments were not new, but dated back at least to 1926, when William Strong, on behalf of Nockels and the CFL, testified before Congress. This commitment to democratic broadcasting also manifested itself in Nockels's constant pleas for rank-and-file participation in labor radio. The CFL secretary never tired of telling Chicago's workers that WCFL was their radio station and that they alone had "the power to determine how it shall be used." He urged workers to listen to the station and "to write to us, making suggestions, comments, and offering criticism." As in all his work for the labor movement, Nockels believed that the catalyst for change, whether in the arena of politics or economics or culture, had to come from the bottom up, not from the top down.[104]

Mollie Friedman of the ILGWU was among the minority of activists who understood and appreciated Edward Nockels's dream. When congratulating him on the establishment of WCFL in 1926, she touched on the vision which drove Nockels for the rest of his lifetime but remained unrealized in 1937. "May your spiritual child," wrote Friedman, "blaze the trail for a large family of labor broadcasting stations."[105]

SEVEN

Labor Radio without Nockels, 1937–46

The New Deal and World War II years marked dramatic trans-
formations in the U.S. political economy. Among these was a new "social
compromise between industrial workers and big business in which each side
recognized certain needs and prerogatives of the other." A new regulatory
state played a vital role in achieving this "corporatist compromise."[1] New
Deal legislation, both in the form of section 7(a) of the National Industrial
Recovery Act (1933) and later the Wagner Act (1935), for example, recognized
the right of workers to organize unions and engage in collective bargaining with leaders of their own choosing. But the relationship between New
Deal reformers and the labor movement remained complex. Militant and
radical workers pushed the Roosevelt administration to make concessions
to America's working class, while New Deal reforms ultimately bolstered
capitalist interests. Throughout the thirties the regulatory state expanded
its efforts to maximize private profits both at home and abroad. When the
United States emerged as the dominant power in the world system after
World War II, the corporatist compromise committed both organized labor and corporate capital to the maintenance of American hegemony.[2]

In Chicago, as elsewhere, the corporatist compromise developed among
trade unions, businesses, and the Democratic party. But this was a slow
process, one characterized as much by stagnation or steps backward as by
leaps forward. New industrial unions emerged under the banner of the
Committee for Industrial Organization, much to the chagrin of the AFL,

which opposed a dual union structure. In many ways, the CIO was far more radical than its craft union rival—both in ideology and in tactics. The developing CIO-AFL battle forced the CFL and WCFL to make difficult decisions that compromised their progressive character. Edward Nockels's death exacerbated this situation.

Julia Wrigley's study of Chicago labor, politics, and public education found that the CFL's growing conservatism during the interwar period derived not from changed leadership but rather from altered circumstances. The failed labor party movement, the open-shop offensive against labor, and government and business cooperation in undermining union organizing efforts weakened the CFL's progressive unionism during the twenties. A decade later the Great Depression, the New Deal, and the splintering of the AFL forced CFL officials to embrace the business and craft unionism of the AFL.[3] The "elderly men" of the CFL, as Joseph D. Keenan recalled, were "pretty staid" by the thirties and "couldn't quite catch up with" the "young" CIO organizers.[4] Nockels's death accelerated these changes in the CFL, especially concerning the development of labor radio. Despite his own turn away from radical options, as manifested in his embrace of Roosevelt's New Deal, Nockels continued to challenge the radio monopoly and the FCC and to demand a clear channel and full power for WCFL. NBC and the AFL both recognized Nockels's radicalism and maintained a safe distance from labor radio when possible. With Nockels gone from the scene, however, these organizations saw their opportunity to increase control over WCFL and to reap the resulting benefits.

The AFL's new interest in labor radio resulted from Nockels's death and from the battle with the CIO. AFL leaders never particularly liked Nockels or his projects. A WCFL without the feisty secretary would be easier for the AFL to manipulate. More important in framing the AFL attitude toward WCFL was the federation's intensifying war with the dissident CIO. During most of radio broadcasting's brief history, the AFL hierarchy rejected the idea of an independent and alternative radio station, favoring instead a cooperative, not antagonistic relationship between labor and capital. William Green's participation on the NBC Advisory Council usually involved praising the "tolerant, broadminded attitude of the National Broadcasting Company in permitting Labor to use its service."[5] The absence of class warfare between workers and business, according to the AFL, made labor radio superfluous. But warfare within labor was another matter. In the context of the struggle with the CIO for the hearts and minds of laborers, employers, and the general public, the AFL leadership discovered not only the significance of WCFL but also the need to expand the federation's use of commercial radio.

Unlike the AFL, which used radio primarily as a public relations tool—a medium for demonstrating organized labor's responsible behavior—the CIO used radio as an organizing tool and as a weapon against recalcitrant employers. Denied access to NBC, CBS, and several regional networks in 1937, CIO leaders vigorously condemned both the industry and the FCC and demanded that Congress investigate corporate broadcasting. More importantly, the union devised a strategy to hook up small independent stations in areas where organizing campaigns were underway. Morris Novik, the program director for WEVD—the low-power New York station created by the Socialist party—became the CIO's adviser on "radio propagandizing." He supplied unions with electrical transcriptions of talks and discussions by prominent pro-labor politicians, trade union leaders, and social activists. Novik helped CIO unions to write, direct, and produce their own programming. To assist in organizing Bethlehem Steel mills, the CIO lined up stations in Baltimore, Maryland, and Johnstown, Allentown, and Harrisburg, Pennsylvania, to broadcast a series of skits performed by steelworkers. "Sandwichmen" paraded outside the mill gates to "advertise" the programs. The CIO arranged similar radio campaigns for workers in Pennsylvania silk mills and Michigan automobile plants.[6]

Officials of the CIO intuitively understood the possibilities of radio broadcasting. When the infamous mayor of Jersey City, New Jersey, Frank Hague, refused to permit the CIO to hold meetings or to congregate in any way in his city, the union continued its organizing campaign and free speech fight by purchasing time over WEVD. Using circulars and other handbills, the union notified city residents of the WEVD broadcasts.[7] The United Automobile Workers' Union (UAW) initiated a "broadcasting barrage" over WJBK in Detroit as part of its effort to organize Ford Motor Company employees in early 1938. The union's Radio Department arranged for volunteers to act out episodes from Upton Sinclair's *The Flivver King,* a novel critical of Henry Ford. In addition, the UAW dramatized important labor news in its "Forward the March of Labor," modeled on CBS's "The March of Time."[8]

Although the CIO made far greater use of radio, and in more innovative ways than the AFL, the older labor body had not ignored the medium altogether. Local AFL affiliates often used small independent stations to get their views across to the public. The Central Labor Union of Bellingham, Washington, for example, used a local one-hundred-watt station to tell its side of the story in industrial disputes. In Washington, D.C., an affiliate of CBS allowed Albert N. Dennis, a labor news editor, to produce the "Labor News Review." The show, which began in 1934, remained on the air for more than a decade. Chester M. Wright, editor of the International Labor News Service, began a weekly talk show over WEVD, which eventually secured a commercial sponsor, Avalon Cigarettes, and became syndicated via electrical transcription. WEVD also provided airtime for programming produced by the ILGWU.[9]

The AFL, with access to the major networks, offered speeches, coverage of union conventions, and an occasional series of programs explaining organized labor's history and principles to radio audiences. But the CIO radio offensive forced the AFL to pay greater attention to radio. In 1938, the AFL signed a contract with Chester Wright to produce "The Labor Parade," which reenacted major labor news events. With a cast of twenty actors, sound effects, and a full orchestra, the once-a-month program captured the drama of AFL Executive Council meetings, union conventions, and the biographies of labor leaders. Each electrically transcribed show dramatized three major news events with one or two short items. A network of fifty-five local stations, including WCFL, signed up to carry the syndicated program. In May 1938, the AFL produced an one-hour show specifically designed to improve its image vis-à-vis the CIO. "The Cavalcade of Labor" concentrated on the war in China rather than on a domestic subject. Sketches, newspaper readings, commentaries, and musical selections created a picture of war-torn China and the plight of Chinese civilians, all in an effort to boost public support for medical and relief aid. Poor production lessened the intrinsic dramatic value of the show's material.[10] But whatever its merits, the program revealed how the AFL had reconsidered its position regarding radio's role in the trade union movement.

Increased CIO organizing activities in Chicago during 1937 worried William Green and Matthew Woll. The death of Edward Nockels, as much as it relieved AFL officers, also concerned them because it removed an important cornerstone from the AFL foundation in the city and threatened the survival of WCFL. Without the strong presence of "the father of labor radio," many local and national union officials feared that an aggressive CIO might gain control of the radio station. Recognizing labor radio's potential role in the war against the CIO, Green told members of the AFL Executive Council that he did not want WCFL "to pass from control of the bonafide Labor Movement." The AFL leadership decided to consult with CFL and WCFL officers on this matter.[11]

In late July 1937, John Fitzpatrick sent William Green newspaper clippings noting the CIO's intention to use radio to further its cause in Chicago and elsewhere. The AFL president dismissed the stories as "ballyhoo." Nevertheless, Green insisted that he fully appreciated the value of radio and invited Fitzpatrick and Illinois Federation of Labor president Victor A. Olander to meet with him to discuss "this radio situation." By September, AFL vice president Matthew Woll admitted that he was "anxious" for Fitzpatrick and Olander to put "together all available documents and materials" on WCFL's status so that "we may in the very near future adopt a plan regarding future arrangements relating to closer cooperation between the AFL and the CFL." Woll saw "a wonderful opportunity for further development of the station." Green, for the first time, assured Fitzpatrick that he valued "highly the fine service which WCFL is rendering labor" under the CFL's direction.[12]

Nockels's death created a void in WCFL that officials found difficult to fill even after ten months of station restructuring. Fitzpatrick put Maynard Marquardt, WCFL's engineer, in charge of operations. Marquardt reorganized the advertising and legal departments, getting rid of advertising manager Carl P. McAssey and station attorney Benjamin F. Goldstein. Although Nockels had served as both WCFL general manager and CFL secretary, Marquardt became general manager and, in September 1937, Joseph D. Keenan was elected CFL secretary. A severe recession and subsequent drop in advertising exacerbated WCFL's financial problems. As late as November, after months of personnel and organizational changes, Fitzpatrick acknowledged that the station was not "out of the woods yet."[13] Neither Fitzpatrick nor Keenan had any clear vision for the station and, as a result, welcomed increased AFL participation.

AFL officials sought more control over WCFL to ensure that the Voice of Labor did not fall into the hands of the hated CIO. Efforts by both NBC and the Hearst organization to secure the 970-kilocycle wavelength alerted Matthew Woll to the value of WCFL. The real danger to the Voice of Labor, however, derived from the possibility that the CIO might apply for and receive WCFL's wavelength. Woll had reviewed WCFL finances and discovered a nine-thousand-dollar operating debt in 1937. Continuing economic problems could create the conditions under which the CFL might lose its radio voice to the CIO.[14]

With an apparent consensus on increasing the AFL's "measure of control over [the] station," labor leaders discussed how to achieve this without creating problems with the FCC or unduly burdening the AFL with WCFL's daily operations. Woll favored forming a new corporation in which the AFL held minority stock ownership and thus minority representation on the board of directors. But former WCFL attorney Benjamin Goldstein pointed out that the plan inadequately addressed the issues of license transfer, taxation, and AFL influence. If the new corporation only held station facilities, it would have to lease those properties to the CFL because only the CFL held the broadcast license. "The corporation would therefore have as its sole purpose to hold the bare legal title to assets, and as such would not solve any problem" that worried the AFL. If, on the other hand, the AFL wanted a body to operate the station, the license would have to be assigned to the corporation. The profit-oriented corporation, unlike the nonprofit CFL, would be subject to federal income and capital gains taxes and franchise laws. As the "real operators" of WCFL, the AFL and the CFL also would assume financial responsibility for the station. These were exactly the financial and legal complications that the AFL sought to avoid. Goldstein warned Woll that without control over the wavelength, "the whole program would be defeated" if "hostile hands" should grab control over the CFL. Under the corporate directorship, the "influence of the A.F.L. is reduced to merely advisory capacity subject to" CFL and Illinois State Federation of Labor (ISFL) policies. "Should their combined wishes be contrary to the A.F.L., they would prevail and yet as far as the world was concerned the A.F.L. would be held morally, if not legally liable for such policies." In a veiled reference to the CIO, Goldstein noted that "hostile parties" intent on destroying the station's "usefulness . . . or its very existence" might take hold of the CFL and ISFL and thereby control WCFL properties.[15]

Having outlined the weaknesses of the corporation proposal, Goldstein suggested a reorganization of WCFL based on a contractual arrangement between the CFL and the AFL. Such a contract would cover the station's operation and future use. The reorganization would create separate departments, one to deal with station properties and one to administer station operations. A board of advisors, consisting of one representative each from the CFL, the ISFL, and the AFL, would control station functions. To guarantee that the board would not take actions inconsistent with AFL policy, the AFL representative would have veto power. Goldstein suggested that because no assets changed hands, there was "no need to stir up any interests" among unions that had invested in the station. He also recommended the funding of station debts in order "to eliminate the possibility of harassment by creditors." These recommendations became the foundation of a contract between the CFL and the AFL.[16]

Some disagreement arose over the details of the contract, but CFL and

AFL officials worked out a compromise that specified the obligations of both parties. For its part, the CFL agreed to form a new corporation for WCFL, to issue stock in its name, and to turn that stock over to a board of trustees. The three trustees—representing the CFL, the ISFL, and the AFL— would control the operation of the station and ensure that management policies adhered to AFL policy. CFL officials agreed that only the corporation could use the wavelength and that the corporation would turn over all income to the CFL, after expenses had been paid. All the trustees had to agree on any sale, transfer, or other disposition of WCFL's wavelength. The AFL consented to use its name, power, and position to further the interests of WCFL and to specify the conditions under which the corporation might use the AFL name in connection with station operations. AFL officials refused to accept any liability for station debts. The AFL Executive Council approved the contract at the end of April. The CFL subsequently approved a resolution instructing Fitzpatrick to create a separate department to manage WCFL's properties and to enter into appropriate contractual relations with the national federation.[17]

AFL officials announced their new arrangement with WCFL on April 29, 1938. On that same day, William Green proclaimed that the newly created Progressive Miners of America would launch an organizing drive in an effort to undercut John L. Lewis, the United Mine Workers, and the CIO. Green specifically noted that WCFL would be available for the new organizing campaign.[18] WCFL's reorganization and its increased adherence to AFL policy thus paralleled the intensified labor war. These developments, however, also coincided with both AFL and CFL efforts to improve labor radio's relations with NBC.

"Enlightened" radio network executives had gradually learned the value of placating conservative trade union leaders. Cooperating with and coopting the trade union elite lessened the potential threat posed by progressive and radical working-class organs in particular and the numerous critics of network radio in general. In this context, NBC vice president Frank M. Russell admonished Roy C. Witmer of NBC's Eastern Division for questioning the efficacy of listing WCFL in the company's standard rate and data sheets. Witmer wondered why NBC and RCA should "tie up so closely with [the] AFL" because "we have a lot of 'antis' among our customers." Russell responded that NBC's affiliation with the AFL had been "beneficial" and that Witmer "ought to be brought up to date on the modern relationship between industry and labor."[19] But Russell and other NBC officers differentiated between the responsible leaders of the AFL and the more radical leaders of the CFL. NBC executives remained wary of WCFL under the control of the CFL and especially under the direction of the impulsive and abrasive Nockels. With Nockels gone, and with the CFL and the AFL restructuring their relationship with regard to labor radio, however, NBC cautiously agreed to meet with WCFL representatives.

Discussions held between NBC and the CFL during the winter of 1937–38 did not fundamentally alter their relationship, yet they reveal much about the growing conservatism of WCFL. Joseph D. Keenan, the CFL secretary and vice president who attended many of the meetings, reassured NBC executives that the "new" WCFL would include AFL representatives. He requested an arrangement between WCFL and NBC "whereby WCFL might receive commercial network programs and get some compensation." Frank Russell, who represented NBC at these preliminary discussions, remained uncommitted. He warned Keenan that the present station management's continued emphasis on labor programs, which garnered "little or no popularity in the Chicago area," precluded any "major tieup" with NBC. The network executive urged Keenan to allow NBC to "program the station and then if later developments justified, we might make arrangements for the station to take network commercial business." Russell reported to NBC president Lenox R. Lohr that "Keenan is a very conservative fellow, understands our problems and is anxious to build up WCFL from a mechanical as well as program standpoint."[20]

After a similar meeting with Keenan in January 1938, NBC's chief executive in Chicago, Niles Trammell, reported that WCFL's new advisors seemed committed to improving the station's technical facilities, programs, and sales. They appeared to understand, according to Trammell, NBC's reluctance "to use WCFL as a network outlet with [its] programs and equipment in their present status." Labor officers also acknowledged the need to minimize the station's "labor propaganda." Trammell, like Russell, explained to Keenan that NBC "would not be interested in WCFL unless we could have complete control of the program and sales activities of the station." NBC found it impossible, under the present management, to increase the station's popularity to the point where network advertisers would find it acceptable. Trammell offered to discuss with CFL officials the possibility of negotiating a long-term arrangement in which NBC would manage the station's programming, sales, publicity, and promotion, but would leave the technical operation in the hands of labor. Keenan felt that his associates might accept this deal and he tried to schedule a meeting with Fitzpatrick, Olander, and Trammell.[21]

NBC-CFL discussions proceeded as WCFL underwent its reorganization. ISFL president Victor Olander met with Trammell in mid-February 1938. He reminded the NBC executive how past labor-capital cooperation in radio had helped to demonstrate the advantages of the American broadcasting system to its critics. Olander contended that continued cooperation between the AFL and NBC could counteract "suggestions, now being made in certain quarters, that the British system of Government ownership be substituted for the American system of private ownership of radio stations." NBC, which had long advertised its harmonious relationship with the AFL hierarchy as a defense of the existing system, took Olander's comments to heart as the FCC moved closer to calling for a complete inquiry into all phases of chain broadcasting. Trying to alleviate any remaining suspicions that NBC might have held regarding WCFL, Olander emphasized to Trammell that "for the first time we [WCFL] now have the wholehearted support and lively interest of the Executive Council" of the AFL. The ISFL president perceptively noted the correlation between NBC's knowledge of the new AFL-WCFL arrangement and its increased interest in the station.[22]

Matthew Woll called NBC president Lohr at the end of April 1938 to inform him of the AFL-CFL agreement to operate WCFL. The AFL vice president stressed that the new WCFL, under the direction of himself, Fitzpatrick, and Olander, wished to establish "closer contact with NBC particularly in selling programs." The new WCFL planned to revise its program policies to "eliminate many objectionable features such as pressure tactics." Labor radio wanted to compete fully and fairly in the radio marketplace and greatly desired NBC's support in this endeavor.[23]

Fitzpatrick, Olander, Keenan, and Woll met with Niles Trammell in late April and devoted "considerable discussion" to the issue of permitting NBC "to manage and operate WCFL." In the end, the labor leaders decided that "it was in the best interests of Labor to continue the operation of the station on its present basis." Despite the temptation, Fitzpatrick and his colleagues saw little real benefit, beyond monetary gain, in abandoning labor radio. They realized that, under NBC management, WCFL could not play a role in the war against the CIO because such partisan warfare would not maximize profits. Having turned down NBC's offer, WCFL's board of directors nevertheless wished to continue searching for some way in which the network could assist in the station's development. "Realizing the importance of keeping on a friendly basis with this station, with a view of some day getting control of it," Trammell offered to have NBC's spot sales department "sell WCFL along with our other" stations. Trammell clarified to NBC chief Lohr that his "only reason for making a suggestion of this kind was to keep our fingers on the situation to prevent an outside group from getting control of the station."[24]

Throughout the thirties, NBC pursued a dual strategy regarding labor and radio. On the one hand, NBC officials co-opted and placated the AFL hierarchy and thus legitimized the status quo in American broadcasting. On the other hand, network executives recognized the importance of making minor concessions to WCFL to ensure an open door to that station. At the appropriate opportunity, NBC might be able to control WCFL's wavelength and thereby vastly increase profits for the network in the Chicago market and also gain access to markets in other areas of the country. For these reasons Trammell and his colleagues agreed that it was a good idea to "keep WCFL tentatively aligned" with NBC. They continued the network practice of feeding WCFL, at no charge, sustaining programs not carried by NBC's affiliates (WMAQ, WENR, and WLS) in Chicago. Trammell's suggestion to have NBC's national sales department sell WCFL to national spot advertisers, however, encountered opposition. Several network executives objected to the duplication in selling (WCFL already had its own agency selling it on a national spot basis) and the potential loss in commissions; they concluded that the proposal was "an unhealthy thing for NBC." Although acknowledging the problems created by his suggestion, Trammell insisted that the task "of holding WCFL" remained paramount. "We must keep our finger in this situation as sone [*sic*] day it may develop to a point where it will be very profitable" to NBC.[25] That day never arrived. WCFL remained an alternate affiliate of NBC until 1942, when the FCC forced NBC to divest itself of one of its networks. The NBC Blue network became the American Broadcasting Company in 1943. The "special" relationship between WCFL and NBC ended and labor radio eventually established an affiliation with ABC.[26]

WCFL's new arrangement with the AFL, like its relationship with NBC, did not develop as its authors had intended. Although CFL and AFL representatives concluded talks regarding their mutual responsibilities and obligations under a new WCFL corporation in April 1938, the CFL Executive Board did not ask for delegate approval until the end of the summer. A prolonged debate among CFL officers and delegates ensued. Several delegates felt that the dramatic shift in WCFL's organization, and especially its redefined relationship with the AFL, required further discussion and consultation with their respective unions. Certainly the AFL's de facto veto over WCFL operations and policy bothered those Chicago unionists committed to continuing the CFL's tradition of democratic decision-making. After considerable discussion, CFL leaders prevailed, defeating an amendment to delay action and then securing a majority vote to approve the new arrangements.[27] On September 1, 1938, the new, not-for-pecuniary-profit WCFL, Inc., met for the first time. Its board of directors included three trustees—Fitzpatrick (CFL), Olander (ISFL), and Woll (AFL)—plus CFL secretary Joseph Keenan, Maurice Lynch, and Leslie Goudie of the Teamsters' Joint Council. Fitzpatrick became president of the corporation, Keenan the vice president, Lynch the treasurer and financial secretary, and Olander the secretary. One of their first actions was to secure the passage of a resolution at the AFL convention asking the AFL and all its affiliates to help attract advertisers to WCFL.[28]

The intricate maneuvering among the AFL, the CFL, and NBC during 1938 came in the context of the intensified war between the AFL and the CIO. The split within organized labor hardened CFL conservatism and adherence to AFL orders and provided an important criterion for establishing who would use WCFL's facilities. Ironically, Fitzpatrick and Nockels had always been strong supporters of industrial unionism and they remained so for their entire lives. Yet the CFL turned its back on the efforts of the CIO to organize industrial unions during the thirties. The CFL leadership's rejection of the CIO reflected, in part, the directives of the AFL.[29] It also reflected the lessons that Fitzpatrick derived from his experiences with William Z. Foster and the communists during the early twenties. Those events had left deep scars on the minds of Chicago labor officials. Fitzpatrick firmly "hated the communists"; he felt that "they were too opportunistic; [that] they were in labor only for the purpose of advancing their own political goals which were destructive of American democracy." Communist participation in the CIO organizing campaigns of the thirties was sufficient reason to earn the wrath of Fitzpatrick.[30] WCFL, of course, did not offer its facilities to CIO organizers. For their part, CIO organizers in Chicago either ignored or attacked WCFL. As Leslie Orear, an organizer in the city's packinghouses, recalled: "WCFL was in the hands of the enemy. And so it never even occurred to us to go to them." Some CIO officials accused the station of engaging in unfair labor practices with its staff artists.[31] The bitter Chicago Newspaper Guild strike of 1938–40 perhaps best illustrates the role of labor radio in the AFL-CIO wars.

Founded in December 1933, the American Newspaper Guild underwent, as Barry Kritzberg has explained, a transformation from "a professional association with trade-union leanings . . . to the craft unionism of the A.F.

of L., and finally . . . the industrial union idea of the newly formed C.I.O."[32] The Chicago chapter formed in 1936, the year in which its parent body affiliated with the AFL. Initially drawing its members from foreign-language and community papers, the Chicago Newspaper Guild (CNG) gradually attracted writers at the principal metropolitan dailies. As an affiliate of the AFL, the CNG received organizing assistance from the CFL. Fitzpatrick, for example, helped the CNG negotiate a contract with Chicago's only liberal newspaper, the *Chicago Times.* Unable to make inroads at the stridently antilabor *Chicago Tribune,* guild officials centered their organizing efforts on the *Chicago American* and the *Chicago Herald Examiner* owned by William Randolph Hearst.[33]

The Hearst chain dramatically cut reporting positions and reduced wages during 1937. Mechanized workers represented by craft trade unions, however, experienced few layoffs and a relatively small pay cut. Hearst officials responded to increased organizing efforts by the CNG by firing 147 workers in the summer of 1937, 139 in January 1938, and 40 branch circulation managers, all CNG members, in November 1938. As a result, nearly 600 CNG members went out on strike against the Hearst Chicago papers on December 5, 1938. The strike quickly became a part of labor's civil war.[34]

In the summer of 1937, the national American Newspaper Guild had voted to leave the AFL and affiliate with the CIO. The AFL moved to issue new charters to those workers in Chicago and elsewhere willing to secede from the American Newspaper Guild. As tensions between the CNG and the Hearst chain increased, so did hostility between the CNG and its old ally, the CFL. Even before the strike, Hearst had encouraged the AFL to challenge the CIO's new jurisdiction at his newspapers by trying to break the CNG. The AFL gladly complied by bringing claims against the CNG before the National Labor Relations Board (NLRB). When the formal strike began in December, the CFL and affiliated AFL unions, including the Teamsters and unions of the printing trades, refused to honor CNG picket lines. As many as twenty-five hundred workers, on orders of the AFL and the CFL, ignored the strike. Teamsters "repeatedly broke the Guild picket lines, clearing the way for AFL newswriters and mechanical employees."[35]

AFL and CFL officials used all the means at their command to vilify the CNG. They red-baited the CNG, insisting that the strike was not a labor dispute, but a communist-led attack against the staunchly anticommunist Hearst press. The CFL expelled a local of the American Federation of Radio Artists for disloyalty to the AFL because it aided the CNG. Fitzpatrick wrote to local business firms that advertised in the Hearst papers, denouncing the CNG as an "outlaw" organization and urging them to continue using the papers. He insisted that the CNG strike was only a jurisdictional dispute and that the CNG had defied the NLRB and the "regular trade unions." A longtime opponent of the ruthless way in which businesses and government had employed the injunction to crush labor, Fitzpatrick nevertheless recommended to William Hearst that he use the injunction to break the strike.[36]

Upon learning that the Chicago Repertory Group had performed a benefit for the CNG at a Hearst plant in late 1938, the CFL withdrew its endorsement of workers' theater. Representatives of the theater appeared at a subsequent CFL meeting and pleaded for reinstatement, explaining that changes in their executive board had brought in people who did not understand the intricacies of Chicago labor. The new executive promised to guard against allowing "subversive elements from making use of the Chicago Repertory Group's name." The CFL voted to reinstate its support for the theater, sending a letter setting forth the requirements that the CFL expected the group to honor.[37]

Not surprisingly, WCFL played an important role in the CFL attack on the CNG and on all CIO organizing campaigns in the city (newspapers, packinghouses, the building industry, and so forth). The station's labor and news programs condemned the CNG strike and supported business and government efforts to crush it. Fitzpatrick, Keenan, and prominent AFL officers used WCFL to review the history of the strike and to order all unions affiliated with the CFL, the ISFL, and the AFL to honor existing contracts. The AFL, said Fitzpatrick and colleagues in a December 1938 broadcast, would not permit its workers "to be manipulated in any alleged strike against the Hearst papers . . . by a few blundering C.I.O. agitators." James F. Barrett, sent to Chicago by William Green to deal with the CNG crisis, told a WCFL audience in November 1939 that the striking group was "headed, led, and directed by Communists" and that this "so-called labor union" used "disgraceful tactics" and "Communist tricks of the trade." At the same time that WCFL aired these attacks, it refused "to sell, let alone give time to the CIO unions."[38]

Virtually cut off from the dominant media in Chicago and denied access to an "alternative" broadcasting outlet, the CNG appealed directly to the public via letters, telephone calls, personal contacts, secondary picketing, a strike newspaper (the *Guild Reporter*), and parades around the Loop.[39] Although innovative and energetic, these efforts failed to match the power and determination of the Hearst empire and a rival labor organ to break the strike. In April 1940, the NLRB sustained nearly all of the CNG's charges against the Hearst chain in Chicago. A settlement to the seventeen-month violent strike quickly followed the ruling. But in September 1940, NLRB-supervised elections at the one remaining Hearst paper, the *Chicago Herald-American*, resulted in a decisive defeat for the CNG and a triumph for AFL-affiliated unions.[40]

WCFL participation in the CNG strike highlighted the tactics typical of labor's civil war. But the station's refusal to allow CIO activists to use its facilities to respond to attacks against them raised troublesome issues of free speech over the air and fair access to the public airwaves. These issues had posed difficulties for WCFL since its early years. While paying lip service to these "rights" and criticizing the radio trust for endangering them, WCFL often fell far short of its own rhetoric. Even under the direction of Edward Nockels, partisan political and labor concerns as well as commercial considerations limited free speech and access on WCFL, as they did on all radio stations in the country. But the inconsistencies and contradictions of these radio rights became exacerbated during the late thirties. In this sense, WCFL was no better or worse than the rest of Chicago radio.

Ira Latimer, the executive secretary of the Chicago Civil Liberties Committee and a former WCFL news commentator, lamented in late 1939 that not one of Chicago's radio stations showed any interest in setting aside "15 minutes to have prominent men in Chicago speak on civil liberties." Weeks earlier, Latimer had asked WGN for time to discuss a speech given by Martin Dies, chairman of what would soon become the House Un-American Activities Committee. Dies had urged restrictions on the civil liberties of so-called undesirable minorities, such as Nazis, communists, aliens, and labor organizers. Latimer characterized the controversial broadcast as a "propaganda address" and asked that WGN make "equal time available for the presentation of a different point of view." WGN manager Quin A. Ryan responded that Dies, as a government officer, had "the right to make a public report on his investigation" and that WGN had no obligation to give time to those who disagreed with the report. WCFL's position regarding controversial issues was little better than that of its bitter rival. "The labor station," complained Latimer, "is very parsimonious about giving time and then they censor all the talks."[41]

By the late thirties, both the CFL and the AFL sought to evade the issue of free speech over the air. At the annual meeting of the NBC Advisory Council in April 1938, NBC president Lenox Lohr raised the problem of how radio should deal with controversial issues. Lohr contended that freedom of speech on the air differed from the freedom of the press. Other radio experts such as WGN attorney Louis Caldwell insisted that there was a legitimate analogy between radio and the press. In any event, William Green, who attended the Advisory Council meeting, found little to say on this matter, even as radio stations across the nation denied labor unions the use of their broadcast facilities. Worried about CIO demands for access to the airwaves, the AFL president remained wary of challenging the status quo.[42]

The prevailing broadcasting environment, however, became more hostile for organized labor in 1939 when the NAB revised its statement of principles for radio and included a section entitled "Labor on the Air." The NAB Code warned that while the broadcasting industry could not ignore the importance of labor, radio stations had to approach labor problems with care because they were "almost always of a controversial nature."[43] Radio station and network officials interpreted this to mean that they could legitimately deny labor groups access to their facilities—for both sponsored and sustained programming—because labor issues were too controversial for the listening public. Individual radio stations quickly embraced the code and eliminated trade unions from the air with impunity. WJW, in Akron, Ohio, for example, canceled its contract with the United Rubber Workers (CIO), explaining that the NAB had instructed member stations to discontinue all sponsored "programs of a controversial nature." The Akron Industrial Union Council shifted its series of roundtable talks on trade union principles and topical issues to a non-NAB local station.[44]

Network executives also moved to deny free airtime to labor bodies. NBC officials tired of complaints that they should set aside time "for a proper discussion of public issues." John F. Royal argued that the definition of a "'public issue'. . . is a matter of opinion" and that NBC did not "permit free *speech* on the air," but rather "free discussion, under radio's editorial judgment."[45] "Editorial judgment" led NBC, in December 1942, to provide free airtime to the American Small Business Organizations, Inc. The association promptly denounced the trade union movement for conducting strikes against war production and recommended the shooting of offending unionists. Union leaders protested the program, explaining that the business sector had easy access to the airwaves—via both sponsored programs and free airtime—and that it frequently used that access to attack organized labor. An assistant NBC manager, however, saw "no reason why labor should have time on the air" to answer business accusations because labor already had a weekly program. If anything, contended NBC, the National Association of Manufacturers should get "free time every week because of the 'Labor for Victory' program."[46]

NBC broadcasted "Labor for Victory," a fifteen-minute program presented alternately by the AFL and the CIO on Sunday afternoons, during World
War II. On the AFL programs, labor officials praised the trade union movement's commitment to wartime production, its no-strike pledge, and its
cooperative relationship with management. CIO programs, on the other
hand, used dramatic reenactments to examine crucial labor issues. This
annoyed NBC officials, who felt that the skits too often touched on controversial subjects. In the spring of 1944, a presidential election year, NBC
battled with the CIO over a program that encouraged voter registration. The
network considered this a controversial theme, but the CIO responded that
any appeal for registration and voting was nonpartisan. Although acquiescing to the CIO on this program, NBC decided to cancel the entire series in
June, arguing that "it wouldn't be fair to give time to any organization which
favors one of the possible candidates even if that organization didn't do any
actual campaigning on the session." The AFL agreed to the decision, the CIO
dissented.[47]

While it was on the air, NBC officials considered "Labor for Victory" a
major concession to organized labor. But this "enlightened" programming
decision by the network did not necessarily translate into local station acceptance of labor programming. Only 35 out of a total of 104 NBC affiliates actually carried "Labor for Victory."[48] Even if a local station aired the
once-a-week show, it barely made a ripple in the ocean of commercial programming and advertising. As the Federated Press reporter Ted Taylor observed in 1942, a labor show on network radio was an accomplishment, "but
15 minutes out of 10,080 minutes is not enough."[49] Indeed, the antilabor bias
of the commercial mass media—both print and broadcast—intensified
during the war. A Federated Press poll in 1943 revealed that 92 percent of
the nation's press was antilabor, a not altogether surprising finding when
one recognizes that as parts of the corporate world, the mass media reflected
business interests and values. Compounding this inherent bias against labor were massive propaganda campaigns initiated by business organizations. During 1943, for example, the National Association of Manufacturers spread antilabor messages in its national weekly radio program and in
the three weekly editions of "Briefs for Broadcasters," which it supplied to
news commentators on 524 radio stations throughout the country.[50]

CFL and CIO officials denounced the capitalist sector's propaganda ex-
ertions and demanded that labor intensify its efforts to get its message to
the public. The American Civil Liberties Union (ACLU) and other organizations agreed that too much radio time went to pro-business and antila-

bor opinion and that labor needed more time to broadcast its views. The ACLU urged the NAB to get its member stations to treat trade unions like they treated business, to invite labor speakers to sustaining shows, to have their commercial features include news and views of labor, and to work out long-range policy with business and labor regarding presentation of controversial industrial problems.[51] Both the CIO and the CFL embraced these proposals, but the AFL remained ambivalent.

The AFL hierarchy had "no grievance against" commercial radio; it endorsed the "American System" and favored the NAB Code. AFL and radio industry officials admitted that the major networks never refused time to the AFL leadership when it wanted it. According to AFL publicity director Phil Pearl, AFL unions were "not interested in using the radio between [election] campaigns" and they "could buy time" during campaigns. The AFL "did not want to organize unions over the radio because [it] considered the radio appeal an emotional appeal." In cases of strikes, Pearl argued, the AFL would seek the support of other unionized industries in the area; it was "not interested in public support, involved in radio speeches."[52]

The CIO, committed to using radio in its organizing campaigns, rejected the NAB Code. CIO general counsel Lee Pressman and other officials protested radio industry discrimination against the newly formed industrial unions. They attacked the NAB Code for providing stations with an excuse to eliminate virtually any discussion of labor issues. "The CIO wants," argued Pressman, "the right to describe itself to the public as a matter of education, not controversy, and not in relation to controversial or special situations." In rhetoric reminiscent of Edward Nockels, Pressman portrayed most advertisers and commentators as "propagandists for employers." The CIO wanted "to meet propaganda with propaganda" and to have the same opportunity, the same right, as business to buy time for the presentation of labor programs and to appear on sustaining shows. Morris Novik, who helped supervise the radio programs of ILGWU locals in New York and UAW programs in Detroit, also opposed the NAB Code "because it interfered with organizing labor unions over the radio."[53]

On the issue of the NAB Code, the CFL echoed the CIO position more than that of the AFL. The CFL objected to the specific NAB Code provisions cautioning against the granting of time to labor unions to discuss strikes. Unlike the AFL, the CFL had effectively used radio in strike and organizing situations throughout the thirties. The NAB warning that stations consider labor strikes controversial and treat them with care amounted, according to WCFL general manager Marquardt, to a "gag" on labor.

Unlike CIO critics of the code, however, Marquardt advanced a market argument: He contended that the NAB's informal, voluntary restrictions against the airing of labor issues might backfire and hinder the radio industry. Labor was the broadcasters' "best customer—your best friend—and is the backbone of that great 'middle class.'" Thus WCFL officials warned that alienating workers could diminish station profits.[54] WCFL's opposition to the NAB Code showed some continuity with the station's past; but it also revealed the market orientation of labor radio's new managers. The heir to Nockels's legacy was the CIO.

CIO efforts to gain access to the airwaves during the late thirties and early forties challenged commercial radio in much the same way that Nockels had done a decade earlier. At the FCC hearings on radio networks and monopoly, the CIO criticized industry discrimination against labor, while the AFL found nothing wrong with the prevailing system.[55] When the FCC investigated newspaper control over radio, the CIO detailed specific instances where its "organizations had been denied time by newspaper-controlled stations" and condemned the FCC's "failure to protect freedom of speech on the air, as it affects labor."[56] The CIO also opposed a 1945 libel bill in the Illinois legislature that held local outlets responsible for broadcasts originating elsewhere and for any extemporaneous libelous statements. Although the CFL and the AFL approved the legislation with some amendments, the CIO opposed the law because it permitted, even required, censorship by individual stations. State CIO officials contended that submitting scripts, a common industry practice, made stations a party to possible libelous statements. "Realizing that, radio stations will bar or severely censor ideas which are not in agreement with the ideas of the station." The CIO maintained its right "to broadcast topics of general public interest, controversial or non-controversial."[57]

Continuous criticism of the NAB Code from local and national CIO unions, the CFL, local AFL affiliates, civil libertarians, and progressive political activists eventually forced a response from the broadcasting system. In early 1944, an NAB committee of program managers met with representatives from the CIO, AFL, ILGWU, ACWA, and ACLU to discuss radio's coverage of labor news. Union officers complained about purchasing commercial time over radio stations and networks and the antilabor bias contained in many sponsored programs. Industry officials cited the difficulty of determining limitations on the sale of airtime to labor bodies and of "culling bona fide demands from the undesirable." Other broadcasting executives contended that many stations offered ample time to trade unions but that "labor prefers to yell about being discriminated against rather than using what is available to them."[58]

The beginning of the end for the NAB Code restrictions on organized labor came in June 1943. Columbus, Ohio, station WHKC sold Local 927 of the UAW a fifty-two-week block of thirty minutes of airtime on Sundays. The union planned a program that would promote good labor-management relations. When the UAW vice president submitted a script praising Franklin Roosevelt but condemning Senator Robert A. Taft and Representative John M. Vorys from Ohio, "WHKC refused to broadcast the speech on the grounds that it contained libelous and slanderous material." The station demanded that the union rewrite the script and omit the controversial statements. Local 927 filed a petition against the station, which was up for license renewal. Subsequent FCC hearings revealed that while WHKC had adhered to the NAB Code clauses dealing with controversial issues, those provisions inadequately protected free speech on the air. As the hearings proceeded in 1944–45, the union and the station reached an out-of-court settlement in which WHKC reversed its position, virtually abandoning the NAB Code. The station agreed to follow a policy of "open-mindedness and impartiality" with regard to controversial public issues and to provide time on both a commercial and sustaining basis "for the full and free discussions of issues of public importance, including controversial issues." Acknowledging the "evil repugnant" nature of censorship, the station promised not to "censor scripts, or delete any matter contained in them." By recognizing this agreement and ending the hearings, the FCC virtually repudiated the provision of the NAB Code dealing with controversial issues.[59]

As the NAB's restrictions on organized labor weakened, local and national unions rushed to make use of the airwaves. In 1944, the CIO's Political Action Committee published its own *Radio Handbook,* something the AFL had never done. The handbook outlined the American public's radio rights and attacked the NAB Code. Its major purpose, however, was to instruct labor leaders and "all those interested in labor education" on "how to obtain time on the air and how to use that time to great advantage for political action." By identifying the best times to broadcast, explaining the different radio formats, and specifying what to do when stations denied labor access to their facilities, the CIO handbook provided an easy guide to using the airwaves.[60] The publication coincided with organized labor's increased use of radio.

By the middle of 1944, more and more local unions of the CIO and the

AFL were "buying time on local stations for regular labor programs geared to their own community" and "for special broadcasts in organizing drives, political action campaigns, and crises where it's important to get labor's point across to the people."[61] In Toledo, Ohio, for example, Local 12 of the UAW started a show entitled "Labor News and Views" on station WHK. New York's Newspaper Guild broadcast a Sunday morning show, "The News and What to Do about It," over WLIB, in which union reporters described stories that "publishers keep out of the papers." Labor unions in Seattle, Cleveland, Chicago, and Hollywood, among other localities, also increased their use of local broadcasting outlets.[62]

With the presidential election behind them, the major networks once again offered sustaining time to the AFL and the CIO, attempting, in the process, to balance the two labor federations' access to the airwaves.[63] The first of three AFL-produced radio series during 1945 was "America United." Carried over the NBC network for thirteen weeks, the program presented leading business, state, and labor leaders discussing vital national problems with the goal of promoting "unity of thought and action" among "labor, business, agriculture and the Government on policies to win the war and the peace." A second series, "Builders of Victory," which aired over the CBS network, dramatized stories of the Seabees (the construction battalions of the Navy's Civil Engineer Corps). It sought to enlighten the public about how AFL members "were doing some of the actual fighting in this war, as well as the hard work." The American Broadcasting Company carried the third AFL series, "Labor, USA," for twenty-six weeks. Subtitled "The American Federationist of the Air," the program offered a radio news-magazine format, "alternating news highlights with feature articles by labor representatives and invited guests on timely subjects of importance and interest to Labor." An AFL report in January 1946 declared that all three series were popular among the federation's own members and the general public and that radio was "the best and most effective medium of reaching the public." It recommended allocating more funds for the development and improvement of radio programming.[64]

CIO productions over the three networks emphasized "simple, popular presentation" and used the latest dramatic techniques, music, and entertainment to hold listeners. The first twenty-six weeks of ABC's "Labor USA" in 1945 and 1946 involved CIO dramatizations of current labor and industrial issues. On NBC's "America United," the CIO followed the weekly forum discussion format that the AFL used, although the focus and perspective of the debates differed. The CIO arranged two thirteen-week series for CBS.

"Jobs for Tomorrow" dramatized industrial reconversion problems, emphasizing the "human-interest" element. "Cross-Section CIO," the second series, featured "on-the-spot interviews with the rank and file of labor." In addition to these sustaining programs on the established networks, several CIO unions filed petitions for FM broadcast licenses in the immediate postwar period.[65]

These efforts by organized labor to gain access to the airwaves became imperative in 1945 and 1946 as a strike wave of "gigantic proportions" spread across the country and as business and state institutions responded with a virulent attack against workers and unions.[66] The ILGWU, the UAW, and numerous other labor bodies discussed the possibility of securing their own broadcasting outlets "to combat anti-labor radio propaganda." In December 1945, the Washington, D.C., Central Labor Union formally asked the AFL to "take the necessary steps immediately to secure a Radio Station for the purpose of broadcasting" to the public "Labor's side of all Labor questions."[67] WCFL management reminded AFL leaders that they already had a broadcasting outlet and offered them, in April 1945, a free half hour on Saturday evenings to air a weekly information program. Warning that the CIO already had applied for as many as nine FM broadcasting stations, WCFL managers urged the AFL to "lose no time in utilizing this opportunity extended by the only station currently owned and operated by labor." Although broadcasting with only 10,000 watts of power, labor radio hoped to apply for 50,000 watts, "which, when granted, will give us a national coverage which will compare favorably with any station in the country." AFL officials considered the offer but never acted on it. They continued to regard WCFL as primarily a local station.[68]

Indeed, despite its concerted efforts to gain greater control over labor radio in 1937–38, the AFL paid very little attention to the station in the ensuing years. Having guaranteed that the CIO would not grab the broadcasting outlet, the AFL hierarchy's interest in the station dissipated. Yet the AFL encouraged a series of changes in business organization, legal structure, personnel, and programming that accelerated the transformation of WCFL into a relatively conventional commercial broadcasting station by 1946.

EIGHT

"Showmanship," 1937–46

The death of Edward Nockels afforded an opportunity to those labor officials in Chicago and Washington who wished to expedite WCFL's transformation into a more competitive commercial broadcaster. Maynard Marquardt, who assumed the role of general manager, outlined new policies for the station in March 1937. The former chief engineer directed labor radio to place more "showmanship" into its programming, to pay more attention to its audience of organized workers, and to take full advantage of its commercial potential.[1] As part of the station's new commercial offensive, George F. Isaac and Melvin Wolens joined the business office. Isaac, the national sales representative, had gained experience working for WGN and several advertising firms. He immediately voiced a desire "to exploit WCFL coverage of the labor market in Chicago." Wolens replaced the station's long-standing commercial manager, C. P. McAssey, in June 1937. A former salesman for WCFL, Wolens had more recently served on the NBC sales staff in Chicago. Promising to make WCFL the number one sales outlet in the Midwest, Wolens noted the need to increase the station's efficiency and to find high-caliber advertisers.[2]

Marquardt and Wolens vowed to place both the commercial and programming departments on a "business basis" and to abandon the "old policy" of giving trade unions virtual free reign over the station. Although both men insisted that WCFL would retain its pro-labor orientation, they indicated that concrete business concerns would dictate future policy. After a failed experiment with an advertising agency, Marquardt chose a former NBC production worker and member of WCFL's staff to supervise programming in early 1938. A more enduring change came as Marquardt and Wolens launched an aggressive "campaign to exploit" the station's labor audience "to both advertising agencies and manufacturers of products for family consumption."[3]

The sales offensive generated encouraging results. Commercial accounts increased over the next year with the addition of new sponsors such as car dealers, jewelers, rug and carpet cleaners, furniture and department stores, a piano company, gasoline and service stations, and a cemetery. Advertising rates rose about 10 percent, although they still trailed the rates of network affiliates and independent stations in Chicago.[4] WCFL staff believed that if the station sold 60 percent of its available airtime, it would achieve self-sufficiency. In January 1939, the commercial department predicted the sale of 235 out of a total of 525 hours for the month, or 45 percent of the available airtime. Within months, labor radio reached a new commercial high with seventy-three sponsored programs in one week. Advertising revenue made up 93–95 percent of WCFL's total income from 1937 through 1940. With a slight decline in 1938—due in part to a recession—station income derived from advertising grew from $314,535 in 1937 to $420,351 in 1940. The percentage of WCFL revenue coming from national advertising also increased—from less than 1 percent in 1936 to over 10 percent in 1939.[5] These favorable results notwithstanding, difficult problems remained for Marquardt and CFL financial secretary Maurice Lynch. WCFL still could not solicit or take on advertising from firms that practiced unfair labor policies—a restriction that eliminated potential sponsors in the Chicago area. In addition, selected businesses refused to buy time over WCFL precisely because of the station's labor affiliation.[6]

Marquardt's staff emphasized the trade union composition of the audience primarily to attract sponsors of consumer goods or services seeking access to relatively well-paid workers. An improved publicity department helped in this effort. By 1939, Chicago newspaper radio editors rated WCFL's public relations efforts as second only to those of WGN.[7] But industry officials remained wary of WCFL publicity. The exact number of "labor families" listening to WCFL, for example, remained unverified. *Variety* reported that only 400,000 families tuned to 970 kilocycles in early 1937; NBC estimated the audience at 1,253,000 families during that summer; and WCFL's own survey in 1939 suggested that approximately 5,700,000 homes listened to the station. Whatever the reliability of these various figures, the general trend, corroborated by the volume of mail to the station, indicated a significant increase in labor radio's listening audience between 1937 and 1940.[8]

WCFL's business office valued Chicago's rank-and-file unionists primarily as consumers, not as direct contributors to labor radio. Station officials dismissed as negligible the trickle of financial contributions from area trade unions. In 1937, for example, union donations amounted to only $635 out of a total station income of $336,000; in 1940, donations reached only $629 out of an income of almost $442,000. The annual WCFL Radio Frolics, which continued throughout the period, provided 2–4 percent (approximately $12,000) of the station's yearly income.[9] As trade union contributions dwindled to insignificance, advertising revenue grew to sufficient totals to cover the bulk of WCFL's operating budget. This gave labor radio officials the financial flexibility to attend to outstanding debts.

To reimburse Laundry and Dye House Drivers' Union Local 712, which had advanced considerable sums to help WCFL in earlier years, the CFL instructed Maurice Lynch to revive the WCFL Park project in 1939. Nockels's dream of selling housing lots from the land surrounding the proposed super-station site at Downers Grove had withered in the reality of the Great Depression. The CFL sold virtually no lots during the thirties and received no payments on those lots already sold. Lynch consulted with the Federal Housing Authority, which agreed to guarantee mortgages up to 90 percent of their value. Holders of unpaid contracts received the option to assume their old obligation, without penalty, back interest, or back taxes. Lynch hired a real estate agent to handle transactions and ordered the construction of a model home. Officials estimated the cost of building a home to range between thirty-five hundred and fifty-five hundred dollars and offered prospective buyers long-term loans as low as twenty-nine dollars per month.[10]

While reviving the Downers Grove real estate project, CFL officers discontinued another part of Nockels's radio design. All work on shortwave station W9XAA ceased by the end of 1937. New FCC regulations required that shortwave transmitters operate with at least five thousand watts. Not wishing to spend the nine to ten thousand dollars that such a power increase would cost, CFL officials decided to abandon a shortwave project that promised to beam "special and highly expensive programming" around the world. The federation instead chose to concentrate its energy and resources on securing increased power for WCFL and improving its reception within the country. After waiting two years for the AFL to decide that it did not want to incur the expense of operating the shortwave station, CFL officials hoped to sell the equipment to a company owned by the Mormon church. The FCC, however, rejected the Mormon petition to engage in shortwave broadcasting, thus scotching the equipment deal.[11]

Abandoning the shortwave component of Nockels's scheme for a national labor radio network made increased power all that more important for WCFL's future development. Throughout the thirties, a lack of funds inhibited WCFL from building its superpower station. As WCFL was increasing its power to only five thousand watts, network and independent stations across the country clamored for authorization to broadcast with five hundred thousand watts. An international agreement on dividing the electromagnetic spectrum—the Havana Treaty (1937)—required that 90 percent of all the radio stations in the United States, including WCFL, change their wavelengths. Fourteen Chicago-area stations shifted their channels; WCFL moved from 970 kilocycles to 1,000 kilocycles at the end of March 1941. The treaty also required that class A stations operate with at least ten thousand watts, which meant that WCFL had to double its power and build additional broadcasting facilities, including a new antenna. The FCC approved WCFL's application for increased power and the station began broadcasting with ten thousand watts in 1942. Four years later, the FCC approved WCFL's petition to increase its power to fifty thousand watts. After more than twenty years, Nockels's dream was on the verge of fruition.[12]

But the realization of a superpower WCFL came at the further erosion of democratic decision-making at the station. Lynch and other labor radio officers found it inefficient to consult with, and seek authorization from, CFL delegates in order to make changes at the station. At their request for greater discretionary powers to respond to FCC rule changes, the Executive Board altered the CFL Constitution and dissolved WCFL, Inc. in 1945–46. Control over WCFL shifted to the CFL board and financial secretary. After the proper consultations, Lynch could increase or decrease funds that had been created for station modernization and expansion. The CFL Constitution restated WCFL's goal of serving the "interests, welfare, and advancement of affiliated unions" and of operating "in accordance with the policies of the" AFL. This latter provision satisfied the AFL hierarchy, which raised no objections to WCFL's altered structure.[13] Increased advertising revenue, the elimination of expenses such as the shortwave station, boosts in power, and the World War II–generated economic boom improved WCFL's financial position. In 1940, for the first time, the station earned a net profit of $20,163. With a new sense of financial stability, federation officials rejected an offer in early 1940 to lease WCFL's facilities to the *Chicago Times* for a period of fifteen years. A few months later, Lynch wrote that the nonprofit WCFL would use its net profits to improve programming and to benefit station employees.[14]

From its inception, labor radio had to reconcile its unique status as both a labor institution and an employer of labor. Station managers were not above engaging in questionable practices as when they refused to pay the actors and writers of two sustaining shows in 1937 while a prospective sponsor "tested" to see which program generated the most listener response.[15] On the other hand, WCFL led the way in hiring union technicians and musicians, in renewing licensing agreements with the American Society of Composers, Authors and Publishers, and in recognizing the union of radio artists. In 1937, the newly formed American Federation of Radio Artists (AFRA) chose to negotiate its first ever contract with WCFL. A December pact officially recognized AFRA as the bargaining agent for station announcers, specified a closed shop, and established basic salaries at forty-five dollars per week, with an eight-hour day, forty-hour week. WCFL informed its nonunion announcers that they would have to join the union or quit their respective shows. AFRA proceeded to secure standard contracts for announcers with other stations. By the summer of 1938, AFRA and WCFL had worked out a contract for actors, writers, singers, and other talent. This agreement also became a model for AFRA pacts with other radio stations.[16]

Union contracts for station employees, while significant in their own right, did not guarantee a larger market share for the Voice of Labor. Despite the growth in the size of WCFL's listening audience, station ratings still lagged behind those of WGN, WBBM, WMAQ, and WENR-WLS. Lynch, Marquardt, and other station officials toiled at improving labor radio's precarious position in the Chicago market by improving programming.[17]

Marquardt and Wolens sought to enhance WCFL's entertainment programs by duplicating the most popular offerings aired over the major networks and using more sustaining programs from NBC Blue. To make way for this entertainment, station staff reduced what commercial radio considered the dull and boring shows "sponsored by churches and other civic and educational groups"; curtailed foreign-language programming; avoided patent medicine, "rupture belt," laxative, and liquor accounts; and eliminated the "stodgy presentation of the labor stuff."[18] Ethnic hours, once the pride of the WCFL schedule, already were in decline by the midthirties and by the end of the decade virtually disappeared from the air. In the 1939

Variety Radio Directory, WCFL specified that it no longer accepted foreign-language programs. Only the noncommercial "Irish Hour" and a half-hour Lithuanian program survived into the forties. Lynch, founder and master of ceremonies for the "Irish Hour," noted that the show had become an "institution" and survived primarily because it served "older folk, especially those . . . 'shut ins' in the various institutions in and about Chicago."[19] Following the network lead, WCFL replaced shows sponsored by religious bodies with religious programs sustained by the station.[20] Having cleared space, station officials turned to developing popular entertainment.

The WCFL staff believed that showmanship entailed, among other things, audience participation in talent shows, promotional contests, advice programs, and quiz shows. A search for "worthwhile talent" gave rise to "The Talent Scout," which premiered in the fall of 1937. The show gave professional performers, who had never broken into radio, the opportunity to avoid auditioning at advertising agencies or networks. Its writer and director, Paul Knapp, insisted that it was a showcase for "reasonably good talent." Amateur hours had been a regular part of WCFL since its inception. With the success of Major Bowes's "Original Amateur Hour," which began on the NBC network in 1934 and moved to CBS in 1936, WCFL continued its own versions of the genre. In the "Master Amateur Hour," for example, the sponsor, Master Jewelers, awarded winners wrist watches and gave them an opportunity to perform on another WCFL program, "Stars of Tomorrow."[21] "Radio Gossip Club," which began a long run in the fall of 1938, featured Eddie Cavanaugh and Fannie Cavanaugh, among radio's oldest "peddlers of 'bits-about-the-stars,'" who answered listeners' questions. Don Norman, a popular WCFL personality, presided over a quiz show and street interview programs during the late thirties. In "Songs in the Making," two composers wrote the words and music for a new song based on a title supplied by the radio audience. Fans of the cooking show "Peekers in the Pantry" participated in recipe competitions. "The Court of Missing Answers," airing in late 1941, invited the home audience to send in general knowledge questions that "Judge George Case," a program director and creator of the program, could ask guest "defendants." A "musical jury" handed out penalties to guests who answered incorrectly.[22] WCFL carried both the NBC variety show "The Breakfast Club" with Don McNeill and its own morning show of musical recordings, discussions of listener mail, and contests. A $450 per week advertising campaign for the latter program paid for billboard messages and trailers in twenty-two neighborhood movie theaters in the spring of 1937.[23]

Despite the station's improved financial condition in the late thirties and early forties, WCFL officials were neither inclined nor prepared to compete with the networks' superior staff and equipment in the area of drama and comedy programming. Labor radio, by and large, did not produce its own soap operas, adventure shows, or "prestige" drama. Throughout the late thirties, Chicago-area theater groups occasionally offered playlets and dramatic readings over WCFL. Transcribed syndicated shows such as "Ports of Call"—a dramatization of the history of foreign nations—also received airtime. But the majority of the station's nonnetwork entertainment programming fell into the categories of gossip-advice-talk and, of course, music.[24]

Music and musical variety shows dominated the WCFL schedule. Night club orchestras, church choirs, symphony orchestras, concert bands, and a variety of soloists offered an assortment of musical options from classical to gospel, country to swing, Latin to jazz. "Golden Melodies" appealed to a general audience with a "quiet evening program of piano melodies" five days a week in 1941–42. Variety shows such as "Curtain Calls" in 1938 and "Tate's Variety Show" in 1942 increasingly combined musical selections with commentary on the entertainment scene or interviews with celebrities.[25]

Throughout this period, WCFL and other independent stations offered disc jockey programs of recorded music. Although this format offered financial advantages for local stations, two obstacles had inhibited its development during the thirties. FCC regulations required that broadcasters frequently identify recorded music as such and these incessant caveats tended to "stigmatize" the use of phonograph records. In addition, recording artists with network contracts unilaterally prohibited stations from using their records for radio broadcast, initiating legal action to guarantee compliance. Both of these obstacles fell in 1940 as the FCC revised its rules, allowing stations to make their own worded announcements every half hour and as a federal court ruled that performing artists' copyright protection ended with the sale of their records. Disc jockey programs consequently multiplied.[26]

Even before the altered legal and regulatory environment, several radio stations had produced recorded music programs. "Make Believe Ballroom," a series begun in 1935 over New York station WNEW, received thousands of letters every month and had a waiting list of potential sponsors. In Chicago, the "Musical Clock," which began as a sustaining show over KYW in 1929, secured the sponsorship of Marshall Field & Co. in 1930. The show's move to the CBS affiliate, WBBM, in late 1934 forced NBC's WMAQ to break its no-phonograph-record policy in order to compete. With the "pleasant voice" of its host, Halloween Martin, and its "snappy music," the "Musical Clock" stimulated other disc jockey shows in the city.[27]

WCFL produced a fair share of these programs by mid-1937. Norman Ross hosted an hour of recorded melodies during the early afternoon, while the versatile Don Norman supervised a late-night show of recordings, time and temperature checks, and small talk.[28] Copying the format of the "Make Believe Ballroom," Eddie Chase created WCFL's "Make Believe Danceland" in late 1937. This thirty-minute, five-day-a-week program created the illusion that a different orchestra leader and accompanying band were right in the studio. The show developed a substantial audience; during one week in the late summer of 1938, for example, an offer to send out a picture of the orchestra leader Shep Fields and his "Rippling Rhythm" band generated twenty-five hundred requests to the program. Service Drug Stores sponsored the "Make Believe Danceland" as well as the "Music Lovers' Hour." On the latter program, which aired six evenings a week at 10:30 P.M., the disc jockey Martin Jacobson skillfully arranged popular, classical, and semiclassical music to produce an "ear-pleasing" hour for both "highbrows" and the "average public." Even *Variety* admitted that the program developed "an almost fanatically loyal audience" and represented "one of the best local programs hereabouts." Indeed, the Chicago Federated Advertising Club honored the "Music Lovers' Hour" as the best locally produced program in 1941. Recognizing that recorded music and transcribed programming would grow in importance, WCFL upgraded its studio phonograph equipment in early 1942.[29]

Sports programming augmented WCFL's live and recorded musical shows. Labor radio, along with several other Chicago stations, carried the home games of the city's two baseball teams. During the 1937 season, over sixty-seven thousand letters arrived at WCFL commenting on some aspect of the station's baseball coverage. Over forty-five thousand letters originated in Chicago with the bulk of the remainder coming from parts of Illinois, Indiana, and Wisconsin. The station also aired Northwestern University's home football games. The sports commentators Hal Totten and Jimmy Evans offered daily sports reviews. In addition to his commentary on professional and college sports, Evans, a former All-American football and baseball player for Northwestern University, reported on Chicago high school sports. Programs that discussed popular pastimes and offered interviews with participants, such as the bowling show "Ten Pin Tattler," attracted strong audience support. In the fall of 1946, WCFL became the only station in the city to broadcast a home game of Chicago's first professional basketball team, the American Gears. Jack Brickhouse, who would later attain fame as the Chicago Cubs' radio and television announcer, did the play-by-play. Sports programming easily secured the commercial sponsorship of brewing companies, automobile dealerships, gas and service stations, life insurance firms, and cigar manufacturers.[30]

The easiest way for WCFL to achieve the quality of network programming was to carry network shows. NBC, with its Blue and Red networks, already had outlets in the Chicago market: WMAQ carried NBC Red programs and WLS and WENR presented NBC Blue shows. WCFL's informal arrangement with the broadcasting giant permitted it to pick up those sustaining and sponsored programs from the Blue network that WLS and WENR did not want or could not take. Labor radio paid nothing for the sustaining shows and regular rates for sponsored programs. A similar arrangement allowed WCFL limited access to Mutual Broadcasting System programs. Although network programming made up an increasing amount of WCFL's schedule—*Variety* estimated that NBC-supplied sustaining shows constituted 13 percent of WCFL's schedule by mid-1939—it did not significantly diversify the station's offerings. The vast majority of NBC shows over WCFL, for example, were light musical or concert programs broadcast during the day or late at night. WCFL carried a small number of popular network soap operas and daytime dramas ("Widder Jones" and "Little Blue Playhouse"), advice programs ("Voice of Experience"), comedy variety ("Danny Thomas"), and adventure shows ("The Lone Ranger"). "Prestige" network shows included special children's concerts and experimental dramas written by the "innovative, original [radio] playwright" Arch Oboler.[31]

Labor radio continued to carry NBC Blue programming even as NBC—in response to an FCC decision ordering the dismemberment of its broadcasting empire—sold the Blue network to Edward J. Noble, "the Lifesaver king," in 1943. WCFL's dependence on network shows became evident in 1944 when the new American Broadcasting Company shifted the long-running variety show "Hall of Fame" from WCFL to the more powerful WENR. WCFL officials wished to continue broadcasting the show because, as *Variety* explained, it "perked up [WCFL's] listening audience to a great extent." ABC officials allowed WCFL to pick up the program without a contract and without any network compensation. WCFL carried a number of ABC sustaining and commercial programs over the next two years: "The Breakfast Club," news reports with Martin Agronsky and H. R. Baukhage, Metropolitan Opera performances, and "Gang Busters." Although WCFL scheduled more live network programs by the spring of 1946 than it had ever done before, its ties with ABC were far from perfect.[32]

As in its earlier network relationship with NBC, WCFL found that the bulk of shows that ABC offered were either untested sustaining programs or dying old series. ABC helped WCFL to produce a sustaining program called "How Do You Pronounce It?" in June 1946. The thirty-minute, Thursday evening show fit the panel quiz–comedy format that had become popular in the postwar period. Panel members—usually newspaper editors and radio comics—challenged each other to give an acceptable pronunciation of a selected word. While mildly amusing, the program never found a sponsor.[33] ABC also attempted to rejuvenate "Club Matinee," a half-hour afternoon variety show that had aired over the NBC Blue and ABC networks for six years. Originating from WCFL's studios on weekdays in July 1946, the renovated program offered "light-weight" comedy sketches depicting soldiers returning to civilian life and parodies of mystery dramas, as well as the requisite musical numbers. "Amateurish reading and . . . weak timing" obstructed the show's few good ideas and it quickly disappeared from the schedule.[34] Occasionally, an ABC sustaining program over WCFL succeeded and remained on the network. "Teen Town," a Saturday morning program aimed at adolescents, aired over WCFL in the spring of 1946. It featured teenage talent, a studio band, playlets written by listeners, comedy patter, and interviews with the studio audience. Renamed "Junior Junction" in the 1946–47 season, the show became a staple on ABC and WCFL for several years.[35]

Music, variety, sports, and informational talk shows, augmented by selected network drama and comedy, made up the bulk of WCFL's popular entertainment programming during the late thirties and the first half of the forties. These programs appeared more polished and professional—demonstrating enhanced showmanship—than those of a decade earlier; they helped to increase the size of the station's listening audience and thus consumed a growing percentage of WCFL's total schedule. But this programming was neither innovative nor creative and failed to distinguish WCFL as a leader in popular entertainment per se. The station's one claim to fame remained its service to the labor movement, the working class, and the general public.

• • •

Even as they accelerated the commercialization of labor radio, station managers reiterated their commitment to allocate a substantial proportion of airtime to civic, labor, and educational groups. In 1937, Marquardt estimated that WCFL annually granted $142,883 worth of free airtime to these organizations. Station staff insisted that the value of free time granted to labor broadcasts alone in 1938–40 ranged from $60,000 to $78,000 per year.[36] But whatever the value of time given to labor and public service programming, the percentage of WCFL's schedule going to this category never reached the 18 percent frequently touted by Marquardt. WCFL's 1944 license renewal application, unlike the 1931 form, for example, no longer included fraternal programming as a separate category, but instead placed labor shows under the "civic" or "news" heading. In addition, WCFL's commercial shows outnumbered sustaining programs by the midforties.[37]

A convergence of commercial, political, and ideological forces explain WCFL's declining responsiveness to progressive and civic organizations between 1937 and 1947. WCFL staff's preoccupation with achieving commercial success dictated that more and more airtime would go to sponsored programming. Manufacturing firms and retail sales outlets, and the advertising agencies that represented them, had more capital to spend on radio programming than organs devoted to political reform or public service, and WCFL increasingly deferred to the big spenders. When the FCC ruled that radio stations needed to provide equal access for all political candidates during election campaigns, WCFL and other broadcasters became reluctant to sell airtime to any public office seekers fearing that this would remove valuable commercial time from program schedules.

The CFL's growing conservatism also necessitated a close monitoring of progressive political activity. War between the AFL and the CIO polarized the thinking of CFL and WCFL officials, leading them to reject any political, cultural, social, or ethnic organization that addressed crucial contemporary issues from a CIO or leftist perspective. This conservatism intensified as the corporatist policy of the AFL gave it a stake in the nation's accession to hegemony during and after World War II. The AFL's eager and total acceptance of cold war ideology led to a narrowing of what organized labor considered the legitimate parameters of political and economic discussion.[38] CFL and WCFL policy changed accordingly, emphasizing organized labor's interest in labor-management cooperation, support for established community institutions, and opposition to any challengers to liberal capitalist society. The combination of these forces inexorably led station staff to reduce the sustaining and commercial time available for liberal and progressive groups.

This policy transformation was neither immediate nor smooth, but rather characterized by small changes and occasional reversals. The ACLU supplied WCFL with weekly radio news scripts, free of charge, during 1939–40. Marquardt, however, refused to use any from "Civil Liberties in the News," offering the weak argument that they lacked "program value" and failed to fulfill "the public interest, convenience and necessity."[39] At the same time, WCFL broadcasted programs produced by progressive and leftist groups that often proved more distinctive in format and content than their popular entertainment counterparts. Labor radio during 1938, for example, aired original radio dramas presented by the Chicago Chapter of the National Lawyers' Guild and shows examining employment opportunities for African Americans produced by the leading black newspaper the *Chicago Defender*.[40]

The CFL and WCFL generally supported the activities of local progressive organs throughout World War II. A new social theater group that emerged in Chicago in 1944, for example, received the backing of the CFL and labor radio. Stage for Action, which had originated in New York with trade union backing, brought together stage, radio, and motion picture talent and technicians to produce short dynamic plays that bolstered the war effort and the peace to come. The group performed its socially relevant plays before neighborhood, civic, religious, and union meetings and over the radio. With the assistance of the CFL Executive Board, Stage for Action contacted local unions, informing them of the group's activities and offering to perform for them. In addition, WCFL considered the possibility of publicizing theater productions. Howard T. Keegan, who replaced Marquardt as station manager in early 1944, proposed studying how to reduce the group's plays to 14.5 minutes for broadcast over WCFL on Saturday evenings. The CFL board approved the idea, but there is no evidence that WCFL aired any of the Stage for Action's plays.[41]

During the last two years of the war WCFL also provided airtime for programs produced by the Independent Voters of Illinois (IVI), one of Chicago's prominent liberal political organizations. An opponent of machine politics and advocate of civil rights, among other causes, the group sponsored a series of forty shows over WCFL during the fall 1944 election campaign. A young lawyer who had written radio plays under the auspices of the Works Progress Administration Writers' Project, acted in the Chicago Repertory Theatre, and helped form AFRA served as scriptwriter and announcer for the programs. Louis "Studs" Terkel helped WCFL's listeners explore the crucial campaign issues of the day from the perspective of independent voters.[42] The IVI sponsored another weekly series of news and commentary programs over WCFL in 1945 with Terkel again examining crucial national and international events. His analysis of the political battle between Henry A. Wallace and Jesse Jones ("Shall Plutocracy or the People Rule in the U.S. of A.?") was so popular that WCFL replayed the commentary twice and reprinted it in the *Federation News*.[43]

With the end of World War II and the onset of the cold war, however, WCFL became more reticent about broadcasting liberal political views. During the election of 1946, the IVI suggested a new series of broadcasts over WCFL, again hoping to examine campaign issues from an independent perspective. This time, however, WCFL declined the request. Outraged CFL delegates wanted to know why a liberal organization such as the IVI had been denied radio time. Maurice Lynch responded that the FCC rule requiring broadcasters to give equal opportunity to all political candidates would force the station to make commercial time available to an array of public office seekers. Luckily, according to Lynch, this regulation did not apply to political parties per se. "If we gave time to IVI, we would have to be shifting around too much" and would lose valuable commercial accounts. Dismissing the IVI's complaint as unjustified, Lynch contended that the organization favored candidates who already had been supported by the Democratic party.[44]

While closing the door to progressive political groups, WCFL responded well to programming requests made by government agencies before, during, and after World War II. Labor radio ran the National Youth Administration's "The Literary Dipper" (1937) and "Youth 'Round the World" (1938). The former show adapted classic literary works and modern books into short radio dramas in an effort to get young people to read. In cooperation with the Social Security Board in 1940, WCFL explained the importance of the Social Security Act through a series of humorous and dramatic stories of ordinary people. The U.S. Employment Service also produced public service programs over the station.[45] During the war, the CFL supported efforts to control commodity prices by the Office of Price Administration. WCFL informed the public about war profiteering and helped organize "neighborhood and community groups" into "consumers' complaint committees to work with the enforcement division of the OPA." The station hoped to educate consumers, especially women, about their obligation to confront and report dealers engaged in overcharging. WCFL produced patriotic shows in cooperation with the public relations offices of the army and navy; "Our American Service Stars," for example, presented "heroic stories of our American boys in action." Spot announcements and short programs aided in the armed forces' recruitment efforts. Like other radio outlets, WCFL donated free time to the Treasury Department for the selling of war bonds and stamps. WCFL management established its own payroll savings plan to help employees systematically purchase war bonds.[46]

The national and international crises of the thirties and forties increased the popularity of broadcast journalism. A desire for quick reports from the battlefields of World War II in particular made Americans turn to their radios rather than newspapers for information. News commentators not only reported on current events but they also enlivened their programs with their own "informed interpretations" of the day's events. A *Variety* survey of radio commentators, published in mid-1945, categorized the vast majority of these broadcasters as "conservatives" or "reactionaries" and only a handful as "liberals."[47] Workers listening to H. V. Kaltenborn, Fulton Lewis Jr., or Rupert Hughes might very well have dismissed these commentators' political and ideological biases, but the cumulative effect of the antilabor propaganda of these and other broadcasters threatened the organized labor movement. As a result, labor radio decided that it needed its own commentators.

During the thirties, Barratt O'Hara, the Reverend J. R. Maguire, and a handful of other speakers offered regular political commentaries with a definite pro-labor orientation. The National Lawyers Guild, the National Urban League, the National Youth Administration, and the *Federation News,* among other organs, sponsored talk and discussion shows over WCFL during 1937–46. Labor, civic, political, and academic representatives covered every conceivable issue from industrial relations to race problems to war and peace. WCFL proudly aired "Montparnasse," a thirty-to-forty-five-minute public discussion forum on Saturday evenings in 1937–38. Modeled after the "The American Town Meeting of the Air," which first appeared over NBC Blue in 1935, "Montparnasse" focused on a different issue each week, with guest experts offering opposing positions and responding to questions and comments from the audience.[48] As informative and stimulating as these programs were, they did not have the impact of news commentaries.

The onset of World War II intensified the efforts of labor radio to expand its own news shows, to carry network news, and to support informed commentators. By the early forties, WCFL was producing nine weekday news reports, seven reports on Saturday, and four news summaries on Sunday. In addition, labor radio carried NBC broadcasts from Europe and commentaries by NBC's experts on foreign affairs. Maurice Lynch inaugurated a regular news commentary segment in his popular "Irish Hour" during the war years, usually ending each brief analysis with an appeal for the purchase of war bonds. WCFL also gave its listeners access to the network news commentaries of Martin Agronsky, Ray Porter, Mark Sullivan, Robert Bellaire, Edward Tomlinson, Max Hill, H. R. Baukhage, and Cary Longmire.[49]

A unique weekly commentary show aired over WCFL for a short period during the summer of 1946. Jesse Albritton, a member of Upholsterers' Local 185, had become, with the support of the CFL leadership, the *Federation News*'s first African-American political columnist in 1942. "Color in the News" offered Albritton's observations on race relations, civil rights, and the general interaction between black workers and the labor movement. The column continued—with a brief interruption when Albritton entered military service—throughout the war and into the postwar period. In June 1946, Albritton went on the air over WCFL for thirteen Sunday mornings. Rejecting the format of playing phonograph records, he instead chose to offer a news commentary on labor and race issues. Like his columns for the *Federation News,* Albritton's radio talks revealed a strong support for AFL policies and a dislike for the leftist CIO. But Albritton also recognized the limitations of AFL policies as they applied to African-American workers. He criticized AFL locals and the national federation for not doing enough to integrate unions and he insisted that CFL and AFL unions sponsor educational programs to deal with racism and the neglect of black labor. Although happy that he received an opportunity to broadcast over WCFL, Albritton observed that organized labor rather than his veteran's organization should have sponsored his radio program.[50]

WCFL boasted another insightful political and labor commentator at the end of World War II. Louis Scofield became the regular announcer for WCFL's "Labor Flashes" in February 1945 and, by the spring, had become "Labor's Own Radio Commentator." Before moving to Chicago in 1939, Scofield had worked for the Crosley Radio Corporation in Cincinnati, where he helped to organize an AFRA local. Once in Chicago, he became a writer for network radio programs and national magazines. He helped to rejuvenate the Radio Writers' Guild of the Authors' League of America, eventually serving as the guild's president in 1943–44. Scofield's radio commentaries aired five nights a week and touched on subjects including public housing, U.S.-Soviet relations, antilabor campaigns by business, and postwar reconversion. In a program devoted to a possible conflict between full employment and the traditional home, Scofield advocated the need for equal opportunity for women in the workplace, publicly funded child care, and shorter hours and higher pay for mothers who worked outside the home. Regarding foreign affairs, Scofield challenged those people "who would preserve the suicidal hatred of Russia." He lashed out against state and national efforts by business organizations "to achieve industrial peace by depriving the unions of their most powerful weapon"—the strike.[51]

The onset of the cold war and the increasing conservatism of WCFL may have led to Scofield's abrupt departure from the station in the summer of 1945. His favorable attitude toward the Soviet Union did not sit well with CFL and AFL officials. The case of Dr. Gerhard Schacher further demonstrates this point. Schacher, a longtime League of Nations correspondent for the *London Chronicle,* presented a news commentary show over Chicago station WIND for five years before moving to WCFL in 1944. Sponsored by the Erie Clothing Company, Schacher's program explored international affairs. Late in 1945, however, WCFL canceled Schacher's contract because he was too sympathetic toward the Soviets. The program's advertising agency as well as its devoted audience denounced the WCFL action. Lynch, CFL financial secretary, defended the decision, citing Schacher's alleged "pro-Russian" and "anti-American" bias.[52]

WCFL's effort to remove potentially embarrassing speakers and programs from its schedule reflected the economic and political realities of the forties. Under AFL guidance, CFL and WCFL officials sought to implement a political and economic agenda that required cooperation with government agencies and the support of corporations. WCFL avoided offending powerful state and business interests and instead sought to demonstrate organized labor's responsible behavior and loyalty to the U.S. political economy. At the same time, WCFL managers wanted to expand the commercial base of their operations and this required securing more advertising. Attracting sponsors meant eliminating all controversy that might inhibit audience growth. WCFL managers contended that they embraced these policies not to maximize station profits per se but to use net revenue to enhance the broadcasting of labor's message.[53]

CFL leaders continued to deem the Radio Frolics as "a very important event" because they contributed to the social well-being of the labor community and to the financial health of WCFL. Charles F. Wills, the *Federation News*'s advertising manager, noted in 1940 that the two-night affair gave "a good time to the members of organized labor and their families"; provided an opportunity for labor "to come together in a fine social event, have a good time and get better acquainted"; and helped the radio station. The Frolics' format—one evening devoted to dancing and one evening to entertainment—changed in 1940, when the event's planners, responding to popular demand, allocated both evenings for entertainment. Organizers recruited Chicago radio and theater artists to perform, while supervising elaborate advertising campaigns. The yearly event brought between eleven and twelve thousand dollars in annual net profits to labor radio in 1938, 1939, and 1940. As the radio station's overall financial situation improved during the early forties, WCFL managers felt confident in dividing the event's proceeds equally between WCFL and the March of Dimes. Contributing to a politically acceptable charity demonstrated organized labor's concern with the welfare of the larger community.[54]

Although the importance of the Frolics as a supplemental source of income for WCFL declined during the forties, the event's social, cultural, and publicity value persisted. This explains why CFL officials became irritated when affiliated unions returned their allotment of Frolic tickets without making an effort to pay for them or distribute them among the rank and file. Organizers of the 1942 event condemned such practice as "inexcusable" and the CFL membership at large criticized local unions who used WCFL but failed to support the station by purchasing Frolics' tickets. The Frolics had become occasions for trade unions "to show their loyalty to the cause of labor."[55]

Labor Day celebrations offered similar occasions to demonstrate labor solidarity. But Chicago's elaborate Labor Day celebrations disappeared by the midthirties and so did WCFL's coverage of the parades, band music, speeches, athletic events, and dances. WCFL continued to broadcast Labor Day speeches by AFL leaders, state and local trade union officials, civic leaders, and sympathetic politicians during the late thirties and throughout the war years. Some speeches came from WCFL facilities and others came via the graces of the NBC or CBS radio network. On Labor Day in 1937, the station recorded afternoon speeches by William Green and Frank Morrison and replayed them in the evening because they originally coincided with WCFL's coverage of baseball games. Occasionally the station recreated "Chicago's previous day parades, before autos and outings" rendered them "passe."[56]

World War II brought to WCFL a new group of staff writers, announcers, and commentators with strong labor sympathies who revived the special Labor Day broadcasts. On Monday evening, September 4, 1944, WCFL presented an one-hour program entitled "The Progress of Labor." Written by Studs Terkel and Louis Scofield, the program dramatized the historical development of the labor movement in America from the days of indentured servants to the present. AFRA members donated their services to fill the more than seventy speaking parts in the "documentary drama." Jack Kelly directed a twenty-five-piece studio orchestra, playing original music composed for the occasion by a WCFL staff member.[57] "The Progress of

Labor" generated a "flood of congratulatory letters" from the Chicago listening area and stimulated interest from people across the nation. Letters came from union and nonunion workers, men and women, the rank and file and union officers; most writers admitted that they rarely corresponded with a radio station about any program. All the letters praised the content of the show and the skill of the participants, calling the production "thrilling" or "outstanding." A worker at the Swift Packing Company plant in Gary, Indiana, commended the actors and writers for their realistic depiction of a racially and ethnically diverse working class. The quality of this "local broadcast" so impressed listeners that they lamented that it "was not heard coast-to-coast."[58] A year later, Terkel and Scofield again collaborated to produce "The Last Bomb," a show that dramatized the ending of the war and labor's recent struggles. The 1946 program "How Straight the Line" combined a short labor drama with music and traditional speeches and commentaries.[59]

These Labor Day radio programs offered a unique perspective on the role that working men and women and their labor organizations played in U.S. history and they served as powerful counterweights to the "malicious propaganda" of the commercial media. Chicago labor officials warned that if rank-and-file workers failed to listen to WCFL or to read the *Federation News* they might very well accept the corporate media's unfair characterizations of organized labor and this, in turn, eventually would undermine the union movement. William L. McFetridge, head of the Chicago Flat Janitors' Union, observed in January 1944 that the general public tended to look down upon trade unions because labor received such poor publicity in the mass media. Making greater use of WCFL might help to alleviate this difficult public relations problem. Alluding to the CIO, McFetridge argued that "if some of our competitors had [WCFL], they would use it to good advantage and probably destroy us with it, so I appeal to you to give serious thought to the public relations problem which is so important." Fitzpatrick, Lynch, and Marquardt agreed with McFetridge's contention that using WCFL was "one of the most important things we can do in the interest of the labor movement."[60]

Station staff believed that the format for presenting labor's message to the public was as important as the message itself. The Labor Day programs in 1944–46 demonstrated that organized labor's message could be presented in an interesting and entertaining format. Hoping that these programs would inspire local trade unions to use WCFL, Station Manager Keegan explained in 1944: "It is our earnest desire that each individual union will recognize the possibilities of a continued series of such broadcasts and will take advantage of the opportunity offered to each of them to dramatize the activities of its own particular organization."[61]

Keegan's call for radio programs that dramatized trade union activities and principles echoed the arguments of station staff who wanted to make labor programs entertaining as well as informative. As part of its 1938 arrangement with NBC, WCFL agreed to reduce and refine the station's labor programming in exchange for sustaining programs and technical assistance from the network. *Variety* frequently complained that WCFL's "stodgy presentation of the labor stuff," with its excessive "dese, dem and dose spiels by fervid spokesmen," had "bored even the partisans." Thus Marquardt and Wolens insisted that they would avoid the "rut of labor speeches" and not return to "the old policy of anything going so long as it was union." Labor programming required "better presentation and more showmanship," including professional dramatizations.[62]

WCFL used both locally and nationally produced labor dramatizations. The station broadcasted the AFL series "The Labor Parade" and "Cavalcade of Labor" during 1938.[63] A Chicago local of the Post Office Clerks' Union sponsored its own dramatic reenactment of the lives of its workers in 1939, portraying how mail carriers might find missing persons or apprehend criminals and closing each show with a message that urged workers and the general public to support important labor legislation. "Manpower," a series produced by the Brotherhood of Boilermakers, aired over WCFL on Thursday evenings during the fall of 1946. Using professional talent, it dramatized workers' lives and workers' role in producing and distributing indispensable commodities and emphasized the union's role in supporting community services.[64]

Another way to make labor's message more palatable for the audience was for trade unions to sponsor popular shows. As a demonstration of both its commitment to WCFL and its belief that radio could provide good publicity for the trade union movement, the Chicago Flat Janitors' Union announced its sponsorship of a comedy-mystery-drama to air over WCFL on Monday evenings in early 1944. The union hired an advertising agency to design the "pure entertainment" show "Whodunit?" President McFetridge explained: "We will attempt to sell our union in much the same manner that any other product or association is sold in first class radio production." Acknowledging that the show was "purely an experiment," he concluded that it might benefit the janitors and the entire labor movement by establishing public confidence in trade unions. McFetridge also hoped that the program would serve as a model for other unions—to help them to use WCFL facilities and to get out the good word regarding labor. He urged delegates to get their friends and families to listen to the show and to make criticisms and suggestions. Chicago union officials sponsored a thirteen-week run for the show, with an option of expanding it nationwide if it proved successful.[65] "Whodunit?" did not air beyond its trial period, but it did serve as a model for future labor programming.

Teamsters' Joint Council 25 took a lesson from both the post office clerks and the janitors when it sponsored a new variety show over WCFL in February 1946. "The Spice of Life" aired on Sunday afternoons in front of a live audience at a neighborhood theater. Each week a different local union presented a show that included drama, music, comedy, and interviews. The first show, which featured Milk Wagon Drivers' Union Local 753, dramatized the story of how Tim McCreery, a teamster, and his horse, Aggie, saved the life of a housewife caught in a burning building. Master of ceremonies Jack Fuller interviewed the union president, who emphasized organized labor's wartime and peacetime contributions to U.S. society. Musical selections by a soloist, choral group, and orchestra rounded out the program. Subsequent shows featured the Taxicab Chauffeurs' Union and the Laundry and Dye House Drivers' Union. *Variety* criticized the inaugural program for a noisy labor audience and the union speakers who engaged in "too much back-slapping." It concluded, however, that the fine orchestra and singers and the overall context of the program "presaged a nice run." The industry magazine also commended labor's effort at public relations—taking a page right out of management's book.[66]

These experiments in combining popular entertainment formats with the union message did not lead to labor's abandonment of straight labor speeches, talks, discussions, and announcements. CFL officials considered WCFL as one of their great labor activities precisely because it served as a direct and immediate source of information and education for Chicago unionists. When invited to give a ten-minute talk over Chicago station WJJD in August 1937, Fitzpatrick declined, explaining that if the CFL did "any broadcasting, it will be over own station."[67] CFL vice president Anton Johannsen preferred straight talks and used the format, in the early forties, to comment on topics ranging from the goals of the union movement to child labor problems to "Nazi terrorism."[68] "Labor Flashes" continued to inform listeners about ongoing strikes, organizing campaigns, boycotts, and union meetings. Through these programs, WCFL served a host of labor organizations ranging from the Chicago Typographical Union to the Women's Trade Union League. Praise for WCFL's service to labor came from all over the city and the Midwest.[69]

WCFL served as the major public relations outlet for the CFL's newly created Federation of Labor School. In the spring of 1937, at the recommendation of the CFL Committee on Education, representatives from the city's various workers' education organizations—including the Chicago Labor College and the CFL School—met to discuss combining their efforts and forming a new school. The new labor institution opened in October 1937 at the headquarters of the Women's Trade Union League. Operating throughout World War II, the school offered low-cost classes in labor law, the history of the labor movement, labor legislation, parliamentary law and public speaking, and labor journalism. Although WCFL made announcements for the new school, it never developed a close relationship with the education project.[70] The policy stressing WCFL's use of professional talent made it impossible for the amateur radio commentators that Sarainne Loewe had trained in her workers' broadcast journalism course to test their skills over labor radio.

A variety of local trade unions used WCFL in their organizing campaigns and labor disputes. Among those unions receiving extensive assistance from WCFL were the printing trades. Since the late twenties, Chicago printing unions had carried on a "perennial struggle" to unionize T. E. Donnelley's Lakeside Press. Donnelley was "the most articulate defender of the open-shop" in Chicago and his company remained the one major printer in the city "outside the union fold."[71] Throughout the thirties and the war years, the Chicago Typographical Union used "Labor Flashes" to announce developments in the campaign. The printing trades unions also produced weekly programs and special shows over WCFL in which they analyzed the company's wage policies and anti-union tactics and explained the boycott of Donnelley publications.[72]

There were limits to WCFL's generosity to the printing trades—and by extension to other trade unions. When he took control of WCFL in 1937, Marquardt explained that just because a trade union made a demand, WCFL would not necessarily ignore other concerns and comply with the request. Indeed, soon after the managerial shift in the spring of 1937, WCFL reminded the pressmen's union that running a radio station entailed "complex problems." The policy of giving time to the printers whenever they asked had interfered with scheduled programming—especially with NBC sustaining shows. This practice therefore stopped and the printers, like all other unions, henceforth complied with a "regular procedure" of requesting the use of station facilities in writing at least two days prior to the desired broadcast.[73]

Chicago's Trades Union Label League, like the printing trades unions, had been a longtime supporter and user of WCFL. Unlike other users of WCFL, however, the Label League experimented with different formats for labor programming, especially under the leadership of Harry Scheck. This effort to find new, effective ways of presenting the union label message via the radio came to a halt in the thirties and the Label League's weekly fifteen-minute program fell into a conventional discussion format. Marquardt's new policy temporarily revived the organization's innovative programming. On the occasion of Union Label Month in October 1937, the Label League developed "Tune Teasers," which aired three times a week and presented musical numbers interspersed with short messages on the union label. The program also conducted a contest that asked listeners to name mystery songs, awarding the winners free passes to area movie theaters. "Tune Teasers" proved so popular that WCFL continued to broadcast the show until the end of November, a month beyond its original expiration date. By the time the program ended, the station had received over twenty-two hundred letters—an average of almost one hundred letters per broadcast.[74] The success of "Tune Teasers," however, did not lead to further Label League experimentation. On the contrary, like many labor bodies, the Label League chose the easy option of relying on talk programs rather than expending time, energy, and money in adapting new radio formats to the service of labor.[75]

During the era of Edward Nockels, labor activists recognized that WCFL could serve not only as a vehicle for conveying trade union information to workers but also as a mechanism for enhancing working-class consciousness and developing a working-class culture. Station programmers and labor organizers attempted to realize these goals by developing new program formats or by adapting popular radio formats to the specific needs of labor. Radio contests made listeners aware of the union label message, while dramatizing the role of organized labor in building American society gave workers a renewed pride in their unions. The vast majority of labor programming, however, remained "talking heads": straight discussion or commentary. In addition, innovative labor programs became less imperative, as labor unions preferred to attach their messages to popular forms of entertainment. WCFL's commercialization turned the original purpose of labor radio on its head.

As late as 1939, WCFL managers continued to argue that WCFL's efforts to expand its commercial operations aimed not at making money, "but with the single thought in mind of financing itself in such a manner as to properly provide for . . . broadcasting labor's message."[76] This meant that WCFL's managers would reinvest the station's surplus earnings to improve studio facilities and transmitting equipment and to enhance employee benefits. But by the midforties, WCFL officials readily admitted that the nonprofit WCFL also used its surplus earnings to fund nonstation activities. Nockels had seen labor radio as a vehicle for spreading trade union messages and building labor solidarity; his successors saw the station as a way to finance other CFL functions and to legitimize the labor movement in the eyes of government and business. The concern with generating net profits raised WCFL's awareness of possible tax difficulties during the forties. The CFL, AFL, WCFL, AFRA, and musicians' union, for example, successfully lobbied against a congressional proposal that would have placed "a most burdensome tax on the gross business of all radio broadcasting, including that done by stations owned and operated by non-profit organizations."[77]

WCFL's success as a commercial operation came at the cost of service to progressive labor and community groups. The forces that altered WCFL had emerged during Nockels's lifetime; indeed, they derived from the inherent contradictions of Nockels's conception of labor radio and its role in American broadcasting. As faulty and contradictory as Nockels's vision and policies might have been, and as powerful as the external pressures created by the AFL, commercial radio, and the FCC were, Nockels, through his strong commitment to developing labor radio as an alternative to the dominant media, tried to hold those forces at bay. This was not the case with WCFL's subsequent managers. By the midforties, the aged and ill John Fitzpatrick had turned over much of the management of the CFL to Vice President William Lee, who embraced the corporatist compromise and appreciated neither Nockels's vision for the station nor his warnings about corporate broadcasting. Fitzpatrick had lost whatever interest he may have once had in the station. His death in September 1946 generated much grief and deeply felt eulogies, but it barely touched the operation of either the labor federation or the Voice of Labor.[78]

William Lee and Commercial Success, 1946–66

As WCFL entered its third decade of broadcasting in 1946, it encountered a political and economic environment far different than the one in which it had been conceived and in which it struggled to survive during the twenties and thirties. Postwar prosperity, consumerism, anticommunism, and the emergence of television deeply affected WCFL's development during the two decades following World War II. At the same time that new opportunities and obstacles faced the Voice of Labor, new individuals and institutions came to direct the station. The young WCFL constantly fought against corporate broadcasters and federal regulators, but these battles subsided significantly after 1945. Whereas Edward Nockels fought AFL leaders to protect WCFL during its formative years, the interests of the city and national federations converged during the postwar period. Chicago politics, which had contributed somewhat to WCFL's early development, took on added importance during the postwar era.

The two decades that followed the end of World War II marked the high point of organized labor in U.S. society. More than one-third of the civilian labor force belonged to unions in 1946 and at least 80 percent of the workers in most basic industries held union cards. As the cold war economy boomed, union workers enjoyed relatively high wages and substantial fringe benefits. Business unionism reigned supreme. "Content to negotiate, sign, and administer labor contracts," labor leaders embraced the capitalist system to such a degree that they ran their own unions like businesses.[1]

The AFL's long-standing hierarchical and centralized structure became a model for Chicago union leaders to emulate.

William Lee became president of the CFL upon John Fitzpatrick's death in 1946. Lee's rise to power and subsequent reign (1946–84) marked a significant shift in the fortunes of both the federation and its radio station. A quest for power and a commitment to business unionism characterized Lee's career, which began in an Irish neighborhood on Chicago's West Side. In 1915, Lee joined Local 734 of the Bakery Drivers' Union and became its business agent a decade later. First elected the local's president in 1929, Lee retained that office for almost three decades. Lee became active in the International Brotherhood of Teamsters, eventually rising to the position of vice president. Although Lee demonstrated little interest in the Chicago central body during the thirties, the powerful Teamsters and building trades supported him as Fitzpatrick's heir apparent. While leading the CFL, Lee remained concerned about the future of the national teamsters' union and, in 1957, joined three other candidates to challenge James R. Hoffa for the presidency. Hoffa's victory placed Lee in an awkward position because of congressional investigations charging Hoffa with misuse of union funds, payoffs, racketeering, and violence. The AFL-CIO voted to expel the teamsters in late 1957. In order to retain his position in the CFL, Lee severed his ties with the teamsters and joined the Building Service Employees' Union headed by his "supporter, ally, and patron," William L. McFetridge.[2]

Quintessential business unionists, Lee and McFetridge favored "negotiations to strikes and conciliation to confrontation" and rarely challenged the economic or political status quo on a local or national level. One Chicago-area union organizer found it impossible to distinguish between these labor leaders and business executives; they all possessed "diamond rings, manicures," air-conditioned luxury cars, and chauffeurs.[3]

Lee and McFetridge collaborated with local government and business in part because of their associations with the Cook County Democratic party and Chicago politician Richard J. Daley. The close personal friendship among McFetridge, Lee, and Daley rested on their similar working-class Irish backgrounds. Daley, who worked his way through law school, won election to the Illinois General Assembly in 1936. Over the next decade the Democratic party stalwart established a pro-labor voting record in the state legislature. Daley's campaign to become Cook County sheriff coincided with Lee's accession to the presidency of the CFL in the fall of 1946. Using his new office, Lee threw labor's weight behind Daley. For the first time in its history, the CFL "unanimously endorsed a candidate for a county office."

Speaking over WCFL, just days before the election, Lee praised Daley as the "greatest friend" that labor, "business and industry and God-fearing people ever sent to the legislature." Lee, the CFL, WCFL, and the *Federation News* supported Daley's subsequent political campaigns, including his run for Cook County clerk.[4]

After five years as county clerk, Richard Daley ran for the Democratic nomination for the mayor of Chicago. Lee brought together 150 labor leaders in early 1955 to form a committee to elect Daley while the CFL passed a motion endorsing Daley for mayor. The labor committee for Daley sponsored a newscast each weekday evening over WCFL. In addition, WCFL aired daily reports on the Daley campaign. Irwin Klass, editor of the *Federation News,* wrote a front-page editorial explaining why organized labor broke tradition and endorsed a candidate in a primary election campaign. Among other things, Klass argued that Daley offered the excellent leadership that the city needed. Daley won the primary and the general election with trade union backing and, within weeks of taking office, appointed Lee as head of the Chicago Civil Service Commission, which guided the city's three hundred thousand employees.[5]

Working closely with Mayor Daley (1955–76), Lee and McFetridge strengthened the Chicago trade union movement's ties to the Democratic party machine and to the city's business leadership. McFetridge, in particular, became known as "Daley's House Man"; whenever the mayor needed a reliable representative on an important committee or commission, he invariably chose McFetridge. One political commentator asserted that "every prince . . . needs his Machiavelli—and McFetridge was Daley's." By the sixties, CFL officials sat on the board of nearly every public body, including the Board of Education, Park Board, Police Board, Public Building Commission, Housing Authority, Board of Health, and the Public Library Board of Directors.[6] Longtime Chicago labor activists feared that the union movement paid too high a price for respectability by collaborating with the political machine. Whenever labor leaders visited city hall in the midsixties, Lew Gibson, staff member of the United Packinghouse Workers of America, worried that "they were gonna pull Mayor Daley's pants down and kiss him."[7]

Chicago thus became a microcosm of corporatism, in which the elites of local labor, business, and government worked together to support the prevailing distribution of economic and political rewards while maintaining labor peace and the image of a cross-class harmony of interests. Lee proudly noted how labor and management in Chicago could sit down together, discuss their differences, negotiate settlements, and get on with "the business of producing goods and services." Organized labor in Chicago and the nation, contended the CFL chief, "actively *defends* the free enterprise system" and did not seek to take over the means of production. Through collective bargaining, productivity, and a free labor and management system, American workers had achieved the world's highest standard of living. Offering his own reading of history, Lee insisted that the CFL had a tradition of "practical idealism" that rejected the "strange and now obscure theories" of labor radicalism. Daley, Lee, and McFetridge did their best to co-opt challengers to their practical arrangement. As Chicago labor dissident Sidney Lens once observed, Lee and his associates simply did not "want unions to grow if they could not control them."[8] In their effort to collaborate with local political bosses and capitalists, Chicago's labor elite discovered a new use for labor radio.

As head of WCFL, Lee, like Edward Nockels, talked of serving organized labor. But Lee's definition of service, and his strategy and tactics for achieving it, diverged from those of the father of labor radio. Lee wished to use WCFL not only to tell labor's story to the general public but, more importantly, to demonstrate labor's contributions to civic affairs, industrial growth, and peaceful employer-employee relations. During the fifties, the CFL expanded its involvement "in every type of community project—health and welfare agencies, improvement of parks and playgrounds, slum clearance and public housing."[9] At a luncheon cosponsored by the Chicago Association of Commerce and Industry and the CFL in July 1957, Lee received a special plaque from the former body recognizing his leadership in creating the city's excellent union-business relationship. In accepting the award, Lee spoke about how labor and management had matured over the years and how each side had come to acknowledge the dignity of the other. He explained that Chicago labor "*knows* that we are *not* a 'working class' that's abusive of our economic system, management and the public interest."[10]

To strengthen the cross-class alliance among labor, business, and government and to enhance the economic and political benefits to city labor leaders, area unions, and the Chicago Democratic party machine, Lee advocated maximizing radio station profits. While ostensibly serving as a vehicle for the enlightenment and entertainment of Chicago's working class, Lee focused on perfecting WCFL's role as a generator of capital. McFetridge acknowledged Lee's abilities as both labor leader and businessman in June 1950 when he nominated his friend for another term as CFL president. Lee shared Nockels's desire to have WCFL generate positive publicity for the labor movement. Providing quality entertainment for a wide audience would help create goodwill for labor among the general public. Nockels also hoped, however, that labor radio's programming would build labor solidarity, offering a labor perspective on crucial contemporary issues and challenging the status quo of bourgeois society. Lee only wished to demonstrate to corporate officials and the public at large that the labor perspective was identical to that of liberal government and big business.[11] The efforts of Lee and his station managers to secure these goals during the fifties and sixties further eroded what remained of Nockels's dream for an alternative and oppositional radio station. Yet, throughout this period, fragments of Nockels's vision remained intact.

• • •

A 1948 study commissioned by Matthew Woll, who still represented the AFL on WCFL's governing board, blasted the Voice of Labor as a weak leader in community affairs and a poor "advocate in the cause of labor." According to the report's author—a person Woll characterized as "fully conversant with radio work"—the station lacked any "outstanding" forums or commentators and aired boring labor programs that avoided controversial topics and failed to champion the local or international issues that the AFL supported.[12] The unnamed radio analyst, however, failed to acknowledge the fine labor-oriented shows such as Rod Holmgren's news commentary or the strike-inspired program "Meet the Union Printers," which aired during 1946–49.

Roderick B. Holmgren replaced Louis Scofield as news commentator on "Labor Flashes" at the end of the summer of 1945. An experienced radio broadcaster and charter member of the American Federation of Teachers Local 635, Holmgren had helped to produce educational and news programs for CBS, NBC, and the Mutual Broadcasting System (MBS) and had provided news commentaries for radio stations in Chicago and Iowa before the war. During the war, he served as assistant deputy chief of the Domestic Radio Bureau in the Office of War Information. After only two months at WCFL, Holmgren transformed "Labor Flashes" into "Labor News Commentary"—a fifteen-minute nightly broadcast that offered labor's "up-to-date analysis of news."[13]

Chicago labor officials thought highly of Holmgren and his commentaries. The *Federation News* repeatedly praised his perceptive analyses of local, national, and international events, his searing exposés of the abuses of corporate capitalism, and his unwavering commitment to working people in Chicago and the nation. CFL vice president Johannsen frequently called CFL delegates' attention to Holmgren's insightful observations. Using a classic line from WCFL publicity promotions of the twenties and thirties, the *Federation News* proclaimed that Holmgren offered his listeners "a feast of reason and flow of soul."[14] When the University of Chicago initiated an eight-week workshop on the theme of labor and public relations early in 1947, Holmgren and Norman Dolnick, a member of the United Packinghouse Workers of America, directed discussions on the press, radio, shop papers, and community relations.[15]

Holmgren's radio commentaries, often reprinted in the pages of the *Federation News,* spanned the spectrum of daily news headlines, from housing and price controls to the bias of the capitalist media, from labor legislation and strikes to the atomic bomb. In an insightful commentary in October 1945, Holmgren questioned the U.S. military's monopoly over atomic energy and argued for civilian and international control of the powerful new force. Holmgren frequently noted the slanted coverage of labor issues by the mainstream press. Why, he inquired in a May 1946 broadcast, did the mass media refer to strikes as "labor trouble" rather than "employer trouble?" Holmgren launched a series of discussions on the Taft-Hartley Act during the summer of 1947.[16]

WCFL managers abruptly dismissed Holmgren in September. When pressured for an explanation, the CFL said that Holmgren had "followed a CIO line."[17] The animosity between AFL and CIO affiliates in Chicago had been deep and occasionally violent during the thirties and early forties. But an atmosphere of calm prevailed by the postwar years.[18] The reference to the "CIO line" served as a euphemism for leftist political leanings. According to Holmgren, FBI agents visited WCFL offices on several occasions to talk about him. Holmgren never learned what information or instructions the FBI passed on to WCFL. It is safe to assume that the CFL aversion to communism—exacerbated by the intensifying cold war—and the station's increasing attention to "balanced" programming led station managers to blacklist the commentator. Only months before Holmgren's dismissal, a *Federation News* article had warned that "Communists are determined to seek access, by means fair or foul, to the radio public and shout their shoddy wares through every radio set in the land." Chicago Typographical Union officials wanted Holmgren to write, produce, and announce shows for them over WCFL in late 1947, but station officials refused to allow Holmgren to set foot inside the studios.[19] Holmgren's dismissal from WCFL generated virtually no discussion within Chicago's broadcasting and labor communities—a reflection of the extent of cold war paranoia and repression. Within weeks, a different controversy consumed the attention of Chicago labor.

The oldest and perhaps most democratic trade union in Chicago began a twenty-two-month strike against the Chicago Newspaper Publishers' Association in November 1947. Chicago Typographical Union Local 16, along with locals of the International Typographical Union from around the nation, battled for improved wage scales and protection against the antiunion and repressive Taft-Hartley Act. By outlawing the closed shop and banning union supervisors, the 1947 law eliminated a large part of "the whole structure of rule and practice which prevails in a union composing room." Printers in Chicago and elsewhere hoped to get publishers to circumvent the act by reaching agreements with them on wages and other issues, but not signing formal contracts. Most newspapers and commercial printing shops in Chicago, however, "were eager to bring the union to its knees" and they continued to publish throughout the strike by using scab labor and introducing new printing techniques into their operations.[20]

During the long and tense strike, the printers found themselves cut off from the public and often from each other because of the enmity of the Chicago mass media. Only WCFL offered the printers an outlet to reach the public. WCFL's "Labor Flashes," which had returned to its old format after Holmgren's dismissal, reported on the growing troubles between printers and newspaper publishers during the fall of 1947. Two weeks after the strike began, the Chicago Typographical Union (CTU) inaugurated a series called "Meet the Union Printers," which WCFL aired until the strike ended in September 1949. During the strike's early months, WCFL broadcasted the show in fifteen-to-thirty-minute periods six evenings a week. CTU president John J. Pilch appreciated the CFL's "wonderful assistance" and praised WCFL's radio programs for reaching "thousands and thousands of listeners." As the strike wore on, however, WCFL cut the broadcasts until, in the summer of 1949, the show aired for only fifteen minutes on Sunday afternoons.[21]

The CTU's publicity committee wanted "Meet the Union Printers" to be both "interesting and informative to the listening audience." Heeding the advice of WCFL's publicity director and professional announcer, Frank McGivern, CTU publicists carefully constructed their scripts, chose articulate speakers, used an interview or dialogue format, and rehearsed. Once a week, selected CTU members became "news reporters," reviewing important developments in the strike, negotiations, court proceedings, and related events "which your daily newspaper has either failed to report at all, or else buried in small paragraphs on inside pages." On other evenings, CTU offic-

ers explained strike policy and benefits; discussed the strike with representatives of the public; presented background information on the history of
the printing trades, the shorter workday movement, and the Taft-Hartley
Act; and answered inquiries from the audience. "Meet the Union Printers"
occasionally offered miniature dramas that juxtaposed a real printer with
some unknown lay person—usually the owner of a small business—who
was naive about corporate capitalism and either hostile, unsympathetic, or
apathetic toward the union cause. After a short discussion with the union
printer, however, the lay character admitted that the strike issues were complex and that the Taft-Hartley Act was a bad piece of legislation. These dramatizations, often accompanied by live organ music, varied in quality, but
demonstrated the potential of labor radio.[22]

Frank McGivern assisted a variety of labor groups in using WCFL. He
urged all participants to make their stories interesting to the public, reminding them that "the problem of the individual union on the air is one of
fundamental public relations." Careful review of program formats and thor-
ough rehearsals would help unions to make efficient use of radio. Retail
clerks, post office employees, airline pilots, and teachers all successfully
explained their struggles over the Voice of Labor. McGivern interviewed
union leaders and state and federal bureaucrats on labor topics. In 1948–
49, the CFL sponsored a series of McGivern interviews with officials of the
Chicago Building Trades Council on the subject of building codes—a dull,
but crucial welfare and safety issue for Chicago's inhabitants. McGivern
helped write and direct "Operation Harmony," a half-hour show that combined union messages and entertainment. A Chicago radio columnist characterized the 1947 show as "the sort of public relations Big Business long
has used." McGivern's 1948 Labor Day program aired over the ABC network
and featured WCFL performers, Chicago labor and political leaders, and the
AFL president. It also marked the official debut of WCFL as a fifty-thousand-watt station. On Mondays during 1949, McGivern's "At Your Service"
profiled the history of Chicago-area unions.[23]

Program directors' commitment to producing labor-oriented shows
continued throughout the fifties, but declined in intensity. WCFL broadcasted public affairs shows such as "Quorum Calls." Moderated by Barratt
O'Hara, a congressional representative from Illinois and a former WCFL
commentator, this series of political discussions aired in 1949–50 and often examined issues of importance to organized labor.[24] "Labor Reports to
the Nation," an AFL-CIO syndicated show, first appeared over WCFL in June
1956. Program topics covered the unification of the labor movement, so-

cial security, national housing problems, right-to-work laws, and labor's fight against communism. Another AFL-CIO program, "Washington Report"—an interview of congressional leaders—premiered in late 1957. WCFL covered the conventions of the AFL and the ISFL when held in Chicago, as well as important meetings of the Building Service Employees' Union, the Teamsters, and other unions. Station reporter Don Graham and *Federation News* editor Irwin Klass reported from the 1957 Teamsters' convention held in Miami Beach, where William Lee provided radio commentary on the corruption and racketeering charges facing the union and the threat of AFL-CIO expulsion.[25] Local unions continued to use WCFL to announce meetings and to convey other messages to the rank and file and the general public. Union organizing drives, such as the effort to organize Montgomery Ward plants in 1953–54, received extensive coverage over WCFL.[26]

General Manager Arthur Harre and Director of Public Relations Fred Herendeen developed "Labor's Own Amateur Hour" in late 1952 to generate labor participation in WCFL. The one-hour, weekday afternoon program (November 1952–February 1953), drew 165 participants representing 86 local unions. Each contestant received a merchandise prize valued at thirty dollars, courtesy of a local retail outlet. WCFL personalities Martin Hogan and Howard Roberts introduced the amateur talent and interviewed audience members. Station staff were delighted that thirty-seven thousand letters—mainly from housewives or other workers at home during the middle of the day—determined the winners of the five thousand dollars' worth of prizes. Although Harre implied that rank-and-file support for this show and the station would benefit labor, it remains problematic whether officials expected this type of program to produce workers' commitment to WCFL.[27]

CFL officers urged cooperation among the federation, affiliated unions, and the radio station, but still lamented that "people outside the labor movement are more familiar with the station than union people"—the "owners of WCFL." During 1949, station managers launched a campaign to publicize WCFL among local trade unions. Program Director Bob Platt and Publicity Director McGivern formed a "flying squadron" to visit area union halls and explain the station's new programming.[28] After a decade of providing only cursory information on WCFL's operations, the *Federation News* resumed publishing a weekly program schedule in May 1949. Throughout the early fifties, CFL officers made it a point to show off WCFL to visiting labor representatives, especially those from foreign countries. Delegates from Iceland, Australia, Great Britain, the Netherlands, Chile, and Costa Rica received the opportunity to talk briefly over labor radio.[29]

Efforts to highlight WCFL's labor orientation confronted a competing policy to reduce or "balance" labor shows, increase popular programming, attract a middle-class audience, expand advertising, and maximize station profits. Even as labor-oriented programs aired, Lee and the WCFL staff moved to tone down the station's labor message and avoid what a radio columnist criticized as labor's "hammer and tongs approach." CFL leaders, hoping to attract a larger audience and hence more advertisers to the station, feared the negative effect that overtly pro-labor or class-conscious programs would have on sponsors and profits. CTU officers, for example, felt somewhat inhibited by the station's refusal to allow militant or radical language on "Meet the Union Printers." WCFL discontinued some labor programs in order to free time slots for popular entertainment as the station apparently did with the weekly program of Chicago Teachers' Federation Local 1 in 1950.[30]

Under the direction of Lee and various station managers, WCFL urged trade unions to sponsor popular programming rather than producing labor shows. Lee suggested that local unions sponsor sporting events and advertise their labor activities. This was not an original concept; several CFL unions had experimented with this format as early as the thirties and many more did so in the fifties. Chicago Teamsters sponsored broadcasts of Notre Dame's 1951 football season while hotel and restaurant workers subsidized coverage of seven local college basketball games from the Chicago Stadium in 1952. In both cases, the unions designed commercials to acquaint the public with their members and the work they did. A typical commercial began: "This is the basketball game with 30,000 sponsors. Every day—seven days a week, 52 weeks a year, somewhere, somehow members of the Hotel and Restaurant Workers are on their various jobs, working with reputable employers to serve you, the public." Lee embraced such efforts to "sell good labor-management relations" and felt certain that "much good will come out of these programs."[31]

WCFL's shifting concern with labor shows also reflected staff changes during the postwar era. Maurice Lynch, the CFL's long-serving financial secretary who had participated in WCFL's operations ever since creating the "Irish Hour" in the early thirties, became general manager in 1945. Although he oversaw WCFL's transition from Fitzpatrick to Lee, a lingering illness forced Lynch to relinquish his role in the station (1948) and in the CFL (1951). Lee and CFL secretary William F. Cleary jointly directed the station

after Lynch's departure, but the executive board decided "to engage a thoroughly experienced and competent radio man" to run WCFL. Art Harre
briefly served as general manager in 1951–52. Martin Hogan, a member of
WCFL's on-air staff since 1948 and a popular disc jockey, sports announcer, and sales representative, eventually took control. Together with Sales
Manager Tom Haviland, Hogan reinforced the new image of labor radio as
"a revenue producer" for the CFL.[32]

Throughout his tenure at WCFL, Hogan adhered to Lee's business unionist and commercial broadcasting philosophy. When introducing a thirteen-
part series on the history of the U.S. labor movement, Hogan explained to
CFL delegates that both the program and the station aimed to "promote
better understanding of labor by the general public and better relations
between employers and employees." Hogan promised that the program
would be as "fascinating as some of the most popular soap operas on the
air" and would stress "what labor's gains have meant to the benefit of industry."[33] The station began avoiding negative reporting—criticizing industrial profits or the power of the wealthy—and instead embraced "a constructive policy—pointing to improved living conditions of our union members,
the homes in which the common people live, the radios, automobiles and
television sets which they own."[34]

Like Nockels, Lee considered WCFL a public relations vehicle for the
labor movement. But WCFL did not necessarily have to produce labor programs to fulfill this goal. Merely broadcasting good music or sports programs would create a positive image for the station and organized labor.
WCFL's popularity in the Chicago radio market derived from its quality
signal, its entertainment schedule, and its general service to the community; this popularity made the station "a power and influence for the good of
the workers and their families." Lee contended that if WCFL acted respon-
sibly, it would generate public goodwill for the trade union movement.[35]

The demand for responsible programming dictated the selection of Rod
Holmgren's replacement. Refusing to accept "speakers of the carping and
ranting kind," the station chose, in June 1949, a journalist who would offer
"balanced" reporting of labor and other news. Victor Barnes had twenty-
five years of experience as a newspaper reporter and editor in Kansas, New
York, and Illinois and as Chicago station KYW's news writer and reader
during the early twenties. An organizer of the American Newspaper Guild
local in Newark, New Jersey, Barnes was fired for his union activity in 1934.
He subsequently worked for the *Chicago Herald-American* and the *Herald
Examiner*. Breaking ranks with the guild because of its alleged ties to the

Communist party and its affiliation with the CIO, Barnes helped found the AFL Chicago Editorial Association. He became the night managing editor of the *Chicago Herald-American* in 1944 and began writing news reports for WMAQ. Barnes continued his newspaper affiliation after joining WCFL.[36]

The *Federation News* described Barnes's style as informal, sincere, and serious. His performance adhered strictly to the "WCFL Style Book," which warned that "labor propaganda must not be permitted to creep into our news broadcasts." A July 1949 study of Barnes's shows concluded that they devoted less time to union issues and covered fewer labor items than the average United Press news roundup. On the other hand, Barnes emphasized favorable aspects of organized labor more often than did the UP. Press services usually reported on labor only during strikes and other controversies, but Barnes frequently discussed national issues from a labor perspective and interviewed union people even when no labor crisis raged. According to Lee, Barnes's audience experienced "the novelty of a newscast on which the organized labor movement is not treated as a shirt sleeved visitor at a banquet."[37]

WCFL's efforts at balancing its coverage of labor disputes extended to giving business officials an opportunity to criticize unions. During the CTU strike, for example, the *Chicago Sun and Times* editor and publisher Marshall Field condemned what he considered "misguided" statements made by CTU president Pilch over WCFL. Lee, taking a neutral stance, noted how both parties had "become entangled in a mess of confusion, doubt and . . . fear engendered by the relatively new and almost incomprehensible Taft-Hartley Act." He praised Field for his "calm approach and courteous attitude" in criticizing Pilch and agreed to print Field's criticism in the newspaper and to read them over labor radio.[38] WCFL's effort to balance news reports, praise U.S. capitalism, and emphasize the achievements of a responsible labor movement coincided with a wave of anti-union propaganda during the late forties.

General strikes and other mass labor disruptions in 1945–46 intensified business anxiety over the power of trade unions. Competitive business sector officials responded with a propaganda offensive designed to "discredit the ideological underpinnings of New Deal liberalism and to undermine the legitimacy and power of organized labor." Oligopolistic corporation leaders, for their part, urged the government to redress, in their favor, what they feared was a balance of power with labor. The resulting unified business attack on labor unions produced an unprecedented wave of anti-union propaganda in the mass media and passage of the Taft-Hartley Act in Congress.[39]

Business attacks on trade unions came from both the print and broadcast media. Through its "Briefs for Broadcasters," distributed to some one thousand radio commentators across the nation, the National Association of Manufacturers defended the private enterprise system and decried labor's power. Business firms also sponsored conservative commentators who came to dominate network airwaves. A survey taken by the weekly newsletter *In Fact* revealed that, by the fall of 1947, only three "liberal" commentators remained on the networks compared to at least seven "reactionaries." The liberals—Cecil Brown and Leland Stowe of MBS and Raymond Swing of ABC—reached a combined audience of 4.5 million over some 155 stations. The reactionary commentators—including H. V. Kaltenborn and Fulton Lewis Jr.—aired over a total of 1,724 stations nationwide, via all four major networks, and reached 31 million listeners. Business-sponsored news commentary and entertainment programs attacked organized labor and the welfare state as fundamental threats to American democracy. They contended that the trade union movement had reached monopoly proportions and wielded far more political and economic power than a divided business community. A 1950 study found that the mass media inadequately treated workers and labor issues. Radio, for example, only covered so-called labor crises in newscasts and discussion programs. Radio drama programs simply ignored "the working man as a central character."[40]

Even business unionists in the AFL and the CFL worried about this vitriolic antilabor campaign. Meeting in mid-June 1947, the CFL Executive Board instructed WCFL to program more spot announcements and to make greater use of "Labor Flashes" to counteract business propaganda. The board also decided to hold a mass protest rally at Soldier Field on Labor Day. WCFL provided daily publicity for the Labor Day program. As was the case during the thirties, CFL officials sought to combine entertainment and public theater with political consciousness-raising. Over 110,000 people attended the celebration and protest, enjoying five hours of circus acts, midget automobile races, musical offerings, and a variety of performers from WCFL and other places. An assortment of union and political officials lambasted the country's antilabor climate with speeches broadcasted over WCFL both locally and nationally.[41]

WCFL became an important vehicle for disseminating information and opinion regarding the Taft-Hartley Act. Immediately prior to his dismissal, Rod Holmgren had presented a series of thoughtful analyses of the law. "Meet the Union Printers" obviously examined the act's detrimental impact on labor. Paul H. Douglas, the University of Chicago economics professor who ran on the Democratic party ticket for the U.S. Senate, discussed the fallacies of the act in a series of talks over WCFL in the spring of 1948. Through WCFL's spot announcements and programs, labor leaders urged area unionists to pressure their congressional representatives to repeal the act.[42]

Stimulated by Taft-Hartley and by the business community's aggressive anti-union media campaign, the AFL hierarchy looked to radio to improve labor's public image.[43] In the spring of 1947, the AFL sponsored three series over ABC and MBS. "The Best Things in Life," a fifteen-minute, weekday afternoon drama on the ABC network, avoided "straight union propaganda" and presented "top-notch" entertainment with talented scriptwriters and actors. "It remained," as a *Variety* reviewer explained, "for the plugs to deliver the anti-Hartley-Taft bill message and, as usual, they were punched across clearly and aggressively." "Lift Your Voices," a half-hour musical variety show that originated in Hollywood and New York, aired over ABC on Thursday evenings and over MBS on Sunday afternoons. The final series, "Labor Must Be Free," presented "outstanding . . . civic, religious, and industrial" leaders who discussed vital social issues on Tuesday evenings over ABC.[44]

This six-week (May–June 1947) intensive radio campaign cost the AFL almost $352,000 and reached approximately 645 stations nationwide. Officials purchased airtime over ABC and MBS, but NBC and CBS—whose affiliates had stronger clear-channel or regional frequencies, better facilities, and larger audiences than those of ABC and MBS—refused to sell time to the AFL on the grounds that the proposed shows would address controversial themes. The two network giants sold airtime to business firms sponsoring anti-union news commentators, but only offered organized labor sustaining time for general discussions of political and economic topics. Despite the networks' double standard, AFL radio consultant Morris Novik maintained that radio was "the last avenue of communications that has some lanes still open to labor."[45]

Seeking to expand their public relations operations in general, and the use of radio in particular, AFL leaders consulted with advertising experts during the summer of 1947. One public relations firm suggested that the AFL use radio to "mould public opinion." Incorporating labor themes into existing radio programs and sponsoring popular entertainment dramatizations of U.S. labor history would reach the "average Mr. and Mrs. America." Sponsoring cultivated, refined programs would "appeal to particular classes, namely, the businessman, the manufacturer, and the so-called elite classes." Buying "time over a national hook-up for such a [cultivated] program," according to the advertising firm, might get labor's "enemies to listen, then to wonder if their attitude toward labor might be slightly wrong, and finally to decide that labor wasn't so bad after all."[46]

AFL officials hired a professional advertising agency in the spring of 1948 rather than build their own public relations office. Owen and Chappell promised to develop and implement, among other things, a full-scale public relations campaign over radio. In its proposal, the firm suggested that the AFL might secure free access to radio by finding a noncontroversial cause to champion and thereby influencing network executives. The agency recommended that the AFL develop "programs designed to fight communism, which is one of [corporate radio's] objectives as well as one of ours." It advised against immediately airing programs that emphasized the importance of labor unions because network management might "feel less sympathetic about" such a topic.[47]

The labor federation hired Owen and Chappell because it found such advice sound and because the firm promised to obtain free network airtime for regular AFL programs, to create a series of transcribed programs for local stations, and to transform a series of fifteen-minute AFL broadcasts over the ABC network into quality entertainment. After four months on the job, however, the advertising agency had failed to deliver on any of its promises. Labor officials terminated the company's services in the fall of 1948 because they tired of spending fifteen thousand dollars on a "soporific music show with a string orchestra and 'messages' without a punch" and because the firm simply could not comprehend either "the basic ideas of the AFL" or what organized labor needed in "an effective public relations program."[48] Despite this unsatisfactory experience, the AFL hierarchy continued to search for ways of using radio "to counteract the evil effects of [antilabor] propaganda."[49]

As the AFL experienced difficulties in producing radio programs that combined both entertainment and pro-union messages, CIO unions and the International Ladies' Garment Workers' Union found effective ways to use the medium. During the 1948 presidential election campaign, for example, the ILGWU produced a four-part radio series that incorporated government officials, Hollywood personalities, and labor leaders. The fifteen-minute shows, which aired over the ABC network on Thursday evenings, combined speeches, music, and comedy. The first program opened with Humphrey Bogart attacking the eightieth Congress for its reactionary policies and urging support for President Harry S. Truman. Secretary of Labor Maurice J. Tobin then praised the ILGWU's public service, especially its efforts to fight communism in Europe, while denouncing the efforts of the Republican Congress to return the United States to a "sweatshop economy." A musical parody entitled "Have a Heart Taft-Hartley, Have a Heart," concluded the program. Participants on subsequent programs included Minneapolis mayor Hubert H. Humphrey, Harry S. Truman, and actors Tallulah Bankhead, Melvyn Douglas, and Ronald Reagan.[50]

In the spring of 1947, the United Electrical, Radio, and Machine Workers of America (UE) began sponsoring a weekly fifteen-minute news commentary program over fifty MBS stations, at an annual cost of $250,000. Leland Stowe, a journalist and commentator with liberal-to-left political views, presided over the first network news analysis series sponsored by a labor union. In the course of presenting "news and general observations on national and international events of importance," Stowe supported New Deal programs, organized labor, and anticommunism, while opposing militarism, corporate monopoly power, red witch-hunts, and antilabor legislation. The UE-sponsored program remained on the air until early 1950 and generated criticism and praise. A Chicago local, for example, was "gratified that [Stowe was] broadcasting in behalf of the working people" and that he offered informative and insightful comments on foreign affairs. On the other hand, the union wanted more time devoted to "such matters as antilabor bills as well as mentioning some victories that the UE" had achieved. Overall, the show demonstrated the potential value of union-sponsored news programming. Although they never acknowledged borrowing the idea from the red-tinged UE, AFL leaders adopted the radio news concept.[51]

In 1949, the AFL Executive Council agreed to join with Labor's League for Political Education to sponsor a nationwide, weekday radio news program with "a good first-class commentator who will give Labor's slant on the news." The AFL would fund 60 percent of the approximately $760,000 needed to broadcast and advertise the news show for one year over MBS. Secretary-Treasurer George Meany admitted that the federation lacked experience in this particular field, but he remained convinced that the proposed program "will attract a lot of attention and . . . will give another side to the picture and maybe compel those [antilabor] commentators to revise their thinking a little."[52]

After auditioning prospective newscasters during the fall of 1949, the AFL chose Frank Edwards, a versatile news and special events reporter with twenty-four years of radio experience, as its commentator. Attracted by his liberal and independent views, as well as his "vivid personality," the AFL hoped that Edwards would offer an attractive alternative to the reactionary commentators who dominated the airwaves. The AFL-sponsored news show began broadcasts in late December 1949 to 147 stations over MBS; eventually 176 stations aired the program. Critics accused Edwards of lacking good sense and good taste, while supporters found him "an outgoing, affable raconteur"; all agreed that he was "outspoken, intelligent, liberal, and informed." William Lee praised Edwards's "splendid job" and stressed that the commentator's "informative well written and well read broadcasts" generated one of WCFL's "highest listening" audiences. "I am hopeful," Lee wrote to AFL officials in early 1954, that "it is your intention to continue this program."[53]

The AFL Executive Council, however, fired Edwards in August 1954 for refusing to adhere to AFL guidelines and failing to distinguish clearly between news and opinion in his broadcasts. George Meany, an able bureaucrat who had risen to the presidency of the AFL upon William Green's death in 1952, sought tighter control over the news commentary show. He installed a formal structure in early August by appointing his man, Charles Herrold, as news editor. Edwards objected to Herrold's "censorship" powers, which included determining all the news items to be aired, checking that opinions expressed conformed with AFL policy, and separating news from opinion.[54]

Although Harry Flannery, a CBS news correspondent, temporarily replaced Edwards, AFL radio consultant Morris Novik and others recommended Edward P. Morgan as the permanent commentator. Morgan, a longtime print journalist, CBS reporter, and director of CBS radio and television news, joined the AFL show in January 1955. "Well trained in the art of shooting down the precise middle," Morgan's first broadcasts in 1955 immediately won commendation for their "good-sense and good-taste tone." The *Federation News* praised Morgan as a reasoned liberal and lauded his "straightforward, intelligent" and "well-rounded view of the world's events." Morgan remained on the air for over twelve years, winning awards for excellence in radio news and the admiration of labor officials and liberal listeners. When Morgan departed from the program in June 1967—in order to participate in the new educational television network—the AFL-CIO hierarchy discontinued regular commercial programming.[55]

The national federation paid five hundred thousand dollars a year for its fifteen-minute, weeknight news commentary show. WCFL supporters pointed out that Chicago's Voice of Labor could broadcast twenty-four hours a day while receiving millions of dollars in advertising revenue.[56]

Nevertheless, questions remained regarding labor radio's role and value in the war for the hearts and minds of the American public. Irwin E. Klass, editor of the *Federation News,* denounced the faulty labor policy of waiting until elections or crises to "leap into the stream of information." The passage of the Taft-Hartley Act and the loss of "liberal candidates" in the 1948 and 1950 elections demonstrated that labor needed to engage in public relations, both locally and nationally, year round. Klass recommended increased use of the CFL's arsenal of public relations weapons. Members of the Cook County Branch of Labor's League for Political Education agreed, urging labor unions to use the *Federation News,* WCFL, and television to "educate our own members and organize the unorganized."[57]

William Lee and WCFL managers did not embrace this strategy. They saw the public relations value of WCFL in the station's ability to attract larger audiences, more advertisers, and enhanced profits. Lee wanted "enough business to meet growing expenses" and to produce surplus revenue for the city federation. By the fifties, no CFL leader advocated a listener-supported or grass-roots radio station. "Let's not kid ourselves," confessed the executive board of the Illinois State Federation of Labor in 1958, "if the station did not solicit and accept advertising, there would be no labor-owned station."[58] Securing adequate advertising in a commercial system dominated by networks and challenged by the new medium of television posed difficulties for WCFL. But labor radio found it surprisingly easy to resolve these problems.

•   •   •

Independent radio always had operated at a comparative disadvantage when trying to compete with the networks' expensive entertainment. By the forties, those stations that remained unaffiliated or, like WCFL, maintained tenuous links with a network abandoned efforts to compete with chain programming. Instead, they produced shows that audiences could not find on the network schedules—in particular, music, sports, and news with a local or regional touch.[59] The ability of stations to develop alternative programming to that of the networks became a crucial element in determining the profitability of radio broadcasters in the age of television.

The advent of television profoundly changed radio's role as a source of entertainment and information for the mass of Americans. As the big three radio networks—NBC, CBS, and ABC—diverted their programming money, talent, and energies toward television, more and more Americans watched the new medium and purchased their own sets. The percentage of all American households that owned a television set grew from 9 percent in 1950 to almost 86 percent in 1959. Television became the entertainment of choice in the evenings and radio lost both listeners and advertisers. When television began its rapid expansion in 1948, the total income of the radio networks and the stations that they owned and operated had reached $18 million; a decade later the radio networks earned no income at all. The percentage of all advertising expenditures in the nation that went into radio fell by 50 percent between 1947 and 1956—from 12 to 6 percent. As radio stations lost their formerly mass evening audiences, the networks gradually eliminated their expensive entertainment programming. By the late fifties, virtually all of radio's top stars had abandoned their shows; several made the transition to television. Network affiliation, once coveted by the nation's radio stations, now became a liability as outlets sought greater freedom to find new and more profitable uses for their wavelengths. In 1947 almost 97 percent of all AM stations in the nation had some network affiliation; in 1956, only 46 percent did.[60]

Although network radio and, in particular, evening radio audiences—and hence profits—declined during the decade following the war's end, the number of radio stations increased. Without even considering the new stations made possible by frequency modulation (FM) broadcasting, the number of AM stations in the country increased from 919 in 1945 to 1,621 in 1948 to 2,331 in 1952. A two-and-a-half-fold increase in the number of AM radio stations combined with a dramatic decline in total radio income meant that individual radio stations received smaller and smaller pieces of a shrinking economic pie.[61]

As the decade of the fifties progressed, most Americans came to look upon the radio as a "supplemental medium, something consumed while they worked or played" or commuted from urban workplace to suburban home. The percentage of households owning radio sets, which had hovered at 80 percent before World War II, reached almost 97 percent by 1954. Radios became a more frequent sight in kitchens and bedrooms, in the workplace, and in automobiles. Approximately 29 percent of all cars contained radio sets in 1947; by 1955, 60 percent did.[62] The first stations to adapt their programming to fit radio's new functions in American society were often the same stations that had abandoned competition with the radio networks in the late forties. WCFL found itself among this group of fortunate broadcasting outlets.

The fifties and early sixties proved to be the most profitable era in the history of the Voice of Labor because officials consciously decided not to compete with network programming. Jack Odell, WCFL program director, bluntly admitted in May 1949 that "there is little to be gained by trying to combat the competition of high-budget network variety and comedy shows with low-budget carbon copies or standard juke-box fare on records." Recognizing that the "phenomenal growth of the television audience in Chicago" would exacerbate WCFL's programming problems, Odell chose a counterstrategy for prime time that emphasized entertainment not offered by Chicago's other AM stations. He believed that the "block-programming of serious music"—especially "concert music, symphonic music and excerpts from operettas and musical comedies"—would prove "a winning formula for the evening audience."[63] WCFL programmers also decided to expand coverage of sporting events. At its height, WCFL aired professional football, baseball, basketball, and ice hockey; college and high school football and basketball; horse racing; and bowling.

WCFL's schedule of music programs included live and recorded performances during the late forties and early fifties. "Music Lovers' Hour," a forty-five-minute, weeknight show of classical music recordings, had begun as a sponsored program in 1938. Supported by a local ice cream company, the show continued well into the postwar period, remaining one of Chicago's best locally produced programs. WCFL provided weekly broadcasts of the Chicago Symphony Orchestra—sponsored by a Chicago finance company. The station's own staff orchestra performed live classical music, with occasional guest vocalists, on the weeknight "Treasury of Music"—supported by a local bank.[64]

Recorded music shows featuring disc jockeys became the standard program format over labor radio and other stations during the fifties. WCFL had a "dazzling array of disc jockey talent" throughout much of the postwar era. These personalities presided over shows that had identical features: The latest record releases, interesting chatter, news and weather reports, and occasional interviews with guest celebrities. Howard Roberts's "zany antics" made his morning disc jockey shows and afternoon man-on-the-street interviews popular. Mal Bellairs maintained the "mythical ballroom" where "his happy talk," interviews with recording artists, and playing of listeners' requests made him a "favorite disc jockey."[65] Patricia Gleason, who had starred on WCFL's "Irish Hour," hosted her own daily show, "That Gal Gleason." When WCFL began broadcasting twenty-four hours a day in the fall of 1949, "The Outer Drive" (12:00–5:00 A.M.) presented Don McCarty reading news and weather reports and spinning "the latest recordings with interesting sidelights on the artists, orchestras, and musical numbers." Art

Hellyer became a popular Chicago disc jockey during the fifties. Combining "wit, charm, and an amazing sense of humor," Hellyer created "an alive, bubbling two hours of daily entertainment." Perhaps his best comedic moment came when he and an aide "'covered' the 1956 Democratic National Convention from a broadcasting booth that was obviously the men's room."[66] WCFL also picked up syndicated disc jockey programs such as "Tommy Dorsey Disc Jockey." By the end of the forties, disc jockey shows and syndicated programs constituted a significant percentage of the schedule. On Thursday, July 20, 1949, for example, 46 percent (495 out of 1,080 minutes) of WCFL airtime derived from recorded music or transcribed programs. This increased to 55 percent when WCFL went to a twenty-four-hour schedule in the fall. Two years later, three-quarters of WCFL's airtime went to recorded music.[67]

Although WCFL sought to create an alternative schedule to that of the networks, the station remained nominally affiliated with ABC and used selected network programs. On Saturday evenings in 1946–47, for example, WCFL listeners could tune in to episodes of ABC's adventure and mystery series: "I Deal in Crime," "Gangbusters," "Sherlock Holmes," "Murder and Mrs. Malone," and "Strange Wills." Even as late as 1951, WCFL aired ABC's "Space Patrol." During the early fifties, WCFL picked up a few syndicated dramatic serials including "Medal of Honor"—a fifteen-minute dramatization of the true stories of wartime medal winners—and "Bold Venture"— a thirty-minute adventure series set in the Caribbean and starring Humphrey Bogart and Lauren Bacall.[68]

WCFL produced some shows for children and adolescents. "Children's Corner," a Sunday morning program of children's records, aimed at a four-to-ten-year-old audience. Vaudeville veteran Malcolm Claire offered stories, anecdotes, and animal imitations on the "Uncle Mal Program" on weekday afternoons in 1947. "Teenage Forum," on Saturdays in late 1946, presented teen opinions on contemporary topics. Sports commentator Jimmy Evans developed a weekday show for teenagers in 1951, in which he played the week's hit songs, mentioned high school activities, and discussed problems identified by students, parents, and teachers. WCFL carried the ABC's "No School Today" for primary school children and "Junior Junction" for high school students.[69]

Talk, interview, and gossip programs remained locally oriented. Guy Savage, host of the evening show "Going Places," visited clubs, theaters, sporting events, and other city attractions during the 1947 season. He interviewed spectators and offered a free watch to the winners of a miniquiz.

Eileen Mack ("Your Sister Eileen") also informed listeners about events around town and interviewed celebrities visiting the city during 1954. Eddie Cavanaugh and Fannie Cavanaugh, the radio gossip team, had a regular fifteen-minute show over WCFL and marked their thirtieth year on radio in March 1952 with a special program. During the summer of 1951, WCFL aired "Movies for the Millions" in which *Chicago Daily News* movie critic Sam Lesner and WCFL disc jockey Myron Barg reported on motion picture news, played music from recent films, and interviewed Hollywood celebrities. A contest asked the audience to call the station and identify the excerpt from a movie soundtrack; winners received record albums. Listeners who called the program also could speak with guest movie stars.[70] Quiz shows, such as "Quick as a Flash" and "Thirty Seconds to Go," were prevalent over WCFL in the fifties. During the fall of 1956, WCFL's morning programs offered daily clues to the location of a one-thousand-dollar bill hidden in a public spot in the metropolitan area. A listener discovered the first treasure in Union Station after two days of hunting.[71]

A popular WCFL daytime program during the late forties was "Talking with Toni." The program premiered in mid-September 1947 and starred a radio actress, magazine writer, and housewife identified only as Toni. Publicity for the show emphasized that the newlywed Toni built "her show around her experiences as a young housewife," but that she knew "everything that happens in the town." Toni's husband, Sherwin R. Rogers, was an advertising executive who produced the series for his agency and played Bob on the program. Sponsored by a food company and a bank, "Talking with Toni" promoted the image of women as housewives and mothers. Toni held weekly "household hint contests" in which the housewives with the best homemaking ideas received tickets to a play of their choice. She provided recipes and "tips on saving for security from the woman's point of view" and interviewed motion picture and theater celebrities. The show proved so popular that, by the fall of 1948, it expanded from three to five days a week. Toni ended the show's run in early April 1949 because she was pregnant with her first child.[72]

Much of WCFL's daytime schedule assumed a large female audience. Disc jockey programs often included advice to help women improve their homes and families. During the spring of 1950, for example, "What's New?" sponsored by a food producer, played "the latest waxings of your favorite artists and orchestras" and provided "recipes, helpful household hints and lively chatter," including interviews with "well known folks." Betty Mattson's 1955 program added fashion discussions to this basic formula.[73] "Marriage License Bureau" began in the summer of 1950 with Martin Hogan recording interviews at the Marriage License Bureau in the Cook County Building, where Richard J. Daley served as county clerk. Hogan interviewed "future brides and grooms," searching for "the lowdown on how they met, wooed, and were won." The weekday program, sponsored by a furniture outlet, remained on the air, with a few changes and hiatuses, for over six years. It drew a large audience because, according to the *Federation News,* "the ladies of the house are interested in other people's romances—and incidentally do most of the buying of furniture and other household goods." Couples interviewed on the show received gift certificates to purchase products from the sponsor.[74]

Labor radio offered limited intellectual fare during the early fifties. "Loyola Seeks an Answer," a half-hour weekend evening program produced with the cooperation of Loyola University, presented faculty members discussing the great ideas of American civilization. During the 1950–51 season, the show analyzed "13 basic American documents which serve as the foundation of the American philosophy of life"; they ranged from the Declaration of Independence to Point Four. Later shows examined the ideas and writings of Oliver Wendell Holmes, William Allen White, Herbert Hoover, and Robert A. Taft.[75]

Together with music programming, sporting events formed the backbone of the WCFL schedule throughout the postwar era. Depending upon the season, WCFL listeners might have heard Jimmy Evans describe the exploits of college and high school basketball stars or listened to Johnny Gottselig recount the skating and scoring prowess of the Chicago Blackhawks or heard Joe Boland detail the football battles of Notre Dame and the Chicago Cardinals or followed Bob Elson's coverage of the pennant efforts of the Chicago White Sox. WCFL also broadcasted tennis championships, daily racing results, and bowling games. All of these live sports broadcasts found ready sponsors in local automobile dealerships, gasoline stations, radio and television manufacturers, cigar makers, brewing companies, soft-drink producers, finance and loan companies, bus firms, and airlines.[76]

Sports commentary shows included Jimmy Evans's daily potpourri of sports news, anecdotes, and biographical sketches; famed Olympian Jesse Owens's "smooth and relaxed microphone technique" that blended "athletic reporting with homey news items" and occasional musical recordings; and bowling authority Sam Weinstein's interviewing of local talent on "Ten Pin Tattler," which began its tenth season in September 1951. WCFL's top sports announcer and commentator remained Bob Elson, who provided play-by-play accounts of baseball and basketball games, offered a daily sports commentary show, and presided over his own daily two-hour disc jockey program. William Lee contended that sports programming had won thousands of new friends for the station and for organized labor.[77] But this programming also generated criticism. In the spring of 1954, local unions complained about the WCFL policy of postponing the commentary of the AFL news analyst in order to air White Sox games. Lee dismissed the complaints, noting that when WCFL carried the baseball games at night, it outdrew all other Chicago stations. The CFL president contended "that we have a greater audience immediately after our ball games for Frank Edwards than we do at any other time of the evening."[78]

With the creation of a department to handle news—especially local events and labor activities—in 1956, Martin Hogan completed labor radio's tripartite foundation: Music, sports, and news. In subsequent years, Hogan arranged for WCFL to use the news-gathering resources—wire services and correspondents—of the *Chicago American*. The weeknight, CFL-sponsored "Invitation to Relaxation and Labor's Daily Report" presented organ music, human interest stories, and reports on labor meetings, activities, and legislation. Hogan also brought AFL-CIO sponsored network programming such as "Labor Reports to the Nation," "Washington Report," and Edward Morgan's news commentary into the schedule.[79]

The strategy of deemphasizing labor-oriented programs and increasing the number of sponsored music shows, sporting events, and news programs aimed at making WCFL financially profitable. Hogan and Haviland pushed the station's commercialization by portraying WCFL "throughout the advertising world as an 'open door' to a huge segment of listeners" in Chicago's lucrative market. They implied that WCFL accepted only legitimate products, that listeners recognized this integrity, and that advertisers appreciated the resultant audience loyalty to WCFL. Always on the lookout for new gimmicks that would increase the station's audience and revenues, Hogan and Haviland arranged for a series of huge billboard signs extending "Seasons Greetings" from WCFL and the CFL to appear in Chicago during December 1954. Months earlier, the CFL had distributed automobile stickers with WCFL's call letters and dial location to area trade unions. Federation officers wished to have "about 200,000 of these stickers moving around Chicago every day." Hogan and Haviland also arranged the participation of WCFL personalities in the radio advertising and merchandising deals of local retailers.[80] Years earlier, Edward Nockels had considered financial problems as necessary evils; resolving them meant achieving the goal of producing quality programs for organized labor and the larger community. For William Lee, however, finances were WCFL's reason for being. The station produced programs and advertisements to generate profits to pay for CFL activities and personnel. WCFL's preoccupation with profits appeared quite clearly in the case of FM broadcasting.

Frequency Modulation radio, developed by Edwin H. Armstrong during the twenties and thirties, offered distinct advantages over Amplitude Modulation.[81] It provided a static-free signal and an increased frequency range, which allowed for high-fidelity broadcasting. An FCC report issued in 1938 verified the technical superiority of FM over AM sound. FM opened the possibility of new channels for prospective broadcasters because the FCC could locate FM stations close to each other on the electromagnetic spectrum. Depending upon frequency allocations, FM could offer as many as two thousand new radio stations in the United States. The FCC authorized commercial operation of FM in May 1940. World War II halted most FM set manufacture and station construction. Despite the freeze, by 1944, the nation had forty-seven operating FM stations, five hundred thousand sets in use, and four hundred FM applications pending.[82] Groups that had been denied access to the dominant AM network broadcasting system looked to FM as an alternative.

Labor unions took advantage of the opportunity offered by FM radio. The ILGWU, in arguments reminiscent of Nockels, urged that labor develop FM radio to stave off the danger of monopolization by corporate interests. Hoping to expand its adult education, cultural, and community service projects, the ILGWU filed applications in 1945 to create stations in New York, Philadelphia, Boston, Chattanooga, Los Angeles, and St. Louis.[83] CIO unions also voiced strong interest in creating labor radio stations. Their battles with recalcitrant industrial leaders and with AFL craft unions led CIO officials to search for their own mass media outlets to public opinion. Although the UE managed to gain access to the AM system with Stowe's news commentary show, other CIO unions turned to FM radio. The United Automobile Workers (UAW) and the Amalgamated Clothing Workers filed applications for FM station licenses in a number of cities. The UAW sought stations in Chicago, Newark, Flint, Cleveland, Los Angeles, and Detroit. In arguing for its own radio outlet in Chicago, the UAW noted how the dominant broadcasting system in the city—including WCFL—blocked CIO access to the airwaves. UAW lawyers attacked WCFL as "an archly conservative station unwilling to broadcast C.I.O. programs and highly discriminatory in its selection of labor programs of any type."[84]

CFL officials automatically filed for an FM broadcast license and just as automatically received one during World War II. WCFL's standard procedure regarding new communication technology was to secure permission to develop and use such technology and then decide whether to do so. The CFL encountered no problems securing an FM license because the FCC, already overburdened trying to regulate the existing radio system, "encouraged AM station owners to take over FM operations and duplicate their programming on these stations." Despite the FCC's acknowledgement that FM offered a potential alternative to AM, the agency relied on the established radio industry to develop guidelines for FM. Not surprisingly, the FCC treated FM "as a service that could only be secondary" to the AM system.[85]

After receiving FCC approval to develop FM broadcasting in 1944 and again in 1947, WCFL officials discussed the potential benefits and drawbacks of the new system. These discussions, which involved corporate radio experts, rarely touched on the issue of programming, but concentrated instead on the cost of FM radio versus its potential profits. CFL secretary Joseph Keenan lamented the "very spotty" and conflicting information regarding FM. The best advice that one industry expert could give Keenan was that FM would develop slowly, but that it could become a "popular and lucrative venture."[86] At a WCFL board meeting in June 1948, station officials weighed the probable costs of FM construction and operations against the increased coverage (seventy-ninety miles), which would bring a "greater sales" area and hence advertising revenue to the station. They talked about giving the FM channel to Loyola University for an appropriate reimbursement. A consulting engineer concluded that "abandoning FM would not severely affect our position in the radio field." The board eventually decided to use its wavelength and construct an FM transmitter. WCFL-FM began operation in early November 1948, broadcasting from 3:00 to 10:00 P.M. and duplicating the programs heard over WCFL-AM.[87]

With a limited financial investment in FM and a continued emphasis on AM radio, WCFL weathered the wave of FM station failures during the early fifties. Weakened by adverse FCC rulings that benefited AM radio and the nascent television industries (often one and the same) and by the phenomenal public interest in television, FM radio proved unable to compete in the commercial broadcasting market. The failure of the three FM stations established by the ILGWU cost the union close to $1.5 million. When the UAW turned its Detroit station, WDET-FM, over to Wayne State University in May 1952, WCFL regained its title as the nation's sole labor radio station.[88]

The labor unions that created FM stations did not have, as the ILGWU explained in 1953, "any illusions about the money-making potential" of their operations. They sought to use the airwaves for the welfare of union members and their communities. Nevertheless, the ILGWU and other unions hoped "to secure, on a carefully selected basis, commercial programs to help out in the maintenance budgets of our stations. The failure of the radio industry to promote FM, however, made the obtaining of paid-for programs increasingly difficult."[89] Experienced WCFL officials knew how to compete in the commercial market and they easily survived the disaster of FM broadcasting.

・ ・ ・

The financial fortunes of WCFL improved considerably during the first fifteen years of William Lee's reign. As 1954 ended, Lee presented to CFL delegates an "inspiring" financial statement on WCFL that showed "a large balance in cash and bonds." WCFL now had sufficient profits to increase the salaries of station personnel and to make necessary improvements in its equipment and facilities. Labor radio's finances were so good in 1954–55 that the station set aside funds to establish a retirement program covering all ninety employees of the CFL, WCFL, and the *Federation News*. In the spring of 1958, Lee announced that the CFL and WCFL would pay for a comprehensive health care plan for all the full-time regular employees of the federation and radio station. Lee also extended WCFL's largess to former CFL employees. Indeed, the CFL Executive Board approved a monthly allowance for the seventy-five-year-old widow of Edward Nockels in 1956. In ill health, Edna Nockels appreciated the aid. Lee explained that the "widows of many of our labor leaders are left without adequate support even though their husbands worked for years to build up" the unions.[90] Prosperity also allowed WCFL to pay its workers "over and above what any other radio station is paying for the same kind of work." By the midfifties, WCFL profits contributed half of the salaries of the CFL president and secretary. At the end of 1959, the Executive Board approved an increase of seven thousand dollars per year for each position, half coming from the CFL and half from labor radio.[91]

On the occasion of WCFL's thirtieth and the CFL's sixtieth anniversary, Lee declared the Voice of Labor the nation's "outstanding independent radio station" and pointed to WCFL's traditional commitment to serving labor, the Chicago community, and the nation. The station's support for community projects, according to the CFL president, reflected organized labor's "interest in education and civic betterment." General Manager Hogan praised the WCFL trinity of news, music, and sports. And Mayor Richard Daley lauded the "alert and intelligent" leaders of the CFL, the *Federation News,* and WCFL for their contributions to the excellent labor-management relations in the city.[92]

At CFL meetings in August and early September 1957, Lee praised WCFL officers—especially Hogan—for their efficient and profitable management of the station. The CFL president described how the station overcame tough competition, especially over sponsors, and how its financial success allowed the CFL to contribute to charities, to establish scholarships and pension funds, and to expand station facilities. Relying on voluntary assessments from local unions would have placed WCFL "in dire straits." Instead, over the past six years, WCFL had attracted 365 advertisers, boosted billings over $1 million a year, and increased salaries of some WCFL employees by 30 percent. Lee attributed much of the station's success to the formation of a ten-state regional network to cover the White Sox baseball games. Despite its commercial and popular program format, WCFL still managed to devote, according to Lee, approximately twenty-seven thousand announcements to the cause of organized labor.[93]

Not everyone concurred with Lee's rosy picture of WCFL. CIO officials in Chicago had long complained of WCFL's hostility toward their unions and few accepted WCFL's title as the Voice of Labor. Dissidents within the CFL also raised questions about WCFL's responsiveness to working-class issues.[94] At the same September 1957 meeting where Lee extolled the baseball network and its advertising conquests, critics provoked a bitter debate over WCFL's accelerated commercialization. Peter Hoban, president of Milk Wagon Drivers' Union Local 753, evoked the sacred images of Nockels and Fitzpatrick when he reminded delegates of WCFL's original goal of promoting "the idealism of labor." He criticized WCFL for becoming "too much of a business-like operation, to the detriment of union philosophy." He lamented that only after his prodding did the station mention how striking state highway maintenance employees confronted scab workers escorted by state police. Joined by jewelry worker William Lennon, Hoban reminded Lee that all affiliated unions had "equity rights in the station and, this being so, WCFL belongs to us and we are not going to let anyone take it away."[95]

The dissenters specifically objected to the failure of Lee to disclose the radio station's financial statement. They demanded to know where the station's money came from and where it went. "Some of this money," according to Hoban, "should flow into the coffers of unions on strike or into those smaller locals who have little funds . . . and not to enrich any individual or group of individuals who think the station is theirs." Lennon pointed out that CFL members did not know whether the station possessed "five cents or $5,000,000."[96] Responding to these criticisms, Lee offered to "take a walk" if the federation's delegates disapproved of his administration of WCFL's affairs. During the ensuing uproar, Lee's supporters quickly passed two votes of confidence for the president, the executive board, and the WCFL staff.[97]

When things quieted down, Lee and other executive board members defended the business operations of WCFL and their decision to keep the station's financial report a secret. On the issue of secrecy, they contended that knowledge of the station's finances might benefit competing radio stations and complicate the delicate negotiations concerning the merger of the AFL and CIO central bodies in Chicago.[98] Lee never clarified the former explanation, and it is debatable how such information might have hindered WCFL's operations in the Chicago market. The latter explanation, however, manifested the latest stage in a long battle between AFL and CIO organizations in the Chicago area.

The national merger of the AFL and the CIO in 1955 presumably would produce cooperation and eventual combination among the two organs' local affiliates. In Chicago, however, merger negotiations between the CFL and the much smaller Cook County Industrial Union Council dragged on for seven years. The opposition to the local merger came from both leadership and the rank and file. Leslie Orear of the United Packinghouse Workers of America had noted that CIO workers held a "we don't need them and they don't need us" attitude toward the merger. For their part, CFL officials remained jealous of their *Federation News* and WCFL "properties." Lee insisted on retaining absolute control over WCFL when the merger was completed and he reminded AFL-CIO officials in March 1956 that only the CFL, and not the AFL-CIO or any other group, owned and managed the newspaper and the radio station. WCFL profits served the political and economic interests of the CFL leadership and Lee refused to share control over WCFL operations and its revenues with either the CIO or the CFL rank and file. Only when the AFL-CIO Executive Council threatened to revoke the charter of unmerged central bodies—thus jeopardizing WCFL's license and profits—did Lee and WCFL management respond. The CFL and the Cook County Industrial Union Council agreed to a merger deal in the fall of 1961 and CFL delegates approved it in January 1962.[99]

With regard to the issue of too much commercialization, Lee argued that as WCFL became more successful and expanded its operations, it required additional facilities, staff, and equipment. WCFL needed funds to win sponsors from "our competitors who have envious eyes on labor's voice." Board member Morris Bialis wondered what was wrong "with unions . . . investing in sound business?" Asking delegates to be fair and practical, Bialis explained that WCFL "would be useless were it not operated on a highly efficient scale, prepared to meet competition, and geared to satisfy the demands of the general listening audience." The words and actions of CFL and WCFL leaders offered a fine defense for business unionism and for commercial broadcasting.[100]

By 1960 the Voice of Labor spoke all too rarely about workers or even trade unionism. "Invitation to Relaxation" still offered a potpourri of organ music and human interest stories and reported on labor meetings, activities, and legislation; and the "Chicago Federation of Labor News on the Air" compiled *Federation News* editorials and stories on events affecting labor and the general community. But within four years, only the retitled "Invitation to Music" presented regular labor news. WCFL carried the AFL-CIO's public affairs programming of commentator Edward Morgan and "Washington Reports to the Nation"—a weekly debate among politicians—through the midsixties. The staff insisted that WCFL now served labor through spot advertisements and claimed that approximately one-half of WCFL's 24,230 public service announcements broadcasted in 1963–64 were labor related. "Buy American" advertisements, for example, warned listeners of cheap foreign imports and urged them to purchase products made by U.S. workers. CFL officials reminded affiliated unions that labor radio would assist them in getting news of strikes or other events to their members. On the occasion of the station's thirty-fifth anniversary, William Lee contended that service to labor remained prominent among WCFL's objectives. Yet labor radio was more likely to meet this commitment through a financial contribution than through programming. In 1961, for example, WCFL and the CFL donated five thousand dollars to the University of Illinois for the construction of the Institute of Labor and Industrial Relations. Lee heralded this contribution as a demonstration of the labor movement's—and WCFL's—interest in workers' education.[101]

When citing its public service accomplishments during the decade, WCFL managers rarely listed the labor unions or progressive organizations that used its facilities. Instead they pointed to the many government, charitable, and business agencies—the U.S. Air Force Recruiting Group, the Salvation Army, the Jewish National Fund, the Chicago Association of Commerce and Industry, and so on—that had used WCFL as an outlet to the public. In 1960, WCFL staff still asserted "that there are many times during the broadcast year that programming in the public interest takes precedence over ratings." Ironically, this assurance referred to WCFL's "open door policy to religious broadcasting" and not to trade union or working-class issues.[102]

Labor radio's news department performed quality service during much of the decade. Howard Roberts, who had joined WCFL in 1943 as an announcer, led a news division that concentrated on local, state, and regional affairs. Three editors and eight reporters, often assisted by the staff of the *Federation News* for labor stories, won citations for excellence in regularly scheduled news shows, documentaries, and special events coverage. WCFL linked with MBS in 1963 primarily to pick up national and international news.[103] The news division's accomplishments included coverage of civil rights issues, a distinction that seemed at odds with general CFL policy.

Although CFL leaders supported federal civil rights legislation and efforts to end racial discrimination in the South, they were "not in the progressive vanguard" when it came to "race issues at home." Since its inception, the CFL had drawn significant support from the overwhelmingly white building trades unions, which had a long history of segregating black workers. Their allegiance with Richard Daley's Democratic party machine also meant that CFL officials had a vested interest in the extant political patronage system. When Dr. Martin Luther King Jr. asked for trade union assistance in ending Chicago's housing segregation in 1966, he received only muted commitments from William Lee and his colleagues and virtual silence from the *Federation News*. WCFL's coverage and analysis of the local and national civil rights movement, however, stood in sharp contrast to that of its parent body.[104]

WCFL had employed African-American entertainers—and exploited racial stereotypes—in its programming since its earliest days. The station expanded coverage of black community issues during the forties and fifties, with the addition of African-American commentators such as Jesse Albritton, Charles Campbell, and Jesse Owens. African-American disc jockeys began to appear on labor radio as the nation's attention concentrated on the issue of racial integration. Sid McCoy, the "silky voiced" Chicago radio veteran, joined WCFL in August 1961, turning the 12:00–5:00 A.M. time slot into one of the best jazz programs in the city. WCFL occasionally aired labor officials who discussed the issue of racial discrimination in the trade union movement. Labor radio reporters carefully followed the civil rights campaign both in the South and in Chicago. The Southern Christian Leadership Conference commended WCFL not only for its "excellent coverage" of the Chicago Freedom Movement but also for "interpreting the significance of our movement here."[105]

The discrepancy between the CFL's ambiguity toward civil rights and WCFL's coverage of the same derived from the public interest, convenience, and necessity standard. When renewing their licenses, radio stations provided information on their news and public service programming to the FCC. Neglecting an important story such as civil rights in Chicago would have raised serious doubts about WCFL's commitment to the community and thereby threatened its license. In addition, the Chicago Freedom Movement's open housing campaign coincided with a CFL attempt to secure a television license. As WCFL argued that its future television station would serve the interests of all groups in the city, a major competitor for the channel promised to serve the specific interests of Chicago's African-American community. WCFL managers had little choice but to cover civil rights stories in the city.

Labor affairs, news, and public service programming notwithstanding, the core of WCFL's program schedule remained, as Tom Haviland proclaimed, sports, "personalities and good music." For the 1961–62 season, WCFL aired college football games, the city's high school basketball championships, and the White Sox. Bob Elson covered baseball games and also played musical recordings and interviewed guest celebrities from the Pump Room afternoons and nights. Milo Hamilton described college football and offered an hour of music each day. An assortment of disc jockeys dominated WCFL's schedule from Sid McCoy's all-night jazz program to the pop tunes and Big Band music of "The Mike Rapchak Show" (9:30 A.M.–1:00 P.M.) to the traffic information, weather, and music of "The Road Show" (4:00–7:00 P.M.).[106] "One of the more quick-witted and imaginative deejays in the business" was Dan Sorkin, who began WCFL's "all-day personality parade" with his 6:15–9:30 A.M. program. When A. C. Nielsen reported that the show drew a relatively small audience, thousands of Sorkin's loyal listeners complained to the ratings company and over six hundred staged a protest demonstration. One advertising executive wrote that he knew "of at least twenty people, all in the advertising business, who constantly listen to WCFL in the morning, many of them while driving to their office."[107] Disc jockeys frequently changed, but the basic music and lively chatter format remained constant.

"Financially," Lee proclaimed in 1961, "we are the richest central body in the nation. We have over 90 employees and well over $2 million in assets as well as Radio Station WCFL which is a valuable property."[108] Indeed, the station had achieved a high point of profitability by the early sixties. Unlike network-affiliated radio stations, labor radio had made a relatively smooth transition into the television age. The very conditions that had made WCFL's first twenty-five years of broadcasting so precarious—its reliance on local music, sports, and discussion programming and its dependence on local advertising—contributed to the station's prosperity in the next decade and a half. Equally important for labor radio's well-being was the corporatist alliance that Chicago labor had reached with the city's government and business elite.

CFL leaders extolled their practical idealism. Acknowledging that differences between labor and capital remained, Lee insisted that "in the larger issues, we are truly interdependent. There can be no isolationism between labor, management and government in American society." Failure to cooperate on common problems inevitably set "the stage for class warfare" and this, asserted Lee, "is foreign to what we know as the American way of life." Labor committed itself to defend capitalism and not one of society's difficult problems could lead it "to make radical changes." CFL and WCFL contributions to the Daley machine and to "civic improvements" benefited Chicago unions in the short-run with lucrative contracts and political patronage.[109]

Lee admitted in 1963 that the CFL maintained only indirect contacts with rank-and-file members: "We try to reach the worker" and the worker's "family through" the *Federation News* and WCFL. He contended that these media outlets spoke for "Chicago area labor on all" political, economic, and social issues. But as WCFL increasingly spoke with the voice of a good corporate citizen, it no longer served as the voice of labor. At best, WCFL represented a small privileged section of Chicago's working class. Its popular entertainment and public service announcements might have promoted the good name of organized labor, but it did little to help unorganized women and minority workers, to strengthen the labor movement, or to resolve the profound structural problems and inequalities that characterized the U.S. political economy.[110]

Labor radio appeared fairly stable for a commercial station in 1966 and CFL officials praised William Lee for the station's progress. During the fall of 1964, WCFL moved its studios and offices out of its home for over thirty years, the Furniture Mart, and into the newly completed Marina City Commercial Building. Millions of dollars from the coffers of William McFetridge's Building Service Employees' Union and the federal government—courtesy of city hall—had financed the construction of Marina City's cylindrical towers on the north side of the Chicago River. WCFL's Radio Frolics continued to raise money, not for the station—because that was unnecessary—but for charity. Mayor Daley proclaimed January 11, 1966, "WCFL Day in Chicago," recognizing labor radio's forty years of "continuous broadcasting and service to the city of Chicago."[111] Despite outward signs of stability, however, WCFL was about to enter its last decade of broadcasting.

TEN

The Fall of Labor Radio, 1967–78

WCFL's demise as labor's voice paralleled the decline of the organized labor movement in the United States. The corporatist bargain among labor, capital, and the state remained viable only as long as its dominant partner reaped its due rewards. By the early seventies, as Alan Dawley has suggested, corporate capitalists faced an increasingly stagnant economy and "began to question the governing system they had sustained over the past four decades." They recognized that "the rising cost of both the 'social wage' and negotiated wage and benefit packages" reduced profits; that "rising demands for nondiscriminatory treatment" threatened corporate prerogatives; that "environmental, safety, and health regulations . . . restricted business"; and that a public questioning of U.S. imperialism weakened the protection of American capitalism overseas.[1] Dismantling the corporatist compromise appeared one way to rectify the situation.

In the early seventies came a new corporate and state assault on the working class and organized labor. Corporations decentralized their production in the industrial North and East, moving to smaller plants in the nonunion Sunbelt and, eventually, low-wage newly industrializing nations. They recruited new workers unfamiliar with union activities and used anti-union management strategies that emphasized worker individualism. At the national level, business organizations fought to deregulate the economy and maximize the prerogatives of capitalists.[2] While corporate and state policies weakened working-class organs, trade union policy itself accelerated the process.

Organized labor's adherence to the bargain with business and government, its dedication to business unionism, and its refusal to challenge the military Keynesianism that defined the U.S. political economy since the late forties made it unable to respond to the initiatives of the corporate sector and to other societal changes. The AFL-CIO leadership, for example, had no coherent policy or strategy for organizing workers—especially millions of women—in lower-wage, service sector employment or for helping "individual unions fighting plant relocation to right-to-work states." Nor could the trade union hierarchy withstand "the increasing willingness of employers to resort to illegal resistance" to labor organizing. Union-busting consulting firms flourished in the late seventies and throughout the eighties. Under their direction, businesses simply fired labor activists, refused to bargain with unions, or violated existing contract agreements. As Mike Davis has pointed out, such flagrant violations of labor rights resulted in a huge backlog in complaints before the NLRB: In 1957 the NLRB ruled that 922 employees had been illegally dismissed for union activity; in 1980, the board ordered the reinstatement of 10,333 illegally discharged union activists.[3]

The commercial mass media system, at worst, aided and abetted in the promulgation of the antilabor environment; at best, it ignored unions, making them invisible to the public. In 1979–80, the International Association of Machinists and Aerospace Workers established a media project to monitor, among other things, what the television networks were "doing *to* workers in America." A project report on entertainment programming revealed that "unions are almost invisible on television." To the extent that these shows presented images of organized labor, they depicted unions "as violent, degrading and obstructive" and unionized workers as "clumsy, uneducated fools who drink, smoke and have no leadership ability." An analysis of television news showed that strikes predominated on network coverage of unions and that strike stories ignored the background and reasons for the disputes. Network news shows rarely sought out official union or working people's positions on national issues.[4]

Things had not changed by the decade's end. Fairness and Accuracy in Reporting, a media advocacy group, commissioned labor reporter Jonathan Tasini to analyze the coverage of working people and their unions by the nation's one hundred largest circulation newspapers and the three nightly network news shows during 1989. Tasini found that "the lives of the 100 million working people . . . are being routinely ignored, marginalized or inaccurately portrayed in the media." During the more than one thousand broadcast minutes in 1989, the three network evening news programs devoted a little more than 2 percent of the total air time . . . to all workers' issues, including child care, the minimum wage, and workplace safety and health. . . . A little more than 1 percent of the total available time . . . dealt with U.S. unions. . . . Workers are virtually never interviewed or portrayed as experts, even though they are the people who know the most about safety and health issues, unemployment or equality in the factory. . . . In the absence of a strike, stories about the campaigns of workers and their unions have, with few exceptions, virtually disappeared from the printed page and TV screen.[5]

These two reports demonstrated that labor's need for alternative media had remained unchanged from the beginning to the end of the twentieth century.[6]

By the seventies, as structural economic changes, corporate ideological warfare, and labor leadership collaborationism wreaked havoc on the trade union movement, the Voice of Labor said and did virtually nothing. Labor radio proved almost irrelevant to the lives of Chicago's working-class families. But for William Lee and his colleagues, WCFL's value to the labor movement derived almost exclusively from the profits and public relations the station generated. The search for ever-higher profits led WCFL to embrace both television and rock music as strategies for success. But labor radio's participation in each marked the station's failure and ultimate death.

· · ·

The growing dominance of television as a source of entertainment and information posed familiar and unique problems for organized labor in the fifties. Some unions believed that corporate control over television threatened workers' interests. In a statement reminiscent of early WCFL advocates, the CIO argued in 1952 that labor's failure to utilize television would leave "the wealthy conservative and big business propaganda agencies . . . to present, uncontested, their reactionary viewpoints." Television also seemed to divert worker attention away from union functions and to weaken class-consciousness. Shipfitters' Local 9 in San Francisco had moved its regular meetings from Wednesday to Tuesday evenings in early 1955 so that members could watch televised boxing matches. But programs with entertainers such as Milton Berle provided other attractions for working-class viewers on Tuesdays. Local 9's secretary suggested, only half in jest, that the union have "a TV set at our meeting and conduct business during commercials." A worried George Meany acknowledged to the AFL Executive Council in 1957 the difficulty of getting workers to attend union meetings once they had purchased a television set.[7]

Spurred by the new medium's challenges and opportunities, organized labor experimented with television programming during the fifties and sixties. "Both Sides," a thirty-minute panel discussion moderated by the liberal commentator Quincy Howe, appeared in the spring of 1953. With this "first venture into television," the AFL hoped to inform the public about current problems and to call "attention to its own contributions to the general welfare in the 'commercial periods' available to the sponsor." A fifty-minute film, *With These Hands,* professionally produced by the ILGWU, aired over television stations in New York, Cleveland, and Chicago in 1952. The film dramatized the rank-and-file struggles of the ILGWU since 1910 as seen through the eyes of an elderly cloakmaker. "Americans at Work," originally made by the AFL-CIO in 1959–60, received airtime from commercial and educational stations during 1959–67. The 104 fifteen-minute episodes depicted how laborers—from bookbinders to potters—did their jobs and aimed to enhance workers' pride and to convince the public of the value of wage earners. Another AFL-CIO public affairs production, "Briefing Session," moderated by Edward P. Morgan, opened with a narrated film on a particular subject, followed by a discussion between guest experts. On the inaugural show in February 1961, advisers from the Eisenhower and Kennedy administrations debated the state of the economy. For Labor Day 1960, ABC televised the AFL-CIO's "Land of Promise," narrated by actor Melvyn Douglas and outlining U.S. economic and labor history. Independent television stations aired an updated version of the film a year later.[8]

These attempts at television programming notwithstanding, the AFL-CIO participation in the popular medium was tenuous at best. Expenditures for television amounted to only a fraction of organized labor's radio operations—and even this spending fell rapidly during the late sixties and early seventies. Between the fiscal years of 1961–62 and 1973–74, for example, total AFL-CIO expenditures for television fell from $70,327.48 to $1,380.39. The AFL-CIO's 1961–62 television budget represented only 14.5 percent of its total spending on radio; by 1973–74, this figure had fallen to only 5.9 percent.[9]

WCFL officials, on the other hand, had a long-standing interest in television, although their understanding of its potential value changed over time. During the late twenties, station engineers experimented with early forms of television as part of their effort to stay in the forefront of broadcasting technology.[10] Financial and technical problems halted much of this tinkering by the early thirties. When television became a viable broadcast medium in the late forties, the CFL once again voiced an interest in it. Officials concluded in 1950 that "television will be just as essential for the protection of Labor's interests as Radio has been." The AFL Executive Council approved, in August 1950, WCFL's bid for a television license. Matthew Woll acknowledged that WCFL was "a valuable asset to Labor" and "worth considerable money" and that it "could sustain itself if given a channel for television."[11]

While preparing its application for a television license, CFL officials tried their hands at programming. In 1952, for example, the CFL joined with the Chicago Building Trades Council and local businesses to sponsor a thirty-minute tribute to the Navy's Construction Battalions. Members of the CFL also participated in "Forum of the Air," a panel discussion program arranged by the Cook County Branch of Labor's League for Political Education. Sponsored by a local appliance store over channel 4, station WBKB-TV, the show aired on Wednesday nights. On one program in early 1952, Peter J. Hoban of the Teamsters and Joseph M. Jacobs, the labor attorney and a permanent member of the program's discussion panel, debated a corporate lawyer on the question "Should the Taft-Hartley Act Be Repealed or Amended?"[12]

The CFL's initial effort to secure a television license failed as the FCC gave priority to educational television. WCFL had applied for channel 11 in 1953, offering to turn over daytime hours to education while retaining the evenings for commercial broadcasting and whatever other purposes it wished to pursue. The following year, however, the FCC awarded the station license to Chicago educational groups. Despite losing this opportunity, the CFL gave financial support and free publicity to WTTW-TV—one of twelve educational stations in the nation by mid-1955. The AFL-CIO also supported educational television by endorsing federal grants for station and production facilities. Labor leaders complained that "commercial channels are loaded with gunslingers, private eyes and soap operas" and that educational television offered unions an opportunity to reach the public. WTTW invited labor to use its facilities, but the CFL never produced a single program for channel 11. The station did televise the AFL-CIO's "Americans at Work" series and "Briefing Session." Lee served as a member of the board of directors of WTTW and considered the station "a vital institution in our community."[13] But the CFL and WCFL wanted their own television outlet.

A new opportunity for WCFL to secure a television license emerged in the early sixties. Responding to pressure from FCC chairman Newton Minow, Congress ordered that television sets manufactured after January 1963 be equipped with ultra-high frequency (UHF) as well as very high frequency

(VHF) receivers. This rule spurred interest in ultra-high frequency broadcasting as more viewers would be able to receive UHF signals and as the available UHF channels far outnumbered desirable VHF channels. During 1964–73, the FCC approved the addition of 111 UHF stations compared to only 47 VHF stations.[14] The executive board of the merged CFL and Cook County Industrial Union Council (CFL-IUC) endorsed Lee's decision to secure UHF-TV channel 38 in Chicago. Promising to spare no effort or expense in preparing the CFL's case for a license, Lee ordered radio and newspaper employees to work on the application. The CFL submitted its request to the FCC at the end of 1964, but soon discovered that it had a competitor for channel 38. Only in 1967 did the FCC grant a license to the federation. But further delays ensued when the competitor for channel 38 appealed the FCC decision.[15] This struggle for television revealed much about Lee's commitment to quality broadcasting as well as WCFL's operations.

Chicagoland TV Company, founded by businessmen Frederick B. Livingston and Thomas L. Davis, challenged the CFL for a UHF-TV license. It wanted a station to offer programs "primarily designed to interest the Negro residents of the station's service area, with a secondary emphasis on matters of especial concern to other groups of identifiable ethnic origin in Chicago." The FCC examiner who investigated the competing applications believed that Chicagoland TV made a stronger case for securing a license than did the CFL. Testimony from ethnic groups and businesses revealed that a significant "minority . . . of foreign extraction" would welcome Chicagoland TV's proposed ethnic shows. African-American community and business representatives also argued "that a television station attuned solely or largely to the concerns of the Negro community . . . [would] not only . . . serve specialized requirements of Negroes as Negroes, but . . . [would also] present to Chicago as a whole the problems and realities of its Negro minority." The CFL offered its own community witnesses who contended that developing special programs for Chicago's blacks would "be wrong and regressive" because it meant segregation rather than integration.[16]

When comparing the management qualifications of the applicants, the FCC examiner again found Chicagoland TV the stronger of the two. Thomas Davis possessed extensive experience in radio management, having served as general manager and president of several stations in the Midwest. If Chicagoland TV received a license, Davis promised to devote his full time to the roles of general manager and sales manager. Frederick Livingston, a public relations expert with experience in radio and television production, testified that he would devote half of his time to the station's public relations, advertising, public service, and live programming. William Lee told the FCC that he too would expend half of his time on the operation of the CFL television station. He testified that he already devoted 50 percent of his time to the affairs of WCFL. Yet "his cross-examination indicated a lack of familiarity with the station's programming and other day-to-day affairs which was uncharacteristic of an operational broadcast executive. He stated that he is a regular listener to WCFL, and it appears that he regarded time devoted to this activity as time spent in the management of the station." Neither Lee nor the WCFL Governing Board appeared to manage the station, leaving that task to hired staff. The FCC examiner concluded that Lee's role in a television station would be similar to his role in WCFL.[17]

Despite a preponderance of evidence indicating the superior merit of the Chicagoland TV application, the FCC examiner recommended that channel 38 go to the CFL. The examiner, and subsequently the FCC, concluded that Chicagoland TV had failed to prove its financial capability to establish and operate a television station.[18] With final FCC approval in June 1968, WCFL-TV, under the direction of General Manager Tom Haviland, arranged for RCA to construct and install a transmitter and antenna at the John Hancock Center. The CFL Executive Board authorized Lee to borrow funds to build and operate a station. In mid-1969, the CFL signed contracts with RCA and an architectural and engineering firm for the construction of WCFL-TV.[19]

Lee's rhetoric on the role of television in the labor movement resembled that of Nockels on the subject of radio. Lee promised in 1969 that television would tell "the union story to all the people in an interesting and colorful style." WCFL-TV would use documentaries to deal with the problems facing labor and the city and would "experiment in television, with programs that will be of special interest to peoples of all ages and economic and social background." Drawing on the legacy of labor radio, Lee declared that just as WCFL "pioneered in many areas of radio broadcasting," WCFL-TV would "add new dimensions to the Chicago television scene."[20] Yet it soon became apparent that CFL leaders had few concrete ideas on how to use television and came to doubt the efficacy of labor television by mid-1970.

The evidence on WCFL's disenchantment with television is sketchy. CFL leaders may have realized that few stations made profits during their first years of operation. According to media consultant and former WGN president Ward L. Quaal, Chicago's major independent television station WGN-TV lost "tens of millions of dollars before we made the first dollar." *Feder-*

ation News editor Irwin Klass recalled that labor television confronted difficult technical and conceptual problems. Whatever the reasons, the CFL Executive Board already had discussed alternative uses for channel 38 by the fall of 1970. At a November meeting, the board recommended that CFL delegates allow officials to negotiate with the Zenith Corporation to take over and develop channel 38 as Chicago's first regular subscription television operation.[21]

Zenith had been advocating pay-TV since the forties, when it designed the "Phonevision" system. Tested in Chicago in the early fifties, the system sent scrambled television programs over the air that viewers could unscramble with a specially purchased telephone-signal device. Drawing on company claims that "pay-TV would provide new kinds of programming," Lee argued that the service had the potential of creating new employment and reviving the stagnating motion picture industry and other depressed entertainment sectors. The Executive Board concluded that this was a better use of the television license than developing a labor station. Although the printed reports of the November meeting contained no reference to finances, there is little doubt that the question of costs and profits entered into the CFL's final decision.[22] In exchange for channel 38, Zenith agreed to reimburse all the "expenses [the CFL] has incurred in the construction of the station up until the consummation of the sale—or $2 million whichever is greater." The deal never materialized, however, because Zenith backed out. Chicago labor officials eventually found a buyer for channel 38. The Atlanta-based religious organ, Christian Communications of Chicagoland, Inc., purchased the station for $850,000, plus the assumption of remaining equipment obligations (another $150,000), in August 1975. The FCC approved the license transfer in early 1976 and WCFL-TV left the television world without broadcasting a program.[23] WCFL's failed television venture coincided with a dramatic alteration in its radio operation, one that enjoyed initial success, but proved disastrous over time.

• • •

Every aspect of the radio industry had changed during the fifties in response to the rapid development and expansion of television. As networks shifted their energy and resources to television programming and advertising, they ignored radio. Local stations affiliated with the networks and dependent on those networks for programming found themselves with more and more free time. Increasingly they duplicated the programming of independent stations of the forties, such as WCFL; that is, they featured music, sports, and news aimed at the widest and largest possible local audience. Other outlets began experimenting with specialized formats. During the fifties radio stations dedicated to country-and-western music, rhythm and blues, classical music, and, in some cases, news expanded. "Top 40," or rock radio, emerged around 1952–54. It revolved around the repeated playing of "hit tunes"—as measured by record sales—incessant jingles, and brief weather and news. The number of rock stations in the country grew from about twenty in 1955 to hundreds by 1960. As the movement toward specialized radio formats intensified, the rock-and-roll genre proved popular among that significant demographic segment known as the postwar baby boomers.[24]

The move to specialized radio audiences in the Chicago market left WCFL with declining ratings and profits by mid-decade. In response to this crisis, General Manager Ken Draper, with Lee's support, altered WCFL's format during 1966. Draper talked about creating "a more aggressive and prestigious image" for labor, but he adopted a genre designed to maximize advertising dollars. With a new Top 40 (all-hit) rock music format, WCFL sought "to capture Chicagoland's 18-to-35-year-old audience, to be Chicago's number one radio station and to enhance the station's profitability." Abandoning the "adult" music and blocks of discussion and interview programs for rock music brought immediate benefits: Audience surveys in the spring of 1967 rated WCFL as Chicago's number one contemporary, non-ethnic radio station. At the same time, WCFL set the highest gross billing record in its history. Lew Witz, who had served as WCFL's general sales manager since February 1968, replaced Draper as station manager in August. The knowledgeable Witz, with ten years of broadcasting experience, accelerated the transformation of WCFL.[25]

By the early seventies, Chicago's ratings war for the rock music audience had intensified. With the assistance of ABC consultants and the introduction of the basic rock music paraphernalia ("an echo chamber, a tight playlist, . . . more personality DJs," and jingles), clear-channel "Musicradio WLS" soon rose to the top of Chicago's pop music ratings. WCFL and WLS became, as one columnist described it, "locked in a death fight for the local rock audience." Witz did his best to win. In 1972, he "pirated" "super-jock" Larry Lujack and program director John Rook away from WLS. Committed to the philosophy of more music and less talk, Witz helped WCFL pull even in the ratings with WLS by 1974.[26]

While embracing WCFL's commercial success, CFL officials insisted that labor radio constituted "a most valuable tool for unions in communicating with their members and the general public." Lee reminded local unions that WCFL newscasts highlighted labor news and that a "Comment Line" allowed listeners to voice their views on any subject to the community at large. Insisting that WCFL remained interested "in your problems and your ideas," Lee urged unions to use the station's facilities and offered the full cooperation of station staff "in preparing the story and timing it for broadcast." The CFL president did not ignore the station's new "youth" orientation and, at an October 1973 CFL meeting, reported that WCFL "continues to draw an ever-growing audience, especially among younger people, whom the trade union movement is trying to reach." But there was never any evidence that Lee used the popularity of WCFL among teenagers and young adults to impart a labor message. AFL-CIO president George Meany, outraged over the station's format change, often questioned what rock and roll had to do with the labor movement and, on at least one occasion, publicly lambasted the station for abandoning the legacy of Edward Nockels.[27]

The rhetoric of Lee and other CFL officials notwithstanding, WCFL's commitment to rock music, "youth power," ratings, and profits all served to further erode the station's remaining public service programs. Managers of Top 40 stations considered FCC obligations to carry local news as bothersome and restrictive. Like his counterparts elsewhere, Lew Witz sought ways to circumvent these public service responsibilities in order to play more music. When WCFL applied for license renewal in 1970, it indicated a plan to reduce its news programming by five hours per week, contending that it still offered fifteen hours of news shows per week, or 9.2 percent of the station's total program schedule. Within a few years, however, WCFL became notorious for broadcasting an excessive number of commercial messages and for falsely logging and classifying entertainment shows as public affairs programs. From 1970 to 1975, Chicago-area citizen groups opposed the renewal of WCFL's license because labor radio "had dealt with its listening public in bad faith."[28]

The Better Broadcasting Council, Inc., the Task Force for Community Broadcasting, and the Illinois Citizens' Committee for Broadcasting asserted that they represented the Chicago radio audience and, in particular, minority group members. They condemned WCFL for its inadequate effort to ascertain the interests of Chicago's minorities and for reinvesting insufficient portions "of its profits and revenues into locally originated and community-oriented programming." Challenging WCFL's classification of telephone call-in shows as public affairs programming, these groups rejected the rationale that the shows gave listeners the opportunity to express their opinions on local, national, and international issues. The critics concluded that even if WCFL aired all the 102 questionable documentaries promised in its renewal application, labor radio's public affairs programming still would account for less than one-half of 1 percent of the station's weekly schedule. Another criticism of WCFL was that it scheduled its public service programs at unreasonable hours. The 1973 license application indicated that WCFL aired approximately five hours of public affairs programming during a week, of which four hours fell between 1:00 and 5:00 A.M. and one hour between 10:00 and 11:00 P.M. From August 15, 1972, to August 15, 1973, WCFL aired 84 percent of its public affairs programs between 4:00 and 5:00 A.M. WCFL responded that it regularly broadcasted a one-hour public affairs program at 10:00 P.M. on Sundays and that it had sufficient editorials, news, documentaries, and religious programs. Station officials also contended that they had a large potential audience of radio listeners at all hours because Chicago's laborers worked around the clock.[29]

Challenges to WCFL's license came to naught. In the fall of 1974 the FCC ruled in favor of WCFL and against the complaining citizen groups. The petitioners appealed the decision and the issue came before an administrative law judge who dismissed all charges against WCFL in the spring of 1975. Like the FCC, the judge found that "program classification is not an easy task" and that "WCFL did not deliberately misrepresent the extent of its public affairs programming."[30] In the process of fending off attacks, WCFL officials offered an important glimpse into the station ideology and strategy.

Upon taking charge of WCFL in 1968, Lew Witz ordered the station to redress its apparently inadequate public affairs programming. Responding to Witz's order, News Director John Webster developed a forum for discussing and debating controversial issues. Webster's "Contemporary News in Depth," which required "an appreciable amount of time and money," aired Sundays from 10:00 to 11:00 P.M. beginning in July 1968. WCFL produced 125 segments of the show and obtained an additional 17 programs from Metromedia News Network during the 1968–70 license period. Poet Allen Ginsberg, musician Duke Ellington, football commissioner Pete Rozelle, civil rights activist Jesse Jackson, and Senator Hubert Humphrey were among the many people interviewed. Discussion topics included Native American issues, the Vietnam war, lead poisoning, the 1968 political conventions and riots, Dr. Martin Luther King, flying saucers, the Cuban revolution, drug addiction, baseball, the Black Panthers, the labor movement, and the environment. "The Big Pitch," broadcasted on January 26, 1969, examined different forms of government propaganda, including armed forces' recruitment advertisements—and the FCC policy of recognizing them as public service programs—and news reporters' collaboration with military, intelligence, and police agencies. This thirty-minute show required eighteen hours of work on the part of two WCFL news staff members.[31]

The Sunday night public affairs documentaries did not last very long. By 1969–70, Witz had begun to replace discussions of contemporary issues with difficult-to-classify informational and entertainment shows. Witz and the program staff proudly unveiled a series of "rockumentaries" beginning in May 1969. These programs, which continued through the early seventies, placed the development of rock music in a superficial historical and social context. Station staff classified them as public affairs programs because, according to Witz, popular music was an art form, an example of an indigenous national culture. The rockumentaries reviewed the development of popular music from jazz to rhythm and blues to contemporary music, describing each stage as a distinct form and demonstrating the logical progression of the various musical movements. WCFL staff argued that "very few of the musical selections used on these programs would normally have been aired as entertainment" because of the station's focus on an audience under thirty-five years of age. A few rockumentaries received advanced preparation (i.e., they were prerecorded and edited) and all of them remained free from commercials and weather or time checks.[32]

The rockumentary series began with "Pop Goes the Music." Airing on Sunday nights from May until late August 1969, the show traced the history of popular music from 1956 to 1968. Host Dick Biondi, who had helped to build a rock audience for WLS during the early sixties, introduced the top records for each year, explained why he had chosen each song, and included a personal anecdote about the music or the performer. A typical show contained about twenty-four minutes of music and five minutes of talk. "Dick Biondi Labels the Blues," an eight-week show, commenced in September 1969 and described the history of the blues and its impact on contemporary music. Biondi selected the records of various African-American artists who had performed during the late forties and early fifties. The prerecorded and edited program had a written script and consisted of one-third talk and two-thirds music. In "This Is Elvis," which replaced the blues program, Biondi offered commentary on the life of Elvis Presley for about 30 percent of the show and played Presley's recordings in the remaining time. The rockumentary "In the Beginning" aired at 1:00 A.M. from May 1970 until May 1972. Biondi again ad-libbed comments on the history of popular music from the late forties through the early sixties. His personal recollections of artists and their music constituted approximately a third of the show, with recordings making up the rest. Witz admitted that station staff had incorrectly classified this rockumentary as public affairs.[33]

Dick Biondi presided over two other questionable public affairs programs. "Dick Biondi and Friend" aired from January 1970 to May 1972 on Sunday nights at 10:00. In this interview program, produced by the station's music department, Biondi supposedly asked guest entertainers about the "current problems facing today's youth and nation." Although "for the most part Mr. Biondi sought to elicit social commentary from his guests," a significant portion of the show allowed entertainers to talk about and to play their music. The "Biondi Vietnam Show," a one-hour afternoon program that began in July 1968 and continued into 1970, offered Chicago-area families the opportunity to send five-minute messages to their relatives serving in Vietnam. Messages included a greeting and a song request, which Biondi played. WCFL staff considered this telephone talk show a public affairs program because Biondi occasionally commented on the Vietnam situation and informed overseas military personnel of events in Chicago. WCFL sent copies of each program to the Armed Forces Network for rebroadcast in Vietnam.[34]

In contrast to these questionable public affairs shows, the news and sports departments provided some quality programs. During the late sixties, for example, WCFL received recognition from the Associated Press for its regularly scheduled noon news show, special events news coverage, and a documentary on the antiwar movement. The AP Awards for Illinois Radio Stations cited WCFL for Best Regularly Scheduled Sportscast, Best Documentary, and Best Enterprise Reporting in 1972. The Illinois Association of Press Broadcasters gave WCFL its Best Local Special Events, Best Sports Show, and Best Sports Documentary awards in 1974. Street reporters such as Jeff Kamen and Carole Simpson also received praise for their work. One-minute editorials addressed important local issues such as antipoverty campaigns, labor organizing and strikes, and jobs for Chicago youth. Talented reporters and quality documentaries notwithstanding, WCFL's image as "Chicago radio's 'sewer' of news and public affairs" steadily grew.[35]

At 8:00 P.M. Chicago time, on August 8, 1974, President Richard Nixon became the first sitting U.S. president to announce his resignation from office. It was a significant news story. WCFL ignored the event, broadcasting music and time checks until 11:30 P.M. Only at that late hour did the news department broadcast a half-hour special on the day's historic events. General Manager Witz later explained that because Nixon's resignation was a foregone conclusion, the actual announcement was not news: "The Chicago radio market-place was provided with more than ample coverage of the whole thing. I figured, why not just continue to program for our very young night audience? . . . We did not interrupt our music. I guess it was an oversight, but I don't think the oversight was that significant."[36] *Chicago Tribune* media critic Gary Deeb considered the oversight an egregious example of Witz's "litany" of "atrocities" that had "transformed WCFL from a bright, civic-minded 50,000 watt rock powerhouse into a sonic slum."[37]

The CFL's gamble to make WCFL profitable as a Top 40 rock music station ultimately failed. WCFL "took a heavy bath in red ink throughout 1975." After a decade fight, WLS emerged as Chicago's sole mass appeal rock station. Witz announced in February 1976 that, effective March 22, WCFL would become a "beautiful music" station. On behalf of the CFL, Witz explained that the station sought to develop programming "more in keeping with the needs of the labor movement and the community at large." Staff employees found the transition from rock to beautiful music painful. Many remained unaware of the station shift until Witz's formal statement. Station managers fired disc jockeys who lacked "no-cut" contracts with one week's severance pay for each year of service to the station. Witz abruptly dismissed two disc jockeys for discussing the impending station changes over the air. WCFL's new public service orientation apparently did not include news. For seven years Witz had slashed both the length and quality of WCFL newscasts. In early March 1976, WCFL's news director, Mike Rollins, resigned after learning that the new "automated Muzak" format did not require a news department.[38]

Although Witz virtually eliminated the station's news department, he did oversee the introduction of new labor-oriented shows into the schedule. Irwin Klass, consulting editor of the *Federation News*, moderated a Sunday evening interview show that first aired in the spring of 1976. WCFL also began a series of daily spot announcements saluting a labor leader or local union or a group of workers. William Lee claimed that "Focus 1000," an evening call-in show, would establish "live dialogue with our listeners on a variety of subjects" and thus draw attention to community problems. In early 1977, a radio news magazine show entered the Sunday schedule before Klass's program.[39] After decades of watching the deterioration of WCFL's labor and public service principles, Lee still contended in 1977 that labor radio "merits broader support from working families than it has been receiving."[40]

WCFL's shift to an automated "beautiful music" format may have served a number of related goals. It slashed station expenses—especially in the areas of programming and personnel—and thereby cut the losses experienced during the latter years of rock radio. Lee and the CFL-IUC hierarchy may have hoped to use the reduced cost of "elevator" music to revive WCFL's capacity to produce revenue for the Chicago area labor movement. If this was so, they were sorely disappointed. The restyled WCFL generated marginal profits at best.[41] Lee may have desired to return to WCFL's glory days as a labor station. He frequently urged CFL-IUC affiliated unions, their members, and their families to use the Voice of Labor and to listen to the labor programs. Whatever the merits of Klass's "Labor Forum," "Focus 1000," the Sunday radio news-magazine program "Weekend 1000," and Chicago Teachers Union president Robert Healy's semimonthly "As We See It," however, they failed to convince local labor or advertisers to tune in to and utilize WCFL.[42]

The most likely goal of the shift to the automated music format was to cut station losses while trying to sell WCFL. The aging and ailing Lee—eighty-one years old in 1976—"felt almost helpless with a board of directors that didn't know the [radio] business [and] with management that obviously wasn't delivering a profit."[43] The city federation's leadership concluded, perhaps as early as the fall of 1975, that it devoted "too much time to the station's problems with too little financial return." Having decided "to get out of the radio business," Lee asked Richard Daley for assistance in selling WCFL.[44]

Mayor Daley, acting as an intermediary for his old friend, contacted Ward L. Quaal in the winter of 1975–76. The former vice president and president of WGN Continental Broadcasting Company (1956–74) headed his own media consulting firm in Chicago. Several months earlier, and at Daley's request, Quaal had assisted WCFL in securing an FCC extension for the completion of the transfer of channel 38 to Christian Communications. Daley told Quaal that Lee needed help finding a buyer for the radio station. Quaal, according to the trade journal *Broadcasting*, became the "man behind [the] scene" in the eventual sale of WCFL. As Quaal later explained, "I took the Chicago Federation of Labor out of broadcasting."[45] But selling WCFL proved a difficult task. The station's "unusually generous union contracts" for its employees produced one snag in sales negotiations. Another obstacle was the federation's asking price, somewhere between $11 and $15 million.[46] With his extensive knowledge of the broadcasting field, however, Quaal identified the Amway Corporation and its recent acquisition, MBS, as a party that might want to own a radio station in Chicago.

Amway, a Michigan-based marketer of vitamins, jewelry, cosmetics, soaps, cleaners, and other household products, approached $1 billion in annual sales by the late seventies and early eighties. Its two founders, Richard DeVos and Jay Van Andel, supported conservative political and social causes—including the right-wing evangelical Christian movement and the antilabor National Right to Work Committee. Amway reflected the values of its owners in its explicitly anti-left and anti-liberal propaganda, its suppression of dissent within its own organization, and its hostility to worker collective action.[47] Amway purchased MBS for $18.5 million in 1977 in part to form an "alternative network" to "restore balance" to the "slanted media." MBS consisted of over eight hundred affiliated radio stations, but it owned no outlets. Quaal suggested that WCFL could provide MBS with a fitting flagship station. Negotiations between the CFL-IUC and Amway proceeded.[48]

With the CFL-IUC Executive Board's approval to take whatever action he deemed appropriate with regard to the station, Lee moved to sell WCFL to MBS. A special meeting of the board convened at 3:00 P.M. on Monday, April 3, 1978; it adjourned at 4:20 P.M. having approved the proposed sale. Lee then consulted with AFL-CIO president Meany, who had long held that "labor should not be involved in business"; he concurred with the sale decision. CFL-IUC delegates attended a special meeting on Friday, April 7 at 7:30 P.M. They heard a summary of the special board meeting; they listened to Lee briefly recall the "rough," "uphill battle" to keep WCFL on the air; and then they voted. Apparently without a dissenting voice, the delegates approved WCFL's sale. Lee lamented for one last time that Chicago had too many professional radio stations, that the CFL was in over its head, and that selling the station would benefit the federation. The entire meeting took seven minutes.[49] The following week, at the NAB convention in Las Vegas, Lee signed the deal with MBS president Edward Little. Amway president DeVos officially announced that MBS had purchased WCFL for $12 million. Lee insisted that WCFL would grow, develop, and expand its services "under the leadership of the world's largest radio network." In any event, the CFL now could "concentrate on our main mission, labor problems," of which there were plenty in 1978.[50]

The announced sale of WCFL coincided with a period of stagnation for Lee and the CFL. Relations between city hall and local trade unions seemed threatened ever since the death of Richard Daley in December 1976. The loss of Lee's personal friend and political ally seriously undermined the quid pro quo that had guaranteed private-sector wage rates for the city's workers and labor leader participation in urban decision-making in exchange for labor peace and labor's support for the political machine. When Jane Byrne became mayor in the spring of 1978, the city hall–labor alliance inexorably fell apart, culminating in Byrne's decision to drop Lee from the politically important Chicago Park District Board in April 1980. In a classic understatement, Lee responded to the mayor's devastating action by observing that "our relations [with city hall] are not as nice as they used to be."[51]

At the same time that the CFL found its ties with local government weakened, it experienced an assault from the federal government and a growing indifference among its own rank and file. Extensive investigations during 1978 detailed labor racketeering and crime-syndicate corruption in Chicago unions. A Justice Department official characterized corruption in the city's unions as "among the worst in the country." CFL leaders responded to these allegations with the weak statement: "We have no control over our affiliates." Lee's failure to address the racketeering problem and his inability to manage the old local corporatist alliance produced no significant movement in the CFL to unseat him. At age eighty-three, Lee won his ninth term as federation president in May 1978. Even acknowledging, as Lee's supporters frequently did, the CFL president's "outstanding" record on behalf of labor, the lack of opposition to the status quo during a period of great upheaval revealed a dispirited and ambivalent rank and file.[52] In this context, the loss of WCFL seemed only to highlight the CFL's dwindling power and prestige.

Questions about labor radio's sale exacerbated the CFL's public relations problems. Accusations of possible MBS "anticompetitive practice in Texas" and an ongoing Federal Trade Commission proceeding against Amway delayed FCC approval of the sale. Lee tried to repel criticisms that both Amway and MBS abhorred labor unions and engaged in anti-union activities. MBS's support for a nonunion shop at its Arlington, Virginia, national news center proved particularly embarrassing to organized labor. The FCC gave its final blessing to the transaction in mid-1979. CFL officials eventually used the $12 million sale price to expand the size of the federation staff and to move CFL headquarters to more spacious surroundings in the new Prudential Building on Michigan Avenue. It is dubious whether these expenditures improved organized labor's position in the city or helped striking printers in the mideighties.[53]

In July 1985, some 240 printers, supported by 760 press operators and mailers, went out on strike against the *Chicago Tribune*. Refusing to abide by a 1975 agreement in which the printers' union secured lifetime employment for its members in exchange for the introduction of labor-saving technologies, the powerful Tribune Company sought "to gain greater control over hiring and assignments in the composing room." Whether the company consciously fomented a strike in order to crush the unions is debatable. But it used the strike to bring in "permanent replacement workers," mostly female and minority males, who received considerably lower wages and benefits than the overwhelmingly white male union workers. The strike lasted forty months, resulted in a defeat for the printers' union, and took place in virtual media silence.[54] Local newspapers carried occasional reports on the conflict, but none allowed the striking unions a public forum. The CFL supported the strikers, but few people outside the labor movement knew of the battle. Unlike their comrades in the forties, the printers of the mideighties did not have access to a broadcasting station willing to carry their message to the public at large.

Labor radio was dead and WCFL soon followed suit. New management did not halt WCFL's decline. MBS shifted WCFL to an all talk/news format in 1978–79, but soon discovered that successful news radio required a capital investment at least 50 percent higher than the $4 million budget. Ratings fell and MBS looked for new ways to generate profits from WCFL. In the fall of 1980, MBS switched the station from nonmusic programming and announced a new commitment to make WCFL into a profitable adult contemporary music station. This decision proved ill-timed because FM radio, with its clearer, sharper signal, had developed as the favorite of music listeners, while AM radio turned more and more to nonmusic formats.[55] WCFL's ratings and profits continued to decline and so did MBS's interest in the station. In 1983, MBS sold WCFL to Statewide Broadcasting, which turned it into a religious music station. WCFL proved no more successful as an evangelical Christian outlet than it had as a news station; it consistently finished near the bottom of the Chicago ratings. To strengthen its financial situation, Statewide merged with Heftel Broadcasting—operator of Chicago FM station WLUP—at the end of 1986. At 12:01 A.M. on Wednesday, April 29, 1987, WLUP-FM assumed management of WCFL-AM. The former Voice of Labor became adult rock station WLUP-AM, "Chicago's the LOOP AM 1000."[56] The last artifact of Chicago labor radio, the call letters WCFL, disappeared from the scene.

The Mixed Legacy of Labor Radio

In the spring of 1930, Roger Baldwin, head of the American Civil Liberties Union, and Upton Sinclair, the radical writer, discussed radio's role as an educational and propaganda tool and, in particular, the activities of the nation's two alternative stations—Chicago's WCFL and New York's WEVD. According to Baldwin, the high cost of operating a radio station necessitated advertising, and the mere acceptance of advertising commercialized the outlet. The public's demand "for entertainment rather than information" required that even alternative radio compete "with other stations on a very low level of so-called entertainment." WCFL and WEVD, contended Baldwin, devoted a large proportion of their programs to "musical entertainment of the jazz variety in order to attract listeners." The "serious stuff" was "fed in small doses in between." Competing with national radio networks compounded these problems. Corporate stations received favorable wavelengths from the state, possessed ample resources to secure highly paid artists, and thus easily commanded "a continuous public hearing" for their propaganda. Small stations, lacking economic and political power, found it "impossible to carry the cost of rival programs of enough merit to attract a similar public." Baldwin also lamented the "difficulty of organizing control of a station so that it does not become the organ of one point of view or party." He accused WCFL and WEVD managers of violating free speech rights over the air and inhibiting the democratic operation of their stations in their effort to serve specific constituencies.[1]

These criticisms of WCFL and WEVD implied that radio stations freed from the commercial obligations of the marketplace might develop an ideological orientation stressing community involvement; produce intellectual, aesthetic, and generally uplifting programming (the "serious stuff"); and practice participatory democracy. Baldwin wanted radio to be open to all citizens and especially those groups traditionally neglected by the established mass media. Other progressives and radicals sought radio that possessed both democratic form and content, where station decision-making practices and procedures were open, and where the final cultural product reflected a diversity of opinions. If alternative radio was to engage in two-way communication and if it was to help the powerless achieve power, it would have to be decentralized—easily controlled by, and readily available to, its users.[2]

Whatever their progressive and democratic orientation, alternative media have had to contend with the daily economic and political constraints of capitalist society. Financial constraints, as Baldwin and others recognized, created a constant tension between alternative radio's ideals and needs. During the first half of the twentieth century alternative radio stations resolved the financial dilemma by seeking the support of listeners or a patron. (Later in the century, limited government sponsorship became an option.) Such support usually meant a "dependency relationship."[3] Political constraints came in the form of regulation and manipulation by state agencies and commercial broadcasters. In addition, the very task of organizing and allocating scarce resources necessitated making a trade-off between internal democratic decision-making and a certain level of efficient operations. The contradiction between alternative radio's ideological orientation and the socioeconomic and political environment in which it operated ultimately shaped the medium, as the case of WCFL has demonstrated.[4]

Nevertheless, Baldwin dismissed WCFL too easily. Edward Nockels believed that labor radio should serve to educate and inform the public, to help organize workers, to entertain listeners, and to challenge the capitalist media. He sought to serve three intersecting groups: Trade unions, workers (and farmers), and the community at large. Using these criteria, the ones that Nockels set for himself and his project, one finds a far more mixed assessment of WCFL than that offered by Baldwin.

Labor radio faced the alternative-media contradiction between its democratic potential and the social constraints of its era. By challenging the capitalist owned and operated broadcasting media, WCFL held democratic potential. As a radio station of workers, their families, and the general public,

WCFL promised to discuss the major economic, social, and political issues of the day; to advance progressive forces of social change; and to open dialogue among members of Chicago's working-class communities. All this was to be achieved with active community participation and support.

The WCFL battle against commercial broadcasting constituted the "good fight," especially when examined within the context of capitalist society and AFL collaborationism. CFL leaders during the first third of the twentieth century struggled against the corporate radio giants and their state servants. While Nockels never had the creativity of a Bertolt Brecht with regard to the two-way functioning of radio, he shared the vision that radio should be a tool for popular education, social justice, and community development.[5] Nockels felt that labor radio had to reach out to a wide audience. He acknowledged, from the very beginning, the importance of popular programming, not as a source of generating revenue, but as a legitimate offering for the listening public. Baldwin and other liberal critics of popular culture lamented radio's failure to present the high cultural and educational programs necessary to uplift the masses. Nockels, never arrogant enough to presume what was best for the working class, argued only that labor deserved the opportunity to receive a wide variety of entertainment, educational, and political programs.

The efforts of Nockels and others to maintain a progressive, independent labor radio station forced them to confront the limitations of a capitalist political economy. As Baldwin correctly observed, the very structure of commercial broadcasting made it difficult for WCFL and other alternative forms of broadcasting to take root and survive. Nockels exacerbated this problem by believing it necessary to play the corporate broadcasting game, to make WCFL into a regional and eventually a national station. But competing with the networks on their terms required massive amounts of capital to purchase sophisticated equipment and hire talented writers, producers, and actors. Securing such finances, especially in the context of a weakened labor movement in the twenties and the Great Depression in the thirties, made it impossible for labor radio to survive as a listener-supported station. Nockels sought a "dependency relationship" with the AFL or NBC, as commercial considerations came to dictate decision-making.

Nockels initially hoped that the AFL would act as WCFL's patron. But such a relationship carried with it great liabilities. AFL business unionists saw radio as another tool in transforming workers into good consumers and in convincing business and government that labor was "responsible." Even if Nockels had been able to win full AFL support and state approval for

WCFL's labor network, labor radio would have been grossly undercapitalized. All this was a moot point because the AFL hierarchy never accepted the need for labor radio. Constantly frustrated by national labor leaders' ambivalence, if not outright hostility, toward WCFL, Nockels returned to the marketplace. WCFL increasingly came to depend on advertising, while attempting to work out financial, marketing, programming, and management deals with NBC and a third major commercial network. Such actions marked the inexorable destruction of labor radio's potential as an alternative to the commercial mass media.

Once WCFL officials shifted the financial base of the station from labor union and community support to advertising, they fundamentally altered labor radio. In its early years WCFL attempted to maintain close contact with its community, seeking local talent for ethnic hours, announcing area labor activities, maintaining a virtual open door for labor and progressive groups, and attempting to develop class-conscious programming. Nockels reluctantly allowed advertising on the station to keep it on the air. The Great Depression–induced financial crises, the rapid rise of powerful commercial radio networks, and Nockels's own grandiose dreams of a national labor broadcasting chain forced WCFL into a second stage of development by the early and middle thirties. Sponsored programming increasingly pushed labor, civic, and educational shows into smaller, less desirable time slots or off the air.

From the midthirties to John Fitzpatrick's death in 1946, WCFL used more and more network programs. The station aired labor shows, especially in the context of the organizing campaigns of the New Deal era. But WCFL staff urged labor to sponsor popular programs and sell unions in commercial slots. Profits became important to stabilize WCFL's financial situation. William Lee's presidency coincided with the apparent triumph of organized labor's corporatist compromise with capital and the state and with the advent of television and the decline of radio. Station officials altered the program format, switching from classical music to sports to rock and roll. WCFL offered fewer labor programs, not only because they generated no profits, but also because, in the context of the labor-capital bargain, such programming seemed superfluous. Even labor union sponsorship of "popular" programming declined. Station managers became preoccupied with maximizing profits. Lee rationalized the policy by arguing that radio revenues supplemented the wages and benefits of CFL and WCFL officials and supported federation projects.

WCFL's commercialization also threatened the participatory democra-

cy that Nockels and Fitzpatrick had championed in the twenties. During
its infancy WCFL opened its broadcast facilities to all parts of Chicago's
progressive and labor community. Station officials responded to executive
board decisions and to delegate votes at CFL meetings. When Nockels unilaterally offered to turn WCFL into a municipally owned and controlled
station in 1927, rank-and-file delegates revolted and secured a resolution
requiring that actions affecting WCFL be put to a referendum vote of the
local unions that had contributed to the station. Such concern for rank-and-
file participation decreased as profits came to define WCFL's existence and
business unionism came to dominate CFL thinking. Nockels's various efforts to secure the survival of WCFL during the early thirties—including
the provisional deal with NBC in 1932—received no discussion at CFL
meetings. To circumvent union participation in radio decision-making, the
CFL executive changed labor radio's organizational and financial structure
in 1934. Under William Lee's direction, CFL officers took absolute control
of WCFL, rejecting the notion that the city central body's members had a
right to know the internal workings of the station. Compared with the
detailed and open discussion that preceded the creation of WCFL in 1926,
the 1978 sale of the station was a quick and quiet affair.

Nockels's opposition to the growing power of the capitalist broadcasting industry led him to advocate a number of alternative plans. While most
of his energy went to support a national labor network, Nockels acknowledged that total public ownership of radio was preferable to corporate
domination. He also suggested, at the beginning and at the end of his radio crusade, that all radio stations should be local stations on low power—
in other words, a decentralized system. Of course this latter plan was not
"efficient" in the context of capitalist broadcasting; but Nockels knew
enough about the dangerous power of centralized media to conclude that
perhaps the American people would prefer democracy over efficiency.

Labor radio emerged during broadcasting's infancy, when anything
seemed possible; yet it failed to develop into a viable alternative to the capitalist media. This resulted, in part, from the ability of corporate capitalists and their state servants to define broadcasting's structure. The onset of
the Great Depression exacerbated the efforts of challengers to commercial
radio. Perhaps most important, however, was the weakness of organized
labor vis-à-vis capital just as broadcasting developed. David Armstrong and
other scholars have suggested that an alternative culture and alternative
media must develop simultaneously. "Activists supply alternative media with
a constituency [and] alternative media provide activists with a sense of

identity and collective purpose."[6] But no militant or radical labor movement thrived during the twenties to create an alternative culture. The CFL's radical phase had passed with the demise of the labor party movement. With some notable exceptions, organized labor was in the doldrums across the nation. Lacking a radical or alternative labor culture, labor radio had difficultly generating rank-and-file support.

As the Great Depression and the New Deal altered economic and political conditions—making them both more conducive and more difficult for labor radicalism to take root—the CFL failed to play a prominent role. The CIO propelled itself to the forefront of labor radicalism, creating, as Lizabeth Cohen has explained, a "culture of unity" and incorporating the mass media along the way.[7] In those few areas where the CFL worked on the cutting edge of organizing and boycotting, WCFL functioned as an alternative medium. Labor Day celebrations, the Radio Frolics, and the work of Sarainne Loewe and the CFL Speakers' Bureau all offered clues on how culture, education, politics, entertainment, and broadcasting could intertwine. But in general, the necessary symbiosis between alternative media and alternative culture never developed. The corporatist compromise of the postwar era killed any hope that the organized labor movement or WCFL would play the role of challenger to the corporate political economy or culture. WCFL management, under William Lee's direction, almost totally divorced the station from its "community" and, to the extent that it concerned itself with the larger socioeconomic and political environment, functioned as a conservative force in Chicago.

Although radio broadcasting's foundation had been set by 1922, important changes occurred in its first decade. In a dynamic situation in which the industry still sought to solidify its position in society, WCFL posed a serious danger to the emerging corporate structure. A vital dialectical process operated here: Nockels wanted to influence a commercial broadcasting environment that ultimately shaped WCFL. Yet Nockels fulfilled the role of an "organic intellectual" because he conceived labor radio as a progressive force for all workers, unions, and the general public. His vision for labor radio saw a station supporting not an individualistic business unionism, but a collective social unionism.[8] This explains why the broadcasting giants, the government, and the AFL hierarchy feared and disliked the CFL secretary. They understood Nockels's dangerous vision and his potentially devastating maneuvers in the legislative and judicial arenas. Corporate broadcasting officials made minor concessions to the conservative AFL, co-opting business unionists such as William Green and Matthew Woll, in an effort to avoid more fundamental alterations in the commercial system. In a similar fashion, NBC and CBS executives allowed Socialist party leader Norman Thomas use of their facilities to demonstrate the openness and fairness of American broadcasting.[9] But the possibility of a radical and militant CFL with its own radio station frightened these same groups and individuals. Nockels correctly recognized all this and did what he thought best to guarantee WCFL's survival during the twenties and thirties. When, in the fifties and sixties, the broadcasting environment again changed with the rise of television and FM radio, William Lee's WCFL made little effort either to challenge the system or to influence its development. Instead, the CFL, firmly ensconced in a corporatist compromise, became a passive participant in commercial broadcasting, using labor radio to generate profits for business unionist goals and strategies.

Nockels had understood, at least intuitively, the crucial link between community and alternative radio. The CFL's experiences with the failed labor party movement of the twenties had taught Nockels a lesson that he applied to the political ferment of the thirties: Independent labor political action must come from the bottom up, from the rank and file, not from the top down.[10] Labor radio began in the early twenties as a grass-roots movement with local unions worried about the propaganda of the capitalist stations and demanding a broadcasting outlet of their own. Nockels took the lead in developing that outlet and, initially at least, building rank-and-file participation. But as the daily economic and political problems mounted, and as more pressing issues sidetracked the attention of both the rank and file and the leadership, decision-making in WCFL became more centralized and labor radio increasingly became a top-down institution. This explains, in part, the recurring lament of CFL officers from the twenties to the seventies that local unions and their members failed to support the Voice of Labor.[11]

• • •

A final assessment of WCFL must acknowledge the importance of radicals and their alternative visions to the larger society. American mass media manipulate and toy with the values, hopes, and aspirations of communities in order to maximize profits and power. When attending to the concerns of workers, they do so in a patronizing way and for their own ends. American capitalism has generated labor-oriented media that are not the products of individual workers or trade unions, but rather the products of advertisers or networks seeking to derive some advantage from labor. Alternative labor media, on the other hand, are produced by labor groups or by organs serving workers' needs; they seek to satisfy workers' cultural, social, and political demands. Labor media must include both the press and broadcasting. Tomasz Goban-Klas has suggested that the print media best defend and expand the rights of specific groups, while the broadcast media best serve those groups' "psychological and cultural needs."[12] Labor broadcasting may help to define and build "a genuine labor movement," as Kim Moody has suggested, by "recapturing the diverse cultures that coexist uneasily within the US working class from their commercialized, alienated, and distorted place in America's uniquely commercialized (and homogenized) popular culture."[13]

Labor alternatives to corporate broadcasting were and are important. WCFL, especially in its first decades of broadcasting, represented an effort on the part of local labor to break its dependence on big business for information and culture. Labor radio reflected labor's interest in producing its own culture through its own institutions. Edward Nockels's ceaseless efforts to win WCFL a clear channel and maximum power accelerated this process by educating rank-and-file workers and their leaders about the importance of mass communications. He assumed the formidable task of wearing down the myths of capitalist broadcasting, of convincing people of the need for alternatives, and of creating open spaces where alternatives might develop.[14] But the post–World War II business unionists were, as longtime CFL secretary Mollie Levitas recalled, a "new breed" of labor leaders who "never had to struggle" and who enjoyed easy living and high salaries.[15] They rejected Nockels's arguments and embraced commercial broadcasting. By playing the corporate broadcasting game these labor leaders abandoned hope for labor alternatives to the capitalist media.

Whatever his inconsistencies and limitations, Edward Nockels deserves credit for challenging the capitalist broadcasting system. He exposed the way in which dominant forces tried to limit debate about the fairness and power of capitalist broadcasting by defining the terms of discussion. Corporate lawyer Louis G. Caldwell, for example, structured the debate about radio free speech in such a way as to dismiss, out-of-hand, those who questioned the proposition that only the capitalist marketplace could guarantee the preservation of free speech. Challengers to the "law of the marketplace" became comparable to the feebleminded who attacked the law of gravity. Capitalist forces sought to construct the meaning of radio's various facets and thereby guarantee their power. NBC executives, FRC commissioners, AFL officials, corporate lawyers, and others found Nockels insufferable because he disputed the meaning of words and actions that they held as self-evident truths. But Nockels, acting as an organic intellectual, revealed the effort of big business and government to create ideological hegemony. He turned their arguments on their head to demonstrate their class origin and intent.[16] Nockels and his colleagues struggled over the "contested terrain" of broadcasting's institutions, economic and political power, and cultural products. That battle continued even after the contested broadcasting territory of the twenties and thirties became surrendered ground in the post–World War II era. During the closing decades of the twentieth century, commercial broadcasting marginalized, at best, and vilified, at worst, workers, their unions, and their communities. But the history of WCFL offers a lesson on how workers and their leaders once struggled with the impact of mass media and culture on their lives, while attempting to use those forces in their own interest.

APPENDIX

Table 1. Distribution of WCFL's Weekly Programming, 1928–32 (minutes)

Programs	Week[a]											Total
	1	2	3	4	5	6	7	8	9	10	11	
Children	0	270	360	315	270	360	270	270	270	360	300	3,045
Comedy	35	0	0	0	210	165	80	60	75	180	90	895
Ethnic hours	0	60	135	30	210	375	350	450	420	300	415	2,745
Farm	165	80	60	90	90	90	90	120	115	90	90	1,080
Labor	200	140	250	210	175	215	170	150	105	210	245	2,070
Music	2,590	1,200	1,940	1,170	1,255	2,075	2,885	3,040	3,215	3,530	3,535	26,435
News/Civic Information/ Education	120	120	15	15	185	295	150	200	130	185	110	1,525
Plays/serials	0	0	0	0	0	0	0	0	30	120	105	255
Religious	405	195	60	195	210	210	60	120	30	255	165	1,905
Sports	0	0	945	570	40	55	135	60	1,035	105	1,020	3,965
Talk	70	950	750	735	825	1,665	2,255	1,410	1,405	1,310	930	12,305
Variety	225	30	255	600	280	345	465	555	610	795	435	4,595
Total	3,810	3,045	4,770	3,930	3,750	5,850	6,910	6,435	7,440	7,440	7,440	60,820

Note: WCFL also broadcast NBC sustaining programs during this period for a total of 2,845 minutes: Week 3: 255; Week 4: 240; Week 5: 270; Week 6: 180; Week 7: 225; Week 8: 270; Week 9: 270; Week 10: 700; Week 11: 435.

a. Week 1: June 2–8, 1928; Week 2: February 9–15, 1929; Week 3: June 29–July 5, 1929; Week 4: October 5–11, 1929; Week 5: January 25–31, 1930; Week 6: March 15–21, 1930; Week 7: November 29–December 5, 1930; Week 8: March 21–27, 1931; Week 9: May 30–June 5, 1931; Week 10: December 26, 1931–January 1, 1932; Week 11: May 28–June 3, 1932.

Sources: *FN*, June 2, 1928, 5, Feb. 9, 1929, 8, 11, June 29, 1929, 5, Oct. 5, 1929, 8, Jan. 25, 1930, 8, Mar. 15, 1930, 8, Nov. 29, 1930, 8, Mar. 21, 1931, 8, May 30, 1931, 8, Dec. 26, 1931, 6, May 28, 1932, 6.

Table 2. Distribution of Major Networks' Programming, 1929–32
(minutes)

Programs	January 1929	January 1930	January 1931	January 1932	Total
Children	0	195	120	225	540
Comedy	90	345	495	840	1,770
Music	2,785	3,450	3,540	4,770	14,545
News/Civic Information/ Education	105	195	435	570	1,305
Plays/Serials	270	510	555	1,080	2,415
Religious	240	270	390	180	1,080
Talk	1,525	900	2,055	1,905	6,385
Variety	210	330	510	825	1,875
Total	5,225	6,195	8,100	10,395	29,915

Source: Harrison B. Summers, *A Thirty-Year History of Programs Carried on National Radio Networks in the United States, 1926–1956* (Columbus: Ohio State University, 1958; New York: Arno Press and The New York Times, 1971), 11–30.

Table 3. Average Distribution of WCFL's Programming,
1931 (percentages)

Program Type	Commercial	Sustaining
Agricultural	0.5	3.0
Educational	0.0	10.0
Entertainment	31.0	43.5
Fraternal	0.0	10.0
Religious	2.0	0.0
Total	33.5	66.5

Source: WCFL License Renewal Application, Nov. 25, 1931, WCFL
1927–34 Folder, FRC, Box 27, FCC Broadcast Bureau, Broadcast
License, RG 173, NARS.

Table 4. Average Distribution of WCFL's Programming,
1944 (percentages)

Program Type	Commercial	Sustaining
Agricultural	0.0	0.5
Civic	0.0	0.5
Educational	0.5	2.5
Entertainment	40.5	27.5
Governmental	2.0	4.5
News	7.5	10.0
Religious	2.5	1.5
Total	53.0	47.0

Source: WCFL License Renewal Application, Jan. 19, 1944, WCFL
1942–48 Folder, Box 130, FCC Broadcast Bureau, Broadcast License,
RG 173, NARS.

NOTES

Preface

1. David Montgomery, *Workers' Control in America* (New York: Cambridge University Press, 1979); David Montgomery, *The Fall of the House of Labor: The*

Workplace, the State, and American Labor Activism, 1865–1925 (New York: Cambridge University Press, 1987); James R. Green, *The World of the Worker: Labor in Twentieth-Century America* (New York: Hill and Wang, 1980); Elizabeth McKillen, *Chicago Labor and the Quest for a Democratic Diplomacy, 1914–1924* (Ithaca: Cornell University Press, 1995); David R. Roediger and Philip S. Foner, *Our Own Time: A History of American Labor and the Working Day* (London: Verso, 1989); George Lipsitz, *Rainbow at Midnight: Labor and Culture in the 1940s* (Urbana: University of Illinois Press, 1994); Kim Moody, *An Injury to All: The Decline of American Unionism* (London: Verso, 1988).

2. Armand Mattelart, *Mass Media, Ideologies, and the Revolutionary Movement,* trans. Malcolm Cord (Atlantic Highlands, N.J.: Humanities Press, 1980), xiv (quote); George Lipsitz, "The Struggle for Hegemony," *Journal of American History* 75, no. 1 (June 1988): 146–50. Studies of radical and labor challenges to the commercial media include Sara U. Douglas, *Labor's New Voice: Unions and the Mass Media* (Norwood, N.J.: Ablex, 1986); Elliott Shore, *Talkin' Socialism: J. A. Wayland and the Role of the Press in American Radicalism, 1890–1912* (Lawrence: University of Kansas Press, 1988); Steven J. Ross, "Struggles for the Screen: Workers, Radicals, and the Political Uses of Silent Film," *American Historical Review* 96, no. 2 (Apr. 1991): 333–67; Steven J. Ross, "Cinema and Class Conflict: Labor, Capital, the State, and American Silent Film," in *Resisting Images: Essays on Cinema and History,* ed. Robert Sklar and Charles Musser (Philadelphia: Temple University Press, 1990), 68–107; Robert W. McChesney, "Labor and the Marketplace of Ideas: WCFL and the Battle for Labor Radio Broadcasting, 1927–1934," *Journalism Monographs* 134 (Aug. 1992): 1–40; Robert W. McChesney, "An Almost Incredible Absurdity for a Democracy," *Journal of Communication Inquiry* 15, no. 1 (Winter 1991): 89–114; Nathan Godfried, "Legitimizing the Mass Media Structure: The Socialists and American Broadcasting, 1926–1932," in *Culture, Gender, Race, and U.S. Labor History,* ed. Ronald Kent, Sara Markham, David Roediger, and Herbert Shapiro (Westport, Conn.: Greenwood Press, 1993), 123–49; Stephen J. Haessler, "Carl Haessler and the Federated Press: Essays on the History of American Labor Journalism" (M.A. thesis, University of Wisconsin at Madison, 1977); and Jon Bekken, "The Working-Class Press at the Turn of the Century," in *Ruthless Criticism: New Perspectives in U.S. Communications History,* ed. William S. Solomon and Robert W. McChesney (Minneapolis: University of Minnesota Press, 1993), 151–75.

3. John Downing, *Radical Media: The Political Experience of Alternative Communication* (Boston: South End Press, 1984), 3.

4. The U.S. media's concentrated nature and problematic rhetoric have been documented in Morris L. Ernst, *The First Freedom* (New York: Macmillan, 1946); Ben H. Bagdikian, *The Media Monopoly* (Boston: Beacon Press, 1983); Gregory Tod Wuliger, "The Fairness Doctrine in Its Historical Context: A Symbolic Approach" (Ph.D. diss., University of Illinois at Urbana-Champaign, 1987); and Noam Chom-

sky and Edward Herman, *Manufacturing Consent: The Political Economy of the Mass Media* (New York: Pantheon Books, 1988).

5. Robin D. G. Kelley, "Notes on Deconstructing 'The Folk,'" *American Historical Review* 97 (Dec. 1992): 1404, 1408; Lipsitz, "Struggle for Hegemony," 146–50.

6. Minutes of the Meeting of Trustees of Debs Radio Fund, Mar. 25, 1927, Miscellaneous Documents, 5619, Folder 4, Box 215, ACWA Records, Labor-Management Documentation Center, M. P. Catherwood Library, Cornell University, Ithaca; *New Leader*, Aug. 6, 1927, 3 (quote); Godfried, "Legitimizing the Mass Media Structure."

7. *Federated Press—Labor Letter*, May 11, 1927, 4 (quote), May 10, 1930, 8; Minutes of the Board of Directors of AFPS, Fifty-Sixth Meeting, Aug. 24, 1925, Fifty-Seventh Meeting, Sept. 23, 1925, and Fifty-Ninth Meeting, Nov. 24, 1925, all on Reel 3, Box 5, AFPS.

8. *Federated Press—Labor Letter*, Feb. 9, 1928, 6, Mar. 8, 1928, 6, Aug. 16, 1928, 6, and Dec. 21, 1929, 4; Dana Frank, "At the Point of Consumption: Seattle Labor and the Politics of Consumption, 1919–1927" (Ph.D. diss., Yale University, 1988), 506; Letter, Mildred Scott Olmstead to Elizabeth G. Flynn, Nov. 17, 1925, Reel 12, Folder 2, Box 18, AFPS (quote).

9. Elizabeth Fones-Wolf, "For Better Listening: Organized Labor and Radio, 1940–1960," paper presented at the North American Labor History Conference, Wayne State University, Detroit, Mich., Oct. 14–16, 1993.

10. Alan Dawley, "Workers, Capital, and the State in the Twentieth Century," in *Perspectives on American Labor History: The Problems of Synthesis*, ed. J. Carroll Moody and Alice Kessler-Harris (De Kalb: Northern Illinois University Press, 1989), 152–66 (quote from 161); Emily Rosenberg, *Spreading the American Dream: American Economic and Cultural Expansion, 1890–1945* (New York: Hill and Wang, 1982).

11. Dawley, "Workers, Capital, and the State," 153.

12. Ibid., 166–82.

13. Eileen R. Meehan, "Critical Theorizing on Broadcast History," *Journal of Broadcasting and Electronic Media* 30, no. 4 (Fall 1986): 393.

14. Susan Douglas, *Inventing American Broadcasting, 1899–1922* (Baltimore: Johns Hopkins University Press, 1987).

15. Robert W. McChesney thoroughly analyzes the radio reform movement in *Telecommunications, Mass Media, and Democracy: The Battle for the Control of U.S. Broadcasting, 1928–1935* (New York: Oxford University Press, 1993).

16. Lawrence W. Levine, "The Folklore of Industrial Society: Popular Culture and Its Audiences," *American Historical Review* 97, no. 5 (Dec. 1992): 1373, 1381, 1384 (quotes); Michael Denning, "The End of Mass Culture," *International Labor and Working-Class History*, no. 37 (Spring 1990): 8.

17. Levine, "Folklore of Industrial Society," 1369–99; T. J. Jackson Lears, "Making Fun of Popular Culture," *American Historical Review* 97, no. 5 (Dec. 1992): 1419, 1422 (quote); "Scholarly Controversy: Mass Culture," *International Labor and Working Class History*, no. 37 (Spring 1990): 2–40.

18. Kelley, "Notes on Deconstructing 'The Folk,'" 1402.

19. Francis G. Couvares, *The Remaking of Pittsburgh: Class and Culture in an Industrializing City, 1877–1919* (Albany: State University of New York Press, 1984); Kathy Peiss, *Cheap Amusements: Working Women and Leisure in Turn-of-the-Century New York* (Philadelphia: Temple University Press, 1986); Roy Rosenzweig, *Eight Hours for What We Will: Workers and Leisure in an Industrial City, 1870–1920* (Cambridge: Cambridge University Press, 1983); George Lipsitz, *Time Passages: Collective Memory and American Popular Culture* (Minneapolis: University of Minnesota Press, 1990).

20. "Scholarly Controversy," 3.

21. George Lipsitz, "'This Ain't No Sideshow': Historians and Media Studies," *Critical Studies in Mass Communication* 5 (June 1988): 157.

Introduction

1. Scott Nearing, "The Control of Public Opinion in the United States," *School and Society* (Apr. 15, 1922): 421–22.

2. Labor capitalism, movies, and press will be examined later in the introduction. On workers' education see Richard J. Altenbaugh, *Education for Struggle: The American Labor Colleges of the 1920s and 1930s* (Philadelphia: Temple University Press, 1990); Julia Wrigley, *Class Politics and Public Schools: Chicago, 1900–1945* (New Brunswick, N.J.: Rutgers University Press, 1982); and Joyce L. Kornbluh, *A New Deal for Workers' Education: The Workers' Service Program, 1933–1942* (Urbana: University of Illinois Press, 1987).

3. Rosenzweig, *Eight Hours for What We Will,* 223.

4. Leo Panitch, "The Development of Corporatism in Liberal Democracies," *Comparative Political Studies* 10 (Apr. 1977): 61 (quote); Rosenberg, *Spreading the American Dream;* William A. Williams, *The Contours of American History* (Cleveland: World Publishing, 1961); Alan Dawley, *Struggles for Justice: Social Responsibility and the Liberal State* (Cambridge, Mass.: Belknap Press of Harvard University Press, 1991), 17–62.

5. See note 4 and William A. Williams, "The Large Corporation and American Foreign Policy," in *Corporations and the Cold War,* ed. David Horowitz (New York: Monthly Review Press, 1969), 71–104; G. William Domhoff, "Corporate-Liberal Theory and the Social Security Act: A Chapter in the Sociology of Knowledge," *Politics and Society* 15, no. 3 (1986–87): 297–330; and Thomas J. McCormick, "Drift or Mastery? A Corporatist Synthesis for American Diplomatic History," *Reviews in American History* 10 (Dec. 1982): 318–30.

6. McCormick, "Drift or Mastery?"

7. Ken Ward, *Mass Communications and the Modern World* (Chicago: Dorsey Press, 1989), 21.

8. Ibid., 35 (second quote); Edwin H. Ford and Edwin Emery, *Highlights in the*

History of the American Press (Minneapolis: University of Minnesota Press, 1954), 263–66; Jon Bekken, "Labor Confronts the Chicago Newspaper Trust," *Journalism History* 18 (1992): 11 (first quote); Margaret A. Blanchard, "Press Criticism and National Reform Movements: The Progressive and New Deal Eras," *Journalism History* 5, no. 2 (1978): 33–37, 54–55.

9. Jack Poggi, *Theater in America: The Impact of Economic Forces, 1870–1967* (Ithaca: Cornell University Press, 1968), xv, 3–27, 253–61.

10. Robert C. Allen, *Horrible Prettiness: Burlesque and American Culture* (Chapel Hill: University of North Carolina Press, 1991), 190 (first and second quotes), 189 (third, fourth, and fifth quotes).

11. Robert Sklar, *Movie-Made America: A Social History of American Movies* (New York: Random House, 1975), 3 (quote); Tino Balio, ed., *The American Film Industry* (Madison: University of Wisconsin Press, 1976), 4–6, 15–16; Russell Merritt, "Nickelodeon Theaters 1905–1914: Building an Audience for the Movies," in *American Film Industry*, ed. Balio, 60–63.

12. Lary May, *Screening Out the Past: The Birth of Mass Culture and the Motion Picture Industry* (New York: Oxford University Press, 1980), 169, 175–99; Jeanne Thomas Allen, "The Decay of the Motion Picture Patents Company," in *American Film Industry*, ed. Balio, 119–34.

13. May, *Screening Out the Past*, 176–77.

14. Ward, *Mass Communications*, 24, 25–26 (quotes).

15. May, *Screening Out the Past*, 182 (first quote), 175 (second quote), 183 (third and fourth quotes), 187, 198, 203, 237 (fifth quote).

16. Robert W. Snyder, *The Voice of the City: Vaudeville and Popular Culture in New York* (New York: Oxford University Press, 1989), xiv–xv, 12.

17. Snyder, *Voice of the City*, xiii–xiv, 12; Allen, *Horrible Prettiness*, 185–89 (quote from 187).

18. Sheila Slaughter and Edward T. Silva, "Looking Backwards: How Foundations Formulated Ideology in the Progressive Period," in *Philanthropy and Cultural Imperialism: The Foundations at Home and Abroad*, ed. Robert F. Arnove (Bloomington: Indiana University Press, 1980), 79.

19. Ross, "Struggles for the Screen," 337.

20. Hiroko Tsuchiya, "'Let Them Be Amused': The Industrial Drama Movement, 1910–1929," in *Theatre for Working-Class Audiences in the United States, 1830–1980*, ed. Bruce A. McConachie and Daniel Friedman (Westport, Conn.: Greenwood Press, 1985), 97–110; Bruce A. McConachie and Daniel Friedman, "Introduction," in *Theatre for Working-Class Audiences*, ed. McConachie and Friedman, 13 (quote).

21. Slaughter and Silva, "Looking Backwards," 79; Joseph R. Conlin, ed., *The American Radical Press, 1880–1960* (Westport, Conn.: Greenwood Press, 1974); Shore, *Talkin' Socialism*; Rebecca Zurier, *Art for the Masses: A Radical Magazine and Its Graphics, 1911–1917* (Philadelphia: Temple University Press, 1988); J. M. Budish and George Soule, *The New Unionism in the Clothing Industry* (New York: Harcourt,

Brace, and Howe, 1920), 233–35. On increased radicalism in the early twentieth century see Philip S. Foner, *The Industrial Workers of the World—1905–1917* (New York: International Publishers, 1965); Paul Buhle, *Marxism in the US: Remapping the American Left* (London: Verso, 1987); James R. Green, *Grass-Roots Socialism: Radical Movements in the Southwest, 1895–1943* (Baton Rouge: Louisiana State University Press, 1978); and Richard W. Judd, *Socialist Cities: Municipal Politics and the Grass Roots of American Socialism* (Albany: State University Press of New York, 1989).

22. Robert Justin Goldstein, *Political Repression in Modern America: From 1870 to the Present* (Cambridge, Mass.: Schenkman, 1978), 107–21 (quote from 107), 125–35, 139–91; Ross, "Cinema and Class Conflict," 82–85; Margaret A. Blanchard, *Revolutionary Sparks: Freedom of Expression in America* (New York: Oxford University Press, 1992).

23. Colin Sparks, "The Working-Class Press: Radical and Revolutionary Alternatives," *Media, Culture, and Society* 7, no. 2 (Apr. 1985): 139, 144; John A. Saltmarsh, *Scott Nearing: An Intellectual Biography* (Philadelphia: Temple University Press, 1991), 185–89; Nearing, "Control of Public Opinion," 422; Lewis Corey, "The New Capitalism," in *American Labor Dynamics: In the Light of Post War Developments,* ed. J. B. S. Hardman (New York: Harcourt, Brace, 1928; New York: Arno and the New York Times, 1969), 62–63.

24. E. W. Morehouse, "Labor Institutionalism: Banking," in *American Labor Dynamics,* ed. Hardman, 310; Corey, "The New Capitalism," 62 (quote); Frank, "Point of Consumption," 356, 357–74.

25. Morehouse, "Banking," 310–11; Frank, "Point of Consumption," 346, 390–92; Louis Levine, *The Women's Garment Workers: A History of the International Ladies' Garment Workers' Union* (New York: B. W. Huebsch, 1924), 450 (quote).

26. Earl D. Strong, *The Amalgamated Clothing Workers of America* (Grinnell, Iowa: Herald-Register, 1940), 247–48; Matthew Josephson, *Sidney Hillman: Statesman of American Labor* (Garden City, N.Y.: Doubleday, 1952), 245, 313–14; Levine, *The Women's Garment Workers,* 359; Frank, "Point of Consumption," 361–70.

27. Frank, "Point of Consumption," 357–90, 378 (quote).

28. Ross, "Struggles for the Screen," 351–52.

29. Budish and Soule, *New Unionism,* 238 (quote); Donald Lazere, ed., *American Media and Mass Culture* (Berkeley: University of California Press, 1987), 17.

30. Shore, *Talkin' Socialism,* 3–5 (quotes), 100–101.

31. Oscar Ameringer, "How Labor Can Build a Daily Press," in *Readings in Trade Unionism,* ed. David J. Saposs (New York: Macmillan, 1927), 379, 380 (first quote); Norman Thomas, "The Labor Daily," in *American Labor Dynamics,* ed. Hardman, 405 (second quote; emphasis in original).

32. Ameringer, "Labor Can Build a Daily Press," 383–84 (second quote); J. B. S. Hardman, "A View of the Trade-Union Press and Its Function," in *American Labor Dynamics,* ed. Hardman, 409 (first quote).

33. Ameringer, "Labor Can Build a Daily Press," 383–84.

34. Budish and Soule, *New Unionism,* 236.

35. AFL, *American Federation of Labor: History, Encyclopedia, Reference Book,* vol. 1 (Washington, D.C.: AFL, 1919), 144.

36. Hardman, "A View of the Trade-Union Press," 409–11.

37. Frank, "Point of Consumption," 378–80 (quote from 379).

38. Budish and Soule, *New Unionism,* 239.

39. Ibid., 245–47 (quote from 247); Strong, *Amalgamated Clothing Workers of America,* 211; Douglas, *Labor's New Voice,* 54; Bekken, "The Working-Class Press." Leftist groups such as the Socialist party and the Industrial Workers of the World also produced oppositional media in the form of newspapers and journals, art, literature, music, songs, plays, and pageants. See Conlin, *The American Radical Press;* Shore, *Talkin' Socialism;* Joyce L. Kornbluh, ed., *Rebel Voices—An IWW Anthology,* rev. ed. (Chicago: Charles H. Kerr, 1988); and Martin Green, *New York 1913: The Armory Show and the Paterson Strike Pageant* (New York: Charles Scribner's Sons, 1988).

40. Budish and Soule, *New Unionism,* 235.

41. AFL, *Encyclopedia,* 1:276.

42. Budish and Soule, *New Unionism,* 235; AFL, *American Federation of Labor: History, Encyclopedia, Reference Book,* vol. 2 (Washington, D.C.: AFL, 1924), 149; George Seldes, *Lords of the Press* (New York: Julian Messner, 1938), 400.

43. Tomasz Goban-Klas, "Minority Media," in *International Encyclopedia of Communications* (New York: Oxford University Press and Annenberg School of Communications, University of Pennsylvania, 1989), 3:30–32; John B. Jentz, "The Forty-Eighters and the Politics of the German Labor Movement in Chicago during the Civil War Era: Community Formation and the Rise of a Labor Press," in *The German-American Radical Press: The Shaping of a Left Political Culture,* ed. Elliott Shore, Ken Fones-Wolf, and James P. Danky (Urbana: University of Illinois Press, 1992), 50 (quote).

44. Ken Fones-Wolf and Elliott Shore, "The German Press and Working-Class Politics in Gilded Age Philadelphia," in *German-American Radical Press,* ed. Shore, Fones-Wolf, and Danky, 63–64.

45. Haessler, "Carl Haessler and the Federated Press," 3, 13 (first quote); A. J. Liebling, *The Wayward Pressman* (Garden City, N.Y.: Doubleday, 1948), 265–75; A. J. Liebling, "The Wayward Press: Do You Belong in Journalism?" *New Yorker,* May 14, 1960, 109 (second quote); AFL, *Encyclopedia,* 1:276 (third quote).

46. Budish and Soule, *New Unionism,* 231 (first quote), 232 (second quote).

47. Oswald Garrison Villard, *Some Newspapers and Newspaper-Men,* 2d ed. (New York: Alfred A. Knopf, 1926); Seldes, *Lords of the Press.*

48. Budish and Soule, *New Unionism,* 233–35.

49. Ross, "Struggles for the Screen," 347–51 (quote from 349).

50. Slaughter and Silva, "Looking Backwards," 80.

51. Wuliger, "The Fairness Doctrine in Its Historical Context," 689; Chomsky and Herman, *Manufacturing Consent,* 298.

52. *Outlook* 136 (Mar. 19, 1924): 465; Orange Edward Means, "The Great Audience Invisible," *Scribner's Magazine*, Apr. 1923, 414 (quote). For histories of radio broadcasting see Erik Barnouw, *A Tower in Babel: A History of Broadcasting in the United States, vol. 1—to 1933* (New York: Oxford University Press, 1966); and Christopher Sterling and John Kittross, *Stay Tuned: A Concise History of American Broadcasting* (Belmont, Calif.: Wadsworth, 1978).

53. Douglas, *Inventing American Broadcasting,* xv–xxiv, xv–xvi (quotes).

54. John F. Kasson, *Amusing the Million: Coney Island at the Turn of the Century* (New York: Hill and Wang, 1978), 5–8; Douglas, *Inventing American Broadcasting,* xxvii, 301–2.

55. Barnouw, *Tower in Babel,* 3–38; Douglas, *Inventing American Broadcasting,* 101, 248–49, 250 (quotes).

56. Douglas, *Inventing American Broadcasting,* 285–91 (quote from 290); Barnouw, *Tower in Babel,* 57–61.

57. Douglas, *Inventing American Broadcasting,* 169–72 (quote from 172); Barnouw, *Tower in Babel,* 25–27.

58. Douglas, *Inventing American Broadcasting,* 293–95; Barnouw, *Tower in Babel,* 25–36.

59. Barnouw, *Tower in Babel,* 27 (quote); Douglas, *Inventing American Broadcasting,* 192–207, 214–15.

60. Douglas, *Inventing American Broadcasting,* 293, 295–99.

61. Ibid., 300–301, 302 (first quote); Daniel J. Czitrom, *Media and the American Mind* (Chapel Hill: University of North Carolina Press, 1982), 67–68, 61 (second quote).

62. Barnouw, *Tower in Babel,* 64–72, 83–84, 88, 90, 107–8; Douglas, *Inventing American Broadcasting,* 320 (quotes).

63. Douglas, *Inventing American Broadcasting,* 250–51, 304 (quote).

64. Ibid., 303–14, 305 (quotes).

65. Ibid., 321.

66. McCormick, "Drift or Mastery?" 323–27; Robert Cox, "Labor and Hegemony," *International Organization* 31 (Summer 1977): 407.

67. AFL, *Encyclopedia,* 1:144–47, 276, 338, 2:149–50.

68. AFL, *Report of the Proceedings of the Forty-First Annual Convention, June 13–25, 1921* (Washington, D.C.: AFL, 1921), 318; AFL, *Report of the Proceedings of the Forty-Second Annual Convention, June 12–24, 1922* (Washington, D.C.: AFL, 1922), 62–63 (quote).

69. Ross, "Struggles for the Screen," 361–62.

70. AFL Executive Council Meeting Minutes, Feb. 15, 1924, George Meany Memorial Archives, Silver Spring, Md.

71. AFL, *Report of the Proceedings of the Forty-Fifth Convention, 1925* (Washington, D.C.: AFL, 1925), 316.

72. Craig Phelan, *William Green: Biography of a Labor Leader* (Albany: State University of New York Press, 1989), 29–47.

73. *American Federationist* 35 (Dec. 1928): 1426–27.

74. Mattelart, *Mass Media and the Revolutionary Movement*, xiv, xxv (quote); Douglas, *Inventing American Broadcasting*.

Chapter 1: The Creation of WCFL, 1925–26

An earlier version of this chapter appeared in *Historical Journal of Film, Radio, and Television* 7, no. 2 (1987): 143–59.

1. AFL, *Report of the Forty-Fifth Convention*, 316.
2. Phelan, *William Green*, 12–13, 29–47 (quotes from 30); Green, *The World of the Worker*, 100–132.
3. *NYT*, May 25, 1926, 23.
4. National Association of Broadcasters, *NAB Code Manual* (Washington, D.C.: NAB, 1939), 15 (quote); Ernst, *The First Freedom*, 145.
5. Sidney Lens, *Left, Right, and Center: Conflicting Forces in American Labor* (Hinsdale, Ill.: Henry Regnery, 1949), 60 (quotes); Eugene Staley, *History of the Illinois State Federation of Labor* (Chicago: University of Chicago Press, 1930); Lewis L. Lorwin, *The American Federation of Labor: History, Policies, and Prospects* (Washington, D.C.: Brookings Institution, 1933); Dana Frank, *Purchasing Power: Consumer Organizing, Gender, and the Seattle Labor Movement, 1919–1929* (New York: Cambridge University Press, 1994).
6. Lens, *Left, Right, and Center*, 61–62 (quote from 64); Lorwin, *American Federation of Labor*, 346–49. State federations retained some important functions, such as lobbying for state legislation. James H. Maurer, "State Federations as Movement Centers," in *American Labor Dynamics*, ed. Hardman, 357–59.
7. John H. Keiser, "John Fitzpatrick and Progressive Unionism, 1915–1925" (Ph.D. diss., Northwestern University, 1965), 155.
8. Moody, *An Injury to All*, xiv.
9. David Brody, *Workers in Industrial America* (New York: Oxford University Press, 1980), 173–257; Irving Bernstein, *The Lean Years: A History of the American Worker, 1920–1933* (Boston: Houghton Mifflin, 1960), 96–97; Keiser, "Fitzpatrick," iii–iv; James O. Morris, *Conflict within the AFL: A Study of Craft versus Industrial Unionism, 1901–1938* (Ithaca: Cornell University Press, 1958), 55.
10. Alan J. Singer, "Class-Conscious Coal Miners: Nanty-Glo versus the Open Shop in the Post–World War I Era," *Labor History* 29 (Winter 1988): 56–57 (quotes); Roediger and Foner, *Our Own Time*, chap. 10; Philip S. Foner, *The T.U.E.L. to the End of the Gompers Era*, vol. 9 of *History of the Labor Movement in the United States* (New York: International Publishers, 1991).
11. Lens, *Left, Right, and Center*, 64 (quote); Steven Sapolsky, "Response to Sean Wilentz's 'Against Exceptionalism: Class Consciousness and the American Labor Movement: 1790–1920,'" *International Labor and Working Class History*, no. 27 (Spring 1985): 35–38; McKillen, *Chicago Labor and a Democratic Diplomacy*, 193–213.

12. Antonio Gramsci, *Selections from the Prison Notebooks,* ed. Quintin Hoare and Geoffrey Nowell Smith (New York: International Publishers, 1971), 3–23.

13. George Lipsitz, *A Life in the Struggle: Ivory Perry and the Culture of Opposition* (Philadelphia: Temple University Press, 1988), 9.

14. Telegram, Morris Sigman to J. Fitzpatrick and Ed Nockels, Dec. 11, 1926, Folder 10, Box 2, Collection 6, Morris Sigman Correspondence, ILGWU Records, Martin P. Catherwood Library, New York State School for Industrial and Labor Relations, Cornell University, Ithaca; Letter, William B. Rubin to L. P. Straube, Mar. 1, 1937, Correspondence 1937, Folder Jan.–Mar., Box 11, William B. Rubin Papers, State Historical Society of Wisconsin Area Research Center, University Archives, University of Wisconsin at Milwaukee (first and second quotes); Transcript of Interview with Leslie Orear, by author, July 2, 1991, Chicago, 7 (third and fourth quotes); Transcript of Interview with Mollie Levitas, by Elizabeth Balanoff, Dec. 22, 1970, 54, OHP.

15. Lipsitz, *A Life in the Struggle,* 10.

16. McKillen, *Chicago Labor and a Democratic Diplomacy,* 46 (quote); Levitas Interview, July 24, 1970, 10; Transcript of Interview with Lillian Herstein, by Elizabeth Balanoff, Oct. 26, 1970, 38–39, OHP; Barbara Warne Newell, *Chicago and the Labor Movement: Metropolitan Unionism in the 1930's* (Urbana: University of Illinois Press, 1961), 24–25, 253; Lens, *Left, Right, and Center,* 64–65.

17. Transcript of Interview with Joseph M. Jacobs, by author, July 2, 1991, Chicago, 3 (quotes).

18. Keiser, "Fitzpatrick," iii–iv.

19. Ibid., 125; Transcript of Oral History Interview with Joseph Keenan, by Joanna Skivenes, Aug. 8, 1970, Oral Histories Folder, Box 1, Joseph D. Keenan Papers, Archives and Manuscript Division, Catholic University of America, Washington, D.C., 13 (first, third, and fourth quotes); Herstein Interview, Oct. 26, 1970, 38 (second quote); McKillen, *Chicago Labor and a Democratic Diplomacy,* 46–48, 84–86.

20. Keiser, "Fitzpatrick," 155.

21. Seldes, *Lords of the Press,* 47–50 (quote from 47); Paul Avrich, *The Haymarket Tragedy* (Princeton: Princeton University Press, 1984), 217–19, 280–81; Bruce C. Nelson, *Beyond the Martyrs: A Social History of Chicago's Anarchists, 1870–1900* (New Brunswick, N.J.: Rutgers University Press, 1988), 186–87, 206–9; Bekken, "Labor Confronts the Chicago Newspaper Trust."

22. *New Majority,* Jan. 4, 1919, 1.

23. Keiser, "Fitzpatrick," 160–63; AFL, *Encyclopedia,* 2:86; Haessler, "Carl Haessler and the Federated Press."

24. Keiser, "Fitzpatrick," 109; McKillen, *Chicago Labor and a Democratic Diplomacy,* 11–12, 48–49; Lens, *Left, Right, and Center,* 3 (quote).

25. Letter, S. Gompers to E. C. Ball, May 31, 1922 (first quote), Federated Press 1922–35 Folder, Box 4, Legislative Reference Files, AFL Papers, SHSW; AFL, *Report of the Proceedings of the Forty-Third Convention, 1923* (Washington, D.C.: AFL, 1923), 134 (second quote).

26. Keiser, "Fitzpatrick," iv–v, 140–54, 187–96; Lens, *Left, Right, and Center,* 64–65, 414; McKillen, *Chicago Labor and a Democratic Diplomacy,* 193–206; Foner, *The T.U.E.L. to the End of the Gompers Era,* 159–69; AFL, *Encyclopedia,* 2:243.

27. Goldstein, *Political Repression,* 170–71, 183–90; Keenan Interview, 14–15; Wilfred Carsel, *A History of the Chicago Ladies' Garment Workers' Union* (Chicago: Normandie House, 1940), 138–59, 169; Royal E. Montgomery, *Industrial Relations in the Chicago Building Trades* (Chicago: University of Chicago Press, 1927), 275–79; Green, *The World of the Worker,* 68, 88, 100–101, 119.

28. Bruce A. Linton, "A History of Chicago Radio Station Programming, 1921–1931: With Special Emphasis on Stations WMAQ and WGN" (Ph.D. diss., Northwestern University, 1953), 45–46, 78–80, 140–41; Barnouw, *Tower in Babel,* 88–90, 99, 130, 196; Lawrence W. Lichty and Malachi C. Topping, *American Broadcasting: A Source Book on the History of Radio and Television* (New York: Hastings House, 1975), 167, 196, 466; Abel Green and Joe Laurie Jr., *Show Biz: From Vaude to Video* (New York: Henry Holt, 1951), 234.

29. *FN,* Mar. 13, 1937, 1–2, 6–7; Levitas Interview, July 24, 1970, 7; Charles Edward Merriam, *Chicago: A More Intimate View of Urban Politics* (New York: Macmillan, 1929), 212. Both Mollie Levitas, CFL secretary, and Lillian Herstein, leader of the teachers' union, acknowledged Nockels's "very rough" language and character. Herstein recalled that the first time she was scheduled to make an announcement at a CFL meeting, Nockels asked Fitzpatrick, "What's that damn skirt here for?" Herstein Interview, Oct. 26, 1970, 39.

30. *FN,* Mar. 27, 1926, 1–2, Mar. 6, 1937, 1; Gary M. Fink, ed., *Biographical Dictionary of American Labor* (Westport, Conn.: Greenwood Press, 1984), 436–37; Erling Sejr Jorgensen, "Radio Station WCFL: A Study in Labor Union Broadcasting" (M.A. thesis, University of Wisconsin, 1949), 31–32; Levitas Interview, July 24, 1970, 7; *Who's Who in Chicago and Vicinity: The Book of Chicagoans, 1931* (Chicago: A. N. Marquis, 1931).

31. Keiser, "Fitzpatrick," 11–12 (quote); *FN,* Mar. 13, 1937, 1, 2, 6, 7.

32. *FN,* Aug. 7, 1926, 3.

33. Letter, Frank Walsh to Ed Nockels, Nov. 24, 1928, Folder Nov. 23–30, 1928, General Correspondence, Box 16, FW.

34. Czitrom, *Media and the American Mind,* 71–72; Douglas, *Inventing American Broadcasting,* 304–12.

35. *Illinois State Federation of Labor Weekly News Letter,* Apr. 26, 1930, 1 (first and second quotes); *FN,* Sept. 2, 1929, 11 (third quote), Oct. 9, 1926, 7; Transcript of Interview with Irwin E. Klass, by author, July 12, 1991, Chicago; Jacobs Interview.

36. *New Majority,* Mar. 24, 1923, 11 (first and second quotes), Apr. 7, 1923, 11, Feb. 9, 1924, 10–11 (third quote).

37. *FN,* Oct. 9, 1926, 7; ISFL, *Proceedings of the Forty-Fourth Annual Convention, September 13–18, 1926, Streator, Illinois,* 156–57, copy in Northwestern University Library, Evanston, Ill.; AFL Executive Council Meeting Minutes, Feb. 15, 1924.

38. ISFL, *Proceedings of the Forty-Fourth Convention*, 157; *FN*, Apr. 18, 1925, 5, Apr. 25, 1925, 11.

39. Minutes of the Board of Directors of the AFPS, Fifty-Fifth Meeting, July 22, 1925, and Fifty-Sixth Meeting, Aug. 24, 1925, both on Reel 3, Box 5, AFPS; Letters, Wm. J. H. Strong to the American Fund for Public Service, Oct. 1, 1925, and Dec. 19, 1925, Reel 29, Folder 4, Box 46, AFPS.

40. *FN*, Oct. 10, 1925, 1, Nov. 21, 1925, 6 (first and second quotes), 8 (third and fourth quotes).

41. John Fitzpatrick, "WCFL—Chicago Labor Broadcasting Station," *American Federationist* 34 (Apr. 1927): 449.

42. *FN*, Nov. 21, 1925, 6 (quotes); Strong to American Fund for Public Service, Dec. 19, 1925.

43. *FN*, Dec. 12, 1925, 11.

44. The 1912 act required that, in order to transmit, all radio stations secure a license from the secretary of commerce and labor. The secretary also had the power to assign wavelengths and time limits. Barnouw, *Tower in Babel*, 31–33, 291–99; and Douglas, *Inventing American Broadcasting*, 234–39.

45. Barnouw, *Tower in Babel*, 94–96, 121–22, 174–75, 177–79; Philip T. Rosen, *The Modern Stentors: Radio Broadcasting and the Federal Government, 1920–1934* (Westport, Conn.: Greenwood Press, 1980), 47–76; Christopher Sterling, *Electronic Media: A Guide to Trends in Broadcasting and Newer Technologies, 1920–1983* (New York: Praeger, 1984), 5, table 170-A.

46. AFL, *Report of the Forty-Fifth Convention*, 316; *FN*, Dec. 12, 1925, 10 (quote).

47. *FN*, Dec. 26, 1925, 10.

48. *FN*, Feb. 13, 1926, 2.

49. *FN*, Dec. 26, 1925, 11.

50. Keiser, "Fitzpatrick," 140–54; *FN*, Feb. 13, 1926, 4, Feb. 27, 1926, 4; AFL Executive Council Meeting Minutes, July 30, 1925. The AFL Executive Council admonished the CFL for supporting the ACWA, reminding the Chicago organ that "as a subordinate branch" of the AFL, it had "to abide in full with all requirements of laws and decisions of" the national federation. AFL Executive Council Meeting Minutes, July 30, 1925.

51. Letter, S. Davis to Nockels, Jan. 13, 1926, in Senate Committee on Interstate Commerce, *Radio Control: Hearings on S. 1 and S. 1754 before the Committee on Interstate Commerce*, 69th Cong., 1st Sess., 1926, part 3, 218.

52. Barnouw, *Tower in Babel*, 174–76; John Tebbel, *An American Dynasty: The Story of the McCormicks, Medills, and Pattersons* (Garden City, N.Y.: Doubleday, 1947), 114.

53. Letter, Nockels to Davis, Jan. 18, 1926, in Senate Committee, *Radio Control*, 218 (quotes); *FN*, Jan. 23, 1926, 6. WEAF's wavelength did not reach throughout the United States. WEAF did operate, however, through a network that covered a fair share of the country. Barnouw, *Tower in Babel*, 143–50.

54. Barnouw, *Tower in Babel*, 72–74, 81–83, 105–14, 143–53, 155–60; Rosen, *Modern Stentors*, 64–69; N. R. Danielian, *AT&T: The Story of Industrial Conquest* (New York: Vanguard, 1939), 123–24 (quote).

55. Joan Hoff Wilson, *Herbert Hoover: Forgotten Progressive* (Boston: Little, Brown, 1975), 112–13 (quote).

56. Senate Committee, *Radio Control*, 218 (quotes); *FN*, Jan. 23, 1926, 6.

57. Senate Committee, *Radio Control*, 219 (first quote), 220 (second quote).

58. Ibid., 199 (quote), 201–2, 205–6. The ACLU protested the Dill bill for its lack of adequate safeguards against monopoly. Letter, Morris Ernst to Forrest A. Bailey, Mar. 1, 1926, Correspondence with Morris Ernst, Federal Legislation 5, Radio Bills, 1926, Reel 45, vol. 301, American Civil Liberties Union Archives 1912–50, New York Public Library, New York.

59. Letter, Wm. J. H. Strong to Robert M. Lovett, Feb. 20, 1926, Reel 29, Folder 4, Box 46, AFPS; ISFL, *Proceedings of the Forty-Fourth Convention*, 158.

60. *Illinois State Federation of Labor Weekly News Letter*, Apr. 10, 1926, 1; ISFL, *Proceedings of the Forty-Fourth Convention*, 159.

61. John R. Schmidt, *"The Mayor Who Cleaned Up Chicago": A Political Biography of William E. Dever* (De Kalb: Northern Illinois University Press, 1989), 80–82, 104–6, 166–67; Wrigley, *Class Politics and Public Schools*, chap. 5; *Chicago Daily News*, Apr. 1, 1926, 5.

62. Fink, *Biographical Dictionary of Labor*, 434; *New Majority*, Feb. 9, 1924, 11; *FN*, Apr. 18, 1925, 5, Apr. 10, 1926, 10; *Chicago Daily News*, Apr. 1, 1926, 5 (quote); ISFL, *Proceedings of the Forty-Fourth Convention*, 159; Alex Gottfried, *Boss Cermak of Chicago: A Study of Political Leadership* (Seattle: University of Washington Press, 1962), 210, 212; Schmidt, *"The Mayor Who Cleaned Up Chicago,"* 166–67; Harvey M. Karlen, *The Governments of Chicago* (Chicago: Courier, 1958), 49.

63. *FN*, Jan. 23, 1926, 10, Feb. 27, 1926, 11, Mar. 13, 1926, 11, Apr. 10, 1926, 10, Apr. 24, 1926, 10, June 26, 1926, 1; *Chicago Daily News*, Apr. 1, 1926, 5; Fitzpatrick, "WCFL," 451; *Illinois State Federation of Labor Weekly News Letter*, Apr. 10, 1926, 1–2.

64. *FN*, Feb. 6, 1926, 8, Feb. 13, 1926, 1–2; Notes, Elizabeth Gurley Flynn to Morris Ernst, Dec. 22, 1925, and Feb. 8, 1926, and Letter, Wm J. H. Strong to Robert M. Lovett, Feb. 20, 1926, all on Reel 29, Folder 4, Box 46, AFPS; Minutes of the Board of Directors of the AFPS, Sixty-Third Meeting, Feb. 24, 1926, Reel 3, Box 6, AFPS. The explanation for rejecting Strong's 1925 request for funds can be found in the Minutes of the Board of Directors of the AFPS, Fifty-Sixth Meeting. The Garland Fund's unsuccessful efforts to create its own radio station are summarized in the Minutes of the Fifty-Seventh Meeting, the Fifty-Eighth Meeting, Oct. 28, 1925, and the Fifty-Ninth Meeting, all on Reel 3, Box 5, AFPS. For a history of the Garland Fund see Gloria Garrett Samson, "Toward a New Social Order: The American Fund for Public Service—Clearing House for Radicalism in the 1920s" (Ph.D. diss., University of Rochester, 1987).

65. *FN*, Feb. 27, 1926, 11; Letter, Fitzpatrick to Affiliated Unions, Mar. 30, 1926, Folder 102, Box 14, JF (first and second quotes).

66. *FN*, Apr. 10, 1926, 10, May 8, 1926, 11.

67. AFL Executive Council Meeting Minutes, Mar. 29, 1926 (second quote); Letter, W. Green to Fitzpatrick, Apr. 2, 1926 (first quote); Letter, Fitzpatrick to Green, Apr. 7, 1926 (third and fourth quotes); and Letter, Green to Fitzpatrick, Apr. 10, 1926, all in Folder 103, Box 14, JF.

68. *FN*, May 24, 1930, 16 (quote), Apr. 13, 1926.

69. *FN*, Feb. 13, 1926, 1 (quote), Feb. 27, 1926, 4, Apr. 10, 1926, 1, May 15, 1926, 5.

70. *FN*, Apr. 24, 1926, 6 (first quote), Mar. 27, 1926, 10 (second quote).

71. *FN*, Jan. 23, 1926, 6.

72. *FN*, May 8, 1926, 11 (first quote), Feb. 27, 1926, 4 (second and third quotes), Mar. 13, 1926, 1, Mar. 27, 1926, 6.

73. *FN*, Apr. 24, 1926, 6.

74. *FN*, May 1, 1926, 6, Dec. 25, 1926, 14 (quote). Lesh also announced plans for the CFL "to sponsor the manufacture of a radio receiving set to bear the union label." *FN*, May 1, 1926, 6.

75. *FN*, Apr. 3, 1926, 1, Apr. 10, 1926, 10, Apr. 17, 1926, 1, Apr. 24, 1926, 10, May 1, 1926, 3 (quote), May 8, 1926, 1–2, June 12, 1926, 10; *WCFL Radio Magazine* 1 (Spring 1928): 58; "List of Organizations—$2 Assessment," Fall 1926, Folder 106, Box 15, JF; ACWA, *Report of the General Executive Board and Proceedings of the Eighth Biennial Convention of the Amalgamated Clothing Workers of America, May 14–19, 1928*, 84, copy in Tamiment Library, New York University, New York; Interview with Frank Rosenblum, by Elizabeth Balanoff, Aug. 14, 1970, 16–17, OHP.

76. Carroll L. Christenson, *Collective Bargaining in Chicago, 1929–30* (Chicago: University of Chicago Press, 1933), 17, table 6; *FN*, Jan. 29, 1927, 11.

77. *FN*, Apr. 24, 1926, 10, June 26, 1926, 11.

78. Barnouw, *Tower in Babel*, 180, 189; Rosen, *Modern Stentors*, 93–94.

79. *FN*, May 1, 1926, 4.

80. Senate Committee, *Radio Control*, 219 (first quote); *NYT*, May 17, 1926, 37 (second quote); *Daily Worker* (Chicago), July 2, 1926, 3.

81. Levitas Interview, July 24, 1970, 8; *NYT*, May 15, 1926, 18; *WCFL Radio Magazine* 1 (Spring 1928): 58; *FN*, June 12, 1926, 4, July 3, 1926, 6; *Daily Worker*, July 2, 1926, 3.

82. Barnouw, *Tower in Babel*, 189–90; *NYT*, July 13, 1926, 18; *FN*, July 17, 1926, 1–4, 8, 13, July 24, 1926, 10–11, July 31, 1926, 3, Aug. 7, 1926, 6–7.

83. *FN*, July 3, 1926, 3, July 31, 1926, 1–2, 6 (quotes).

84. *FN*, Aug. 21, 1926, 6, Sept. 11, 1926, 6, Oct. 2, 1926, 6 (quotes), Oct. 16, 1926, 8, June 22, 1963, 5; John Fink and Francis Coughlin, *WGN: A Pictorial History* (Chicago: WGN, 1961), 10–19.

85. *FN*, Aug. 14, 1926, 7 (quotes), Sept. 18, 1926, 8, Oct. 23, 1926, 1; J. Fred MacDonald, *Don't Touch That Dial: Radio Programming in American Life from 1920 to 1960* (Chicago: Nelson-Hall, 1979), 2–13; Linton, "History of Chicago Radio Programming."

86. *FN,* July 24, 1926, 1 (first quote); Strong, *Amalgamated Clothing Workers of America,* 201–3 (second and third quotes).

87. Michael Kazin and Steven J. Ross, "America's Labor Day: The Dilemma of a Workers' Celebration," *Journal of American History* 78 (Mar. 1992): 1294–1323.

88. *FN,* Mar. 13, 1926, 1 (first quote), Mar. 27, 1926, 10 (second quote).

89. *FN,* July 31, 1926, 1–2.

90. For a selection of these addresses and speakers see *FN* issues published between Aug. 7, 1926, and Jan. 8, 1927.

91. *FN,* Aug. 21, 1926, 6 (first quote), Sept. 11, 1926, 11 (second quote), Oct. 9, 1926, 15, Oct. 23, 1926, 14.

92. Letters, Ed Nockels to Abe Baroff, June 22, 1927 (quote); Baroff to Nockels, July 7, 1927; and Nockels to Baroff, July 11, 1927, all in Folder 10, Box 2, Collection 6, Morris Sigman Correspondence, ILGWU Records.

93. *FN,* Apr. 10, 1926, 1; Levitas Interview, July 24, 1970, 8–9; ISFL, *Proceedings of the Forty-Fourth Convention,* 158. In mid-1927, the International Labor News Service's affiliated labor newspapers became clearinghouses for labor news to be sent to Chicago for broadcast. Local editors determined which news was "of sufficient importance to be put on the air." Joseph A. Wise articles, Aug. 1927 and July 21, 1927, WCFL Scrapbook, CFL Papers, CHS.

94. *FN,* Jan. 8, 1927, 11. Anton Johannsen had been "a leading anarcho-syndicalist" and leader in the free-speech fights of the Industrial Workers of the World. He strongly advocated labor solidarity and worker ownership and operation of all industry. Richard Schneirov and Thomas J. Suhrbur, *Union Brotherhood, Union Town: The History of the Carpenters' Union of Chicago, 1863–1987* (Carbondale: Southern Illinois University Press, 1988), 96–97.

95. *FN,* July 24, 1926, 11, Sept. 11, 1926, 9, Oct. 9, 1926, 7, Jan. 8, 1927, 10–11.

96. Ameringer, "Labor Can Build a Daily Press," in *Readings in Trade Unionism,* ed. Saposs, 384.

97. *FN,* Oct. 30, 1926, 9, Nov. 13, 1926, 14, Nov. 20, 1926, 6, Dec. 25, 1926, 14.

98. *FN,* Nov. 13, 1926, 8.

99. *FN,* Jan. 1, 1927, 8.

100. *FN,* Oct. 9, 1926, 15 (quotes), Oct. 23, 1926, 14, Nov. 27, 1926, 10, Dec. 4, 1926, 1–2, 7, 8, Dec. 11, 1926, 8–9, Dec. 18, 1926, 1–3, 7.

101. *FN,* Aug. 7, 1926, 1, 3, 11, Dec. 18, 1926, 1–2; Telegram, Morris Sigman to Fitzpatrick and Nockels, Dec. 11, 1926, Folder 10, Box 2, Collection 6, Morris Sigman Correspondence, ILGWU Records; *Labor Age* 16 (Jan. 1927): 23.

102. *FN,* June 12, 1926, 6, Aug. 7, 1926, 3, 11, Oct. 10, 1925, 1; AFL, *Report of the Proceedings of the Forty-Sixth Convention, 1926* (Washington, D.C.: AFL, 1926), 247–48 (quote).

103. "Ask Aid for Labor Radio," *Federated Press—Labor Letter,* Mar. 30, 1927, 8, Reel 9145, *Labor Letter* 1927 Folder, FP Papers, Rare Books and Manuscript Library, COLU; Letter, Victor Olander to Ed Nockels, May 24, 1927, Folder May 18–24, 1927, Box 10, Victor A. Olander Papers, CHS.

Chapter 2: The Promise of Labor Radio, 1927–28

1. Federal Radio Commission, *First Annual Report, 1927* (Washington, D.C.: GPO, 1927), 10–11; Rosen, *Modern Stentors,* 101–2; Barnouw, *Tower in Babel,* 189–90.

2. *FN,* Jan. 1, 1927, 6, Jan. 29, 1927, 6; McChesney, *Telecommunications, Mass Media, and Democracy,* 16–17.

3. *FN,* May 1, 1926, 4.

4. Senate Committee, *Radio Control,* 201–2, 205–7 (quote from 206).

5. *FN,* Dec. 4, 1926, 6 (first, third, and fourth quotes), May 8, 1926, 6; Rosen, *Modern Stentors,* 83, 85, 95–96; Senate Committee, *Radio Control,* 199; Letters, H. M. Merrill, the Schenectady Trades Assembly, to Frank Morrison, AFL Secretary, Feb. 11, 1926 (second quote), Wallace H. White to H. M. Merrill, Feb. 13, 1926, Frank Morrison to White, Feb. 19, 1926, and Morrison to White, Mar. 9, 1926, all in Radio Miscellaneous Folder, Box 51, Departmental File 1917–27, Wallace H. White Papers, Manuscript Division, Library of Congress, Washington, D.C.; "Radio Commission to Review Labor Station," *Federated Press—Labor Letter,* Mar. 2, 1927, 2, Reel 9145, *Labor Letter* 1927 Folder, FP Papers.

6. McChesney, *Telecommunications, Mass Media, and Democracy,* 17.

7. Barnouw, *Tower in Babel,* 195–99 (quotes from 198), 201; Rosen, *Modern Stentors,* 11, 104–6; McChesney, *Telecommunications, Mass Media, and Democracy,* 17–18.

8. "WCFL Radio Broadcast Station," Application for Radio License, ca. May 1927, Folder 11, Box 2, Collection 6, Morris Sigman Correspondence, ILGWU Records (quotes); *FN,* Mar. 12, 1927, 10, Apr. 23, 1927, 6.

9. *FN,* Apr. 23, 1927, 6; "WCFL Radio Broadcast Station" (quotes).

10. *FN,* Mar. 12, 1927, 10; Barnouw, *Tower in Babel,* 171, 211–12, 214; Lawrence W. Lichty, "The Impact of FRC and FCC Commissioners' Backgrounds on the Regulation of Broadcasting," *Journal of Broadcasting* 6 (Spring 1962): 99.

11. *FN,* Apr. 9, 1927, 1.

12. McChesney, *Telecommunications, Mass Media, and Democracy,* 20 (first quote); Rosen, *Modern Stentors,* 12–13 (second quote).

13. Orestes H. Caldwell, "The Reminiscences of Orestes H. Caldwell," 1951, 10–11, 12 (first quote), Oral History Collection, COLU; Rosen, *Modern Stentors,* 214 (second quote).

14. "Labor Offers Its Radio to Chicago Civic Hall," no. 2128, Mar. 18, 1927, and no. 2133, Mar. 24, 1927, Reel 9152, Press Releases Mar. 1927 Folder, FP Papers; *FN,* Mar. 19, 1927, 1 (quote), Mar. 26, 1927, 11; Letter, from Victor A. Olander, et al., Mar. 3, 1927, Folder Mar. 1–5, 1927, Box 9, Olander Papers.

15. *FN,* May 28, 1927, 6, June 4, 1927, 6.

16. *FN,* May 14, 1927, 5.

17. Sapolsky, "Response to Sean Wilentz," 35–38 (quote from 37).

18. *FN,* Sept. 1, 1928, 14, 60, June 25, 1927, 11.

19. *WCFL Radio Magazine* 1 (Spring 1928): 17 (quotes), 52.

20. *FN*, Mar. 24, 1928, 1–2.

21. *FN*, June 25, 1927, 11 (first, second, and third quotes); Letter, Nockels to William Green, Aug. 10, 1927, Folder 112, Box 15, JF (fourth quote).

22. *FN*, May 21, 1927, 10, June 11, 1927, 6, Aug. 13, 1927, 10–11 (quotes).

23. *WCFL Radio Magazine* 1 (Spring 1928): 9, 59; *FN*, June 23, 1928, 14; Letter, E. Nockels to Sam Pickard, Feb. 13, 1928, Folder 117, Box 16, JF (quotes); Letters, John Fitzpatrick and Ed Nockels to Abe Baroff and Morris Sigman, May 2, 1927, and ILGWU to Fitzpatrick, May 3, 1927, Folder 10, Box 2, Collection 6, Morris Sigman Correspondence, ILGWU Records.

24. *FN*, Feb. 4, 1928, 2 (quote), Feb. 11, 1928, 4, Feb. 25, 1928, 11; FP Chicago Weekly Letter, no. 2621, Dec. 29, 1928, Reel 9154, Press Releases Dec. 1928 Folder, FP Papers. Chain broadcasters used telephone or telegraph wires to broadcast simultaneously the same program over radio stations in different parts of the nation. Steven P. Phipps, "The Commercial Development of Short Wave Radio in the United States, 1920–1926," *Historical Journal of Film, Radio, and Television* 11, no. 3 (1991): 215–27.

25. *FN*, June 16, 1928, 3, June 23, 1928, 1, 14, Sept. 1, 1928, 21. WCFL received authorization to experiment with television for one hour each day in October 1928. Letter, Sam Pickard to Edward Nockels, Oct. 9, 1928, WCFL 1927–34 Folder, Box 27, FCC Broadcast Bureau, Broadcast License, RG 173, NARS; *NYT*, Mar. 12, 1930, 26.

26. *FN*, Feb. 19, 1927, 1, 3, Feb. 26, 1927, 14 (quote), Mar. 12, 1927, 10, Apr. 30, 1927, 1.

27. *FN*, Apr. 30, 1927, 1; *Variety*, May 4, 1927, 64 (advertisement), May 11, 1927, 51 (quotes), May 18, 1927, 52.

28. William Albig, "The Content of Radio Programs, 1925–1935," *Social Forces* 16, no. 3 (Mar. 1938): 338–49, esp. 344 (table 1).

29. *FN*, June 2, 1928, 5.

30. *FN*, Dec. 10, 1927, 11 (first quote), Apr. 16, 1927, 6 (second quote).

31. *FN*, June 4, 1927, 1, 3, Jan. 14, 1928, 6; *Radio Digest—Illustrated*, Sept. 1927, 11.

32. Letters, Mrs. R. E. Riggle to John H. Walker, Jan. 17, 1927, Walker to Riggle, Jan. 18, 1927, and Walker to Nockels, Jan. 18, 1927, Folder 238, General Correspondence, John H. Walker Papers, Illinois Historical Survey Library, University of Illinois at Urbana-Champaign; Letters, John McIntyre to ISFL, May 21, 1927, Folder May 18–24, 1927, Box 10, and V. Olander to John McIntyre, n.d., Folder May 25–31, 1927, Box 11, both in Olander Papers; *FN*, Jan. 28, 1928, 3, Apr. 21, 1928, 5, Apr. 28, 1928, 3.

33. *FN*, July 2, 1927, 1 (quotes), Aug. 6, 1927, 1–2.

34. *FN*, Feb. 25, 1928, 1 (quotes); MacDonald, *Don't Touch That Dial*, 10–11.

35. *FN*, May 26, 1928, 2, July 14, 1928, 8, Dec. 31, 1927, 8, July 2, 1927, 5, May 7, 1927, 1; *Variety*, May 11, 1927, 51.

36. *Radio Digest—Illustrated*, Sept. 1927, 11; *FN*, Apr. 21, 1928, 8, June 9, 1928, 4, June 30, 1928, 6, July 28, 1927, 5 (quotes), Aug. 4, 1927, 9.

37. *FN,* June 18, 1927, 6, Sept. 24, 1927, 1–2 (first quote), 7, Oct. 1, 1927, 1–3; ISFL, *Proceedings of the Forty-Fifth Annual Convention, Sept. 12, 1927,* 98, 100 (second quote), copy in Northwestern University Library.

38. *Radio Digest—Illustrated,* Sept. 1927, 11.

39. *FN,* June 11, 1927, 6, June 18, 1927, 6, June 25, 1927, 6, July 9, 1927, 6, Oct. 8, 1927, 6.

40. *FN,* Oct. 22, 1927, 2, Nov. 5, 1927, 1, Dec. 3, 1927, 3; Lizabeth Cohen, *Making a New Deal: Industrial Workers in Chicago, 1919–1939* (New York: Cambridge University Press, 1990), 76, 441n58; James R. Barrett, *Work and Community in the Jungle: Chicago's Packinghouse Workers, 1894–1922* (Urbana: University of Illinois Press, 1987), 105–7 (quote from 106).

41. *FN,* Aug. 27, 1927, 10, Sept. 10, 1927, 1, 6, Aug. 25, 1928, 1, 15; *Radio Digest—Illustrated,* Sept. 1927, 11; Kazin and Ross, "America's Labor Day," 1300–1310.

42. *FN,* Sept. 3, 1927, 1, Sept. 10, 1927, 1–3, 8, Feb. 4, 1928, 2, Aug. 4, 1928, 1–2, 15, Aug. 11, 1928, 1, Aug. 18, 1928, 8–9, Sept. 8, 1928, 1; Kazin and Ross, "America's Labor Day," 1301.

43. *FN,* Apr. 7, 1928, 14.

44. *FN,* May 14, 1927, 1–2, 5, Nov. 26, 1927, 3; Senate Committee on Interstate Commerce, *Commission on Communications,* 71st Cong., 1st Sess., 1929, 2:2079 (quote).

45. *FN,* Jan. 1, 1927, 2, July 23, 1927, 9, Nov. 19, 1927, 5, Nov. 17, 1928, 9; WCFL Application for Modification of Station License, Oct. 30, 1928, Docket 342, Box 70, FCC Docket Section, RG 173, NARS; *FN,* May 14, 1927, 6, 8, Mar. 5, 1927, 1, Nov. 10, 1928, 8; "Preacher Broadcasts Attack on Present Order," *Federated Press—Labor Letter,* Mar. 29, 1928, 4, Reel 9146, *Labor Letter* 1928 Folder, FP Papers.

46. *FN,* Jan. 22, 1927, 7; Joseph A. Wise, "Labor Paper Editors Quick to Recognize Importance of Hookup with Station WCFL," Aug. 1927, and "Nation-Wide Labor News Service Starts at Chicago," July 21, 1927 (quote), both in WCFL Scrapbook, CFL Papers; *FN,* Apr. 16, 1927, 8, Apr. 7, 1928, 15, June 2, 1928, 5, Oct. 6, 1928, 19, Oct. 13, 1928, 3.

47. *FN,* Apr. 16, 1927, 8, July 2, 1927, 11 (third quote), Oct. 29, 1927, 2 (fourth quote), Nov. 19, 1927, 11 (second quote), Dec. 15, 1928, 15, Jan. 19, 1929, 5–6 (first quote).

48. *FN,* May 21, 1927, 2, Aug. 13, 1927, 11, Sept. 10, 1927, 10.

49. Letters, Ed Nockels to William Green, Aug. 10, 1927, Nockels to Richard Wolff, Aug. 10, 1927, John H. Walker to Nockels, Aug. 11, 1927, all in Folder 112, Box 15, JF; *FN,* Apr. 16, 1927, 1, 9, Apr. 23, 1927, 1, 2, Jan. 28, 1928, 3, Nov. 19, 1927, 5, Nov. 24, 1928, 13.

50. Letters, Edward Nockels to Abe Baroff, June 22, 1927, Baroff to Nockels, July 7, 1927, and Nockels to Baroff, July 11, 1927, all in Folder 10, Box 2, Collection 6, Morris Sigman Correspondence, ILGWU Records.

51. *FN,* Feb. 4, 1928, 9, Feb. 18, 1928, 11.

52. *FN*, Apr. 7, 1928, 6 (first, second, and third quotes), Apr. 28, 1928, 2 (fourth quote), May 5, 1928, 5.

53. *Federated Press—Labor Letter*, Apr. 19, 1928, 4; Levitas Interview, July 24, 1970, 9 (quote); *FN*, Feb. 18, 1928, 6, Mar. 3, 1928, 1, Mar. 10, 1928, 1–2, Mar. 24, 1928, 1–2; *WCFL Radio Magazine* 1 (Spring 1928): 45.

54. *FN*, Apr. 7, 1928, 15; *Federated Press—Labor Letter*, Apr. 19, 1928, 4; *WCFL Radio Magazine* 1 (Spring 1928): 45.

55. *FN*, Oct. 29, 1927, 2, Dec. 10, 1927, 10 (first quote), Feb. 25, 1928, 11, Mar. 10, 1928, 11, May 26, 1928, 15, Sept. 15, 1928, 3 (second quote).

56. *FN*, Apr. 7, 1928, 15; Letter, Cecelia Galewski to WCFL, Mar. 7, 1928, Folder 118, JF; Letter, Harry B. Miller to J. Fitzpatrick (quote), Folder 119, Box 16, JF; Letters, Elmer Brader to WCFL, May 21, 1930, Mrs. E. Erisman to WCFL, June 26, 1930, Dan Niksic to WCFL, May 19, 1930, and Mrs. E. Lakowski to WCFL, June 27, 1930, all in Folder 127, Box 18, JF.

57. *Radio Broadcast*, May 1927, 15–16, July 1927, 138–40, Aug. 1927, 203–4 (quote from 204), July 1928, 144; *Radio Digest—Illustrated*, Feb. 15, 1927, 3.

58. James L. Palmer, "Radio Advertising," *Journal of Business* 1 (Oct. 1928): 495–96 (quotes); Susan Smulyan, *Selling Radio: The Commercialization of American Broadcasting, 1920–1934* (Washington: Smithsonian Institution Press, 1994), 7.

59. "Great Lakes Broadcasting Company Report on Survey of Chicago Radio Station Preference," Nov. 12, 1928, Docket 881, Box 167, FCC Docket Section, RG 173, NARS; FRC, *Annual Report to Congress, 1928* (Washington, D.C.: GPO, 1928), 118.

60. Claude S. Fischer, *America Calling: A Social History of the Telephone to 1940* (Berkeley: University of California Press, 1992), 108–13, 146–47, 180. A 1924 study of 884 families of unskilled and semi-skilled workers in Chicago showed that only 20 percent lived in households with a telephone. As early as 1905, however, 66 percent of Chicago's "elite" population lived in households with a telephone. Ibid., Appendix D, 287–88.

61. Linton, "History of Chicago Radio Programming," 45, 140; FRC, *Annual Report to Congress, 1928*, 118.

62. *FN*, Apr. 7, 1928, 15 (quote), Aug. 13, 1927, 11.

63. *FN*, Jan. 28, 1928, 2.

64. *FN*, Feb. 25, 1928, 11.

65. *FN*, Jan. 8, 1927, 10, 11 (quote), Jan. 29, 1927, 8, Feb. 26, 1927, 15.

66. *FN*, Apr. 9, 1927, 10.

67. *FN*, May 14, 1927, 5, Jan. 29, 1927, 8, Nov. 26, 1927, 3; Barnouw, *Tower in Babel*, 93, 207; *Variety*, Aug. 10, 1927, 53. During its first months on the air, WCFL did not adhere to the silent night tradition. An irate listener, known only as "R.K.K.K."—presumably the Radio Ku Klux Klan—demanded that WCFL "sign off at 7 pm on Monday night so as not to interfere with the program of WEAF, New York." *FN*, July 31, 1926, 6; *Daily Worker*, Aug. 2, 1926, 2. WCFL observed silent nights until January 1928, when it began signing off at 10:00 P.M. It abandoned the ritual in June. *FN*, Jan. 7, 1928, 5, June 2, 1928, 5.

68. Stuart Chase, "An Inquiry in Radio," *Outlook* 148 (Apr. 18, 1928): 617–18 (first quote from 618); Letter, M. L. Lyon to J. Fitzpatrick, Nov. 4, 1927, Folder 114, Box 16, JF (second quote); Transcript of Address by Dr. P. L. Clark, July 11, 1928, Docket 342, Box 70, FCC Docket Section, RG 173, NARS (third quote); *FN*, June 23, 1928, 15 (fourth quote).

69. *New Leader*, Jan. 8, 1927, 3, Feb. 12, 1927, 2; *FN*, Jan. 1, 1927, 8, Jan. 8, 1927, 11 (quotes).

70. *FN*, July 23, 1927, 9, Nov. 26, 1927, 11; "Thompson's Radio Talks Suppressed," *Public Ownership* 9, no. 11 (Nov. 1927): 176; *NYT*, Nov. 20, 1927, 17; *Chicago Daily News*, Nov. 19, 1927, 3 (quote); Forrest McDonald, *Insull* (Chicago: University of Chicago Press, 1962), 257–58.

71. "Freedom of Speech on Labor's Radio Upheld," Nov. 21, 1927, no. 2316, FP Chicago Bureau, Reel 9152, Press Releases Nov. 1927 Folder, FP Papers (quote); *FN*, Nov. 26, 1927, 11.

72. *FN*, Nov. 26, 1927, 11.

73. *FN*, Sept. 10, 1927, 10, Nov. 26, 1927, 11 (quote).

74. *WCFL Radio Magazine* 1 (Spring 1928): 9, 59; Letter, Ed Nockels to Sam Pickard, Feb. 13, 1928, Folder 117, Box 16, JF; *FN*, Feb. 25, 1928, 11, June 16, 1928, 3, June 23, 1928, 1, Sept. 1, 1928, 21; Letter, Sam Pickard to Ed Nockels, Oct. 9, 1928, WCFL 1927–34 Folder, Box 27, FCC Broadcast Bureau, Broadcast License, RG 173, NARS.

75. E. N. Nockels, "WCFL 50,000 Watt Station," *WCFL Radio Magazine* 1 (Spring 1928): 9; Letter, Ed Nockels to M. Woll, Nov. 6, 1928, Folder Nov. 1–13, 1928, General Correspondence, Box 16, FW; *New Leader*, July 6, 1929, 3.

76. Thomas T. Eoyang, *An Economic Study of the Radio Industry in the United States of America* (New York: RCA Institutes, 1937; New York: Arno Press, 1974), 179, 181; Barnouw, *Tower in Babel*, 189–93, 235–39, 250–53; Laurence Bergreen, *Look Now, Pay Later: The Rise of Network Broadcasting* (Garden City, N.Y.: Doubleday, 1980); *FN*, Jan. 8, 1927, 10–11, Feb. 4, 1928, 6, Oct. 20, 1928, 18.

77. Letter, R. L. Redcliffe to F. Lundquist, May 31, 1927, Folder 109, Box 15, JF; *Federated Press—Labor Letter*, Aug. 16, 1928, 2; Press Release, no. 2219, July 8, 1927, Reel 9152, Press Releases Apr.–July 1927 Folder, FP Papers; *FN*, Feb. 27, 1926, 11, Jan. 8, 1927, 10–11, Jan. 22, 1927, 11, Mar. 12, 1927, 11, June 11, 1927, 2, July 23, 1927, 10–11, May 26, 1928, 15; Letter, E. Nockels to Matthew Woll, Nov. 6, 1928, Folder Nov. 1–13, 1928, General Correspondence, Box 16, FW (quote); Newell, *Chicago and the Labor Movement*, 198.

78. Vita Lauter and Joseph H. Friend, "Radio and the Censors," *Forum* 86 (Dec. 1931): 360; *Federated Press—Labor Letter*, Mar. 8, 1928, 6 (quotes).

79. *FN*, Mar. 12, 1927, 10 (first quote), June 25, 1927, 11 (second quote).

80. "Ask Aid for Labor Radio"; Letter, R. L. Redcliffe to F. Lundquist, May 31, 1927, Folder 109, Box 15 (first and second quotes); Redcliffe to Fitzpatrick, Sept. 7, 1927, Folder 113, Box 16; and Redcliffe address, 1927, Folder 115, Box 16 (third quote), all in JF.

81. *FN,* Mar. 17, 1928, 4.

82. *FN,* Mar. 12, 1927, 11 (first quote), Mar. 17, 1928, 4 (second quote), Aug. 13, 1927, 10–11, Feb. 25, 1928, 11.

83. *FN,* Oct. 13, 1928, 2. For background on the Farmer-Labor party see Mc-Killen, *Chicago Labor and a Democratic Diplomacy,* 15–16, 152–53, 217–20.

84. *FN,* Jan. 1, 1927, 2, Jan. 22, 1927, 7, Mar. 12, 1927, 1–2, 10–11, Apr. 23, 1927, 6; Smulyan, *Selling Radio,* 61 (quote).

85. *FN,* Aug. 13, 1927, 10–11.

86. *FN,* Oct. 13, 1928, 1–2; Senate Committee, *Commission on Communications,* 1st Sess., 2:2082.

87. *FN,* Aug. 11, 1928, 14–15; *Federated Press—Labor Letter,* Aug. 16, 1928, 2; Senate Committee, *Commission on Communications,* 1st Sess., 2:2082.

88. *FN,* Aug. 11, 1928, 14.

89. *FN,* Mar. 12, 1927, 10, Nov. 12, 1927, 11, Oct. 20, 1928, 18, Oct. 26, 1929, 11.

90. *FN,* Dec. 25, 1926, 14, Nov. 19, 1927, 2 (quote), Nov. 26, 1927, 3, Dec. 10, 1927, 1, 3, Dec. 24, 1927, 15, Feb. 4, 1928, 2, Oct. 20, 1928, 18.

91. *FN,* May 21, 1927, 3, July 23, 1927, 10–11, Oct. 20, 1928, 18, Jan. 14, 1928, 9, Jan. 21, 1928, 2, Mar. 10, 1928, 3, 5, July 14, 1928, 8, Oct. 20, 1928, 8, 13, Nov. 17, 1928, 10, Nov. 24, 1928, 13; Script of "Early Risers" program, Nov. 2, 1928, Docket 342, Box 70, FCC Docket Section, RG 173, NARS.

92. Rosen, *Modern Stentors,* 133–34; McChesney, *Telecommunications, Mass Media, and Democracy,* 21–29; "Thirty Years in Broadcasting," Oral History of William S. Hedges, Oral History Project Folder, Box 2, William S. Hedges Papers, SHSW; Lichty, "FRC and FCC Commissioners' Backgrounds," 97–110.

93. Rosen, *Modern Stentors,* 134–37; McChesney, *Telecommunications, Mass Media, and Democracy,* 29–37.

94. *FN,* Sept. 29, 1928, 4, Oct. 6, 1928, 1; *NYT,* Oct. 7, 1928, 12.

95. *FN,* Oct. 13, 1928, 3, 6. Nockels did not make much of the last point because commercial radio firms used it to rationalize permanent claims on broadcast frequencies and licenses.

96. *FN,* Dec. 8, 1928, 9.

97. *FN,* Oct. 13, 1928, 3, 6, Dec. 7, 1929, 15 (quotes). Nockels understood that a revolving door connected the FRC with corporate broadcasters. Commissioners Sam Pickard and Henry Bellows, for example, became executives for CBS after brief terms on the FRC. Bergreen, *Look Now, Pay Later,* 62; Barnouw, *Tower in Babel,* 247, 251, 273. William S. Hedges, WMAQ manager and NAB official, aided in formulating an industry reallocation proposal that partly became FRC policy. He admitted that his "first interest was in the WMAQ. . . . I wanted to see it come out with a 670 kilocycles full-time clear channel. That was my objective. I don't feel any qualms about that because I felt that our station was doing a high grade of public service." "Thirty Years in Broadcasting."

98. *FN,* Dec. 7, 1929, 13, Jan. 12, 1929, 2–3 (quote from 3); AFL, *Report of the Pro-*

ceedings of the Fifty-First Annual Convention, October 5–15, 1931 (Washington, D.C.: AFL, 1931), 469.

99. *FN*, Mar. 30, 1929, 6, 14 (quotes).

100. *FN*, Oct. 13, 1928, 6 (quotes), Nov. 17, 1928, 1; "Chicago Fights Tribune Radio Control," Mar. 11, 1929, no. 2701, FP Washington Bureau, Reel 9154, Press Releases Mar. 1929 Folder, FP Papers.

101. *FN*, Oct. 13, 1928, 6, Nov. 17, 1928, 1, May 4, 1929, 2; Letter, Ed Nockels to Frank Walsh, Feb. 24, 1932, Folder Feb. 18–29, 1932, General Correspondence, Box 19, FW (quote).

102. AFL Executive Council Meeting Minutes, Jan. 17, 1927 (quote), and Apr. 24, 1928; Letter, Victor Olander to Edward Nockels, May 24, 1927, Folder May 18–24, 1927, Box 10, Olander Papers.

103. "Ask Aid for Labor Radio"; AFL, *Report of the Proceedings of the Forty-Seventh Convention, 1927* (Washington, D.C.: AFL, 1927), 378 (first and second quotes), 379 (third quote).

104. McKillen, *Chicago Labor and a Democratic Diplomacy.*

105. AFL Executive Council Meeting Minutes, Oct. 18–19, 1928.

106. Letter, Matthew Woll to Ed Nockels, Nov. 3, 1928, Folder Nov. 1–13, 1928, General Correspondence, Box 16, FW. Nockels did appear before Congress as the AFL's radio advocate. Senate Committee, *Commission on Communications*, 1st Sess., 2:2074.

107. Letter, Ed Nockels to Matthew Woll, Nov. 6, 1928, Folder Feb. 1–13, 1928, General Correspondence, Box 16, FW.

108. Ibid.

109. AFL Executive Council Meeting Minutes, Nov. 18, 1928.

110. Ibid. *WCFL Radio Magazine* 2 (Summer 1929): 14–15; *FN*, Dec. 1, 1928, 1; AFL, *Report of the Proceedings of the Forty-Eighth Annual Convention, November 19–28, 1928* (Washington, D.C.: AFL, 1928), 115 (first quote), 116, 215 (second and third quotes), 254–55. CFL's willingness to abide by AFL policies seemed particularly ironic at the 1928 convention. AFL officials unilaterally outlawed the Brookwood Labor College, condemning it as a haven for communists. Fitzpatrick, who served as one of the college's directors, protested the AFL's undemocratic action. AFL, *Report of the Forty-Eighth Convention*, 86–87; FP Chicago Weekly Letter, Nov. 17, 1928, Reel 9154, Press Releases Nov. 1928 Folder, FP Papers; *Federated Press—Labor Letter*, Dec. 6, 1928, 2; *Federated Press—Labor Letter*, Dec. 20, 1928, 1–2.

111. AFL, *Report of the Forty-Eighth Convention*, 254 (first quote), 115–16, 215; *American Federationist* 35 (Dec. 1928): 1426, 1427 (second quote).

112. Barnouw, *Tower in Babel*, 204–6 (second quote from 205); Advisory Council of the National Broadcasting Company, *The President's Report—Committee Reports*, Second to Sixth Meetings, Mar. 1928, Jan. 1929, Jan. 1930, 1931, Feb. 1932, Folders 1–10, Box 107, NBC Records, SHSW; AFL Executive Council Meeting Minutes, Oct. 23, 1928 (first quote).

113. Douglas, *Inventing American Broadcasting*, 315–17.

114. *FN*, Dec. 10, 1927, 11.

Chapter 3: Clear-Channel and Other Battles, 1929–32

1. McChesney, *Telecommunications, Mass Media, and Democracy*, 36.

2. Ibid., 38–150; George H. Gibson, *Public Broadcasting: The Role of the Federal Government, 1912–76* (New York: Praeger, 1977), 19–23; Barnouw, *Tower in Babel*, 259–63, 265; Erik Barnouw, *The Golden Web: A History of Broadcasting in the United States, vol. 2—1933 to 1953* (New York: Oxford University Press, 1968), 23; Letter, Professor B. B. Brackett to P. Armstrong, Apr. 27, 1931, NAEB-Add. General Correspondence 1929–31 Folder; Letters, Brackett to T. M. Beaird, Feb. 2, 1932, and T. M. Beaird to J. F. Wright, Feb. 25, 1932, General Correspondence 1932 Folder, all in Box 1A, General Correspondence 1929–50, National Association of Educational Broadcasters Papers, SHSW.

3. House Committee on Merchant Marine and Fisheries, *Hearings on H.R. 15430, Federal Radio Commission*, 70th Cong., 2d Sess., 1929, part 1, 234–35 (first quote from 235), 238 (second quote), 243.

4. *FN*, Dec. 22, 1928, 1, 3, 11; Letters, J. Fitzpatrick and Nockels to Abe Baroff (ILGWU), Dec. 15, 1928, and Jan. 24, 1929, Resolution Re: Application of CFL to FRC, Jan. 28, 1929, and Letter, Hope Thompson to A. Baroff, Jan. 30, 1929, all in Folder 11, Box 2, Collection 6, Morris Sigman Correspondence, ILGWU Records; Meeting of the Executive Board of ILGWU, Jan. 23, 1929, General Executive Board, ILGWU—Minutes of Meetings, Collection 16, ILGWU Records; *FN*, Jan. 12, 1929, 1–3.

5. *NYT*, Jan. 20, 1929, sec. 9, p. 23. Several progressive senators—including George W. Norris (Nebraska), Smith W. Brookhart (Iowa), and Thomas J. Walsh (Montana)—naturally joined the attack on the radio trust and the FRC. "Norris in Radio and Power Trust Battle," Nov. 17, 1928, no. 2611, FP Washington Bureau, Reel 9154, Press Releases Nov. 1928 Folder, FP Papers; *NYT*, Nov. 17, 1928, 10.

6. Letter, Ed Nockels to all City Central Bodies, Apr. 4, 1929, Folder Apr. 1–17, 1929, General Correspondence, Box 16, FW; Telegrams, FRC Docket 342 (WCFL), Box 70, FCC Docket Section, RG 173, NARS.

7. National Women's Trade Union League of America, *Proceedings: Eleventh Convention, Washington, D.C., May 6–11, 1929*, 46–47 (quote from 47), 113–14, copy in Tamiment Library. See also Missouri State Federation of Labor, *Proceedings of the Thirty-Third Annual and Third Biennial Convention of the Missouri State Federation of Labor, May 27–30, 1929, St. Joseph Missouri*, 51–52, copy in Northwestern University Library. Labor radio also received backing from the Socialist party. Letter, M. H. Barnes to James Oneal, June 29, 1929, Reel 12, Series 1, Correspondence and General Records, National Office Papers, Socialist Party of America Papers, SHSW; and *New Leader*, Jan. 19, 1929, 10.

8. *WCFL Radio Magazine* 2 (Summer 1929): 14; *NYT*, Apr. 17, 1929, 32; Transcript

of FRC Hearings, Apr. 19, 1929, Docket 342, Box 70, FCC Docket Section, RG 173, NARS (first and seventh quotes); "Radio Loot—Who Has It?" Apr. 19, 1929, no. 2734, FP Washington Bureau, Reel 9154, Press Releases Apr. 1929 Folder, FP Papers (second through sixth quotes).

9. *WCFL Radio Magazine* 2 (Summer 1929): 15.

10. *Chicago Daily News,* Apr. 18, 1929, 39–40; *WCFL Radio Magazine* 2 (Summer 1929): 14–15 (quote from 14); *NYT,* Apr. 17, 1929, 32, Apr. 19, 1929, 31; *FN,* May 4, 1929, 1–2, May 18, 1929, 2, 10.

11. Transcript of FRC Hearings, Apr. 19, 1929 (quote); Transcripts of WCFL programming, Feb. 12–19, 1929, Docket 342, Box 70, FCC Docket Section, RG 173, NARS.

12. Laurence Todd, "The Washington Scene," Apr. 16, 1929, no. 2731, FP Washington Bureau, Reel 9154, Press Releases Apr. 1929 Folder, FP Papers.

13. ISFL, *Proceedings: Forty-Ninth Annual Convention, September 14–19, 1931,* 162, copy in Northwestern University Library.

14. Transcript of FRC Hearings, Apr. 19, 1929.

15. Todd, "The Washington Scene" (quotes); "Class Struggle in Radio Won't Be Glossed Over," Apr. 18, 1929, no. 2733, FP Washington Bureau, Reel 9154, Press Releases Apr. 1929 Folder, FP Papers; *Labor's News* 17 (Apr. 27, 1929): 3.

16. *FN,* May 25, 1929, 1, 6, June 8, 1929, 1, 8, June 15, 1929, 1–2, 17; Letter, Ed Nockels to Edwin P. Thayer, Secretary of U.S. Senate, June 14, 1929, Sen 71A-J37 Folder, Box 174, RG 46, NARS.

17. *WCFL Radio Magazine* 2 (Summer 1929): 37; *FN,* June 8, 1929, 1, Aug. 10, 1929, 3 (quote), 9; Senate Committee, *Commission on Communications,* 1st Sess., 1:126–28, 130.

18. Laurence Todd, "Radio Czars O.K. Air Gag on Union Labor," *Labor's News* 17 (July 27, 1929): 3; *FN,* Aug. 10, 1929, 1, 3 (quotes), 9. Numerous cases of commercial radio station censorship of progressive, radical, and labor opinion arose during this period. See, for example, *Federated Press—Labor Letter,* Mar. 1928, 6; Lauter and Friend, "Radio and the Censors," 359–65; and Letters, Clarence Senior to G. August Gerber, Oct. 18, 1929, and Clarence Senior to Ed Nockels, Oct. 18, 1929, Reel 12, Series 1, Correspondence and General Records, National Office Papers, Socialist Party of America Papers.

19. Todd, "Radio Czars," 3.

20. AFL Executive Council Meeting Minutes, May 27, 1929, 94–95; "Labor Radio Rights Up to Council," May 23, 1929, no. 2762, FP Washington Bureau, Reel 9154, Press Releases May 1929 Folder, FP Papers; *NYT,* June 7, 1929, 28 (quotes); *FN,* June 15, 1929, 1–2.

21. *NYT,* June 26, 1929, 29; *FN,* July 13, 1929, 3 (quote); Caldwell, "Reminiscences of Orestes H. Caldwell," 23. Congress eventually repealed the Davis Amendment, which forced the FRC to assign frequencies in proportion to state populations.

22. *NYT,* June 26, 1929, 29; *FN,* July 13, 1929, 3 (first, second, and third quotes), 8 (fourth quote); *Illinois State Federation of Labor Weekly News Letter,* Apr. 5, 1930, 3.

23. *FN*, July 13, 1929, 3, 8; Senate Committee, *Commission on Communications*, 1st Sess., 1:68; Caldwell, "Reminiscences of Orestes H. Caldwell," 19 (quotes; emphasis in original).

24. *FN*, July 6, 1929, 1 (second quote), 7 (third quote), July 13, 1929, 8 (first quote).

25. Harvey O'Connor, "Flashes from the Labor World," *Labor Age* 18 (Aug. 1929): 25.

26. AFL, *Report of the Proceedings of the Forty-Ninth Annual Convention, October 7–18, 1929* (Washington, D.C.: AFL, 1929), 291–92, 103 (quote; emphasis added); AFL Executive Council Meeting Minutes, Feb. 20, 1929, 42–43, May 27, 1929, 94–95, and Aug. 15, 1929, 28–31.

27. *FN*, Nov. 2, 1929, 2.

28. *FN*, Feb. 23, 1929, 15.

29. G. William Domhoff, *Who Rules America?* (Englewood Cliffs, N.J.: Prentice-Hall, 1967), 111–14.

30. Women's Trade Union League, *Proceedings: Eleventh Convention,* 46 (first quote); *FN*, Oct. 12, 1929, 1; William Hard, "A Woman Senator?" *Review of Reviews* 81 (Mar. 1930): 64–65 (second and third quotes); U.S. Senate, *Biographical Directory of the United States Congress, 1774–1989,* 100th Cong., 2d Sess., 1989, S. Doc. 100–34, 895, 1066; *FN*, Nov. 9, 1929, 20 (fourth quote).

31. *FN*, Feb. 1, 1930, 2 (quotes), Feb. 8, 1930, 1; Senate Committee, *Commission on Communications,* 1st Sess., 2:1886–97.

32. Senate Committee, *Commission on Communications,* 1st Sess., 2:2074–82 (quote from 2:2080).

33. Senate Committee on Interstate Commerce, *Commission on Communications,* 71st Cong., 2d Sess., 1930, part 12, 1603–4 (first quote from 1604), 1642 (second quote), 1643 (third quote); part 15, 2362 (fourth and fifth quotes); part 13, 1744–45.

34. Letter, Nockels to John Walker, Nov. 5, 1929 (first quote), Folder 325, General Correspondence, Walker Papers; *FN*, Nov. 9, 1929, 20, Nov. 16, 1929, 8, Nov. 23, 1929, 24 (quotes), Dec. 7, 1929, 20, Dec. 28, 1929, 8, Feb. 15, 1930, 9; *NYT*, Nov. 24, 1929, sec. 11, p. 14.

35. *FN*, Dec. 22, 1928, 15, June 15, 1929, 8, June 2, 1928, 5, Feb. 9, 1929, 8, 11; Letter, William Rubin to F. Lundquist, Mar. 26, 1930, Correspondence 1930, Folder Jan.–Mar., Box 7, Rubin Papers.

36. Edward Nockels, "The Voice of Labor," *American Federationist* 37 (Apr. 1930): 414–16 (third and fourth quotes from 416), 419; Edward Nockels, "Voice of Labor," *Illinois State Federation of Labor Weekly News Letter,* Apr. 26, 1930, 1 (first and second quotes), 3 (fifth quote). The arguments found in these articles were drawn from Nockels's testimony before the Senate Committee on Interstate Commerce in January 1930. Senate Committee, *Commission on Communications,* 1st Sess., 2:2074–82.

37. *Federal Reporter: Second Series* 41 (July–Sept. 1930): 422–23 (third and fourth

quotes from 423); "Decisions," *Air Law Review* 1, no. 3 (July 1930): 419 (first and second quotes).

38. Ralph Miliband, *The State in Capitalist Society* (New York: Basic Books, 1969), 72–73.

39. *Program: Formal Dedication of Radio Station,* Sept. 25, 1931, Radio Station WCFL Folder, Miscellaneous, CFL Papers; AFL, *Report of the Proceedings of the Fiftieth Annual Convention, October 6–17, 1930* (Washington, D.C.: AFL, 1930), 241–42, 379–80.

40. *FN*, Feb. 28, 1931, 1 (first quote), Mar. 14, 1931, 1, 6–7, Sept. 19, 1931, 1–2, Jan. 31, 1931, 9, Mar. 28, 1931, 14 (second and third quotes); Paul Hutchinson, "Is the Air Already Monopolized?" *Christian Century* 48 (Apr. 1, 1931): 441; Ruth Brindze, *Not to Be Broadcast: The Truth about Radio* (New York: Vanguard Press, 1937), 156; McChesney, *Telecommunications, Mass Media, and Democracy,* 128–39.

41. *Radio Broadcast,* Sept. 1926, 375–76, Oct. 1926, 475 (second quote), July 1927, 139–40, Sept. 1929, 273 (first and third quotes). See McChesney, *Telecommunications, Mass Media, and Democracy,* 107–20, for details of the industry's position.

42. *Radio Broadcast,* Jan. 1930, 142.

43. The views of NAB officials frequently appeared in trade journals such as *Radio Broadcast* and *Broadcasting.* Officials also testified before various congressional hearings. In 1933, the NAB brought together its "analyses" of the American radio system in one publication. See NAB, *Broadcasting in the United States* (Washington, D.C.: NAB, 1933), 16, 56 (first quote), 168 (second and third quotes), 172–74; McChesney, *Telecommunications, Mass Media, and Democracy,* 108–11; and David R. Mackey, "The Development of the National Association of Broadcasters," *Journal of Broadcasting* 1, no. 4 (Fall 1957): 305–25.

44. "Thirty Years in Broadcasting"; *WCFL Radio Magazine* 1 (Spring 1928): 46 (first quote); *FN*, Feb. 9, 1929, 14–15 (second and third quotes), Dec. 7, 1929, 9, 13 (fifth quote), 15 (fourth quote). For background on the NAB see David R. Mackey, "The National Association of Broadcasters—Its First Twenty Years" (Ph.D. diss., Northwestern University, 1956).

45. *CT,* July 6, 1926, Editorial; *FN*, Mar. 24, 1928, 14, Apr. 4, 1931, 16; Tebbel, *An American Dynasty,* 110, 118, 121, 215; Seldes, *Lords of the Press,* 41–42, 47–52; Letter, Robert R. McCormick to Hatcher Hughes, Dec. 30, 1932 (quotes), vol. 513, Correspondence on Federal Legislation, Reel 88, ACLU Archives, New York Public Library.

46. O. H. Caldwell, "The Administration of Federal Radio Legislation," *Annals of the American Academy of Political Science* 142 (Mar. 1929): supp., 47 (first quote); *FN*, Nov. 9, 1929, 20, Jan. 31, 1931, 9; Senate Committee, *Commission on Communications,* 1st sess., 1:25; Frank C. Waldrop, *McCormick of Chicago: An Unconventional Portrait of a Controversial Figure* (Englewood Cliffs, N.J.: Prentice-Hall, 1966), 201–2 (second quote); Llewellyn White, *The American Radio: A Report on the Broadcasting Industry in the United States from the Commission on Freedom of the Press* (Chicago: University of Chicago Press, 1947), 148n4 (third and fourth quotes); *Radio*

Broadcast, Oct. 1928, 340; C. B. Rose Jr., *National Policy for Radio Broadcasting: Report of a Committee of the National Economic and Social Planning Association* (New York: Harper and Brothers, 1940), 81–82.

47. *Education by Radio* 2, no. 26 (Nov. 10, 1932): 104 (quote); Transcript of Interview with Ward L. Quaal, by author, Aug. 10, 1990, Chicago.

48. *Radio Broadcast,* Oct. 1928, 340; Louis G. Caldwell, "Three Years of the Federal Radio Commission," *Radio Broadcast,* Mar. 1930, 270–72 (first quote from 270; second quote from 272); Louis G. Caldwell, "Appeals from Decisions of the Federal Radio Commission," *Journal of Air Law* 1 (July 1930): 274–320; Louis G. Caldwell, "Recent Decisions under Radio Act of 1927," *Air Law Review* 1 (July 1930): 295–330; Louis G. Caldwell, "Who Owns the Ether?" *Radio Law Bulletin of the School of Law* (Catholic University of America) 17, no. 5 (Aug. 1931): 1–14; Ward L. Quaal and James A. Brown, *Broadcast Management: Radio, Television,* 2d ed. (New York: Hastings House, 1976), 442; Quaal Interview.

49. Letter, Ed Nockels to F. Walsh, Feb. 24, 1932, Folder Feb. 18–29, 1932, General Correspondence, Box 19, FW; *Chicago Daily News,* Sept. 18, 1930, 32.

50. *CT,* Dec. 16, 1930, 1 (third quote), Dec. 17, 1930, 14; *FN,* Jan. 31, 1931, 9 (first and second quotes).

51. *FN,* Apr. 25, 1931, 9; *NYT,* Apr. 16, 1931, 34 (quote), Apr. 17, 1931, 32; *Chicago Daily News,* Apr. 18, 1931, 16.

52. *NYT,* Apr. 19, 1931, 22 (quotes); *New Leader,* Apr. 25, 1931, 8.

53. *Labor's News* 19, no. 26 (Dec. 27, 1930): 4 (quote); Nockels, "Voice of Labor," 419.

54. Barnouw, *Tower in Babel,* 261; *Radio Digest* 27, no. 4 (Sept. 1931): 54. On the ABA's involvement in radio issues see Robert W. McChesney, "Free Speech and Democracy! Louis G. Caldwell, the American Bar Association, and the Debate over the Free Speech Implications of Broadcast Regulation, 1928–1938," *American Journal of Legal History* 35 (Oct. 1991): 351–92.

55. ABA, *Report of the Fifty-Fourth Annual Meeting of the American Bar Association, Atlantic City, New Jersey, September 17–19, 1931* (Baltimore: Lord Baltimore Press, 1933), 381–89, 97–104 (quote from 104); *The American Bar: A Biographical Dictionary of Contemporary Lawyers, 1933* (Minneapolis: James C. Fifield, 1932); *The American Bar: A Biographical Dictionary of the Leading Lawyers of the United States and Canada, 1941* (Minneapolis: James C. Fifield, 1941), 1085–86, 862; J. C. Schwarz, ed., *1937,* vol. 1 of *Who's Who in Law* (New York, 1937), 142–43, 373. Before 1931, ABA committees favored repeal of antimonopoly clauses of the 1927 Radio Act and passage of provisions that would guarantee private property rights on the air. *FN,* Nov. 9, 1929, 20–22; *NYT,* Sept. 3, 1929, 24; Senate Committee, *Commission on Communications,* 1st Sess., 1:66.

56. ABA Standing Committee on Communications, Transcript of Open Meeting, Sept. 16, 1931, Atlantic City, N.J., 1–2, 21–22, 27 (quote), Northwestern University Law School Library, Chicago.

57. Letters, Walter V. Woehlke to Marcy B. Darnell, July 31, 1931; H. O. Davis to Editor, *Iroquois County Times,* Sept. 25, 1931; David Sarnoff to M. H. Aylesworth, Oct. 21, 1931; and Aylesworth to Sarnoff, Oct. 23, 1931, all in Folder 65, Box 5, NBC Records. On the press-radio competition see McChesney, *Telecommunications, Mass Media, and Democracy,* 57–62, 136–37.

58. ABA Standing Committee on Communications, Transcript of Open Meeting, 34–37 (quote from 36).

59. Ibid., 36.

60. *Education by Radio* 1 (Aug. 27, 1931): 101.

61. Telegram, Frank Walsh to Ed Nockels, Sept. 14, 1931, Folder Sept. 14–30, 1931, General Correspondence, Box 18, FW.

62. ABA Standing Committee on Communications, Transcript of Open Meeting, 3–5.

63. ABA, *Report of Fifty-Fourth Meeting,* 107–9.

64. Ibid., 111–13 (quote from 111); *NYT,* Sept. 19, 1931, 6, Sept. 25, 1931, 24.

65. Letters, Tracy F. Tyler to Walsh, Nov. 23, 1931, L. Caldwell to Walsh, Dec. 21, 1931, Folder Nov. 13–30, 1931, General Correspondence, Box 18, FW; Letter, Walsh to Nockels, Apr. 5, 1932, Folder Apr. 1–12, 1932, General Correspondence, Box 19, FW (quote).

66. *FN,* Feb. 15, 1930, 9, June 21, 1930, 8, Jan. 3, 1931, 8, June 20, 1931, 2, 8, Sept. 26, 1931, 5; AFL, *Report of the Fifty-First Convention,* 470 (quotes).

67. *Education by Radio* 1 (Feb. 12, 1931): 1, 1 (Mar. 26, 1931): 25–28 (first and second quotes from 28), 1 (June 18, 1931): 73–78, 2 (Mar. 31, 1932): 49–52 (third quote from 50); Letter, B. B. Brackett to T. M. Beaird, Feb. 2, 1932, NAEB-Add. General Correspondence 1932 Folder, Box 1A, National Association of Educational Broadcasters Papers; McChesney, *Telecommunications, Mass Media, and Democracy,* 47–52, 93–95, 129–30.

68. AFL, *Report of the Fifty-First Convention,* 344.

69. Barnouw, *Tower in Babel,* 261–62; McChesney, *Telecommunications, Mass Media, and Democracy,* 52–56; Rosen, *Modern Stentors,* 166; Letter, Levering Tyson to Neville Miller, Dec. 9, 1938, Folder 66, Box 62, NBC Records (quotes); *School and Society,* May 17, 1930, 666–67, Mar. 28, 1931, 428.

70. *FN,* Apr. 30, 1932, 1–3; Letter, M. Woll to Nockels, Apr. 18, 1932, in Letter from M. Lynch to V. Olander, Apr. 20, 1932, Folder Apr. 16–20, 1932; and Letter, Woll to Nockels, Apr. 23, 1932, Folder Apr. 21–26, 1932, all in Box 52, Olander Papers. The AFL tried to link WCFL with the NACRE. Letter, Spencer Miller to John Fitzpatrick, May 22, 1930, Folder 127, Box 18, JF.

71. *Congressional Record,* 72d Cong., 1st Sess., 1932, vol. 75, part 2:1555, 1997.

72. *FN,* Jan. 16, 1932, 1, 3.

73. Letter, Ed Nockels to Frank Walsh, Feb. 17, 1932, Folder Feb. 1–17, 1932, General Correspondence, Box 19, FW.

74. Ibid.

75. *NYT,* Mar. 17, 1932, 16; *Education by Radio* 2 (Apr. 21, 1932): 57–60.

76. *Broadcasting,* Apr. 1, 1932, 25.

77. Ibid.

78. *FN,* Mar. 26, 1932, 1, 6 (quotes); Senate Committee on Interstate Commerce, *Hearings before the Committee on Interstate Commerce: To Amend the Radio Act of 1927.* 72d Cong., 1st Sess., 1932, 23–26; *Broadcasting,* Apr. 1, 1932, 25.

79. *Education by Radio* 2 (Apr. 21, 1932): 57–60.

80. *Broadcasting,* Apr. 15, 1932, 14; McChesney, *Telecommunications, Mass Media, and Democracy,* 146–47.

81. Letter, Ed Nockels to W. B. Rubin, Apr. 14, 1932, Folder Apr. 13–30, 1932, General Correspondence, Box 19, FW.

82. Letters, Olive G. Recker to Members of ABA Committee on Communications, Feb. 1, 1932; L. Caldwell to Nockels, Apr. 8, 1932 (first quote); Nockels to Walsh, Apr. 14, 1932 (second quote); Nockels to W. B. Rubin, Apr. 14, 1932 (third quote); and Walsh to Nockels, Apr. 21, 1932 (fourth and fifth quotes), all in Folder Apr. 13–30, 1932, General Correspondence, Box 19, FW; *FN,* May 7, 1932, 6 (sixth and seventh quotes).

83. *Broadcasting,* June 1, 1932, 28; American Bar Association, *Advance Program, Fifty-Fifth Annual Meeting, Washington, D.C., October 12–15, 1932,* 146, Law Library, Northwestern University, Chicago.

84. Letter, P. Armstrong to Dr. R. P. Raup, Mar. 22, 1932, Folder 1129, Container 58, Payne Fund, Inc. Records, Western Reserve Historical Society, Cleveland, Ohio; McChesney, *Telecommunications, Mass Media, and Democracy,* 147.

85. *FN,* June 4, 1932, 6.

86. *New Leader,* Jan. 19, 1929, 10.

87. Letters, M. Woll to V. Olander, Mar. 29, and Olander to Woll, Apr. 5, 1932, both in Folder Mar. 29–31, 1932, Box 51, Olander Papers; *FN,* May 21, 1932, 3 (quote).

88. Letter, H. D. Hatfield to W. Green, Folder 16, Box 80, Congressional Correspondence, Collection 1, AFL-CIO Department of Legislation, Meany Archives.

89. *FN,* Oct. 26, 1929, 11–13, June 21, 1930, 12–14, July 30, 1932, 1, 5, Aug. 6, 1932, 1–2, 5, Sept. 3, 1932, 5.

90. *FN,* May 10, 1930, 1 (quotes); *Labor's News* 18, no. 19 (May 10, 1930): 8.

91. *FN,* Apr. 4, 1931, 16.

92. *New Leader,* Jan. 19, 1929, 10.

93. *FN,* Jan. 16, 1932, 1 (quotes), Oct. 8, 1932, 5.

Chapter 4: *"Something Different into Our Lives"*

1. *Radio Broadcast,* July 1927, 138, Aug. 1927, 204, Jan. 1930, 142.

2. Newell, *Chicago and the Labor Movement,* 32–41, esp. table 4 (third quote from 32); Cohen, *Making a New Deal,* 214–49; *FN,* Mar. 22, 1930, 21 (first and second quotes).

3. Ventura Free Press, *American Broadcasting: An Analytical Study of One Day's Output of 206 Commercial Radio Stations Including Program Contents and Advertising Interruptions* (Ventura, Calif.: Ventura Free Press, 1933), 1–2, 9, 15.

4. Albig, "The Content of Radio Programs," 338–49, esp. table 1.

5. Harrison B. Summers, *A Thirty-Year History of Programs Carried on National Radio Networks in the United States, 1926–1956* (Columbus: Ohio State University Press, 1958; New York: Arno Press, 1971), 11–30.

6. Judith C. Waller, *Radio: The Fifth Estate,* 2d ed. (Boston: Houghton Mifflin, 1950), 72, 90; Waldo Abbot, *Handbook of Broadcasting: How to Broadcast Effectively* (New York: McGraw-Hill, 1937), 362; Sydney W. Head, *Broadcasting in America: A Survey of Television and Radio* (Cambridge, Mass.: Riverside Press, 1956), 200–202.

7. Summers, *History of Programs,* 19–23; McChesney, *Telecommunications, Mass Media, and Democracy,* 29–30; Smulyan, *Selling Radio,* 131.

8. WCFL Application for License Renewal, Nov. 25, 1931, WCFL 1927–34 Folder, Box 27, FCC Broadcast Bureau, Broadcast License, RG 173, NARS; *FN,* Mar. 21, 1931, 8, May 30, 1931, 8, Dec. 26, 1931, 6.

9. Smulyan, *Selling Radio,* 96.

10. *FN,* Dec. 22, 1928, 9, Sept. 2, 1929, 12, Nov. 9, 1929, 8, Aug. 16, 1930, 9. See table 1 in the appendix.

11. *FN,* May 28, 1927, 5, Jan. 5, 1929, 1, 3 (quotes); Copeland Smith League Booklets, *Radio Broadcasts by Copeland Smith,* Radio League Leaflets, nos. 3–17, n.d., CHS; Transcript of Smith's "Question Box," Feb. 17, 1929, FRC Docket 342 (WCFL), Box 70, FCC Docket Section, RG 173, NARS; Copeland Smith League, "Biographies in Bronze" Scripts no. 1–10, CHS; Transcript of "Biographies in Bronze," Feb. 14, 1929, FRC Docket 342 (WCFL), Box 70, FCC Docket Section, RG 173, NARS.

12. WCFL occasionally aired educational talks by civic and women's groups and Chicago-area museums. Transcript of talks by Chicago Women's Club and Margaret Cornell of the Field Museum, Feb. 18, 1929, FRC Docket 342 (WCFL), Box 70, FCC Docket Section, RG 173, NARS. Children's programs included "The Fable Lady—Stories for Children" (1926–27) and the "Aeroplane Club" (1931–32), which used popular music recordings to awaken children in the morning. *FN,* Sept. 11, 1926, 6, Sept. 18, 1926, 8, Jan. 31, 1931, 8, July 16, 1932, 6; *Variety,* Apr. 29, 1931, 82.

13. *FN,* Dec. 15, 1928, 3 (quote), 7, Jan. 26, 1929, 7, Feb. 2, 1929, 7, July 20, 1929, 5, Sept. 2, 1929, 65, Dec. 14, 1929, 7, Dec. 21, 1929, 2, Aug. 30, 1930, 19, Nov. 15, 1930, 18; Transcripts of "Junior Federation Club" programs, Feb. 12–16, 18–19, 1929, FRC Docket 342 (WCFL), Box 70, FCC Docket Section, RG 173, NARS.

14. *FN,* Dec. 22, 1928, 7, Dec. 29, 1928, 3, Jan. 5, 1929, 7, Apr. 13, 1929, 7, Nov. 23, 1929, 20, Mar. 29, 1930, 9.

15. *FN,* Nov. 23, 1929, 24.

16. *FN,* Dec. 14, 1929, 7, Dec. 21, 1929, 1, 10, 11, Dec. 28, 1929, 2, Jan. 4, 1930, 2, Jan. 11, 1930, 17 (quote), Aug. 30, 1930, 19.

17. *FN*, Nov. 29, 1930, 9, Dec. 20, 1930, 9, Jan. 3, 1931, 1, Jan. 24, 1931, 16, Mar. 22, 1930, 21 (quote).

18. *FN*, Oct. 5, 1929, 9, Nov. 23, 1929, 2, Jan. 25, 1930, 8, Aug. 30, 1930, 27, Nov. 8, 1930, 8, Feb. 21, 1931, 8, May 9, 1931, 8.

19. Transcript of "Early Risers," Nov. 2, 1928, FRC Docket 342 (WCFL), Box 70, FCC Docket Section, RG 173, NARS; *FN*, Apr. 23, 1932, 6; Summers, *History of Programs*, 11–30; see tables 1 and 2 in the appendix.

20. *FN*, May 10, 1930, 8, June 21, 1930, 9, May 23, 1931, 11, Nov. 9, 1929, 8; *Variety*, June 9, 1931, 56, 60, Jan. 28, 1931, 79 (quote).

21. *FN*, Sept. 21, 1929, 8, Feb. 1, 1930, 10, Feb. 8, 1930, 8 (quote), Feb. 15, 1930, 8, June 14, 1930, 9, Aug. 30, 1930, 11; Jan. 17, 1931, 8, Sept. 3, 1932, 7; *Radio Digest*, Mar. 1930, 68–69; *Variety*, May 20, 1931, 136, Aug. 25, 1931, 52, Jan. 5, 1932, 58.

22. *Variety*, Aug. 25, 1931, 52 (first and third quotes), Dec. 29, 1931, 159, Feb. 9, 1932, 52 (second quote); MacDonald, *Don't Touch That Dial*, 91–132.

23. *FN*, Nov. 30, 1929, 8, Jan. 25, 1930, 8, Aug. 30, 1930, 43, Nov. 8, 1930, 8; *Radio Digest*, Feb. 1931, 68–69; *Variety*, Feb. 25, 1931, 66 (quotes).

24. *Variety*, Dec. 29, 1931, 159 (quote); *FN*, Dec. 26, 1931, 6, May 28, 1932, 6.

25. Irving Zeidman, *The American Burlesque Show* (New York: Hawthorn Books, 1967), 80 (first quote); *Variety*, Dec. 8, 1931, 58 (second, third, and fourth quotes); *FN*, May 16, 1931, 11 (fifth quote), May 23, 1931, 11.

26. *Variety*, Sept. 1, 1931, 58.

27. Smulyan, *Selling Radio*, 111–24; MacDonald, *Don't Touch That Dial*, 25–28, 50–51; Summers, *History of Programs*, 11–30.

28. *FN*, Feb. 7, 1931, 8, May 23, 1931, 11 (first quote); *Variety*, May 27, 1931, 96 (second and third quotes).

29. *FN*, July 18, 1931, 6 (first quote); *Variety*, July 14, 1931, 50 (second and third quotes), Feb. 16, 1932, 74; *FN*, Dec. 26, 1931, 6. A show similar to "Hello, Marie" but called "Hello, Peggy" aired over the NBC network in 1937. Frank Buxton and Bill Owen, *The Big Broadcast, 1920–1950* (New York: Viking Press, 1972), 109.

30. *FN*, Sept. 24, 1927, 1–2, 7, Mar. 2, 1929, 1, May 11, 1929, 1, Oct. 5, 1929, 8, May 24, 1930, 8; Jorgensen, "Radio Station WCFL," 90–91; *FN*, July 20, 1929, 5; Senate Committee, *Commission on Communications*, 1st Sess., 2:1887.

31. John M. Allswang, *A House for All Peoples: Ethnic Politics in Chicago, 1890–1936* (Lexington: University of Kentucky Press, 1971); Keenan Interview, 5–6; Cohen, *Making a New Deal*, 94–96.

32. McKillen, *Chicago Labor and a Democratic Diplomacy*, chaps. 1, 4.

33. *FN*, Dec. 15, 1928, 6, Mar. 1, 1930, 8, Aug. 23, 1930, 9, Apr. 4, 1931, 8, Dec. 12, 1931, 6, Apr. 2, 1932, 7; Clippings from German-language newspaper, 1928, WCFL Scrapbook, CFL Papers; *FN*, Nov. 22, 1930, 8; *Variety*, Jan. 21, 1931, 71 (quotes); Joseph Migala, *Polish Radio Broadcasting in the United States* (New York: Columbia University Press, 1987), 126, 129, 132–33, 214; *FN*, July 26, 1930, 14, Aug. 16, 1930, 10, Sept. 13, 1930, 8, Nov. 1, 1930, 8, Sept. 17, 1932, 8.

34. *FN,* Mar. 1, 1930, 8, Mar. 29, 1930, 8, Apr. 12, 1930, 8, July 5, 1930, 9, July 26, 1930, 8, Mar. 14, 1931, 8, May 16, 1931, 16; *Variety,* May 6, 1931, 64 (quote). WCFL also carried a religious program called the "Jewish Hour" via the NBC network. *FN,* Mar. 8, 1930, 8.

35. *FN,* July 5, 1930, 9, Aug. 2, 1930, 5, 8, Mar. 5, 1932, 1–2, Apr. 2, 1932, 7, Aug. 13, 1932, 8 (first quote), Jan. 6, 1934, 6, Sept. 6, 1937, 67 (fourth quote), June 23, 1956, 3, June 22, 1963, 5; *Variety,* June 30, 1931, 55 (second and third quotes). Lynch and Nockels hoped to broadcast the "Irish Hour" via shortwave to Ireland. *FN,* Apr. 1, 1933, 6.

36. James R. Grossman, *Land of Hope: Chicago, Black Southerners, and the Great Migration* (Chicago: University of Chicago Press, 1989), 242.

37. *FN,* July 28, 1928, 5 (first quote), Nov. 16, 1929, 8, July 25, 1931, 6 (second and third quotes), Dec. 12, 1931, 6 (fifth quote), Nov. 26, 1932, 6; *Variety,* July 14, 1931, 50 (fourth quote), Feb. 9, 1932, 52 (sixth quote); MacDonald, *Don't Touch That Dial,* 75–76, 327–46; Michele Hilmes, "Invisible Men: *Amos 'n' Andy* and the Roots of Broadcast Discourse," *Critical Studies in Mass Communication* 10, no. 4 (Dec. 1993): 301–21; Melvin Patrick Ely, *The Adventures of Amos 'n' Andy: A Social History of an American Phenomenon* (New York: Free Press, 1991).

38. *FN,* Jan. 4, 1930, 8 (quote), Feb. 22, 1930, 8.

39. *FN,* Dec. 31, 1927, 8 (first quote), Mar. 10, 1928, 12, Mar. 24, 1928, 6, Dec. 20, 1930, 8 (second and fourth quotes), Oct. 17, 1931, 6, Oct. 24, 1931, 6 (third quote); Dempsey J. Travis, *An Autobiography of Black Jazz* (Chicago: Urban Research Institute, 1983), 413; William Howland Keeney, *Chicago Jazz: A Cultural History, 1904–1930* (New York: Oxford University Press, 1993), 17–18, 156–57.

40. *FN,* Aug. 13, 1932, 8, Sept. 6, 1937, 67, June 8, 1929, 5, Aug. 24, 1929, 8, Sept. 2, 1929, 5, Dec. 21, 1929, 11, Feb. 13, 1932, 6 (quote).

41. Keeney, *Chicago Jazz,* 156–57; Travis, *Autobiography,* 413–23 (quote from 415); Transcript of WCFL program, Feb. 14, 1929, FRC Docket 342 (WCFL), Box 70, FCC Docket Section, RG 173, NARS.

42. *FN,* June 14, 1930, 8–9, Aug. 30, 1930, 11, May 14, 1932, 6, Jan. 3, 1931, 8 (first quote), Jan. 31, 1931, 8 (second quote), Mar. 16, 1929, 8 (third quote), Oct. 25, 1930, 8 (fourth quote).

43. *FN,* Apr. 13, 1929, 2, 3, July 20, 1929, 5, Aug. 30, 1930, 46; *Variety,* Apr. 5, 1932, 57; *FN,* June 29, 1929, 5, Sept. 28, 1929, 8, Oct. 5, 1929, 8, Nov. 7, 1931, 7 (quote); Harold Seymour, *Baseball: The Golden Age* (New York: Oxford University Press, 1971), 451–53. The Cubs lost the series in five games.

44. *FN,* Apr. 19, 1930, 8, Sept. 27, 1930, 8.

45. *FN,* July 4, 1931, 6, Apr. 18, 1931, 8, June 11, 1932, 6.

46. Transcripts of WCFL programming, Feb. 12–19, 1929; *FN,* June 29, 1929, 5, Jan. 25, 1930, 8, Nov. 29, 1930, 8, Oct. 11, 1930, 8, Oct. 18, 1930, 8, Dec. 13, 1930, 8, May 9, 1931, 8.

47. See table 1 in the appendix.

48. *FN*, Mar. 23, 1929, 1–2 (first quote), Jan. 11, 1930, 1–2 (second and third quotes).

49. *FN*, Oct. 13, 1928, 1–2 (first quote); Letter, Clarence Senior to E. N. Nockels, Aug. 15, 1929, Reel 12, Series 1, Correspondence and General Records, National Office Papers, Socialist Party of America Papers (second and third quotes); *FN*, Apr. 18, 1931, 8, May 2, 1931, 6.

50. *FN*, Mar. 16, 1929, 4 (first and second quotes), Mar. 7, 1931, 8, Mar. 21, 1931, 8, Dec. 26, 1931, 6; *Variety*, Jan. 5, 1932, 58; Letter, Meyer Fink to Ed Nockels, Apr. 18, 1932 (third quote), enclosed in Letter, Nockels to Victor Olander, Apr. 21, 1932, Folder Apr. 21–26, 1932, Box 52, Olander Papers.

51. *FN*, Oct. 22, 1932, 3; Herstein Interview, May 12, 1971, 268–71, OHP; Transcript of WCFL programming, Feb. 18, 1929, FRC Docket 342 (WCFL), Box 70, FCC Docket Section, RG 173, NARS; *FN*, Mar. 23, 1929, 1–2; Letter, William B. Rubin to L. P. Straube, July 28, 1932, Correspondence 1932, Folder Mar.–Oct., Box 8, Rubin Papers; Letters, F. C. E. Lundquist to Rubin, Feb. 23, 1931, Rubin to Lundquist, Feb. 24, 1931, both in Correspondence 1931, Jan.–June Folder, Box 8, Rubin Papers; *Variety*, Apr. 8, 1931, 66.

52. Letters, William Rubin to Victor Olander, Feb. 15, Mar. 3, 1930, and Olander to Rubin, Mar. 1, 1930, both in Correspondence 1930, Folder Jan.–Mar., Box 7, Rubin Papers; Letters, Paul Bern to Rubin, Sept. 11, 1931, and Rubin to Bern, Sept. 14, 1931, both in Correspondence 1931–33, Folder July 1931–Feb. 1932, Box 8, Rubin Papers. Tom Mooney, a San Francisco labor leader, was falsely convicted of a bombing and sentenced to death: the sentence was later commuted to life imprisonment. Nockels supported efforts to free Mooney during the twenties and thirties.

53. Letter, Clarence Senior to Morris Hillquit, Aug. 22, 1929 (quote); Letter, Mable H. Barnes to Morris Hillquit, Aug. 29, 1929; Telegrams, Edward Nockels, C. Senior, and M. Hillquit to Ramsay MacDonald, Aug. 29, 1929, M. Hillquit to C. Senior, Aug. 28, 1929, and Mable H. Barnes to M. Hillquit, Aug. 28, 1929, all on Reel 12, Series 1, Correspondence and General Records, National Office Papers, Socialist Party of America Papers; *FN*, Mar. 15, 1930, 2.

54. *FN*, Mar. 2, 1929, 3 (quote), Feb. 14, 1931, 8, Jan. 4, 1930, 8, July 12, 1930, 8, Dec. 13, 1930, 10, Feb. 27, 1932, 1, June 20, 1931, 8, July 16, 1932, 6, July 9, 1932, 6; *Variety*, May 17, 1932, 50.

55. *FN*, Apr. 27, 1929, 6, June 29, 1929, 5, Mar. 21, 1931, 8, May 16, 1931, 8 (first quote), Oct. 3, 1931, 6, Mar. 19, 1932, 6 (second quote), July 16, 1932, 6.

56. Transcript of Winnick talk, Feb. 13, 1929, FRC Docket 342 (WCFL), Box 70, FCC Docket Section, RG 173, NARS; *FN*, Mar. 9, 1929, 5, May 4, 1929, 9, Mar. 15, 1930, 8; *Variety*, June 7, 1932, 58.

57. *FN*, Nov. 30, 1929, 18, June 29, 1929, 18 (quote), July 13, 1929, 22.

58. *FN*, Apr. 18, 1931, 18.

59. *FN*, Feb. 7, 1931, 16, Apr. 25, 1931, 16 (quote).

60. *FN*, Aug. 29, 1931, 6, June 14, 1930, 14, May 28, 1932, 2, 7–8.

61. *FN*, July 13, 1929, 21 (quote), June 29, 1929, 5, Oct. 5, 1929, 8, May 10, 1930, 2, Dec. 6, 1930, 1, Dec. 13, 1930, 2; May 7, 1932, 1–2, 7.

62. *FN*, Oct. 6, 1928, 19; Transcript of Scheck programs, Feb. 12, 18, 1929, FRC Docket 342 (WCFL), Box 70, FCC Docket Section, RG 173, NARS; *FN*, Apr. 4, 1931, 8, Aug. 29, 1931, 6; *Variety*, Jan. 19, 1932, 58 (quotes), June 7, 1932, 58.

63. *FN*, June 20, 1931, 8 (first quote), July 16, 1932, 6; *Variety*, May 17, 1932, 50 (second quote).

64. *FN*, June 2, 1928, 13, Feb. 23, 1929, 13, Apr. 19, 1930, 3.

65. *Variety*, June 23, 1931, 58, 60 (quote).

66. Kazin and Ross, "America's Labor Day," 1312–13.

67. *FN*, Feb. 8, 1930, 16.

68. Haessler, Lloyd, and O'Connor worked for the "radical" Federated Press; Nearing was a noted pacifist and radical. Jessie Lloyd O'Connor, Harvey O'Connor, and Susan M. Bowler, *Harvey and Jessie: A Couple of Radicals* (Philadelphia: Temple University Press, 1988); Haessler, "Carl Haessler and the Federated Press"; Scott Nearing, *The Making of a Radical: A Political Biography* (New York: Harper and Row, 1972).

69. *FN*, Jan. 2, 1932, 1, 3, Jan. 9, 1932, 3.

70. *FN*, Nov. 21, 1931, 3, Jan. 9, 1932, 1, Jan. 16, 1932, 3; WCFL Application for License Renewal, Nov. 25, 1931.

71. Levitas Interview, July 24, 1970, 8–9; ISFL, *Proceedings of the Forty-Fourth Convention*, 158; Fannia M. Cohn, "Again the Labor Press: It Should Appeal to Worker's Family," *Labor Age* 17 (Nov. 1928): 22–23; *FN*, Apr. 4, 1931, 8, Aug. 29, 1931, 6, Jan. 19, 1929, 5–6; Letters, Nockels to William Green, Aug. 10, 1927, Nockels to Richard Wolff, Aug. 10, 1927, and John H. Walker to Nockels, Aug. 11, 1927, all in Folder 112, Box 15, JF.

72. Transcript of "CFL Bulletin Board," Feb. 12–19, 1929, FRC Docket 342 (WCFL), Box 70, FCC Docket Section, RG 173, NARS.

73. Hearing before FRC, Apr. 17, 1929, FRC Docket 342 (WCFL), Box 70, FCC Docket Section, RG 173, NARS (emphasis added).

74. *FN*, Feb. 7, 1931, 16.

75. *FN*, Sept. 13, 1930, 16 (first quote), May 24, 1930, 16 (second quote).

76. *FN*, May 24, 1930, 16.

77. *FN*, Apr. 12, 1930, 20, May 10, 1930, 5 (quotes; emphasis added).

78. *FN*, May 10, 1930, 5 (quote), May 24, 1930, 16, Nov. 22, 1930, 2, 10.

79. *FN*, Dec. 1, 1928, 4, Dec. 8, 1928, 9 (first quote), July 13, 1929, 21 (second quote), Feb. 16, 1932, 1.

80. *FN*, May 14, 1927, 5.

81. *FN*, Oct. 26, 1929, 11–13, June 21, 1930, 12–14, Dec. 20, 1930, 16–18.

82. *FN*, Oct. 26, 1929, 11–13, June 21, 1930, 12–14, Dec. 20, 1930, 16–18, Jan. 24, 1931, 17, Feb. 7, 1931, 16, Mar. 7, 1931, 17, Apr. 4, 1931, 16, May 23, 1931, 12.

83. *FN*, Feb. 23, 1929, 14, Mar. 23, 1929, 16, Mar. 8, 1930, 1, 5, Mar. 22, 1930, 21

(quote), Jan. 24, 1931, 16, Feb. 21, 1931, 1, Mar. 21, 1931, 16, Feb. 13, 1932, 1, 8, Apr. 9, 1932, 3.

84. *FN,* June 8, 1929, 16, 17, June 21, 1930, 12.

85. *FN,* Aug. 30, 1930, 7 (first and second quotes), Sept. 5, 1931, 7 (third quote), 18.

86. Chomsky and Herman, *Manufacturing Consent,* 14; Shore, *Talkin' Socialism,* 94–114; *FN,* Aug. 30, 1930, 7 (quote); Letter, W. Rubin to F. Lundquist, Mar. 26, 1930, Correspondence 1930, Folder Jan.–Mar., Box 7, Rubin Papers; *FN,* Apr. 4, 1931, 17.

87. *FN,* Mar. 16, 1929, 15, Sept. 5, 1931, 7, 18 (quote).

88. *FN,* Apr. 9, 1932, 3 (quote), Nov. 22, 1930, 10.

89. Transcripts of Leiter program, Feb. 12, 15, 19, 1929, FRC Docket 342 (WCFL), Box 70, FCC Docket Section, RG 173, NARS; *FN,* Nov. 8, 1930, 8, Nov. 29, 1930, 8, Feb. 21, 1931, 8, Mar. 21, 1931, 8, Nov. 21, 1931, 6, Apr. 16, 1932, 6.

90. *Variety,* May 20, 1931, 136.

91. *Variety,* June 23, 1931, 58 (quotes); *FN,* Sept. 5, 1931, 6.

92. *FN,* Oct. 26, 1929, 11–13, June 21, 1930, 12–14, Dec. 20, 1930, 16–18.

93. Letters, Meyer Fink to Ed Nockels, Apr. 18, 1932 (second quote), and Nockels to Fink, Apr. 21, 1932 (first quote), in Letter, Nockels to Victor Olander, Apr. 21, 1932, Folder Apr. 21–26, 1932, Box 52, Olander Papers.

94. *FN,* Aug. 30, 1930, 7 (quotes), Sept. 5, 1931, 14.

95. *FN,* May 9, 1931, 17, Aug. 29, 1931, 1, 3, Oct. 3, 1931, 2; CFL, *Program: Formal Dedication of Radio Stations,* Sept. 25, 1931, Radio Station WCFL, Miscellaneous, CFL Papers; *FN,* Feb. 14, 1931, 9, Apr. 4, 1931, 14.

96. *FN,* Nov. 16, 1929, 8, Sept. 13, 1930, 9; AFL Executive Council Meeting Minutes, Sept. 12, 1930; *FN,* Jan. 24, 1931, 8, Mar. 14, 1931, 7.

97. *WCFL Radio Magazine* 1 (Spring 1928): 9, 59; *FN,* Mar. 2, 1929, 9, June 15, 1929, 5, June 22, 1929, 9, July 27, 1929, 7.

98. *WCFL Radio Magazine* 1 (Spring 1928): 9, 59; *FN,* Mar. 2, 1929, 9, June 15, 1929, 5, June 22, 1929, 9, 16, July 27, 1929, 7. On the ACWA's housing program see Strong, *Amalgamated Clothing Workers of America,* 220–26.

99. *FN,* June 22, 1929, 3 (first and second quotes), 9 (third and fourth quotes).

100. *New Leader,* July 6, 1929, 3.

101. *FN,* July 27, 1929, 7.

102. *FN,* July 27, 1929, 21, Aug. 17, 1929, 3.

103. *FN,* June 11, 1932, 1, 3, Aug. 6, 1932, 1–2, 5, Aug. 20, 1932, 4, Aug. 27, 1932, 2; CFL, *Program: Formal Dedication of Radio Stations,* Sept. 25, 1931, Radio Station WCFL, Miscellaneous, CFL Papers (quote).

104. Letter, Ed Nockels to Michael J. Flynn, July 3, 1933, Folder July 1–10, 1933, General Correspondence, Box 20, FW; *Variety,* Feb. 24, 1937, 4; WCFL, *Official Program: WCFL Annual Radio Frolics, "Varieties of '47,"* Apr. 1947, CFL Papers.

105. Nockels's 1932 Labor Day article in the *Federation News* proclaimed "WCFL—Organized Labor's Great Publicity Agent." *FN,* Sept. 3, 1932, 5.

106. *FN*, Jan. 25, 1930, 17.

107. *FN*, Feb. 15, 1930, 1, Mar. 1, 1930, 20, Mar. 8, 1930, 1, 5, 10, 16.

108. *FN*, Mar. 22, 1930, 21.

109. *FN*, Jan. 24, 1931, 16 (first quote), Feb. 21, 1931, 20 (second quote).

110. Kazin and Ross, "America's Labor Day," 1311 (quote); *FN*, Sept. 7, 1929, 24, July 5, 1930, 20, July 12, 1930, 17, Aug. 9, 1930, 2, Aug. 23, 1930, 1, Sept. 6, 1930, 1–2, Sept. 13, 1930, 1, Oct. 11, 1930, 17, May 30, 1931, 12, June 13, 1931, 11, Aug. 1, 1931, 1, 3, Sept. 12, 1931, 1, 2, 10.

111. Cohen, "Encountering Mass Culture," 20 (quote); Cohen, *Making a New Deal.*

Chapter 5: Tangled Web, 1932–37

1. Letters, P. Armstrong to Dr. R. P. Raup, Mar. 22, 31, 1932, Folder 1129, Container 58; and Letters, Walter V. Woehlker to S. Howard Evans, May 4, 1932 (first quote) and Evans to Woehlker, May 9, 1932 (second quote), Folder 1166, Container 60, all in Payne Fund, Inc. Records.

2. Roger Biles, *Big City Boss in Depression and War: Mayor Edward J. Kelly of Chicago* (De Kalb: Northern Illinois University Press, 1984), 22.

3. Letters, Herbert L. Pettey to CFL, July 1, 1933 (first quote), and Nockels to Michael Flynn, July 3, 1933 (second quote), both in Folder July 1–10, 1933, General Correspondence, Box 20, FW.

4. Irving Bernstein, *Turbulent Years: A History of the American Worker, 1933–1941* (Boston: Houghton Mifflin, 1970), 1–11, 29–36; Newell, *Chicago and the Labor Movement*, 44; Cohen, *Making a New Deal*, 283–89; Green, *The World of the Worker*, 133–34 (quote), 140–43.

5. John Kennedy Ohl, *Hugh S. Johnson and the New Deal* (De Kalb: Northern Illinois University Press, 1985), 113, 115, 137, 196–97 (quote); William E. Leuchtenburg, *Franklin D. Roosevelt and the New Deal, 1932–1940* (New York: Harper and Row, 1963), 57–58, 64–71.

6. Newell, *Chicago and the Labor Movement*, 46–48; Cohen, *Making a New Deal*, 277–78.

7. Letter, Nockels to Walsh, Sept. 23, 1933, Folder Sept. 22–30, 1933, General Correspondence, Box 21, FW; National Industrial Recovery Administration, "Hearing on Code of Fair Practices and Competition Presented by Radio Broadcasting Industry," Sept. 27, 1933, 113–14, 126–47, National Association of Broadcasters Library, Washington, D.C.; *Broadcasting*, Oct. 1, 1933, 11–13; National Recovery Administration, *Codes of Fair Competition, Nos. 111–150*, vol. 3 (Washington, D.C.: GPO, 1934), code no. 129, p. 354–64.

8. Minutes of the Code Authority for the Radio Broadcasting Industry, Minute no. 9, Feb. 8–9, 1935, Folder 54, Box 39, NBC Records.

9. Herstein Interview, May 12, 1971, 275.

10. *FN*, July 9, 1932, 1, 5; Letter, Wm. Rubin to James B. Farley, Oct. 19, 1932, Correspondence 1932, Folder Mar.–Oct., Box 8, Rubin Papers (quote).

11. Newell, *Chicago and the Labor Movement*, 44–53; Wrigley, *Class Politics and Public Schools*, 236–40; *FN*, Nov. 4, 1933, 1, 6, Nov. 11, 1933, 1, 3, 6, Nov. 18, 1933, 1, 7.

12. *FN*, Mar. 3, 1934, 7, Mar. 31, 1934, 1, 8, Apr. 7, 1934, 1, 4, Apr. 14, 1934, 1, 9, 10. Nockels lost the primary.

13. Telegram, Edward Nockels to Frank Russell, June 1, 1936 (quote); Letter, Ed Nockels to George M. Harrison, June 8, 1936; and Letter, Martin P. Durkin to Nockels, June 13, 1936, all in Folder 140, Box 20, JF.

14. Letters, Nockels to Michael Flynn, and Nockels to F. Walsh, both dated July 3, 1933, Folder July 1–10, 1933, General Correspondence, Box 20, FW (quotes). FDR appointed Walsh to the New York State Commission to Recodify the Public Service Law in 1929 and chairman of the State Power Authority in 1931. Walsh organized the National Progressive League for Roosevelt in 1932. *The Nation*, May 13, 1939, 547; Fink, *Biographical Dictionary of Labor*, 571–72.

15. Letter, Ed Nockels to Frank Walsh, Nov. 7, 1933, Folder Nov. 1–8, 1933, General Correspondence, Box 21, FW.

16. Barnouw, *Golden Web*, 7–8; Hugh Carter Donahue, *The Battle to Control Broadcast News: Who Owns the First Amendment?* (Cambridge, Mass.: MIT Press, 1989), 20.

17. McChesney, *Telecommunications, Mass Media, and Democracy*, 177–96; Rosen, *Modern Stentors*, 174.

18. *FN*, Feb. 24, 1934, 2, 5.

19. Senate Committee on Interstate Commerce, *Hearings before the Committee on Interstate Commerce on S. 2910*, 73 Cong., 2d Sess., 1934, 197–99 (Nockels), 184–92 (Harney). On Harney and WLWL see McChesney, *Telecommunications, Mass Media, and Democracy*, 196–200; and Robert W. McChesney, "Crusade against Mammon: Father Harney, WLWL, and the Debate over Radio in the 1930s," *Journalism History* 14 (Winter 1987): 118–30.

20. McChesney, *Telecommunications, Mass Media, and Democracy*, 196–206; Barnouw, *Golden Web*, 23–26; Gibson, *Public Broadcasting*, 24–27. Commercial radio supporters held that the "amendment was conceived in the interest of *labor.*" Letter, Levering Tyson, NACRE, to Nevill Miller, NAB, Dec. 9, 1938, Folder 66, Box 62, NBC Records (emphasis in original).

21. *FN*, Apr. 7, 1934, 6 (quotes); Memorandum, Frank M. Russell to R. C. Patterson, Nov. 13, 1934, Folder 29, Box 26, NBC Records.

22. *FN*, Apr. 7, 1934, 6, Sept. 3, 1934, 26; *NYT*, May 10, 1934, 3; House Committee on Interstate and Foreign Commerce, *Hearings before the Committee on Interstate and Foreign Commerce on H.R. 8301: Federal Communications Commission*, 73d Cong., 2d Sess., 1934, 344–49 (first, second, and third quotes from 347; fourth quote from 349), 147–63; McChesney, *Telecommunications, Mass Media, and Democracy*, 200–208.

23. Letter, Edward Nockels to Robert F. Wagner, May 18, 1934, Folder 1489, Box 223, Legislative Files 1934, Robert F. Wagner Papers, Georgetown University Library Archives, Washington, D.C.

24. Letter, Nockels to Louis M. Howe, May 23, 1934, including Letter, Nockels to Roosevelt, Folder June 1–19, 1934, General Correspondence, Box 21, FW.

25. Letters, Ed Nockels to Frank Walsh, both dated June 1, 1934, Folder June 1–9, 1934, General Correspondence, Box 21, FW.

26. NAB, *Broadcasting in the United States.*

27. *Congressional Record,* 73d Cong., 2d Sess., 1933, vol. 78, part 8:8830–32 (first quote from 8830), 8837, 8843–45 (second quote from 8845); McChesney, *Telecommunications, Mass Media, and Democracy,* 196–210.

28. *Congressional Record,* 73d Cong., 2d Sess., 1933, vol. 78, part 8:8829–32, 8835, 8844, 8846, part 10:10319; *NYT,* May 16, 1934, 29, 31; McChesney, *Telecommunications, Mass Media, and Democracy,* 196–210.

29. Barnouw, *Golden Web,* 25–26; McChesney, *Telecommunications, Mass Media, and Democracy,* 208–12; Gibson, *Public Broadcasting,* 27; Donahue, *Battle to Control Broadcast News,* 28–29; Letter, Levering Tyson to Neville Miller, Dec. 9, 1938, Folder 66, Box 62, NBC Records; *NYT,* May 20, 1934, sec. 9, p. 9.

30. McChesney, *Telecommunications, Mass Media, and Democracy,* 210–14; Gibson, *Public Broadcasting,* 27–28; Barnouw, *Golden Web,* 26–27; *NYT,* Aug. 19, 1934, sec. 8, p. 15 (quotes).

31. NAB, *NAB Reports* 2, no. 42 (Aug. 22, 1934).

32. FCC, *Official Report of the Proceedings before the FCC, Hearing in re: Before the Broadcast Division of the FCC on Section 307(c) of the Communications Act of 1934, Oct.–Nov. 1934,* 579, 584–87, Transcript of hearing, copy in New York Public Library, New York. See McChesney, *Telecommunications, Mass Media, and Democracy,* 213–25, for an analysis of the hearings.

33. FCC, *Official Report of the Proceedings,* 598, 667–71. Bellows proudly offered a letter from the Minnesota State Federation of Labor to station WCCO, which he managed in 1928–29. The labor group thanked WCCO for making it possible "for us to carry on to the radio audiences information as to the activities and problems of this Federation and the American labor movement." Ibid., 670.

34. Ibid., 11212–11215 (quote from 11214). CBS occasionally offered airtime to AFL officials. AFL Executive Council Meeting Minutes, July 15, 1932, 19.

35. FCC, *Official Report of the Proceedings,* 12288-A7 to 12288-A32, 12288-A391 to 12288-A396 (first quote from 12288-A391; second quote from 12288-A395).

36. *Variety,* Oct. 2, 1934, 57, 66; *NYT,* Oct. 14, 1934, sec. 10, p. 11; Letter, Carl Menzer to Harold G. Ingham, Aug. 22, 1934, NAEB Correspondence 1925–37 Folder, Box 1, National Association of Educational Broadcasters Papers; Letter, L. Tyson to N. Miller, Dec. 9, 1938, Folder 66, Box 62, NBC Records; McChesney, *Telecommunications, Mass Media, and Democracy,* 211–13, 216–19, 221–23; Gibson, *Public Broadcasting,* 28–31.

37. *FN,* Sept. 3, 1934, 26, 36, Oct. 6, 1934, 1, 3, 12; *Variety,* Sept. 18, 1934, 37.

38. AFL, *Report of the Proceedings of the Fifty-Fourth Annual Convention held at San Francisco, 1–12 October 1934* (Washington, D.C.: AFL, 1935), 611 (first quote), 617 (second quote), 635–36; *FN,* Oct. 6, 1934, 1, 3, 12. A fifth resolution recommended that the Executive Council prepare at least thirty programs to dramatize labor history and to discuss problems of labor. AFL, *Report of the Fifty-Fourth Convention,* 200, 611–12.

39. AFL, *Report of the Fifty-Fourth Convention,* 612, 635–36; Letter, Tracy F. Tyler to William Green, Nov. 2, 1934, Folder 866, Container 45, Payne Fund, Inc. Records; *Education by Radio* 4 (Nov. 8, 1934): 49 (quote).

40. FCC, *Official Report of the Proceedings,* 13667–13673.

41. *Broadcasting,* Oct. 15, 1933, 26. For Green's comments on radio advertising see *NYT,* Feb. 21, 1932, sec. 8, p. 14.

42. FCC, *Official Report of the Proceedings,* 13744–45, 13753–58.

43. McChesney, *Telecommunications, Mass Media, and Democracy,* 223–25.

44. Workers' Education Bureau of America, *Labor Speaks for Itself!* (New York: Workers' Education Bureau Press, 1936); *FN,* Jan. 2, 1937, 2. WCFL did not air the series because it was not an affiliate of CBS. *FN,* Nov. 9, 1935, 7.

45. Even after the 1932 deal, the AFL leadership repeatedly rejected Nockels's offer for a closer association with labor radio. AFL Executive Council Meeting Minutes, Oct. 19, 28, 1932, 4–15, 53–54.

46. *FN,* Dec. 7, 1929, 9, 13, June 20, 1931, 9; Senate Committee, *Commission on Communications,* 1st Sess., 2:2074–79 (first, second, and third quotes); Letter, Nockels to F. Walsh, Nov. 7, 1933, Folder Nov. 1–8, 1933, General Correspondence, Box 21, FW (fourth quote).

47. NBC Interdepartmental Correspondence, Frank M. Russell to A. L. Ashby, Jan. 9, 1933, and Memo, Ashby to P. G. Parker, Jan. 13, 1933, both in Folder 77, Box 99, NBC Records; Letters, Maynard Marquardt to Raymond F. Guy, June 20, 27, and Aug. 1, 1934, Guy to Marquardt, June 25, 1934, and Russell to P. J. Hennessey, July 12, 1934, all in Folder 60, Box 24, NBC Records.

48. Letter, Niles Trammell to Frank M. Russell, Apr. 6, 1933, Folder 77, Box 99, NBC Records.

49. Josephine Young Case and Everett Needham Case, *Owen D. Young and American Enterprise: A Biography* (Boston: David R. Godine, 1982), 192–96, 200–206; Ida M. Tarbell, *Owen D. Young: A Type of Industrial Leader* (New York: Macmillan, 1932), 140–58; Rosenberg, *Spreading the American Dream,* 93–95.

50. Letter, Norman Thomas to M. H. Aylesworth, Oct. 2, 1931, Folder 1, Box 4, NBC Records (first and second quotes); H. V. Kaltenborn, "The Future of Radio," *Education by Radio* 1 (May 14, 1931): 53 (third quote); "Thirty Years in Broadcasting"; Ventura Free Press, *The Empire of the Air: The Story of Exploitation of Radio for Private Profit, with a Plan for the Reorganization of Broadcasting* (Ventura, Calif.: Ventura Free Press, 1932), 70–71, 77.

51. Letter, Glenn Snyder (WLS) to Niles Trammell, Mar. 2, 1934; Memoranda, Trammell to R. C. Patterson, Mar. 27, 1934 (quotes); and A. L. Ashby to F. Russell and Trammell, May 25, 1934, all in Folder 40, Box 100, NBC Records.

52. Memo, Trammell to Patterson, Mar. 27, 1934, Folder 40, Box 100, NBC Records.

53. Ibid.; Memoranda, F. Russell to R. C. Patterson, Mar. 29, 1934, and A. L. Ashby to Russell and Trammell, May 25, 1934, Folder 40, Box 100, NBC Records.

54. Memoranda, C. W. Horn to R. C. Patterson, June 15, 1934, Trammell to Ashby and Russell, June 22, 1934, Trammell to Frank E. Mason, July 10, 1934, Trammell to Patterson, Aug. 17, 1934, Trammell to Patterson, Sept. 20, 1934; Letter, Niles Trammell to Burridge D. Butler, June 22, 1934; and Telegram, Patterson to Trammell, Sept. 12, 1934, all in Folder 40, Box 100, NBC Records.

55. Memorandum, Frank M. Russell to R. C. Patterson, Mar. 29, 1934, Folder 40, Box 100, NBC Records (quotes); Letter, Edward Nockels to H. L. Pettey, June 1, 1934, Folder June 1–9, 1934, General Correspondence, Box 21, FW.

56. Memorandum, Frank M. Russell to R. C. Patterson, Nov. 13, 1934, Folder 29, Box 26, NBC Records (emphasis added).

57. Letter, M. H. Aylesworth to David Sarnoff, Aug. 17, 1934, Folder 27, Box 26, NBC Records.

58. Letter, Nockels to H. L. Pettey, June 1, 1934, Folder June 1–19, 1934, General Correspondence, Box 21, FW; Telegram, E. Nockels to M. H. Aylesworth, Sept. 23, 1934, Folder 28, Box 26 (first quote); and Telegrams, Aylesworth to Nockels, Sept. 25, 1934, Folder 43, Box 30 (second and third quotes), both in NBC Records.

59. *Broadcasting*, Nov. 15, 1934, 46 (first and second quotes); Memorandum, Frank Russell to R. C. Patterson, Nov. 13, 1934, Folder 29, Box 26, NBC Records (third quote).

60. Telegram, Frank Russell to R. C. Patterson, Nov. 12, 1934 (first quote); and Memorandum, Russell to Patterson, Nov. 13, 1934 (second through sixth quotes), both in Folder 29, Box 26, NBC Records.

61. Memorandum, M. H. Aylesworth to R. Patterson, Nov. 16, 1934, Folder 29, Box 26, NBC Records.

62. Memo, Mark Woods to Edgar Kobak, Dec. 6, 1934, Folder 60, Box 24, NBC Records; Memo, R. C. Patterson Jr. to David Sarnoff, Jan. 8, 1935, Folder 77, Box 99, NBC Records.

63. Memoranda, M. Woods to R. C. Patterson Jr., Dec. 11, 1934, and Patterson to D. Sarnoff, Jan. 8, 1935, both in Folder 77, Box 99, NBC Records.

64. Memo, M. H. Aylesworth to R. C. Patterson Jr., Dec. 18, 1934, Folder 77, Box 99, NBC Records.

65. Memoranda, A. L. Ashby to R. C. Patterson Jr., Dec. 18 (first quote), 27 (second quote), 1934, Ashby to Mark Woods, Jan. 31, 1935, Woods to Patterson, Apr. 12, 1935, and Ashby to Patterson, Apr. 15, 1935, all in Folder 77, Box 99, NBC Records.

66. Memorandum, Woods to Patterson, Apr. 12, 1935, Folder 77, Box 99, NBC Records.

67. *Variety,* Feb. 20, 1935, 34, Mar. 6, 1935, 40, May 1, 1935, 25; *Broadcasting,* Sept. 1, 1934, 18; *FN,* June 6, 1936, 8.

68. *FN,* June 17, 1934, 10.

69. Letters, William Green to M. H. Aylesworth, Jan. 7, 1935 (first quote), Green to Aylesworth, Jan. 24, 1935, and Aylesworth to Green, Jan. 29, 1935 (second and third quotes), all in Folder 31, Box 37, NBC Records.

70. Letter, Aylesworth to Green, Apr. 23, 1935, Folder 31, Box 37, NBC Records.

71. *FN,* Apr. 9, 1927, 10.

72. *FN,* Aug. 12, 1933, 5, 7, May 12, 1934, 8, May 26, 1934, 2, June 17, 1934, 10, Oct. 13, 1934, 2, 7; *Billboard,* Sept. 20, 1934, 10.

73. One of the remarkable aspects of the WCFL-NBC deal was that not one word of it was ever reported either at a CFL meeting or in the *Federation News.*

74. Memorandum, William S. Hedges to Niles Trammell, Dec. 7, 1937, Folder 77, Box 99, NBC Records.

75. *NYT,* Mar. 11, 1933, 15, 1; Robert W. McChesney, "Press-Radio Relations and the Emergence of Network, Commercial Broadcasting in the United States, 1930–1935," *Historical Journal of Film, Radio, and Television* 11, no. 1 (1991): 41–57.

76. Letter, Ed Wynn to Ed Nockels, Mar. 23, 1933, Folder Mar. 27–31, 1933, General Correspondence, Box 20, FW; and Letter, Nockels to F. Walsh, Sept. 23, 1933, Folder Sept. 22–30, 1933, General Correspondence, Box 21, FW (quote); *NYT,* Sept. 10, 1933, sec. 2, p. 4, Sept. 24, 1933, sec. 10, p. 7, Sept. 26, 1933, 19, Oct. 26, 1933, 22, Oct. 29, 1933, 31, Nov. 30, 1933, 39, Dec. 2, 1933, 9; Barnouw, *Golden Web,* 31n8; *Broadcasting,* Oct. 1, 1933, 14; *Variety,* Oct. 10, 1933, 33.

77. Letter, Frank E. Mason to Niles Trammell, June 20, 1935, Folder 26, Box 37, NBC Records (first quote); *Billboard,* Sept. 30, 1933, 17; *Variety,* May 29, 1934, 31, June 26, 1934, 41; *Broadcasting,* July 1, 1934, 12; *Variety,* Oct. 30, 1934, 31, 37 (second quote). George B. Storer, the owner of several midwestern radio stations developed contacts between WCFL and the proposed Amalgamated Broadcasting System in the summer of 1934. *Broadcasting,* July 15, 1934, 6, Sept. 15, 1934, 10.

78. Letter, Ota Gygi to John F. Royal, June 1, 1935, Folder 26, Box 37, NBC Records.

79. Letter, Ota Gygi to Frank E. Mason, June 17, 1935, Folder 26, Box 37, NBC Records.

80. *Variety,* Sept. 18, 1934, 37, Oct. 23, 1934, 35, Nov. 27, 1934, 32, Dec. 25, 1934, 31, Jan. 1, 1935, 81, Jan. 8, 1935, 45 (quote); Letter, Ota Gygi to John F. Royal, June 1, 1935, Folder 26, Box 37, NBC Records.

81. Letter, Gygi to Mason, June 17, 1935, Folder 26, Box 37, NBC Records.

82. Ibid.; Letter, Gygi to Royal, June 1, 1935, Folder 26, Box 37, NBC Records (quote). Gygi remained committed to the "sectional radio chain" concept even as he desperately looked for work as a staff radio musician in mid-1935. Letters, Gygi to Royal, June 1, Gygi to Mason, June 17, Mason to Gygi, June 20, Mason to Niles Trammell, June 20, Gygi to Mason, June 24, Gygi to Mason, Sept. 9, Mason to Gygi,

June 25, and Mason to Gygi, Sept. 13, 1935, all in Folder 26, Box 37, NBC Records. Gygi eventually became vice president in charge of operations for the Affiliated Broadcasting Company, headed by former Chicago utility magnate Samuel Insull. *Broadcasting*, Mar. 15, 1936, 13, May 1, 1936, 12.

83. *FN*, June 20, 1936, 8, Sept. 7, 1936, 51, Dec. 19, 1936, 2, 6, Jan. 2, 1937, 2; Edward Nockels, "The Last of the Public Domain," *American Federationist* 44 (Jan. 1937): 22–29 (quote from 22).

84. *FN*, Sept. 7, 1936, 51.

85. Memorandum, Niles Trammell to Lenox R. Lohr, Nov. 19, 1936, Folder 40, Box 100, NBC Records.

86. Memoranda, Frank M. Russell to Lenox R. Lohr, Dec. 15, 1936, and Feb. 13, 1937, Folder 77, Box 99, NBC Records; *Broadcasting*, Jan. 15, 1937, 9, 66, Feb. 1, 1937, 14, 75; Edward N. Nockels, "Labor's Radio Battle Continues," ca. Feb. 1937, Folder 1, Box 4, JF.

87. *Broadcasting*, Jan. 15, 1937, 9 (first quote), Feb. 1, 1937, 75; *Variety*, Feb. 24, 1937, 44 (second quote).

88. Memorandum, Frank P. Russell to Lenox R. Lohr, Feb. 13, 1937, Folder 77, Box 99, NBC Records.

89. FCC Engineering Department, *Report on Social and Economic Data Pursuant to the Informal Hearing on Broadcasting, Docket 4063, Beginning October 5, 1936* (Washington, D.C.: GPO, 1938), 1.

90. Ibid., 82–85 (quotes from 83), 90–91.

91. Ibid., 115–16. Nockels reproduced his entire testimony in "Last of the Public Domain," 22–29 (quote from 22).

92. Nockels, "Last of the Public Domain," 24.

93. FCC Engineering Department, *Report on Social and Economic Data*, 115.

94. Ibid., 116.

95. Ibid.

96. Ibid., 16–18 (first quote from 16; second quote from 17).

97. Ibid., 18 (emphasis in original).

98. Barnouw, *Tower in Babel*, 263–64, 279–83; Rosen, *Modern Stentors*, 161–74; McChesney, *Telecommunications, Mass Media, and Democracy*, 214; Erik Barnouw, *The Sponsor: Notes on a Modern Potentate* (New York: Oxford University Press, 1978); Godfried, "Legitimizing the Mass Media Structure."

99. ACLU, Minna F. Kassner, comp., *Radio Is Censored: A Study of Cases Prepared to Show the Need of Federal Legislation for Freedom of the Air* (New York: ACLU, 1936). See also Letter, Minna F. Kassner to Hazel Rice, Dec. 1, 1937, Reel 148, vol. 1011, 1937, ACLU Archives.

100. FCC Engineering Department, *Report on Social and Economic Data*, 19 (emphasis added).

101. *National Association of Broadcasters: Eighth Annual Convention of the NAB, 17–19 November 1930, Cleveland, Ohio* (Washington, D.C.: NAB), 73 (first quote);

Illinois State Federation of Labor Weekly News Letter, Apr. 26, 1930, 1 (second and third quotes).

102. Louis G. Caldwell, "Freedom of Speech and Radio Broadcasting," *Annals of the American Academy* 177 (Jan. 1935): 182.

103. Ibid., 179–207 (quotes from 182n11; emphasis added); Quaal Interview; McChesney, "Free Speech and Democracy!" Caldwell opposed the "public interest, convenience, and necessity" standard and state intervention in the marketplace. Yet, when the radio networks launched an assault on clear-channel stations in the late thirties, Caldwell insisted that the FCC adopt regulations in the public interest. In this case, the clear-channel stations represented the public interest—because they provided direct service to millions of people—while the networks represented the interest of private companies. Memorandum, Frank M. Russell to Lenox R. Lohr, June 2, 1939, Folder 21, Box 68, NBC Records.

Chapter 6: Labor Radio and Working-Class Culture, 1932–37

1. *FN,* Sept. 7, 1936, 51.

2. *FN,* Nov. 12, 1932, 3. The CFL executive board eventually decided not to suspend publication of the newspaper. *FN,* Nov. 26, 1932, 3.

3. *FN,* Sept. 3, 1932, 5, Oct. 8, 1932, 5 (first quote), Oct. 15, 1932, 1 (second quote), Oct. 22, 1932, 1, 5, Nov. 5, 1932, 6, Nov. 12, 1932, 1–2.

4. *Variety,* Oct. 16, 1934, 33, 38, Aug. 28, 1934, 33, 36.

5. *Billboard,* Sept. 30, 1933, 17; *Variety,* Oct. 30, 1934, 31, 37, Jan. 1, 1935, 81, Jan. 8, 1935, 45; *FN,* Sept. 2, 1935, 36, 37, 38 (quotes).

6. *FN,* Sept. 24, 1932, 8, Dec. 9, 1933, 6, Jan. 13, 1934, 6, June 9, 1934, 6, Dec. 29, 1934, 6, Jan. 26, 1935, 6, Mar. 23, 1935, 6; MacDonald, *Don't Touch That Dial,* 26, 134; Summers, *History of Programs,* 47–48; *Billboard,* Feb. 9, 1935, 7; Buxton and Owen, *The Big Broadcast,* 171; *CT,* Oct. 19, 1936, 19.

7. *Variety,* Sept. 5, 1933, 62; *FN,* Sept. 2, 1935, 67 (first quote), 36 (third quote); *CT,* Jan. 3, 1936, 14, Jan. 1, 1936, 26, Feb. 16, 1937, 17; Ely, *Adventures of Amos 'n' Andy,* 131 (second quote); Buxton and Owen, *The Big Broadcast,* 57; *FN,* Mar. 23, 1935, 6.

8. *FN,* June 9, 1934, 6, Mar. 23, 1935, 6, Sept. 2, 1935, 67; *CT,* Feb. 17, 1937, 19; *FN,* Nov. 17, 1934, 6; *Billboard,* Dec. 1, 1934, 10, Dec. 8, 1934, 9, Apr. 13, 1935, 11, Nov. 23, 1935, 11.

9. Arnold Passman, *The Deejays* (New York: Macmillan, 1971), 69; *FN,* Oct. 18, 1930, 8; *Variety,* Jan. 24, 1933, 41.

10. *FN,* Mar. 11, 1933, 6, Sept. 24, 1932, 8, Dec. 16, 1933, 6; *Variety,* Oct. 16, 1934, 32; *FN,* Dec. 14, 1935, 11; Passman, *Deejays,* 58 (quote).

11. *FN,* Jan. 13, 1934, 6, June 9, 1934, 6, Nov. 3, 1934, 6; *Variety,* Sept. 25, 1934, 40 (first quote); *CT,* Sept. 1, 1936, 20, Sept. 2, 1936, 24, Sept. 3, 1936, 26, Sept. 4, 1936, 32, Sept. 5, 1936, 21, Sept. 6, 1936, sec. 3, p. 4; Cohen, *Making a New Deal,* 326–28, 362–68 (second quote from 363).

12. *Variety,* Aug. 23, 1932, 41; *FN,* Oct. 15, 1932, 8, Apr. 1, 1933, 6, Apr. 15, 1933, 6; *Variety,* Oct. 16, 1934, 32; *FN,* Nov. 3, 1934, 6, Dec. 29, 1934, 6, Mar. 23, 1935, 6; *Billboard,* May 25, 1935, 11; *CT,* Jan. 2, 1936, 12, Apr. 17, 1936, 24, July 19, 1936, sec. 3, p. 2, Sept. 3, 1936, 26, Sept. 5, 1936, 21.

13. *FN,* Dec. 3, 1932, 8, Jan. 14, 1933, 6, Jan. 21, 1933, 6, Apr. 1, 1933, 6, Dec. 9, 1933, 6, Dec. 16, 1933, 6, Jan. 27, 1934, 9, Mar. 23, 1935, 6, Dec. 7, 1935, 9, Feb. 3, 1936, 11, Nov. 21, 1936, 3; Robert C. Allen, *Speaking of Soap Operas* (Chapel Hill: University of North Carolina Press, 1985), 108–10, 139–40; *Billboard,* Mar. 18, 1933, 14, Feb. 8, 1936, 7; *Variety,* May 20, 1936, 32; *CT,* Jan. 1, 1936, 26, Apr. 17, 1936, 24.

14. *FN,* Dec. 10, 1932, 6.

15. Summers, *History of Programs,* 35, 64–65; Allen, *Speaking of Soap Operas,* 101–19 (first quote from 103; second quote from 112).

16. Allen, *Speaking of Soap Operas,* 105 (first quote); *Billboard,* Dec. 9, 1933, 13; *FN,* Jan. 28, 1933, 6, 8; *Billboard,* Nov. 10, 1934, 10; MacDonald, *Don't Touch That Dial,* 50–60 (second quote from 56).

17. *FN,* Nov. 19, 1932, 8, Dec. 24, 1932, 6, Mar. 11, 1933, 6; *Billboard,* Mar. 18, 1933, 14, Apr. 6, 1935, 8, Nov. 10, 1934, 10; *FN,* Dec. 9, 1933, 6, Dec. 16, 1933, 6, June 18, 1932, 6, June 25, 1932, 6, July 2, 1932, 6; *Variety,* Aug. 23, 1932, 41; *FN,* Jan. 14, 1933, 6, July 25, 1936, 7 (quotes).

18. Memorandum, A. L. Ashby to M. H. Aylesworth, Mar. 31, 1933, Folder 7, Box 100, NBC Records; Minutes of the Code Authority for the Radio Broadcasting Industry, Minute no. 9; Columbia Broadcasting System, *Listening Areas Second Series* (New York: CBS, ca. 1933); J. Pusateri, "FDR, Huey Long, and the Politics of Radio Regulation," *Journal of Broadcasting* 21 (Winter 1977): 85–95.

19. *FN,* Sept. 7, 1936, 51 (quotes), Jan. 23, 1937, 1.

20. *FN,* Aug. 27, 1932, 2, Sept. 3, 1932, 17, Apr. 15, 1933, 6, June 3, 1933, 6, Dec. 16, 1933, 6, Apr. 14, 1934, 6, Sept. 3, 1934, 26, Apr. 13, 1935, 12, May 11, 1935, 2; *Broadcasting,* June 15, 1933, 26.

21. *FN,* June 23, 1934, 10, Oct. 13, 1934, 2 (quotes).

22. *FN,* July 27, 1935, 2 (quote), Sept. 2, 1935, 12.

23. *FN,* Jan. 14, 1933, 6, Jan. 21, 1933, 6; *Billboard,* Mar. 18, 1933, 14; *FN,* Feb. 4, 1933, 6, Mar. 11, 1933, 6.

24. *Variety,* Apr. 3, 1934, 37. Chicago radio stations WLS and WGN received top ranking because of their showmanship.

25. *Variety,* Oct. 3, 1933, 38.

26. *FN,* Jan. 21, 1933, 6, Sept. 2, 1933, 18 (first quote), 45 (fifth and sixth quotes), 46, Sept. 3, 1934, 9, Sept. 2, 1935, 36; *Broadcasting,* Oct. 1, 1933, 66 (second, third, and fourth quotes).

27. McChesney, *Telecommunications, Mass Media, and Democracy,* 87–88, 94–97, 101–2, 122–23; Smulyan, *Selling Radio,* 125–53.

28. *FN,* Sept. 2, 1935, 33 (quotes), Sept. 7, 1936, 51.

29. *FN,* Jan. 14, 1933, 6, Aug. 5, 1933, 6 (first and second quotes), Sept. 2, 1933, 18 (third and fourth quotes), 45–46, Sept. 3, 1934, 9, Sept. 2, 1935, 36.

30. Barnouw, *Tower in Babel,* 239–45; Barnouw, *Golden Web,* 9–17, 111–12; Bergreen, *Look Now, Pay Later,* 54–60 (first quote from 60); *FN,* Nov. 11, 1933, 6 (second through seventh quotes).

31. *FN,* Sept. 2, 1935, 37 (first quote), Feb. 17, 1934, 6, Dec. 10, 1932, 6 (second quote), Dec. 24, 1932, 6, Sept. 2, 1933, 18 (third quote).

32. *FN,* Sept. 3, 1934, 9, Dec. 19, 1936, 6.

33. *FN,* Sept. 3, 1932, 36, Dec. 24, 1932, 6, Feb. 25, 1933, 3, 7, 8, Mar. 4, 1933, 6, Dec. 9, 1933, 6, Dec. 16, 1933, 6, Aug. 18, 1934, 6, Sept. 3, 1934, 9, June 2, 1934, 1, Sept. 7, 1936, 52, Dec. 19, 1936, 1, 3, 9.

34. *FN,* Dec. 8, 1934, 11, Dec. 22, 1934, 8, Jan. 19, 1935, 12, Jan. 26, 1935, 12, Feb. 2, 1935, 1, 12.

35. *FN,* Sept. 3, 1932, 1, Sept. 10, 1932, 8, Sept. 24, 1932, 8, Nov. 17, 1934, 12.

36. *FN,* June 3, 1933, 6, Jan. 13, 1934, 6, Apr. 21, 1934, 4, May 12, 1934, 1, 7, June 2, 1934, 1, 2, June 9, 1934, 6, May 25, 1935, 2, 3, Apr. 6, 1935, 6; Newell, *Chicago and the Labor Movement,* 147, 233.

37. *FN,* Apr. 22, 1933, 2 (quote), May 6, 1933, 2, June 3, 1933, 2, Mar. 24, 1934, 2, Sept. 26, 1936, 1, Nov. 7, 1936, 5; "Radio Speech of Barratt O'Hara," Transcript, June 3, 1935, Folder 134, Box 19, JF.

38. *FN,* Mar. 24, 1934, 2, Apr. 21, 1934, 1, 7.

39. *FN,* Mar. 24, 1934, 2.

40. *Billboard,* Mar. 16, 1935, 10; *FN,* Apr. 6, 1935, 6, 7, June 22, 1935, 6, Aug. 17, 1935, 6; Letter, Nockels to Harry Fultz, May 3, 1935, Folder 133, Box 19, JF (quote).

41. *FN,* Apr. 13, 1935, 12, Apr. 20, 1935, 6, Oct. 19, 1935, 6 (quote).

42. *FN,* Oct. 26, 1935, 6, Nov. 2, 1935, 6, Apr. 27, 1935, 6 (quotes).

43. *FN,* May 25, 1935, 6 (first quote), Nov. 23, 1935, 6 (second quote), Feb. 8, 1936, 6 (third through fifth quotes), Mar. 14, 1936, 6.

44. *FN,* May 25, 1935, 6.

45. *FN,* Nov. 10, 1934, 2 (quotes), 9, Oct. 26, 1935, 3.

46. Newell, *Chicago and the Labor Movement,* 123.

47. *FN,* Sept. 15, 1934, 3, Nov. 10, 1934, 9, Dec. 15, 1934, 1 (first quote), June 1, 1935, 9, July 6, 1935, 9, July 13, 1935, 10, Sept. 2, 1935, 10 (second and third quotes).

48. *FN,* July 27, 1935, 2.

49. *FN,* Sept. 15, 1934, 3.

50. Ibid.

51. *FN,* Jan. 4, 1936, 12.

52. *FN,* Dec. 15, 1934, 1, 3, Jan. 12, 1935, 9, Apr. 20, 1935, 9 (third quote), May 4, 1935, 9, May 11, 1935, 9 (first and second quotes). About fifty Chicago-area unions helped to create the Chicago Labor College in the spring of 1934. Supervised by Lillian Herstein and Joseph M. Jacobs, the college offered courses on public speaking, parliamentary law, labor law, and labor history. "The splendid work of the Women's Trade Union League College and the Speakers' Bureau" set the set stage for the new college. *FN,* Oct. 12, 1935, 5. See also *FN,* May 12, 1934, 8, May 26, 1934, 2, Oct. 13, 1934, 9, 12, Nov. 3, 1934, 14, Nov. 10, 1934, 2, Sept. 2, 1935, 10, and Oct. 12, 1935, 8.

53. *FN,* May 25, 1935, 9 (quote), Oct. 12, 1935, 12, Oct. 19, 1935, 11, Nov. 14, 1936, 9.

54. *FN,* June 8, 1935, 9, June 22, 1935, 8, 9, Jan. 25, 1936, 12 (quotes).

55. *FN,* Feb. 3, 1936, 11 (first quote), May 2, 1936, 9 (second and third quotes).

56. *FN,* Jan. 25, 1936, 12, Mar. 14, 1936, 10, May 2, 1936, 9, May 16, 1936, 11, May 23, 1936, 3 (quote). The bureau's radio program returned to a "traditional" format in the fall of 1936 with talks by Agnes Nestor, Sam Levin, Victor Olander, Fitzpatrick, and other labor leaders. *FN,* Oct. 24, 1936, 2.

57. Mordecai Gorelik, "Theatre Is a Weapon," *Theatre Arts Monthly* 18 (June 1934): 420–23; McConachie and Friedman, "Introduction," 3–15; Daniel Friedman, "A Brief Description of the Workers' Theatre Movement of the Thirties," in *Theatre for Working-Class Audiences,* ed. McConachie and Friedman, 112.

58. Colette A. Hyman, "Women, Workers, and Community: Working-Class Visions and Workers' Theatre in the 1930s," *Canadian Review of American Studies* 23 (Fall 1992): 15–37 (first and second quotes from 16); Friedman, "Brief Description of Workers' Theatre Movement," 112–15, 117 (third quote).

59. Ira A. Levine, *Left-Wing Dramatic Theory in the American Theatre* (Ann Arbor: UMI Research Press, 1985), 97 (first, second, and third quotes), 98, 178; Karen Malpede Taylor, *People's Theatre in Amerika* (New York: Drama Book Specialists, 1972), 68–71; *NYT,* Oct. 20, 1935, sec. 10, p. 2, Sept. 5, 1937, sec. 10, p. 1 (fourth and fifth quotes).

60. *New Theatre,* Apr. 1934, 10–11, May 1934, 11–12, 22; *Billboard,* Dec. 1, 1934, 3, 10; *FN,* Sept. 28, 1935, 6, Oct. 19, 1935, 6, 7, Dec. 14, 1935, 6.

61. *FN,* Sept. 28, 1935, 6.

62. *FN,* Mar. 21, 1936, 6 (second, fourth, and fifth quotes), Sept. 28, 1935, 6, Oct. 19, 1935, 6, 7, Sept. 19, 1936, 7, Dec. 5, 1936, 7 (first quote), Dec. 26, 1936, 8 (third quote), Jan. 23, 1937, 11, Apr. 24, 1937, 1, May 8, 1937, 9.

63. *FN,* Sept. 12, 1936, 2, Oct. 17, 1936, 6 (quotes), Nov. 21, 1936, 5.

64. *FN,* Sept. 28, 1935, 6 (first quote), Oct. 12, 1935, 6, Oct. 19, 1935, 6, 7, Oct. 26, 1935, 6 (second quote), Nov. 2, 1935, 6, Dec. 14, 1935, 6.

65. Merrill Denison, "The Actor and Radio," *Theatre Arts Monthly* 17 (Nov. 1933): 851.

66. *Billboard,* Mar. 14, 1936, 10; *FN,* Oct. 12, 1935, 6, May 2, 1936, 9, Sept. 19, 1936, 7, Feb. 6, 1937, 11, Feb. 13, 1937, 2; John O'Connor, "The Federal Theatre Project's Search for an Audience," in *Theatre for Working-Class Audiences,* ed. McConachie and Friedman, 171–83; Colette A. Hyman, "Politics Meet Popular Entertainment in the Workers' Theater of the 1930s," in *Radical Revisions: Reconsidering 1930s Culture,* ed. Bill Mullen and Sherry Lee Linkon (Urbana: University of Illinois Press, 1996), 208–24.

67. Jerrold H. Lapham, "What Hope Radio Drama?" *Theatre Arts Monthly* 18 (Jan. 1934): 44, 50; Denison, "The Actor and Radio," 850–51 (third quote); Ralph Rogers, *Dos and Donts of Radio Writing* (Boston: Associated Radio Writers, 1937), 12 (first and second quotes).

68. New York station WEVD developed a much closer relationship with workers' theater than did WCFL. In 1934, WEVD presented "The People's Theatre," a one-hour talk show that publicized the work of the Theatre Union and explained the purpose of social plays. WEVD and the Theatre Union joined forces in 1935–36 to present a series entitled "Social Plays of the Past Decade." The thirty-minute sustaining program aired on Sunday nights. *Variety*, May 1, 1935, 30; Edith J. R. Isaacs, "Communal Theatre," *Theatre Arts Monthly* 20 (July 1936): 494; Mark W. Weisstuch, "The Theatre Union, 1933–1937: A History" (Ph.D. diss., City University of New York, 1982), 174–75.

69. *FN*, Jan. 21, 1933, 3, Feb. 25, 1933, 10–11, Mar. 4, 1933, 1, 3; *Billboard*, Mar. 11, 1933, 14.

70. *FN*, Jan. 13, 1934, 3, 8 (quote), Feb. 17, 1934, 1, 7, Jan. 26, 1935, 6, Mar. 2, 1935, 12, Mar. 9, 1935, 1, 2, 7, Mar. 23, 1935, 6.

71. *FN*, Feb. 1, 1936, 12, Feb. 29, 1936, 1, Jan. 23, 1937, 1, 5, Feb. 13, 1937, 1, 5.

72. *FN*, Sept. 3, 1932, 22.

73. *FN*, Sept. 3, 1934, 30–31, Sept. 8, 1934, 1, 6.

74. *FN*, June 15, 1935, 9 (quotes); Dawley, *Struggles for Justice*, 403–4. For background on Coughlin see Alan Brinkley, *Voices of Protest: Huey Long, Father Coughlin, and the Great Depression* (New York: Alfred A. Knopf, 1982).

75. *FN*, Sept. 14, 1935, 2 (quote), 10; Charles J. Tull, *Father Coughlin and the New Deal* (Syracuse: Syracuse University Press, 1965), 100.

76. Letter, E. Nockels to Father Charles E. Coughlin, May 23, 1935, Folder 133, Box 19, JF; Transcript of Radio Speech, Barratt O'Hara, June 3, 1935; Letter, Nockels to Father Coughlin, June 4, 1935; Transcript of Radio Speech, Barratt O'Hara, June 21, 1935; and Letter, Nockels to William Green, June 18, 1935, all in Folder 134, Box 19, JF; *FN*, June 22, 1935, 11; Brinkley, *Voices of Protest*, 200–201, 319n13; Neil Betten, *Catholic Activism and the Industrial Worker* (Gainesville: University Presses of Florida, 1976), 90–107.

77. *FN*, Sept. 14, 1935, 2 (quotes), 10. The CFL unanimously supported Coughlin's free speech rights, believing that free speech and assembly were crucial for organized labor. Leftists within the CFL reminded their more conservative colleagues that free speech should apply to everyone, not just right-wing advocates. *FN*, June 15, 1935, 9.

78. *FN*, Aug. 10, 1935, 12, Aug. 17, 1935, 12, Sept. 7, 1936, 1, Sept. 12, 1936, 1, 8.

79. George Rawick, "Working-Class Self-Activity," in *Workers' Struggles, Past and Present: A "Radical America" Reader*, ed. James Green (Philadelphia: Temple University Press, 1983), 145–46; Green, *The World of the Worker*, 133–73; Bernstein, *Turbulent Years*, 400–431; Phelan, *William Green*, 107–56; Christopher L. Tomlins, "AFL Unions in the 1930s: Their Performance in Historical Perspective," *Journal of American History* 65 (Mar. 1979): 1021–42.

80. Letters, M. Bialis to David Dubinsky, Jan. 16, 1936, Dubinsky to Edward Nockels, Jan. 18, 1936, and Ed Nockels to Dubinsky, Jan. 22, 1936, all in Folder 2, Box 212, Collection 2, David Dubinsky Correspondence, ILGWU Records.

81. Letters, Fred W. Smith to WCFL, Aug. 8, 1936, Charles Sand to Ed Nockels, Aug. 18, 1936 (first and second quotes), and Nockels to Smith, Aug. 19, 1936 (third quote), all in Folder 142, Box 20, JF.

82. WCFL Form, Folder 142, Box 20, JF.

83. Letter, Joseph M. Jacobs to author, Aug. 6, 1991, in the possession of the author; *FN*, May 26, 1934, 10.

84. Jacobs Interview (second quote); Radio Speech, Joseph M. Jacobs, Oct. 10, 1935, transcript in the possession of the author, courtesy of Joseph M. Jacobs (first quote). For a brief description of some of Jacobs's activities, see Newell, *Chicago and the Labor Movement*, 108–9, 148–49.

85. *FN*, Sept. 3, 1932, 32, Apr. 8, 1933, 10, Nov. 3, 1934, 15, Apr. 20, 1935, 10, Mar. 6, 1937, 10 (quote); *Broadcasting*, Aug. 1, 1934, 8.

86. *FN*, Nov. 16, 1935, 10; "Discussion of Recent Decisions," *Chicago-Kent Review* 14, no. 2 (Mar. 1936): 171–74; "Notes," *Air Law Review* 7, no. 2 (Apr. 1936): 243–46.

87. *FN*, Sept. 26, 1936, 1, 5, Nov. 7, 1936, 1, 5, Dec. 12, 1936, 8, Jan. 16, 1937, 8, Jan. 23, 1937, 5, Jan. 30, 1937, 2, Mar. 27, 1937, 11.

88. *FN*, Mar. 18, 1933, 3, Apr. 8, 1933, 2, Apr. 29, 1933, 1, Apr. 14, 1934, 11, Nov. 3, 1934, 6, Mar. 23, 1935, 6.

89. *FN*, June 16, 1934, 6.

90. *FN*, May 13, 1933, 2, May 20, 1933, 1, 8, June 10, 1933, 1, Jan. 13, 1934, 1, Apr. 21, 1934, 4 (quotes). The court acquitted the union of racketeering charges in May 1934. *FN*, May 12, 1934, 1, 7.

91. MacDonald, *Don't Touch That Dial*, 48–49 (quotes); Buxton and Owen, *The Big Broadcast*, 191, 193, 247; Thomas A. DeLong, *Quiz Craze: America's Infatuation with Game Shows* (New York: Praeger, 1991), 11–21.

92. *FN*, Jan. 16, 1937, 8, Jan. 23, 1937, 5, Jan. 30, 1937, 2, Feb. 6, 1937, 8, Feb. 20, 1937, 11, Mar. 27, 1937, 11, Apr. 10, 1937, 3.

93. Newell, *Chicago and the Labor Movement*, 112–13 (first quote); *FN*, Mar. 14, 1936, 3, Mar. 21, 1936, 3 (second quote); *Broadcasting*, July 1, 1936, 98.

94. James Curran, Anthony Smith, and Pauline Wingate, eds., *Impacts and Influences: Essays on Media Power in the Twentieth Century* (London: Methuen, 1987), 223.

95. Goban-Klas, "Minority Media," 32.

96. Ibid., 30–31.

97. Cohen, *Making a New Deal*, 325–33 (quotes from 329–30).

98. Barnouw, *Golden Web*, 168–74.

99. Letter, Edward Nockels to William Green, Feb. 24, 1937, Folder 146, Box 21, JF; *Chicago Sunday Times*, Feb. 28, 1937, 2; *FN*, Mar. 6, 1937, 1, Mar. 13, 1937, 2; *Broadcasting*, Mar. 15, 1937, 56.

100. Telegrams, F. Walsh to John Fitzpatrick and Walsh to Marvin H. McIntyre, Feb. 27, 1937, Folder Feb. 16–27, 1937, General Correspondence, Box 23, FW.

101. *FN*, Mar. 13, 1937, 1.

102. Letter, William B. Rubin to L. P. Straube, Mar. 1, 1937, Correspondence 1937, Folder Jan.–Mar., Box 11, Rubin Papers (first and second quotes); FCC Engineering Department, *Report on Social and Economic Data,* 16 (third quote).

103. *FN,* May 4, 1929, 2.

104. FCC Engineering Department, *Report on Social and Economic Data,* 116; Nockels, "Last of Public Domain," 29; Senate Committee, *Radio Control,* 201–7; *FN,* Sept. 2, 1935, 33 (quotes), May 26, 1934, 5.

105. Telegram, Mollie Friedman to Ed Nockels, Dec. 11, 1926, Folder 11, Box 2, Collection 6, Morris Sigman Correspondence, ILGWU Records.

Chapter 7: Labor Radio without Nockels, 1937–46

1. Dawley, "Workers, Capital, and the State," 167–73, (first quote from 166–67; second quote from 172); Rosenberg, *Spreading the American Dream,* 169–70, 176–228.

2. Green, *The World of the Worker,* 133–34; Lipsitz, *Rainbow at Midnight;* Rosenberg, *Spreading the American Dream;* Thomas J. McCormick, *America's Half-Century: United States Foreign Policy in the Cold War* (Baltimore: Johns Hopkins University Press, 1989).

3. Wrigley, *Class Politics and Public Schools,* 244–45.

4. Keenan Interview.

5. Advisory Council of the National Broadcasting Company, *Committee Reports,* Second Meeting, 36 (quote), 1928, Folder 2, Box 107, NBC Records.

6. *Variety,* May 19, 1937, 35, May 26, 1937, 27, 31, July 21, 1937, 35, Sept. 1, 1937, 34, Oct. 20, 1937, 42, Jan. 12, 1938, 28 (quote).

7. *Variety,* Dec. 8, 1937, 25; Richard J. Connors, *A Cycle of Power: The Career of Jersey City Mayor Frank Hague* (Metchen, N.J.: Scarecrow Press, 1971), 98–100.

8. *Variety,* Jan. 12, 1938, 28; *Billboard,* Jan. 1, 1938, 38; Upton Sinclair, *The Flivver King: A Story of Ford-America* (Pasadena: Upton Sinclair, 1937; Chicago: Charles H. Kerr, 1987). "The March of Time," a quasi-news program, dramatized recent events.

9. *FN,* Jan. 23, 1937, 7, Feb. 20, 1937, 3, July 21, 1945, 4, 9; *Variety,* May 19, 1937, 35; Letter, Morris Novik to Charles Zimmerman, Mar. 17, 1934, Folder 8, Box 37, Charles S. Zimmerman Correspondence, ILGWU Records; Publicity fliers for ILGWU program and "Talk by David Dubinsky over Station WEVD," Apr. 6, 1934, Folder 8, Box 49, Collection 2, David Dubinsky Correspondence, ILGWU Records.

10. *FN,* Mar. 5, 1938, 1, 6, June 18, 1938, 1, 8; *Radio Daily,* May 31, 1938, 5, 7.

11. AFL Executive Council Meeting Minutes, May 28, 1937, 100–101.

12. Letter, J. Fitzpatrick to W. Green, July 28, 1937, Folder 152, Box 22, JF (first and second quotes); Letter, Green to Fitzpatrick, Aug. 7, 1937, Folder 153, Box 22, JF; Letters, M. Woll to Fitzpatrick, Sept. 14, 1937 (third through sixth quotes), and Green to Fitzpatrick, Sept. 23, 1937 (seventh quote), both in Folder 154, Box 22, JF.

13. *Variety,* Mar. 17, 1937, 40; Letters, J. Fitzpatrick to F. Walsh, Nov. 10, 1937,

Folder Nov. 1–17, 1937 (quote), and Walsh to Fitzpatrick, Nov. 19, 1937, Folder Nov. 18–29, 1937, both in General Correspondence, Box 23, FW; Keenan Interview, 8. CFL secretary Mollie Levitas recalled that while Keenan had the support of the Chicago building trades unions, "he had never really taken an active part in the" CFL. Throughout the forties, he was preoccupied serving as a labor representative in various federal offices. Levitas Interview, Dec. 22, 1970, 48–49, 51; Francis X. Gannon, *Joseph D. Keenan, Labor's Ambassador in War and Peace: A Portrait of a Man and His Times* (Lanham, Md.: University Press of America, 1984).

14. AFL Executive Council Meeting Minutes, Feb. 8, 1938, 205.

15. Ibid., 206–7; "B. F. Goldstein—Analysis given to Mr. Woll, April 8, 1938," Folder 14, Box 17, Collection 2, William Green Papers, Meany Archives (quotes); Telegram, B. Goldstein to M. Woll, Apr. 13, 1938, enclosed in memorandum, Goldstein to Thea Glenn, Apr. 14, 1938, Folder 1, Box 14, Collection 3, Office of the President William Green, Meany Archives; Memorandum, Niles Trammell to L. R. Lohr, Dec. 30, 1937, Folder 77, Box 99, NBC Records.

16. "Goldstein—Analysis."

17. AFL Executive Council Meeting Minutes, Apr. 29, 1938, 101–3; Resolution for CFL, enclosed in memorandum, B. F. Goldstein to Thea Glenn, Apr. 11, 1938, Folder 1, Box 14, Collection 3, Office of the President William Green, Meany Archives; *FN*, Apr. 23, 1938, 7.

18. AFL Executive Council Meeting Minutes, Apr. 29, 1938, 101; *FN*, Apr. 23, 1938, 7, May 14, 1938, 1; *CT*, Apr. 30, 1938, 5; *NYT*, Apr. 30, 1938, 16; *Variety*, May 4, 1938, 38; *Billboard*, May 14, 1938, 10; Walter Galenson, *The CIO Challenge to the AFL: A History of the American Labor Movement, 1935–1941* (Cambridge, Mass.: Harvard University Press, 1960), 209–10.

19. Memoranda, William S. Hedges to F. M. Russell, Nov. 29, 1937, and Russell to Hedges, Dec. 1, 1937, Folder 77, Box 99, NBC Records.

20. Memorandum, F. M. Russell to L. R. Lohr, Jan. 19, 1938, Folder 77, Box 99, NBC Records.

21. Memorandum, Niles Trammell to L. R. Lohr, Jan. 21, 1938, Folder 77, Box 99, NBC Records.

22. Letter, V. Olander to J. Fitzpatrick and J. Keenan, Feb. 16, 1938, Folder 160, Box 23, JF. On the FCC inquiry see Barnouw, *Golden Web*, 115–16.

23. Telegram, L. Lohr to N. Trammell, Apr. 29, 1938, Folder 77, Box 99, NBC Records.

24. Memorandum, Niles Trammell to Lenox Lohr, Apr. 29, 1938, Folder 77, Box 99, NBC Records. Trammell's reference to "an outside group" having interest in WCFL may have meant either CBS or the Hearst organization.

25. Memoranda, Wm. S. Hedges to N. Trammell, Dec. 7, 1937, Trammell to Roy C. Witmer, May 3, 1938, Witmer to Trammell, May 5, 1938, Trammell to Witmer, May 7, 1938 (third and fourth quotes), Hedges to Trammell, May 11, 1938 (first and sec-

ond quotes), and Witmer to Trammell, May 12, 1938, all in Folder 77, Box 99, NBC Records; *Variety,* Mar. 9, 1938, 34. Rumors persisted into the summer that NBC would purchase WCFL. *Billboard,* July 23, 1938, 7.

26. Barnouw, *Golden Web,* 170–71, 187–90; *Variety Radio Directory, 1937–1938* (New York: Variety, 1937), 443; *Broadcasting Yearbook, 1942* (Washington, D.C.: Broadcasting Publications, 1942).

27. *FN,* Aug. 27, 1938, 2.

28. *FN,* Nov. 6, 1938, 9, Feb. 4, 1939, 10; AFL Executive Council Meeting Minutes, Feb. 9, 13, 1939, 208–10, 279, 329; Letter, Green to J. Keenan, Dec. 20, 1939, Folder A.F. of L., William Green, President, JF.

29. Keiser, "Fitzpatrick"; Newell, *Chicago and the Labor Movement,* 182–96, 253; Phelan, *William Green,* 129–56; Levitas Interview, July 27, 1970, 26–27.

30. Jacobs Interview, 3 (quote); McKillen, *Chicago Labor and a Democratic Diplomacy,* 194–205; Herstein Interview, Oct. 26, 1970, 44, 67; Nathan Fine, *Labor and Farmer Parties in the United States, 1828–1928* (New York: Rand School of Social Science, 1928; Berkeley: Center for Socialist History, 1984), 429–36.

31. Orear Interview, 3 (quote); *Variety,* Apr. 7, 1937, 30.

32. Barry Kritzberg, "An Unfinished Chapter in White-Collar Unionism: The Formative Years of the Chicago Newspaper Guild, Local 71, American Newspaper Guild, A.F.L.-C.I.O.," *Labor History* 14, no. 3 (Summer 1973): 399–400.

33. Kritzberg, "Unfinished Chapter," 400–402; Newell, *Chicago and the Labor Movement,* 187–88.

34. Kritzberg, "Unfinished Chapter," 402–5; Newell, *Chicago and the Labor Movement,* 189–90.

35. Kritzberg, "Unfinished Chapter," 404–5; Galenson, *The CIO Challenge,* 558 (quote).

36. Newell, *Chicago and the Labor Movement,* 190, 192; *Guild Reporter,* Jan. 15, 1939, 4, May 1, 1939, 1; Galenson, *The CIO Challenge,* 558; Wrigley, *Class Politics and Public Schools,* 242–43; *Variety,* July 19, 1939, 23.

37. *FN,* Dec. 24, 1938, 5, Feb. 25, 1939, 8 (quote).

38. *FN,* Dec. 10, 1938, 1 (first quote), 7, Nov. 18, 1939, 5 (second through fifth quotes), 11; Letter, Ira Latimer to Hazel L. Rice, Dec. 12, 1939, vol. 2104: Radio Correspondence—Censorship, 4, WGN, Reel 173, ACLU Archives (sixth quote); Memorandum, A. L. Ashby to Frank E. Mullen, Mar. 10, 1941, Folder 77, Box 99, NBC Records; Jorgensen, "Radio Station WCFL," 124; Edgar Bernhard, Ira Latimer, and Harvey O'Connor, *Pursuit of Freedom: A History of Civil Liberties in Illinois, 1787–1942* (Chicago: Chicago Civil Liberties Committee, 1942), 49, 196.

39. Kritzberg, "Unfinished Chapter," 406; *Guild Reporter.*

40. Kritzberg, "Unfinished Chapter," 408–10; Bernhard, Latimer, and O'Connor, *Pursuit of Freedom,* 196; Galenson, *The CIO Challenge,* 558.

41. Letters, Ira Latimer to Radio Station WGN, Nov. 25, 1939 (second and third

quotes), Quin A. Ryan to Latimer, Dec. 1, 1939 (fourth quote), and Latimer to Hazel L. Rice, Dec. 12, 1939 (first and fifth quotes), all in vol. 2104: Radio Correspondence—Censorship, 4, WGN, Reel 173, ACLU Archives.

42. Memorandum of Minutes of the Eleventh Meeting of the Advisory Council of the National Broadcasting Company, Apr. 12, 1938, Folder 5, Box 17, Collection 6, Reference Files, Miscellaneous, Green Papers; "Memorandum for Mr. Thomas, February 26, 1936. RE: Freedom of the Air," Bethuel M. Webster Jr. to Norman Thomas, vol. 913, Radio Correspondence, 1936, Reel 134, ACLU Archives.

43. NAB, *NAB Code Manual,* 15–17 (quote from 15).

44. *Variety,* Nov. 8, 1939, 21 (quote), Nov. 22, 1939, 38, Dec. 20, 1939, 26; Fones-Wolf, "For Better Listening," 6–7.

45. Letter, John F. Royal to Janet MacRorie, Aug. 21, 1939, Folder 77, Box 70, NBC Records.

46. *FN,* Dec. 26, 1942, 10 (quotes); Fones-Wolf, "For Better Listening," 7–8.

47. *Variety,* May 24, 1944, 23, June 7, 1944, 23 (quote); Barnouw, *Golden Web,* 230–31.

48. Gilbert Seldes, *The Great Audience* (New York: Viking Press, 1950), 133; Barnouw, *Golden Web,* 230–31.

49. Ted Taylor article, Apr. 30, 1942, Reel 9111, Radio 1940–42 Folder, FP Papers.

50. *FN,* Apr. 3, 1943, 2, 3, Apr. 24, 1943, 9.

51. *FN,* Apr. 3, 1943, 2, 3, Apr. 24, 1943, 9, Aug. 14, 1943, 4.

52. Letter, Janet MacRorie to N. Trammell, Apr. 6, 1939, Folder 78, Box 70, NBC Records (first quote); Emanie N. Arling, Report on NAB Code, Feb. 1, 1940, vol. 2212, Radio Correspondence—NAB, Reel 186, ACLU Archives (second through sixth quotes).

53. Letter, MacRorie to Trammell, Apr. 6, 1939, Folder 78, Box 70, NBC Records; Arling, Report on NAB Code (quotes); CIO, *Proceedings of the Fourth Constitutional Convention of the Congress of Industrial Organizations, Detroit, Michigan, Nov. 17–22, 1941* (Washington, D.C.: CIO, 1941), 69–70, 291; Cohen, *Making a New Deal,* 341, 343; Fones-Wolf, "For Better Listening," 8.

54. *FN,* Sept. 2, 1939, 53 (quotes). See also Cohen, *Making a New Deal,* 356–57.

55. MacRorie to Trammell, Apr. 6, 1939; FCC, *Report on Chain Broadcasting* (Washington, D.C.: GPO, 1941).

56. CIO, *Proceedings of the Fourth Convention,* 70.

57. *FN,* Apr. 21, 1945, 2, May 5, 1945, 1, July 7, 1945, 2–3; "Accuse McCormick of Trying to Censor Radio," June 20, 1945, "McCormick Radio Libel Bill Passed," July 3, 1945, and "McCormick's Radio Libel Bill Becomes Law," July 25, 1945 (quotes), all on Reel 9112, Radio 1945–46 Folder, FP Papers.

58. *Variety,* Jan. 12, 1944, 37, June 14, 1944, 22 (quotes).

59. CIO, *Proceedings of the Seventh Constitutional Convention of the Congress of Industrial Organizations, Chicago, Illinois, Nov. 20–24, 1944* (Washington, D.C.: CIO, 1944), 237–38; Jorgensen, "Radio Station WCFL," 6–11 (first quote from 7); FCC, *Federal Communications Commission Reports: April 2, 1943, to June 30, 1945* (Wash-

ington, D.C.: GPO, 1947), 515–18 (second through fifth quotes from 516–17); Fones-Wolf, "For Better Listening," 15–17.

60. CIO Political Action Committee, *Radio Handbook* (1944), Meany Archives.

61. "Federated Press Survey Shows Unions on the Air from Coast to Coast," June 27, 1944, Reel 9112, Radio—Use by Labor 1940–44 Folder, FP Papers.

62. Ibid. (quote); Press Release, Sept. 7, 1944, Reel 9111, Radio 1943–44 Folder, FP Papers; *FN*, July 8, 1944, 1.

63. "America Goes for Labor's Radio Shows," Feb. 16, 1945, Reel 9112, Radio—Use by Labor 1945–47 Folder, FP Papers.

64. "Report on Radio," in AFL Executive Council Meeting Minutes, Jan. 31, 1946, 135–36.

65. CIO, *Proceedings of the Eighth Constitutional Convention of the Congress of Industrial Organizations, Atlantic City, New Jersey, Nov. 18–22, 1946* (Washington, D.C.: CIO, 1946), 66 (quotes); Fones-Wolf, "For Better Listening," 28–29.

66. Lipsitz, *Rainbow at Midnight*, 100. For details on the post–World War II strike wave see Lipsitz, *Rainbow at Midnight*, 99–154.

67. "Washington AFL to Buy Radio Station," Aug. 5, 1946, Reel 9112, Radio—Use by Labor 1945–47 Folder, FP Papers (first quote); AFL Executive Council Meeting Minutes, Jan. 21, 1945, 17 (second and third quotes). On labor's FM stations see Fones-Wolf, "For Better Listening," 22–26.

68. Letter, Howard T. Keegan to Matthew Woll, Apr. 12, 1945, in AFL Executive Council Meeting Minutes, May 3, 1945, 38–39.

Chapter 8: "Showmanship," 1937–46

1. *Radio Daily*, Mar. 9, 1937, 3, Mar. 23, 1937, 5; *Broadcasting*, Mar. 15, 1937, 56.

2. *Variety*, Mar. 3, 1937, 34 (quote), June 23, 1937, 51; *Broadcasting*, Mar. 15, 1937, 56; *Radio Daily*, June 22, 1937, 1, 6; *FN*, Sept. 6, 1937, 66.

3. *Variety*, Nov. 10, 1937, 31 (first and second quotes), Mar. 17, 1937, 40 (third and fourth quotes), May 19, 1937, 34, June 23, 1937, 51, Jan. 12, 1938, 35; *FN*, Sept. 6, 1937, 66; *Radio Daily*, Apr. 22, 1937, 6, May 26, 1937, 6, June 22, 1937, 1, 6.

4. *Variety*, Nov. 10, 1937, 31; *Radio Daily*, May 6, 1938, 5, Sept. 29, 1938, 13; Arthur J. Todd, William F. Byron, and Howard L. Vierow, *Commercial Recreation*, vol. 2 of *The Chicago Recreation Study 1937* (Chicago: Northwestern University, 1938), 121.

5. AFL Executive Council Meeting Minutes, Feb. 9, 1939, 210–11; *Variety*, June 7, 1939, 18; CFL Application for FM Station, Oct. 16, 1941, Docket 7139, Box 2559, FCC Docket Section, RG 173, NARS; *FN*, Sept. 2, 1939, 35.

6. *FN*, Sept. 2, 1940, 54, 91.

7. *Billboard*, Mar. 25, 1939, 9.

8. *Variety*, Mar. 17, 1937, 40; Memorandum, William S. Hedges to Niles Trammell, Dec. 7, 1937, Folder 77, Box 99, NBC Records; *FN*, Sept. 2, 1939, 35; AFL Executive Council Meeting Minutes, Feb. 9, 1939, 210–11.

9. CFL Application for FM Station, Oct. 16, 1941; *FN,* Mar. 27, 1937, 6, Nov. 27, 1943, 4, Sept. 2, 1940, 54.

10. *FN,* July 27, 1940, 1, Sept. 2, 1940, 54, Sept. 21, 1940, 3, Feb. 9, 1946, 4. By 1950, CFL officials had abandoned the Downers Grove project and only wanted to sell the land to the highest bidder. The federation retained eighty acres hoping that continued home construction in the area would increase land prices for a retail shopping center. *FN,* Feb. 18, 1950, May 13, 1950, 5.

11. *FN,* Nov. 12, 1938, 10, Sept. 23, 1939, 1–2 (quote from 2); *Variety,* Feb. 22, 1939, 36. The Mormon church wanted shortwave facilities to send "'American culture' into 'Latin American ears.'" *Variety,* Feb. 22, 1939, 36.

12. *Radio Daily,* June 21, 1938, 1, 3; *FN,* Aug. 24, 1940, 12, Sept. 2, 1940, 53, Feb. 8, 1941, 1, Mar. 8, 1941, 8, Mar. 29, 1941, 1, 3; ISFL, *Proceedings: Sixty-First Convention, September 20, 1943, Springfield, Illinois,* 99, copy in Northwestern University Library; *FN,* Aug. 25, 1945, 2, Sept. 21, 1946, 2.

13. *FN,* Nov. 11, 1944, 4, Nov. 10, 1945, 5, Feb. 9, 1946, 4–5 (quotes), Feb. 23, 1946, 2. The reorganization in 1945 also derived from a concern over WCFL's tax status. AFL general counsel Joseph Padway worried that the Bureau of Internal Revenue would rule "that all money earned over and above operating expenses," regardless of the CFL's ownership of all stocks and regardless "that earnings, if any, will go to the union for the purpose of furthering union principles, is subject to the payment of taxes in the same manner as though the corporation were [an] independent commercial concern." Letter, Padway to M. Woll and M. Lynch, Apr. 25, 1944, Folder 168, Box 25, JF.

14. Draft Proposal by Chicago Times, Inc., Jan. 27, 1940, Folder 167, Box 25, JF; *FN,* Sept. 2, 1940, 91, Sept. 6, 1941, 1; ISFL, *Proceedings: Sixty-First Convention,* 99.

15. *Variety,* Apr. 7, 1937, 30.

16. *FN,* Apr. 4, 1931, 8, Apr. 25, 1931, 17; *Variety,* Dec. 4, 1940, 34, Nov. 3, 1937, 31, Dec. 8, 1937, 25; "Contract between . . . WCFL and AFRA," Dec. 1937, Folder 158, Box 23, JF; *Broadcasting,* Feb. 15, 1938, 18; *Billboard,* Mar. 26, 1938, 6, July 23, 1938, 7.

17. *CT,* May 19, 1937, 16.

18. *Radio Daily,* Sept. 7, 1937, 1 (first quote), 3 (second quote), Sept. 13, 1937, 2; *Variety,* Mar. 17, 1937, 40 (third quote), Nov. 10, 1937, 31.

19. *Radio Daily,* Oct. 4, 1937, 6; *CT,* Feb. 20, 1938, sec. 3, p. 4; *Variety Radio Directory, 1939–1940* (New York: Variety, 1939), 625; *FN,* Sept. 6, 1937, 67 (quote), Sept. 3, 1938, 54, Sept. 2, 1946, 57.

20. *Radio Daily,* Sept. 7, 1937, 3; Summers, *History of Programs,* 78, 87, 119, 135.

21. *Radio Daily,* Sept. 7, 1937, 3; *Variety,* Nov. 10, 1937, 31; *Radio Daily,* Oct. 22, 1937, 7 (quote), Feb. 16, 1937, 2, Sept. 19, 1938, 4; *Broadcasting,* Nov. 15, 1937, 55; MacDonald, *Don't Touch That Dial,* 47–48, 80; Buxton and Owen, *The Big Broadcast,* 149–50.

22. *Billboard,* Nov. 19, 1938, 10 (quote); *Radio Daily,* Sept. 7, 1937, 3, Oct. 22, 1937, 1, May 5, 1938, 4, July 25, 1938, 5, Aug. 30, 1938, 7; *Broadcasting,* July 15, 1937, 62; *FN,* Aug. 9, 1941, 11, Dec. 6, 1941, 12.

23. *Variety,* May 5, 1937, 42; *Broadcasting,* July 15, 1937, 62.

24. *Radio Daily,* June 24, 1937, 5, Sept. 29, 1938, 13, Mar. 29, 1938, 5, Aug. 26, 1938, 3, June 17, 1938, 4, Mar. 2, 1939, 6; *Billboard,* Nov. 19, 1938, 10.

25. *Radio Daily,* Mar. 30, 1937, 7, July 27, 1937, 7, Mar. 14, 1938, 6, June 30, 1938, 8, Aug. 25, 1938, 5, Sept. 28, 1938, 6, Nov. 14, 1938, 8; *FN,* Dec. 13, 1941, 15 (quote), Nov. 14, 1942, 1; *Billboard,* June 4, 1938, 9.

26. Barnouw, *Golden Web,* 217.

27. Ibid., 217–18; Passman, *Deejays,* 50, 52, 53–54 (quotes), 56–57. The "Musical Clock" moved in 1944 to WCFL, where it remained for two years.

28. *Radio Daily,* Sept. 7, 1937, 3.

29. *Radio Daily,* Aug. 25, 1938, 5; *Billboard,* Apr. 29, 1939, 7; *Variety,* Sept. 18, 1940, 24 (quotes), Nov. 27, 1940, 38; *FN,* Dec. 20, 1941, 3, Feb. 21, 1942, 8; Buxton and Owen, *The Big Broadcast,* 29. WCFL's "Make Believe Danceland" remained on the air even after Chase left over a contract dispute in 1939. He began a competing show, "Mythical Ballroom," on station WAAF.

30. *FN,* Sept. 3, 1938, 53; *Radio Daily,* Apr. 1, 1937, 2, Apr. 28, 1937, 4, Sept. 8, 1937, 5, Sept. 14, 1937, 5, Jan. 21, 1938, 1, 3; *CT,* July 1, 1938, 23, July 5, 1938, 19; *Radio Daily,* Apr. 7, 1938, 6, Sept. 23, 1940, 8; *FN,* Apr. 11, 1942, 8, Dec. 14, 1946, 10.

31. WCFL Application for License Renewal, Nov. 28, 1941, WCFL Period (Feb. 1, 1942 to Nov. 24, 1948) Folder, Box 130, FCC Broadcast Bureau, Broadcast License, RG 173, NARS; *Variety,* June 7, 1939, 18; *CT,* July 1, 1938, 23, Feb. 16, 1938, 12, Feb. 17, 1938, 20; *FN,* Aug. 1, 1942, 1–2, Aug. 22, 1942, 3, Oct. 10, 1942, 8, 9, Oct. 17, 1942, 1, 5, Dec. 26, 1942, 10; MacDonald, *Don't Touch That Dial,* 57 (quote).

32. Barnouw, *Golden Web,* 187–90 (first quote from 187); *Variety,* Feb. 23, 1944, 33, Mar. 8, 1944, 37 (second quote); *FN,* Jan. 12, 1946, 9, Jan. 19, 1946, 3; *Variety,* May 1, 1946, 47–48.

33. *Variety,* June 26, 1946, 34; MacDonald, *Don't Touch That Dial,* 49; Summers, *History of Programs,* 142.

34. *Variety,* July 24, 1946, 36 (quotes), 40; Summers, *History of Programs,* 136; Buxton and Owen, *The Big Broadcast,* 54.

35. *Variety,* Apr. 24, 1946, 30; Summers, *History of Programs,* 146, 190.

36. *FN,* Sept. 2, 1939, 35, Sept. 6, 1937, 66, Sept. 2, 1940, 53; AFL Executive Council Meeting Minutes, Feb. 9, 1939, 210–11.

37. In its 1941 renewal application, WCFL officials estimated that during the typical 18.5 hour weekday, the station broadcasted 11 hours and 16 minutes of commercial programs and 7 hours and 14 minutes of sustaining programs; 58 minutes of commercial hours and 3 hours and 16 minutes of sustaining time went to educational and fraternal matters. WCFL Application for License Renewal, Nov. 28, 1941. See tables 3 and 4 in the appendix.

38. For studies detailing AFL complicity in the cold war see Howard Schonberger, "Labor's Cold War in Occupied Japan," *Diplomatic History* 3 (Summer 1979): 249–72; and Carolyn Eisenberg, "Working Class Politics and the Cold War: American

Intervention in the German Labor Movement, 1945–1949," *Diplomatic History* 7 (Fall 1983): 283–306.

39. Letters, Maynard Marquardt to Thomas D. Eliot, June 22, 1939 (quote), Marquardt to Ira Latimer, Aug. 7, 1939, Marquardt to ACLU, July 12, 1940, and Roger Baldwin to Station Managers, Sept. 9, 1940, all on Reel 186, vol. 2214, Radio Correspondence—Committee Matters, ACLU Archives.

40. *Radio Daily,* Apr. 28, 1937, 8, July 8, 1938, 5, July 13, 1938, 5, Aug. 3, 1938, 4, Aug. 23, 1938, 5.

41. *FN,* Sept. 23, 1944, 2–3, Oct. 14, 1944, 9, Mar. 10, 1945, 3.

42. *FN,* Sept. 23, 1944, 2, Jan. 20, 1945, 2; James T. Baker, *Studs Terkel* (New York: Twayne, 1992), 11–19.

43. *FN,* Jan. 20, 1945, 2, Feb. 3, 1945, 2.

44. *FN,* Nov. 9, 1946, 2.

45. *FN,* June 26, 1937, 10, Feb. 17, 1940, 12; *Radio Daily,* June 21, 1938, 7, June 6, 1938, 4.

46. *FN,* Oct. 31, 1942, 8, May 22, 1943, 2 (first and second quotes), Sept. 20, 1941, 10, Feb. 28, 1942, 3, May 16, 1942, 2, July 4, 1942, 5 (third quote), July 18, 1942, 6, Aug. 22, 1942, 1, 3, Sept. 5, 1942, 35, 55, Sept. 4, 1943, 55, Nov. 25, 1944, 2, 4; Press Release, Mar. 9, 1943, Reel 9112, Radio—Use by Labor 1940–44 Folder, FP Papers.

47. MacDonald, *Don't Touch That Dial,* 288–92; *Variety,* July 25, 1945, 26, 30; Irving E. Fang, *Those Radio Commentators!* (Ames: Iowa State University Press, 1977), 17–43, 199–215.

48. *Radio Daily,* Apr. 28, 1937, 8, Oct. 5, 1937, 6; *FN,* June 26, 1937, 10, July 3, 1937, 6, Feb. 26, 1938, 8, 11, Feb. 6, 1943, 5, Apr. 7, 1945, 8–9, Feb. 6, 1937, 5; *Broadcasting,* Oct. 15, 1937, 64; MacDonald, *Don't Touch That Dial,* 289–90.

49. *FN,* May 25, 1940, 11, Jan. 2, 1943, 3, Mar. 6, 1943, 3, Sept. 4, 1943, 55, Sept. 18, 1943, 1–3, Sept. 25, 1943, 8; Buxton and Owen, *The Big Broadcast,* 173; Summers, *History of Programs,* 102, 112, 118–19, 122, 129.

50. *FN,* Feb. 13, 1943, 10, July 10, 1943, 2, 3, Nov. 6, 1943, 6, Apr. 22, 1944, 9, Apr. 20, 1946, 11, June 29, 1946, 11, Sept. 28, 1946, 10.

51. *FN,* May 5, 1945, 3, Mar. 31, 1945, 3, May 5, 1945, 3 (first quote), 5, May 26, 1945, 10, July 28, 1945, 2 (second quote), 3.

52. *Variety,* May 15, 1946, 29, June 12, 1946, 36 (quotes).

53. ISFL, *Proceedings: Fifty-Seventh Annual Convention, September 18, 1939,* 93, copy in Northwestern University Library.

54. *FN,* Mar. 5, 1938, 1, 2, 6, Feb. 25, 1939, 1, Jan. 13, 1940, 3, 8 (quotes), Mar. 8, 1941, 1, Mar. 14, 1942, 1, 3, Feb. 13, 1943, 8, Mar. 25, 1944, 2, Mar. 23, 1946, 1; *Variety,* Mar. 15, 1944, 42; CFL Application for FM Station, Oct. 16, 1941.

55. *FN,* Feb. 19, 1939, 1 (second quote), Apr. 12, 1941, 8, Mar. 21, 1942, 3 (first quote), Mar. 11, 1944, 3.

56. *FN,* Aug. 7, 1937, 6, Sept. 18, 1937, 9, Sept. 17, 1938, 3 (quote), Sept. 12, 1942, 1, Sept. 11, 1943, 1, 3.

57. *FN,* Sept. 2, 1944, 3, 55; *Variety,* Sept. 6, 1944, 24.

58. *FN,* Sept. 30, 1944, 12 (quotes); "Labor Radio Program in Limelight," Sept. 28, 1944, Reel 9112, Radio—Use by Labor 1940–44 Folder, FP Papers.

59. *FN,* Sept. 15, 1945, 1–2, Sept. 22, 1945, 3, Sept. 2, 1946, 1.

60. *FN,* May 10, 1941, 2, Jan. 22, 1944, 3 (quotes), Sept. 2, 1944, 55.

61. *FN,* Sept. 2, 1944, 55.

62. Memoranda, Niles Trammell to Lenox Lohr, Jan. 21, 1938, and Apr. 29, 1938, both in Folder 77, Box 99, NBC Records; *Variety,* Mar. 17, 1937, 40 (first, second, third, and sixth quotes), Nov. 10. 1937, 31 (fourth and fifth quotes).

63. *FN,* Mar. 5, 1938, 1, 6, Aug. 13, 1938, 8, Sept. 3, 1938, 53.

64. *FN,* Sept. 2, 1939, 35, Aug. 10, 1946, 5, Oct. 12, 1946, 9, Dec. 7, 1946, 15.

65. *FN,* Jan. 22, 1944, 3 (third quote), Jan. 29, 1944, 1 (first and second quotes), Mar. 25, 1944, 8; Press Release, May 8, 1944, Reel 9112, Radio—Use by Labor 1940–44 Folder, FP Papers.

66. *FN,* Feb. 9, 1946, 4, Feb. 23, 1946, 5, Mar. 2, 1946, 1, Mar. 9, 1946, 3, Mar. 16, 1946, 1; *Variety,* Feb. 27, 1946, 36 (quotes).

67. Keenan Interview; Letters, Marjorie Nesbit to J. Fitzpatrick, Aug. 3, 1937, and Fitzpatrick to Nesbit, Aug. 5, 1937 (quote), both in Folder 153, Box 22, JF.

68. *FN,* Feb. 28, 1942, 2–3, Oct. 16, 1943, 3, June 3, 1944, 8.

69. *FN,* Nov. 13, 1937, 2, 7, Aug. 14, 1937, 3, Oct. 23, 1937, 8, June 7, 1941, 2, July 12, 1941, 12, Dec. 12, 1942, 2.

70. *FN,* June 26, 1937, 11, Sept. 6, 1937, 85, July 26, 1941, 2, Oct. 3, 1942, 6, Sept. 18, 1943, 1, Feb. 9, 1946, 3.

71. Newell, *Chicago and the Labor Movement,* 27 (third quote), 189 (first quote), 228 (second quote).

72. *FN,* May 7, 1938, 2, Aug. 13, 1938, 2, 11, Aug. 20, 1938, 5, Oct. 22, 1938, 10, Mar. 18, 1939, 11, Mar. 25, 1939, 8, Mar. 20, 1943, 6, Apr. 24, 1943, 10, Nov. 25, 1944, 1.

73. WCFL Form, Aug. 1936, Folder 142, Box 20, JF; Announcement on "Labor Flashes," May 8, 1937, and Letter, WCFL to Hugh Crambert, May 12, 1937, both in Folder 150, Box 22, JF.

74. *FN,* Oct. 16, 1937, 3, Oct. 23, 1937, 3, Oct. 30, 1937, 3, Nov. 13, 1937, 13, Dec. 18, 1937, 3.

75. *FN,* Oct. 15, 1938, 9, Sept. 14, 1940, 10, Mar. 1, 1941, 10, Dec. 26, 1942, 11.

76. ISFL, *Proceedings: Fifty-Seventh Convention,* 93.

77. *FN,* Aug. 23, 1941, 2, 5 (quote), Sept. 6, 1941, 1, Sept. 27, 1941, 1; Letter, J. Padway to Woll and Lynch, Apr. 25, 1944, Folder 168, Box 25, JF.

78. *NYT,* Sept. 29, 1946, 60; *Chicago Daily News,* Sept. 28, 1946, 5.

Chapter 9: William Lee and Commercial Success, 1946–66

1. Moody, *An Injury to All,* 41–69 (quote from 56); Green, *The World of the Worker,* chap. 7.

2. *CT,* June 17, 1984, sec. 3, p. 8; *NYT,* June 18, 1984, B14; Michael Kilian, Connie Fletcher, and F. Richard Ciccone, *Who Rules Chicago?* (New York: St. Martin's Press, 1979), 241–42; William J. Grimshaw, "The Daley Legacy: A Declining Politics of Party, Race, and Public Unions," in *After Daley: Chicago Politics in Transition,* ed. Samuel K. Grove and Louis H. Masotti (Urbana: University of Illinois Press, 1982), 64, 68; Levitas Interview, Dec. 22, 1970, 52–53; *FN,* Apr. 22, 1933, 5, Sept. 28, 1957, 1, Nov. 9, 1957, 6–7, Oct. 18, 1958, 7, Nov. 8, 1958, 5; Robert D. Leiter, *The Teamsters Union: A Study of Its Economic Impact* (New York: Bookman Associates, 1957), 35, 53, 117–18; Sam Romer, *The International Brotherhood of Teamsters: Its Government and Structure* (New York: John Wiley and Sons, 1962), 26, 130; David Greenstone, *Labor in American Politics* (Chicago: University of Chicago Press, 1977), 94 (quote).

3. *CT,* June 17, 1984, sec. 3, p. 8 (first quote); Studs Terkel, *Division Street: America* (New York: Pantheon Books, 1967), 131 (second quote).

4. *FN,* Nov. 2, 1946, 20 (quotes), Oct. 28, 1950, 10; Len O'Connor, *Clout: Mayor Daley and His City* (Chicago: Henry Regnery, 1975), 71, 93.

5. *FN,* Jan. 8, 1955, 1, 6, Jan. 29, 1955, 1, Feb. 5, 1955, 1 (quote), Feb. 17, 1955, 1, Feb. 26, 1955, 1, Mar. 5, 1955, 5–6, Apr. 9, 1955, 1, May 21, 1955, 1; O'Connor, *Clout,* 84–85, 128.

6. O'Connor, *Clout,* 133–34 (quotes); *FN,* Mar. 23, 1963, 5.

7. Gibson quoted in Terkel, *Division Street,* 131.

8. Greenstone, *Labor in American Politics,* 93–97; Kilian, Fletcher, and Ciccone, *Who Rules Chicago?* 241–42; Grimshaw, "The Daley Legacy," 64, 68; Len O'Connor, *Requiem: The Decline and Demise of Mayor Daley and His Era* (Chicago: Contemporary Books, 1977), 3, 37; *FN,* July 13, 1957, 4 (first and second quotes; emphasis in original), Sept. 3, 1956, 2 (third and fourth quotes), Sept. 1, 1958, 3; Sidney Lens, *Unrepentant Radical: An American Activist's Account of Five Turbulent Decades* (Boston: Beacon Press, 1980), 135–38, 139 (fifth quote), 211–12; Terkel, *Division Street,* 130–31.

9. *FN,* Sept. 4, 1948, 53, May 24, 1952, 4, Mar. 7, 1953, 7, Sept. 3, 1956, 2 (quote), Oct. 11, 1958, 4.

10. *FN,* June 29, 1957, 1, July 13, 1957, 4 (quote; emphasis in original).

11. *FN,* Sept. 4, 1948, 53, June 17, 1950, 11, Mar. 7, 1953, 7.

12. Memorandum in Letter from Matthew Woll to Joseph Keenan, June 10, 1948, Series 3, Box 3, Folder 5, Keenan Papers.

13. *FN,* Sept. 29, 1945, 1.

14. *FN,* Nov. 29, 1945, 1 (quote), Jan. 12, 1946, 2, Apr. 6, 1946, 11, Aug. 10, 1946, 2, Nov. 30, 1946, 7; WCFL, *"Varieties of '47"; FN,* Mar. 15, 1947, 3.

15. *FN,* Dec. 14, 1946, 7.

16. *FN,* Oct. 20, 1945, 1, 10, Nov. 3, 1945, 2, Jan. 12, 1946, 10, Feb. 2, 1946, 2, May 18, 1946, 10 (quotes), July 12, 1947, 8.

17. Holmgren's dismissal was never noted in the *Federation News* or discussed publicly by union officials. The only testimony on the incident is Holmgren's own account, which John Cogley included in his *Radio-Television,* vol. 2 of *Report on Blacklisting* (New York: Fund for the Republic, 1956), 82–83.

18. Orear Interview.

19. Cogley, *Radio-Television,* 82–83; *FN,* Apr. 12, 1947, 9 (quote). Holmgren worked for the Progressive party in 1948, an organization that one Chicago labor leader identified as controlled directly by the Communist party and Joseph Stalin. *FN,* June 5, 1948, 3. Holmgren's name appeared in the infamous broadcasting blacklist, American Business Consultants, *Red Channels: The Report of Communist Influence in Radio and Television* (New York: American Business Consultants, June 1950), 79. The authors tied Holmgren to two alleged communist front bodies— Chicago's Abraham Lincoln School and the National Labor Conference for Peace in Chicago. Although Holmgren wrote scripts for the CTU and briefly participated in programming for another Chicago station, his radio career was finished. He found employment on the editorial staff of the *Union,* published by the International Union of Mine, Mill, and Smelter Workers.

20. Freeman Champney, "Taft-Hartley and the Printers," *Antioch Review* 8 (Spring 1948): 49–62 (quotes from 53–54); Lipsitz, *Rainbow at Midnight,* 157–81; Lloyd Wendt, *Chicago Tribune: The Rise of a Great American Newspaper* (Chicago: Rand McNally, 1979), 680–81; *Business Week,* Aug. 16, 1947, 90, 92, Sept. 6, 1947, 84, 86–87, Dec. 6, 1947, 114–16, Dec. 11, 1948, 97–99.

21. *FN,* Dec. 13, 1947, 1, Mar. 13, 1948, 3 (quotes), Sept. 4, 1948, 54, 57; "Meet the Union Printers," Scripts, Series 5, Publicity 1939–51, Boxes 64–66, Chicago Typographical Union no. 16 Papers, CHS; *FN,* Sept. 17, 1949, 1.

22. *FN,* Sept. 4, 1948, 57 (first quote); "Meet the Union Printers," Scripts, Feb. 14, 21 (second and third quotes), Mar. 22, 29, 31, and Apr. 5, 14, 15, 1948, Series 5, Publicity 1939–51, Boxes 64–66, Chicago Typographical Union no. 16 Papers; Tape recordings of "Meet the Union Printers" shows are in the possession of Franklin Rosemont, Chicago.

23. *FN,* Sept. 4, 1948, 54, 57 (first quote), Jan. 31, 1948, 8, Feb. 1, 1947, 10, Mar. 8, 1947, 10 (second quote), June 12, 1948, 2, Apr. 17, 1948, 7, Aug. 7, 1948, 3, Aug. 21, 1948, 3, Jan. 22, 1949, 3, Sept. 11, 1948, 10, Nov. 5, 1949, 6, Mar. 19, 1949, 2.

24. *FN,* July 2, 1949, 7, Feb. 11, 1950, 8, Feb. 25, 1950, 7.

25. *FN,* May 15, 1948, 7, June 12, 1948, 2, Oct. 9, 1948, 12, Apr. 16, 1955, 1, Sept. 5, 1955, 51, June 16, 1956, 1, June 23, 1956, 1, June 30, 1956, 2, July 14, 1956, 6, Aug. 11, 1956, 8, Oct. 19, 1957, 1, Nov. 30, 1957, 1; Klass Interview.

26. *FN,* Aug. 14, 1948, 3, Mar. 7, 1953, 7, Apr. 9, 1955, 4.

27. *FN,* Oct. 18, 1952, 8–9, Nov. 22, 1952, 6, Feb. 21, 1953, 6, Mar. 7, 1953, 7, Sept. 14, 1957, 7.

28. *FN,* Oct. 13, 1951, 8 (first and second quotes), Nov. 12, 1949, 4 (third quote).

29. *FN,* May 7, 1949, 9, June 23, 1951, 3, Aug. 4, 1951, 6, Nov. 10, 1951, 10, Apr. 5, 1952, 6, Aug. 2, 1952, 8, Apr. 4, 1953, 1.

30. *FN,* Mar. 8, 1947, 10 (quotes), Jan. 14, 1950, 7; Jorgensen, "Radio Station WCFL," 120.

31. *FN,* Sept. 15, 1951, 1, 6, Oct. 13, 1951, 8, Oct. 25, 1952, 6, Jan. 19, 1952, 1, Feb. 9,

1952, 6 (second and third quotes), Feb. 16, 1952, 5 (first quote), Mar. 22, 1952, 6, Sept. 6, 1954, 53. Locals of the United Packinghouse Workers and the United Automobile Workers in Waterloo, Iowa, sponsored broadcasts of the University of Iowa football games in 1947. One-minute commercials addressed issues such as high prices, organized labor's contributions to the community, the history of the CIO, and antilabor laws. Typical spot announcements proclaimed that "football is a great American sport and organized labor is a great American institution." During halftime, a local union representative gave a three-minute "neighborly talk." "Iowa Gets Football Broadcasts with Labor Plugs," Oct. 31, 1947, Reel 9112, Radio 1947–48 Folder, FP Papers.

32. *FN*, Aug. 11, 1951, 2 (first quote), Oct. 13, 1951, 7, Nov. 17, 1951, 7; ISFL, *Proceedings: Seventieth Convention, October 13, 1952, Peoria, Illinois,* 98 (second quote), copy in Northwestern University Library; *FN*, June 25, 1949, 9, July 23, 1949, 2, Apr. 7, 1951, 6, Oct. 8, 1960, 2, Nov. 25, 1961, 6. Hogan remained general manager until late in 1960, when he resigned due to illness.

33. *FN*, Mar. 7, 1953, 7.

34. ISFL, *Proceedings: Sixty-Ninth Annual Convention, October 8, 1951, Springfield, Illinois,* 111 (quote), copy in Northwestern University Library; *FN*, Oct. 13, 1951, 2, July 2, 1960, 4.

35. *FN*, Apr. 18, 1953, 7 (quotes), Sept. 5, 1955, 3.

36. *FN*, July 23, 1949, 1–2, Sept. 10, 1949, 6, Oct. 13, 1951, 2 (quote); Jorgensen, "Radio Station WCFL," 137–40.

37. *FN*, July 23, 1949, 1–2, Sept. 3, 1949, 47 (second quote), Sept. 10, 1949, 6, Mar. 11, 1950, 1, June 17, 1950, 10, Feb. 17, 1951, 8; Aug. 25, 1956, 7; Jorgensen, "Radio Station WCFL," 136 (first quote), 155, 160.

38. *FN*, Mar. 8, 1947, 10; Letters, Marshall Field to William Lee, Feb. 2, 1948 (first quote), and Lee to Field, Feb. 4, 1948 (second and third quotes), both in Folder 1938–42 Undated Items, Box 83, Olander Papers; ISFL, *Proceedings: Sixty-Ninth Convention,* 111.

39. Fones-Wolf, "For Better Listening," 17 (quote), 18–20; Fones-Wolf, *Selling Free Enterprise,* 32–63; Lipsitz, *Rainbow at Midnight,* 157–81.

40. "Survey Shows Radio Nets Sell Out to Big Business," Oct. 13, 1947, Reel 9112, Radio 1947–48 Folder, FP Papers; Fones-Wolf, "For Better Listening," 18–21; Fones-Wolf, *Selling Free Enterprise,* 32–63; *FN*, Nov. 11, 1950, 8 (quote).

41. *FN*, July 12, 1947, 2, July 19, 1947, 1, July 26, 1947, 2, Aug. 16, 1947, 1, Sept. 6, 1947, 1–4, Sept. 13, 1947, 3.

42. *FN*, May 1, 1948, 8–9, Apr. 16, 1949, 2, Sept. 3, 1949, 47.

43. AFL, *Report of the Proceedings of the Sixty-Seventh Annual Convention 1947* (Washington, D.C.: AFL, 1947), 221, 562, 667–68. Labor's response to the Taft-Hartley Act can be found in Lipsitz, *Rainbow at Midnight,* chap. 7; and Green, *The World of the Worker,* 198–209. Douglas, in *Labor's New Voice,* 22–29, summarizes the AFL's public relations during this period.

44. Morris S. Novik, "Labor on the Air," *American Federationist* 54, no. 6 (June 1947): 8–9 (fifth quote); *Variety,* June 4, 1947, 36 (first through fourth quotes).

45. "Billing Time for A.F.L. Radio Campaign, May 5–June 9, 1947," Folder 6, Box 7, Collection 7, Office of the Secretary-Treasurer George Meany, Meany Archives; Novik, "Labor on the Air," 8–9, 15 (quote).

46. "Suggested Program of Public Relations for the American Federation of Labor," Aug. 15, 1947, in Letter, Omar H. Odle to George Meany, Feb. 18, 1948, Folder 11, Box 5, Collection 7, Office of the Secretary-Treasurer George Meany, Meany Archives. The public relations firm Bozell and Jacobs proposed that getting a radio program such as the "George Burns and Gracie Allen Show" to address labor themes would help make the average citizen aware of anti-union legislation. "Gracie Allen in her naive way" could ask about the Taft-Hartley Act, "getting a bit mixed up in her nouns and adjectives, then finally being convinced that [it] was a terrible thing." Ibid.

47. Letter, Matthew Woll to George Meany, Mar. 15, 1948, Folder 10; "Owen and Chappell Proposal for AFL," Mar. 1948, Folder 12 (quotes); and Letter, John H. Owen to G. Meany, Mar. 26, 1948, Folder 10, all in Box 5, Collection 7, Office of the Secretary-Treasurer George Meany, Meany Archives.

48. Phil Pearl, Memorandum on Owen and Chappell, ca. Sept.–Oct. 1948, Folder 10, Box 5, Collection 7, Office of the Secretary-Treasurer George Meany, Meany Archives.

49. AFL Executive Council Meeting Minutes, Aug. 17, 1949, 90.

50. ILGWU's 1948 Campaign Committee, Tape Recordings, Museum of Television and Radio, New York. Reagan, who appeared on the second show of the series, criticized the Republican Congress, lamented the decline in workers' wages and the rise in corporate profits, and sneered at marketplace solutions to inflation.

51. Contract, Leland Stowe and United Electrical, Radio, and Machine Workers of America, Apr. 7, 1947 (first quote); newspaper clippings, all dated Apr. 1947; and Topics of Broadcasts, 23 Apr.–18 June 1947, all in Radio Broadcasts: Union-Sponsored Contract, Clippings, Broadcasts 1947–50 Folder, Box 6, Leland Stowe Papers, SHSW; Letters, Thomas F. Flanagan, UE District 6 (Sharon, Penn.), to Julius Emspak, UE Gen. Sec. and Treas., May 20, 1947, and Sam Kushner, UE Local 1119 (Chicago) to L. Stowe, May 24, 1947 (second and third quotes), both in Radio Broadcasts: Union-Sponsored Fan Mail Apr.–Oct. 1947 Folder, Box 6, Leland Stowe Papers; Fones-Wolf, "For Better Listening," 29–30; Steve Rosswurm, "Introduction: An Overview and Preliminary Assessment of the CIO's Expelled Unions," in *The CIO's Left-Led Unions,* ed. Steve Rosswurm (New Brunswick, N.J.: Rutgers University Press, 1992), 1–17.

52. AFL Executive Council Meeting Minutes, Aug. 17, 1949, 91 (first quote), 92 (second quote).

53. *FN,* Dec. 24, 1949, 1 (first quote), Dec. 31, 1949, 1; Douglas, *Labor's New Voice,* 30; Letter, Don Connery to Edward P. Morgan, Jan. 3, 1955, Correspondence File

1955–57 Business, Box 37, Edward P. Morgan Papers, SHSW; *Business Week,* Aug. 21, 1954, 32 (second quote); *The Nation,* Aug. 21, 1954, 141 (third quote); *FN,* Apr. 29, 1950, 6; Letter, William Lee to William F. Schnitzler, Jan. 29, 1954, Folder 9, Box 37, Collection 8, 6—Miscellaneous Correspondence, AFL, AFL-CIO, Office of the President George Meany, Meany Archives (fourth through eighth quotes); Transcript of Interview with Morris S. Novik, by author. Dec. 7, 1991, New York.

54. Memoranda, George Meany to F. Edwards, William Schnitzler, et al., Aug. 2, 1954, and George Meany to F. Edwards, M. Novik, et al., Aug. 4, 1954, both in Folder 11, Box 37, Collection 8, 6—Miscellaneous Correspondence, AFL, AFL-CIO, Office of the President George Meany, Meany Archives; Letter, G. Meany to William R. Perrin, Sept. 1, 1954, Folder 10, Box 37, Collection 8, 6—Miscellaneous Correspondence, AFL, AFL-CIO, Office of the President George Meany, Meany Archives; Frank Edwards's Statement, n.d., Folder 11, Box 37, Collection 8, 6—Miscellaneous Correspondence, AFL, AFL-CIO, Office of the President George Meany, Meany Archives (quote). Novik recalled that Edwards had a fascination with "flying saucers," which did not improve the image of the AFL. Novik Interview.

55. *FN,* Aug. 21, 1954, 6, Jan. 8, 1955, 6; Letter, A. F. Monroe to Morgan, Jan. 4, 1955 (first quote), and Letter, Don Connery to Morgan, Jan. 3, 1955 (second quote), both in Correspondence File 1955–57 Business, Box 37, Morgan Papers; Novik Interview; *FN,* Feb. 12, 1955, 4 (third and fourth quotes); Letters, Charlotte Rosenfeld to Meany, Dec. 3, 1957, Morris H. Ruben, Editor, *The Progressive,* to Meany, Dec. 5, 1957, C. J. Haggerty, California State Federation of Labor, to Meany, Sept. 24, 1957, and William Benton, Publisher of *Encyclopedia Britannica,* to Meany, Nov. 14, 1957, all in Folder 12, Box 37, Collection 8, 6—Miscellaneous Correspondence, AFL, AFL-CIO, Office of the President George Meany, Meany Archives; Letters, Leon Pearson, NBC News, to Meany, Sept. 3, 1958, Senator Wayne Morse to Meany, May 24, 1958, and Anne E. Queen, YMCA, University of North Carolina, to Meany, Dec. 15, 1958, all in Folder 7, Box 37, Collection 8, 6—Miscellaneous Correspondence, AFL, AFL-CIO, Office of the President George Meany, Meany Archives.

56. *FN,* Dec. 11, 1954, 8.

57. *FN,* Nov. 11, 1950, 4 (first and second quotes), Nov. 18, 1950, 1 (third quote). At a 1950 meeting in Waukegan, Illinois, sponsored by the AFL Lake County Trades and Labor Council and conducted by the University of Illinois's Institute of Labor and Industrial Relations, union representatives agreed on the importance of public relations for organized labor. They discussed several options, but never explored the use of radio or television. *FN,* Nov. 25, 1950, 3.

58. ISFL, *Proceedings: Seventieth Convention,* 98 (first quote); ISFL, *Proceedings: Seventy-Sixth Convention, October 6, 1958, Peoria, Illinois,* 126 (second quote), copy in Northwestern University Library.

59. MacDonald, *Don't Touch That Dial,* 86–87.

60. James L. Baughman, *The Republic of Mass Culture: Journalism, Filmmaking, and Broadcasting in American since 1941* (Baltimore: Johns Hopkins University Press,

1992), 66; Sterling and Kittross, *Stay Tuned,* 535 (table 9), 516–17 (table 4), 512–13 (table 2); Sydney W. Head and Christopher H. Sterling, *Broadcasting in America: A Study of Electronic Media* (Boston: Houghton Mifflin, 1990), 73–74.

61. Sterling and Kittross, *Stay Tuned,* 511 (table 1B); Head and Sterling, *Broadcasting in America,* 74.

62. Baughman, *Republic of Mass Culture,* 66 (quote); Sterling and Kittross, *Stay Tuned,* 533 (table 8).

63. *FN,* May 28, 1949, 6 (first, second, and fourth quotes), June 4, 1949, 6–7 (third and fifth quotes).

64. *FN,* Sept. 4, 1948, 56, May 28, 1949, 6, June 4, 1949, 6–7, June 25, 1949, 9, July 23, 1949, 1–2, Feb. 4, 1950, 6, Aug. 5, 1950, 6, Sept. 16, 1950, 6.

65. *FN,* July 23, 1949, 1–2 (first quote), Feb. 8, 1947, 10, Mar. 22, 1947, 11, May 7, 1949, 9, Nov. 19, 1949, 6, June 30, 1951, 6, Apr. 7, 1951, 6, Aug. 18, 1951, 6 (second, third, and fourth quotes), Apr. 24, 1954, 6, Aug. 27, 1955, 6.

66. *FN,* Feb. 15, 1947, 10, Jan. 24, 1948, 10, June 5, 1948, 2, May 7, 1949, 9, Oct. 8, 1949, 6 (first quote), May 26, 1951, 6, June 19, 1954, 6 (second and third quotes); Passman, *Deejays,* 198, 199 (fourth quote).

67. *FN,* May 31, 1947, 12, Jan. 10, 1948, 10, Feb. 14, 1948, 11, Feb. 28, 1948, 10, July 16, 1949, 9, Oct. 8, 1949, 6, Aug. 18, 1951, 6.

68. *FN,* Dec. 7, 1946, 15, Jan. 18, 1947, 6, Oct. 8, 1949, 7, Feb. 11, 1950, 6, Dec. 2, 1950, 1, Jan. 27, 1951, 6, Mar. 17, 1951, 6, Apr. 7, 1951, 6, Aug. 18, 1951, 6, Mar. 29, 1952, 6.

69. *FN,* Dec. 7, 1946, 15, Dec. 28, 1946, 7, Feb. 22, 1947, 10, Sept. 4, 1948, 56, Aug. 5, 1950, 6, Feb. 24, 1951, 6, Aug. 18, 1951, 6.

70. *FN,* Jan. 4, 1947, 7, July 3, 1954, 6, July 31, 1954, 6, Aug. 7, 1954, 6, Sept. 6, 1954, 53, Mar. 29, 1952, 6, June 30, 1951, 6, July 7, 1951, 5.

71. *FN,* Jan. 7, 1950, 6, June 26, 1954, 6, Sept. 15, 1956, 5, Sept. 29, 1956, 1.

72. *FN,* Sept. 13, 1947, 12 (first and second quotes), Nov. 29, 1947, 5 (third quote), Feb. 14, 1948, 11, Oct. 9, 1948, 5 (fourth quote), Dec. 18, 1948, 11, Feb. 26, 1949, 8, Apr. 9, 1949, 3.

73. *FN,* Mar. 18, 1950, 6 (quotes), Apr. 29, 1950, 6, Mar. 26, 1955, 6.

74. *FN,* Aug. 5, 1950, 6 (first and second quotes), Feb. 3, 1951, 6, Feb. 9, 1952, 6, June 14, 1952, 6, July 10, 1954, 6, July 7, 1956, 6 (third quote).

75. *FN,* Nov. 4, 1950, 6 (quote), Nov. 25, 1950, 5, Feb. 3, 1951, 6, May 5, 1951, 6, May 26, 1951, 6, Oct. 6, 1951, 6.

76. *FN,* Dec. 14, 1946, 10, Sept. 11, 1948, 3, Sept. 25, 1948, 1, Oct. 16, 1948, 3, Feb. 25, 1950, 6, June 17, 1950, 6, Nov. 25, 1950, 6, Apr. 21, 1951, 6, Aug. 18, 1951, 6, Sept. 3, 1951, 6, June 14, 1952, 6, Jan. 17, 1953, 6, Feb. 28, 1953, 6, Sept. 19, 1953, 6, June 30, 1956, 6, Mar. 2, 1957, 1, Apr. 13, 1957, 2, Sept. 27, 1958, 2, Sept. 12, 1959, 3, Dec. 12, 1959, 7, Mar. 19, 1960, 7, Oct. 7, 1961, 3, Mar. 2, 1963, 7, Nov. 30, 1963, 7, June 27, 1964, 3.

77. *FN,* Aug. 4, 1951, 6, Oct. 14, 1950, 6, Mar. 7, 1953, 6 (quotes), Oct. 14, 1950, 6, Sept. 8, 1951, 6, Feb. 28, 1953, 6, May 23, 1953, 6, Sept. 19, 1953, 6, Sept. 6, 1954, 53, Dec. 11, 1954, 2, Sept. 5, 1955, 51, Oct. 10, 1959, 8.

78. *FN,* June 5, 1954, 7–8.

79. *FN,* June 30, 1956, 1, 6, Nov. 30, 1957, 1, Jan. 4, 1958, 1, Sept. 1, 1958, 62, Sept. 7, 1959, 59; *Broadcasting,* Jan. 6, 1958, 104–5; *Sponsor* 13 (Aug. 15, 1959): 46–47, 14 (Dec. 26, 1960): 48–49.

80. *FN,* May 19, 1951, 6 (first quote), Jan. 1, 1955, 1, May 8, 1954, 1, 8, June 5, 1954, 7 (second quote), Apr. 13, 1957, 1, May 17, 1958, 6.

81. Lawrence Lessing, *Man of High Fidelity: Edwin Howard Armstrong* (Philadelphia: Lippincott, 1956); Barnouw, *Golden Web;* Vincent Mosco, *Broadcasting in the United States: Innovative Challenge and Organizational Control* (Norwood, N.J.: Ablex, 1979), 50–69.

82. Mosco, *Broadcasting in the United States,* 52, 54, 55; Barnouw, *Golden Web,* 130.

83. Frederick F. Umhey, "Radio Stations Run by Labor," *American Federationist* 52, no. 12 (Dec. 1945): 10; ILGWU, *Report of the General Executive Board to the Twenty-Sixth Convention, June 16–24, 1947,* 207–9, copy in New York Public Library.

84. Contract, Leland Stowe and United Electrical, Radio, and Machine Workers of America, Apr. 7, 1947, and Clippings File, Apr. 1947, both in Radio Broadcasts: Union-Sponsored Contract, Clippings, Broadcasts 1947–50 Folder, Box 6, Stowe Papers; FP News Items, Oct. 9, 1945, Feb. 14, 1946, and Mar. 17, 1947, all on Reel 9112, Radio—Use by Labor 1945–47 Folder, FP Papers; Chicago FM Hearings before FCC, June 5, 1945, quoted in Jorgensen, "Radio Station WCFL," 124 (quote); CIO, *Proceedings of the Eighth Constitutional Convention of the CIO, Atlantic City, New Jersey, Nov. 18–22, 1946* (Washington, D.C.: CIO, 1946), 66, 305–6.

85. Letter, Maurice Lynch to Joe Keenan, Oct. 6, 1944, Series 3, Box 2, Folder 6, Keenan Papers; Mosco, *Broadcasting in the United States,* 52–53, 62 (first quote), 54 (second quote); Barnouw, *Golden Web,* 41–42, 242, 283.

86. FP News Item, Nov. 16, 1944, Reel 9111, Radio 1943–44 Folder, FP Papers; FP News Item, Mar. 17, 1947, Reel 9112, Radio—Use by Labor 1945–47 Folder, FP Papers; Letters, Frank M. Folsom to Henry C. Herman, Nov. 5, 1947 (second quote), Keenan to F. Folsom, Nov. 11, 1947 (first quote), both in Series 3, Box 2, Folder 16, Keenan Papers.

87. Minutes of Meeting of WCFL Governing Board, June 11, 1948, Series 4, Box 4, Folder 11, Keenan Papers; Jorgensen, "Radio Station WCFL," 117.

88. Mosco, *Broadcasting in the United States,* 50–69; FP News Items, June 2, 1951, and Apr. 3, 1952, Reel 9112, Radio—Use by Labor 1948–54 Folder, FP Papers; ILGWU, *Report of the General Executive Board to the Twenty-Eighth Convention, May 18, 1953,* 19–20, copy in New York Public Library; *FN,* Feb. 9, 1952, 6.

89. ILGWU, *Report to the Twenty-Eighth Convention,* 20. For a study of an alternative FM station that survived the fifties, see the story of the Pacifica Foundation's radio station KPFA in San Francisco in David Armstrong, *A Trumpet to Arms: Alternative Media in America* (Boston: South End Press, 1981), 74–76; and Downing, *Radical Media,* 74–80.

90. *FN,* Dec. 11, 1954, 7 (first and second quotes), May 7, 1955, 6, Apr. 5, 1958, 5, June 9, 1956, 5, 6 (third quote); Letter to John P. Fitzpatrick, Aug. 20, 1956, Folder 8, Box 3, JF.

91. *FN,* May 7, 1955, 6 (quote), May 11, 1957, 6, Dec. 11, 1954, 7, Nov. 7, 1959, 5.

92. *FN,* June 9, 1956, 6 (first quote), June 23, 1956, 1 (second quote), 3, June 30, 1956, 1, Sept. 3, 1956, 9 (third quote).

93. *FN,* Sept. 14, 1957, 6 (quote), 7; *Chicago Daily News,* Sept. 4, 1957, 27.

94. Orear Interview; Jorgensen, "Radio Station WCFL," 124; *FN,* Mar. 6, 1954, 7.

95. *FN,* Sept. 14, 1957, 7 (quotes); *Chicago Daily News,* Sept. 4, 1957, 27; *CT,* Sept. 4, 1957, sec. 2, p. 4.

96. *FN,* Sept. 14, 1957, 7–8 (quotes); *CT,* Sept. 4, 1957, sec. 2, p. 4. Hoban and Lennon were upset at news of the WCFL yacht. In May 1956, General Manager Hogan purchased a forty-two-foot, 160-horsepower yacht for $15,000. Lee and WCFL officials used the *Big Pedro* to entertain clients and station managers. During the winter of 1956–57, Hogan took the yacht to Florida to entertain executives of the eighteen Florida radio stations that participated in WCFL's White Sox network. After Hogan's return to Chicago, WCFL sold the yacht for $21,000. Hogan wanted to purchase another one because WBBM, WIND, and other Chicago stations had yachts. *Chicago Daily News,* Sept. 4, 1957, 27.

97. *FN,* Sept. 14, 1957, 7–8; *CT,* Sept. 4, 1957, sec. 2, p. 4 (quote); *Chicago Daily News,* Sept. 4, 1957, 27.

98. *FN,* Sept. 14, 1957, 7–8; *CT,* Sept. 4, 1957, sec. 2, p. 4.

99. *FN,* Oct. 7, 1961, 4, Dec. 2, 1961, 1; Greenstone, *Labor in American Politics,* 99; Derber, *Labor in Illinois,* 237–38; Orear Interview, 8 (quote); Levitas Interview, July 27, 1970, 27–28; *FN,* Mar. 10, 1956, 6, Mar. 17, 1956, 6, Nov. 30, 1957, 6–7, Dec. 5, 1959, 5, Oct. 28, 1961, 1, Nov. 11, 1961, 5, Jan. 13, 1962, 1.

100. *FN,* Sept. 14, 1957, 7–8 (quotes); *CT,* Sept. 4, 1957, sec. 2, p. 4.

101. *FN,* Sept. 1, 1958, 62, Nov. 29, 1958, 1, Jan. 7, 1961, 3, 8, Feb. 11, 1961, 7, Oct. 7, 1961, 4, Sept. 3, 1962, 5, Mar. 16, 1963, 6, Nov. 9, 1963, 6, Sept. 7, 1964, 50, Sept. 5, 1966, 50, June 17, 1961, 2, Apr. 15, 1961, 1.

102. *FN,* Oct. 7, 1961, 3, June 22, 1963, 5, June 24, 1961, 5, Sept. 3, 1962, 55, July 1966, 6, May 6, 1961, 1, June 17, 1961, 2, 4 (first quote); Telegram, WCFL to George Meany, Apr. 1, 1960, Folder 8, Box 37, Collection 8, 6—Miscellaneous Correspondence, AFL, AFL-CIO, Office of the President George Meany, Meany Archives (second quote).

103. *FN,* Apr. 27, 1963, 3, June 22, 1963, 5, July 1966, 6, Oct. 1966, 14.

104. *FN,* Sept. 5, 1966, 50, Oct. 1966, 14; James R. Ralph Jr., *Northern Protest: Martin Luther King, Jr., Chicago, and the Civil Rights Movement* (Cambridge, Mass.: Harvard University Press, 1993), 70–72, 145 (quote from 71); Philip S. Foner, *Organized Labor and the Black Worker, 1619–1981,* 2d ed. (New York: International Publishers, 1981), 362–65.

105. *FN,* June 30, 1951, 6, Aug. 12, 1961, 3, July 1966, 6; William Barlow, "Sounding Out Racism: Commercial and Noncommercial Radio," in *Split Image: African*

Americans in the Mass Media, ed. William Barlow and Janette L. Dates, 2d ed. (Washington, D.C.: Howard University Press, 1993), 236 (first quote); *FN,* Mar. 30, 1957, 3, Sept. 5, 1966, 50 (second and third quotes).

106. *FN,* Oct. 7, 1961, 3 (quote), Aug. 5, 1961, 5, Jan. 13, 1962, 6, Mar. 9, 1963, 6, June 22, 1963, 5, Mar. 14, 1959, 1, Mar. 12, 1960, 1.

107. *FN,* Aug. 19, 1961, 3, Oct. 7, 1961, 3 (first quote); Pressman, *Deejays,* 268 (second quote), 269 (third quote), 270; *NYT,* Mar. 27, 1963, 5.

108. *FN,* Sept. 23, 1961, 1–2 (quote), Oct. 7, 1961, 5.

109. *FN,* Sept. 3, 1956, 2, Sept. 1, 1958, 3, Oct. 11, 1958, 4, Aug. 5, 1961, 1, Mar. 23, 1963, 5 (quotes).

110. *FN,* Aug. 5, 1961, 1, Mar. 23, 1963, 5, Sept. 2, 1963, 5 (quotes).

111. *FN,* Oct. 5, 1963, 5, Oct. 3, 1964, 5, Nov. 28, 1964, 1, Dec. 5, 1964, 5–6, Jan. 19, 1963, 3, Jan. 1966, 2 (quote); O'Connor, *Clout,* 133.

Chapter 10: The Fall of Labor Radio, 1967–78

1. Dawley, "Workers, Capital, and the State," 179. See Moody, *An Injury to All,* and Mike Davis, *Prisoners of the American Dream: Politics and Economy in the History of the US Working Class* (London: Verso, 1986), for details on the dismantling of the corporatist deal.

2. Davis, *Prisoners of the American Dream,* 129; Moody, *An Injury to All,* 128.

3. Davis, *Prisoners of the American Dream,* 129 (first quote), 131n36 (second quote).

4. Douglas, *Labor's New Voice,* 83 (first quote; emphasis in original), 85 (second quote), 86 (third and fourth quotes).

5. Jonathan Tasini, *Lost in the Margins: Labor and the Media* (New York: FAIR Report, 1990), 2–3.

6. See Geoff Walsh, "Trade Unions and the Media," *International Labour Review* 127, no. 2 (1988): 205–20; William J. Puette, *Through Jaundiced Eyes: How the Media View Organized Labor* (Ithaca: ILR Press, 1992).

7. Douglas, *Labor's New Voice,* 32 (first quote); *FN,* Feb. 26, 1955, 5 (second quote), June 1, 1957, 6.

8. *FN,* Mar. 7, 1953, 2 (quotes), Apr. 12, 1952, 1, Sept. 1, 1952, 55; AFL-CIO, *Report of the Executive Council, November 14–20, 1963,* vol. 2 of *Proceedings of the Fifth Constitutional Convention* (Washington, D.C.: AFL-CIO, 1963), 276–78; AFL-CIO, *Report of the Executive Council, December 9–15, 1965,* vol. 2 of *Proceedings of the Sixth Constitutional Convention* (Washington, D.C.: AFL-CIO, 1965), 247; AFL-CIO, *Report of the Executive Council, December 7–12, 1967,* vol. 2 of *Proceedings of the Seventh Convention* (Washington, D.C.: AFL-CIO, 1967), 269; *FN,* July 4, 1959, 1, July 11, 1959, 5, Jan. 7, 1961, 3, Feb. 18, 1961, 5, Sept. 8, 1962, 3, Jan. 5, 1963, 2, Aug. 27, 1960, 1, Sept. 4, 1961, 54.

9. AFL-CIO, *Report of the Executive Council, 1963,* 20; AFL-CIO, *Report of the*

Executive Council, October 2–7, 1975, vol. 2 of *Proceedings of the Eleventh Constitutional Convention of the AFL-CIO* (Washington, D.C.: AFL-CIO, 1975), 25; Douglas, *Labor's New Voice,* 31–32.

10. *FN,* June 16, 1928, 3, June 23, 1928, 1, Sept. 1, 1928, 21.

11. Memorandum in Letter, M. Woll to Keenan, June 10, 1948, Series 3, Box 3, Folder 5, Keenan Papers; *FN,* May 13, 1950, 5 (first quote); AFL Executive Council Meeting Minutes, Aug. 11, 1950, 54–55 (second, third, and fourth quotes).

12. *FN,* Apr. 19, 1952, 2, Feb. 2, 1952, 2, Mar. 15, 1952, 3, 6, May 3, 1952, 3.

13. *FN,* Mar. 7, 1953, 7, Dec. 11, 1954, 7, Mar. 17, 1956, 5 (second quote), Apr. 1, 1961, 8 (first quote), Mar. 18, 1961, 7.

14. Sterling and Kittross, *Stay Tuned,* 356–59, 381, 417.

15. *FN,* Oct. 31, 1964, 5, Feb. 6, 1965, 5–6, Oct. 1966, 12, Oct. 1967, 9.

16. FCC, *Federal Communications Commission Reports, January 5, 1968, to March 22, 1968,* vol. 11, 2d series (Washington, D.C.: GPO, 1969), 119–38, 120 (first quote), 121 (second, third, and fourth quotes).

17. Ibid., 130–33 (quote from 131).

18. Ibid., 101–8, 137–38. A dissenting member argued that the FCC had applied unfair financial qualifications to Chicagoland TV. He also pointed out that the examiner had "found Chicagoland to be superior to the [CFL] in the significant and important criteria of diversification and integration." Ibid., 109–18 (quote from 109n1).

19. *FN,* Jan. 1968, 1, June 1968, 1, Oct. 1968, 8, Aug. 1969, 4.

20. *FN,* Sept. 1969, 1.

21. Quaal Interview, 15 (quote); Klass Interview; *FN,* Nov. 1970, 7.

22. Sterling and Kittross, *Stay Tuned,* 258–59, 326 (quote); *FN,* Nov. 1970, 7. The CFL's assessment of the Zenith system was faulty. Industry experts agreed by the late sixties that pay-TV via cable, rather than over the air (the Zenith system), seemed most likely to succeed. Although the FCC approved the Zenith system for operation in the early seventies, the first over-the-air pay stations did not begin broadcasting until the spring of 1977. Sterling and Kittross, *Stay Tuned,* 431, 382–83.

23. *Broadcasting,* Aug. 23, 1971, 37; *FN,* Oct. 1973, 4–5; *Broadcasting,* Aug. 11, 1975, 30, Feb. 2, 1976, 52; Quaal Interview; FCC, *Federal Communications Commission Reports, July 25, 1975, to September 5, 1975,* vol. 54, 2d series (Washington, D.C.: GPO, 1976), 471–76.

24. MacDonald, *Don't Touch That Dial,* 88; Sterling and Kittross, *Stay Tuned,* 338–39; David T. MacFarland, "Up from Middle America: The Development of Top 40," in *American Broadcasting,* ed. Lichty and Topping, 399–403; Rick Sklar, *Rocking America: How the All-Hit Radio Stations Took Over* (New York: St. Martin's Press, 1984), xi–xii, 25–29.

25. FCC, *Federal Communications Commission Reports, July 1, 1966, to September 23, 1966,* vol. 4, 2d series (Washington, D.C.: GPO, 1967), 492–94; *FN,* Sept. 1967,

36 (quotes), Dec. 1968, 8, Sept. 1968, 12, July 1969, 4; FCC, *FCC Reports, July 25, 1975, to September 5, 1975,* 480.

26. Sklar, *Rocking America,* 146 (first quote); *FN,* Oct. 1973, 4, 6; Gary Deeb columns, *CT,* Dec. 17, 1973, sec. 1A, p. 15 (second through fifth quotes), May 8, 1974, sec. 3, p. 18; *Broadcasting,* Jan. 29, 1973, 52, Feb. 18, 1974, 70.

27. *FN,* Mar. 1968, 6, Aug. 1970, 3 (first through fourth quotes), June 1972, 3, Oct. 1973, 4, 6 (fifth quote); Passman, *Deejays,* 138; Orear Interview; Transcript of Interview with Ralph Helstein, by Leslie Orear, Jan. 14, 1981, Chicago, 102–3, Illinois Labor History Society, Chicago.

28. Sklar, *Rocking America,* 90, 97; FCC, *Federal Communications Commission Reports, Dec. 1, 1972, to Feb. 2, 1973,* vol. 38, 2d series (Washington, D.C.: GPO, 1974), 424; *Broadcasting,* Sept. 21, 1970, 50, Dec. 4, 1972, 8, Jan. 8, 1973, 11, Dec. 31, 1973, 22 (quote).

29. *Broadcasting,* Apr. 8, 1974, 42–43, July 22, 1974, 19 (quote), Nov. 4, 1974, 25; FCC, *FCC Reports, Dec. 1, 1972, to Feb. 2, 1973,* 417–29; FCC, *FCC Reports, Apr. 12, 1974, to May 31, 1974,* vol. 46, 2d series (Washington, D.C.: GPO, 1975), 16; FCC, *FCC Reports, July 25, 1975, to Sept. 5, 1975,* 482, 492; FCC, *FCC Reports, Aug. 16, 1974, to Oct. 18, 1974,* vol. 48, 2d series (Washington, D.C.: GPO, 1976), 1175–78.

30. *FCC Reports, Aug. 16, 1974, to Oct. 18, 1974,* 1174–80; FCC, *FCC Reports, July 25, 1975, to Sept. 5, 1975,* 498–501 (first quote from 500; second quote from 501); *Broadcasting,* Nov. 25, 1974, 31–32, June 23, 1975, 38; Gary Deeb, "The Dark Side of the Medium," *CT Magazine,* Mar. 4, 1979, sec. 9, p. 27.

31. FCC, *FCC Reports, July 25, 1975, to Sept. 5, 1975,* 484–88 (quote from 487). "Contemporary News in Depth" began under the direction of John Webster. When Webster left WCFL in April 1969, Assistant News Director Michael Rollins supervised the show.

32. Ibid., 488.

33. Ibid., 489–90; Passman, *Deejays,* 256. WCFL purchased "The Elvis Presley Story" from a California company, broadcasting it in 1971 and 1972. The new series provided a more in-depth study of Presley and his music than WCFL's own program on the subject. Witz defended the classification of this program as public affairs. FCC, *Reports, July 25, 1975, to Sept. 5, 1975,* 498.

34. FCC, *Reports, July 25, 1975, to Sept. 5, 1975,* 490 (first quote), 491 (second quote), 484.

35. Ibid., 492; *FN,* Oct. 1966, 14, June 1967, 7, July 1967, 2, Oct. 1967, 2, June 1972, 2, 6, Sept. 1972, 40, May 1974, 9, July 1966, 6; *CT,* Jan. 6, 1987, sec. 5, p. 1; Darlene Clark Hine, ed., *Black Women in America: An Historical Encyclopedia* (Brooklyn, N.Y.: Carlson, 1993), 1037; Deeb column, *CT,* Feb. 16, 1976, sec. 6, p. 9 (quote).

36. Deeb column, *CT,* Sept. 18, 1974, sec. 3, p. 11.

37. Deeb, "Dark Side of the Medium," 27.

38. *Broadcasting,* Sept. 27, 1976, 53–54; Deeb columns, *CT,* Feb. 11, 1976, sec. 3, p. 12 (first quote), Mar. 3, 1976, sec. 3, p. 12; *FN,* Feb. 1976, 1 (second quote); *CT,* Mar.

4, 1979, sec. 9, p. 34, Feb. 16, 1976, sec. 6, p. 9; Tape Recording, "Wally Phillips Show," WGN, Mar. 4, 1976; "Interview of Disc Jockeys Fired by WCFL," both in Paige Box 2, William A. Lee Papers, CHS.

39. *FN,* May 1976, 10, June 1976, 1, Oct. 1976, 7 (quote), Jan. 1977, 1, May 1977, 5.

40. *FN,* Nov. 1977, 6 (quote); *Broadcasting,* Aug. 8, 1977, 5; *CT,* Apr. 11, 1978, 3.

41. *CT,* Apr. 11, 1978, 3.

42. *FN,* May 1976, 10, June 1976, 1, Oct. 1976, 7, Jan. 1977, 1, May 1977, 5, June 1977, 4, Nov. 1977, 6.

43. Quaal Interview.

44. "Kup's Column," *Chicago Sun-Times,* Apr. 11, 1978, 66 (first quote); *CT,* Apr. 11, 1978, 3 (second quote).

45. Quaal Interview, 8 (second quote); *Broadcasting,* Apr. 17, 1978, 7 (first quote).

46. *Broadcasting,* Aug. 8, 1977, 5 (quote); *CT,* Apr. 11, 1978, 3.

47. *Chicago Sun-Times,* Apr. 12, 1978, 13; Stephen Butterfield, *Amway: The Cult of Free Enterprise* (Boston: South End Press, 1985), 1–2, 140–41, 143, 153–62.

48. *Chicago Sun-Times,* Apr. 12, 1978, 13 (quotes); *Broadcasting,* Apr. 17, 1978, 52; Quaal Interview.

49. *FN,* Apr. 1978, 8; Special Meeting of CFL-IUC, Apr. 7, 1978, Tape Recording, Paige Box 2, Lee Papers (quotes).

50. *CT,* Apr. 11, 1978, 3; *Broadcasting,* Apr. 17, 1978, 52 (first quote); "Kup's Column," *Chicago Sun-Times,* Apr. 11, 1978, 66 (second quote).

51. *CT,* Apr. 2, 1980, sec. 1, p. 17 (quote), Sept. 15, 1978, sec. 1, p. 1, Sept. 16, 1978, sec. 2, p. 2, Sept. 18, 1978, sec. 1, p. 3, Sept. 23, 1978, sec. 3, p. 13; Derber, *Labor in Illinois,* 240–41.

52. *CT,* Apr. 30, 1978, sec. 1, p. 22 (quote), May 4, 1978, sec. 3, p. 8, May 6, 1978, sec. 1, p. 10 (editorial), May 17, 1978, sec. 3, p. 2, May 19, 1978, sec. 3, p. 2.

53. *Chicago Sun-Times,* Apr. 12, 1978, 13; *Broadcasting,* Sept. 11, 1978, 30 (quote); *FN,* May 1978, 6; *Broadcasting,* June 11, 1979, 19.

54. *CT,* Jan. 4, 1986, sec. 1, p. 5, July 18, 1986, sec. 2, p. 4 (second quote), Nov. 5, 1988, sec. 2, p. 8, Nov. 21, 1988, sec. 2, p. 4 (first quote), Nov. 25, 1988, sec. 2, p. 2.

55. *CT,* Aug. 22, 1978, sec. 2, p. 8, July 30, 1980, sec. 3, p. 12, Aug. 19, 1980, sec. 2, p. 6, Aug. 22, 1980, sec. 2, p. 14.

56. *CT,* Nov. 4, 1983, sec. 3, p. 14, Apr. 29, 1987, sec. 3, p. 3; *Broadcasting,* May 11, 1987, 86.

Conclusion

1. Letters, Upton Sinclair to Roger Baldwin, May 2, 1930, and Baldwin to Sinclair, May 27, 1927 (quotes), both on Reel 12, Folder 2, Box 18, AFPS.

2. William Barlow, "Community Radio in the US: The Struggle for a Democratic Medium," *Media, Culture, and Society* 10 (Jan. 1988): 81, 83; Armstrong, *A Trumpet to Arms;* Mattelart, *Mass Media and the Revolutionary Movement;* Downing, *Radical Media.*

3. WEVD established just such a relationship, first with the Socialist party and then with the *Jewish Daily Forward*. See Godfried, "Legitimizing the Mass Media Structure."

4. Barlow, "Community Radio," 81, 83, 101–3; Armstrong, *Trumpet to Arms*, 23–24.

5. Brecht, writing in 1930, argued that radio receivers should have the capacity to become transmitters and that radio should be a system of "communication" rather than "distribution." Bertolt Brecht, "Radio as a Means of Communication: A Talk of the Function of Radio," in *Liberation, Socialism,* vol. 2 of *Communication and Class Struggle,* ed. Armand Mattelart and Seth Siegelaub (New York: International General, 1983), 169–71.

6. Armstrong, *Trumpet to Arms*, 24.

7. Cohen, *Making a New Deal*, 333–53.

8. Moody, *An Injury to All*, xiv–xv.

9. Godfried, "Legitimizing the Mass Media Structure." WGN's attorney, Louis Caldwell, defended WEVD's right to exist because it offered no threat to corporate radio; on the contrary the station's continuation on the air served to legitimize commercial broadcasting. Caldwell, however, despised WCFL and vilified the station and its managers because he viewed them as threats to the private capitalist system.

10. *FN,* May 26, 1934, 5.

11. See, for example, *FN,* June 25, 1927, 11, Oct. 13, 1951, 8, June 1972, 3.

12. Goban-Klas, "Minority Media," 30–31 (quote), 32; Downing, *Radical Media,* 156.

13. Moody, *An Injury to All*, 341.

14. Downing, *Radical Media,* 359; Barlow, "Community Radio," 103–4.

15. Levitas Interview, Dec. 22, 1970, 52–57 (quotes from 56).

16. Denning, "The End of Mass Culture," 10, 13–14, 17; Kelley, "Notes on Deconstructing 'The Folk,'" 1400–1408; Lipsitz, "The Struggle for Hegemony," 146–50; Lipsitz, *A Life in the Struggle.*

SELECTED BIBLIOGRAPHY

Manuscript Collections

American Civil Liberties Union. Archives. New York Public Library. New York, N.Y.

American Federation of Labor. Papers. George Meany Memorial Archives. Silver Spring, Maryland.

American Fund for Public Service. Records, 1922–41. Rare Books and Manuscripts Division. New York Public Library.

Federal Communications Commission. Broadcast Bureau. Broadcast License. RG 173. National Archives and Records Service. Washington, D.C.

Federated Press. Papers. Rare Books and Manuscript Library. Columbia University Libraries. New York.

Fitzpatrick, John. Papers. Chicago Historical Society.

Hedges, William S. Papers. State Historical Society of Wisconsin. Madison.

International Ladies' Garment Workers' Union. Records. Martin P. Catherwood Library. New York State School for Industrial and Labor Relations. Cornell University. Ithaca.

Keenan, Joseph D. Papers. Archives and Manuscript Division. Catholic University of America. Washington, D.C.

Lee, William A. Papers. Chicago Historical Society.

National Association of Educational Broadcasters. Papers. State Historical Society of Wisconsin. Madison.

National Broadcasting Company. Records. State Historical Society of Wisconsin. Madison.

Olander, Victor A. Papers. Chicago Historical Society.

Payne Fund, Inc. Records, 1924–72. Western Reserve Historical Society. Cleveland, Ohio.

Rubin, Willam B. Papers. State Historical Society of Wisconsin Area Research Center. University Archives. University of Wisconsin at Milwaukee.

Socialist Party of America. Papers, 1897–1964. State Historical Society of Wisconsin. Madison.

Thomas, Norman. Papers. Manuscript Division. New York Public Library.

Walker, John H. Papers. Illinois Historical Survey Library. University of Illinois at Urbana-Champaign.
Walsh, Frank P. Papers. Manuscript Division. New York Public Library.

Reports and Proceedings

American Bar Association. *Report of the Fifty-Fourth Annual Meeting of the American Bar Association, Atlantic City, New Jersey, September 17–19, 1931.* Baltimore: Lord Baltimore Press, 1933.
American Federation of Labor. *Report of the Proceedings of the Annual Convention.* Washington, D.C.: AFL, 1924–50.
Congressional Record. Various sessions of Congress.
Congress of Industrial Organizations. *Proceedings of the Constitutional Convention.* Washington, D.C.: CIO, 1941–46.
Federal Communications Commission. *Federal Communications Commission Reports.* Washington, D.C.: GPO, 1943–78.
——. *Official Report of the Proceedings before the FCC, Hearing in re: Before the Broadcast Division of the FCC on Section 307 (c) of the Communications Act of 1934, October–November 1934.* Transcript in New York Public Library. New York.
——. Engineering Department. *Report on Social and Economic Data Pursuant to the Informal Hearings on Broadcasting, Docket 4063, Beginning October 5, 1936.* Washington, D.C.: GPO, 1938.
House Committee on Interstate and Foreign Commerce. *Hearings before the Committee on Interstate and Foreign Commerce on H.R. 8301: Federal Communications Commission.* 73d Cong., 2d Sess., 1934.
Illinois State Federation of Labor. *Proceedings: Conventions.* 1926–51.
Senate Committee on Interstate Commerce. *Commission on Communications: Hearings before the Committee on Interstate Commerce.* 71st Cong., 1st Sess., 1929.
——. *Commission on Communications: Hearings before the Committee on Interstate Commerce.* 71st Cong., 2d Sess., 1930.
——. *Hearings before the Committee on Interstate Commerce on S. 2910, March 1934.* 73d Cong., 2d Sess., 1934.
——. *Hearings before the Committee on Interstate Commerce: To Amend the Radio Act of 1927.* 72d Cong., 1st Sess., 1932.
——. *Radio Control: Hearings on S. 1 and S. 1754 before the Committee on Interstate Commerce.* 69th Cong., 1st Sess., 1926.

Oral Histories/Interviews

Caldwell, Orestes H. "The Reminiscences of Orestes H. Caldwell." 1951. Oral History Collection. Columbia University Libraries. New York.
Herstein, Lillian. Interview by Elizabeth Balanoff. Transcript. Oct. 26, 30, 1970, May

7, 12, 1971. Roosevelt University Oral History Project in Labor History. Roosevelt University Library. Chicago.

Jacobs, Joseph M. Interview by author. Transcript. July 2, 1991. Chicago.

Klass, Irwin E. Interview by author. Transcript. July 12, 1991. Chicago.

Levitas, Mollie. Interview by Elizabeth Balanoff. Transcript. July 24, 27, 1970, Dec. 22, 1970. Roosevelt University Oral History Project in Labor History. Roosevelt University Library. Chicago.

Novik, Morris S. Interview by author. Transcript. Dec. 7, 1991. New York.

Orear, Leslie F. Interview by author. Transcript. July 2, 1991. Chicago.

Quaal, Ward L. Interview by author. Transcript. Aug. 10, 1990. Chicago.

Rosenblum, Frank. Interview by Elizabeth Balanoff. Transcript. Aug. 14, 1970. Roosevelt University Oral History Project in Labor History. Roosevelt University Library. Chicago.

Periodicals

American Federationist. 1924–50.
Broadcasting. 1932–87.
Chicago Tribune. 1925–87.
Daily Worker. 1925–47.
Education by Radio. 1931–41.
Federation News. 1924–89.
Labor Age. 1926–33.
New York Times. 1924–87.
Variety. 1933–50.

Books

Armstrong, David. *A Trumpet to Arms: Alternative Media in America.* Boston: South End Press, 1981.

Barnouw, Erik. *The Golden Web: A History of Broadcasting in the United States, vol. 2—1933 to 1953.* New York: Oxford University Press, 1968.

———. *A Tower in Babel: A History of Broadcasting in the United States, vol. 1—to 1933.* New York: Oxford University Press, 1966.

Barrett, James R. *Work and Community in the Jungle: Chicago's Packinghouse Workers, 1894–1922.* Urbana: University of Illinois Press, 1987.

Cogley, John. *Radio-Television.* Vol. 2 of *Report on Blacklisting.* New York: Fund for the Republic, 1956.

Cohen, Lizabeth. *Making a New Deal: Industrial Workers in Chicago, 1919–1939.* New York: Cambridge University Press, 1990.

Czitrom, Daniel J. *Media and the American Mind.* Chapel Hill: University of North Carolina Press, 1982.

Douglas, Sara U. *Labor's New Voice: Unions and the Mass Media.* Norwood, N.J.: Ablex, 1986.

Douglas, Susan. *Inventing American Broadcasting, 1899–1922.* Baltimore: Johns Hopkins University Press, 1987.

Downing, John. *Radical Media: The Political Experience of Alternative Communication.* Boston: South End Press, 1984.

Dubofsky, Melvyn, and Warren Van Tine, eds. *Labor Leaders in America.* Urbana: University of Illinois Press, 1987.

Foner, Philip S. *History of the Labor Movement in the United States.* Vol. 8, *Postwar Struggles, 1918–1920.* New York: International Publishers, 1987.

Fones-Wolf, Elizabeth A. *Selling Free Enterprise: The Business Assault on Labor and Liberalism, 1945–1960.* Urbana: University of Illinois Press, 1994.

Frank, Dana. *Purchasing Power: Consumer Organizing, Gender, and the Seattle Labor Movement, 1919–1929.* New York: Cambridge University Press, 1994.

Green, James R. *The World of the Worker: Labor in Twentieth-Century America.* New York: Hill and Wang, 1980.

Lens, Sidney. *Unrepentant Radical: An American Activist's Account of Five Turbulent Decades.* Boston: Beacon Press, 1980.

Lipsitz, George. *A Life in the Struggle: Ivory Perry and the Culture of Opposition.* Philadelphia: Temple University Press, 1988.

———. *Rainbow at Midnight: Labor and Culture in the 1940s.* Urbana: University of Illinois Press, 1994.

Mattelart, Armand. *Mass Media, Ideologies, and the Revolutionary Movement.* Trans. Malcolm Cord. Atlantic Highlands, N.J.: Humanities Press, 1980.

McChesney, Robert W. *Telecommunications, Mass Media, and Democracy: The Battle for the Control of U.S. Broadcasting, 1928–1935.* New York: Oxford University Press, 1993.

McKillen, Elizabeth A. *Chicago Labor and the Quest for a Democratic Diplomacy, 1914–1924.* Ithaca: Cornell University Press, 1995.

Milton, David. *The Politics of U.S. Labor: From the Great Depression to the New Deal.* New York: Monthly Review Press, 1982.

Montgomery, David. *The Fall of the House of Labor: The Workplace, the State, and American Labor Activism, 1865–1925.* New York: Cambridge University Press, 1987.

Moody, Kim. *An Injury to All: The Decline of American Unionism.* London: Verso, 1988.

Mosco, Vincent. *Broadcasting in the United States: Innovative Challenge and Organizational Control.* Norwood, N.J.: Ablex, 1979.

Newell, Barbara Warne. *Chicago and the Labor Movement: Metropolitan Unionism in the 1930's.* Urbana: University of Illinois Press, 1961.

Roediger, David R., and Philip S. Foner. *Our Own Time: A History of American Labor and the Working Day.* London: Verso, 1989.

Rosen, Philip T. *The Modern Stentors: Radio Broadcasting and the Federal Government, 1920–1934.* Westport, Conn.: Greenwood Press, 1980.

Schudson, Michael. *Discovering the News: A Social History of American Newspapers.* New York: Basic Books, 1978.

Shore, Elliott. *Talkin' Socialism: J. A. Wayland and the Role of the Press in American Radicalism, 1890–1912.* Lawrence: University of Kansas Press, 1988.

Williams, Raymond. *Television: Technology and Cultural Form.* New York: Schocken Books, 1975.

Wrigley, Julia. *Class Politics and Public Schools: Chicago, 1900–1950.* New Brunswick, N.J.: Rutgers University Press, 1982.

Articles and Chapters in Books

Barlow, William. "Community Radio in the US: The Struggle for a Democratic Medium." *Media, Culture, and Society* 10, no. 1 (Jan. 1988): 81–105.

Dawley, Alan. "Workers, Capital, and the State in the Twentieth Century." In *Perspectives on American Labor History: The Problems of Synthesis,* ed. J. Carroll Moody and Alice Kessler-Harris. De Kalb: Northern Illinois University Press, 1989. 152–200.

Denning, Michael. "The End of Mass Culture." *International Labor and Working-Class History,* no. 37 (Spring 1990): 4–18.

Godfried, Nathan. "Legitimizing the Mass Media Structure: The Socialists and American Broadcasting, 1926–1932." In *Culture, Gender, Race, and U.S. Labor History,* ed. Ronald Kent, Sara Markham, David Roediger, and Herbert Shapiro. Westport, Conn.: Greenwood Press, 1993. 123–49.

Klee, Marcus. "'Hands-Off Labour Forum': The Making and Unmaking of National Working-Class Radio Broadcasting in Canada, 1935–1944." *Labour/Le Travail* 35 (Spring 1995): 107–32.

Lipsitz, George. "The Struggle for Hegemony." *Journal of American History* 75 (June 1988): 146–50.

———. "'This Ain't No Sideshow': Historians and Media Studies." *Critical Studies in Mass Communication* 5 (June 1988): 147–61.

McChesney, Robert W. "An Almost Incredible Absurdity for a Democracy." *Journal of Communication Inquiry* 15, no. 1 (Winter 1991): 89–114.

———. "Labor and the Marketplace of Ideas: WCFL and the Battle for Labor Radio Broadcasting, 1927–1934." *Journalism Monographs* 134 (Aug. 1992): 1–40.

McKillen, Beth. "The Corporatist Model, World War I, and the Public Debate over the League of Nations." *Diplomatic History* 15 (Spring 1991): 171–97.

Meehan, Eileen R. "Critical Theorizing on Broadcast History." *Journal of Broadcasting and Electronic Media* 30, no. 4 (Fall 1986): 393–411.

Montgomery, David. "Thinking about American Workers in the 1920s." *International Labor and Working-Class History,* no. 32 (Fall 1987): 4–24.

Ross, Steven J. "Cinema and Class Conflict: Labor, Capital, the State, and American Silent Film." In *Resisting Images: Essays on Cinema and History,* ed. Robert Sklar and Charles Musser. Philadelphia: Temple University Press, 1990. 68–107.

————. "Struggles for the Screen: Workers, Radicals, and the Political Uses of Silent Film." *American Historical Review* 96, no. 2 (Apr. 1991): 333–67.

Sapolsky, Steven. "Response to Sean Wilentz's 'Against Exceptionalism: Class Consciousness and the American Labor Movement: 1790–1920.'" *International Labor and Working-Class History*, no. 27 (Spring 1985): 35–38.

Sparks, Colin, ed. Special Issue. "The Working-Class Press." *Media, Culture, and Society* 7, no. 2 (Apr. 1985): 131–255.

Dissertations and Theses

Haessler, Stephen J. "Carl Haessler and the Federated Press: Essays on the History of American Labor Journalism." M.A. thesis, University of Wisconsin at Madison, 1977.

Jorgensen, Erling Sejr. "Radio Station WCFL: A Study in Labor Union Broadcasting." M.A. thesis, University of Wisconsin, 1949.

Keiser, John H. "John Fitzpatrick and Progressive Unionism, 1915–1925." Ph.D. diss., Northwestern University, 1965.

Mackey, David R. "The National Association of Broadcasters—Its First Twenty Years." Ph.D. diss., Northwestern University, 1956.

Samson, Gloria Garrett. "Toward a New Social Order: The American Fund for Public Service—Clearing House for Radicalism in the 1920s." Ph.D. diss., University of Rochester, 1987.

Wuliger, Gregory Tod. "The Fairness Doctrine in Its Historical Context: A Symbolic Approach." Ph.D. diss., University of Illinois at Urbana-Champaign, 1987.

INDEX

Nathan Godfried has previously published *Bridging the Gap between Rich and Poor: American Economic Development Policy toward the Arab East, 1942–1949* and articles on labor, radicals, and broadcasting. He is an associate professor of history at the University of Maine.